SPAIN

HOW TO USE THIS GUIDE

The first section consists of useful general information—Facts at Your Fingertips—designed to help you plan your trip, as well as local facts, business hours, local holidays, time zones, and customs that will be of use while you are traveling.

Next are essays to help you with the background of the area that this Guide covers—the cultural scene, some historical insights, regional food and drink, and so on.

Following these essays comes the detailed breakdown of the area, geographically. Each chapter begins with a description of the place or region, broadly describing its attraction for the visitor; this is followed by Practical Information to help you explore the area—detailed descriptions, addresses, directions, phone numbers, and so forth for hotels, restaurants, tours, museums, historical sites, and more.

Two vital ways into this book are the Table of Contents at the beginning and the Index at the end.

FODOR'S TRAVEL GUIDES

are compiled, researched, and edited by an international team of travel writers, field correspondents, and editors. The series, which now almost covers the globe, was founded by Eugene Fodor in 1936.

OFFICES
New York & London

FODOR'S SPAIN:

Area Editor: HILARY BUNCE

Editorial Contributors: ROBIN DANNHORN, ANDREW HERITAGE, FRANCES HOWELL, AILSA HUDSON, PETER SHELDON, DAVID TENNANT

Executive Editor: RICHARD MOORE

Assistant Editor: THOMAS CUSSANS

Photographs: PETER BAKER, J. ALLEN CASH, SPANISH NATIONAL TOURIST OFFICE

Drawings: BERYL SANDERS

Cartography: ALEX MURPHY, BRYAN WOODFIELD

FODOR'S

SPAIN
1984

(Excluding the Canaries)

FODOR'S TRAVEL GUIDES
New York

All the following Guides are current (most of them also in
the Hodder and Stoughton British edition.)

CURRENT FODOR'S COUNTRY AND AREA TITLES:

- AUSTRALIA, NEW ZEALAND
  AND SOUTH PACIFIC
- AUSTRIA
- BELGIUM AND
  LUXEMBOURG
- BERMUDA
- BRAZIL
- CANADA
- CARIBBEAN AND BAHAMAS
- CENTRAL AMERICA
- EASTERN EUROPE
- EGYPT
- EUROPE
- FRANCE
- GERMANY
- GREAT BRITAIN
- GREECE
- HOLLAND
- INDIA
- IRELAND
- ISRAEL
- ITALY
- JAPAN
- JORDAN AND HOLY LAND
- KOREA
- MEXICO
- NORTH AFRICA
- PEOPLE'S REPUBLIC
  OF CHINA
- PORTUGAL
- SCANDINAVIA
- SCOTLAND
- SOUTH AMERICA
- SOUTHEAST ASIA
- SOVIET UNION
- SPAIN
- SWITZERLAND
- TURKEY
- YUGOSLAVIA

CITY GUIDES:

- BEIJING, GUANGZHOU, SHANGHAI
- CHICAGO
- DALLAS AND FORT WORTH
- HOUSTON
- LONDON
- LOS ANGELES
- MADRID
- MEXICO CITY AND ACAPULCO
- NEW ORLEANS
- NEW YORK CITY
- PARIS
- ROME
- SAN DIEGO
- SAN FRANCISCO
- STOCKHOLM, COPENHAGEN,
  OSLO, HELSINKI, AND
  REYKJAVIK
- TOKYO
- WASHINGTON, D.C.

FODOR'S BUDGET SERIES:

- BUDGET BRITAIN
- BUDGET CANADA
- BUDGET CARIBBEAN
- BUDGET EUROPE
- BUDGET FRANCE
- BUDGET GERMANY
- BUDGET HAWAII
- BUDGET ITALY
- BUDGET JAPAN
- BUDGET MEXICO
- BUDGET SCANDINAVIA
- BUDGET SPAIN
- BUDGET TRAVEL IN AMERICA

USA GUIDES:

- ALASKA
- CALIFORNIA
- CAPE COD
- COLORADO
- FAR WEST
- FLORIDA
- HAWAII
- NEW ENGLAND
- PENNSYLVANIA
- SOUTH
- TEXAS
- USA (in one volume)

FOREWORD

People have been calling their unattainable dreams "castles in Spain" for nearly six hundred years—since, at least, the days of England's medieval poet Chaucer. But in only the last tiny fraction of that time, around twenty-five years, has the world of romantic mystery that Spain represented become solid reality for hundreds of thousands of holidaymakers. Suddenly holidays in the sun at a price everyone could afford came within everyone's grasp. The fountain-singing courtyards of Moorish Granada, the long somnolent beaches of the Costa del Sol, the twisted flames of El Greco's paintings, the dusty plains where Don Quixote rode to do battle with his vision-enemies—all these found their places in travel agents' brochures, and the rush to enjoy relaxation and romance at bargain-basement prices was on.

That this boom could take place at all was largely dependent upon the availability of cheap labor, both for the building of the concrete jungle of hotels that sprung up along the coasts, and for the staffing of them once they had raised their ugly heads. But, with the death of General Franco, the political scene changed dramatically and the national work force, until then only a few steps removed from medieval peasantry, began to insist upon its rights in the scheme of things.

The result of this fundamental change in Spain's way of life is that the country is no longer the budget destination it was. The attractions that drew millions of visitors there are no less magnetic, but they now have a slightly higher price tag on them than they used to. (We have, for example, found a marked change in the availability of budget eating places). This does *not* mean, we must stress, that Spain has reached the same insensate price bracket that, say, Britain and Belgium enjoy. It has simply risen a notch or two from its former place as a budget travel target. For those who find vast crowds antipathetic, this may be no bad news, and certainly, although such sought-after sites as Toledo still get swamped at the height of the season, you may find yourself a little less jostled as you seek out Spain's magic— and the castles are as romantic as ever.

* * *

We would like to thank Sr. José Antonio López de Letona, Director of the Spanish National Tourist Office in London, Heather Wildman and Linda Bartellot for their help and courtesy. We would also like to thank the directors and staff of the regional and local offices of the National Tourist Organization in Spain for their constant assistance and interest. We are grateful to Robin Dannhorn for his advice. We would like to thank, especially, Hilary Bunce for the enthusiasm and care she brings to her task of Area Editor; without her understanding and attention to detail this edition would not have been possible.

* * *

All prices quoted in this Guide are based on those available to us at time of writing, mid-1983. Given the volatility of European costs, it is inevitable that changes will have taken place by the time this book becomes available. We trust, therefore, that you will take prices quoted as indicators only, and will double-check to be sure of the latest figures.

We would like to stress that the hotel and restaurant listings in this Guide represent a selection only of the wealth of establishments available. But errors are bound to creep into any publication. When a hotel closes or a restaurant's chef produces an inferior meal, you may question our recommendation. Let us know, and we will investigate the establishment and the complaint. Your letters will help us to pinpoint trouble spots.

Our addresses are:

in the USA, Fodor's Travel Guides, 2 Park Ave., New York, N.Y. 10016;

in Great Britain, Fodor's Travel Guides, 9-10 Market Place, London W.1.

CONTENTS

ix

CONTENTS

SUPPLEMENTS

EUROPE AND
DON'T MISS

Now you can sail the legendary QE2 to or from Europe—
and fly the other way, free! That means you can begin or
end your European vacation with five glorious days and
nights on the last of the great superliners. And get a free
British Airways flight between London and most major
U.S. cities. (Specially reserved flights of the Concorde are
open to QE2 passengers at incredible savings.)

Only the QE2 offers four top restaurants and five
lively nightspots. A glittering disco, a glamorous casino,
and a 20,000-bottle wine cellar. The famed "Golden
Door" spa, with saunas and Jacuzzi® Whirlpool Baths.
And your choice of yoga, aerobic dance, jogging, swimming, hydrocalisthenics and massage.
• Regular crossings between England and New York,
some also calling at other U.S. ports. Sail roundtrip at big
savings.
• Cunard's choice European tours—varying in length,
attractively priced, either escorted or independent—all
include a QE2 crossing.
• Big discounts at all of Cunard's London hotels—
including the incomparable Ritz.
• Enchanting QE2 European cruises, which may be combined with a crossing.

For all the facts, including any requirements and
restrictions, contact your travel agent or Cunard, P.O. Box
999, Farmingdale, NY 11737; (212) 661-7777.

CUNARD

Certain restrictions apply to free airfare and Concorde programs. See
your travel agent.

THE QE2:
THE MAGIC.

British Registry

FACTS AT YOUR FINGERTIPS

Planning Your Trip

WHAT IT WILL COST. Though the days when Spain was the bargain basement of Europe are certainly well in the distance, the country is still relatively inexpensive compared to other places like France, Germany or the Scandinavian countries. In both food and lodgings, there is a very wide range of prices. But, in contrast to other parts of Europe, you can often find excellent value and modern facilities in a modest three-star hotel or two-fork restaurant. Moreover, though prices may be similar to, say, England, you often get more for your money in way of comfort and amenities.

Spain offers great luxury for those willing to pay for it. For others, a carefully planned trip can provide ideal vacationing at inexpensive rates, especially if you're willing to eat in the simpler local restaurants, use buses and the 'metro' instead of taxis and rented cars, and explore the out-of-the-way towns and the mountain provinces rather than the more fashionable areas.

For the independent traveler, the cities and regions around Valencia, Alicante, Murcia and Almería tend to be cheaper than the Costa del Sol or the Costa Brava. In the south, the Costa Blanca round Cartagena and the Costa de la Luz from Tarifa to the Portuguese border are fairly unspoilt and hence still reasonably priced. On the northern coast, you can still find relatively unexploited coastal villages in Santander, Asturias and Galicia provinces, where your dollar and pounds will stretch further.

The top resort of Marbella is now as expensive as Barcelona and Madrid in anything from buying an apartment to buying candy, though less expensive restaurants and hotels can be found. The cities of Santander and La Coruña on the north coast are also high-priced. Inland, prices usually level off and even in such major tourist attractions as Toledo, El Escorial, Segovia, and the Andalusian cities of Granada, Seville, Cádiz, Málaga and Córdoba there is enough choice in hotels and restaurants to go either in international style or on a shoestring.

Spain has long been the mecca of the all-inclusive tour. Majorca, and numberless resorts along the Costa Brava, the Costa Blanca and the Costa del Sol are easily available to those who are happy with packaged holidays. The value for money of most of these tours is simply incredible and, simply as vacations in the sun, they are extremely hard to beat. Conversely, if you're one of those people who dislike package holidays and meeting the people you see at home, these are the places to avoid.

Though hotel prices are more or less uniform throughout Spain, there is a tendency for hotels in Madrid and Barcelona especially, and certain other major

3

cities like Seville, to be more expensive than elsewhere. Many of the modern 3-star hotels in popular coastal resorts offer extremely reasonable rates, due probably to their working in close liaison with package tour agencies. For this very reason you may find they are totally booked throughout the high season, but that outside of July and August, you have a good chance of finding high standards of accommodations at a very reasonable price.

Restaurants too, in Madrid and Barcelona, tend to be expensive, unless you can find, and are willing to brave, the back street *económicos* patronized by students. Whereas restaurants in coastal resorts now frequently offer very inexpensive set menus (*menu del día*), even where their *à la carte* prices compare with those in major cities. On the Costa Blanca, for example, you will find plenty of restaurants offering a *menu del día* for 400–500 ptas., whereas in Barcelona you will be hard pressed to find one for 700 ptas.

In shopping, there's usually more for the money in department stores such as *Galerías Preciados* and *El Corte Inglés* which have branches in most major cities, rather than in boutiques and tourist shops. On the other hand, the local grocer, baker etc. is cheaper for many items than supermarkets.

Coins are: 1 peseta, 5, 25, 50 and the new 100 ptas. coin; bills are of 100, 500, 1,000 and 5,000 ptas. As of mid-1983, the exchange rate was around 130 ptas. to the dollar and 200 ptas. to the pound sterling.

Traveler's checks are still the standard and best way to safeguard your travel funds; and you will usually get a better exchange rate in Europe for traveler's checks than for cash, though the commission charge will also be higher. In the U.S. *Bank of America, Citicorp* and *Republic Bank of Dallas* issue checks only in U.S. dollars; *Thomas Cook* issues checks in U.S., British and Australian currencies; *Barclays Bank* in dollars and pounds; and *American Express* in U.S., Canadian, French, German, British, Swiss and Japanese currencies. Our experience has been, however, that Spanish shops want dollar or sterling traveler's checks—and may actually refuse checks in pesetas. The best-known British checks are those of Cook, Visa (Barclays), Lloyds, Midland and National Westminster.

Major credit cards are accepted in most large hotels, restaurants and shops though Visa is much more widely accepted in Spain than Access/MasterCard. Note also that many Spanish hotels limit the amount you can charge to a credit card (see under Hotels).

A typical day might cost two people:	ptas.
Hotel (moderate) double room with bath	3,750
Lunch	2,000
Dinner	3,250
Transport (2 taxis, 2 buses)	575
Evening entertainment (average)	1,400
2 coffees	180
4 beers	240
Miscellaneous	800
	12,195

SAMPLE COSTS. Canned goods and meat are expensive in Spain, tobacco and liquor are not. In a supermarket a liter of *Gredos* wine can cost as little as 70 ptas., a liter of *Valdepeñas* wine 180 ptas., a bottle of good *Rioja* from 300 ptas., Scottish whiskies start around 950 ptas., Spanish whiskey such as *Dyc,* 350 ptas., local brandy such as *Fundador* or *Soberano* 350 ptas., Bacardi 425 ptas., Gordon's gin 750 ptas., Larios gin 400 ptas.; an American-style cocktail costs around 225 ptas. A haircut costs 400 ptas., a hairdresser about 1500 for a shampoo and blow-dry; a cinema ticket is around 250 ptas., a ticket to the opera costs from 800–1,500 ptas. A local newspaper is 35 or 40 ptas., a phone call 5 ptas. and an ice-cream cone will set you back about 45 ptas.

SPANISH NATIONAL TOURIST OFFICES. You can get a great deal of information and advice to help you plan your trip from one of the offices of the Spanish National Tourist organization. The main addresses are:

In the U.S. 665 Fifth Ave, New York, N.Y. 10022
845 North Michigan Ave, Water Tower Place, Chicago, Ill. 60611
1 Hallidie Plaza, Suite 801, San Francisco, Calif. 94102
Casa del Hidalgo, Hypolita and St. George, St. Augustine, Fla. 32084
PO Box 463, Fortaleza 367, San Juan, Puerto Rico, 00902
4800 The Galleria, 5085 Westheimer, Houston, Tex. 77056
In Canada. 60 Bloor St. W., Suite 201, Toronto, Ontario
In Great Britain. 57-58 St. James's St., London SW1

CLIMATE. The tourist season in Spain lies approximately between the first of April and the end of October as it does in most other countries, and for the same reason—it is then that most Europeans and Americans take their vacations. However, parts of Spain may well be too hot for many visitors during the height of summer. It is best to try and avoid Madrid, Córdoba and Seville in July and August when the heat can be stifling and many places close for the day at around 1.30 or 2 P.M.

The best places to go if you come to Spain at this season are seaside spots or mountain resorts like the Pyrenees, Picos de Europa, Sierra Nevada, etc. The northern coast (San Sebastián, Bilbao, Santander, La Coruña) is pleasant from late June to early October. The east coast (the Costa Brava, Barcelona, Valencia) and the Balearic Islands are at their best in spring and fall. The southeastern Costa del Azahar and Costa Blanca and Andalusia's Costa del Sol and Costa de la Luz have a much longer season which spans the winter months. In fact balmy January and February weather is quite common not only on the coast but even in Madrid and Barcelona. Though be warned that Madrid can also be unbearably cold in winter, and that heavy rain is not unknown all over Spain even as late as early May. When it does rain in Spain, it often does so in abundance so come well prepared. Madrid is best visited in the late spring or autumn, preferably in May. Seville is at its best in April and May; in full summer it is unbearably hot.

Average max. daily temperatures in Fahrenheit and Centigrade:

Madrid	Jan.	Feb.	Mar.	Apr.	May	June	July	Aug.	Sept.	Oct.	Nov.	Dec.
F	48	52	59	64	70	81	88	86	77	66	55	48
C	9	11	15	18	21	27	31	30	25	19	13	9
Málaga												
F	63	63	64	70	73	81	84	86	81	73	68	63
C	17	17	18	21	23	27	29	30	27	23	20	17

OFF-SEASON TRAVEL. This has become increasingly popular in recent years as tourists have come to appreciate the advantages of avoiding the crowded periods. Transatlantic fares are slightly cheaper and so are hotel rates. Even where prices remain the same, available accommodations are better; the choicest rooms in the hotels, the best tables in the restaurants have not been pre-empted, nor are you harried by fellow tourists at every turn. Moreover, if you really want to get under the skin of a country, the time to do it is when its inhabitants are going about their daily routines, not when they're all away on vacation, too.

Spain is an ideal country for the off-season tourist, because there is no time of year at which some region is not pleasant to visit. Spain presents wide differences of climate, since the normally warm Mediterranean winters are affected by its mountainous nature, which provides cool, high-altitude areas. The outlying provinces also constitute holiday spots which enjoy comparatively good weather all year round.

 SPECIAL EVENTS. It is difficult to appreciate the essence of Spain until you have shared in one of its multitude of fiestas. It doesn't matter, essentially, if you choose the saint's day of a local village or one of the great celebrations in Seville or Santiago. The basic quality of intense and yet joyful participation is the same.

Below we list some of the more famous of Spain's many traditional events. The dates given below are only an indication, the exact days are often not known until a few weeks before the festival; always check.

Jan. *San Sebastián,* 19–20. Tamborrada, drummer processions.

Feb. *Bocairente* (Valencia), 1–6. Festival of Moors and Christians, fantastic costumes, fireworks.

Cádiz, carnival festivities.

Ciudad Rodrigo (Salamanca). Traditional festival, bullfights.

Mar. *Valencia,* 12–19. Fallas of San José, parades, bonfires, dancing.

Castellón de la Plana. Romería to St Mary Magdalene.

Easter. The most famous of Spain's pageants, its Holy Week processions, are best in Seville, Málaga, Granada, Córdoba, Cuenca and Valladolid.

Apr. *Avilés* (Oviedo), 7. Fiesta del Bollo. Variety of events, river races, folklore groups.

Pola de Siero (Oviedo), 8. Painted Easter egg festival, huge folklore parade.

Seville, .3rd or 4th week of month. April Fair. Cavalcades of riders, flamenco dancing and singing, all-night entertainment in fairground tents. Good bullfights.

Andújar (Jaén), 23–26. Romería to Our Lady of the Cabeza at top of Sierra Morena.

Murcia, 20–26. Blessing of the Orchards; Battle of Flowers; Burial of the Sardine.

Alcoy (Alicante), 23–24. Moors and Christians festival. Spectacular street battles.

May. *Córdoba,* 1–12. Festival of decorated patios.

Jerez de la Frontera (Cádiz), 13–17. Horse Fair, flamenco, bullfights, livestock and agricultural machinery exhibitions.

Madrid, mid month. San Isidro festivals. 10 days of the best bullfights, fiestas in the Plaza Mayor.

Almonte (Huelva). Whitsun. Romería del Rocío, most famous pilgrimage in Andalusia.

June. *San Feliú de Pallarols* (Girona), 5–9. Major festival, ancient dances.

Calella (Barcelona), 1st or 2nd Sun. Sardana dance and music festival.

Corpus Christi (Thurs. after Trinity Sunday). Magnificent processions in *Toledo;* flower-strewn streets and processions in *Sitges* (Barcelona).

Alicante, 21–30. Hogueras de San Juan. Cavalcades, bonfires of effigies, fireworks.

Irún (Guipúzcoa), 30. Alarde de San Marcial, commemorating the battle.

San Lorenzo de Sabucedo (Pontevedra), 4–6. A Rapa das Bestas. A kind of round-up in which horses are caught, broken and branded.

July. *Pamplona,* 6–14. Fiesta de San Fermín, running of bulls through the town, parades, fireworks, bullfights.

Pontevedra, 11. San Benitiño de Lerez romería, Galician music and song.

Olot (Girona), 13. Sardana dance festival.

Villajoyosa (Alicante), 24–31. Fiesta of the Moors and Christians, battles on land and sea.

Santiago de Compostela, 24–25. Pilgrimage to tomb of St James the Apostle, with celebrations of great pomp.

Cangas de Onís (Oviedo), 25. Festival of the Shepherds.

Luarca (Oviedo), 27. Cowherds of Alzada Festival, very colorful.

Aug. *Vitoria,* 4–9. Patron Saint Festivals of the White Virgin. Traditional processions, fireworks, music.

Llanes (Oviedo), 12–31. San Roque Festivals. River boat processions and battle of flowers, regional dances, fair.

Elche (Alicante), 14–15. Mystery play. Also at many other places.

La Alberca (Salamanca), 15–16. Feast of the Assumption celebrations.

Villafranca del Panadés (Barcelona), 29–2 Sept. Feast of San Felix Martyr. Medieval folk dances, processions, human castles contests.

Sept. *Villena* (Alicante), 4–9. Moors and Christians festival.

Jerez de la Frontera (Cádiz), 9–13. Grape harvest festival. Carnival queens, processions and lots of sherry drinking.

Oviedo, 19. "America Day in Asturias".

Mieres (Oviedo), 27. Romería to the Martyr Saints Cosme and Damian.

Oct. *Zaragoza,* 10–15. Fiestas del Pilar. Float parades, jota dance contests, sports.

El Grove (Pontevedra), 14. Shellfish festival. Galician dances, exhibition of live shellfish and shellfish cuisine.

Mondoñedo (Lugo), 18–20. As San Lucas Festival. Important horse, mule and donkey sale, also craftwork on sale.

Dec. *Labastida* (Alava), 24. Midnight Mass celebrations.

 WHERE TO GO. Unless you travel on a packaged tour, with a fixed itinerary, it's unlikely that you will follow unchanged any detailed plans you make in advance. Nevertheless, it is advantageous to rough out your trip and the Spanish National Tourist Offices, in most major cities, can send you brochures and catalogs to help you do so (see above for addresses). This lets you decide how much you can comfortably cover in the time at your disposal and to relate the extent of your travels to the limits of your pocketbook.

HIGHLIGHTS. Perhaps the number one tourist attraction of Spain is the Alhambra at Granada. Following close behind it in the same category of sights, that of architectural wonders in cities that are also gems, come the mosque of Córdoba and the Alcázar and cathedral of Seville.

Santiago de Compostela is a museum city and Avila a historic walled town. Madrid, the capital, contains one of the greatest art collections in the world, and the nearby Escorial Monastery is another of Spain's great sights; the excursion can be combined with a visit to the Valley of the Fallen memorial.

Barcelona, the capital of Catalonia, has a charm and vitality quite its own. Synagogues and El Greco paintings can be seen in Toledo, a marvellous medieval city.

There are literally hundreds of beach resorts. In the north there is San Sebastián in the Basque country, Spain's former summer capital. Further to the west are Santander and, over on Spain's strip of the Atlantic, La Coruña, a long time favorite of British visitors, and the island of La Toja near Vigo. In the northeast is the popular Costa Brava. Further south, around Alicante, is the Costa Blanca, its largest center being Benidorm. South again is the famous Costa del Sol. This stretches more or less from Almería to Algeciras and contains resorts such as Torremolinos, Fuengirola, Marbella and Estepona. From Cádiz to Huelva on the Portuguese border is the recently developed Costa de la Luz. Off Spain's Mediterranean coast are the Balearic Islands, Majorca, Minorca and Ibiza.

Two special highlights are the spectacular caves at Drach on Majorca and those at Nerja near Malaga. In Santander province the Altamira caves, famous for their prehistoric wall paintings, may well be open to limited groups of tourists in 1984.

PILGRIMAGES. Spain's chief place of pilgrimage is an ancient one; Compostela, site of the tomb of St. James the Apostle, was second only to Rome and Jerusalem in the Middle Ages. The feast of St. James is on July 25, and a Holy Year is kept whenever this date falls on a Sunday.

Also important are the pilgrimages to the Black Virgin of the Monserrat monastery near Barcelona, on April 27 and September 8. The cathedral of Valencia claims possession of the Holy Grail (or at least one of them!). Conveniently near Madrid is Avila, St. Teresa's city, with relics of the saint. Other important shrines are those of the Virgin of Guadalupe in Caceres province and of the Virgin of the Pillar in Zaragoza's basilica.

Further information about pilgrimages is available from *Catholic Travel Office*, 1019 14th St., NW, Washington, DC 20036.

WHAT TO TAKE. The first principle is to travel light, and fortunately for the present-day traveler, this is really possible, due to lightweight luggage, and drip-dry fabrics for clothing. If you plan to fly across the Atlantic, airline baggage allowances are now based on size rather than weight.

Porters are increasingly scarce in Europe nowadays and you will sometimes face delays. Motorists need to be frugal, too: limit your luggage to what can be locked into the trunk or boot of your car when you make daytime stops. At night, everything should be removed to your hotel.

CLOTHING. If you are wisely limiting yourself to two average-size suitcases, it's obvious that your clothes must be carefully selected. The first considerations are the season of the year and the countries you plan to visit. You must also bear in mind the altitude at which you plan to stay. Sea-level resorts may be fine for summer wear, but warmer evening clothes are essential for places only a few kilometers inland at a higher altitude. What you choose to take in the way of clothes will depend greatly upon your type of travel: generally speaking, dress is informal and unless you plan to stay at luxury hotels and visit the ultra chic nightspots, formal evening dress is not necessary. In Madrid and Barcelona, especially in the winter season, Spaniards tend to dress up for the top restaurants, theater and opera; elsewhere and during the summer, dress tends to be very informal and an ever increasing number of casual, even downright scruffy, dressers now throng the streets of all major cities. On Spanish beaches where not so long ago to appear in a bikini was considered scandalous, the scantiest of attire is quite acceptable, and topless and nude sunbathing is not unknown in many places.

Remember that the weather can be sizzling in summer and very chilly in winter, although neither extreme is likely to be as great as transatlantic visitors might expect.

MISCELLANY. Kleenex are useful when traveling, and are usually much more expensive abroad. Toilet rolls never come amiss, especially in country districts; these, of course, can be bought en route though. Although towels are supplied in European hotels, soap is sometimes not, so bring a tablet or two to carry you on until you can stock up in the shops.

Remedies for headaches, constipation, seasickness etc., are best brought with you because, though readily available, they may not suit you so well as the ones you are used to. Prescriptions for special medicines and for spectacles should always be carried. In Spain, there are pharmacies *(de guardia)* open all the night.

TRAVEL DOCUMENTS. British, United States and Canadian citizens need only a passport, no visa, to visit Spain.

Apply for passports several months in advance of your expected departure date. U.S. residents may apply in person to U.S. Passport Agency Offices, at selected Post Offices and county courthouses. They will need 1) proof of citizenship, such as a birth certificate; 2) two identical photographs, in either black and white or color, on non-glossy paper and taken within the past six months; 3) $35 for the passport itself plus a $7 processing fee if applying in person (no processing fee when applying by mail) for those 18 years and older, or if under 18, $20 for the passport plus a $7 processing fee if applying in person (again, no extra fee when applying by mail). Adult passports are valid for 10 years, others for five years; 4) proof of identity such as a driver's license, previous passport, any governmental ID card, or a copy of an income tax return. When you receive your passport write down its number, date and place of issue separately; if it is later lost or stolen, notify either the nearest American Consul or the Passport Office, Department of State, Washington, D.C. 20524, as well as the local police.

Canadian citizens entering Spain must have a valid passport, application forms for which may be obtained at any Post Office and then sent to the Canadian Passport Office at 40 Bank Street, Ottawa, with a remittance of $10.

British subjects should apply on a form obtainable from travel agencies or main post offices. Send this form to the Passport Office for your area at least 4 weeks before the passport is required. The fee is £11, validity 10 years.

A British Visitor's Passport, cost £5.50 and valid for one year, can be obtained straight from main post offices.

MEDICAL SERVICES. The *I.A.M.A.T.* (International Association for Medical Assistance to Travelers) offers you a list of approved English-speaking doctors who have had post-graduate training in the U.S., Canada or Britain. Membership is free; the scheme is worldwide with many European countries participating. Fees are: office call, $20; house call, $30; night and weekend call, $35. For information apply in the U.S. to 736 Center St., Lewiston, N.Y. 14092; in Canada, 123 Edward St., Suite 275, Toronto, Ontario M5GIE2.

A similar scheme with an initial membership fee of $6 per person, or $10 for a family is *Intermedic,* 777 Third Ave, New York, NY 10017; fees are somewhat higher than those of *I.A.M.A.T.* In Spain, *I.A.M.A.T.* has 31 correspondent clinics, *Intermedic* has 23.

Europ-Assistance Ltd. offers unlimited help to its members. There are two plans: one for travelers using tours or making their own trip arrangements, the second for motorists taking their cars abroad. Multilingual personnel staff a 24-hour, seven-days-a-week telephone service which brings the aid of a network of medical and other advisers to assist in any emergency. Special medical insurance is part of the plan. Write to 252 High St., Croydon, Surrey CRO ÍNF for details. (Available for British residents only.)

Unlike Britain, there is *no* free medical treatment in Spain.

In case of an emergency, contact your hotel reception or the police.

 TRAVEL FOR THE HANDICAPPED. Major sources of information are: *Access to the World: A Travel Guide for the Handicapped,* by Louise Weiss, available from Facts on File, 460 Park Ave. South, New York, N.Y. 10016 at $14.95 postpaid. *Travelability,* by Lois Reamy, published by Macmillan; the *International Directory of Access Guides,* a listing of publications describing access facilities in specific countries and cities, published by *Rehabilitation International,* 1123 Broadway, New York, N.Y. 10010; the lists of commercial tour operators who arrange travel for the disabled published by the *Society for the Advancement of Travel for the Handicapped,* 26 Court St., Brooklyn, New York 11242; and the *Travel Information Center,* Moss Rehabilitation Hospital, 12th St. and Tabor Rd., Philadelphia, Penn. 19141.

Information on Europe is also available from *Mobility International,* 43 Dorset St., London W.1., England; the *National Society for Mentally Handicapped Children,* 117 Golden Lane, London E.C.4; the *Across Trust,* Crown House, Morden, Surrey, England. But the main source in Britain for all advice on handicapped travel is *The Royal Society for Disability and Rehabilitation,* 25 Mortimer St., London W.1.

Getting To Spain

From North America

BY AIR. *Iberia,* the Spanish national airline, and *TWA* have frequent flights between New York and both Madrid and Barcelona. Iberia also has flights between Miami and Montreal and Madrid. Other major Spanish cities are easily reached from Madrid on Iberia's extensive internal air network.

Air fares are in a constant state of flux, and we advise you to consult a travel agent for up-to-date information on fare structures, rules governing various discount plans (advance booking, minimum and maximum stay requirements, etc.), off-season low prices, charter flights and package tours. There are now basically four fares for crossing the North Atlantic to Europe. On scheduled flights there is first class, business or Club, and economy with various divisions within the last (including APEX); then there are charter flights.

First and business classes are expensive: the 1984 return fares from New York to Madrid are likely to be around $3,000 and $1,400 respectively. APEX (Advance Booking Excursion) tickets are likely to range around the $750 to $900 mark according to the time of travel. All tickets in the cheaper range have various restrictions including advance purchase (usually 21 days) and no change in dates without financial penalty. Spain is well served by charter services and by package tour operators. Packages are worth investigating even if you do not wish to use the tour's other services (hotels, meals, etc.) as block booking can bring the cost of a package to below that of a separately booked air fare. There are currently no 'stand by' fares to Spain from North America.

Children between the ages of 2 and 12 travel at half the adult tariff, but are entitled to a full luggage allowance. Infants under 2 not occupying a seat and accompanied by an adult are charged only 10% of the full fare. Although they are not entitled to a free luggage allowance, their food, clothing, and other supplies needed in flight are not weighed. Most airlines provide special bassinets if notified in advance.

BY SEA. The possibilities of crossing the Atlantic by boat diminish each year, on both ocean liners and cargo boats. For many, the leisurely tempo is as appealing as the land part of a trip. Crossing time is from 5 to 11 days depending on the route and speed of the vessel.

Stylish and comfortable, *Cunard's* Queen Elizabeth II provides the only regular transatlantic service, and calls at French and English ports. *Royal Viking* operates a cruise service from Fort Lauderdale, Florida, and New York City to Malaga, Spain (as well as to Funchal, Portugal) every April: Royal Viking, 630 Fifth Avenue, New York, N.Y. 10111 or P.O. Box 1612 Vika, Oslo 1, Norway.

A few freighters provide relatively comfortable one-class accommodations for up to 12 people, and they are booked several years ahead. Passages on Polish and Russian boats are currently not available to citizens of the United States. Those wishing to travel by freighter should consult: *Air Marine Travel Service,* 501 Madison Ave., New York, N.Y. 10022, publisher of the *Trip Log Quick Reference Freighter Guide;* or *Pearl's Freighter Tips,* 175 Great Neck Road, Great Neck, N.Y. 11201.

From Great Britain

BY AIR. *Iberia* has the largest number of services from London (Heathrow) to main Spanish cities and resorts. *British Airways* flies from Gatwick to Madrid, Barcelona, Bilbao, Valencia, Alicante and Málaga. There are also some flights from other British cities including Manchester, Birmingham and Edinburgh.

Although fares on scheduled flights to Spain can be high there has been a rationalization in these by both British Airways and Iberia in the last two years. They now offer low cost APEX (Advance Booking) fares on many routes, e.g. London to Madrid for 1984 is likely to be around £130, to Barcelona about £105, to Málaga around £130. Club (business) class fares are much higher e.g. £310 to Barcelona.

In the last year or two there has been an increase in the number of charter flight tickets from many U.K. airports to Spain: sometimes these are sold with "basic" accommodation which you need not take up, sometimes as straight "fares only". Sample fares: Gatwick to Málaga £95, to Palma £85, to Ibiza £90, all return. Tour operators such as Thomson, Intasun, Cosmos and Falcon offer these; details from travel agents. Although decreasing in numbers thanks to the charter flight outlets, tickets are also available on both scheduled and charter flights via "bucket shops". These outlets are not members of the British Association of Travel Agents nor do they hold International Air Transport Association licenses. Details are in the classified advertisements of many newspapers and magazines. Double check on the tickets and their validity.

BY TRAIN. In the last few years, train services to Spain have all been improved considerably. For the independent traveler Paris is the main starting point, although there are one or two special trains run by the British and continental tour operators from Channel ports (and also West Germany) to the Franco-Spanish frontier.

From Paris there are two main routes, one going southwest toward the Atlantic coasts of France and Spain, thence to Madrid, the other going toward the Mediterranean and Barcelona. The first one goes via Bordeaux to Hendaye and Irún, the border towns. Here routes go south to Madrid, or west to Portugal via Burgos, Valladolid and Salamanca. Local services also run along the north coast.

A convenient train on this route from Paris is the *Puerta del Sol* (Gate of the Sun) which leaves Paris (Austerlitz) at 5.50 P.M. and travels via Bordeaux and the frontier, reaching Madrid the following morning at about 10. 2nd class couchettes and both 1st and 2nd class carriages are available all the way to Madrid. The wheels, believe it or not, are changed at the frontier by an ingenious if somewhat noisy contraption, Spanish rail gauges being wider than those in the rest of Europe. A dining car runs from Paris to the frontier and another from Miranda de Ebro to Madrid itself.

There is a daylight service to San Sebastián in northern Spain from Paris. This is the *Sud Express* which leaves Austerlitz at 9 A.M. and reaches San Sebastian at around 6 P.M. You change trains at the frontier. A train with beds and couchettes leaves Paris at 10.50 P.M., connecting at Irún with the 8.55 A.M. *Iberia Express* which reaches Madrid at 5.48 P.M.

However, the best train on the Paris-Madrid route is undoubtedly the deluxe *Talgo* service. This is an all-sleeper express with 1st and 2nd class and tourist class sleepers and a dining car all the way. It leaves Paris at 8 P.M. and arrives at Madrid at about 9 the following morning.

The other main route from Paris goes via Toulouse and Perpignan in France to Cerbère/Port Bou on the French/Spanish border and from there on to Barcelona in Spain. There is a through train from Paris every day, though you must change trains at the border.

The best Paris/Barcelona train is the splendid *Barcelona Talgo*. This Spanish-designed train is an all-sleeper express with 1st-, 2nd- and special tourist-class (four-berth) sleepers and both a dining and a buffet car all the way. The wheels are altered at the frontier by another ingenious but quieter method. Inclusive rail and sleeper tickets are issued for this train. It leaves Paris at 9 P.M. and arrives at Barcelona at 8.30 the next morning.

Spanish railways operate self-drive car hire services at main line stations in the principal cities. They also have a network of car-carrying trains by night and some by day also.

BUDGET RAIL FARES. A *Eurailpass* is a convenient, all-inclusive ticket that can save you money on over 100,000 miles of railroads, and railroad-operated buses, ferries, river and lake steamers, hydrofoils, and some Mediterranean crossings in 16 countries of western Europe. It provides the holder with unlimited travel at rates of—15 days, $322; 21 days, $400; 1 month, $500; 2 months $655; 3 months, $840.

In addition children under 12 get half fare in all cases and those under four go free of charge if accompanied by a Eurailpass holder on a ratio of one to one.

May be purchased and used *only* if you live outside Europe and North Africa. The pass must be bought from an authorized agent before you leave for Europe. Apply through your travel agent; or the general agents for North America: French National Railroads, Eurailpass Division, 610 Fifth Avenue, New York, N.Y. 10020; or through the German Federal Railroad, 11 West 42nd Street, New York, N.Y. 10036 and 45 Richmond Street, W., Toronto M5H 1Z2, Ontario, Canada.

BY BUS. Bus travel has become an increasingly popular way to get to Spain, if only because of the extremely reasonable rates. However, long bus trips, especially in hot weather, can be uncomfortable and the great number of cut-price air fares to Spain has begun to make the prospect of a 36-hour-plus trip by bus seem a little pointless. Bear in mind also that the need to take food along makes the trip more expensive than it might appear at first sight.

The main regular bus line operating between England and Spain is *Euroways,* who in conjunction with Wallace Arnold and several Spanish bus companies, run thrice weekly services from London's Victoria Coach Station to San Sebastián, Vitoria, Burgos, Madrid, Córdoba, Málaga, Torremolinos, Fuengirola, Marbella and Algeciras. They also have thrice weekly services to Girona, Barcelona, Valencia, Benidorm and Alicante stopping at many intermediate coastal resorts. Fares are no cheaper than charter flights. For reservations contact Euroways/Evan Evans, 73 Russell Sq., London WC1 OJZ (tel. 01-837-6543) or Victoria Coach Station direct.

BY SEA. *Brittany Ferries* operate the only regular sea link to Spain from the U.K. on their Plymouth-Santander route. There are two sailings weekly and the trip takes around 25 hours. Cabins are available. Though prices are fairly high, the mere fact of not having to make the lengthy and hence expensive drive through France makes this trip well worth while, especially for families.

BY CAR. The easiest trip to Spain by car is via *Brittany Ferries'* twice weekly service to Santander in northern Spain (see above). All other car journeys to Spain from the U.K. involve cross channel trips and consequently a lengthy drive through France. This rather slow drive is not recommended for those in a hurry; you may find the return journey in particular long and tiring, especially if you are rushing to catch your ferry.

However, if you are going to drive across France to Spain, the best ferry routes over the Channel are those from Southampton, Portsmouth and Weymouth to Le Havre, Cherbourg and St. Malo. *P.&O., Townsend Thoresen* and *Sealink* all have frequent sailings on these routes; journey times are between 4 and 7 hours. The shorter and less expensive crossings between Dover and Ramsgate and Calais and Boulogne add significantly to the total driving time and consequently can be more expensive than they might at first sight appear. For driving routes to Spain from France, see below.

From The Continent

BY AIR. *Iberia* links not only Madrid and Barcelona but many other major Spanish cities with a considerable number of European destinations including Lisbon, Rome, Milan, Geneva, Zurich, Amsterdam, Brussels, Copenhagen, Vienna, Athens, Moscow, Frankfurt, Paris and most other principal European cities. A large number of continental airlines also serve Madrid, Barcelona, Palma and other Spanish cities from their capitals.

BY TRAIN. Services to Spain from continental Europe are good. The best services are mostly those from Paris, details of which are listed above. However, other train services to Spain include the following routes:

From the French Riviera, there is a direct service along the coast. To reach Spain by train from other European countries, travelers from Scandinavia, Benelux or northern Germany should go first to Paris. From Geneva, go via Lyon, joining the French Riviera route at Tarascon. From southern Germany, western Austria and central Switzerland, go either via Geneva–Lyon, or via Lucerne, Milan and Ventimiglia, where you pick up the line from the French Riviera. From Rome there is a through train via Genoa and Nice, along the French Riviera to either Port Bou or Irún. From Florence, go via Genoa, and from Venice, via Milan. From Vienna, go via Venice.

BY SEA. The Danish Line *DFDS Seaways* now run the *M/S Dana Corona* on a weekly service between Genoa (Italy), Palma de Mallorca and Motril on the Costa del Sol. *Canguro Iberia* lines run ferries three times weekly between Genoa (Italy) and Barcelona, saving you 980 km of road travel. Trip takes 21 hours.

BY BUS. All the major European buslines operate services to Spain but these are usually all-inclusive tours. *Atesa Marsans,* a major Spanish tour and bus company, has many excellent tours (see page 20). It cooperates closely with *Europabus. Intercar Alsa,* Juan Ramón Jiménez 28-30-D, Madrid 16, runs a twice weekly service from Paris to San Sebastián, Burgos and Valladolid, then on to Salamanca or to Santiago de Compostela via Orense. *Iberbus* runs six services a week from Paris to Valencia via Barcelona, and twice weekly via Zaragoza. Thrice weekly this service continues on to Murcia. Its Paris office is at the Gare Routière Stalingrad; in Spain, their offices are at Bailén 2, Valencia; Vergara 2, Barcelona; Canarias 17, Madrid. *Via Tourisme,* Place Stalingrad 8, Paris, runs a thrice weekly service to Girona, Barcelona, Valencia, Alicante and Murcia.

BY CAR. From the countries lying north and northeast of France, the route to Spain can begin with the auto-route running between Paris, Liège and the German network. After that, A10 goes direct to the west side of the Pyrenees, and A20 to Toulouse, whence there is a choice of continuing on it over the mountains close to Andorra, or taking the road to Narbonne to enter Spain near its east coast. From southern Germany and Switzerland make for the Autoroute du Sud at Châlons or Lyon, down to Perpignan and the border at Le Perthus on the toll-road to Barcelona. Italian autostrada link up with the French to bring one to the same point, while from England it is best to make one's way to Bordeaux for west or central Spain or to Limoges and Toulouse to Narbonne for the Mediterranean side.

Paris–Madrid via Hendaye. The A10 is direct; the distance to the frontier is 787 km (489 miles). From Hendaye to Madrid is another 515 km (319 miles). It is one of the most interesting French roads, passing through both the château and the wine country, but is heavily trafficked. A tourist "route verte" is signed on minor roads.

Paris–Barcelona via Toulouse. The best route to Barcelona is via Toulouse. At Toulouse there are two possibilities. The first and more direct is via Foix, crossing the border at Bourg-Madame. Route 20 goes direct to Bourg-Madame and the total distance from Paris to the border is 900 km (559 miles), or 1,139 (709 miles) to Barcelona. This route cuts through the Pyrenees and passes so close to Andorra that most motorists will wish to turn off for a visit.

From Toulouse, an alternative route skirts the Pyrenees via Carcassonne, joins the toll-road at Narbonne, continuing via Perpignan, and the border town of Le Perthus. This route is slightly longer yet quicker.

Paris–Barcelona via Lyon. A splendid, longer but faster route via Sens, Lyon, Avignon, Nîmes, Montpellier, Beziers, Perpignan and Le Perthus, totals around 1,126 km (700 miles). It increases costs and mileage slightly but reduces time greatly by using motorways all the way.

Arriving in Spain

CUSTOMS. You can bring into Spain anything intended for your personal use, but be reasonable about it. There will be no duty on nylons if you're not overloaded with them; nor on one camera and one cine-camera (8 or 16 mm) per person, but it's doubtful whether you will get by free with more; you are allowed up to 5 rolls of film; 200 cigarettes or 50 cigars or 250g tobacco; 1 liter of hard liquor or 2 liters of fortified or sparkling wine, and 2 liters of still table wine, but theoretically you are not supposed to bring in more than that. You may take out purchases up to 25,000 pesetas without payment of export duty. However, on this matter, as on all matters of prices, it would be safer to inquire at the time of traveling, as such things are always subject to revision from time to time.

PHOTOGRAPHY. Those once-in-a-lifetime holiday films are vulnerable to the X-ray security machines on airports. At some, such as London's Heathrow, extra-powerful equipment is used; on most the machines are of the "low-dose" type. Both can cause films to be "fogged", and the more often the film passes through such machines, the more the fog can build up.

Warning notices are displayed sometimes, and passengers are advised to remove film—or cameras with film in them—for a hand check. But many airport authorities will not allow hand inspection and insist that all luggage pass through the detection devices.

There are two steps you should follow. First, ask for a hand-inspection whenever you can. Second, buy one or more *Filmashield* lead-laminated bags. These will help to protect films from low-dosage X-rays, but should not be relied on against the more powerful machines. The bags are also available in Britain.

Bring plenty of film with you; film in Spain is very much more expensive than in the U.S., and slightly dearer than in Britain.

Staying in Spain

MONEY. You may not legally acquire more than 100,000 pesetas outside Spain, so you will not be able to bring more into the country. You may only take out 20,000 pesetas in cash. However, you can bring in any amount of foreign currency in bills or travelers' checks and you can take out however much you have left when you leave. Although in theory you should keep a record of every exchange transaction, hotel cashiers rarely bother with a receipt and you are never asked for one at the border.

Generally speaking, you should get a better rate of exchange in banks than in hotels, shops or restaurants. However, many Spanish banks now charge such a high rate of commission that you may well be no worse off changing money in an hotel.

HOTELS. Spanish hotels are a good buy for the tourist, not least because of the strict regulations imposed upon them by the Spanish government. These are designed to prevent abuses and sharp practices. Consequently, if you should come across any irregularities, have no scruples in reporting the hotel concerned to the Spanish National Tourist Office.

Hotels are officially classified from 5-star to 1-star; hostels and pensions are classified from 3-star to 1-star. These grades equate roughly with our classifications of deluxe (L), expensive (E), moderate (M) and inexpensive (I). Prices are set by the government and, by law, must be prominently displayed in all rooms. As prices can vary considerably within the various classifications, the number of stars a hotel has is usually but *not always* a guide to its price.

Ask to look at your room before you take it to ensure that you are completely sure of the price. Be sure also to check whether meals are included in the price and whether you will be required to pay for them even if you don't eat them. This applies especially to breakfast.

Approximate prices for a double room are shown below. A single person in a double room will be charged 80% of the full price. Many of the larger new hotels have double rooms only. Many hotels now also levy a 4% tax (ITE) on top of the prices quoted. If you are planning to pay your hotel bill with a credit card, check in advance with reception; at presstime only 20,000 ptas. could be charged to a Visa card and 25,000 ptas to American Express or Diners.

HOTEL PRICES: DOUBLE ROOMS

Category	Major city	Major resort	Provincial capital	Budget resort
5-star; Deluxe	10,000	7,000	7,000	5,800
4-star; Expensive	6,000	4,600	5,750	4,500
3-star; Moderate	4,000	3,500	3,750	3,000
2-star; Inexpensive	3,000	2,500	2,500	2,400
1-star	2,350	2,000	2,000	1,750

Important. We must stress that these prices are subject to change and are only indicative. Also, variations within each category can be considerable—for example between Torremolinos and Marbella, which are both major resorts, with Marbella the more expensive of the two. Be very sure to check either with your travel agent or with the Spanish National Tourist Office for the latest rates.

 PARADORES, ALBERGUES AND REFUGIOS. The government operates a number of hotels, motels and hostelries called *paradores, albergues, refugios* and *hosterías.* The *paradores,* often historic castles in magnificent settings, are well furnished and equipped and all have restaurants. *Albergues,* principally for motorists, are more functional but very comfortable and they also have restaurants. *Refugios* are simple but adequately equipped shelters in remote or mountain districts. No restaurants. *Hosterías* are rustic, local speciality restaurants in places of touristic interest. No sleeping accommodations.

We highly recommend the paradores and have had many delighted reports from readers. Some tour operators run special parador tours; they include

Mundi Color, 276 Vauxhall Bridge Rd., London S.W.1. who do a fly-drive holiday to the paradores of Andalusia; and *Atesa Marsans,* 500 Fifth Ave., New York, N.Y. 10010 and 35 Piccadilly, London W.1., who have a 14-day coach tour to the paradores of Santander, Oviedo, La Coruña, Santiago, León, Salamanca, Extremadura, Seville, Córdoba and Granada, starting from and ending in Madrid. *Brittany Ferries,* Millbay Docks, Plymouth, England, also offer parador holidays. These are go-as-you please motoring holidays. You sail with your car from Plymouth to Santander and then stay at whichever of the 66 paradores you choose for between 5 and 14 days.

The Secretary of State for Tourism runs about 20 different parador tours, some of which also take in one or two of the National Parks of Spain. These tours are listed in a brochure *(Rutas Turisticas)* which is obtainable from the Spanish National Tourist Office.

In many paradores, advance reservations are essential, though we advise these in any case. Rates are usually higher at Christmas and Easter and in high season. Reservations can be made by contacting the establishment directly or through the *Centro de Reservas de los Paradores de España,* Almagro 36, Madrid 4. In the U.S. it would be sensible to approach your parador holiday through *Marketing Ahead,* 515 Madison Ave., New York, N.Y. 10022. They not only facilitate the booking of paradores (not always easy to do direct), but provide excellent information and other services for their clients.

Note that many paradores are closed in January and February for refurbishing.

Below is a list, in alphabetical order, town by town, of the paradores, with the name of the parador in italics.

Selected paradores

Aiguablava (Girona): *Costa Brava,* 80 rooms.
Alarcón (Cuenca): *Marqués de Villena,* 11 rooms.
Albacete: *de la Mancha,* 70 rooms.
Alcañiz (Teruel): *La Concordia,* 12 rooms.
Almagro (Ciudad Real): *Almagro,* 55 rooms.
Antequera (Málaga): *Antequera,* 17 rooms.
Arcos de la Frontera (Cádiz): *Casa del Corregidor,* 21 rooms. Closed at presstime for restoration.
Argomaniz (Alava): *Argomaniz,* 54 rooms.
Arties (Lérida): *Don Gaspar de Portola,* 40 rooms.
Avila: *Raimundo de Borgoña,* 27 rooms.
Ayamonte (Huelva): *Costa de la Luz,* 20 rooms.
Bailén (Jaén): *Bailén,* 40 rooms.
Bayona (Pontevedra): *Conde de Gondomar,* 128 rooms.
Benavente (Zamora): *Rey Fernando II de León,* 30 rooms.
Benicarló (Castellón): *Costa del Azahar,* 108 rooms.
Bielsa (Huesca): *Monte Perdido,* 16 rooms.
Cádiz: *Atlántico* (hotel), 48 rooms.
Calahorra (La Rioja): *Marco Fabio Quintiliano,* 67 rooms.

Cambados (Pontevedra): *Albariño*, 63 rooms.
Cardona (Barcelona): *Condes de Cardona*, 65 rooms.
Carmona (Seville): *Alcazar Rey D. Pedro*, 55 rooms.
Cazorla (Jaén): *Adelantado*, 22 rooms.
Cervera de Pisuerga (Palencia): *Fuentes Carrionas*, 80 rooms.
Chinchón (Madrid): *Chinchón*, 38 rooms.
Ciudad Rodrigo (Salamanca): *Enrique II*, 28 rooms.
Córdoba: *La Arruzafa*, 56 rooms.
El Ferrol (Coruña): *El Ferrol del Caudillo*, 27 rooms.
Fuente Dé (Santander): *Río Deva*, 78 rooms.
Fuenterrabía (Guipúzcoa): *El Emperador*, 16 rooms.
Gijón (Oviedo): *Molino Viejo*, 6 rooms.
Granada: *San Francisco*, 26 rooms.
Guadalupe (Cáceres): *Zurbarán*, 20 rooms.
Jaén: *Castillo de Santa Catalina*, 43 rooms.
Jarandilla (Cáceres): *Carlos V*, 43 rooms.
Javea (Alicante): *Costa Blanca*, 60 rooms.
Málaga: *Gibralfaro*, 12 rooms.
Mazagón (Huelva): *Cristóbal Colón*, 20 rooms.
Melilla: *Don Pedro de Estopiñán*, 27 rooms.
Mérida (Badajoz): *Vía de la Plata*, 45 rooms.
Mojácar (Almería): *Reyes Católicos*, 99 rooms.
Navarredonda (Sierra de Gredos) (Avila): *Gredos*, 77 rooms.
Nerja (Málaga): *Nerja*, 40 rooms.
Olite (Navarre): *Príncipe de Viana*, 39 rooms.
Oropesa (Toledo): *Virrey Toledo*, 47 rooms.
Pajares (Oviedo): *Puerto de Pajares*, 29 rooms.
Pontevedra: *Casa del Barón*, 47 rooms.
Puebla de Sanabria (Zamora): *Parador Nacional*, 18 rooms.
Puerto Lumbreras (Murcia): *Puerto Lumbreras*, 13 rooms.
Puertomarín (Lugo): *Puertomarín*, 10 rooms.
Ribadeo (Lugo): *Ribadeo*, 47 rooms.
Salamanca: *Salamanca*, 108 rooms.
El Saler (Valencia): *Luis Vives*, 40 rooms.
Santillana del Mar (Santander): *Gil Blas*, 24 rooms.
Santo Domingo de la Calzada (La Rioja): parador of same name, 27 rooms.
Segovia: *Segovia*, 80 rooms.
Seo de Urgel (Lerida): *Seo de Urgel*, 85 rooms.
Sierra Nevada (Granada): *Sierra Nevada*, 32 rooms.
Sigüenza (Guadalajara): *Castillo de Sigüenza*, 82 rooms.
Soria: *Antonio Machado*, 14 rooms.
Sos del Rey Católico (Zaragoza): *Fernando de Aragón*, 66 rooms.
Teruel: *Teruel*, 42 rooms.
Toledo: *Conde de Orgaz*, 58 rooms.
Tordesillas (Valladolid): *Tordesillas*, 73 rooms.
Torremolinos (Málaga): *Golf*, 40 rooms.

Tortosa (Tarragona): *Castillo de la Zuda,* 82 rooms.
Túy (Pontevedra): *San Telmo,* 16 rooms.
Ubeda (Jaén): *Condestable Davalos,* 25 rooms.
Verín (Orense): *Monterrey,* 23 rooms.
Vich (Barcelona): *Vich,* 31 rooms.
Viella (Lérida): *Valle de Aran,* 135 rooms.
Villafranca del Bierzo (León), 41 rooms.
Villalba (Lugo): *Condes de Villalba,* 6 rooms.
Zafra (Badajoz): *Hernán Cortés,* 28 rooms.
Zamora: *Condes de Alba y Aliste,* 19 rooms.

Albergues

Manzanares (Ciudad Real), Madrid–Córdoba–Seville road: 50 rooms.
Santa María de la Huerta (Soria), Madrid–La Junquera road: 40 rooms.
Villacastín (Segovia), Avila–Segovia road: 13 rooms.

Refugios

Ojen in the Sierra Blanca (Málaga): *Refugio de Cazadores de Juanar,* 17 rooms.

Hosterías

Alcalá de Henares (Madrid): *El Estudiante.*
Cáceres: *El Comendador.*
Pedraza (Segovia): *Pintor Zuloaga.*

VILLA RENTAL. A villa for six can be rented for around $250 a week in off-season and $350 a week in July and August. *At Home Abroad Inc.,* 405 East 56th St., New York, N.Y. 10022, has properties in Spain, Portugal, Majorca and Tangiers as well as six other countries. *Rent-a-Villa Ltd.,* 422 Madison Ave., New York, N.Y. 10017, operates on the Mediterranean coast of Spain. *Air India* rents apartments in Madrid. *Villas International,* 213 East 38th St., New York, N.Y. 10016, have a number of properties along the Mediterranean coast of Spain.

Variety Leisure, 1701 Walnut St., Philadelphia, Pa 19103, specializes in renting exclusive properties (many belonging to royalty and/or celebrities) in Spain and elsewhere.

Travelseekers Ltd, 296–300 St John St, London EC1V 4PA, have a wide range of villas on the Costa del Sol and in Minorca. *Interhome Villas,* 10 Sheen Rd., Richmond, Surrey, have a wide choice of villas in every part of the Mediterranean coast and in Majorca and Ibiza. *Villas Abroad,* 322 Croydon Rd., Beckenham, Kent, have villas on the Costa Brava, Costa del Sol and Costa Dorada, in Majorca, Ibiza and Tenerife, and some delightful houses in the mountain village of Cazorla in Jaen.

CAMPING. Camping sites in Spain are government controlled and there are over 530 sites. Most have their own mailbox and supermarket and will take both coach parties and caravans. The weather in Spain being so good, the camping season is long; April to late Sept. or Oct. is normal, but some sites are even open all year. Camping carnets are not essential but are nonetheless recommended, and foreigners must show passports or identity cards when registering. As might be expected, the heaviest concentration of camps is along the Mediterranean coast.

Further information can be obtained from *American Youth Hostels Inc.,* 1332 (Eye) St., N.W., 8th Floor, Washington D.C. 20005; *Canadian Youth Hostels Association,* National Office, 333 River Rd., Vanier City, Ottawa, Ont.; *Camping Club of Great Britain and Ireland,* 11 Lower Grosvenor Place, London, S.W.1.

 RESTAURANTS. As with hotels, all Spanish restaurants are classified under strictly adhered to Government regulations. The classification "symbol" is the fork, as opposed for example to the star, and runs from 5-forks to 1-fork. As a general rule, 5- and 4-fork restaurants are rare outside major cities and you will normally find that you get a good meal at a 3-fork restaurant. A 2-fork restaurant is an average everyday spot. There are, nonetheless, many delightful restaurants in this category.

Our grading system is slightly simpler: (L) for Deluxe, (E) for Expensive, (M) for Moderate and (I) for Inexpensive. The relative approximate cost of a meal for one would be: Major centers—Deluxe, 3,000–4,500 ptas., Expensive 2,250–3,250 ptas., Moderate, 1,250–2,200 ptas., Inexpensive 750–1,200 ptas. These prices are for *à la carte* meals and include wine. Outside major centers you can expect prices to be rather lower.

Most restaurants offer a *menu del día* which more or less answers to the description of a tourist menu *(menu turístico).* By law this must include soup or appetizer, one or two main courses, bread, dessert and, sometimes, mineral water, wine or beer. Tea or coffee are never included. Prices vary according to the class of restaurant, but 500–800 ptas. per person is fairly average.

Don't be put off Spanish cooking by stories of how it comes swimming in olive oil; this is no longer the case, except possibly in humbler establishments very much off the beaten track. Generally Spanish food is well cooked and well presented, and there is always a wide choice of dishes.

Meals are habitually taken much later in Spain than in any other country in Europe. It's hard to get lunch before 1.30 P.M. and 3 P.M. is considered quite normal. Dinner before 8 P.M. is almost unheard of; 10 P.M. is the usual hour. Madrid tends to keep even later hours than the rest of the country, but the Balearics' hotel dining rooms usually close at 10 P.M.

TIPPING. Service charges are rarely included on Spanish hotel bills so leave the chambermaid 300 ptas. a week, and tip the porters 35 ptas. a bag. At the end of your stay, leave something for your waiter in the hotel dining room, say 500 ptas., though this is only customary if you have stayed a week or more. Only tip the hotel receptionist if he has provided you with special service.

Except in tip-top establishments, Spanish restaurants rarely include a service charge on their checks. If you are satisfied, you should leave at least 5% (10% is plenty), even when the menu says "service and tax included" as is usually the case with the *menu del día.* In cafés and bars it is customary to leave loose change on the saucer; at least 5 ptas. for a coffee or beer, and considerably more if you have spent a pleasant evening and the barman has been friendly, though this custom is beginning to die out.

Tip taxis 10% when they use the meter, otherwise nothing. Station porters operate on a fixed rate, usually 35 or 40 ptas. a bag. Cinema and theater ushers get 10 ptas. At nightclubs or flamenco shows doormen get 25 ptas., coat-check attendants 10 ptas. and waiters 25 ptas. a drink, or more, depending on the kind of establishment. Restroom attendants everywhere get 5 ptas., no matter how humble the facilities.

MAIL. Current rates for letters are 46 ptas. to the U.S., 33 ptas. to the U.K. and the rest of Europe. Within Spain letters cost 14 ptas. Postcards to the U.S. cost 36 ptas., 23 ptas. to Europe and 9 ptas. within Spain.

Hotel delivery is safe, but you may find it easier to receive mail at the *Lista de Correos* (Poste Restante), a special counter in all post offices in the country, where mail is held for you free of charge. Upon claiming your letters, simply present your passport or other identification. Also providing a free mail-deposit service are the American and British embassies, provided you are a national of either country.

CLOSING TIMES. Shops open in the morning between 9 and 10 to either 1.30 or 2. In the afternoon they open from approximately 4 to 7 in winter, and 5 to 8 in summer. In some cities, especially in summer, they close on Saturday afternoons. Tourist shops in seaside resorts and the *Corte Inglés* and *Galerías Preciados* department stores mostly stay open throughout the siesta. Banks are open 9.30 to 2, Mon.-Fri., and 9.30 to 1 on Saturdays. A few banks open at 9. Most churches and museums close for the siesta; some museums open mornings only.

NATIONAL HOLIDAYS. January 1 and 6, March 19, Maundy Thursday, Good Friday, May 1, Ascension Day, Corpus Christi (second Thursday after Whitsun), June 29, July 18 and 25, August 15, October 12, November 1,

December 8 and 25. In addition every town and village has its own local fiesta when everything will be closed.

 DRINKING WATER. Drinking water is perfectly safe all over Spain except perhaps in a very few out of the way places. However, many Spaniards still tend to drink mineral water in preference to tap water, not least because it is actually much nicer. If you ask a waiter for water, he will bring mineral water unless you specify tap water. Mineral water comes in two types; still *(sin gas)* or fizzy *(con gas)*. *Gaseosa* is a fizzy, sweet water similar to English lemonade or *7 Up,* and is often mixed with red wine.

CONVENIENT CONVENIENCES. There are few public facilities in Spain but restrooms are plentiful in hotels, restaurants and cafés. In the better hotels and restaurants they are cared for by a special attendant whom it is customary to tip 5 ptas. upon leaving restrooms.

Restrooms are usually identified by a picture of a man or a woman, otherwise the words *Señoras* (ladies) and *Caballeros* (men) tell you which way to head. The name for the restroom is usually *aseos, servicios* or simply W.C. Ask for, *"los servicios"* or *"los aseos."*

 SPORTS. The range of sporting activities available to visitors is in direct relation to the amount of tourist development in any particular area. Tennis, golf and much more are most easily indulged in where a high density of hotels and villas is found. The farther you get from these centers, the less there is available, until you reach, for example, the wilder mountains, where all you will be able to indulge in is shooting.

Fishing. Spain, with its nearly 3,220 km (2,000 miles) of coastline and its more than 74,000 km (46,000 miles) of rivers and streams, together with the many dams and reservoirs scattered around the country, offers magnificent possibilities for those interested in any kind of fishing.

Contact the Spanish National Tourist Office, which will tell you how to go about obtaining a license, where one is needed.

Golf. This has become one of Spain's main attractions and there are over 80 courses most of which have been carefully planned to take account of the best local scenery. Marbella on the Costa del Sol has 14 excellent courses and there are several good courses on the Costa Brava and on the Costa Blanca such as La Manga's splendid complex near Murcia, and around Madrid. Many other courses are located along the Atlantic and Mediterranean coasts as well as inland at Zaragoza, Córdoba and Seville. In the Balearics, there are 4 courses on Majorca, including the *Son Vida* and *Punta Rotja* clubs, 4 on Minorca and the *Rocallisa* club at Sta Eulalia del Rio on Ibiza.

Scuba diving. To dive in Spain every foreigner, regardless of whether he is a member of a diving club or not, must have a license and a permit for the relevant area. Details can be obtained from the Spanish Tourist Office. Apply at least 2 months in advance.

Skiing. Spain has some excellent winter sports areas. By far the best equipped are the Pyrenees resorts from Burguete and Isaba in Navarre, Astun, Candanchú, Cerler, El Formigal, Guarrinza and Panticosa in Aragón, to Espot, La Molina, Nuria, Port del Compte, Salardú and Viella in Catalonia. In the Sierra Nevada, only 35 km from Granada, is the big Sol y Nieve complex, one of the most fashionable regions. 50 km from Madrid are the Guadarrama mountains with resorts at Navacerrada, Valcotos and Pinilla; and in the north in the Picos de Europa are the resorts of Pajares, San Isidro, Reinosa and Alto Campóo.

Tennis. Nearly all the large tourist complexes and many major hotels have their own tennis courts. There is Lew Hoad's famous tennis club in Fuengirola on the Costa del Sol, while the newly developed complex at La Manga in Murcia boasts several splendid courts.

NATURIST BEACHES. It was only a few years ago that the Spanish government announced that certain beaches would be designated as official naturist (i.e. nudist) beaches. Spanish reaction to this has been somewhat mixed—small wonder in a country where until as late as the mid-70s for a girl even to appear in a bikini was regarded by many as little short of mortal sin. At time of writing there are two official naturist beaches on Ibiza, at Playa d'Aigua Blanca in the northeast, and at Playa d'Es Cavallet in the southeast. On Formentera the naturist beach is at Playa de Illetas in the northwest of the island.

On the mainland there is a naturist resort and complex with room for 400 in Almería province on the road between Vera and Garrucha. 4 km away there is a naturist beach. A naturist camp has also been planned for the Almerimar development near Dalia. On the Costa del Sol 3 km west of Estepona there is a vast naturist complex and beach which will eventually have room for 12,000.

The above are all "official" naturist beaches; if you hunt around a bit, there are also plenty of "unofficial" nudist beaches in most coastal areas.

POLLUTION. According to a recent report, over one-third of Spanish beaches represent a potential health hazard. Worst affected are those in the Basque province of Guipuzcoa, followed by those in Santander, La Coruña and Valencia, all highly industrialized regions. As a general rule the sea and sand of the Costa Blanca resorts tend to be cleaner than those of the Costa del Sol. The cleanest beaches are in Huelva and Murcia provinces.

Traveling in Spain

 BY TRAIN. Extensive electrification, the construction of new lines and the upgrading of others, the provision of new rolling stock and locomotives and the modernization of many stations as well as the installation of a more efficient booking system have all helped the Spanish State Railroads *(Red Nacional de Ferrocarriles Españoles* or *RENFE)* to reach those standards of efficiency found in most other west European countries. The dirty, inefficient, slow and altogether unreliable Spanish train system of modern memory is, at last, a thing of the past.

Because of the country's geography, the main rail routes radiate from Madrid, the sole exception being the line down the Mediterranean coast which runs through Barcelona, Valencia and Alicante. Consequently, Madrid is linked by fast trains to practically all the principal Spanish cities.

Basically there are three types of express in Spain. The first is the TALGO, a unique, deluxe train which gives a very smooth ride. Next, there is the *electrotrén* or ELT which, as its name implies, is electric. The third type of train is the TER. Various catering facilities from full dining cars to mini-buffets are available on all of these. Seat reservation is almost always obligatory, and advisable in any case. These trains, together with *Corail* and *InterCity,* all require fare supplements but are well worth the extra cost. Other trains are confusingly known as *rápidos* or *expresos* (not always the case) and carry both first and second class. A few 'special' 2nd-class trains are also operated, again involving a small supplement. Many overnight services have sleeping cars (including new airconditioned units) again with both 1st and 2nd class, as well as 2nd-class couchettes on many routes.

It is more usual in Spain to buy your ticket and make your advance bookings in the RENFE office in the center of town and not at the railroad station, though tickets are readily available at both. Expect to stand in line for a long time at either place. Seat reservation can be made up to 60 days in advance. An electronic network connects the reservation offices of RENFE all over the country.

If you wish to take your car by train there is a system of car-sleeper services connecting Madrid with the main provincial cities, plus a through Bilbao-Barcelona service. Either sleeping car or couchette car services are available on these routes. In addition your car can travel overnight and the passengers by day if more convenient.

Couchettes for journeys within Spain cost a flat 800 ptas. and sleepers have a two-tiered price system depending on whether your journey is above or below 550 km. First-class compartments with only one or two beds are very much more expensive than the second-class 3-berth compartments where a bed costs 1,000 ptas. for under 550 km. and 1,150 ptas. for over 550 km. Should the train be airconditioned then beds cost 1,250 and 1,400 ptas. respectively. Sleeping car services are available on most long overnight journeys from Madrid and Barcelona to other major Spanish cities as well as to Paris and Lisbon and on the Irún-La Coruña-Vigo line and the Orense-Paris line.

Note. Left luggage facilities have been withdrawn from all railroad stations.

BUDGET BUYS. You can obtain a "Blue Days" *(Díaz Azules)* leaflet from any RENFE office or station which shows the days on which you can travel at reduced rates—approximately 300 'blue' days a year! The best Blue Day reductions are 25% reduction on round trip fares; 50% discount for those of 65 and over; 50% discount for children 7–14 in family groups; discounts on Madrid-Barcelona journeys; reduced rates for taking your car on Auto-Expreso.

Another good budget rail buy is the *Chequetren,* available from any main station or RENFE office. This is a book of coupons that allows you 20,000 ptas. worth of rail travel at a cost of only 17,000 ptas. or 25,000 ptas. worth of rail travel for only 21,250 ptas. It can be used on any kind of train and in both 1st and 2nd class and by up to six different people.

BY BUS. The public bus network in Spain is extensive and many places not served by the railroad can be reached by bus. Fares are slightly cheaper than trains. Many of the larger towns have modern depots but in others buses leave from different places depending on their destination; best ask the local tourist office. Advance reservations are not essential. Bus travel is becoming increasingly popular and is both economical and efficient. Most bus depots still also provide left luggage facilities.

BY AIR. The main internal airline in Spain is *Iberia.* This connects Madrid with all the major Spanish cities as well as having flights both to and within the Balearics. *Aviaco,* the domestic airline, also flies to many of the principal Spanish cities and to the Balearics. Both Iberia and Aviaco have a number of flights between Barcelona and the principal Spanish cities.

Iberia also operates a shuttle service *(puente aéreo)* between Madrid and Barcelona. There are hourly, or in some cases half hourly, flights in both directions between 6 or 7 A.M. and midnight.

At presstime left luggage facilities had been withdrawn from all airports.

BY BOAT. *Compañía Transmediterránea* has frequent sailings from Barcelona, Valencia and Alicante to the Balearic Islands of Majorca, Ibiza and Minorca. Their handling agents in Britain are *Meliá Travel,* 12 Dover St., London W.1., and their offices in Spain are at Alcalá 63, Madrid; Via Layetana 2, Barcelona; Avda. Manuel Soto 15, Valencia; and Expl. España 2, Alicante.

Tickets can be bought from the above offices or from Avda. Ramón Carranza 26 in Cádiz. It is now possible to buy a combined rail and boat ticket from destinations on the mainland to the Balearics; details from RENFE offices.

There is a service along the Cantabrian coast—fortnightly from Pasajes and weekly from Bilbao—calling at Gijón, Villagarcía and Vigo. The return journey calls at Vigo, Gijón and Santander. Details from *Compañía Aucona* in the relevant ports or at Alcalá 63 or Pedro Muñoz Seco 2, Madrid.

Inter-island sailings in the Balearics are frequent; inquire locally.

Compañía Transmediterránea also have sailings from Almería and Málaga to Melilla and Ceuta on the North African coast. There are several ferry crossings and hydrofoil services each day from Algeciras to Melilla, Ceuta and Tangiers in Morocco.

 BY CAR. As with their railways, the Spanish have improved their road system greatly over the last few years. Roads are classified as A for *autopista* (toll motorway), N for *nacional* (main road) and C for the rather indeterminate small roads that can be found throughout the country. Those that have neither numbers nor letters are better avoided. Bear in mind, however, that these designations are sometimes a little confusing as parts of what is marked as an A road may well be an older and slower N road.

The autopistas from the French border down the Mediterranean coast to Cartagena, and from Irún on the French Atlantic border, to Bilbao and all those around Madrid are worth every peseta you'll pay in tolls as the traffic on the alternative N roads is dictated by slow moving trucks heading immense columns of cars in permanent traffic jams.

Driving is on the right and horns may not be used in cities, nor dipped headlights; neither may children ride in the front seats. City speed limits are signed, otherwise they are 120 kph (74 mph) on motorways, 90 kph (56 mph) elsewhere. The wearing of front seat belts is compulsory.

Spanish mechanics are excellent, but spare parts for some British or American cars are difficult to obtain. Documents required are: international driving permit and valid US or UK license, and international insurance certificate.

Gasoline (petrol) costs for 1983 were 86 ptas. a liter for *extra* (98 octane, at certain pumps only), 80 ptas. for *super* (96 octane), and 76 ptas. for *normal* (90 octane). Gas prices are set by the government and are uniform throughout mainland Spain.

Note: You are strongly advised not to leave *anything* in your car that might attract thieves.

Insurance. ASTES state-run tourist insurance, giving usual coverage plus legal defense (cheaper than a bail bond), is available through *Trafalgar Insurance Co. Ltd,* Trafalgar House, High St, Leatherhead, Surrey, or Nuñez de Balboa 101, Madrid. *Note:* Both the AA and the RAC advise members to take out a bail bond when motoring in Spain.

Car hire. *Avis,* with 40 car rental stations around the country, also has depots at all Spanish airports. *Hertz* is adequately represented as well; both offer their usual efficient service.

The cheapest car you can hire is a Seat Fura L or a Seat Panda. From *Avis* or *Hertz* these cost about 1,800 ptas. a day plus 16.5 ptas. per km. Alternatively, for approx. 16,000 ptas. you can hire the same car, with unlimited mileage for a commercial week (Mon. to Fri.).

Other car rental firms include *Ital, Europcar,* and *Budget,* all with offices throughout the country. Their rates are slightly lower than *Avis* or *Hertz.* For a Seat Panda the cheapest daily rate is *Ital's* at 1,300 ptas. plus 11.5 ptas. per km. Best rate for a commercial week is *Budget's* at 11,500 ptas.

ATESA has the most complete and modern car hire service in Spain, whether for chauffeur driven or self drive cars. Their offices are found throughout the country and their driver-mechanics not only know the country well but speak English. ATESA's main offices are at Batalla de Belchite 15, Madrid and Gran Vía 59, Madrid. They also have many offices at airports. They can also arrange supplementary services such as hotel reservations, transfers etc.

Rates in the Balearic islands are lower than in mainland Spain.

From Britain *Iberia* airlines offer Fly-Drive holidays in conjunction with *Atesa* car hire. *British Airways* will reserve an *Avis* car for you when you book on one of their flights to Spain.

Leaving Spain

 CUSTOMS. If you propose to take on your holiday any *foreign-made* articles, such as cameras, binoculars, expensive time-pieces and the like it is wise to put with your travel documents the receipt from the retailer or some other evidence that the item was bought in your home country. If you bought the article on a previous holiday abroad and have already paid duty on it, carry with you the receipt for this. Otherwise, on returning, you may be charged duty (for British residents, VAT as well).

Americans. U.S. residents may bring in $400 worth of foreign merchandise as gifts or for personal use without having to pay duty, provided they have been out of the country more than 48 hours and provided they have not claimed a similar exemption within the previous 30 days. Every member of a family is entitled to the same exemption, regardless of age, and the exemptions can be pooled.

The $400 figure is based on the fair retail value of the goods in the country where acquired. Included for travelers over the age of 21 are one liter of alcohol, 100 cigars (non-Cuban) and 200 cigarettes. Any amount in excess of those limits will be taxed at the port of entry, and may additionally be taxed in the traveler's home state. Only one bottle of perfume trademarked in the U.S. may be brought in. However, there is no duty on antiques or art over 100 years old—though you may be called upon to provide verification of the item's age. Write U.S. Customs Service, Washington D.C. 20229 for information regarding importation of automobiles and/or motorcycles. You may not bring home meats, fruits, plants, soil or other agricultural items.

Gifts valued at under $50 may be mailed to friends or relatives at home, but not more than one per day (of receipt) to any one addressee. These gifts must not include perfumes, tobacco or liquor.

If you are traveling with such foreign made articles as cameras, watches or binoculars that were purchased at home, it is best either to carry the receipt for them with you or to register them with U.S. Customs prior to departing. This will save much time (and potential aggravation) upon your return.

Canadians. In addition to personal effects, Canadians may bring into Canada duty-free: a maximum of 50 cigars, 200 cigarettes, 2 pounds of tobacco and 1 quart of liquor and 1 quart of wine, after being out of Canada for 7 days; and upon written declaration, may claim an exemption of $300 a year on duty-free articles. Lesser allowances for shorter trips. For mailed personal gifts, the same as for the U.S. except that the value allowed is $25. For full details ask for the Canada Customs leaflet 'I Declare'.

British subjects. There is now a two-tier allowance for duty-free goods brought into the UK, due to Britain's Common Market membership. The Customs and Excise Board warn that it is not advisable to mix the two allowances.

If you return from an EEC country (Belgium, Denmark, France, W. Germany, Holland, Ireland, Italy, Luxembourg, Greece) and goods were bought in one of those countries, duty-free allowances are:

300 cigarettes (or 150 cigarillos, or 75 cigars, or 400 g tobacco); 1.5 liters of strong spirits (over 38.8 proof), or 3 liters of other spirits (under 38.8 proof) or fortified or sparkling wines, plus 4 liters of still table wine; 75 g perfume and .375 liter toilet water; gifts to a value of £120.

If you return from a country outside the EEC, such as Spain, *or if the goods were bought in a duty-free shop on ship, plane or airport* the allowances are less:

200 cigarettes (or 100 cigarillos, or 50 cigars or 250 g tobacco); 1 liter of strong spirits (or 2 liters of other spirits or fortified wines) plus 2 liters of still table wine; 50 g perfume and .25 liter toilet water; plus gifts to a value of £28.

THE
SPANISH
SCENE

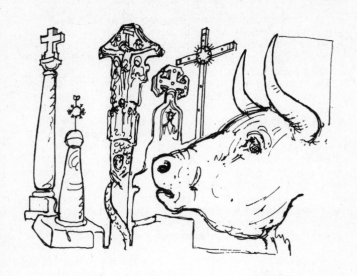

INTRODUCING SPAIN

The Land and Its People

South of the great barrier of the Pyrenees, accessible by road through only ten mountain passes, is the square-shaped Iberian Peninsula, picturesquely referred to in one ancient political treaty as the 'bull's hide'. Larger than France, nearly twice the size of the British Isles, the peninsula spreads out over 230,393 square miles and, although one geographical unit, is politically divided into two nations, Spain and Portugal.

Spain covers a territory six times that of Portugal and offers every type of climate and topography from the scorched bare hills of the south to the snow-capped Pyrenees in the northeast; from the sandy beaches of the Mediterranean to the rocky coast of the Atlantic; from ruddy Andalusia, with endless rows of ancient olive trees, to the tawny La Mancha tableland, dotted with windmills, and the austere Castilian

plateau, parched in summer and swept by cold winds from the Guadarrama mountain range in winter; from the rich low region around
Valencia, with its rice swamps and well-irrigated farms, to the sparsely
populated plains of Extremadura; from the lush sugar-cane area of
Motril to the fertile, verdant Basque region.

This remarkable variety in land and climate partly explains the
contrasts in regional character, physical aspect and customs of the
Spanish people. Nonetheless Spaniards have many fundamental characteristics that constitute a national spirit, and due to modern communications and television, some of these regional differences are
slowly disappearing.

Seven centuries of Holy Wars against the Moors, the counter-Reformation and a mysticism inherent in the Spanish character are among
the factors that contributed to make Spain a nation in which religious
fervor often nears fanaticism. The country of St. Teresa of Avila, St.
Ignatius Loyola and St John of the Cross has achieved a religious unity
stronger than that of other nations.

Another basic Spanish characteristic is pride, the fierce pride that
urged Don Quixote on to his famous exploits. And yet another is a form
of introspection, or *insimismo,* which accounts for many frequently
contradictory, often inexplicable Spanish attitudes.

Before the opening of Spain to tourism there was a wide belief that
the Spanish were fanatic, cruel and lazy, probably due to ingrained
ideas on the Spanish Inquisition, the Civil War, the tradition of
bullfighting, and the long siesta. Today's tourist will doubtless modify
these ideas when he sees the industrial upsurge in the north and in
many of the larger cities. Bullfights he can avoid, fanaticism and civil
strife he can compare with other countries today.

Marginal Europe

A prominent Spanish historian, Pedro Lain Entralgo, once defined
his country as "marginal Europe". And, until twenty years ago, the
definition held good. More than a hundred years of misrule, followed
by the devastating Civil War of 1936–9, with isolation during World
War II and in its wake, kept Spain literally cut off from the rest of the
world. Since the 'fifties, however, the face of Spain has changed. The
opening of the country's frontiers to new ideas and methods, and an
influx of foreign capital and tourists have brought comparative prosperity and, as a result, this nation has become a fast-moving and integral
part of modern Europe.

Spain's economy was on the verge of bankruptcy not too long ago,
until a pact for mutual defense and aid was signed with the United
States by which Spain ceded air and naval bases to the United States

and received in exchange some 450 million dollars and a billion dollars' worth of foodstuffs (due to the geography of the country and poor cultivation in the past, Spain has to import a large proportion of her food), bringing a speedy economic and industrial recovery as a result in its wake. New industries were set up throughout the country. Industrial plants already in existence were overhauled. Foreign money and know-how were welcomed into Spain.

All this triggered off a chain reaction that brought deep changes in the country's social structure and individual approach. It was then that Spain's tycoons of today, selfmade, ambitious businessmen, first came to the fore. They include men like Eduardo Barreiros, an able Galician in his fifties, who began with only a small, one-man mechanic's repair shop and now runs a successful auto and truck empire that has more than 26 branches throughout the country; Pedro Durán, who started from scratch and currently operates the country's largest shipbuilding business; José María Aristrain, a former bank employee who went into business on his own selling scrap iron and now has plants that produce more than 60,000 tons of steel per year; or José Meliá, who started with a modest travel agency after the war and now owns a chain of national and international hotels, travel agencies and car rental offices on the scale of the Hiltons and Sheratons. In the days of "marginal European Spain", there were no such opportunities for industrious, alert men unless they were born with silver spoons in their mouths.

Along with the economic boom, Spanish frontiers were opened to international tourism. Attracted by the slogan "Spain is different", tourists and vacationers by the million (36 million in 1980) began pouring into the country to discover a new land and bask in the sun in what Spaniards delightedly call a "pacific invasion". They brought money, new customs, and new trends, and they carried off unforgettable experiences and souvenirs. They also introduced new styles that broke down the age-old traditions of formality and conservative garb. It wasn't too long ago that the bikini was strictly taboo on all Spanish beaches, without exception. Today, whether worn by Spanish or foreign girls, it attracts little attention. Spanish girls don the latest styles; boys adopt internationally trendy clothes and hair styles, "massage parlors," sex shows, nudist beaches, and soft-core porn abound.

Prosperity has brought important sociological changes based on a far more solid foundation than that evidenced through mere superficial facts such as the tremendous leap Spaniards have made from the coal stove to bottled gas, from the family Vespa sidecar to the Seat 127 auto and bigger models, from the time-honored methods of threshing in the fields to the use of modern machinery, or from the mere fact that they are eating and dressing better.

A major change was brought by television, which has given Spaniards a wider outlook on life. Traveling around the country, the visitor will be amazed to see TV antennae perched atop the thatched roofs of adobe huts in a precarious yet nonetheless efficient way.

New Look in the Economy

In 1964, for the first time in her history, Spain ceased to be primarily an agricultural country, and today many more people are employed in industry than in the fields. This brought a basic change in Spain's population pattern, as some 400,000 men and women a year flocked to industrial centers in search of better wages, despite the general improvement, while others went abroad to work for higher wages than they would get at home, mostly to France, Belgium and Germany, at the rate of 30,000 a year.

The main industrial magnets that draw workers from rural areas, where machines have taken over the work on the land, are the Basque region, Avilés and Gijón in Asturias (heavy industries), around Barcelona (textiles, chemicals, automobiles), Cádiz (shipping), Valladolid (automobiles), and numerous mineral mines throughout the country. Madrid, once a quiet, drowsy city of sidewalk coffee houses and easy tempo, has become a bustling metropolis with an industrial belt some 32 km (20 miles) deep encircling it and changing its skyline.

With an automobile industry that started to boom in the late 1960s and continued through the 1970s, Spaniards are moving about as never before. Gone are the days when the average Spaniard's weekly pleasure trip consisted of a subway ride to the bullfight or the soccer stadium. With new mobility the Spaniard is not only getting out of the city on weekends, traveling, both at home and abroad (around 18 million Spaniards traveled outside Spain per year in the early 1980s), but he is taking to outdoor sports—fishing, hunting, golf and tennis—all sports that until recently were enjoyed only by a handful of wealthy people.

But the new face of Spain also includes endless political jockeying, constant strikes, inflation, unemployment, a significant increase in crime, and persistent political terrorism no longer contained in the Basque region but spilling over into other parts of the country.

THE SPANISH WAY OF LIFE

Old Folklore, New Outlook

Spanish life has undergone a profound and rapid change in the last two decades, and the processes of transformation and modernization, which began in the big cities and the coastal regions, are penetrating into the hinterland of a country that was formerly one of the least advanced in Europe. All over Spain, the sense of eagerness for change is evident, and as a consequence the Spanish way of life, once thought immutable, is assuming a different aspect. Sociologists, historians, politicians and economists have their own explanations for the transformation, but even the casual visitor can witness the fascinating drama of an entire nation, once backward, pushed on by an irrepressible urge to make up for lost time.

In the big cities, and especially among the younger generation, Spain now has very little catching-up to do. In Madrid, Barcelona and certain provincial capitals you will see people whose lifestyles and appearance proclaim the impact of Progress in all its aspects, especially the material ones. Among such as these, the only distinguishing and unmistakably Spanish characteristic is the national personality, made up of gaiety, conviviality, excitability and a confidence which can easily be mistaken for aggressiveness or brashness.

Yet modern ways have by no means worked through the whole population. The big cities still have colorful quarters—and not all of these are tourist-traps—where the old life is still being lived. Here, and in the rural areas, the old Spain lingers on, to the accompaniment of a wealth of religious and folkloric events unsurpassed by any other European country.

In the rural areas, the ass and the mule, still in evidence, symbolize the old ways, and the old customs die hard. Nevertheless, these people are aware of what has been happening in the world outside them.

Only some twenty years ago, coffee house and bar life "for men only" was common; smoking in public, for a girl, was considered little less than a crime, and so was going out without a chaperon. But, as their country emerged from self-centered preoccupations, young men left the dusty clubs, dark coffee houses and smoky taverns for outdoor life, taking up sports and dating, American-style, while the girls burst forth from their protective cocoon, protected by eagle-eyed *dueñas,* to take advantage of life.

The career girl now takes her part in Spanish life along with the salesgirls, waitresses, seamstresses and typists who have been familiar for years. Daughters of middle-class families often take a university course and graduate. Many of them work in laboratories, libraries, research institutes and business. A number of women have also been successful as doctors, lawyers, journalists, writers, painters and musicians. They are in diplomacy, law, the police force, business management, and even in the Cortes, the Spanish Parliament. The image of the Spanish woman whose only aim in life is to catch a husband and raise a large family of children is disappearing, to be replaced by that of an enterprising, energetic young woman; the latter is inclined to devote less time to the hairdresser's shop and gossip in a coffee house and more to the office and outdoor sports, while her children attend public schools and outdoor camps.

In a like vein, the image of the lazy, dark-suited, patent-leather-shod young man lounging against a corner street lamp or playing dominos and cards inside a smoky coffee house has been replaced by that of an ambitious youth in jeans and loafers grabbing life by the horns, in true *torero* style, and trying hard to master it.

Chivalry and Hospitality

Nonetheless, old customs, manners and traditions have not faded away completely; they are merely being blended with a new way of life. Most Spaniards still feel it's no compliment to tell a girl she is intelligent or learned; the only fit compliment for any woman, the majority feel, is to tell her she is beautiful. Girls are still brought up to expect that—just as boys, even if they plan to go in for an office career or scientific research in a lab, are still reared to consider physical prowess as the badge of manhood. This helps to account for the girl's self-assurance; she has been told since babyhood that she is *guapa*. It also accounts for much of the boy's bravado, since his aim is to live up to the reputation of being *macho*.

Hospitality and courtesy to foreigners was at one time so widespread that you could almost travel around the country without opening your wallet, if you didn't mind taking advantage of the situation. This is hardly the case today. Nonetheless, much of the old *galantería*, or chivalry, has survived and, as a rule, Spaniards are always happy to help a stranded foreigner. If your car breaks down while you're touring the country, you may find the entire nearby village will turn out to give you a helping hand, and you'll have a hard time paying them back for whatever they may have done for you. As in all countries geared to an influx of tourists, tips are now hoped for and expected in Spain but, unless you are helped by a doorman or one of the many others who make their living by such personal services, it's not always essential to tip with money. A cigar or a cigarette is often acceptable. In the country areas a cash tip is still considered abasing: a hearty hand-shake and a smiling *gracias,* or, if the case calls for it *muchísimas gracias,* will do the trick and prove far more effective. Obviously this does not apply to gypsies, who may pester you anywhere, particularly in the southern part of the country; they may be safely ignored even if they threaten to "put a curse" on you. As for beggars, their numbers had begun to drop, but now with today's problems of unemployment, many are again appearing on the streets of larger cities like Madrid and Barcelona.

Other typical Spanish ways are either on the way out or remain visible only on the surface of daily life, for the sake of appearances. One, for instance, is the age-old custom of never seeming to be in a hurry or to move under pressure. Things in Spain today are getting done, and done well. Highways and factories are being built, and modern apartment houses, public buildings and luxury hotels are going up, changing the skyline of every town. Thermal and nuclear power stations are in production, with more being planned. All these works are efficiently maintained by their industrious builders. But, when pushed, the Spaniard comes to a stubborn halt.

Social Life and the Siesta

The life of the coffee house, another aspect of Spanish life that played such a prominent role in Spain's intellectual and political history, has undergone a significant transformation but gives no indication of expiring. Most of the smoke-laden, plush-upholstered, spacious coffee houses, featuring strong black coffee and strong anise liqueur, have now given way to shiny American-modeled cafeterias offering malted milk, doughnuts and hot dogs. The cafeteria, too, serves as a rendezvous for the *tertulia* (literally, "chat") crowd, which moves out onto the sidewalk in summer, the *tertulistas* mingling with loafers and jointly ogling the pretty *señoritas* passing by.

Although in the past you were unlikely to be invited into a Spanish home on short acquaintance, in the larger cities like Madrid and Barcelona, with their modern, functional apartment houses and the example of the rest of Europe, the younger generation is now opening its streamlined homes to guests with cocktail parties and buffet suppers but in the smaller cities and towns, the center of social life is still the coffee house, where the forgotten art of conversation still lives on.

Even the siesta, that typically Spanish institution, with fame so farflung that it holds its own place in English language dictionaries, is becoming a thing of the past. For centuries, Spain's daily routine was based on exceptionally late eating hours, possibly because of the warm climate. Nevertheless, Spanish workers do not get up any later in the morning than workers in any other southern European country. Factories open at eight in the morning, offices at nine. But lunch is usually around 2 P.M. and dinner rarely before ten in the evening. Obviously, with such late hours, Spaniards never get to bed until hours after the eleven o'clock deadline of other societies. Outside Madrid movies and theaters start at about ten o'clock in the evening. Therefore, if a theatergoer wants to get to work the next morning, he has no more than six or seven hours' sleep. Recurrently over the past few years, there have been official attempts to cut out the siesta, with a call for a continuous eight-hour day's work and earlier entertainment hours. But they have not yet been successful.

The growth of Spain's big cities, with their wide suburban belts and long distances from home to place of work, plus insufficient public transportation and an acute shortage of parking space in town, is now cutting the siesta to a much more limited time. Offices and shops may still close from 1.30 to 4.30 in the afternoon, but the three-hour break, once quite enough for a relaxed lunch and peaceful siesta, now gives one barely time to reach home, eat, nap a bit, and get back to work. Spanish dietitians who claim that the post-prandial nap and a lack of exercise are responsible for many digestive complaints say that the decline of the siesta, along with a revival of popular sports (up to now Spaniards were chiefly sports spectators and not participants), have brought a notable decrease in liver and gall bladder ailments, once the major complaints of the middle and upper classes.

Another aspect of Spanish life that has undergone a drastic change is domestic service. In former times, no Spanish housewife, no matter how humble her station, would have found life worth living without at least one maid, or *criada*. As the education level rises, and factory and office jobs become more abundant, servants are more expensive and harder to get. The cloistered mentality of the village girl of the past, who was content to find a family that would lift her out of poverty, clothe her, house her, and feed her, in addition to paying her a small sum of spending money, is disappearing. Wages for servants are sky-rocketing, and in the supermarkets (another innovation that has brightened the life of Spanish women) it's practically impossible to distinguish the maid from the housewife in dress and manner.

One facet of life in Spain today that the unwary visitor should be warned about is the noise. It is quite possible to go to bed in an attractive small-town hotel, hoping to be bright-eyed and bushy-tailed for the next day's sightseeing, only to have all hell break loose in the square outside when the youth of the town decide to try out their motor-cycles. It may go on for hours, so try to ensure in advance that you get a quiet room.

Abundance of Folklore

You cannot be anywhere in Spain for longer than a week without encountering some form of folk festival, and, if you are to understand and enjoy it in all its many colorful and strange manifestations, you must first realize that it is not a case of the natives dressing up in order to put on a "quaint" show for your benefit. They don their local costumes and dance their centuries-old dances because they are proud of the costumes and enjoy the dances. They go on pilgrimages for spiritual benefit; on Good Friday the penitents walk barefoot in black pointed hoods because they are, for the moment, sharing emotionally and directly in the sufferings of Christ.

This tremendous simplicity and sincerity imbues with vitality the many thousands of *romerías, verbenas, ferias, fiestas, fallas,* processions and Passion Plays, which occur literally all over the country almost throughout the year. Perhaps the real secret of the passionate reality of their presentation lies in the fact that no Spaniard is ever self-conscious or embarrassed—in fact there is no word for it in their language, "ashamed" or "timid" being the nearest.

The motive power behind nearly all these manifestations of popular custom is religious, though in many cases it is not difficult to see that the Catholic Church is its early centuries frequently adapted local pagan customs and shrines. Having, for example, discovered that they could not prevent certain villagers from paying their respects to the nymph or dryad of some particular freshwater spring, the Church metamorphosed the spirit into the Virgin Mary, and re-named the spring the Fountain of Our Lady of such-and-such, thus encouraging instead of forbidding the villagers to continue their existing reverence for the place. As a result you will find countless Christian shrines at freshwater springs, particularly in Andalusia, that were objects of superstition or worship long before the birth of Christ.

The realism which is such a striking characteristic of Spaniards and makes them accept without any sophistication the fact that man is composed of body and soul results in material jollifications being mingled with religious ceremonies on the feast days of saints and other liturgical occasions. Bullfights, dancing, music, fireworks, picnicking and other pleasures are the order of the day, except in Holy Week, when people go into mourning for the death of Christ and solemnity prevails.

It would not be out of place if we mentioned that the tremendous spectacle of the *Semana Santa* (Holy Week) really does mean a great deal to those taking part, and to the Spanish onlookers, so be careful not to offend by laughing, smoking or talking, or by failing to take off your hat while a procession is passing. But for the following festivals, while religion provides the excuse, it does not set the tone.

The chief types of Spanish celebrations are these:

Romería. An English dictionary translates this as "a picnic excursion to some shrine or beauty spot" and although it is a pity that in English we have to use nine words instead of one, the translation is fair. These, with their long cavalcades of horsemen, belong essentially to the country districts.

The most famous romería is the gypsy pilgrimage to El Rocío, southeast of Almonte in the province of Huelva, held during Whitsun. In the church is a small statue of the Virgin Mary, believed to have miraculous powers.

For a week before Whitsun, roads in Andalusia leading to Almonte and El Rocío are crowded with men on horseback, escorting white covered wagons garlanded with flowers, Manila shawls and paper streamers, and containing such of the womenfolk as are not riding pillion behind the men. A separate cavalcade sets out from each town where there is a Lodge of the Brotherhood of the Virgin of El Rocío, and at the head of each is the special "sinless" cart of the Virgin, covered with white silk, embroidered with gold.

As they make their way slowly through the endless olive groves of Andalusia, there is the continual sound of singing, castanets, guitars and laughter. After religious ceremonies on Whit Sunday morning, the rest of the day is spent in dancing, resting and bullfighting, and, on Monday, the slow journey home is begun.

Verbena. Translated in the dictionary as "a night festival on the eve of a religious holiday". These are associated with towns or separate districts in large cities. Being open-air affairs, demanding the still, purple-velvet nights of high summer, they reach a peak around August 15—the day of the Assumption of the Virgin Mary.

Falla. In medieval times a bonfire of the accumulated wood shavings of the carpenters' guilds, burned on St. Joseph's day; it is now a festival for which effigies are made solely for burning. Fallas are the speciality (though not exclusively so) of Valencia, the best known, which is held from March 12 to 19. All pretense at serious work is laid aside, most offices and some shops close after lunch, and all wheeled traffic is diverted from the streets and squares where monumental, cleverly painted figures of cardboard, papier mâché and wood have been erected. Some of these are caricatures of famous people, and some are of less popular officials of the community.

Amid scenes of revelry that would undoubtedly surprise St. Joseph by their abandonment the figures are set afire on the last night of the week's celebrations and, by the light of these fires, there is all-night dancing in attractive local costumes. There are also floats decorated with thousands of carnations, enthroning "Queens of Beauty" wearing the *mantilla* over a high comb; fireworks, illuminated balloons, bullfights, a dozen orchestras all playing different (but always fortissimo) music, battles of flowers—anything in fact that can be relied upon to make the loudest possible noise, for to all Spaniards, since they are extroverts, happiness and noise are only different words for the same thing.

Feria. Meaning Fair, this may suggest commercial activities, but you will see little buying or selling of anything other than drinks, though in some rural areas they are the occasion for horse and cattle markets.

The Seville feria, at the end of April, is probably the most famous, though that of Jerez de la Frontera at the beginning of May is more spectacular. Jerez is in the land of the horse-lover, and cavalcades of magnificent animals are one of the features. The men wear short, tight-fitting jackets, soft leather boots and wide brimmed Córdoban hats, while the women, bowered in flowers, ride in smartly turned-out open carriages, wearing the high comb and lace mantilla on their heads, and the huge, flounced, brightly colored skirts that are traditional in Andalusia. Naturally there are bullfights, horse races, dancing in the streets, and the best sherry and the second-best cognac in the world for a few pesetas a glass, always assuming that the notoriously hospitable Andalusians will let you pay.

The Corpus Christi fiestas held on the second Thursday after Whitsun all over the country include a religious procession, but religion seems to be the excuse for, rather than a restraint upon, the holiday spirit. Particularly grandiose Corpus Christi fiestas are staged in Toledo and Granada. A charming one takes place in Sitges on the Catalan shore. On the eve, girls go from house to house with huge baskets collecting flowers and, this being both June and Spain, they soon have tens of thousands of blooms, principally carnations and the purple bougainvillaea. Early on next morning every family, from grandma to the smallest child, sets to work using the petals of these flowers to form intricate and beautiful designs on the narrow stretch of road outside their front door. Later, money prizes are given for the best designs.

No foot may disturb these works of art until the Blessed Sacrament is carried at the head of a long procession over this mile or so of flowery carpet, the long line of gaily dressed men and women falling to their knees on the pavement as it passes with its escort of chanting priests, banners and religious statues. Once the procession has passed, bells clash, fireworks explode, and rings are formed to dance the *sardana*. The 6-meter-high (20-foot) plaster figures of King Ferdinand and Queen Isabella, wearing crimson velvet and their golden crowns, can then be seen jiggling around among the other dancers on the shoulders of the local strong men. Queen Isabella's long, flowing locks are real, having been donated by penitents. Soon Their Majesties, having opened the dance, return with dignity to the Town Hall.

Mystery Plays *(camuñas)* are performed at Toledo during Corpus Christi, but at Elche, 42 kilometers (26 miles) from Alicante, a particularly interesting and ancient one is performed on August 14 and 15, with 13th-century music of great beauty. Each role in the play is the property of a particular local family, which must produce a member to play that part or lose this jealously guarded privilege.

Processions and Pilgrimages

The Semana Santa (Holy Week) is celebrated by processions of varying magnificence and fame in every town, village and hamlet in Spain. Those that take place in Seville have attracted tourists from all over the world for many years, since Andalusia is at its colorful best in spring and Seville, as the capital, provides comfort and a wide choice of amusements. This is a good enough reason for choosing Seville, though if you want to see a version of the same thing from the Spanish rather than the tourist point of view, Granada offers a more moving spectacle.

From Maundy Thursday until Saturday night some people wear black; most cinemas, theaters and other places of amusement are closed, and even private cars, trams and buses are not permitted to circulate in some or all of the streets. Images of saints or, more often, tableaux representing scenes from the last days before the Crucifixion, often with a macabre emphasis upon suffering and pain, are carried through the darkened streets on Friday night. Hundreds of candles, however, illuminate the gold, jewels and priceless silks and brocades worn by such famous figures as Seville's Vírgen de la Macarena, and in single file on either side of the procession march the bare-footed penitents, their eyes glinting through the narrow slits in their high, pointed black or white hoods.

In Granada the only sound is the tolling of the cathedral bell as for the dead, the sharp dramatic beat of a single drum to set the pace of the procession, and the occasional sound of weeping.

Pilgrimages are obviously of a purely religious character. Two of the most famous are those to the Black Virgin, wooden image supposedly carved by St. Luke, and located in the Benedictine Monastery on the sacred mountain of Montserrat, 51 km (32 miles) from Barcelona, which take place on April 27 and on September 8; and that to the tomb of Spain's patron, Santiago (St James) in Santiago de Compostela, 66 km (41 miles) from La Coruña, on July 25.

Costumes

No less striking than the pronounced contrasts in climate, scenery, language and racial origin in different areas of Spain are the differences in regional costumes worn at the fiestas. Not only has every province completely distinctive costumes for both men and women, but often those of individual villages in the same province, only a score of miles apart, will be found to bear no resemblance to one another. Except for the familiar Andalusian costume of high comb, mantilla, sleeveless bodice and wide flounced skirts with large white spots, it is safe to say that nearly all Spanish regional costumes clearly reveal Moorish influence.

In some districts, particularly in the north, this influence is not immediately obvious; in others, as with the embroidered linen cloths with which the women of La Alberca in Salamanca almost completely cover their chins and mouths, the *yashmak,* or veil, of Islam is unmistakable. In almost all cases the head is covered, as are the heads of Moorish women, with embroidered cloths. The men's costumes are, for the most part, more sober, and have a practical value for their owners as shepherds, horsemen, mountaineers or land workers, but, when it comes to the question of male splendor, do not forget the bullfighter's costume of tight-fitting silken hose, knee-length pants and stiff bullion-encrusted jacket, known as the *traje de luces,* or, quite simply, the "suit of lights."

Folk Music and Dancing

Nearly all countries possess traditional songs and dances that have been preserved from ancient times, but Spanish folk music is still developing, with new *sardana* and *flamenco* tunes being composed, played and danced to throughout the country. The tourist would perhaps not recognize the new from the old, as the traditional form is jealously retained by public opinion.

As for Spanish dancing, there is no lack of partisans for the *muneira* of Galicia, the *giraldilla* of León, the *fandango* of Almería, or the *jota* of Aragón. All are dances of individuality and charm, each with its own distinctive music, but two styles of Spanish folk music and dancing are outstanding. These are the Andalusian flamenco, both the *cante jondo* and *cante grande*—fiery, passionate, strongly suggestive of Moorish influence—and the lively but subtle Catalan sardana.

Nearly all the best flamenco is to be seen and heard in spontaneous performances by nomadic gypsies near their campfires, or in some obscure *taberna.* However, for those who have neither the time nor the inclination to wait for such fortuitous circumstances, flamenco is included in almost every Spanish music-hall show or nightclub entertainment, and there is always plenty of it at any Andalusian fiesta or feria. The dance, with its fierce stamping of heels and rattle of castanets, is more or less familiar to everyone, but few foreigners realize the supreme importance of the sinuous hand, finger and wrist movements, which almost recall the Balinese ritual dancer, whose hands alone relate the story.

The music accompanying the cante jondo, the deep song describing the singer's emotions, is usually provided by a guitar—harsh and intense music, with an underlying sultry beat, that seems to be that of the gypsy's own pulse, emphasized by the rhythmic clapping of hands. The song often begins with a single long-drawn-out cry at the maximum pitch of the lungs, overwhelmingly recalling the *muezzin,* the first cry of the Moslem *imam* from his high minaret, calling the faithful to prayer.

The sardana is about as different from flamenco as is possible. The reed pipe, flute, oboe or woodwind, with its clear but nasal whine, at times almost resembling bagpipes, is dominant in the sardana music, which, however, is intensely vital and often plaintive.

The dance is strangely intricate, involving a fixed number of steps to every bar of music, and the changing of the position of the hands every so many bars. It is danced with hands joined in a circle. Once a circle of four or five forms, it may be enlarged to forty or so in a matter of moments, as more and more people join in and other circles often form within or around the first one. The greater part of the dance does not move the individual from his place, though all the time he is carrying out his intricate toe and heel pattern and then suddenly, as the music becomes louder, the rings begin to spin, often in different directions and one within another, but always still maintaining the same step, so that you may see a thousand heads rise and fall together in swift rhythmical movement.

The sardana is at its best in the open, and you can see it danced in the streets of any Catalan town or village during its Fiesta Mayor, in Cadaqués, and before Barcelona's cathedral at noon every summer Sunday. There are competitions during August in the beautiful Costa Brava town of S'Agaró.

SPAIN'S GRANDIOSE HISTORY

A Record Written in Blood and Gold

When you pass through Castile, the land of castles, and the wind-swept plains of La Mancha, where Don Quixote and his squire met with their adventures, or when you visit Seville and Granada, with their magnificent Moorish palaces, Córdoba of the Caliphs, El Cid's Valencia, Toledo and Madrid, the past and present capitals, you cannot fail to be touched by a sense of Spain's colorful history. Any attempt to understand the Spanish people would fail without some knowledge of their background and of the historical events and deeds inside and outside the country, which shaped it over the centuries.

The Beginnings

It is impossible to identify with any degree of certitude the very earliest inhabitants of Spain, but in the early Stone Age two quite separate cultures flourished concurrently: one was in the Cantabrian–Pyrenean region, the other in the Mediterranean area. The people of these cultures reached a certain degree of civilization and sensitivity; they left as evidence various examples of cave art, notably the paintings at Altamira, near Santander on the north coast. After them came a succession of cultures, identifiable through the different artifacts brought to light by archeology.

The earliest tribes in Spain for whom there is a definite historical record were the Iberians and the Celts, who left all manner of visible testimony of their passage. Many present-day Spanish settlements trace their origins back to these founding fathers.

About 3,000 years ago, the seafaring Phoenician and Greek traders began to settle and build cities along the Mediterranean coast of Spain. The earliest was Cádiz and subsequently other ports were established, notably Barcelona, Málaga and Denia (Phoenician), Valencia and Rosas (Greek). Ampurias, on the Bay of Rosas, is the finest excavation of these and the Roman developments (see Costa Brava chapter).

By the 3rd century B.C., the Carthaginians were established in Spain, and the second Punic War arose from Rome's jealousy of their expansion on the peninsula. Hannibal destroyed the Roman-allied town of Sagunto in 218 B.C., whereupon Rome declared war, thus leading to Hannibal's famed crossing of the Pyrenees and Alps into Italy. In 210, Scipio Africanus landed at Ampurias, and the following year he captured New Carthage (Cartagena), the Carthaginian capital on the Iberian Peninsula. This event and Hannibal's death ended the Carthaginian ascendancy, and around 201, the Roman colonization of Spain began; it was to last for several centuries.

The Romans

The inhabitants of early Spain began by fiercely resisting the Roman invaders, and none more so than the people of Numancia, near Soria. In 134 B.C., this city held the Roman legions at bay for eight months, before firing their buildings and committing mass suicide in the flames rather than submit to Rome. The remains of the Roman-rebuilt city can still be seen.

Roman civilization left a deep mark on Spain, affecting above all the language, laws, and architecture. Roman bridges (Alcántara), arches (Medinaceli), aqueducts (Segovia) and roadbeds are still in existence

today. Spain provided the Roman Empire with an impressive array o
emperors, poets and philosophers, including Trajan, Martial and Sene
ca.

Christianity and the Visigoths

From the 1st century A.D., Christianity attracted fervent converts i
Spain. Traditionally, it was St. James the Apostle who preached th
Gospel there. During the period of the Roman persecutions, countles
Spanish martyrs died for their faith, which only acquired more celebri
ty as a result, drawing more followers.

In the 3rd century the barbarians living in the territories to th
northeast began invading the Roman Empire. By the 5th century th
Visigoths had spread to Spain, conquered the Vandals, and establishe
a rule that was to last until the Moors arrived in 711. The Visigoth
were Arians: to put an end to the religious disputes between Goths an
Hispano-Romans King Reccared in 587 announced his Catholicism
followed by most of his court, members of the heretic priesthood, an
the Visigothic population. After 600, all Jews had to accept baptism
which is one of the reasons why they later welcomed the Moslem
invasion. Despite the Visigothic rule, Roman tradition and organiza
tion survived generally, and Latin was the vernacular language.

In 711 the Visigothic period ended abruptly. Disintegration had se
in internally: the elective system of monarchy and the disaffection o
many segments of population, notably the serfs and the Jews, mad
collapse inevitable. The invasion came from the south, and the last o
the Goths, King Roderick, died (it is thought) fighting Tarik's Moorish
army at the battle of the Guadalete.

The conquest was almost immediate and total. Resistance survived
in isolated pockets, but the only one to go down to history lay in the
northern mountains of Asturias. There, in a cave at Covadonga, nea
Cangas de Onís, the Hispano-Gothic survivors met to elect Pelayo a
their king. They defeated a punitive Moorish expedition in 718, and the
Reconquest was launched; it was to end with the capture of Granada
in 1492.

Moors and Christians

The Moors boldly fought their way across the Pyrenees into France
where their advance was halted by Charles Martel's Frankish army in
732. The Franks entered Spain during the reign of Charlmagne, one o
whose campaigns was concluded by the disastrous battle at Roncesvalles (778) which inspired much medieval literature, including the
Song of Roland. Charlemagne ultimately conquered northeastern

Spain and set up Marches, or boundaries, against the Moors, Barcelona becoming independent early in the 9th century.

The Moors of Spain were ruled from the Caliphate of Baghdad until 756, when Abd al-Rahman proclaimed himself an independent emir. He made Córdoba his capital, and built the famous mosque. In 929, Abd al-Rahman III became caliph, and made Córdoba one of the largest, richest and most illustrious intellectual centers of its time.

The various Christian kingdoms grew out of nuclei of resistance. They conquered and recolonized more and more territory and thrust their way southwards, León to the Duero, Navarre to the Ebro. Aragón and the county of Barcelona toward the Mediterranean. The colonists defended their new lands with castles, and from this comes the name of the County of Castile, which separated from the mother-kingdom of León under Count Fernán González in the 10th century and was to grow to pre-eminence in the peninsula.

But there was much internal discord in the Christian communities. Different rulers also warred with other monarchs, dissipating their energies and seriously impeding the Reconquest. The Moorish leader al-Mansur turned the tide, striking terror into the hearts of the Christian colonists with his *razzias*, looting campaigns in the Christian lands. He captured Santiago de Compostela, the great pilgrimage shrine reputed to hold the remains of Spain's patron, St James, and sacked Barcelona, Burgos and León.

After his death Moslem unity began to disintegrate, and their territories split into small autonomous kingdoms known as *taifas*. The once dazzling splendor of the Caliphate of Córdoba became but a dim memory. The Christian kings were able to take advantage of the situation to play off one Moorish ruler against another, and to make vassals of many of them.

El Cid and the Reconquest

The great semi-legendary hero of the Spanish Reconquest was Rodrigo (or Ruy) Díaz de Vivar (c. 1043–99), better known as El Cid Campeador. A knight of Burgos, whose cathedral holds his tomb and that of his wife Jimena, he fought for both Castile and the Moors, eventually becoming ruler of Valencia. He became the national hero of Spain, and his deeds, much romanticized, have been told by various writers throughout the centuries. The earliest version is probably the *Cantar de mio Cid,* dating from the early 13th century.

The Castilians won a key victory when Alfonso VI regained Toledo in 1085; the Aragonese won Zaragoza, whilst Catalonia took Lérida and Tarragona. The union of Aragón and Catalonia was achieved through the marriage of Petronilla, heiress to the Aragonese throne, with Ramón Berenguer IV, Count of Barcelona.

In the face of the Christian advance, the taifa kings sought aid from Morocco, and the warlike, fanatically religious Berber tribesmen known as the Almoravides came, soon claiming sovereignty over the Spanish Moors.

The Almoravides posed a real threat to the Christian Reconquest, and they were followed by another wave of Berber invaders, the Almohades. Now the Moslem opposition was reunited and extended its hold over southern Spain. They routed Alfonso VIII at Alarcos in 1195, but in 1212 Alfonso enlisted the newly formed military orders, the Knights of Santiago and Calatrava, to win the great battle of Las Navas de Tolosa.

Two Great Kings

The two great monarchs of the 13th-century Reconquest were Ferdinand III (St. Ferdinand), King of Castile and León (1230–52) and Jaime I of Aragon (1213–76). Jaime won the island kingdom of Majorca in 1229, and in 1238 recovered Valencia, ceding Murcia to Castile.

Ferdinand brought the same energy and fervor to the Castilian war effort. He added Córdoba, Jaén and Seville to his kingdom, began the codification of Spanish law, and refounded the University of Salamanca. He was canonized in 1671.

But the old rivalries and dissensions delayed the completion of the task of Reconquest for another two and a half centuries. Alfonso X, the Wise, was much more effective as a thinker than as a statesman; the 14th- and 15th-century rulers wasted most of their energies on internal strife. Henry of Trastámara, by the assassination of his half-brother Peter the Cruel, gained the throne, and his son John I, after his defeat at Aljubarrota in 1385, was forced to recognize Portugal's definitive independence. In the next century the reign of Henry IV was fraught with scandal—he was variously accused of impotence and homosexuality—and with bloody civil wars over the question of the right of his daughter to succeed to the throne. She was nicknamed La Beltraneja, because of her resemblance to the royal favorite Don Beltrán de la Cueva, and the throne went to Henry's half-sister Isabella on his death in 1474. Her marriage to Ferdinand, heir to the Aragonese throne, finally united the two great kingdoms of Castile and Aragón in 1479.

Culture in the Middle Ages

The Middle Ages in Spain are considered to have begun with the invasions of the barbarian hordes and to have ended with the reign of the Catholic monarchs. But the period is far too intricate for it to lend itself to a summary judgment. It may be said to have been accompanied at the beginning by the almost total eclipse of all culture, right after the fall of the Roman Empire. During the early years of the Reconquest, the cultural life of the Christian population was meagre. In contrast, the Arabs excelled in the study of arts, letters, and sciences, and enjoyed highly sophisticated patterns of social life. From the standpoint of civilization, the Spanish Moors were indeed on an advanced level, superior not only to that of the peninsular Christian kingdoms but also to those of other European nations.

As the Reconquest proceeded, urban population grew, relationships between the Christian kingdoms became more stable and there were truces with the Moors; customs, accordingly, became much less barbarous with the progress of culture. In the monasteries, where the traditions of ancient learning were kept alive, arts, letters, and even some sciences were cultivated. Universities were founded, some of them attaining great renown, such as those of Salamanca, Montpellier (then in Aragón) and Barcelona.

Alfonso the Wise, son of St. Ferdinand, lent a tremendous impetus to culture. In his School of Toledo, he pooled the resources of Christian, Hebrew and Arabic learning, contributing to the advance and dissemination of culture throughout Europe. His name is linked with those of Gonzalo de Berceo (the first known Castilian poet); of Juan Ruiz, the Archpriest of Hita; of Raimundo Lulio, or Llull, the Illustrious Doctor; and of the Marquis of Santillana; of the Infante Juan Manuel; and of Ausias-March, all of whom in their time were eminent exponents of Christian learning in the Castilian, Galician and Catalan idioms. In the Arab kingdoms, many famous names stand out, both Arabs and Jews having contributed immeasurably to the furtherance of universal culture. The Cordoban Maimónides and the Arabo-Andalusian poets are among the most outstanding examples. Spectacular progress was made in the fields of medicine, astronomy, mathematics and history. Córdoba and, later on, Toledo were centers for the promulgation of learning.

Of all the arts, architecture left the most traces. Only a very few Visigoth churches survive, curious rather than impressive, but the Moors erected splendid fortresses, palaces and mosques, the wonders of their age like the great mosque of Córdoba and the Alhambra of Granada. The Christians followed as the Reconquest gathered momentum, first converting what they found, but soon building great Romanesque monasteries and churches, while most of the castles bear the imprint of the Gothic.

In the economic domain, the times were too troubled, locally and nationally, to favor steady development, and with the very complicated tariff restrictions on trade it is surprising that industry was able to grow at all. Agriculture suffered from unfair competition with stock-raising; the guild of sheep-farmers, known as the Mesta, was able to drive and graze their migrant flocks almost wherever they wished in the kingdom. This privileged industry, and the introduction of the fine-wooled Merino breed of sheep from Africa, gave rise to Castile's supremacy in the wool-trade and ultimately to an important wool-processing industry in some Castilian towns. Sea trade grew: on the north coast the important port of Bilbao was founded, and in the Mediterranean Barcelona became a vitally important commercial and harbor city, maintaining numerous consulates along Mediterranean shores.

Catholic Kings and Spanish Expansion

The reign of Ferdinand and Isabella, the Catholic Monarchs, saw the end of the great task of the Reconquest when the state of Granada fell to the Christians. The last Moorish king, Boabdil, handed the keys to his city over in an emotional ceremony in 1492. This was Spain's *annus mirabilis,* for the same year an explorer and seafarer whose birthplace and nationality remain controversial to this day, Christopher Columbus, plied the ocean in Castilian ships with Castilian seamen, discovered America, and claimed it in the name of his sponsors, the Catholic Monarchs. On October 12, an ordinary seaman named Rodrigo de Triana descried land from his perch high in the crow's-nest, and this day is celebrated throughout the Spanish-speaking world.

Also during this reign, the structure of the Spanish state acquired a definitive form, attaining the summit of its power and glory. Administrative and legal systems were organized, the nobles and the army were brought into line, and the life of the country received a powerful new nationwide stimulus. But at the same time, the Inquisition flourished, instituted by Isabella and organized by Torquemada, notorious for his cruelty. In their fervent religious zeal, the Catholic Monarchs decreed the expulsion of all Jews who refused baptism and conversion to Catholicism. This policy resulted in an exodus that portended far-reaching political, cultural and economic consequences.

Isabella died in 1504, but Ferdinand reigned on, although without full powers in Castile. Navarre became part of the kingdom in 1512, and meanwhile the new Empire in the West was being opened up.

The Habsburg Dynasty

Spain may be said to have reached the very height of its splendor and brilliance during the 16th century, when for half a century or more it became the most powerful country in the world. However, the struggles that the Habsburg House of Austria forced the Spanish to engage in, plus the worries, responsibilities, and wasting of resources required for implementing an active political program on a European scale, and the new enemies that this automatically created, gradually began to sap Spain's strength.

Charles I, who lived from 1550 to 1558, was the son of Mad Queen Joanna, daughter of Ferdinand and Isabella. His father was Philip of Burgundy, called the Fair. His father's early death and his mother's insanity brought Charles to the throne as sole monarch on Ferdinand's death in 1516. He also inherited the Low Countries from his father, and in 1519 he was elected to succeed his grandfather, Maximilian, as Holy Roman Emperor Charles V.

Two dominating events colored Charles' reign: the Protestant Reformation, begun in Germany by Martin Luther, and the Council of Trent, which led to the Catholic Counter-Reformation and the formation of the Jesuits by the Spaniard St. Ignatius Loyola. Charles V railed against the Protestant princes in Germany, fought in both Italy and France against his deadly foe, Francis I of France, soundly defeated the Moslem pirates of Tunis and Algeria, and in 1556 abdicated in favor of his son, Philip II. He then withdrew to seclusion in the solitary monastery of Yuste, in the remote mountain fastnesses near Plasencia.

Philip II, although not inheriting the Holy Roman Empire, ruled Spain, the Low Countries, parts of Italy and France, and most of the New World. Portugal was annexed to Spain in 1580, and only recovered her independence in 1640. Philip continued his father's European policies faithfully; he also found time to marry four times, his second wife being Mary Tudor, Queen of England. Spain's special role was that of defender of the Catholic church, right arm and financial provider in the fight against Protestantism. As the major world power, her adversaries were the English, the French, and latterly the Dutch; the theaters of military operations were principally Flanders, Italy, France and the high seas.

The Turks had been threatening the safety of Europe since their seizure of Constantinople in 1453, and the forces of Christendom, led by the Spanish fleet, and under the command of the king's bastard brother, Don John of Austria, won the great sea battle at Lepanto, in Greek waters, in 1571. (A lowly soldier named Miguel de Cervantes lost a hand in this victory over the Turks.) But a great reverse came when Philip sent his mighty fleet, the invincible Armada, to fight and invade England in 1588. This defeat marked the beginning of the end of Spain's European hegemony.

Explorations and Conquests

During the first part of the Habsburg rule the actual conquest and colonization of America was undertaken. The conquering of the New World was one of the heaviest tasks ever assumed in the history of mankind. Cortés subjected Mexico, Pizarro overcame Peru, and Balboa sailed across the Isthmus of Panama to claim the Pacific Ocean for the King of Spain. The list would indeed be endless if it were to include all the names of those intrepid *conquistadores*. Although afflicted with all the usual shortcomings of their fellow men, they excelled in bravery, endurance and valor, to the extent that they were able to perform incredible exploits and accomplish miraculous discoveries that continue to dazzle us even today.

A Spanish expedition in 1519, led by a Portuguese navigator named Magellan, reached South America via the straits that now bear his name and sailed on to discover the islands of Oceania. When Magellan met death in a fight with the natives in the Philippines, a Basque mariner, Juan Sebastián Elcano, took command. Only a single ship, the *Victoria,* returned to Seville after completing what was history's first round-the-world cruise. Of the 240 men who had originally sailed in the five-vessel fleet only 18 returned.

In succeeding years, the Amazon was explored and the foundations were laid for Buenos Aires, Lima and Santiago de Chile. But a gradual decline of Spain marked the reigns of Philip III and IV, who strove to perpetuate the policies of their forebears but lacked those men's ability and energy. Spain was torn by an endless succession of wars, followed by peace treaties that deprived her of more and more territories. Spanish supremacy waned in Europe while France and England rose to the ascendancy. These two countries, with the assistance of Holland, launched attacks against Spain's American colonies and against Spanish ships that plied the seas carrying American gold and silver, and the goods of the world's trade.

Spain's domestic economy had been shaken: there was an enormous loss of life from the staggering wartime casualties, and thousands of Spaniards had emigrated to the New World, or had met untimely deaths in some wild exploration scheme. Nevertheless, it was precisely at this time that arts and literature flourished at a level that has never again been reached. This was Spain's artistic Golden Age.

The House of Austria, the most brilliant of the Spanish dynasties, ended with the deformed, half-witted Charles II, nick-named "the

Bewitched". When it became certain that he would die without issue, the European courts watched and plotted to claim the Spanish crown.

The House of Bourbon

The end came in 1700 and brought a war of continental proportions. The Archduke Charles of Austria and Philip of Bourbon, the grandson of the almighty Louis XIV of France, were the chief pretenders to the Spanish crown. England, determined to prevent any possible union of the French and Spanish crowns, became involved; this was the war in which John Churchill won his great victories, his dukedom of Marl-borough and his great palace of Blenheim. Finally the Treaty of Utrecht brought peace, installed the Bourbon as Philip V, diminished Spanish territories still further, and ceded Gibraltar to Britain.

Of the descendants of Philip V, the outstanding ruler was Charles III (1759–88). The Bourbons claimed to be revitalizing the structure of the country that they ruled with the support of ministers who sought to impose what was designated as enlightened despotism. The chief Bourbon achievement lay in the centralization of the state, and in a rather limited development of communications, commerce, industry and education. Charles III sponsored an extensive program of public works. But oversubmissiveness to French international policy led Spain to sign agreements that were detrimental to her and to find herself subsequently involved in wars and disputes from which she derived absolutely no benefit.

Charles IV was a weak-willed ruler, possessed of only moderate intelligence. His queen and her favorite, Godoy, actually ran the affairs of state, Godoy's ambitions being infinitely greater than his abilities. The paintings of a great artist, Goya, bear eloquent and implacable witness to the sad state of Charles IV and his entourage.

Having set himself up as the arbiter for Europe, Napoleon assumed that Spain, under the rule of this inept king, would prove an easy prey for his own ambitions. He had no trouble sneaking the Imperial Army into Spain and luring the king and the royal family over the border to Bayonne. Playing on the enmity between the king and his eldest son, Napoleon forced both to abdicate and placed his own brother, Joseph Bonaparte, on the throne of Spain. Supported by collaborationist Span-ish ministers and by a segment of the ruling classes, Joseph installed himself in Madrid as José I, although the Spanish people christened him *Pepe Botella,* or Joe Bottle Paunch.

The Spanish refused to bow to the invaders, and the people of Ma-drid, aided by Spanish troops, staged an uprising on the famous Second of May 1808. This was cruelly repressed, as Goya's stark painting illustrates, but the insurrection spread and grew into the full-scale War of Independence (or Peninsular War).

The French army was defeated at Bailén. Meanwhile, the British expeditionary force under Sir Arthur Wellesley (later Duke of Wellington) landed in Portugal, defeated the French at Vimeiro, and continued into Spain. They were forced to retreat at Corunna (under Sir John Moore), but in 1812 Wellington won the battle of Salamanca, and the French defeat at Vitoria in 1813 finally forced them back over the Pyrenees. The war was characterized by desperate sieges (Gerona, Zaragoza), and by fierce fighting by the Spanish guerrillas, as well as the pitched battles in which Wellington's forces played the major role.

In March 1814, the lawful monarch, Ferdinand VII, the son of Charles IV, was restored. He immediately abolished the liberal constitution of 1812, and ruled autocratically, although not without liberal resistance, until his death in 1833.

Civil Strife and the End of an Empire

The Napoleonic crisis gave Spain's American colonies the chance to seize their independence, which the mother country could scarcely oppose. Bolívar and San Martín set in train a series of revolutionary movements, and there was little that Spain could do to prevent the formation of the several Latin-American republics. Thereafter they went very much their own way, although sharing a common heritage with their once-great parent.

At home, Ferdinand's death left a great dynastic problem. One part of the country supported the regent, Queen María Cristina, governing in the name of her infant daughter Isabella II, while a strong reactionary element invoked the disputed Salic Law preventing female succession and supported the claims of Don Carlos, the late king's younger brother. The Carlist civil wars split the country throughout the 1830s and 1870s, and Carlism, an ultra-Catholic traditional conservatism, continued to be a force into the 20th century, especially in Navarre.

During the long regency and the reign of Isabella II, party politics developed into a struggle between Moderates and Progressives. There were frequent *pronunciamientos,* or seizures of power by the military, and generals ran the country for long periods. Modernization, in the form of railroads and heavy industry, came to Spain, but slowly, and late. Isabella's confused reign ended in her abdication; there followed a brief liberal monarchy (Amadeo of Savoy), the First Republic, and then a pronunciamiento at Sagunto installed Isabella's son, the short-lived King Alfonso XII (1874–85).

He was to be followed by his posthumous son, Alfonso XIII, who reigned as king from 1902. During the Regency, Spain's brief and disastrous war of 1898, against the United States of America, cost her the remains of her colonial empire, Cuba, Puerto Rico and the Philippines.

The 20th Century

The growth of Republicanism and working-class movements in the 20th century was boosted by a growing public awareness of corruption and inefficiency, especially in the army. Spain remained neutral in World War I, but her troops became engaged in fighting in Spanish Morocco. In 1923 General Primo de Rivera's military coup halted the breakdown of public order at home, and the General quickly brought the Moroccan insurgents to heel. His seven-year dictatorship gave Spain stability and progress, but at the cost of political and much personal liberty. Then, a year after Primo de Rivera's fall from power in 1930, Alfonso, finally persuaded of the unpopularity of the monarchy, went into voluntary exile with his queen, the granddaughter of Queen Victoria. He never returned.

The make-up and the constitution of the Second Republic had been planned already during the dying days of the Monarchy, by a group of politicians who met secretly at San Sebastián. On the king's departure after the municipal elections of April 1931, these men were all ready for their great moment. The Republic came in, under the Presidency of Niceto Alcalá Zamora, with great optimism and high expectations. Its program of economic, social, and educational reform gave hope to Spain's great numbers of poor and dissatisfied people, but it polarized attitudes between Right and Left.

Within the new government, the bourgeois Republicans were competing with Socialists, Conservatives, Catalan, Basque, and even Galician separatists. These, and the groups outside the government—Communists, Trotskyists and Anarcho-syndicalists among the urban population and the landless laborers of Andalusia—made very improbable colleagues.

To the Right, various populist movements, owing a great deal to Fascism, were developing, and attracting much support. They were to come together under the charismatic personality of José Antonio Primo de Rivera, the son of the late dictator, whose own party, the Falange, won great popularity among the urban young. José Antonio was executed, aged thirty-three, in a Republican jail in Alicante early in the Civil War; his movement, the Falange, merged with two other groups, formed the basis of Franco's post-war National Movement. This helps to explain why during the Franco era virtually every town in Spain had a street named after him. (In many towns these streets are now reverting to their original name.)

Also to the Right in the forthcoming struggle would be the Church and landowning establishment, and the large corps of military and naval officers. The seeds of the great conflict were already sown. During the Second Republic's short life of five years, rebellions from both Right and Left were contained, the second of these, in the mining area of Asturias, being put down with great severity by a young officer who had made a great reputation for himself in the Moroccan wars, General Francisco Franco.

In February 1936 the Popular Front of Republican and left-wing parties was elected with a large majority. With increasing tension and unrest, violence and arson, particularly of churches, the army—as so often in the past—prepared to intervene. The arrest of José Antonio, and the assassination of a prominent right-wing politician, José Calvo Sotelo, in July, brought matters to a head.

While the mainland army prepared, General Franco, in a chartered English aeroplane, flew incognito from his post in the Canary Islands to Morocco, to raise the Army of Africa. At 5 P.M. on July 17 1936, the Spanish Civil War was under way.

The Nationalist forces, under Franco, quickly overran most of Andalusia; a hastily organized militia was no match for them. An early civilian casualty in the south was the great playwright and poet Federico García Lorca, senselessly executed near Granada. In the north, particularly in Old Castile and Navarre, army garrisons rose for Franco. He had become undisputed leader of the rebellion, and ultimately Head of the Nationalist State, with his headquarters at Burgos, after the death in an aircraft accident of the only other possible contender, General Sanjurjo.

On the Republican side, Manuel Azaña, now President, was losing control of the diverging forces that were threatening to destroy such superficial unity as there was. He appointed the Socialist leader Largo Caballero as Prime Minister. Meanwhile, the Nationalists advanced. Their supporters wanted to march on the capital, but Franco insisted they should go to the help of the young army cadets in the Alcázar of Toledo. This was a Nationalist island in a Republican zone, and Colonel Moscardó was defending it against the Republican besiegers. The Nationalist army was able to reach the famous city in time to raise the siege and boost Nationalist morale, but Moscardó's son, held as a hostage, was executed.

By now, worldwide passions had been aroused. In response to Italian and German military aid to the Nationalists, including personnel, the USSR supplied the Republicans, and volunteers poured into Spain from France, Britain, America and many other places, most of them to fight against Franco in the famous International Brigades. One such was the writer George Orwell, whose account *Homage to Catalonia* gives a lucid picture of the conduct of the war and of the turmoil among factions on the Republican side. By now Juan Negrín was Prime Minister, and Communists took control of the Republican government.

1937 saw the Nationalists make great gains in the north and northeast, including the fiercely republican Basque country—at the price of the infamous destruction by bombing of the historic Basque town of Guernica by Nazi aircraft. The world's diplomats decreed non-intervention, but they could do nothing to stop the flow of arms from Germany and Italy. By now the Nationalists had control of important industrial areas in the north, although the Republicans held Spain's three largest cities until the end.

Fierce campaigns were fought at Brunete, near Madrid, and in Aragón. The Republican Popular Army at last seemed to be able to hold Franco, but its great weakness was shown by its inability to follow up and capitalize on a successful initiative. The Aragonese campaign of the bitter winter of 1937 seemed, indeed, to herald a Republican revival. However, the Republicans failed to keep their hold on Teruel, and in April 1938 Franco's troops at last broke through to reach the Mediterranean, and split the dwindling Republican territory into two.

At this crucial point, Franco elected to attack in the direction of Valencia, now the seat of the Republican government. The Republicans made a great counterattack at the River Ebro in the summer, but the Popular Army, still inferior to the Nationalist forces in experience and professionalism, could not sustain the advance.

The final phase of the war was the Nationalist campaign in Catalonia. Barcelona fell in January 1939; the International Brigades were sent home. On March 28, the Nationalists entered the starving city of Madrid where, undoubtedly, many Fifth Columnists (as General Mola had termed them) had been preparing a welcome.

Three days later the Republicans capitulated; what was left of the Republican government fled from Valencia to carry on, in Mexico, as a government-in-exile. Meanwhile, Franco declared the Civil War officially over. Thousands of refugees fled into France to escape the repression which, with good reason, they expected to follow. The country and its economy were in ruins. Total casualties of the war, civilian and military, and the post-war reprisal purges, were probably around one million.

Post-War

Spain's attitude during World War II was, officially, that of a non-belligerent, despite considerable sympathy in Nationalist circles for the German cause, and the presence of the Blue Legion, who fought on the Russian front. After the Allied victory, there began a very difficult period for Spain. She was barred from membership of the most important international associations, and her trading partners were discouraged from doing business with her. Social conditions, even long after the end of the Civil War, were still desperate. Industry was still in shreds, and almost half the active population depended for their living on the land, earning microscopic wages.

Franco's ability to survive the period of ostracism gave further proof of his tenacity and shrewdness. The corner was finally turned when, in 1953, President Eisenhower came to Madrid to meet Franco and sign the Spanish-American defense and trade agreements. Investment in Spanish industry soon followed, and the Spanish government launched the first of three major Development Plans. Meanwhile, the growth of mass tourism was beginning to show the beaches and countryside of Spain to great numbers of European and American visitors. Yet political, civil and artistic liberties scarcely existed.

The constitutional future of the state was carefully controlled by Franco. The 1947 referendum had decided that Spain was to be a kingdom, but that Franco was to continue indefinitely as regent, and would designate his own successor, who would be King and Head of State on Franco's death or inability to carry on.

As the country's industry developed, large numbers of people flocked from rural areas into the cities, in search of work. Still there was not enough, and many left the country to work for long periods in more prosperous European countries, helping their dependants and the national economy with regular remittances.

In 1956, Spanish Morocco was given independence, in the wake of the French decision to free their former colony. Relations between Spain and its southern neighbor proved uneasy, especially during Franco's last years.

The ageing Head of State announced, in 1969, that his successor was to be the young prince Juan Carlos of Bourbon, son of the legitimate Pretender Don Juan, and grandson of Alfonso XIII. Soon after, Franco delegated some of his powers by appointing his first Prime Minister, or President of the Government, Admiral Carrero Blanco, who was assassinated by Basque terrorists in December 1973. He was succeeded by Carlos Arias Navarro.

Franco's long terminal illness coincided with a serious crisis in relations between Spain and Morocco over the status of the potash-rich Spanish Sahara. In the face of the threatened Green March, a plan to occupy the territory with Moroccan civilians, the Spaniards ceded it to King Hassan, and hostilities were averted.

After Franco

In November 1975, at the age of 82, Franco finally died. He was succeeded as Head of State by King Juan Carlos. His reign has so far been by no means trouble free, but he has proved wrong all those who referred to him upon his accession as "Juan el Breve"—Juan the Brief.

The King's principal goal has always been the restoration and protection of democracy in Spain. In this, he was enormously aided by his first Prime Minister, Adolfo Suárez. Indeed, Suárez proved an indispensible partner in the potentially fraught transition from dictatorship to democracy.

The first problem faced by the King and Suárez was to reconcile those who favored a swift move towards democracy with an ultra-conservative right wing, who were deeply suspicious of all attempts at liberalization and of democracy in general. But in addition, a number of other pressing problems needed to be faced and solved.

First, the already unsound economy was exacerbated by the world recession of 1976 and 1977. At the same time, certain regions of the country were pressing hard for autonomy; and in this, they were prepared to reinforce their demands with violence. The Basques have consistently been the most vocal and determined of these groups, with Catalonia and Andalusia only a little less insistent. This issue was, and remains, complicated also by the hostility it arouses among the right, in particular the police and army, who have been only too willing to meet violence with violence.

In attempting to balance these complex opposing forces, political reforms were of necessity introduced only gradually and carefully. In April 1977 the Movimiento Nacional, the only political organisation permitted under Franco, was disbanded. At the same time, the numerous *de facto* political parties were able to apply for legal recognition. Despite an increase in terrorist activity and unrest in the armed forces over the legalization of the Communist Party, Spain held its first general election for forty years on June 15th 1977.

The Center Democratic Union, headed by Prime Minister Suárez, was returned to continue its moderate policies, although the Socialist and regional parties did gain many seats. A hefty devaluation of the peseta (over 20%) helped exports and increased tourism, although this also led to high unemployment. At the same time, negotiations for entry into the EEC were intensified, but even now the date of entry may be some years off, largely the result of French reluctance. Spain's efforts to join NATO have proved more successful. In May 1982 she became a full member, despite the question mark hanging over the future of Gibraltar.

In 1977 the right to strike was accorded, and trade unions, legalized in April that year, grew in strength. Further liberalizing measures followed in 1978 with the relaxation of censorship and the restriction of the power of the Church, military and police. On December 29 1978, after approval in a national referendum, a new Constitution appeared, restoring civil liberties and providing the basis for Spain's way forward.

In the general election of March 1979 Suárez's party was again returned—but without an overall majority—the Socialists led by Felipe González gaining heavily. In the municipal elections that followed the Socialists took control of many of the big cities, though the Center Democratic Union did hold on to the rural areas.

Nonetheless, progress continued to be made, especially in meeting demands for regional autonomy. Statutes of Autonomy were voted for in many of Spain's regions, those for the Basques and the Catalans being accepted by 90% of voters in the referendum of October 1979. Under the Oak of Guernica the Basque government in exile, home after 42 years, formally abolished itself in favor of the new autonomous Council.

By late 1979, however, the popularity of the Suárez régime began to wane significantly. Increasing unemployment and the state of the economy drew criticism from both left and right. A simultaneous upsurge in violence by organisations such as ETA, the Basque separatist movement, provoked strong reaction from the right towards these movements. Political opinions were polarizing, and in January 1981 Suárez resigned.

During the following weeks, certain elements of the army, long critical of the government, took advantage of the ensuing leadership crisis to attempt a military coup. The coup of February 23, led by Colonel Antonio Tejero, failed largely due to the expert handling of the crisis by King Juan Carlos. In the end only one army general, Millans del Bosch in Valencia, rose in support of Tejero. The failure of the coup was an undoubted triumph for Spain's new democracy.

Differences over the election of a new Prime Minister, were put aside, and Leopoldo Calvo Sotelo was eventually voted to power with a large majority. But it was now clear that major efforts had to be put into protecting democracy. Acts of terrorism increased and although the majority of the Spanish people still backed a democratic Spain, factions composed of high-ranking army and civil guard officials became more and more dissatisfied with the government's handling of the terrorist issue. Strict new anti-terrorist measures were passed in parliament, these being aimed partly at pacifying the army. The frailty of Spanish democracy had been glimpsed and the maintenance of harmonious relations with the army has remained a priority of the Spanish government.

On August 27 1982 Sotelo dissolved his parliament and called for new elections to be held on October 28. By calling the elections early, rather than at the constitutionally scheduled time of Spring 1983, Sotelo gave his opponents less time to organize and campaign. However, in spite of this, the Spanish Socialist Party (PSOE) won a landslide victory under their leader Felipe González.

Prior to the election González had pledged that the Socialists would not join forces with the Communists, and indeed the first three months of his government saw no nationalization and no major shake-ups. He introduced moderate policies and brought to an end the drift that had become the norm during the last three years of centrist rule. Terrorism in the Basque country has continued to fall over this year, and fears of an army coup have subsided. The government's mildly conservative economic policy of wage restraint and monetary caution is nudging Spain's inflation downwards, and although this is unlikely to enable González to keep his pledge of creating 800,000 jobs, Spain should avoid an economic crisis of French proportions.

The regional and municipal elections held in May this year saw another victory for the Socialists. González's six-month old government, which has looked secure and sensible, won a strong endorsement from the voters for its mild-mannered reformist plans, with the Socialists winning 43% of the vote. Their chief rival—Manuel Fraga's right-wing Popular Alliance—trailed far behind with only 26% of the vote.

It is indisputable that González, the youngest European Prime Minister, has won wide popularity, but the task he is faced with is not an easy one. He has to keep his own party satisfied with the moderate policies he is pursuing in his attempt to resolve Spain's economic difficulties, as well as safeguarding democracy by not alienating the right-wing and the military. In addition, in foreign affairs he is at present having to contend with the growing anti-NATO feeling of the left, and the debate over whether Spain, with its Latin-American ties, should move towards a policy of Third World or European alignment.

Picasso
Manuel de Falla

CREATIVE SPAIN

Arts and Letters with a Passion

The Spaniard of today enjoys a cultural heritage of great breadth and depth. It is the product of many civilizations and influences. The peninsula has undergone a series of invasions, warlike and peaceful, and the old commonplace that art and literature in Spain are home-made, outside the traditions of the rest of the world, should not be taken seriously. But there is an element of truth in it. Down the ages, Spain has led some artistic fashions and absorbed others, but almost always the Spanish genius has been able to impart individual flavor to each incoming movement.

Since most people agree that Spain's most impressive contribution to the world's culture has been in the visual arts, it is right to begin with the prehistoric cave paintings of Santillana, on the north coast. Here can be seen the most remarkable prehistoric paintings of animals, birds and fish of the Magdalenian Period, but other engravings are from even earlier periods. The roofs and walls are covered with large frescos of extraordinary realism, as the natural form of the rock face was used to emphasize the muscles and body hollows of the animals. The bison, horses, boar and deer, colored in shades of yellow and red, and outlined in black, look as fresh as though recently painted. Sadly, the needs of conservation have made it necessary to close the caves to tourists.

The influence of Greek, Phoenician, or Carthaginian art in Spain was not long lasting because they limited their colonization to cities along the coast. An example of Greek-inspired Spanish art is the beautiful sculptured head known as the Lady of Elche, in Madrid's Archaeological Museum.

Rome and the Visigoths

According to Pliny, the Romans built 829 cities in Spain. Of the remarkable work they did in their time, much has survived; nearly every Spanish province has some vestige of ancient Rome to show. Among the finest examples of Roman architecture is Segovia's aqueduct, with its 128 arches, built in huge blocks of granite from the nearby Guadarrama mountains. Alcántara's bridge, built by Trajan in A.D. 106, although destroyed and restored several times during Spain's long history, is another excellent example, with its triumphal arch in the center and temple at one end. Roman ruins are most numerous in Tarragona, Sagunto (near Valencia), Itálica (near Seville) and Mérida, near Badajoz. Ampurias, on the Costa Brava, has Greek and Roman remains side by side.

After 150 years of Roman conquest and 400 years of Roman colonization, Spain became the most truly Romanized province in the empire outside Italy. Roman law, architecture, culture, the Latin language, and Christian religion were almost universally adopted by the Spaniards. Spain contributed great teachers and writers as well as material resources and manpower to the empire: the list includes the Senecas, Martial, Quintilian and Juvenal.

Visigothic art, strongly influenced by Rome and Byzantium, left its mark mainly in architecture. A good example is the tiny church of San Juan de Baños de Cerrato, near Palencia. This is the oldest Christian church in Spain, built by King Recceswinth in A.D. 661. Other relics of the Visigoths' 300-year stay in Spain can be seen in Córdoba's cathedral, where some of the Corinthian capitals exhibit Visigothic work. The magnificent gold crowns and crosses set with precious stones now in the armory of Madrid's Royal Palace are typical of Visigoth craftsmanship.

Hispano-Moorish Architecture

With their invasion of Spain in A.D. 711, the Moors brought their
architecture from the East, and in the following centuries it flourished
and developed into major phases under the successive dynasties. The
co-existence of two entirely different cultures, Moslem and Christian,
resulted in many of the grandiose buildings to be seen in Spain today.

Built in 785 on the foundation of the Visigoth church of St Vincent,
Córdoba's mosque, with its forest of 850 columns, is the most splendid
example of early Moorish architecture. The small Toledo mosque also
belongs to this period. Among its characteristics are the horseshoe-
shaped arches, the alternating red and white keystones of brick and
stone, doors surmounted with blind arcades, and polylobed arches. The
Koran forbade the representation of human or animal form, and the
only decoration was based on horizontal Kufic script, geometric and
conventional floral designs.

The Almohad buildings (12th–13th century), of which the Giralda
in Seville is a fine example, were constructed of brick, with wide bands
of decoration in relief, arches were pointed, and both interior and
exterior walls were lined with *azulejos* (glazed pottery tiles) with geometric motifs.

Moorish architecture reached its peak in Granada during the 14th
and 15th centuries, in a period of high sophistication. Simplified arch
outlines appeared, but with ever more intricate lacework carving
around them; ceramics and stucco were used to decorate outside walls.
The Alhambra is the outstanding example of this period.

However, during the later stage of the Reconquest, Moorish work
became incorporated with Spanish architecture. As various towns were
retaken, the Moors were allowed to stay and to continue their traditional work, the form becoming known as *mudéjar.* Buildings were remarkable for their brickwork in towers and apses, and for the ornate carved
wooden *(artesonado)* ceilings.

Mudéjar architecture is to be found only in Spain, and can be seen
at its best in the Alcázar in Seville, in Granada, and particularly in
Toledo. And it was in Toledo that the Mudéjares, skilled in working
ivory, enamel, silver, and gold, as well as excelling in mosaics, leatherwork and ceramics, developed the art of damascening. Their method
of encrusting steel with gold and silver is still used in Spain today and
is called Toledo work.

Gothic and Renaissance

While Moorish architecture was flourishing in the south of Spain, in the north, among the Christians, the Romanesque style gained favor, especially in the province of Catalonia. Its general features are like those in France, and the main difference lies in the general plan of the churches more than in construction or decoration. Of the many Romanesque churches in Spain, San Isidoro in León and San Pedro in Huesca are considered the purest examples. A notable feature of some Catalonian churches is their Byzantine-flavored interior decoration.

With the 13th century, Gothic architecture was imported from France. The best examples of this are the cathedrals of Toledo, León, Seville and Burgos. Spanish cathedrals compete architecturally with those of France, and surpass them in the abundance and beauty of ecclesiastical furniture of the Gothic period—wrought-iron work, carved stalls, monstrances, paintings, tombs and above all the magnificent reredos. The Gothic style lingered long in Spain, even into the 16th century.

At the end of the 15th century, the Italian influence began to enter Spanish architecture, resulting in a less ornate Renaissance style and, in contrast, lavish decoration in the *plateresque* Gothic buildings. In this, the stonework is so finely chiseled as to resemble a silversmith's rather than a mason's work. The façade of the University of Salamanca is a particularly fine example of the work. Plateresque architecture continued into the 18th century, merging with baroque to result in the flamboyant decoration so loved by the Spanish, and known there as *Churrigueresque.*

The marvelous flowering of Spain's fortunes after the conquest of Granada and the achievements of the explorers led, in the time of the powerful Spanish Habsburgs, to a great period for Spanish art and architecture. At this time the Gothic and Renaissance styles meet, as in the cathedral of Granada, the work of three architects. Pure Renaissance work is to be found in the unfinished palace of Charles V, inside the Alhambra at Granada. A major part of the Alcázar of Toledo, almost totally destroyed early in the Civil War but now restored, belonged to this time. So also does the huge grid-shaped monastery of El Escorial, near Madrid, built for Philip II by Juan de Herrera and completed in 1584.

The replacement of the Habsburgs by a French royal house is reflected in the architecture of the 18th century, especially in the palace of La Granja, north of Madrid, and in the capital's Royal Palace. In the 19th and 20th centuries, Spanish architecture has been less memorable than in the golden days. But an exception should be made for the work of an eccentric Catalan genius, Antonio Gaudí, whose unfinished Church of the Holy Family in Barcelona is quite unforgettable in its originality.

Until the 15th century, sculpture, as a separate art, was practically ignored in Spain, being considered only as an accessory to architecture. But a major sculptor of the late 15th century was Diego de Siloé, the best example of whose work can be seen in the Carthusian monastery of Miraflores, outside Burgos.

The Great Spanish Art: Painting

Like sculpture, the art of painting was slow to develop in Spain, despite an early flourishing of primitives in Valencia and Catalonia. The 14th- and 15th-century painters followed the models of French, Italian and Flemish artists, and their works can be seen in several major cathedrals.

But in the 16th and early 17th centuries Italian painters, lured by the liberal patronage of the Spanish kings, came to Spain to work. Along with Spaniards who had, in turn, studied in Italy, like Navarrete, Ribalta and particularly Ribera, they formed the Spanish school that also includes the great names of Velázquez, Murillo and El Greco.

Ribera, born near Valencia in 1591, had the greatest influence in forming the Spanish school. He went to Italy when young, settled in Naples, where he earned renown as the "Spagnoletto," and died there in 1652. He painted an immense quantity of pictures, nearly all religious, and reveled in gloomy scenes of martyrdom and execution.

Spain's most representative painter in the 16th century was not a Spaniard by birth. Domenikos Theotocópulos, born in Crete, studied in Italy in one of Titian's studios, and later came to Spain. In 1577, at the age of 28, he settled in Toledo and, known as El Greco, painted there almost exclusively until he died in 1614, two years before Cervantes and Shakespeare. El Greco, with his masterly use of line and shape and gleaming white against somber backgrounds, achieved the aspiration of the Spain of his day to spiritualize earth and raise it up to heaven. The elongation of figures, typical of his painting, responds to El Greco's inner vision and his longing to express something that is on a higher plane than the merely terrestrial. El Greco symbolizes in Spanish painting the ideals of pure spiritual mysticism, yet he did not take his place among the great Spanish painters until half a century ago.

The 17th century saw a flowering of great painters in Spain, headed by Diego Velázquez (1599–1660), who is regarded by many as Spain's greatest painter. Velázquez, from Seville, represents the opposite side of the Spanish character to the spiritualistic El Greco: shrewd and penetrating detail, both psychological and real. One of Spain's most prolific painters, rich, admired and successful, Velázquez painted few religious pictures; his work is filled with Bacchuses, drunken youths and contemporary episodes of astonishing virtuosity. He was the first painter in Spain to paint a female nude, the *Rokeby Venus* (now in London's National Gallery). He was a master of space, light and shade, and a remarkable portraitist, preserving for all time the decadent brilliance of the court of his patron, Philip IV (see the section on the Prado Museum in *Exploring Madrid*).

Stern realism, vanities transformed into moralities, and portraiture were the hallmarks of this great age of Spanish painting. Landscapes, until now reckoned to be a lower form, were given some respectability by Velázquez and his son-in-law Mazo, and especially by Bartolomé Murillo, also an important and distinctive painter of religious subjects. Alonso Cano and Francisco de Zurbarán were other major painters of this period. Cano, also a sculptor, was much influenced by Zurbarán; both were chiefly inspired by religious themes.

Claudio Coello (1642–93), who became court painter in 1684, is considered to be the last great painter of the school of Madrid, and of the Golden Age. His outstanding work is *Charles II adoring the Blessed Sacrament* (Sacristy of the Escorial).

Francisco de Goya

The 18th century produced no major artists in Spain until the arrival of the Aragonese Francisco de Goya. He was born near Zaragoza in 1746, at Fuendetodos, of peasant farmer parents (the house can be visited), and left Spain in a hurry, with the Inquisition on his trail, to emerge as a court favorite in the years before the Napoleonic invasion. His brilliantly cruel portraits of Charles IV, his Queen María Luisa, and her bull-like boy friend, Godoy, are unrivaled, and his nude portrait (believed by some to have been the Duchess of Alba) known as *La Maja Desnuda,* is both highly original and strangely ambiguous. Following a serious illness which led to complete deafness (the comparison with Beethoven, a contemporary, is hard to resist), his entire style changed; the *Executions of Spaniards on the Third of May* and the series of etchings known as *The Horrors of War* are as frightening and true today as they were originally. Again, his *Black Paintings* are the supreme pictorial expression of the macabre. He died in exile at Bordeaux, France, in 1828.

From Goya to Today

Fortuny (1838–74) was a dominant influence on Spanish art before the rise of the Impressionists, and married into the Madrazo family of portrait painters. Landscape painting appeared again with Sorolla and Zuloaga. Both lived into the 20th century, Zuloaga until 1945.

In our own day, some of the most famous and influential painters have been Spaniards. Pablo Picasso, one of the many Catalan artists (though born in Málaga), lived most of his life after 1905 in Paris. During his long life (1881–1973) he produced a tremendous number of canvases in his progressive styles. He is, undoubtedly, the most influential figure in 20th-century painting. There is a museum of his work in Barcelona. Two other great Catalans are Joan Miró and Salvador Dalí, born in 1893 and 1904 respectively, the first Spanish Surrealists.

In modern times, the long-lasting struggle between figurative and abstract painting continues. Popularly acclaimed contemporary artists are Antonio Tapiès and Modesto Cuixart, leaders of the innovatory Catalan school, and in Madrid the 'El Paso' group, headed by Millares and Canogar; other painters with reputations are Sempere, Pepe Ortega and Feo Reinado. The most important contemporary sculptor is undoubtedly Eduardo Chillida (born 1924).

The rise in the art market, and the fact of many Spaniards and foreigners turning to paintings and sculpture as an investment, sparked off the opening of new galleries, especially in Madrid and Barcelona. Modern Spanish art now fetches high prices, not only in Spain, but in top galleries throughout Europe and the United States.

Literature

A literature that is recognizably Spanish was born with the emergence of the Castilian language, which descends (like all the other languages of the peninsula, except Basque) directly from Latin. During the Middle Ages, the Church had an almost complete monopoly of learning, and thereby dominated culture and education. Naturally, this resulted in a strong Christian element in Spanish literature, with more than a hint of mysticism. But the Latin tradition takes its place alongside those of two other cultural traditions and schools, Moslem and Hebrew.

The Castilian vernacular literary art begins with epic poetry. There is a great wealth of this early Spanish poetry, and scholars still argue fiercely about the dates of the most famous compositions and the methods by which they were handed down. The first major epic composition was the *Cantar de Mío Cid,* of the 13th century. It narrates, in assonantal rhyme, the heroic deeds of Spain's great hero of the Reconquest, Rodrigo Díaz de Vivar, El Cid. The author is unknown, but he has a realistic technique that makes his landscapes and personages forceful and compelling.

The reign (1252-84) of Alfonso the Wise is the vital time for the establishment of Castilian as the major language of Spain, since this king made it the language of scholarship and the Court. He attracted a great school of scholars to Toledo, and under his patronage a great quantity of scientific and literary work was produced.

The major work of the 14th century is the famous *Libro de Buen Amor,* by the Archpriest of Hita, Juan Ruiz. The same period saw the appearance of Don Juan Manuel's series of cautionary tales, many of which were based on Eastern folklore. Later came another, rather different, work of fiction, *La Celestina.* This was a dramatic novel written about the year 1500, probably by Fernando de Rojas. Showing the influence of the Italian Petrarch, it was to be enormously influential in the following centuries. Original, but in a different form, was the short, anonymous tale *Lazarillo de Tormes,* the first example of that typically Spanish genre, the picaresque novel. It has been translated into English under the title *Blind Man's Boy.*

The Golden Age

With the 16th century begins Spain's literary Golden Age, in verse, prose and drama. It took many facets; lyricism and erudition in poetry contrasted strikingly with blunt realism of prose works such as *Lazarillo* and *Don Quijote.*

Taking poetry first, we begin with Garcilaso de la Vega, the great lyric poet of the time of Charles V. He was a typical Renaissance Universal man, a poet and a man of action. He spent the latter part of his short life (1501–36) in Italy. His output was small but very intensive, consisting of three eclogues, or pastoral poems.

The greatest verse of the mid-period of the Golden Age was the work of Quevedo (1580–1645) and, above all, Góngora (1561–1627). Spanish verse of the Renaissance period, like its Italian models, is rich in complicated metaphor and allusions, and Góngora's *Soledades,* his most famous metaphysical poems, have been likened to the work of his English contemporary John Donne.

In the realm of prose, many writers were active, but only one need detain us: Miguel de Cervantes, born at Alcalá de Henares in 1547 and dying in the same year as Shakespeare, 1616. In *Don Quijote* Cervantes gave Spain not only one of the world's great works of literature, but an eternal representation, in Don Quixote and Sancho Panza, of the Spanish character, ever oscillating between idealism and materialism.

Cervantes' personal life was one of dreams, delusions and suffering. He lost his left hand at the Battle of Lepanto, and was twice imprisoned (by the Moors in Algiers and by his own countrymen in Seville). Cervantes was keenly aware of the cultural problems of his day, but his *Don Quijote* is certainly not a philosophical manual. Every episode touches the deepest problems of humanity, with the contrasting reaction of earthy, life-loving Sancho and idealistic, day-dreaming Quixote.

The stage, too, had its Golden Age in the late 16th and 17th centuries. Lope de Vega (1562–1635) was a phenomenally prolific writer, who claimed to have written more than 1,800 plays. Of those that survive, the quality is uneven, but some, at least, such as *El caballero de Olmedo, El castigo sin venganza* and *Fuenteovejuna,* entitle him to rank among the greatest European playwrights.

Tirso de Molina, Lope's contemporary, has gone down to fame as the creator of the character Don Juan, the hero—perhaps the villain—of his moralistic play *El burlador de Sevilla.* Lope's mantle was assumed by another dramatist of international stature, Pedro Calderón de la Barca (1600-81), best known for *La vida es sueño* (Life's a Dream) and *El alcalde de Zalamea.*

These great heights of creativity were not maintained in the 18th century, when most aspects of Spanish cultural life seemed to lose their originality.

The 19th Century—Romantic and Realistic

The revival of the 19th century was led from across the Pyrenees; interestingly enough, Spain provided a background that was the inspiration of many foreign writers and composers, notably Victor Hugo and Prosper Mérimée (the author of *Carmen*). Later, both Verdi and Puccini used Spanish romantic plays as bases for opera libretti. The best-known Spanish writers of this century were Gustavo Adolfo Bécquer and José Zorrilla, whose *Don Juan Tenorio* is still staged by many Spanish theaters around All Saints' Day. One mighty novelist, fit to be ranked and compared with Balzac and Dickens, was at work in 19th-century Madrid. This was the realist Benito Pérez Galdós, born in the Canary Islands in 1843; he died in 1920. He is remembered for his long series of historical novels, the *Episodios Nacionales,* and among his works of purely creative fiction, *Doña Perfecta,* and the vast *Fortunata y Jacinta.*

The 20th Century

As far as Spanish culture is concerned, the 20th century began two years early, in 1898, the year of the great military and naval catastrophe, the Spanish-American war. Defeat, loss of the remainder of the empire, and national soul-searching inspired a wide-ranging and fruitful movement of regenerationism in the national life, especially in politics and literature.

Membership of the "Generation of '98" included the Basque Miguel de Unamuno (1864–1937), one of the most vigorous spirits of modern times. A professor of Greek, novelist, essayist, philosopher, and poet, his most important work is *The Tragic Sense of Life,* in which he explores the conflict between reason and man's longing for immortality. Ramón del Valle-Inclán was an eccentric and iconoclastic Galician novelist and playwright, Pío Baroja a prolific novelist, and Azorín a skilled and perceptive analyst of his country's character.

The poets of the twentieth century include Juan Ramón Jiménez, the Nobel Prize-winner of 1956, the brothers Antonio and Manuel Machado and, in a class by himself, Federico García Lorca (1898-1936). This abundantly talented Andalusian is probably the major figure of twentieth-century Spanish literature. His brief life ended early in the Civil War when he was shot by Nationalist partisans. Fortunately he was able to leave the world a series of moving and gripping plays— *Blood Wedding* and *The House of Bernarda Alba* are the most famous —and several collections of haunting poetry, notably the *Gypsy Balladeer.* A talented musician, he took great inspiration from Andalusia, especially its gypsy folklore. His stay at Columbia University led to his collection *A Poet in New York.*

Miguel Hernández, who died in jail in 1942, and Rafael Alberti, elected to the Spanish Parliament in 1977, were two important poets of the Civil War period.

Post-War

The post-war years were characterized by a certain stagnation and pessimism and by an obsession with national and domestic issues. Censorship and official cultural policy were to blame for this state of affairs, which restricted the creative talents of this gifted nation. However, the new cultural freedom and the abandonment of censorship in the post-Franco era have begun to take effect and this change in the climate is strikingly obvious to anyone who cares to glance at Spanish bookshops and newsstands.

Among other developments, this ideological shift has meant that major writers of the war period such as Lorca and Hernández are now widely read and appreciated. But the restrictions on artistic freedom have taken their toll nonetheless and of all the literary genres, perhaps the theater has suffered most. For a long time, the commercial stage in both Madrid and Barcelona was forced to rely heavily on translations of plays from London and New York, despite the presence of some important and successful indigenous dramatists. Today, however, the Spanish stage is much more healthy and an important reason for its current vigor was the creation in late 1978 of the Centro Dramático Nacional. This regularly puts on works of a high standard, both native and imported, at its María Guerrero Theater in Madrid. Such well-known figures as Nuria Espert and José Luis Gómez have been among its early directors and plans are afoot for the CDN to form a traveling company to complement its Madrid-based company.

Among Spanish novelists, the best-known are J. M. Gironella, writer of enormous novels dealing with the war years, Miguel Delibes, Carmen Laforet, and the most important and controversial, Camilo José Cela, the variously witty, caustic and erudite author of books ranging from novels and travel to essays on subjects such as Madrid slang and eroticism. He was thought to be a strong candidate for the 1977 Nobel Prize which went, to the surprise of many, to the poet Vicente Aleixandre.

José Ortega y Gasset, who died in 1955, was the last Spanish philosopher to gain a European reputation. In our own time a great impact on the ideology of the national life has been made by the radical economist Ramón Tamames.

Music

Spanish music of the early days is not well known outside its country of origin, with the possible exception of Tomás Luis de Victoria or Vitoria (1549–1611), who published a great number of beautiful religious choral compositions. But the turn of the last century saw a great surge in Spanish music. Chief among these composers were the Catalans Isaac Albéniz (1860–1909) and Enrique Granados (1867–1916). They were soon joined by the Andalusian Manuel de Falla (1876–1946), composer of the Ritual Fire Dance, from *El Amor Brujo*. All three were inspired by native folkloric melody and rhythms, and made great reputations as local colorists.

Since Falla's day, Spain's younger composers have broken with the past, turning to European atonal, electronic and serial music. Internationally known exponents are Luís de Pablo, Ernesto and Cristóbal Halffter (the latter the composer of the Cantata for the United Nations), Tomás Marco, Anton García Abril and Ramón Barce.

In the performance of music, Spain's great contribution has been in the domain of the guitar. The octogenarian Andrés Segovia is still the great master, bringing to worldwide concertgoers the works of, among others, Fernando Sor and Joaquin Rodrigo *(Concierto de Aranjuez)*. Carlos Montoya, Narciso Yepes and Paco Peña are world-famous

flamenco guitarists. Spain has also produced some great virtuoso singers—Victoria de los Angeles, Montserrat Caballé, Teresa Berganza,
Pilar Lorengar and Plácido Domingo (Spanish-born, although raised
in Mexico).

So far as pop music is concerned, Spain has yet to produce anyone
of international stature, with the exception of Julio Iglesias, and for the
most part the country is in the grip of "Euro-disco-pop." For what it
is worth, however, native singers in vogue include Manolo Escobar,
Rocío Jurado (Spain's top girl singer) and the *rockero* Miguel Bosé.
Rock Andaluz, an unusual phenomenon, is led by the group Triana.
There are jazz festivals every year at Barcelona, Sitges and San Sebastián.

Although cultural freedom has brought a downturn in the influence
of protest song, it is still surprisingly popular, especially among students and intellectuals. Its theme is now largely social, rather than
political. Leaders are Antonio Labordeta, Lluis Llach, María del Mar
Bonet and Luis Eduardo Aute.

The Cinema

Like all recent Spanish history, the story of the cinema is uneven. A
small native cinema emerged in the early years of this century, and by
1932 *Cipesa,* a Hollywood-style studio, was established, producing
gypsy and bullfighting sagas for the home market on low budgets, tight
schedules and using unskilled actors. The critical magazine *La Gaceta
Literaria* (1927-33) frequently bemoaned the absence of an intelligent
national cinema comparable to those of France, Germany or Russia.
Among its contributors was Luis Buñuel (1900–83), who for many
remains the master of the Spanish cinema.

Un Chien Andalou (1928, in collaboration with Salvador Dalí), and
L'Age D'or (1930) were Buñuel's two early masterpieces. Both were
made in Paris, and remain seminal Surrealist works. Returning to
Spain, Buñuel directed a bitter social documentary, *Land Without
Bread* (1932), while attempting to establish a native film industry.
During the Civil War Buñuel joined the Republican government in
Paris, and so began his exile; nonetheless, Spain remained the background of his films, in which he used the devices of Surrealism, especially the intrusion of the irrational into everyday existence, as a basis
for moral and poetical expression. Working briefly in the US, Buñuel
finally settled in Mexico in 1947, where he made *Los Olvidados* (1950),
about urban juvenile delinquency, and *Robinson Crusoe* (1952). With
Archibaldo de la Cruz (1955) and *Nazarin* (1958) his more persistent
themes were crystallised: the capacity of obsession to release the imagi-

nation, and a spirited contempt for the Church and the powerful middle-class.

In 1960 his reputation was such that he was invited to film in Spain. The result, *Viridiana,* was immediately suppressed by the authorities, and had to be smuggled out of the country. From then to his death in 1983 he concentrated on the neuroses of a wealthy bourgeois and the absurdities of political and ecclesiastical power in a series of masterful but progressively stylized films.

During the Franco era all media were rigidly controlled. A single, state-run TV channel exists to this day. Foreign films were censored and dubbed, and home-produce tended to glorify the army or concentrate on trite comedy. Some co-productions were made with other countries, such as *A Fistful of Dollars* (1964), European producers being attracted to Spain by the locations and low production costs.

By the 1970s there were signs of considerable life in the movie industry, not least in the films of Juan Bardem, Carlos Saura (*La Caza, Peppermint Frappé, Raise Ravens,* and the TV film of Lorca's *Blood Wedding*), and the romantic pessimist Boreau (*Poachers, La Sabina*). International awareness of this development was underlined by the success of Victor Erice (*Spirit of the Beehive, The South*).

Maybe it is not surprising that the promise of the 1970s has not shown dividends on the international circuit. In the wake of Franco's death Spanish film makers turned back on the last 40 years in an intense attempt to make sense of them. The few international successes have funded a thriving industry which is now truly native, and ranges from the highly commercial to the avant garde work of Alvaro del Amo (*Dos*), or the historical analyses of Manuel Aragón (*Los Sonámbulos, Demons in the Garden, Maravillas*). The recent past can now be dealt with in a direct fashion, such as Pedro Almodovar's *Pepi, Luci, Bom and Other Girls,* set in the pop culture of the 1970s, Luis Berlenga's *National Shotgun* and *National Patrimony,* lampooning National Service, or the two-part documentary *Afterwards . . .* by Cecilia and Juan José Bartolomé.

The recent relaxation of censorship led to a predictable proliferation of sex cinemas, although some films still provoke a hostile reaction from the authorities, such as Pilar Miró's *El Crimen de Cuenca,* which implied that the Civil Guard used torture. It says something about the current strength of the Spanish cinema that this film, temporarily banned, proved to be the largest grossing film in Spain of 1981 (outstripping even *Superman II!*)

The major international festival is at San Sebastián (Sept.), although others are held at Madrid (Sci-Fi, March), Barcelona (Oct.), Seville (Oct.), Sitges (Fantastic Cinema, Oct.) and Bilbao (Nov.).

Bull fight in a Village by Goya

BULLFIGHTING FOR
BEGINNERS

How to Watch a Bullfight

Anglo-Saxons, on their first introduction to bullfighting customarily voice an objection to it that indicates their lack of understanding of its basic nature. They consider that it is unfair. It is a contest between a man and a bull, in which the bull always dies. There is something wrong, they feel, in a sport in which the identity of the winner is fixed in advance.

So there would be, if bullfighting were a sport. But bullfighting is not a sport. Bullfighting is a spectacle. In a sense it is a play, with a plot. The plot calls for the bull to die. To object to that is as pointless as to object that the plot of *Julius Caesar* calls for Caesar to die. In another sense, it is a ballet. One of its essential features is the performance of

81

stylized traditional movements, and a byproduct of their accurate performance is grace. In still another sense, it is an exhibition of physical dexterity, with the risk of injury or death accepted as the penalty for clumsiness, like the art of a trapeze performer. But in its essence, it is a demonstration of the mastery of a human over two living organisms —over the bull, for the point of the torero's art is to maneuver a thousand pounds of recalcitrant, malevolent armed muscle according to his will—and over himself, for perhaps the basic meaning of the bullfight is that it is an ordeal of the quality most prized by Spaniards, courage. The bullfighter must master his own fear before he can master the bull.

The brave man is not the one who does not feel fear; he is the man who feels fear and still faces the danger that frightens him. Bullfighters are invariably afraid when they enter the ring. Make no mistake about that. They are afraid, and they are right to be afraid. They know that their chance of dying in the ring is one in ten. They know that their chance of dying or being crippled is about one in four. They know, usually, what the horn ripping through the flesh feels like; no bullfighters finish their careers completely unscathed.

The bull may always die (he can avoid that fate by refusing to fight, but this is rare), but he does not always lose. In that sense, bullfighting *is* a sport. But you will understand it better if you cease to regard it as a sport and look upon it instead as a spectacle—a spectacle to which death does not put an end, but is itself an intrinsic element.

The Plot

Bullfighting is a highly ritualized affair. All its details have been developed over a long period into a pattern that now never varies, each one ticketed with its own label in the extensive vocabulary of bullfighting. To begin with, the bullfight is not a fight—it is a *corrida,* a "running" of the bull. It is divided, like most plays, into three acts, the *tercios*—the act of the picadors, the act of the banderillas, and the act of death. There is also a curtain-raiser, the parade across the ring, in which all the participants in the coming spectacle take part, even to the men who will drag the dead bulls out of the arena.

The act of the picadors has scenes—the *doblando,* the first luring of the bull with the capes; the matador's first playing of the bull; the arrival of the mounted picadors to attack the bull with their lances; and the *quites*—which is the work of the matadors in luring the bull away from the picador after the former has reacted in natural fashion to the bite of the lance. The fine points of these maneuvers will be explained in a moment.

The act of the banderillas also usually has three scenes, in the sense that three pairs of gaily decorated darts are ordinarily thrust into the bull's shoulders, but each of these scenes is the same.

The act of death, the *faena,* has two scenes—first, the playing of the bull with the small red flannel *muleta,* which replaces the billowing capes at this stage of the fight—and the killing with the sword—the moment of truth.

All of this you will see in every bullfight, good, bad or indifferent. How is a novice to know whether the manner in which it is performed is skillful or clumsy?

You may be surprised, at your first bullfight, to hear the crowd roar its approval for a maneuver that, to you, looks no different from those that preceded it, and were allowed to pass in silence. You may be baffled when seat cushions start flying into the ring, hurled by an angry crowd whose method of showing its ire is to attempt to trip up the matador and give the bull a chance at him. The fine points that arouse the admiration or the contempt of the crowd (and the crowd, at a Spanish bullfight, provides a spectacle second only to what is going on in the ring) cannot be expected to be obvious to a newcomer. You will undoubtedly know whether the performance you are watching is, in general, skillful or clumsy, for deft movements are graceful and awkward ones are not and it takes no expert to appreciate the difference between the single clean thrust of the sword that sends the bull down as though he had been struck by lightning and the blundering butchery marked by thrust after thrust, with the sword spinning into the air as it strikes the shoulder-blade of the bull instead of piercing through the opening that leads to the heart. But in order to know why a performance is good or bad, you will need some coaching in what to look for.

What to Look For

The three elements by which the critics judge bullfighters (and the bullfight critic, in Spain, is a highly respected individual, whose verdicts can make or break a matador's career) are *parar, mandar* and *templar.* Parar is style, and consists in standing straight firmly planted, unyielding, bringing the bull past in a thundering rush with a gracefulness that gives no ground. Mandar is mastery of the bull, controlling his every move and spinning him about like a puppet. Templar is timing, and the acme of skill in this respect is to perform the maneuvers of the fight in slow motion. The more slowly the bull is moving as he passes the matador, the longer the time of dangerous propinquity lasts, and the more opportunity is granted to the animal to change tactics and go for the man instead of the cape.

Watch the matador's feet. He should not move them as the bull thunders past. If he really has control of the animal, he will make it avoid him; he will not have to move to avoid it. Watch how closely he works to the bull. Obviously his mastery of the beast must be more exact if he lets the horn graze his chest than if he pulls it by a foot away. Closeness can be faked. If the torero holds his arms with the cape far out from his body, if he leans well forward so that, without moving his feet, he can still bring the upper part of his body back when the bull reaches him, then he is not showing the same skill as the man who stands ramrod straight and maneuvers the bull without budging himself.

Some grandstand plays are really dangerous. Some aren't. Kneeling really is, because it reduces the mobility of the bullfighter. Passes in which the cape swings over the head of the torero are dangerous because it makes him lose sight of the bull at a critical moment. Passes in which the cape is held behind the bullfighter's body are also dangerous, obviously. Passes in which the bull, charging towards one side of the torero, is drawn across his body to pass on the other side are dangerous.

Psychology of the Bull

On the other hand, standing with one's back against the fence, which looks dangerous, often isn't. It depends on the bull. Most bulls have no desire to bang their heads against a hard wooden wall. It is often more dangerous, close to the fence, to allow the bull to pass between it and the bullfighter; bulls have a tendency to swerve outward from the fence. If you notice that the bull returns habitually to a certain spot in the arena after his various charges, it is more dangerous to fight him in that part of the ring than elsewhere; he has elected it, by some mysterious instinct, as his home ground, and he is fiercer on it. It is more dangerous for the matador to taunt him into charging outward from this territory than into it. When he is returning to his base, he is intent upon getting back 'home'. He is paying no attention to the man who may happen to be standing on the edge of the path he is following. Bullfighters know that and sometimes take advantage of the bull's rush past to draw applause from spectators who haven't grasped the situation.

Paradoxically, the bull who looks most dangerous to you is the one who looks least dangerous to the torero—the one who comes charging into the ring full of fight and makes a vicious dash for the first bullfighter he sees. The type of bull that is out to kill is the type of bull the torero can handle. He has a one-track mind; and a bull with a one-track mind, like a man with a one-track mind, is predictable. You can tell what he will do. Therefore you can control him. Bullfighters like a fighting animal, one that is going to charge hard—and straight.

You know now some of the things to look for. In order not to miss them, you should know when to be on the alert.

When the bull first charges into the arena, one of the bullfighters will wave his cape at him and very probably, at the bull's rush, will dart behind one of the bulwarks that guard the openings into the corridor behind the barrier. Don't mark him down as a coward for that. It is all part of the ritual. The bull is not yet actually being played. He is being studied. Perhaps the first cape will be waved by the man closest to him, to find out if his near vision is good. Then a man on the other side of the ring will try, to test his vision at a distance. The matador is watching how he charges, and whether he has a tendency to hook to the left or the right. Upon his correct interpretation of the bull's reaction to these preliminary flaggings will depend his success in the rest of the fight.

After these opening evolutions, the matador comes out to demonstrate his skill with the cape. This is your first real chance to witness the art of the bullfighter. If, in reading bullfight stories, you have come across the term *verónica,* and wondered what it meant, it is probably what you are watching now. The verónica is the simplest and most basic of the various passes *(pases),* and it is almost always the one with which the matador begins. The torero holds the cape before him, more or less gathered into folds, his profile towards the bull, and as the animal charges, he spreads the cloth before the animal's snout, swings it by his body, and the bull follows it past. Ordinarily, as the bewildered bull turns, he swings him by again, then perhaps a third time, each time a little closer, as he becomes acquainted with the animal's reactions and acquires *mandar,* and perhaps finishes by gathering the cape in against his body in a half verónica as the bull passes. This usually stops the bull short, and the matador can turn his back disdainfully on the horns and walk away, a display of mastery over the bull that always brings a roar of *"Olé".*

The Picador

With the end of this scene, the picadors appear—the mounted bullfighters with lances. The object of this part of the fight is to launch an offensive against that tremendous hump of flesh on the top of the bull's neck, the tossing muscle. Until that has been tired, so that the bull will drop his head, he cannot be killed with the sword. The way to the animal's heart is opened only when the front feet are together and the head dropped.

The picador attacks the tossing muscle by meeting the bull's charge with his lance, which he digs into it. The role of the horse is to be tossed—not to be gored. He wears a mattress to protect him from goring and the management, which has to pay for the horses, sincerely hopes that it will succeed. But the bullfighters want the horse to be tossed. A bull whose tossing muscle has hoisted three heavy horses into the air is a bull beginning to be tired. There is also a second motive, to maintain the bull's combativity. He will not go on indefinitely charging into yielding cloth and empty air. He has to be allowed to hit something solid or he won't play.

There is perhaps one exception to the statement that the bullfighters want the horse to be tossed. The picador, though it is part of his job, isn't happy about it. When his horse is tossed, he goes down. The picador, unlike the horse, has no mattress. He does have a heavy piece of armor on the leg which is going to be on the side from which the bull will charge, and it is so heavy that when he goes down he can't easily get up unaided. He depends on his colleagues to draw the bull away.

Years ago, of course, the picador was even more vulnerable, because his horse had no protection at all against the bull. Everything depended on the picador's skill at holding off the bull with his lance. So many horses were gored, however, that the *peto* or mattress was prescribed. This last grew longer and longer until finally it began to scrape the ground. Picadors grew careless and sometimes jabbed away at a bull until he was half-dead from lance wounds alone. Recently the size of the *peto* has been limited to about 60 pounds (instead of 90 or more), thus making the horse somewhat vulnerable and restoring a certain degree of skill to the picador's task. Horses are occasionally gored again, and the next phase of this debate remains to be seen. But back to our bullfight.

Watch closely now, for here it is probable that you will have an opportunity to see some dexterous capework. The usual bullfight program calls for the killing of six bulls by three matadors. Although each matador has two bulls definitely assigned to him for the kill, at this stage of the fight all three will probably intervene. It is usual for the picadors to appear three times. The three matadors take turns in drawing the bull off, and in demonstrating their mastery of the animal. Thus this portion of the fight takes on the aspect of a competition among the three, and you may see exceptional brilliance displayed at this juncture.

Now you are likely to see some of the most intricate passes—though the chances are that at your first fight they will all look much alike. One pretty effect is to end a series of verónicas by holding the cloth of the cape to the waist and twirling as the bull passes, so that it stands up like the skirt of a pirouetting dancer. This is called a *rebolera*. In the *chicuelina,* a rather dangerous pass, the matador gathers in the cloth just as the bull is passing, wrapping it around his own body. He hopes the bull's rush will carry him past, in spite of the sudden removal of his target. Usually it does. This pass is named for the bullfighter who first used it. So is the *gaenera,* which starts like a *verónica,* but in which the cape is thrown up over the head as the bull is passing. So is the *manoletina,* in which the cape or muleta is held behind the matador's back while the bull is invited to charge only an arm's length away.

The planting of the banderillas—the pairs of decorated darts that are thrust into the bull's shoulders—comes next. This is a spectacular feat to the uninitiated, but it is in fact one of the least dangerous parts of the fight. Watch closely, however, if you see the matador himself preparing to perform this maneuver, instead of entrusting it to the banderilleros, which is the normal course. That means he is particularly expert with the darts, and you may see an extra twist added.

The Climax

The last stage of the fight is the final playing of the bull and his killing. This is when the matador, at least if he feels he had a good bull, a responsive animal, bold and aggressive, will put on his best show. If, before advancing into the ring, he holds his hat aloft and turns slowly round, to salute the whole audience, it is your cue to miss nothing. It means that he is dedicating the bull to everyone, and that is done only when the torero believes he has an opportunity to give a particularly fine performance with all the extra, spectacular flourishes.

This is also the most dangerous part of the fight. For the large cape, the muleta is now substituted, a small piece of red cloth that offers a much less conspicuous target for the bull's attention than the matador's body. It is now that his skill will be exerted to its utmost and now that you will want to follow most closely every movement of the torero until at last the great black bulk of the bull goes crashing down onto the sand.

You may think that the quality of the bullfighting has suddenly decreased at the beginning of the faena, for there may not be much grace in the opening passes. That is because their object is to attain complete mastery over the bull. His will to fight is being broken, and it is done by violence rather than by grace. It is at this stage that you will see the faena's counterpart of the opening act's *verónica,* that is to say the most simple pass of this part of the fight, the *natural.* This consists in presenting the muleta, held out in one hand to the left side of the matador, and swinging it before the bull's muzzle as he charges. This is more dangerous when done with the right hand *(un natural con derechazo).*

Once the bull has been shown again who is master, however, you may see some of the most daring and elegant passes of the whole corrida. Passes in which the matador stands erect holding the muleta with both hands, as though flagging the animal by, are called 'statues'—*estatuarios.* It is at this stage that you may see the manoletina, mentioned above, and some overhead passes *(pases por alto).* The most dangerous pass you are likely to see now is the *arrucina,* in which the muleta is held behind the body. Also risky is the *pendulo,* in which the cloth is swung back and forth behind the matador's legs.

At the end of this demonstration, the time comes for the kill. First, it is necessary to square *(cuadrar)* the bull—that is, to maneuver him into a head-on position with the two front feet together. We had a lesson in the importance of that point at Bilbao, where we saw a bull squared seven times. Each time he shifted his feet as the matador lunged forward with the sword, and each time the blade struck bone and flew high into the air. The bull was killed on the eighth attempt, by which time the ring was carpeted with seat cushions thrown by furious fans.

The Kill

With the bull fixed, the matador drives the sword in over the horns with his right hand, while his left, with the muleta, sweeps under his eyes and pulls his head down. It is a moment as dangerous for the man as for the bull; if the swing of the muleta fails to hold that head down, instead of sword into bull it will be horn into man. But if the matador has judged correctly, the bull crumples to the ground after a few moments' agony.

What the president of the fight, whose judgment is usually much influenced by the reaction of the crowd, thinks of the bullfighter's performance will be indicated now. If the matador did well, he is awarded an ear; exceptionally well, both ears; and for a really superlative performance, the ears and the tail. This is ordinarily as far as recognition goes, but there have been occasions on which a hoof or two has been added, and the all-time record is probably held by Carlos Arruza, who in Málaga was awarded the whole animal, at the end of a fight in which he had once been tossed. The dead bull may be dragged around the ring and cheered in tribute to his courage. This in no way reflects upon the performance of the matador—indeed, quite the contrary.

Now for a few odd items of information:

When you buy a ticket for a bullfight, you will be asked if you prefer *sol* or *sombra*—the sunny side of the ring or the shady side. The sunny side of the ring is cheaper, for reasons that will be obvious to you once you have become acquainted with the Spanish sun. Sometimes you may be offered the intermediate choice of *sol y sombra* when the ring is so located that, as the sun sinks, broilers in the sun will be afforded some relief. Ringside seats are *asientos de barrera.* A sign over the box office reading *"No quedan localidades"* means that the seats are sold out, and if it continues, *"ni entradas,"* there is no standing room either. But Spain has ticket speculators, so this does not mean that you cannot get in, only that you can't get your ticket at the box office. Bullfights and Mass are the only things in Spain that start on time, so be sure to get there early; once the corrida has started, the arena doors are closed.

If you want to go to the bullring in any Spanish city, ask for the Plaza de Toros. The fence around the arena is the *barrera,* the corridor behind it, before the seats begin, the *callejón,* the shields that guard the openings in the barrera are the *burladeros.* A bullfighter is a *torero* (never, except in *Carmen,* a toreador) and only the star, who kills the bull, is a *matador.* The matador and his attendant group, which works together as a unit, is the *cuadrilla. Novilladas* are fights with young bulls and aspirant matadors.

You will want to identify the matadors at the beginning, to follow the fight. They will be the men walking in front of the opening procession into the arena, just behind the mounted escort. The senior will be on the right and will kill the first and fourth bulls, the youngest in the center, and will kill the third and sixth bulls.

The bullfight season in Spain runs from the end of March through October. Madrid is naturally the place where the most famous fighters are to be seen most often and the best fights are staged here for the San Isidro fair in May. Madrid's Plaza de Toros, which seats 25,000, is the main ring. There is always a fight on Sunday, and often on Thursday as well; starting times have altered recently because of daylight saving and tend to be around 6 or 7 P.M. Barcelona also has a great season. The second most important place and time is Seville during the fair week that begins in late April. Pamplona is the place where the bulls run through the streets before the fights on July 7–14 and Bilbao stages its biggest fights in the middle of August. Bullfights are also staged at most regional festivals during the same seasons.

That strange phenomenon Manuel Benítez (El Cordobés) is now retired. Among the undeniably best toreros are Angel Teruel, Paco Camino, Curro Girón, and Diego Puerta. Recently the *rejoneador* has made an important comeback to the Spanish bullring, reviving the old style of bullfighting in which each phase of the contest is performed by the rejoneador, mounted on a beautiful Arab horse which, needless to say, is kept out of contact with the bull's horns.

If, after this exposition on bullfighting, any reader still feels strongly opposed to the spectacle, he may wish to contact the *International Council Against Bullfighting,* 13 Graystone Rd., Tankerton, near

Whitstable, Kent CT5 2JY; the *Association for Prevention of Cruelty in Public Spectacles,* Vico 21, Barcelona 6.; the *World Society for the Protection of Animals,* 29 Perkins St., Jamaica Plain, Mass. 02130, U.S.A.; or Mrs. M. Mashinter, 340 Mill Rd., Appt. 304, Etobicoke, Ontario N9C1Y8, Canada.

SPANISH FOOD AND DRINK

Paella and Squid, Sherry and Brandy

Eating in Spain can be a delightful adventure or a sad disappointment. The traveler who has the good sense to hunt out local delicacies and to choose carefully the restaurants where he eats then can enjoy his trip to Spain for the food alone. But many hotels, particularly in the popular coastal areas, put on their version of an Anglo-Saxon meal, which is usually disastrous.

Spanish cuisine is neither so dainty nor so varied as the French or, perhaps, the Italian, but it has virtues of its own. It is substantial and plentifully served and still has its light and delicate dishes for hot weather. One virtue for the traveler is that eating in Spain is still as economical as anywhere in Western Europe today.

Spaniards do not like their food very hot. They say it has no taste that way. Those who like their food piping hot should insist with the waiter that it be served *muy caliente.*

In general, the food is not highly seasoned—as so many visitors expect it to be—like Mexican cooking. Only a few dishes are highly spiced or peppery. Olive oil is the basis of cooking, and when well used you will hardly notice it. Each region has its own specialties, and in all of them good seafood is to be found.

The abundance of fresh fish and other sea products all over Spain is one of the best organized features of the country. Fast trucks drive all night to bring them even to the center of the country no later than the morning after they have been landed. All along the roads in the country you will see fish peddlers with flat boxes of fresh fish strapped on their bicycles for delivery to the surrounding villages. *Merluza* (hake) is found everywhere and is served well, though it is not the most interesting of fish. In San Sebastián, above all in Bilbao, and in some of the fishing ports, fresh sardines, grilled or fried, are popular.

Tuna fish is served fresh in the north, cut into steaks and cooked in a rich tomato and onion sauce. It is even more plentiful on the Atlantic coast between Gibraltar and Cádiz. Trout and salmon can also be had in season.

A dish likely to be strange to Anglo-Saxon visitors is squid, or cuttlefish, but it is well worth sampling. Known as *calamares,* or if small, *pulpitos* or *chipirones,* they are at their best in the Basque country and Catalonia but are eaten everywhere. They are served "in their ink," in a dark sauce, or cut up and fried crisp, in which case their flavor is light and delicate. Also found in the Basque country and farther west in Galicia, is a huge crab *(centolla)* from which the meat is usually taken, chopped up and cooked in the shell with a highly spiced sauce. It is also eaten boiled. Lobster, crayfish and Dublin Bay prawns are both plentiful and delicious.

One of the basic elements of Spanish diet is pulses—dried beans, lentils and chick peas. They are cooked in all sorts of ways and the dishes have different names in each part of the country. The Basques like white or red beans stewed with *chorizo*—a peppery red sausage— and blood sausage. Farther west, Asturias is famous for *fabada,* a sort of simplified cassoulet of white beans with salt pork and sausage. Each region has its bean dish. Madrid's specialty is *cocido,* made with big yellow chick peas. Boiled beef, boiled chicken, boiled bacon and other choice bits are served with a great dish of peas, preceded by a broth made with the water they have been cooked in. It is a meal all by itself.

An excellent hors d'oeuvre found everywhere is *jamón serrano,* or mountain ham. The ham is laid out in the sun on the snow of the mountains, for the sun to cure it, while the snow keeps it from spoiling.

It is a fine dark red in color and, sliced thin, is translucent. With it one often eats *lomo embuchado,* a long strip of loin of pork cured with paprika and garlic, also at its best if sliced thin. Mountain ham with ice-cooled melon also makes an excellent first course.

As for dessert let's face it: Spanish pâtisserie is a far cry from what Central Europe has to offer. The Moorish-inspired dry cakes, like *polvorones, manoletes, yemas,* etc., are too sweet for the Anglo-American palate. You can always fall back on the ubiquitous crême caramel *(flan).* There is no need to despair however: Spanish oranges and melons, Almería grapes, Alicante dates, wonderful peaches from Aragón and the world-famous dried raisin of Málaga more than make up for this gap in Spanish gastronomy. There are tasty cheeses, too, of a simple sort, nearly everywhere, a good sharp one being *Manchego.* And if the Italians make the best espresso machines, it's the Spaniards who know how to use them. If you want your coffee black, say *solo,* while *con leche* means "with milk".

Gazpacho and Paella

Gazpacho deserves special mention. It is strictly a summer item, ice-cold soup made basically with oil and vinegar, though there is nothing oily about a properly made gazpacho. In it are finely strained tomatoes, garlic, bread crumbs, finely chopped cucumber, green pepper and sometimes onion. *Croutons* are put into it as it is served, and few things are so refreshing at the end of a long hot day. Originally the food of poor Andalusian peasants, it has become popular all over Spain and most tourists are delighted with it.

Paella, another dish that delights nearly all visitors, is much served in Madrid, though everybody seems to agree that for some reason it is never so good anywhere else as in Valencia. Its foundation is rice, flavored with saffron, and in it are mixed many tidbits of seafood: prawns, flakes of fish, tender bits of calamares, small clams, and anything of the sort that suits the chef's fancy. Small bits of meat and pieces of chicken are included and the whole is decorated on top with strips of sweet red pimento and with green peas. Properly, it should be served in the shallow iron pan in which it has been cooked. Paella is made to order, and takes from 20 minutes to cook. So, it is not a dish for those in a hurry. A tourist unwilling to wait can telephone ahead to the restaurant of his choice and order his meal for a given time.

Catalan Cuisine

Though *everybody* believes rice dishes are best in Valencia, the Catalans, farther up the coast, claim that theirs are just as good. Purists say that paella without chicken is not paella, but the Catalans insist that it is better that way. In any case, it is one of the Spanish dishes that has had most success abroad.

Catalonia is less marked for its special dishes than some other regions, but all its cooking is notable for liberal use of garlic. Tomatoes and peppers also are used lavishly and Spaniards say that many of the dishes served in France *à la Provençal* are Catalan dishes introduced by the Spanish-born Empress Eugénie and baptized with French names to avoid offending national susceptibility.

For real garlic-lovers, they produce a relish made principally of garlic, on the style of the French *aioli,* but it is a little powerful for many foreigners.

One of Catalonia's boasts is that the meat is usually better there than in most other parts of Spain, because, in the foothills of the Pyrenees, there is good grazing, though it is even better in Spain's northwestern provinces of Asturias and Galicia. Castile's pride is its roast lamb and roast suckling pig *(cochinillo asado),* at their best when prepared in a baker's oven. In Segovia and other country places pieces (chunks) of dried meat are hanging overhead and you can make your own choice.

Basque Cuisine

The Basques have the reputation of being great eaters, and the food of the Basque country is among the best in Spain. It is one of the few regions where good beef can usually be found, though the traveler who insists on steaks may be disappointed as veal is the Basques' own preference. They like hearty dishes and usually eat several at a meal. One of their specialties that has spread all through Spain is salt codfish cooked with fresh tomatoes—*bacalao a la Vizcaina*—and another is the same fish cooked very slowly *(pil-pil)* in olive oil.

In winter their great luxury is *angulas,* baby eels, cooked whole and served in sizzling hot olive oil with garlic and pieces of red-hot peppers. It takes nerve to try them the first time and it remains an acquired taste.

The fortunate traveler who has a Basque friend to invite him to one of the eating clubs will have a unique experience. These clubs, which exist only in the Basque country, are strictly for men. There are no servants. The members, ranging from the mayor to simple fishermen, but strictly limited in number, bring in the food and prepare it themselves. Staple supplies are kept on hand, and the members help themselves and drop the money to pay for what they have taken into a box. Each club includes a large "library"—the wine cellar—from which members help themselves and guests to quantities of *chacolí,* a local white wine with a slight sparkle and an equally slight alcoholic content, or to cider.

They make a fish soup *(sopa de pescado)* that is by no means inferior to French *bouillabaisse,* though less complicated. It is the staple food of the fisherman, and with prawns, tiny clams, and other dainties, it becomes a restaurant delicacy. *Zarzuela* is a variation on the same theme, but here the fish are fried before being cooked in a sauce made up of onions, garlic, tomatoes, wine and laurel. Clams are served magnificently, a small, hard-shelled variety, steamed with a sauce of garlic and olive oil and finely chopped parsley, as *almejas marinera.* Sometimes it is varied with a meat-stock sauce.

Meals—Better Late than Never

Meal hours in Spain startle many travelers, and some find them hard to get used to. They vary with the region, but in general Spaniards eat much later than in other Western countries, and later in the south of Spain than in the north. A normal dinner hour for any part of Spain is 10 P.M., though in Madrid and farther south the hour is more likely to be 10.30 P.M. It is difficult anywhere to have dinner before nine, except in the State-operated paradores and albergues, where food can be obtained, literally, at any hour of the day or night. Lunch is eaten anytime from 1.30 P.M. on. In Madrid 2.30 P.M. is a normal lunch hour and 3 P.M. is not unusual. Lunch is the main meal, dinner much lighter.

It is rare to find a restaurant that serves meals out of hours, but there are some. For those who find it hard to hold out until meal time, there are numerous cafés that serve tempting snacks *(tapas).* Shrimps are a great favorite, either boiled or grilled. Seafood of one sort or another— shrimps, prawns, crayfish, crab—are the most usual, but there are sandwiches as well and a great variety of sausages. With these Spaniards drink beer or wine.

At about six o'clock, the many coffee houses and pastry shops are filled with women having their *merienda* of coffee or chocolate with cakes and pastries, for which they have an astonishing capacity.

In Vino Felicitas

Although Spaniards consume a good deal of beer, which is usually good though light, this is essentially a wine-drinking country, and sherry is the principal product. Its name is the anglicized version of the town Jerez (pronounced *kherez*), from which the wine was first shipped to England in 1608, around which time English buyers settled in Jerez (hence such partnership names as González-Byass). Today, Britain buys about 75% of all sherry exports.

The area where genuine sherry is produced covers about 25,000 acres, but there are hardly any vineyards in the immediate vicinity of

Jerez. The 50 million or so vines are planted far from the main roads in chalky soil and have a lifetime of between 17 and 20 years. Young cuttings *(cepas)* start bearing grapes after about five years. The vintage usually begins in the first half of September. The harvest is laid out for a day or so, varying upon its nature, then taken to large stone troughs where, since the advent of mechanization, the grapes are pressed scientifically.

There are good and bad years, but no vintage sherries. Quality is ensured by a control system, called *solera:* young wines replace—but only partially—the wine drawn off for sale. It takes a period of three years to make sherry, but it takes more than twenty years to make a great sherry. There are four main types of sherry: *fino,* very pale and very dry, about 15% alcohol; *amontillado,* dry, richer in body and darker in color, about 12% alcohol; *oloroso,* medium, full-bodied, fragrant and golden; *dulce,* sweet.

A bare 24 kilometers (15 miles) to the west of Jerez, the historic city of Sanlúcar de Barrameda is the home of another type of sherry, the *manzanilla* (the Spanish word for *camomile,* because of its straw-color). Lighter (13–14% alcohol), and drier than the wine of Jerez, it is sold mostly in Spain. Call at the Town Hall *(Ayuntamiento),* and a man will show you around the beautifully patioed buildings (leave a small tip).

Montilla-Moriles, a blended dry wine, comes from the Córdoban hills between Montilla and Lucena, and is also produced under the solera system. It has more body and a different flavor than a fino from Jerez.

If you apply in advance to one of the shippers, it is possible to visit one of the *bodegas* (above-ground wine store) in Jerez. Large casks of heavy oak—mostly from America—containing the precious liquid are stocked in pillared and arcaded buildings that are not without a certain grace. Ventilation and a constant temperature of about 20°C (68°F) are ensured by highly placed large windows.

The fino sherries are the principal apéritifs in Spain, and some of the best known are Tío Pepe, San Patricio, Carta Blanca, Pando, Viña AB and Fino Coquinero, in decreasing dryness. Manzanilla is also drunk as an apéritif, as are the amontillados and Montilla-Moriles. The sweet, dark olorosos are generally drunk as a dessert wine and few people want many glasses at one sitting.

In towns near Jerez there are often local finos that are not eligible to be sold as sherry, but anywhere in that region by asking simply for fino one can usually get a cheap and refreshing drink of dry white wine, weaker than sherry.

In San Sebastián a favorite is chacolí, a "green" wine, slightly sparkling and a little bit sour, rather than dry. Cocktails are likely to prove a bad mistake except in large hotels or smart bars. The nearest approximation in a smaller place usually is a *combinación*, a mixture of about two parts of vermouth to one of gin, or a *cuba libre*, a Bacardi and Coke.

A good hot-weather drink, much drunk in Madrid, though it might shock sherry connoisseurs abroad, is the *Andaluza*, made of equal parts of dry sherry and orange juice, with crushed ice and a squirt of soda. The increasingly popular *sangría* consists of red table wine, *gaseosa*, lemon, ice and sugar. Sometimes a bit of brandy is added.

Table Wines

Of table wines, the principal ones are the *Riojas* and *Valdepeñas*, named for the regions where they are produced. In general, Rioja, from the region around Logroño in the northeast, resembles the French Bordeaux, though it is less delicate. It varies from vineyard to vineyard, and unfortunately sometimes from bottle to bottle of the same brand, being less successfully standardized than the French wines. There are many brands, but among the better known ones are Marqués de Riscal, Marqués de Murrieta, Viña Albina and Montecillo, all of them good.

Valdepeñas is a rougher wine, but pleasant and hearty. Unfortunately, a good many others are often sold as Valdepeñas, and it will be found at its best in the region where it is grown, midway between Madrid and Córdoba.

In Catalonia the *Ampurdan* and *Perélada* wines tend to be heavy and those that are not rather sweet are harsh. *Alella Marfil*, produced near Barcelona, is a white wine that purports to be a hock type but it is on the sweet side. Well chilled, it is pleasant in summer. *Alicante*, also good, is dryer and stronger, really a light apéritif. In addition to its *tinto* and *blanco* (red and white), Oliveda produces an all-purpose rosé that is astonishingly cheap for its quality.

As a general principle, it is wise to try the unbottled wine of the house *(vino de casa)*. It is much cheaper than the bottled wines and even in small places is usually, in fact nearly always, a perfectly good, drinkable table wine.

Among the many brands of sparkling wines known locally as champagne *(champán)*, the best brands are Cordorniú and Freixenet, dry or semi-dry. The majority of Spanish sparkling wines are sweet and fruity, and they serve as main ingredients to champagne cocktail, much favored by tourists.

Spanish *brandy* is as different from French as Scotch whisky from Irish. It is relatively cheap, and pleasant for a change, though most brandy drinkers find it a little on the sweet side. The dryest, probably, is Soberano. Others are Fundador, Domecq, Terry (rather sweet) and

103, which is smoother. All the same houses put out better grades under other names. Among the best are the Lepanto of González-Byass, Bobadilla Gran Reserva, Carlos Primero and Larios 1866. But if you plan to end your restaurant meal with a glass *(una copa)* of good quality brandy *(coñac)* you would be well advised to check the price; mark-ups can be astonishing.

For those who want mineral water, Spain has several good ones, and in small towns it may be wiser to drink them rather than the local water. One of the most popular brands is *Lanjarón* which comes from the town of the same name in the Sierra Nevada mountains. It can be either still or fizzy. *Mondariz* is fizzy and slightly salty. *Vichy Catalán* is almost exactly like French Vichy. *Malavella* is slightly effervescent (very pleasant) and *Font Vella* is still. Ask for *agua mineral con gas* (effervescent) or *sin gas* (still).

SPORTS IN SPAIN

Fun in the Sun

The Spanish are passionately interested in sports; both those that are common to all Europe and those that, if not peculiar to Spain, may be considered as particularly Spanish because they flourish here more than elsewhere.

Of the international sports, the one Spaniards follow more avidly than any other is the great mass spectator sport of almost everywhere in Europe—football. The Real Madrid team is internationally known, and the Atlético is second in fame. Every Sunday from September until May modern stadiums all over Spain are packed with 40,000 or 50,000 fans (135,000 in Madrid and 100,000 in Barcelona) to witness matches between the different city teams, and the same enthusiasm is to be found, on a smaller scale, at village games. The Spaniards play a more intricate game than you will ordinarily see in Britain, but it is clean and skillful, and you will not be disappointed, if you decide to see a match between any of the better teams.

Baseball *(beisbol)* is just being "discovered" by the Spaniards, and teams have sprung up all over the country during the past few years. Basketball, too, reached Spain only after the end of the war, but the Spaniards have taken to it more rapidly than baseball. Best ask your hotel porter about match venues and times.

Horse racing has never been as popular in Spain as in America, Britain and France, but there are good race courses outside Madrid, at the Hipodromo de la Zarzuela (spring and fall); at San Sebastián, at the fine Lasarte course in August at Barcelona, Seville and Santander. There is a bigger following, however, for the jumping trials and exhibitions, in which officers in the crack cavalry regiments take part, and in this particular sport Spanish teams have competed successfully of late with British, Italian and Austrian experts. The pure white Spanish-Arab horse, bred chiefly in Andalusia in the south, is admitted to be one of the best in the world. There are riding establishments in several areas, but particularly in Andalusia: at Pino Rojo (Málaga), in the San Antón urbanization (English owned); also at Andalucía La Nueva (km 181 to Cádiz), Los Alamos, El Ranchito and Antonio's, all in Torremolinos.

For golf enthusiasts, there are many good courses in Spain, some designed by American golfers, and mostly well sited around the coasts, but Madrid's Puerto de Hierro club is one of the oldest, most fashionable and expensive. In Barcelona there are two good clubs.

The Costa del Sol is the most advanced golf area, with a superb course at Sotogrande, near La Linea, and others at Andalucía La Nueva, Málaga, Torremolinos, Guadalmina and Los Monteros. On the Costa Blanca there are courses at Alicante, Valencia and the fine two-course golf complex of La Manga some twenty minutes' drive from Murcia. European Ferries, who own the complex, are developing its sporting facilities and accommodations considerably and have appointed Severiano Ballesteros as the club's tournament professional. His brother Manuel Ballesteros is the club's resident golf professional. Along the rainier north coast there are good golf courses, notably at San Sebastián, Bilbao, Santander, La Coruña and Fuenterrabia.

The booming popularity of golf in Spain has been given even greater impetus by the international successes of such young players as Severiano Ballesteros, winner of several major international competitions. Most courses are 18 holes, and the championship ones are mainly in Andalusia. Also, several of the large modern hotels have their own golf courses.

Tennis has increased in popularity over the last couple of decades with the international successes of such brilliant players as Manuel

Orantes, Juan Gisbert and José Higueras. Their flair has given this sport further impetus. In Spain, with its dry climate, the preference is for hard courts. Tennis is perhaps more widely played in Catalonia than elsewhere, but recently Andalusia has come to the fore. In the north, tournaments are held at San Sebastián, Santander, La Coruña, and there are courts in Bilbao and La Toja. On the Costa Blanca, the La Manga golf club also boasts a major tennis complex including thirteen hard courts, two championship grass courts and a stadium with a capacity for 3,000 spectators. In Andalusia, among the best clubs is Lew Hoad's Tennis Club at Fuengirola, which also has a restaurant and accommodations for 40 people. Other good tennis courts are provided by many hotels in the area, and in larger towns elsewhere.

Pelota

Not quite exclusively Spanish, for it is Basque, and is played on the French side of the frontier as well. Pelota is often described as the fastest game in the world. Spain may perhaps claim it as a little more peculiarly her own than can the Basques of France, for it has spread in Central and South America.

Pelota, more correctly called *jai alai* (happy festival), is a fast, skillful, and attractive game to watch, played on a large cement court known as a *frontón,* sometimes in the open, but more often indoors by artificial light, and between 5.30 P.M. and 9.00 P.M. There are frontones in most big Spanish cities—Barcelona has two and Madrid one. But to see it at its most brilliant, visit the frontones of any Basque city, where the highly paid professionals play. If you want to see it as the Basques know it from childhood, wander through a small town or village on a fine day.

The game is vaguely similar to squash-rackets or fives, though the court is much larger—some 10 metres wide by 60 metres long (35 ft by 200 ft). The players, usually two on each side, wear a foot-long curving basket *(cesta)* as a kind of extended glove in which they catch the hard ball, and hurl it back above a marked line on the back wall. The impact is like a machine-gun bullet, the ball traveling with tremendous speed off the hard cement, and the game is so strenuous that any player over 30 years of age is a veteran.

Betting is fast and furious and the bookmakers stand with their backs to the game (but with one eye on the scoreboard) and facing the audience. The spectators are protected from the ball by a wire net which, however, does not interfere with visibility.

Hunting, Fishing and Sailing

Spain is better provided with game than any other country in Western Europe. The tourist department has established game preserves in various parts of the country and, through it, it is possible to arrange for what the Americans call a hunting, and the British a shooting, trip. Licenses for hunting and fishing can be obtained through any government tourist office, or through your travel agent.

In addition to chamois, both the Pyrenees and the Picos de Europa mountains (on the frontiers of the northern provinces of Santander and Asturias), there are wild boar, lynx, wolf and deer. Brown bear, common in Asturias, may not be shot. From the Parador de Gredos, over 1,676 metres (5,500 feet) above sea level in central Spain, you can also go after the ibex, found nowhere else in Spain, which is known as "Capra Hispánica".

Duck shooting, outside Valencia and in the southwestern province of Huelva, is the best to be found with the sole exception of the delta of the Danube, and it is also excellent on the Balearic island of Majorca. Partridge bags of three hundred birds to six guns are not unusual in the area of the Gredos mountains near Madrid or around Toledo. Capercailzie and woodcock are plentiful in the province of León.

The tourist department has also established salmon fishing preserves on the Sella, Eo, Narcea and Dova-Cares, all in the northern provinces of Asturias and Galicia. There is a trout-fishing preserve on the River Tormes in the province of Avila, for which stretches can be rented through the tourist department.

The less aristocratic deep-sea fishing is easy and plentiful in the Mediterranean, and from the northwestern province of Galicia you can go after tuna, which may weigh up to 270 kilograms (600 pounds).

Underwater fishing has become so popular in recent years that various legal restrictions have been introduced, and any ardent hunters are advised to obtain full information from the Spanish National Tourist Office nearest their home town. Briefly, a permit is required, issued by the Naval Commandant of the Maritime Province where you want to operate; the use of oxygen equipment for underwater fishing is forbidden, as is fishing between sunset and sunrise. However, once having a permit in your hand and an understanding of the rules, you'll find some of the best underwater fishing in Europe, particularly off the Costa Brava. At Torremolinos there is an Aqualung Diving School, with English or English-speaking instructors.

With her tremendously long coastline, it is not surprising that sailing is popular in Spain. The regattas run by the Royal Yacht Clubs in San

Sebastián, Santander, La Coruña and Bilbao (Santurce) are for the big stuff, but there are races for the Snipe class as well.

Winter Sports

There are four main skiing areas in Spain: in the Guadarrama mountains 50 kilometers (30 miles) from Madrid; in the south in the Sierra Nevada where a big winter sports complex has been developed only 32 kilometers from Granada; in the Picos de Europa in northern Spain in the Braña Vieja and Alto Campo regions of Santander province; and finally in the Aragonese and Catalan Pyrenees bordering France where the largest winter sports resorts are to be found. In the Pyrenees, La Molina and El Formigal are the most popular resorts.

The season in the Pyrenees is from December until April and while the enjoyable Super-Molina runs are considered good enough for international competitions, there are plenty of runs for the less expert skiers. A cabin and a ski lift take you right up to the Tossa d'Alp (2,536 metres, 8,322 feet) from which you can make a difficult or more simple run down. Three chair lifts and a second cabin lift rise to the easier slopes. Not far from La Molina are Camprodón and Nuria which, though less highly organized, have adequate facilities. La Molina is linked with the electric railway that connects Toulouse in France with Barcelona.

THE
FACE
OF
SPAIN

Velasquez

MADRID

Life in a Modern Capital

An old Madrid adage claims that there is only one place better than
the capital to be in—Heaven, which itself can be improved only by
having a loop-hole through which to look down at Madrid. Admittedly
most cities possess such bits of local chauvinism, but Madrid's boast
of a magnificent life-style has been substantiated by countless travelers
and residents who would not hesitate to recommend it as one of the
most pleasant capitals in Europe.

Madrid, the teeming capital of Spain, rises like a mirage out of the
desert tablelands, an oasis of color and bustle surrounded by vast,
lonely stretches of slaked sand, thyme-scented brush, and granite
mountains that ensnare the Castilian sun's fire and hoard it through the
summer months. Ever since the 16th century when Philip II was struck
with the fancy of making the sleepy, inconsequential town his capital,

107

Madrid has been considered the bulwark of Spanish virtues and traits. For many years the Madrid court was held to be the most austere in Europe; however, over the past centuries the city has evolved into a fun-loving capital with few peers in the world. Not many cities can vie with it for the sheer crackling liveliness of its thronged streets, its delightful, bustling cafés, its taverns bursting with boisterous drinkers and congenial gourmands; in few cities is it so hard to find a table in a good restaurant at 10 P.M. and in none do theaters, concerts and movies invariably start at 10.30 P.M. Whatever other qualities the city may have, certainly its most outstanding is the contagious verve of daily life and the gusto its inhabitants have for going out and enjoying themselves.

The Lost Siesta

It takes the visitor time to get accustomed to the strange time-table, extreme even for Spain, by which Madrileños, as the denizens of Madrid are called, regulate their lives. For the pace is built into the very fabric of the city. Efforts have been made over the past five years to introduce more "rational" and "European" schedules, but most have been doomed to languish under bureaucratic sloth. Recently some of the big department stores did decide to stay open during the three-hour lunch break. And a law was passed that all cafés and restaurants had to close by 1.30 A.M. in the winter. But there is still no indication that any more radical changes will be forthcoming in the near future. Madrileños enjoy their tempo, even if it means having four rush hours a day instead of two and sleeping only six hours at night, though few people now have time to go home and sleep the traditional siesta at midday, for distances between work and home are increasing and traffic is excruciatingly slow.

The long working hours and the fact that many Madrileños have two jobs dispels the calumny of laziness that has been hurled at Spaniards for so many centuries; anyone seeing the crowds and traffic jams in the streets at 8 A.M. can have no further doubts of the truth that Spaniards do work long hours. The *mañana* attitude is largely a thing of the past. Now harried businessmen with attaché cases in their hands and ulcers in their stomachs flit about as singlemindedly as in Frankfurt or Milan. Domestic help is far less common than ten years ago, and labor-saving appliances are helping to polish off domestic chores as hundreds of thousands of women take to careers of their own choice.

But few minions of finance, or success-obsessed executives or bustling office and blue-collar workers will dispense with the traditional *aperitivo* in the late afternoon at their favorite café. Before heading home Madrileños love to go out and you will find that most cafés are jammed between seven and nine. The taste for going on the town also explains the huge number of cinemas and restaurants in the city. Most Madrileños find ample time to catch a leisurely movie once a week which means reserved seats (at first-run theaters) and a coffee break between the short subject and the feature film; or they may drive to El Pardo or any number of outdoor restaurants, *mesones* and *merenderos* on the outskirts of Madrid for lunch or midnight dinner during the summer. Or perhaps they will opt for a stroll in the Retiro at sunset, or a bit of browsing through the bookstalls on the Cuesta Moyano. On Sundays, for lunch, you will be hard-pressed to find an empty table at restaurants between two and four in the afternoon. Like Paris and Buenos Aires, Madrid is ideally suited for strolling and loafing. The parks, cafés, shops and museums seem custom-made for it.

Madrid Now

Those who knew Madrid a couple of decades ago lament its rapid industrialization. Some of their complaints are justified, though only incurable romantics will claim that everything was better in what they describe as the halcyon days, which in truth were days of fierce political oppression, economic and cultural penury, hardship and narrow-minded traditionalism.

Physically, Madrid has grown enormously. In 1900 its population was a mere 300,000 and it pretty well ended at the Puerta de Alcalá. Now the city's population is over ten times that (the population of greater Madrid in December 1977—the latest count—was 3.8 million), and most of the growth has come since 1960. In fact, Madrid has doubled its population in the last twenty years and is expected to hit the four million mark soon. As the city expanded it gobbled up the surrounding suburbs and villages such as Fuencarral, Hortaleza, Getafe and Vallecas. Even Alcalá de Henares and San Lorenzo del Escorial are now virtual adjuncts of the capital, with commuters traveling back and forth daily. In 1955, the city ended at around the Plaza de Lima. Now the Castellana region beyond there, is one of the most important business, residential and gastronomic areas of Madrid; it stretches north to the Chamartín Railroad Station, the La Paz Hospital, the Palace of Congresses and other important new landmarks which have risen over the past decade. A new complex, called the Azca Center, which will eventually include cinemas, shopping centers, recreational facilities and underground garages opened in 1980.

Meanwhile, the outskirts, once bleak expanses dotted with shanty towns, have been covered with middle- and lower-class apartment blocks to accommodate the exploding population. You will see these tenements on any highway leading out of the capital. Even the poorest of the complexes is usually embellished with terraced apartments, greenery and a number of cafés.

An Exploding Population

One of the reasons for the vast increase in Madrid's population is the influx of workers from other parts of Spain, and even from Portugal and Morocco and South America, who are attracted by Madrid's job opportunities, comparatively high wages, and easy life-style. Many of the Madrileños you see have actually migrated from Galicia or Asturias in the north, or from the surrounding Castilian provinces of Guadalajara, Cuenca, Soria, Toledo, Segovia and Avila, or from the still predominantly agricultural areas of Andalusia.

Also contributing to the swelling population has been the arrival of a sizable foreign community. Americans, Britons, Frenchmen, Germans, Latin Americans and others have helped to lend a more cosmopolitan touch to the capital by opening restaurants, founding cultural institutions and even starting a magazine and a newspaper in English. They range from engineers to foreign correspondents, retired Yanks living on a pension or working at the Torrejón Air Base, to writers and actors who find Madrid a congenial and convenient base.

The days when we could say that "one of the factors that attracts foreigners to Madrid is its very low crime rate" and that "women walk home unaccompanied in the wee small hours of the morning without giving their safety a second thought" are sadly gone. Madrid has joined most other large Western cities in its ration of violence, though still not high on the list. The city now has a police force, where once it made do with traffic police and a riot squad, and now has a growing reputation for purse snatching and such like popular pastimes. Robbery on the streets is an increasingly unpleasant fact of life in many of Spain's cities and Madrid comes in for its share. As we say elsewhere in this book, you would be very unwise to walk about with easily snatched bags, purses, cameras or other goodies festooned about your person, they are an invitation to the snatch artist plying his trade on the busy streets, keeping a watchful eye open for the passing visitor.

Madrid's Changing Face

The great urban expansion has inevitably taken its toll in venerable old buildings and tree-lined boulevards. Worse, Madrid is now one of the most polluted cities in Europe. But where trolley tracks have been torn up and streets widened for the mounting traffic, new trees have usually been planted and new parks and green areas provided, since any urban innovations and changes are always hotly debated in the press. Thus when a flyover across the Castellana was built at the Calle Juan Bravo, City Hall had the good sense to build an outdoor sculpture museum under it and provide benches and a fountain to beautify the area. When the huge statue of Columbus standing on a pillar was removed from the Plaza de Colón, it was subsequently placed in a pretty park where the old Mint formerly stood. The lower reaches of the Castellana, near Cibeles, which for ten years were little better than dust and desolation, are now lined with flower shops and cafés. And when underground garages were built at the Plaza Mayor, the Plaza de España, the Plaza de Santa Ana, and countless other squares, the city left them more attractive than before, with benches, greenery, and flowers to enhance their appearance.

Among the "typical" relics of the past that have vanished are the oldtime cafés with their afternoon tertulias, or conversations, where men sat for hours reading the paper and arguing about books, art and politics. They have been replaced by elegant cafeterías, which are basically coffee shops with table service. The gaslights are gone, as are the quaint donkeys laden with crockery, and the gypsy hurdy-gurdies; even the *serenos* or night watchmen who opened the house doors on each street have been retired, to the chagrin of some and the satisfaction of others. The *porteras,* or doorwomen, still hold gossipy court at the entrance to houses, but they are slowly being replaced by intercoms which are less expensive and neither nosy nor meddlesome.

Society Relaxes

This inevitable change has affected many customs and attitudes towards formerly sacrosanct subjects. Only fifteen years ago you could get a fine for kissing a girl in a park, and a young lady home later than 10 P.M. was considered to have dubious morals. Now young men and women in jeans are seen enjoying themselves at all hours of the night; discothèques and nightclubs offer the rhythms of a generation which considers the traditional Castilian values of reserve and austerity as remote and antiquated as the Escorial.

Though family structures are still fairly tight by comparison with other European countries or the United States, the influence of travel, television, cinema and a spate of liberalizing books and magazines has been such that it would be hard to differentiate a Spanish university student from his French or Italian counterpart. Censorship in questions of morality and sex, not to mention politics, has eased considerably and imitations of *Playboy* abound, as do Spanish films with nude scenes in them, more outspoken articles in a plethora of new magazines, books on sex education, Karl Marx, Freud and Marcuse.

A new pop-oriented culture with fast cars and a taste for imported Scotch whisky has largely replaced the demure, self-conscious Spaniard of old. Now the latest literary, philosophical, and scientific trends are quickly snapped up and translated into Spanish for publication. Given this universalist influence impinging upon Spaniards for years, the supposedly inherent Castilian traits such as reserve, austerity and even bigotry, are hard to detect, though those with a penchant for making generalizations will doubtless find examples to feed their pet theories on national characteristics.

A Widening Choice

The disappearance of vestiges of the past is offset by the advent of new facilities which certainly make the city more comfortable for the tourist. Among them are the dozens of new Spanish and international restaurants which serve Chinese, Japanese, Italian, Indian, Russian and American foods unheard of only twenty years ago in Madrid, when travelers often had to resign themselves to either insipid hotel food or unpalatable oily local fare. The quality and range of Spanish restaurants in Madrid has greatly improved. The choice now runs from the humblest students' and workers' *restaurante económico,* with its tiled walls, moist napkins, blaring televison set, home cooking and slow waiters, where you can still get a complete meal very cheaply, to the *haute cuisine* of posh international favorites, where the tab is comparable to the best restaurants in New York or London.

For the shopper there are now a dozen large department stores. Often they are easier for the tourist to grapple with than the local stores where each item has to be sought separately and where English is often not spoken. Many comfortable new theaters now show films in the original language, and transportation around the city is by clean, comfortable buses, subways and taxis, not the rickety tramcars and tatty doubledeckers of old. An efficient bus links the modernized airport with the city and one of the most modern railway stations in Europe greets rail travelers coming from the north.

Business practices too have been streamlined and the use of checking accounts has become widespread, as Spanish banks blossom forth on virtually every street corner of the city. Madrid continues to have some of the finest hotels in the world, with service that matches their elegance. The Ritz and the Villa Magna are in a class by themselves and others such as the Meliá Madrid, the Monte Real, the Eurobuilding and the Princesa Plaza are welcome additions.

Seeing the Sights

Madrid offers several attractions that can be found nowhere else in the world. The chief of these for tourists is bound to be the Prado Museum which despite frequent overcrowding, bad ventilation, a terrible restaurant and inadequate lighting must still be considered one of the top sights in Europe. (Plans have been approved for new installations, including air-conditioning.) Here is your opportunity to view works by Goya, Velázquez, Murillo, El Greco, Bosch, and Zurbarán which have made the Prado a mecca for art lovers throughout the centuries.

Those who can only take great picture galleries in small doses might alternate with several other really excellent museums, especially the Lazaro Galdiano, a magnificent storehouse of *objets d'art,* the Archeological Museum, which has a first-rate collection ranging from prehistoric times to the medieval period, and the Royal Palace, a compendium of museums including the palace itself, an armory, a coach museum, an old apothecary and a library.

Perhaps the most fascinating attraction, however, is just to stroll through the streets and squares of the city, especially in the area around the Puerta del Sol, the Gran Vía and the Plaza Mayor, observing the old streets, houses and shops, stopping for a *café con leche* or a *vino tinto.*

The pace can be changed by visiting the Egyptian Temple of Debod, near the Plaza de España, the Convent of the Descalzas Reales, off Preciados, or the Wax Museum on the Plaza de Colón.

You might spend the late afternoon just relaxing in an outdoor café sipping a dry sherry accompanied by a plate of shrimp, and watching the passers-by. These outdoor cafés can be found all over Madrid. Sitting on the Gran Vía tends to be hectic with its car fumes and noise. A better choice is the trafficless Plaza Mayor, or any of the parks. Better still, head towards the Paseo de Rosales where ten blocks of cafés line the Parque del Oeste and there is usually a breeze in the summer. Actually, sipping and seeing can be enjoyed almost anywhere in the city; even the lowliest suburb will have a bar with some chairs and tables placed outside and an assortment of tapas (tidbits) placed on the counter to accompany your glass of beer or wine. And *never* will anyone every hurry you to pay. In fact, the problem usually is to catch the waiter's eye.

Tasca-hopping

The alternative attraction is to go *tasca*-hopping, one of the great pastimes that Madrid—and Spain in general—has to offer. Tascas are small taverns which are clustered mostly around two areas. The first is behind the Puerta del Sol, starting from the Calle Echegaray, running across to the Plaza de Santa Ana, and then down to the Calle Victoria and thereabouts. The other good area for tasca-hopping is off the Plaza Mayor, down the Arco de Cuchilleros, where you'll find a dozen mesones (taverns) jammed full with munching customers, strumming guitarists and an occasional *tuna* group of university minstrels dressed in the garb of Philip II, now serenading tourists for money instead of the traditional sweethearts of old for love.

The usual tasca trip, best done with three or four friends, might start, say, at the Casona on the Calle Echegaray, with an order of shrimp, squid, mushrooms or *tortilla* (potato omelet), washed down by a glass of beer *(caña)* or wine *(chato de vino tinto);* then you press on to another tavern, trying a different specialty such as octopus or mussels; then to a third for clams and barnacles and oysters and so on until you have tried most of the tidbits and are ready for a proper meal. In fact, many people do the tasca rounds in lieu of a meal. If it is your first time in Spain and you are gastronomically adventurous, trying so many types of new food will prove an exhilarating experience.

At night you have the choice of a flamenco show, a movie in English, a fast game of jai-alai (pelota), a discothèque or maybe just a coffee in the Plaza Mayor. If the weather is inclement, one can turn to the innumerable cocktail lounges and American-type bars, most of the better ones in the Generalísimo area. Those in search of nostalgia can ensconce themselves in the Café Gijón or the Café Comercial for smoke, talk and a coffee and brandy. Others may prefer to sip cocktails and mingle with the show business crowd at Oliver's.

Still another suggestion is to have dinner under the stars in one of the restaurants outside the city, on the road to La Coruña or to Burgos or Barcelona, where charcoal-broiled baby lamb cutlets are the specialty, their superlative taste unequaled anywhere in the world.

Weather Matters

The way you spend your sojourn in Madrid will partially depend on the month of the year you have decided to come. Generally the best time to visit Madrid is in the spring or autumn. If we were to pick the best two months, they would be May and October. April is still a bit too early and tends to be cold and rainy, though the Holy Week processions are well worth seeing. They are not as famous as those in Seville, Cuenca, Valladolid, Málaga and Zamora, but are nonetheless impressive, especially La Procesión del Silencio on Good Friday.

By May the city blossoms with flowers and the weather is usually mild and sunny, perfect for *al fresco* dining and excursions to the surrounding cities. The countryside is then bespeckled with poppies and the grass is still green and aromatic. Even the humblest restaurants serve seasonal specialties such as fresh asparagus and strawberries with whipped cream. May is also the month of Madrid's celebrated activities in honor of its patron saint, San Isidro, meaning two weeks of top bullfights, fireworks, street festivals, contests and concerts.

June is still usually very pleasant, though often it will bring the first heat wave, with temperatures soaring to the 90s. The climate of Madrid, it should be emphasized, is very dry and thus bearable even when hot, since the city lies at an altitude of over 600 metres (2,000 feet) and is surrounded by a virtual desert.

July and August are the hottest months of the year, the former usually far worse than the latter. In August the city is semi-deserted, since most Madrileños have a month's vacation which they usually take at the seaside or in the mountains. Most of the restaurants are closed, and there are virtually no cultural activities except perhaps the Festivales de España, organized by the Tourist Ministry. Relatively little traffic hampers you from moving along the streets and the city completely shutters itself against the pressing heat that lasts from midday till the time the sun starts to sink behind the Guadarrama mountains. Many office workers who stay behind switch to a schedule that ends at 3 P.M. At night Madrid revives again; the streets fill with people and the cafés draw idlers who sip cool drinks till the early hours, catching the evening breeze as the city cools off; sometimes it even gets chilly during the starry August nights.

After the summer vacations, activities don't resume until mid-September, when the music and theater seasons start up again. October is a very lively tourist time and rooms are at a premium. Numerous conventions invade the city as Madrid swings back into its usual pace.

With November the rains and cold weather set in. By cold we mean temperatures in the low 'forties. Rarely does it drop below freezing in Madrid. Winter, in fact, can be very pleasant and often surprisingly mild. It is not uncommon, for example, to be able to sit outdoors in the Retiro in January, or walk about without an overcoat. Snowfalls are usually limited to a half-hour of flurries per year; any snow that sticks is quickly photographed by assiduous newsmen before it melts.

In the pre-Christmas season, the city is decked in lights and decorations, especially down the Gran Vía and around the Puerta del Sol;

trees and Nativity scene figures are sold in the Plaza Mayor, and parades and religious services fill the calendar from about mid-December till Epiphany, January 6.

The Library of El Escorial,
gaudily frescoed, with 40,000
books—many of them priceless
treasures

The serene cloister of San
Juan de los Reyes Monastery
in Toledo, built in thanksgiving
for victory over the Portuguese

**The façade of Gaudí's
fantastic Sagrada Familia
Church in Barcelona**

The picturesque Basque town
of Ondarroa, near San
Sebastian. A quiet landscape,
in the rugged northern
mountains of León

El Greco

EXPLORING MADRID

A Little History and a Lot of Wandering

Until the 16th century Madrid slumbered as an obscure little village with little to recommend it. In 1561, King Philip II decided to move the capital from Valladolid to Madrid. Philip III tried in vain to have the capital revert to Valladolid in 1601, but in 1607 the court was back in Madrid again, this time for good.

At first courtiers were not happy living in the dusty, unsalubrious town, torrid in the summers, freezing in the winters, with gusts of cold air blowing down from the Guadarrama mountains in those days before good heating, and with no river worthy of the name flowing through it—for the Manzanares has always been more of a joke than a river. Nonetheless, thanks to Spain's Golden Age, Madrid blossomed forth intellectually in the 16th and 17th centuries with such protean talents as Cervantes, Lope de Vega, Calderón de la Barca, Quevedo,

117

Rojas, Tirso de Molina and others gracing its somewhat austere streets, and painters like Velázquez, El Greco and Zurbarán decorating its palaces and churches.

Bourbons and Napoleon

After the reign of the Habsburg dynasty, the Bourbon kings made some improvements in the city, especially King Carlos III, an Italian. Spain's decline in its fortunes in the 18th century was followed by the reign of the ludicrous Carlos IV, whose ineptness was aptly chronicled by the brush of Francisco Goya. The country then fell briefly into the hands of the French. Napoleon's brother, Joseph, was installed on the throne. Though much maligned by the Spaniards, who called him Pepe Botellas due to his reputed love of liquor, Joseph was instrumental in modernizing the city. The Bonapartes were driven out by an allied Anglo-Spanish force during the Peninsular War (called in Spain the War of Independence), though not before the Spaniards rose against the French Mameluke soldiers in the Puerta del Sol on May 2 1808, a scene which inspired Goya's famous painting on the subject.

What followed was almost worse than the French, for the rule of King Fernando VII, probably the most despicable monarch in Spanish history, is remembered as one of oppression and tyranny. After over thirty years of persecuting his subjects, Fernando finally died in 1833 and was succeeded by Queen Isabel II, not exactly a paragon of virtue either. Innumerable changes in government, *pronunciamientos* by ambitious generals and two civil wars followed between Isabel's backers, the liberal *cristinos* and the supporters of the pretender Carlos, until the question of succession was finally settled by the defeat of the Carlists and the advent of Alfonso XII in 1874. After his death and a period of regency by his mother, he was succeeded by Alfonso XIII who ruled till 1931. He went into exile in Italy when the Republic was declared. The present king, Juan Carlos, is Alfonso's grandson.

Madrid in the Civil War and After

Through all these years Madrid had been evolving. By 1900 the city was fast becoming more cosmopolitan as good hotels and restaurants sprang up to cater to the burgeoning tourist trade; railroads linked virtually all the major cities to the capital, a subway was built and an intellectual renaissance occurred with the advent of the "Generation of '98".

Throughout almost all of the Civil War Madrid remained loyal to the Republic. The battle front against General Franco's Nationalist troops was only a mile away from the center of the city, beyond the university grounds, in the Casa de Campo Park. The Telephone Building on the Gran Vía, the main observation point for the Republicans, was piled stories high with sandbags. Yet despite three years of turmoil, relatively little damage was done to the city, except in the area around the Paseo de Rosales and the University City. When it was all over, the names of many major streets were changed and a triumphal arch built at the northern entrance to the city. (Many of the streets renamed by General Franco have recently reverted to their original names.) Shortly, work was begun on the mammoth cross in the Valley of the Fallen, near El Escorial, where the Generalísimo is now buried.

In 1959, Spain's currency was finally stabilized after decades of economic chaos accompanied by privations and hardships on the part of Spaniards. The tourist flood began, bringing with it foreign currency, foreign tastes and prosperity in the form of television sets, cars and installment buying. Madrid benefited greatly from this influx, both directly as a showpiece of Spanish culture, and indirectly through the funds that were funneled into the capital from other tourist regions and from Spanish workers who had gone abroad (still totaling an estimated one million).

It was largely thanks to this artificially imposed centralization that Madrid quickly made strides in evolving from a merely bureaucratic center to one of the major industrial hubs of the country, matching and often surpassing its traditional rival, Barcelona. Now Madrid is not only the financial capital of Spain, but it is also a center for car manufacturing, aircraft construction, entertainment, food processing, advertising, publishing, research, education, chemical and cosmetics industries, pharmaceuticals and furniture making.

Discovering Madrid

To do Madrid ample justice, the tourist should plan to stay a minimum of three days, after which another day or two can be dedicated to excursions to Toledo, Segovia, Aranjuez, El Escorial, the Valley of the Fallen and Avila.

With the exception of the sprawling Generalísimo area of the city, Madrid is still a fairly compact capital and you can usually walk from one tourist attraction to another and be assured that enough sights will line your way to prevent boredom. When there is little traffic, the main part of the city can be sped through in fifteen minutes. With the usual traffic jams, however, it will take you an hour. So, whenever possible, it is best to walk. If you get tired, simply take a bus or cab back to your hotel.

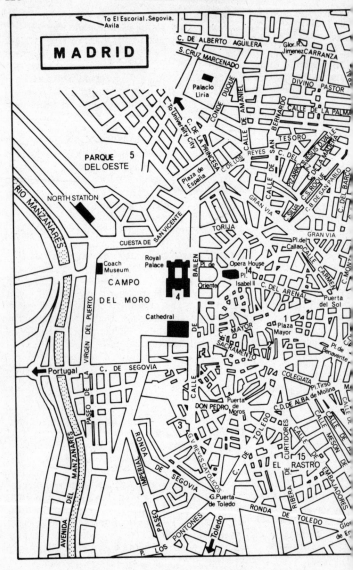

To El Escorial, Segovia, Avila

MADRID

C. DE ALBERTO AGUILERA
S. CRUZ MARCENADO
Glor. R. Jimenez CARRANZA
DIVINO PASTOR
Palacio Liria
CONDE DUQUE
CALLE DE AMANIEL
CALLE DE SAN BERNARDO
CALLE DE LA PALMA
C. DE LA PRINCESA
To University City
TESORO
REYES
C. DEL PEZ
C. DE SAN ROQUE
C. B. DE SAN PABLO
C. DE BARCO
PARQUE DEL OESTE 5
Plaza de España
C. DE LOS
GRAN VIA
SILVA
NORTH STATION
RIO MANZANARES
CUESTA DE SAN VICENTE
TORIJA
GRAN VIA
Pl. del Callao
GRAN VIA
CALLE
CARMEN
C. MONT
Coach Museum
Royal Palace
BAILEN
Pl. de Oriente
Opera House
14.
Pl. Isabel II
C. DEL ARENAL
Puerta del Sol
CAMPO DEL MORO
4
CALLE DE
1 Plaza Mayor
MAYOR
Cathedral
SACRAMENTO
Pl. de Peñavente
Portugal
C. DE SEGOVIA
PASEO DE LA VIRGEN DEL PUERTO
COLEGIATA
Pl. Tirso
C. D. DE ALBA de Molina
Puerta DON PEDRO de Moros
TOLEDO
CALLE DE CURTIDORES
CALLE MESON
3
G. V. REYES CATOLICOS
C. DE
15
EL RASTRO
CALLE DE
RONDA DE
SEGOVIA
IMPERIAL
G. Puerta de Toledo
RONDA DE TOLEDO
AVENIDA DEL MANZANARES
PONTONES
Toledo
P. LOS
Glor. de En

KEY

1   Plaza Mayor
2   Cuchilleros Arch
3   San Francisco Church
4   Royal Palace
5   Debod's Temple
6   Prado Museum
7   Neptune Fountain
8   Cortes Españolas
9   Cibeles Fountain
10   Post Office
11   Alcalá Gate
12   Atocha Railway Station
13   Archeological Museum
14   Opera House
15   Rastro

The Prado as Starting Point

Since the attraction most tourists head for first upon arrival in Madrid is the Prado Museum, we will start our tour of the city from this world-famous art gallery, one of the great storehouses not only of Spanish art, but of Flemish and Italian masterpieces.

Located on the Castellana (here called the Paseo del Prado), the Prado can be entered either from the Paseo del Prado, where you'll see a statue of the painter Diego Velázquez, or from a side entrance, where there is a rather inadequate parking lot and a statue of Francisco Goya.

The Prado was originally opened in 1823 and has since been superbly stocked with the works of Velázquez, Murillo, Zurbarán, Ribera, Valdés Leal, Alonso Cano, El Greco, Berruguete as well as with a fine collection of Titian, Rubens, Raphael, Botticelli, Correggio, Mantegna and Bosch which were transferred from the Escorial Monastery outside Madrid where King Philip II had originally housed them. Both he and his father, Emperor Charles V, were avid collectors and brought many art treasures from southern Italy and the Netherlands, both at that time part of the Spanish empire.

To view the Prado's many paintings, statues, tapestries, frescos, numismatic collection and other treasures properly would take weeks. But the highpoints most popular with tourists are usually the El Greco, Goya, Velázquez and Bosch galleries.

The Prado provides a unique opportunity to see the full diversity of Goya's styles. One room is dedicated entirely to the *Caprichos,* well over a hundred of them. Adjacent is a room displaying two of the artist's most famous works, the *2nd of May,* showing the uprising of the Spaniards in 1808 against the French Mamelukes in the Puerta del Sol, and the *3rd of May,* which depicts the execution of patriots by a French firing squad which has the same intensity of reaction to its subject as the later *Guernica* by Picasso. Passing on, you come to a room containing various works from the artist's "black" period, when he was already deaf and living outside the city. The most startling are *The Pilgrimage to San Isidro, Meeting of Witches* and *Saturn.* In another room hang the famous *Naked Maja* and *Clothed Maja,* as well as several portraits of the royal family, including the superb *Family of Carlos IV, Blind Man's Buff* and lighthearted works such as *The Mannikin.*

One of the most highly regarded Spanish painters over the centuries, Diego Velázquez, also has several rooms set aside for him. In one hangs the *Surrender at Breda.* Make sure to see *The Drunkards* and his famous series of four dwarfs. *Las Meninas,* perhaps his most famous work, has been placed in a room by itself, with a strategically placed mirror to help you appreciate its extraordinary complexities.

The main gallery and adjoining rooms contain El Grecos, Riberas, Rubens, Titians and Murillos. You should not leave before visiting the astounding collection of Hieronymus Bosch paintings displayed in the Flemish wing, which includes his famous *Garden of Earthly Delights,* the triptych *The Hay Wagon,* and Pieter Breughel's *Triumph of Death.*

In the fall of 1981 Picasso's *Guernica* was brought to Spain after its years of exile in New York. Its arrival in Madrid was the highlight of that year's celebrations of the centenary of the artist's birth. It is now housed permanently in the Casón del Buen Retiro, an annex right behind the Prado.

From the Retiro to Cibeles

After a bout with the Prado, you can either take a stroll through the rather dull adjacent Botanical Gardens, opened in 1774 in the reign of Carlos III, or better still go to the Retiro Park, two streets away.

Madrid's prettiest and most popular park, the Retiro dates back to the 15th century, though it was not opened to the public until 1876. Among the park's attractions are a dozen or so outdoor cafés, two nightclubs, a lake for rowing, playgrounds for children and shady lanes, often decorated with statues and monuments and fountains, ideal for strolling. In spring and summer, band concerts are held on Sunday mornings, and members of the Catalan colony in Madrid meet and solemnly dance the sardana. The Retiro plays host annually to a dog show, art exhibitions in the 19th-century glass-and-iron Crystal Palaces, and puppet shows; even outdoor theatrical performances are sometimes staged here.

In addition to the large lake with its huge monument to Alfonso XII, there are two smaller ones, stocked with ducks and swans and surrounded by weeping willows. Fountains, statues and busts, beautiful flower arrangements and a delightful rose garden all help to make the Retiro a welcome haven from the city's bustle. In summer you can enjoy the park till about 10.30 at night.

Leaving the Retiro at its main exit, the Plaza de la Independencia, you'll see a large arch, the Puerta de Alcalá, built in 1778 by Sabatini in Carlos III's reign. The arch was formerly one of the gates to the city, with an adjoining customs' station; beside it stood the old bullring, which was later moved to its present location on the Calle de Alcalá at Ventas.

Running along the side of the park is the Calle Alfonso XII; near its southern end it crosses the Cuesta Claudio Moyano, the site of the secondhand book fair; further on, at the corner, you come to the

Ethnological Museum, of no particular interest. A right turn leads to the Atocha Railroad Station, a colorful 19th-century glass-and-steel structure. Crossing under the ugly flyover and proceeding up the Calle de Atocha, you will enter an old working-class area, worth a stroll for those seeking off-beat neighborhoods and local color.

If at the Plaza de la Independencia you turn down the Calle de Alcalá, you will come to the Plaza de Cibeles, named after the Greek goddess Cybele (daughter of Uranus) who stands mounted on a chariot. The fountain has become the unofficial emblem of the city. Cibeles, as the square is known to Madrileños, is the great crossroads of the city, the intersection of the Calle de Alcalá and the Castellana. Two large outdoor cafés on the southern corners are perennial favorites, and a shady promenade with a small playground, trees and benches make the area between Cibeles and the Neptune fountain an especially inviting place to rest after sightseeing.

Cibeles to Gran Vía

On the southeast corner of Cibeles rises the huge, cathedral-like Palacio de Communicaciones, or Main Post Office (1918) providing telephones and all the usual services.

On the southwest corner of Cibeles is the Banco de España, analogous to the Federal Reserve Bank in the US. In the bank's underground vaults are stored Spain's gold reserves. The building was finished in 1891.

At the northwest corner stands the Ministry of the Army building, surrounded by lush gardens and guarded by soldiers. It was originally the palace of the Marquis of Linares, built at the turn of the century. Opposite, on the northeast corner, is the Palacio de Buenavista, built for the Duke of Alba in 1769. It was slated to be torn down, like so many other palaces lining the Castellana, but in 1976 a reprieve came from the government who declared it a national monument.

Progressing down the Calle de Alcalá, on the right, is the church of San José, finished in 1742. At the Dolar Cafetería we branch right into the Gran Vía, Madrid's bustling shop and cinema-lined Great White Way. On the left side you will see the Grassy jewelry store, which has a clock museum in its basement well worth a visit; on the right, Chicote's bar, a favorite meeting place during pre-war days and much frequented by Hemingway and other writers. Chicote's famous bottle collection of 10,500 bottles from all over the world, formerly housed in the basement of this bar, has now been moved to the Torres de Jerez in the Plaza Colón. It reopened in May 1982.

Around the Puerta del Sol

The small traffic circle we come to next is the Red de San Luis. You can here branch left down the Calle Montera which will take you to the Puerta del Sol, or go toward the right up the Calle Hortaleza or the Calle Fuencarral. The latter is lined with inexpensive shoe shops, and ultimately links up with the "boulevards," a network of avenues skirting the center, which start at Colón and end at the Parque del Oeste. Continuing up Fuencarral you come to a popular entertainment section lined with cinemas as well as the *Drugstore* and Café Comercial. On the way notice the impressive Churrigueresque façade sculpted by Pedro de Ribera in 1722 on what was formerly a hospital. Now the building houses the recently reopened Municipal Museum. It had been closed for 21 years.

Back at the corner of the Gran Vía and the Calle Valverde you'll see the Telephone Building (La Telefónica), at one time the highest structure in the city. Walking on past the movie theaters with their large marquees, you come on the left to the Plaza del Callao. The main building of the Galerías Preciados department store, together with its annex, takes up most of the square. Two pleasant shopping streets, which are closed to traffic and where benches and flowers have been installed, the Calle de Preciados and the Calle del Carmen, both lead down to the Puerta del Sol. At the lower end of Preciados is the original Corte Inglés department store, which now has branches all over Madrid. If instead you branch down the Calle Preciados toward the Plaza de Santo Domingo you come to several excellent restaurants.

The Plaza de España

Continuing down the Gran Vía past Callao, we pass on the right the Sepu budget store as well as numerous cafeterias, movie theaters, airline offices, hotels, travel agencies and shops. Cross the Calle de San Bernardo (which toward the right takes you to the old university building, the Music Conservatory and then links up with the boulevards) and a few streets on you come to the large, spacious Plaza de España, flanked by two skyscrapers, the Edificio España, (the highest in Spain, 100 metres—333 feet) and the Torre de Madrid. The former contains the Plaza Hotel, while the latter houses the Tourist Bureau Information Office.

A large, three-storey garage was built under most of the Plaza de España, but the square, as all others where similar facilities were built, was then tastefully redone. Now the Plaza is a delightful place for lounging, reading or having a refreshment. Around the fountain, tourists sun themselves and hippies strum guitars. In the middle of the park stands the statue of Don Quixote and Sancho Panza, as well as a monument to the Discovery of America.

From this square, should you proceed straight ahead up the Calle Princesa, you'll first see on the left a conglomerate of shops and restaurants huddling in the large courtyard of an office building, which has become a popular meeting place for young Madrileños. In addition to cafeterias and the Cerebro nightclub and discothèque, there's also a pub, El Bolo, with a miniature bowling alley in it.

On the right of Calle Princesa stands the Palacio de Liria, privately owned by the Duke of Alba and not open to the public. Work on it began in 1770. After being badly damaged during the Civil War, it was subsequently rebuilt. A pleasant café and a mesón-restaurant in the small park in front of the palace make ideal resting places.

Continuing up the street on the left is the Meliá Madrid hotel. Further up we come first on the right to the Princesa Plaza hotel, then on the corner of the boulevards another Corte Inglés department store; there are shopping arcades on either side of the street. Beyond, as far as the Triumphal Arch, is an area popular with students from the University of Madrid, who come here for squid sandwiches and beer.

At the Plaza de España you can take an alternative route. Walk to the other side of the park, cross the Calle Ferraz, and enter the park, formerly the Cuartel de la Montaña (a barracks) and you'll come to the Temple of Debod, an authentic Egyptian temple which formerly stood in the Aswan area of the Nile. It was transported stone by stone to Madrid from Egypt when the Aswan area was flooded. The temple and its pleasant surroundings and palm-tree landscaping are well worth a visit. A stone's throw away is the Los Porches restaurant, set in the delightful Parque del Oeste, for *al fresco* dining or luncheons.

From the Cerralbo Museum to the Zoo

Crossing over to Ferraz, we come to the Cerralbo Museum, formerly the private mansion of the Marquis of Cerralbo. The building is crammed full of paintings, furniture, personal mementos and is rather less museumlike than the Lázaro Galdiano Museum. Visiting it is akin to paying a call on a nobleman's private quarters at the turn of the century. The mansion was built by the traditional-minded marquis in 1876.

Returning to the Parque del Oeste across the street, you continue up the Paseo de Rosales (named after a 19th-century bohemian painter from Madrid). Lining the paseo are countless outdoor cafés, delightful in fine weather. The park is well cared for. Especially beautiful is a large rose garden, with bowers, a fountain and benches.

At the corner of Rosales and Marqués de Urquijo (the end of the boulevards) is an excellent ice cream parlor with dozens of exotic flavors. Next door the Pickwick Pub is nice for a drink or a dart game. Across, at the corner beside the children's playground, is the end station of the cablecar *(teleférico)* which takes you over the Manzanares river to the Casa de Campo Park. It is a trip well worth making, for it affords some breathtaking views of the city and the Royal Palace. At either end of the cablecar are restaurants, the one on the Casa de Campo side with outdoor selfservice facilities. Buses run regularly from the cablecar station to the excellent zoo and the amusement park. The zoo, by the way, opened in 1974, in addition to the usual outdoor animals, also features a children's zoo, camel and boat rides, puppet shows and a good restaurant.

Old Madrid

A tour of Old Madrid can best be started from the Plaza Mayor, a few streets down from the Puerta del Sol. This, the oldest section of the city, was built during the rule of the Habsburg dynasty, prior to the mid-18th century. Old Madrid is a warren of narrow streets, silent churches and small squares, a welcome respite from the hectic pace and fumes of the city, an area ideal for the cursory wanderer who will let whim dictate his steps and so encounter charming vistas, streets and buildings at each turn. Getting lost here is part of the fun, for you are sure to come out eventually at some imposing monument or church which will act as a landmark.

The Plaza Mayor

The Plaza Mayor measures approximately 110 by 90 meters (360 by 300 feet) in length and width and is one of the most beautiful and also one of the most representative squares in the city. Work on it was begun by Juan Gómez de Mora in 1617 in Philip III's reign and when it was completed in 1620 eight days of merrymaking followed. Fires gutted parts of the structure in 1631, 1672 and 1790; complete restoration was not undertaken till 1853.

In the 17th century the square was used for bullfights and also for *autos da fé* and the burning of heretics, with the king watching from the section called the Panadería (Bakery) in the center of the northern side, while the 476 balconies were full of nobles and dignitaries enjoying the fun. The square was also used for the canonization of San Isidro, San Ignacio de Loyola, San Francisco Javier, Santa Teresa de Jesús and

San Felipe Neri. In it were held masked balls, firework displays and plays, among them those of Lope de Vega.

In 1629 the square was lavishly decorated for 42 days to celebrate the marriage of the Infanta María and the King of Hungary. Here also was celebrated the arrival in 1623 of the Prince of Wales, the future Charles I. During his reign, King Philip V turned the square into a market; and in 1810 triumphal arches were raised to receive the Duke of Wellington; later, in 1812 the square's name was changed to the Plaza de la Constitución. And in 1847 the last bullfights were held here to commemorate the marriage of Queen Isabel II.

Until 15 years ago the Plaza Mayor was a bustling, commercial square, with buses and trolley cars and traffic noisily clanking through it. But with the crush of tourists invading Madrid, the city decided to close it to traffic and keep it as a haven of peace and sun for pedestrians. Around 1970 a large parking lot was built under the square, but the cobblestones and the statue of Philip III by Juan de Bolonia, made in 1616, were dutifully replaced. The cafés could now spread out and strollers relax without being bothered by traffic fumes and noise.

Though the day-to-day vitality of the Plaza Mayor is gone, it is still lined with old shops and taverns; the most famous of the former are the hat and uniform shops where an extraordinary selection of headgear can be bought—anything from a pith helmet to a cabby's tweed cap. Three good restaurants with tables and chairs placed outdoors provide a pleasant opportunity for outdoor lunching or dining. In summer, theatrical performances and the Festivales de España are sometimes held here; before Christmas the square fills with stands selling decorations, noisemakers and Nativity scenes, while all around fir and pine trees are placed on sale. On Sunday mornings the square fills with stamp and coin collectors who cluster on the sidewalks and cobblestones as they buy, sell and swap parts of their collections.

Researching the Mesones

Walking down the time-worn steps under the Arco de Cuchilleros, beside the El Púlpito restaurant, you come to one of the most picturesque tourist areas in the city. The two streets leading from the Calle Mayor down to the Plaza de Puerta Cerrada (marked by a stone cross), the Calle Cuchilleros and the Cava de San Miguel, are lined with taverns and mesones which at night are a-bustle with a merry crowd spearing tapas and drinking beer and wine. Tourists mix easily with natives in a congenial babble of languages, with the glasses of beer and wine acting as a common denominator for friendship. To make the taverns still more enticing, many owners hire guitarists and accordion-players to liven things up. Especially on Saturday nights, the area has a touch of carnival about it as tourists and locals spill out into the streets and the noise reaches a boisterous pitch.

The Cuevas de Luis Candelas, one of the oldest of the mesones, has an old barrel-organ to provide the music. The Cuevas is named after a famous bandit (1806–37) whose exploits passed into the realm of folklore over the years. In an effort to prove its authenticity, the tavern has hired a doorman and dressed him up in a bandit's costume. Some wags feel that it is the tourists instead of the coach travelers who are now being fleeced; but apocryphal or not, the Cuevas is always a fun spot for roving visitors.

From Luis Candelas' you can proceed to the Mesón de Drácula, the Mesón de la Tortilla, or a half-dozen other mesones, each specializing in local foods, which are usually recognizable in their windows where you may see mushrooms frying in oil or omelets being flipped into the air. Most of the taverns are more suited for a drink or a tapa than a full-course Spanish meal. For that, you can go to Botín's on Cuchilleros, one of the quaintest old restaurants in town which makes a determined effort at being picturesque on its three stories crammed with wooden furniture and Castilian knick-knacks. The prices are moderate, the rooms oozing with charm, and the crowd of tourists usually impenetrable.

Around the corner at the Puerta Cerrada lurks another oldtime haunt, Casa Paco, unbeatable for its thick, juicy steaks served on sizzling plates. The simple home-spun décor is lorded over by Paco and his wife who, unless you have a reserved table, will make you wait in the bar up front, a not altogether unpleasant fate.

The Royal Palace

Bearing right, the narrow, curvy Calle de San Justo takes you to the Plaza del Cordón and the Casa de Cisneros, originally built in 1515 and restored in 1915. The house once belonged to the son-in-law of Cardinal Gonzalo Ximenez de Cisneros, Primate of Spain and Inquisitor General, much maligned abroad for his role in the Inquisition.

A sharp right takes you up the Calle del Cordón to the Plaza de la Villa, the site of Madrid's City Hall (Ayuntamiento) and the Torre de los Lujanes, where King Charles V supposedly kept his main European rival, François I of France, prisoner for a while after winning the Battle of Pavia. The building is now used by the Hemeroteca Municipal, or Municipal Newspaper Archives, open to researchers and public.

Continuing down the Calle Mayor, past the Consejo de Estado y Capitanía (Council of State and Captaincy) on the left we come to the Calle Bailén on which is the Royal Palace, one of the great sights of Madrid. Beside it stands the stark Cathedral of La Almudena, a modern afterthought which has been ignominiously doomed to be shrugged off by Madrileños, who consider it an intrusive pastiche. Construction remains incompleted.

The Royal Palace, a magnificent Bourbon structure, stands on the site of the former Alcázar, or fortress, which burned down in 1734. The first stone of the palace was laid in 1737 in Philip V's reign using plans drawn up by Juan Bautista Sachetti, but it wasn't completed until 1764, under Carlos III's rule. The palace provided a stylish abode for Spanish monarchs for almost two hundred years. Even Napoleon's brother, Joseph, was sumptuously housed in it in the early 19th century. After the French were ousted, King Fernando VII moved into the palace. The building remained a royal residence until the coming of the Second Republic in 1931 when King Alfonso XIII left it for exile in Italy.

Though General Franco sometimes used the palace for official state receptions and audiences, he lived in the El Pardo Palace just outside the city, leaving most of the Royal Palace as a museum. King Juan Carlos presently lives in the less ostentatious Zarzuela Palace, also outside the city.

A tour of the Royal Palace takes several hours, and includes visits to the Pharmaceutical Museum, the Royal Armory and the Library. The Coach Museum is at the other end of the gardens and must be entered from that side, a five-block walk away.

Outside the palace is the spacious Plaza de Oriente, enhanced by large stone statues of pre-unification kings and warriors. Originally 108 of them were intended to adorn the roof, but their weight was so great it was considered more prudent to place them in this park and in the Retiro. The Plaza de Oriente has traditionally been used for demonstrations for and against the regimes in power. Across from the palace you can see the Opera House, which after decades of neglect was refurbished and regally opened in 1966 as a concert hall.

San Francisco el Grande

If you continue southward over the viaduct bridge, a favorite place for suicides in the old days, down the Calle de Bailén, passing the pleasant Vistillas Park on the right and the nearby excellent Las Brujas flamenco club, you come to the biggest and most important church in Madrid, San Francisco el Grande, begun in 1761 by Fray Franciso de las Cabezas and completed in 1784 by Francisco de Sabatini.

The inside decorations date from 1881. Outstanding is the large dome which can be seen from many points in the city. It measures 29 meters (96 feet) in diameter, larger than St Paul's in London. Paintings in the chapels include works by Goya, Claudio Coello and Lucas Jordán. The fifty splendidly carved choir stalls originally stood in El

Paular Monastery outside Madrid. The fine English organ dates from 1882.

A few streets ahead along a rather bleak section takes you to the Puerta de Toledo, an arch built in 1827 under Fernando VII's rule by Antonio Aguado. Nearby, at the Plaza de Gabriel Miró, you can visit the painter Ignacio Zuloaga's studio.

Double back up the Calle Bailén and then right to the Carrera de San Francisco, formerly the scene of lively summer verbenas or street festivals during the celebrations in honor of La Paloma, which takes you to the Puerta de Moros square, opposite the Cebada market. The present "barley market" is a relatively new structure and replaced the steel-and-glass one long a landmark of the city. Beyond the Plaza de la Cebada and crossing the Calle de Toledo, go down the Calle de Maldonadas and you come out at the Plaza de Cascorro, the threshold of the Rastro.

The Flea Market

The Rastro, or Flea Market, especially on Sunday mornings, is something which should not be missed by tourists, even if they decide to buy none of the tempting wares that clutter the shops and sidewalks. It is a sprawling indoor and outdoor emporium that attracts gypsies and art connoisseurs, tourists and hippies, where you can find anything from a rusty flintlock rifle to a new puppy dog. Despite the fact that decades of bargain-hunters and professional antique dealers have raided the Rastro, new objects turn up constantly, and bargains are still occasionally found if you know what you're after. Some of the wares are wildly overpriced, so watch your step. It really takes repeated visits before you get the hang of it and know which sections to hunt in. Though the most active time is Sunday mornings, the better antique shops are open every day of the week, but not the street stands.

The main thoroughfare of the Rastro is the steep hill of the Ribera de Curtidores, which on Sundays is jammed full with pushcarts, stands and hawkers and gypsies selling trinkets, plastic toys, records, camping equipment, new furniture and foam rubber mattresses. The better wares are usually kept inside the stores on either side of the street.

Those seeking antiques, though hardly at bargain prices, might enter the two sections off the Ribera de Curtidores, about halfway down the length of the street. On the left, the Galerías Piquer is renowned for its choice art pieces, and on the right another Galería is equally reputable. The Galerías each consist of a large courtyard surrounded by a dozen or so antique stores on two levels. To pick through the Galerías carefully takes hours.

Also leading off from the Ribera de Curtidores on the left are two narrow streets, one specializing in the sale of modern paintings and the other selling birds, fish, puppies and other pets.

At the bottom of the Ribera, where the iron junk market starts, you turn right down the Calle Mira el Sol one block and come out on the Campillo del Mundo Nuevo, a square with a park in its center, where midst other stands and items spread on tables and blankets, you'll find a book and record fair where bargains can occasionally be found. The Rastro sprawls across the Ronda de Toledo, to the other side of the road, but that section of it is mostly reserved for electrical appliances, old bicycles and spare machinery parts.

Instead walk back up one of the steep narrow streets such as the Calle Carlos Arniches or the Calle Mira el Rio Baja, lined with junk shops and stands, a good bargain-hunting area. Wind up at the Plaza General Vara del Rey, another recommended area surrounded by antique shops and jammed on Sundays with stands of every description.

Vendors start putting away their wares and locking their shops around 2 P.M. at which time you can dip into some tapas at one of the taverns on the Plaza del Cascorro. Favorites are the snails and *chorizo* at the 18 de Cascorro or the succulent chicken and seafood at the adjacent Esquinita.

Another Stroll from the Prado

Back at our starting point at the Prado Museum, another itinerary takes us across the Paseo del Prado, up past the Palace Hotel to the Carrera de San Jerónimo; on the right stands the Cortes Españolas (Parliament) opened in 1850, in front of which crouch two lions cast from the molten metal of cannons captured in the war with the Moroccans in 1860. At the back of the Cortes is the Teatro de la Zarzuela where Madrid's opera season as well as many dance recitals, zarzuelas and shows are staged.

Crossing the small park in front of the Cortes, and going down the Calle de San Agustín, you come to the Calle Cervantes, upon which stands the house where Spain's famous playwright Lope de Vega lived and died (in 1635). After visiting it, return to the Calle del Prado, leading out of the Plaza de las Cortes, and lined with some good antique shops. On the right, note the Atheneum, containing a research library and rooms where lectures, film shows and exhibitions are regularly held. Membership can be applied for on a monthly basis for a small fee.

Straight ahead you come to the Plaza de Santa Ana, where you'll see the Teatro Español, the government-subsidized theater where Spanish classics are staged in season. It burned down partially a few years ago but has now been refurbished. Across the square is the Simeón department store, and above it the Victoria Hotel. The wood-paneled Cervecería Alemana on one side of the square used to be a popular rendezvous for literati, and in recent years became for a while a bohemian haunt. Today it is a favorite with tourists.

A short walk down the Calle Príncipe, or the Calle de la Cruz, past Seseña, the store specializing in capes, takes you to the Carrera de San Jerónimo, on the corner of which stands the large Banco Hispano-Americano. Going around the building on the Calle de Sevilla and turning right on the Calle de Alcalá leads you to the San Fernando Fine Arts Academy, which contains several rooms of rather badly lit galleries with works by Goya, Zurbarán and Murillo.

The Puerta del Sol

A few steps more lead you into the Puerta del Sol (Gate of the Sun), along the major crossroads of Madrid and, indeed, of all of Spain. Kilometer distances in the country are still measured from this zero point. Formerly, the Puerta del Sol was famous for its bustling, all-night cafés and hectic traffic. Around it and on the Calle de Alcalá and Calle Arenal a generation of artists and intellectuals thrashed out the problems and theories of an as-yet non-industrial Spain in endless tertulias and talk-sessions. Unfortunately none of the cafés are now left, and much of the action has moved on to other parts of town. However the square is still a very lively intersection and on December 31 it fills with people cheering in the New Year as they watch the golden ball on top of the Ministerio de la Gobernación building (Interior Ministry) descending at midnight. Most still follow the old custom of trying to swallow one grape at each stroke of the clock. The large ministry building is now police headquarters. On one corner, the old Paris Hotel overlooking the square still keeps its vigil. On another is the perennially popular La Mallorquina bakery to which Madrileños with a sweet tooth have been flocking for pastries and sweets for decades. The tea-room upstairs commands a good view of the square.

The Puerta del Sol has been the scene of many stirring events and its history is closely linked to that of the country. The most famous incident that occurred here was the uprising in 1808 against the French, depicted in Goya's painting.

Chocolate and the Sisters of Santa Clara

Proceeding on the Calle Arenal, you come on the left to the old Teatro Eslava, and next to it the Church of San Ginés. Between the two is an outdoor second-hand bookshop, and in the alley directly behind it the best-known of the old *chocolaterías,* still a favorite for early risers wanting to get *churros* and thick Spanish hot chocolate. In the old days the San Ginés *chocolatería* was often the final destination for revelers after a night of talking and drinking, before they finally went home to bed.

Branching right off the Calle Arenal along the Calle San Martin, we come to the Convent of the Descalzas Reales, founded in the 16th century by Princess Joan of Austria, daughter of Charles V and the Queen of Portugal. In 1559, the Franciscan sisters of Santa Clara moved into the building. Since then it has been lived in by many famous scions of royalty and to this day contains cloistered nuns in one part of the convent. Tours through other sections of the building are provided so that tourists can now admire the superb tapestries and assorted paintings by El Greco, Velázquez, Titian and Breughel the Elder that decorate its historical walls.

The building across the refurbished square (again with an underground garage) houses the Montepío, or Government Pawnbrokers Office; on another side of the Plaza de las Descalzas is a Portuguese fado restaurant and an excellent antiquarian bookshop, Luis Bardón.

Leaving the square at another exit, along the Calle de Trujillos, you come out on the Plaza de Santo Domingo. Turn left on Calle de la Bola, then right at the third street and come out at the Plaza de la Marina Española where you'll see a large building which was the Spanish Parliament in 1820. Originally it housed the Colegio de Doña María de Aragón, one of the earliest university-type institutions in Madrid. The building is now used by the Falange.

You can then continue on to the Plaza de España, previously described.

Museums and Lexicography

Returning once again to our starting point at the Prado Museum, we can visit a cluster of other museums in the area. Adjacent to the Post Office you'll find the Navy Museum, small but well furnished, with ship models, nautical instruments and Juan de la Cosa's famous map of the New World. Also nearby is the Army Museum, fronted by a terrace covered with vintage cannons and mortars. The museum has a good collection of weapons, armor, flags, maps and paintings, all of them well-labeled. Nearby is the Casón del Buen Retiro, opposite the Retiro Park, used now for 19th-century Spanish paintings and the new home of Picasso's *Guernica*. On one side of the small square in front of it rises the Royal Academy of the Spanish Language, the learned body charged with safeguarding the Castilian language. It re-edits its monumental dictionary every ten years or so.

The Salamanca Neighborhood and Beyond

The area northeast of Cibeles, the Salamanca neighborhood, is named after the financier José Salamanca who started building this then-new residential area in the 1870s. The *barrio* or neighborhood is bounded on the south by the Calle de Alcalá and the Calle Goya, the latter a busy shopping street lined with shops and two large department stores.

We can now proceed north either along the Castellana or the Calle Serrano, the latter being the most elegant and expensive shopping street in the city. The surrounding streets parallel and perpendicular to Serrano are the domain of elegant shops and boutiques as well. Mainly try Claudio Coello, Lagasca, Castelló, Velázquez, Oretga y Gasset, Juan Bravo and Diego de León.

Going up Serrano from the Plaza de la Independencia (Puerta de Alcalá) we first come on the left to the Archeological Museum, a large, sprawling building with sections dedicated to Greek, Roman, prehistoric and Christian and Moorish cultures. Here you can see a reproduction of the Altamira prehistoric caves in Santander, a worthwhile visit since visits to the caves themselves are limited. Beside the museum till recently stood the old Mint, which has now been torn down to make room for a huge esplanade decorated with olive trees, sculptures by Vaqueros Turcios, allegorical of the Discovery of America, and the statue of Columbus high up on a pillar, which formerly stood in the center of the Colón square. Underneath is the airport bus depot as well as arcades, shops and a theater.

Crossing the Calle Goya, you come on the right to the Celso García department store and then on the left to the large Sears department store. After passing many sidewalk cafés and art galleries, as well as the American Embassy and the British ambassadorial residence and dozens of boutiques, you finally reach the Lázaro Galdiano Museum.

Housed in what was formerly the luxurious private villa of José Lázaro Galdiano, writer, journalist and antique collector of the early 20th century, the museum contains a magnificent collection of *objets d'art*, all tastefully displayed, which ranges over clocks, paintings from Spanish and foreign masters, armor, furniture, tapestries, enamels and jewels—in all a really splendid array which is well worth a visit.

If instead of going up the Calle Serrano you proceed north on the Castellana from Cibeles, you first pass on the left several streets of promenade lined with flower shops. The Café Gijón on the left is one of the old literary standbys. In summer, the café places tables and chairs in the garden area outside. Meals are also served here. On the right side of the Castellana you pass the sumptuous Banco Hipotecario, formerly the home of the Marquis of Salamanca. Then, also on the right, comes the National Library, which usually features exhibits and art shows in some of its salons. Foreigners can use the library by simply showing their passports and paying a tiny fee.

Coming up to the Plaza Colón, you can visit the Wax Museum in the recently built Centro Colón office complex, on the left. Around the corner, and up a flight of stairs, is a pleasant cafeteria called Riofrío, with good views and a comfortable terrace. Across the street are two large office buildings, the Torres de Jerez, much criticized in Madrid for their graceless obtrusiveness and architectural non-style. Curiously enough, they were built from the top down, using a narrow central tower as a support. They now house the 10,500 bottles of Chicote's famous collection.

Excursions from Madrid

El Pardo, about 14 kilometers (9 miles) from Madrid, is notable for its royal palace. Built in the 15th century, it was, like so many of Spain's palaces, destroyed by fire and then rebuilt. It now contains tapestries, frescos and paintings of great worth. The palace was the residence of General Franco and is now open to the public.

Northwest: El Escorial and the Valley of the Fallen

Fifty kilometers (31 miles) from Madrid, at the foot of the Guadarrama mountains, is San Lorenzo del Escorial, burial place of Spanish kings and queens. It is a monastery, erected in a barren and severe setting by Philip II as a memorial to his father, Charles V, "to offer respect and honor to death", and to commemorate Spain's victory at Saint Quentin in 1557.

The building was begun by Juan Bautista de Toledo and finished by Juan de Herrera, making him one of Spain's best-known architects and establishing a new architectural trend. Everything is on such a large scale that the edifice seems cold and drab from a distance; it is only when it is studied at close range that the beauty of the classical ornamentation and of its gardens and pools is seen. You may wander freely about the courts and patios, but tickets must be purchased for the endless suite of rooms and other buildings.

This monastery-palace is eloquent testimony to the acute religious mania that clouded Philip's brain during the years before his death in 1598. The building is a vast rectangle 206 meters (676 feet) long by 160 meters (526 feet) wide, containing no less than 16 courts, 88 fountains, three chapels, 15 cloisters, 86 staircases, 300 rooms, 1,200 doors and 2,673 windows.

The combination of truly royal grandeur with monastic austerity has resulted in something unique in the world, from the small, bare and poorly furnished cell in which Philip chose to die, to the fabulously beautiful carpets, porcelain and tapestries (all specially made by the Royal Factory at Madrid) with which his less austere successors decorated the rest of the building.

The church is in the shape of a Greek cross; large, with many chapels. On either side of the main chapel are statues of Charles V and Philip II with their wives. The choir rests on a vault without apparent support, a masterpiece of Herrera, who also designed the stalls. In the trans-choir is a famous cross by Benvenuto Cellini. The museum and vestry contain paintings by Velázquez, Ribera, El Greco, and Flemish artists. The library is a gold mine for book lovers, with its 40,000 rare volumes, frescoes and rich wood-carvings. Among the treasures are Teresa of Avila's diary, illuminated manuscripts including the *Codex Aureus* with its gold lettering, and a great globe which once belonged to Philip II.

Hidden away, and reached by long winding halls, is the private apartment of Philip, remaining as it was when he was alive. Here is no luxury, but rather Spartan surroundings. His bed was so placed, above and to one side of the high altar, with a small window overlooking it, that he could take part in the mass without rising from his pillow when ill.

The Pantheon is reached by a stairway leading to the crypt, which is divided into several chambers. The Royal Pantheon is of black marble and bronze, with an altar in the center, its walls are lined with urns of uniform design containing the remains of the kings of Spain from Charles V to Alfonso XIII. Only two are buried in other places— Philip V and Ferdinand VI. The body of Alfonso XIII who died in Rome in 1941 was finally brought to rest in the Escorial in January 1980.

As an antidote to a cold and eerie experience, climb up the mountains to "Philip's Chair" and sit on the rocky steps, walk out to the Prince's Lodge, built in the 18th century, and then come back to stroll in the Jardín de los Frailes (Friars' Garden) amid the cut boxwood, rose bushes and shrubs.

The Valle de los Caídos can be included in your trip to the Escorial, as it's only a few miles further on. Set in a state park, with magnificent views, it is an extraordinary architectural concept which serves as a memorial to Spain's Civil War dead. It is also the last resting-place of General Franco. Like a modern-day Valhalla, the crypt is cut through 260 meters (853 feet) of living rock and surmounted by a 150-meter

(429-foot) cross of reinforced concrete faced with stone (with an elevator to the top). A Benedictine monastery and school complete the memorial.

East: Alcalá

Alcalá de Henares, 34 kilometers (21 miles) from Madrid, is a birthplace of learning and of famous people. It was here that Cardinal Cisneros founded, in 1498, the Colegio Mayor de San Ildefonso, which was the origin of the University of Madrid. Moved to the nation's capital in 1836 Alcalá University has now been restored and houses, among other institutions, the new Civil Servants Training Center. Among those who first saw the light of day in Alcalá are Cervantes, Catherine of Aragón, and Emperor Ferdinand brother of Charles V. You can visit the Archbishop's Palace (now an archive), with its Renaissance façade and plateresque stairway, and the house where the author of *Don Quijote* was born. He was baptized in the church of Santa María la Mayor, destroyed, like all Alcalá's religious buildings between 1931 and 1939. (The baptistery has been rebuilt and the priests still preserve Cervantes' birth certificate.) The first Polyglot Bible (the Complutensian) was written here, under the direction of Cardinal Cisneros.

South: Aranjuez

The Palace of Aranjuez, only 48 kilometers (30 miles) from Madrid (main road south), was begun by Philip II, but the garden and the cascade that fall into the Tagus river date from the 18th century. Here in 1808, the meeting took place that saw the overthrow of Godoy, adviser to Queen María Luisa.

First see the palace, with its lavishly furnished rooms filled with priceless art treasures, and then lunch at one of the outdoor restaurants that border the river. When the sun is low, visit the *Casa del Labrador* (farm house), built by Charles IV in imitation of Versailles' Trianon, and walk through the *Jardín del Príncipe.* There's a miniature train which will take you to the Casa del Labrador, a picturesque ride for those short on time.

The palace is notable for its harmonious extension into the town by way of graceful arcades round the huge square, and especially for its gardens. The Queen's Garden and the Island Garden, both filled with valuable statuary, are the last word in the forgotten art of formal landscape designing, though somewhat neglected. The tiny Casa de

Labrador here is a perfect example of the artificial elegance associated with that period—complete with a lavatory walled in platinum and gold!

PRACTICAL INFORMATION FOR MADRID

 HOW TO GET ABOUT. The least expensive way to travel from the airport to the city center is to go by bus. The 13 km journey to the Plaza Colón Terminal in the heart of town takes 10 minutes. Yellow, airconditioned buses leave the international and national arrival terminals every 15 minutes from 6 A.M. to 11 P.M.; the fare is 100 ptas. A taxi between the airport and the city center will cost the meter reading (700-900 ptas.), 100 ptas. surcharge, 15 ptas. per suitcase, plus 30 ptas. on Sundays, fiestas or at night. Check that meter is on.

BY METRO. The subway is the easiest and quickest way of getting around Madrid. There are ten lines and over 100 stations. The metro runs from 6 A.M. to about 1 A.M. Fares are 25 ptas., whatever distance you travel. Subway maps are available from ticket offices, hotel receptions and the tourist office. Plans of the metro are displayed at every station. A book of ten single tickets (a *taco*) is on sale at ticket offices and costs 240 ptas. A *taco* of ten round trip tickets costs 360 ptas. but these are only available for outward rides made before 9 A.M.

BY BUS. City buses are red or blue and white and run from 5.30 A.M. to between 11 P.M. and 2 A.M., depending on the line. The fare is 30 ptas., or 35 ptas. for a transfer. Microbuses, which are airconditioned, cost 35 ptas. Plans of the route followed are displayed at bus stops, and a map of all city bus routes is available free from the EMT kiosk in Plaza Cibeles. A *bono-bus,* good for ten rides, costs 210 ptas. and can be bought from an EMT (Empresa Municipal de Transportes) kiosk or office. Books of 20 tickets valid for microbuses are available from the kiosk on Plaza Cibeles or at EMT headquarters, Alcántara 26, cost 605 ptas.

A good way to get acquainted with the city is to ride the *Circular* bus, marked with a red C. Its route passes several monuments and a number of the main streets, and a ride will cost you only one ticket. Another good ride is on bus 27 along the Paseo del Prado, Paseo Recoletos and the Castellana.

BY TAXI. Taxi fares start at 50 ptas. and the rate is 26 ptas. per kilometer. Supplements are 30 ptas. on Sundays and holidays, 30 ptas. between 11 P.M. and 6 A.M., 30 ptas. when leaving bus or railway stations and to and from bullrings, swimming pools and football matches, and 15 ptas. per suitcase. Taxis available for hire display a *"Libre"* sign during the day and a green light at night. Always check the driver puts his meter on when you start your ride. Taxis hold three or four passengers.

RAILROAD STATIONS. There are two main stations. *Chamartín* in the north of the city, is the departure point of all major trains to the northwest, north and northeast, including those to Irún, Paris, Gijón, Bilbao, Santander, San Sebastián, Valladolid, Zaragoza and Barcelona. *Atocha* at the far end of Paseo del Prado is the departure point for trains to the Levante (Valencia), Andalusia, Extremadura and Lisbon. An underground line connects Atocha with Chamartín. Trains to local destinations such as El Escorial, Avila, Segovia, Guadalajara and Alcalá de Henares, can be boarded at either station.

The *Estación del Norte* (North Station or Príncipe Pío), just off the Cuesta de San Vicente, has trains to Salamanca, Fuentes de Oñoro, Santiago de Compostela and La Coruña, and all other destinations in Galicia.

For train information and tickets in advance go to the RENFE office at Alcalá 44, any station above *(Norte* is the least crowded), or call 733 3000.

BUS STATIONS. Travel by bus is far cheaper than by train, and in many cases it is also quicker as a result of the meandering nature of many Spanish railroad lines. There are two main bus stations, the *Estación del Sur,* Canarias 17, (tel. 468 4200), and *Auto-Res,* Fernández Shaw 1, (tel. 251 6644). Buses to Aranjuez and Toledo and many destinations in the south leave from the Estación del Sur; to Cuenca and Salamanca from Auto Res. Buses to El Escorial and the Valley of the Fallen leave from Isaac Peral 10 and Paseo de Moret 7. Buses to Avila leave from Toledo 143 and Martín de los Heros 4, near Plaza de España. To Segovia they leave from Paseo de la Florida 11.

STREET NAMES. Many of Madrid's street names have been changed in the past six years and this affects bus routes as well as the addresses of many hotels and restaurants mentioned in this book. We have used the new names throughout, and by now most of the tourist maps and literature have been updated too, but a few old maps are still in circulation. We hope the following will be of help. Avda José Antonio Primo de Rivera is now Gran Vía; Avda del Generalísimo is now an extension of Paseo de la Castellana (though the surrounding area is still known as the Generalísimo area); Paseo de Onésimo Redondo is now Cuesta de San Vicente; García Morato is now Santa Engracia; General Sanjurjo is now José Abascal; Paseo de Calvo Sotelo is now Paseo de Recoletos; and General Mola is now Príncipe de Vergara.

HOTELS. Madrid offers a wide range of hotels, all the way from the millionaire Villa Magna to modest little pensions where you can live and eat remarkably well, for 1,000 pesetas a day. For a capital city Madrid's accommodations are very reasonably priced and standards are mostly high. Many hotels are fully booked at Easter and around July and August. There are hotel accommodation services at Chamartín and Atocha stations and at both the national and international airport terminals.

Super Deluxe

Ritz, Paseo del Prado 5 (tel. 221 2857). Conservative, aristocratic and very quiet, with beautiful rooms and large suites. It has long been the choice of foreign diplomats and wealthy Spanish families.

Villa Magna, Paseo de la Castellana 22 (tel. 261 4900). The most exclusive of hotels and Madrid's international rendezvous. With restaurant, bars, banquet rooms and garage. Décor is elegant and tasteful, and the hotel is fronted by a pleasant garden.

Deluxe

Alameda, Avda de Logroño 100 (tel. 747 4800). Opposite Barajas airport with pool, restaurant and bar. Free transportation to airport and city. Attractive rooms, but readers have complained of noise and poor service.

Barajas, Avda de Logroño 305 (tel. 747 7700). A mile from the airport and recent, with 230 rooms, pool, gardens and nightclub.

Eurobuilding, Padre Damián 23 (tel. 457 1700). An enormous hotel with two entrances; one on Padre Damián and one on Juan Ramón Jiménez. It has a pool, gardens, several bars, nightclub, *Balthasar* restaurant and *Le Relais* coffee shop. Popular with Americans and business men.

Luz Palacio, Paseo de la Castellana 57 (tel. 442 5100). Tastefully decorated with restaurants, cocktail lounge, garage and all amenities.

Meliá Madrid, Princesa 27 (tel. 241 8200). 25 stories and 266 rooms featuring every modern convenience. Close to the Plaza España with its own garage. Elegant and modern; recommended.

Miguel Angel, Miguel Angel 31 (tel. 442 0022). Modern, luxurious hotel with elegantly appointed public and private rooms. Conveniently located in smart area and has fast become a favorite with discerning travelers. Topnotch *Zacarias* restaurant-disco.

Mindanao, San Francisco de Sales 15 (tel. 449 5500). In residential area with indoor pool and sauna. *Domayo* restaurant offers regional Spanish dishes and French cuisine. The *Keynes* bar is a favorite aperitif spot for Spanish society. Openair pool, bars, etc.

Monte Real, Arroyo Fresno 17 (tel. 216 2140). In the Puerta de Hierro section out of town and the last word in ritzy elegance. Quiet and dignified, with all amenities.

Palace, Plaza de las Cortes 7 (tel. 429 7551). Dignified turn-of-the-century hotel opposite the Cortes. A slightly poorer step-sister of the Ritz and long a favorite of politicians and journalists; hosts many conventions.

Princesa Plaza, Princesa 40 (tel. 242 3500). Modern hotel on busy central avenue, usually well thought of.

Wellington, Velázquez 8 (tel. 275 4400). A modern hotel, attracting a solid, conservative clientele.

Expensive

Alcalá, Alcalá 66 (tel. 435 1060). Convenient to Retiro Park and Serrano shopping area. Well praised by readers for its good value.

MADRID Metro

Arosa, Calle de la Salud 21 (tel. 232 1600). Recent and close to Gran Via; recommended.

Calatrava, Tutor 1 (tel. 241 9880). Private garage, disco; close to Plaza de España.

Convención, O'Donnell 53 (tel. 274 6800). A huge hotel; opened in 1978 and near the Goya shopping area. Self-service cafeteria, direct-dial phones.

Emperador, Gran Vía 53 (tel. 247 2800). Comfortable; very central, pool.

Emperatriz, Lopez de Hoyos 4 (tel. 413 6511). Modern and pleasant; recommended.

Escultor, Miguel Angel 3 (tel. 410 4203). Beautiful, luxurious apartments, just off Castellana, but rather geared to businessmen and tour groups.

Florida Norte, Paseo de la Florida 5 (tel. 241 6190). Opposite the North Station, uphill walk to Plaza de España.

Los Galgos, Claudio Coello 139 (tel. 262 4227). Comfortable with well appointed rooms, most with balcony; near Serrano shopping area and American Embassy.

Gran Hotel Velázquez, Velázquez 62 (tel. 275 2800). Oldish, but comfortable and spacious. Rooms facing front are rather noisy.

Liabeny, Salud 3 (tel. 232 5306). Modern hotel very centrally located in the Plaza del Carmen, close to shops, Gran Vía and Puerta del Sol.

Mayorazgo, Flor Baja 3 (tel. 247 2600). Pleasant hotel tucked away in a side street off the Gran Vía.

Menfis, Gran Vía 74 (tel. 247 0900). Pleasant and old fashioned; on Madrid's main street.

Principe Pío, Cuesta de San Vicente 14 (tel. 247 8000). Only a 3-star hotel, but pleasant and quiet, and the dining room, food and service are especially recommended.

Suecia, Marqués de Casa Riera 4 (tel. 231 6900). A small, modern and elegant hotel, very centrally located near Cibeles. Highly recommended.

Moderate

Abeba, Alcántara 63 (tel. 401 1650). 90 rooms; pleasantly appointed off Ortega y Gasset.

Anaco, Tres Cruces 3 (tel. 222 4604). Small modern, comfortable hotel just off Plaza del Carmen, very central.

Carlos V, Maestro Vitoria 5 (tel. 231 4100). Pleasant old hotel, very centrally located just off main shopping street.

Casón del Tormes, Río 7 (tel. 241 9745). Older hotel; near Plaza de España.

Colón, Dr. Esquerdo 117 (tel. 274 6800). Pool, disco and shops among the many amenities of the 4-star hotel. Reasonable rates, but rather far from center.

Conde Duque, Plaza Conde del Valle de Suchil 5 (tel. 447 7000). A pleasant hotel in a square off Alberto Aguilera but service not always up to scratch.

Gran Vía, Gran Vía 25 (tel. 222 1121). 163 rooms, good service and very central, though rates are rather high for this category.

Inglés, Echegaray 10 (tel. 429 6551). A good, small hotel; 58 rooms. Located in the older part of town near Puerta del Sol.

Marquina, Prim 11 (tel. 222 9010). 21 rooms, modern and comfortable; just off Paseo Recoletos. Reader recommended.

Moderno, Arenal 2 (tel. 231 0900). Good hotel, though a bit noisy; just off Puerta del Sol.

Montesol, Montera 25 (tel. 231 7600). 52 rooms. Pleasant, old-style hotel in central street between Puerta del Sol and Gran Vía.

Opera, Cuesta Santo Domingo 2, (tel. 241 2800). 86 rooms; in the old part of town close to Opera and only a short walk from Royal Palace.

Victoria, Plaza del Angel 7, (tel. 231 4500). Stylish, old-world hotel; long a favorite of bullfighters and *aficionados.* Good service and well recommended.

Zurbano, Zurbano 81 (tel. 441 5500). Modern and elegant with high standards; in fashionable area.

Inexpensive

Alexandra, San Bernardo 29 (tel. 242 0400). 69 rooms; fairly central.

Asturias, Sevilla 2 (tel. 429 6670). Old world charm but on rather busy intersection.

Francisco I, Arenal 15 (tel. 248 0204). Old hotel with modernized décor, half way between Puerta del Sol and Opera. Top floor restaurant is recommended.

Internacional, Arenal 19 (tel. 248 1800). Old world charm and friendly service. Some excellent rooms, others rather scruffy.

Lar, Valverde 16 (tel. 221 6592). A 3-star hotel with good value rates; central location but on a rather noisy street.

París, Alcalá 2 (tel. 221 6496). A delightful hotel, full of elegant, old world charm, right on Puerta del Sol.

Regente, Mesonero Romanos 9 (tel. 221 2941). A 3-star hotel with low rates. Very central location just off Callao; quiet and close to shops.

MOTELS

Los Angeles (M) on the N-IV to Andalusia (tel. 696 3815). 46 rooms, 14 km from town; pool and tennis.

Avion (M), Avda. Aragón 345 (tel. 747 6222). Convenient for those driving in from Barcelona. 14 km out of town with restaurant, bar and pool.

Los Olivos (M), on the N-IV to Andalusia (tel. 695 6700). 12 km out, 100 rooms, pool. Praised by readers.

 RESTAURANTS. If Madrid is your first stop in Spain, you may feel ravenous before you see any signs of food on the way; normal meal hours in the capital are even later than in the rest of Spain, where they are already later than anywhere else in Europe. No one thinks of eating lunch in the capital before 2 P.M., 3 P.M. is quite normal, 3.30 not at all unusual; and while most Spanish diners begin to eat at 10, 10.30 is about the earliest for Madrileños and 11 is normal. If you can't wait, a few restaurants and several hotels open their dining rooms earlier for the benefit of foreigners, but you won't find any Spaniards in them. Otherwise, you can obtain snacks, and even meals, in any of the numerous cafeterias around town which are open from early morning till midnight or later.

Madrid is plentifully provided with restaurants of all classes and of all types, and can give you French, German, Italian, Chinese, Mexican, Japanese, Moroccan, Russian or American cooking as well as Asturian, Basque, Galician, Valencian or Catalan, and, of course Castilian.

All restaurants are required to offer a *menu del día,* (although not all of them do) a 3-course fixed price set meal including tax and service and sometimes wine or mineral water. This, however, does not cover extras. There is often a choice but unless the fixed meal happens to be exactly what you want, perhaps you will prefer to compound your own menu though this is almost certain to prove more expensive. In practice this set menu is becoming less and less common.

Incidentally it is customary to give an additional tip of five per cent even if the tab says service is included.

If you want to be really economical, look for a *taberna*—a small café dispensing drinks in the front room, with a few tables tucked away in the back, or a *restaurante económico.* At the bottom of the scale in price, but not in quality, many will give you a fine meal for 450 pesetas, and there is no obligation to order a full-course dinner.

A word of warning: many of the best-known establishments close for a month in summer. Many restaurants close on Sunday and some also close one other day during the week; be sure to check.

For an approximate guide to prices see page 23.

Deluxe

El Amparo, Puigcerdá 8 (entrance Jorge Juan 10) (tel. 431 6456). Elegant restaurant with the emphasis on Basque traditional and *nouvelle cuisine.* Imaginative dishes and pleasing décor. Closed Sat. lunch, Sun., Easter week and Aug. No credit cards.

Clara's, Arrieta 2 (tel. 242 0071). Superb food in classic setting. Chef formerly of Maxim's and Villa Magna. Set in fine old building, Clara's is considered one of the very best gourmet attractions in town.

Club 31, Alcalá 58 (tel. 221 6622). International cuisine and Spanish regional dishes. Specialty of the house is lobster in champagne. Closed Aug.

Horcher, Alfonso XII 6 (tel. 222 0731). One of Madrid's most famous—and expensive—restaurants. Service is excellent, ladies are even brought a cushion to rest their feet on! Specialties are Central European dishes and game. Well praised by readers. Closed Sun.

Jockey, Amador de los Ríos 6 (tel. 419 2435). A long standing favorite and one of the best. Try the smoked salmon or *lubina* with aubergines. Closed Sun. and Aug.

Ritz Hotel, Paseo del Prado 5 (tel. 221 2857). The garden of this deluxe hotel is probably the most attractive place to dine in summer, though the food does not always equal the setting.

Zalacaín, Alvarez de Baena 4 (tel. 261 4708). In a private villa with elegant décor and topnotch food; highest recommendations. Closed Sat. lunch, Sun., Easter week and Aug.

Expensive

Al-Mounia, Recoletos 5 (tel. 255 0642). Moroccan specialties and an oriental tea room. One of the best restaurants in town.

Bajamar, Gran Vía 78 (tel. 248 5903). Offers some of the best seafood in town in its downstairs dining room, but watch those prices.

Escuadrón, Tamayo y Baus 8 (tel. 419 2830). Small, intimate and exclusive. Wonderful game in season. Impeccable food and service.

El Gran Chambelán, Ayala 46, tel. 431 77 45. Elegant restaurant with superb cuisine. Try their *menu estrecho y largo,* literally "narrow and wide"—a little of everything, it's delicious.

Gure Etxea, Plaza de la Paja 12 (tel. 265 6149). An excellent Basque restaurant.

Nuevo Valentín, Concha Espina 8 (tel. 259 7555). One of the six Valentin restaurants in town. Waiters in red tuxedos, candlelight and an elegant bar.

Nicolasa, Velázquez 150 (tel. 261 9985). Top Basque dishes served by owners of its namesake in San Sebastián.

O'Pazo, Reina Mercedes 20 (tel. 253 2333). An elegant Galician restaurant.

Platerías Comedor, Plaza Santa Ana 11 (tel. 429 7048). Superb French dishes in lovely setting in this delightful square.

Príncipe de Viana, Manuel de Falla 5 (tel. 259 1448). Fashionable restaurant with Basque, Navarre and international dishes.

Riscal, Marqués de Riscal 11 (tel. 419 7580). Valencian specialties. Its *paellas* have been famous for years.

Sakura, Apolonio Morales 1 (tel. 458 1588). Good Japanese restaurant.

Las Tres Encinas, Preciados 33 (tel. 232 3112). Specializes in seafood. The special potpourri with oysters, clams, shrimps, crabs, lobster and crayfish is especially good.

El Ultimo Cuple, Palma 51 (tel. 222 0087). Pleasant setting in old café. Live entertainment by old stagers from Spanish operetta.

Valentín Los Porches, Pintor Rosales 1 (tel. 248 5197). Set right in the Parque del Oeste, near the Plaza España. It features international dishes in a spacious dining room with a large garden for outdoor dining.

Moderate

Alkalde, Jorge Juan 10 (tel. 276 3359). Cave-like rooms, pleasant atmosphere, excellent food and service. One of Madrid's most consistently good restaurants.

La Barraca, Reina 29 (tel. 232 7154). One of the best restaurants for Valencian cooking. Excellent *paella.*

Bistroquet, Conde 4 (tel. 247 1075). A popular French restaurant on the corner of Calle Segovia. There is a terrace for outdoor dining and a cozy dining room inside. Particularly good onion soup, steaks and *fondu bourgignon.*

Boguí, Barquillo 29 (tel. 221 1568). Lovely setting but limited choice of dishes.

Casa Botín, Cuchilleros 17 (tel. 266 4217). Just off the Plaza Mayor this is Madrid's oldest restaurant. Catering to diners since 1725 it was a great favorite with Hemingway. Dinner here is a must for every tourist. It opens as early as 8 P.M. but be sure to book. Singers later in the evening.

Casa Lucio, Cava Baja 35 (tel. 265 8217). Atmospheric restaurant near the Plaza Mayor, serving topnotch Spanish fare (steaks, lamb, eels, etc.) in mesón setting in a maze of small rooms. Personalized service, excellent value.

Casa Paco, Puerto Cerrada 11 (tel. 266 3166). This atmospheric old tavern is a perennial favorite. Famous for steaks. Limited space and there is nearly always a line.

Las Cuevas de Luis Candelas, Cuchilleros 1 (tel. 266 5428). Atmospheric restaurant built inside part of the old walls of Madrid. At the bottom of the steps leading out of Plaza Mayor. A bit of a tourist trap but fun.

El Cosaco, Alfonso VI 4 (tel. 265 3548). An American-owned Russian restaurant with charming old Russian décor. Portions can be a bit skimpy.

Edelweiss, Jovellanos 6, just behind the Cortes. Substantial portions of German food. Opens for dinner at 7 P.M. Reservations are not accepted so best go early.

Fado, Plaza de San Martín 2 (tel. 231 8924). Portuguese food and singing.

La Gran Tasca, Ballesta 1 (tel. 231 0044). Old stand-by specializing in home-cooked Castilian dishes. Small, cozy and delightful with top food.

Hogar Gallego, Plaza Comandante Morenas 3 (tel. 242 1174). Galician restaurant specializing in seafood. Outdoor dining in summer.

House of Ming, Castellana 74 (tel. 261 9827). Excellent Chinese delicacies in a luxurious setting.

El Locro, Trujillos 2 (tel. 222 4382). Argentinian restaurant, so good steaks of course. Specialties are *parrilladas* and *churrascos.* Live folk music.

Mesón del Corregidor, Plaza Mayor 8 (tel. 266 3024). Touristy but pleasant.

Mesón de San Isidro, Costanilla de San Andrés 16 (tel. 265 1164). Good food in Toledo setting.

Mesón de San Javier, Conde 3 (tel. 248 0925). Nicely tucked away in a corner behind the City Hall. Serves good roast pork and lamb. Downstairs is a typical bodega, upstairs a cozy restaurant.

Mikado, Pintor Juan Gris 4 (tel. 270 1033). Japanese restaurant featuring *sukiyaki* and *tempura.*

Sacha, Juan Hurtado de Mendoza 11 (tel. 457 7200). Cozy with exquisite décor and outdoor dining in summer. Wide variety of Spanish dishes.

Shangri-La, Leganitos 26 (tel. 241 1173). Chinese restaurant serving good sweet and sour pork and delicious fried bananas.

Sixto Gran Mesón, Cervantes 28 (tel. 468 6602). Excellent food in typical setting. Specialties are lamb from Avila and roasts. Also good seafood.

La Toja, Siete de Julio 3 (tel. 266 4664). Just off the Plaza Mayor and specializing in seafood. A good place to try *paella.* Open for dinner at 8 P.M.

La Valenciana, Gran Vía 44 (tel. 232 0150). Valencian restaurant, specializing, of course, in *paella.*

Valentín, San Alberto 3 (tel. 259 7555). Another of the famous six. Longtime rendezvous of the influential and the famous from all walks of life, from bullfighters to literati. Intimate décor, good service, standard Spanish dishes.

Zarauz, Fuentes 13 (tel. 247 7270). Just off Calle Arenal, this serves wonderful fish and a great variety of seafood. Try their *chacoli* wine.

Inexpensive

La Argentina, Válgame Diós 9 (tel. 221 3763). Attractive décor and very popular; you may have to wait in the bar. Good pasta and roast lamb.

La Bola, Bola 5 (tel. 247 6930). Plenty of old world charm with local specialties.

Casa Ciriaco, Mayor 84, (tel. 248 5066). Atmospheric; an old stand-by.

Casa Domingo, Alcalá 99 (tel. 226 1895). Opposite the Retiro; unpretentious sidewalk lunching. Meat dishes from north of Spain.

Casa Gades, Conde de Xiquena 4 (tel. 232 3051). Owned by dancer Antonio Gades. Lively and often crowded. Italian dishes with *osso bucco* a specialty.

Casa Ricardo, Fernando el Católico 31 (tel. 446 0100). Only open for lunch. Excellent home cooking and Castilian dishes.

La Hoja, Moratín 7 (tel. 239 8179). Small and intimate, with specialties of *cangrejo* (crab) soup, lobster thermidor, and sizzling steaks.

Jada, Corredera Baja de San Pablo, tel. 222 9667. Good Chinese food.

Mesón Theo, Infantas 26 (tel. 232 0129). Good food in typical mesón atmosphere.

Paris, Huertas 66. Decoration is sparse but clean. Attracts a lively neighborhood clientele. Reader recommended.

Terra a Nosa, Cava San Miguel 3 (tel. 247 1175). A small Galician bistro, good for *lacón y grelos* (ham and turnip tops) and heady Galician wines.

CAFETERIAS. For snacks or American-type meals, a good place to go is any of the numerous cafeterias, by which we do not mean the self-service type of establishment which one finds in the United States, but a restaurant with table service. In these, you can order sandwiches, fruit juices, soft drinks, coffee, pastries, simple meals, etc. They are on the whole very clean and excellent value. The following is a partial list:

California. There are several in town, all known for their good food and pastries. Two are on Goya, one at number 21, the other at 47, further up past Velázquez. Others at Gran Vía 39 and Salud 21. Try the strawberry tarts or pancakes with chocolate syrup.

Manila, one of the best known cafeterias in town, branches at Gran Vía 16 and 41, Carmen 4 (now known as *Kenia*), Génova 21, Diego de León 41, and Juan Bravo, off Príncipe de Vergara; good for quick lunches.

Morrison, at Gran Vía 43, Arapiles 13 with an outdoor terrace, Capitán Haya 78, Avda. Felipe II 18. Good for breakfast and snacks.

Nebraska, Alcalá 18, Bravo Murillo 109, Gran Vía 32 and 55.

TRADITIONAL CAFÉS. Café Comercial, Glorieta de Bilbao 7. An old-time café that has not changed much over the last 30 years, always crowded.

Café Gijón, Paseo de Recoletos 21. The best and most famous of the remaining cafés of old. It is still a hang-out for writers and artists, carrying on a tradition which dates back to the turn of the century when it was a meeting place of the literati. In summer they have tables outside on the main avenue.

Café Lyon, Alcalá 57. Charming, old fashioned décor, just up from Cibeles.

Café Metropolitano, Glorieta de Cuatro Caminos. Student atmosphere.

The Embassy, corner of Castellana and Ayala. Elegant pastry shop and tea room with a vast assortment of sandwiches, canapés and pastries.

La Mallorquina, in the Puerta del Sol between Mayor and Arenal. An old world pastry shop with a tea salon; incredible but probably doomed tea ritual 6–7 P.M.

FAST FOODS. *Burger King,* Gran Vía 40 and 68, Princesa 5 and 61, Fuencarral 121, Lagasca 48, Orense 4, Conde de Peñalver 96, Arenal 4, San Bernardo 123. *Foremost,* ice-cream parlor, on Goya opposite Galerías Preciados. *McDonald's,* Gran Vía 52, Montera 47, Fuencarral 125, Duque de Alba 15, Alcalá 396. *Wendy's,* Plaza de España, Plaza Callao and in the Glorieta del Emperador Carlos V opposite Atocha station. *Pizza Hut,* Orense 11, Plaza de Santa Bárbara 8.

BARS. If you want to spend an enjoyable, typically Spanish evening, then go bar-hopping in any of the following areas. You'll find numerous bars and cafés where you can sample the local wine, have a glass of beer and choose from any number of tapas.

The **Malasaña** area around Bilbao, Fuencarral and San Bernardo is the "in" place for Madrid's youth, students and hippies. There are any number of lively, trendy bars open till the small hours, around the Plaza Dos de Mayo and Calles Ruiz, San Andrés and Vicente Ferrer.

The mesones area between the **Puerta Cerrada** and the **Plaza Mayor** has long been famous. Do the rounds of the mesones with names like the *Tortilla, Champiñon, Gamba, Cochinillo,* etc. and you may well be able to listen to the locals strumming their guitars and singing, which can become quite a spectacle especially on Friday and Saturday nights.

The old, narrow streets between the **Puerta del Sol** and the **Plaza Santa Ana** are packed with crowded, colorful tapa bars. You can sample something different in every bar. Wander along Espóz y Mina, Victoria, Nuñez de Arce and Echegaray and go into any bar that takes your fancy. *Las Cuevas de Sésamo* on Príncipe 7 is an atmospheric bar with good piano music. In the Plaza Santa Ana the *Cervecería Alemana* is a popular German beer hall well patronized by tourists.

For the oldest mesones in Madrid, try the area in the streets around the **Rastro.** Here you will find such long standing names as the *Mesón de Paredes, Jesús y María, Magdalena, Cascorro* and *La Esquinita,* a bar with magnificent tapas, beer in mugs, and roasted chicken.

NIGHTLIFE. Since Franco's death, the nightclub scene has flung off all restraint and Madrid now abounds in shows featuring striptease, topless dancers, gay spectacles, transvestitism and similar entertainments. Pick-up bars ranging from the old-time stand-bys to flashy, elegant new places in the Generalísimo area, have multiplied enormously over the past few years. Travelers who knew the tame Spain of a few years ago will be amazed at the difference; all censorship has been discarded.

El Biombo Chino, Isabel la Católica 6 (tel. 248 5081). Dancing and show nightly.

Cleofas, Goya 7, tel. 276 4523. Discothèque followed by orchestra, dancing and a show.

Florida Park in the Retiro, tel. 409 5408. Expensive dinner club with dancing and entertainment. Traditional favorite. Closed at presstime.

Lido, Alcalá 20 (tel. 232 3139). Dancing to an orchestra and two shows nightly.

Molino Rojo, Tribulete 16 (tel. 239 4080). Dancing to an orchestra; shows.

La Scala, Rosario Pino 7, tel. 450 4500, in the Meliá Castilla hotel. Tops. Dinner, dancing, cabaret. Second nightly show cheaper.

Xairo, Paz 11 (tel. 231 2440). Dancing and music hall shows on Saturdays.

Xenon, Plaza Callao, tel. 231 9794. Discothèque, orchestra and cabaret.

DISCOS. These are numerous and very popular in Madrid. Some charge an entrance fee, usually starting around 700 ptas., which includes your first drink; others just charge for your drinks. Gay discos and transvestite clubs also abound. For a complete listing, see the weekly *Guía del Ocio*. The following are just a few of the better known ones.

Bocaccio, Marqués de la Ensenada 16. Smart place, upstairs are art-nouveau nooks and booths; the action takes place downstairs.

Cerebro, Magallanes 1. Features live music and records. This is one of the swinging places for Spanish youth.

Cleofás, Goya 7. Popular disco with good shows on certain nights.

Macumba, Chamartín Station. With a grill, crêperie and pizzeria open till 3.

Rock Ola, Padre Xifre 5. Very trendy with lots of live music.

FLAMENCO. Madrid has some of the best flamenco shows in the country. Entrances 1,300-1,700 ptas, including one drink; most serve dinner for 3,500-4,500 ptas. Open around 9.30 P.M. till 3 A.M. Be sure to reserve.

Arco de Cuchilleros, Cuchilleros 7 (tel. 266 5867).

Las Brujas, Norte 15 (tel. 222 5325). One of the best; also serves dinner.

Café de Chinitas, Torija 7 (tel. 248 5135). Good show and top food, but much more expensive than most.

Los Canasteros, Barbieri 10 (tel. 231 8163).

Corral de la Morería, Morería 17 (tel. 265 8446).

Corral de la Pacheca, Juan Ramón Jiménez 26 (tel. 259 1056). A bit touristy but fun. Folk dancing as well as flamenco.

Torres Bermejas, Mesonero Romanos 15 (tel. 231 0353). One of the best for serious flamenco.

Venta del Gato, Avda de Burgos 214 (tel. 202 3427). 7 km north on road to Burgos. Very authentic flamenco. Other flamenco dancers in the audience.

THEATER. If your Spanish is not very good, the legitimate theater is likely to be a complete loss to you. However, you won't need Spanish to enjoy a *zarzuela* or a musical revue. They're good fun. The best bet for non-Spanish-speaking visitors is the *Zarzuela,* Jovellanos 4, where you may see the top dance groups, operas, operetta and, of course, *zarzuela,* if it's the season. The *Teatro Español* at Príncipe 25, in Plaza Santa Ana, shows Spanish classics. The second of the state-sponsored theaters, usually showing plays of interest, is the *Teatro María Guerrero,* Calle Tamayo y Baus 4.

Most theaters in Madrid have two curtains, at 7 and 10.30 P.M. They close one day during the week, usually Mondays. Tickets are very inexpensive and on the whole easy to obtain. With a few exceptions it is not at all unusual to buy tickets on the night of the performance.

CINEMA. Most foreign films shown in Spain are dubbed into Spanish, but there are about half a dozen cinemas in Madrid showing films in their original language with Spanish subtitles. Consult the local press, *El País* or *Guía del Ocio,* where these films will be marked "v.o." for *version original. El País* also lists cinemas showing subtitled films. A good cinema to try for films in English, is the Alphaville (with four screens, entrance in Martín de los Heros) just off Plaza España. There is an official *Filmoteca* showing different films each day, always in their original language with Spanish subtitles. At presstime these showings were split between the Círculo de Bellas Artes, Marqués de Casa Riera 2 and the Museo de Arte Contemporáneo, Avda Juan de Herrera in the University City. Most movie houses have three performances a day at roughly 4.30, 7.30 and 10.30. Tickets cost 200-300 ptas.

MUSIC. The modern *Teatro Real* (conveniently located opposite the palace, entrance in Plaza Isabel II) is now exclusively dedicated to concerts. Tickets cost 400–1,000 ptas; the performances in the luxuriously decorated *Opera* tend to be good. Concerts are also given one Wednesday a month by the Orquesta de la Radio-Televisión Española in the *Teatro de la Zarzuela,* seats costing 300 to 600 ptas. There are also concerts in the auditorium of the *Fundación March* on the Calle Castelló 77, and at the *Sala Fénix,* Paseo de la Castellana 37. Check the local papers for programs and times.

At the *British Institute,* there are also sometimes concerts, plays and movies. Address is Almagro 5. The *French Institute* on the Calle Marqués de Ensenada is better for literary lectures, though record concerts are also given. All institutes have libraries, the one at the British Institute being particularly fine. The latter permits books as well as records to circulate to members. Concerts of chamber music at musical conservatory, Plaza de Isabel II.

The *Washington Irving Center*, San Bernardo 107, run by the US government, often has interesting lectures and concerts with some film showings. The *Italian Institute*, Calle Mayor 86 offers similar activities.

 MUSEUMS. The opening times and entrance charges given below hold good at time of writing, but are subject to frequent changes. Museums belonging to the *Patrimonio Nacional* are closed Mondays and are free for Spaniards but not foreigners. Holders of ISIC cards may get in free.

Bullfighting Museum (Museo Taurino), Ventas Bullring, 10–1, closed Mon. Admission 10 pesetas.

Cerralbo Museum, Ventura Rodriguez 17. 9–2, closed Tues., and throughout August. Entrance 100 pesetas. Tapestries, painting and some of the loveliest old porcelain to be seen anywhere. Housed in the Cerralbo mansion, with many personal bric-à-brac still left in place. A good place to see the aristocratic setting of a turn-of-the-century villa.

Convent of the Descalzas Reales, Plaza de las Descalzas Reales, open Mon. to Thurs. 10.30–1.30 and 4–6; on Fridays, Saturdays and Sundays from 10.30–1.30 only. Admission 100 pesetas includes entrance to nearby Museum of the Encarnacíon. The convent, founded in the 16th century, has a good collection of medieval paintings. It is still used as a convent, so only part of it can be visited.

Ethnological Museum, Paseo de Atocha 11. 10–1.30, closed Mon. Entrance 50 pesetas. Closed in August. Primitive artifacts, weapons etc. from the Philippines and Africa, with several interesting mummies.

Goya Pantheon, in the Hermitage of San Antonio de la Florida, Paseo de la Florida, 11–1.30, 3–6; holidays 11–1.30. Closed Wed. In summer 10–1, 4–7; holidays 10–1. Entrance 25 ptas. Not to be missed. Here are the frescos which the irrepressible Goya painted depicting some of the more respectable court officials hobnobbing with some of the less respectable ladies of his considerably varied acquaintance. Goya (headless) is buried here. Nobody knows what happened to his head, which disappeared between his burial in Bordeaux in 1828 and the exhumation of his body for transfer to Spain in 1888.

Lazaro Galdiano Foundation, Serrano 122. Open 10–2, closed Mon and in August. Admission 50 ptas. This museum is a "must". It is housed in an old, aristocratic mansion, and besides containing a magnificent collection of paintings, furniture, clocks, armor, jewels, artifacts, weapons etc., it is a delight, thanks to the impeccable and tasteful arrangement of its treasures. There is a sizeable collection of English painting, too. The best collection in Europe of ivory and enamel; works by El Greco, Zurbarán, Velázquez and Goya.

Lope de Vega's House, Cervantes 11. Open 11–2, closed Mon. The great playwright's house and garden skillfully restored. Admission 35 pesetas. Closed July 15 to Sept. 15.

Municipal Museum, Fuencarral 78. Several rooms depicting Madrid's past, including a model of Madrid in 1830. Open 10–2 and 5–9; Sun. 10–3. Closed Mon.

Museum of the Americas, Reyes Católicos 6. 'America' refers to Latin America of course, but for a time that included some of the present United States. Entrance 50 pesetas. Open 10–2 daily, closed Mon. Excellent displays with many replicas.

Museum of Archeology, Serrano 13. Open 9.30–1.30. Closed Mon. Entrance 100 pesetas. This much-neglected museum contains an excellent archeological collection. The Greek vases and Roman artifacts are particularly fine. Also includes large collection of medieval furniture and art: a good ceramics collection and the little-known (to tourists) treasures of Iberian Spain. Well worth a visit. Entrance fee entitles you to visit a replica of the Altamira Caves. This museum now houses the famous Dama de Elche.

Museum of the Army, Méndez Núñez 1, 10–5, closed Mon. Entrance 50 pesetas. Contains a vast collection (three stories) of trophies, weapons and documents. A special section dedicated to the Civil War. This is one of the few museums in Spain where all articles are meticulously indexed and labeled. Highly interesting.

Museum of Contemporary Arts, a new museum near the University City, Avda. Juan de Herrera, 375 paintings, 200 sculptures, including Picassos and Mirós; set in pleasant gardens; well worth a visit. Open weekdays 10–6, Sundays 10–3. Admission 100 ptas. Closed Mon.

Museum of Decorative Arts, Montalbán 12. Open 10–5, Sat. and Sun. 10–2, closed Mon. Entrance 50 pesetas. Closed in August. Fine collections of Spanish ceramics, crystal and furniture.

Museum of the Navy, Montalbán 2. 10.30–1.30; closed Mon. Ship models, nautical instruments etc. The most famous exhibit is Juan de Cosa's original map, used by Columbus on his first voyage to the New World.

Museum of the Railroad, at the Calle San Cosmé y San Damián 1. Presents a modest but well-arranged assortment of models, rails, switches, engravings, lamps and a fullsized old locomotive. Free entrance. Open 10–1.30. Closed Mon.

The Prado, Paseo del Prado. Open Tues.-Sat. 10–6 (10–5 in winter); Sun. and holidays 10–2. Closed Mon. Admission 200 ptas includes entrance to the **Casón del Buen Retiro** annexe, home of 19th century Spanish painting and of Picasso's *Guernica.* If you can't visit both on the same day, hang on to your ticket as it will still be valid for the part you haven't seen. The Prado is universally acknowledged as one of the world's greatest art collections. If your time is limited, the greatest treasures (Velázquez, El Greco, Murillo, Bosch though not Goya) are one floor up and can be reached directly by a flight of steps from the outside, thus bypassing the ground floor and, incidentally, the long lines that often form at the lower entrance! Once inside you have access to both floors, though not necessarily to special exhibitions which are charged separately. The Prado is always horribly crowded, especially at weekend, and, as its modernization program involving the installation of air conditioning and better lighting is not yet complete, can get unbearably stuffy.

The Casón del Buen Retiro is open the same hours as the Prado except on Wed. when it opens from 3–9. Entrance to *Guernica* is round the back in Alfonso XII.

Royal Academy of San Fernando Museum. Temporarily housed at Paseo Recoletos 20 in same building as Archeological Museum and National Library. Open weekdays 10–2. Collection of Spanish paintings including works by Goya and Zurbarán.

Royal Palace, Plaza de Oriente. Entrance through vast courtyard and door on right. Summer hours (May-Sept.) are roughly 10–1.30 and 4–6.15; in winter, 10–12.45 and 3.30–5.15. Sundays and holidays 10–1.30 only. Different tickets are available depending on how much you want to see; the full visit is 310 ptas.

Royal Coach Museum, Royal Palace gardens. Same hours as palace. Admission 30 ptas.

Royal Tapestry Works, Fuenterrabía 2. Open 9.30–12.30. Entrance 25 pesetas. Closed Sat. and Sun. and in August. A visit to these workshops is highly recommended.

Sorolla Studio and Museum, General Martínez Campos 33. The famous painter's house, with a number of his works. Open 10–2. Closed Mon. and from August through September 15. Entrance 100 pesetas.

Temple of Debod. A large Egyptian temple brought stone by stone from Egypt, and now beautifully placed in a park near the Plaza de España (off Calle Ferraz). Admission 5 ptas. Open 10–1, 5–8. Sun. 10–3.

Wax Museum, Centro Colón. Excellent "panels" representing scenes and personages out of Spanish history, as well as latter-day international personalities ranging from Gary Cooper to President Kennedy. Admission 250 ptas. adults, 100 for children. Open 10.30–2, 4–9.

 PARKS. The main two parks in the city are the *Retiro* (see page 123) and the *Parque del Oeste* where you can visit the Temple of Debod and enjoy a stroll on summer evenings. You might also enjoy a visit to the *Moncloa Park,* home of the University City. This was the scene of fierce fighting during the Civil War when most of the buildings were destroyed. The university has been rebuilt and is now Spain's most important as well as enjoying considerable European standing.

On the edge of town is the vast *Casa del Campo* Park where Madrileños flee to at weekends. A great attraction here is the very popular Amusement Park which is well kept and clean with many wonderful rides, a restaurant and several snack bars. It is open 4–9.15 on weekdays, 12–10.45 on Saturdays, and 11–10.15 on Sundays and holidays and, in winter, at weekends only (mid October through March). Admission is 50 ptas. for adults and 20 ptas. for children under 10. The rides cost between 10 and 50 ptas., you can pay individually or buy books of tickets. You can reach the Amusement Park by taking the metro to Batán or the 33 bus from Plaza Isabel II. Another way of getting to the amusement park is to take the cablecar that runs from the Paseo de Rosales to the park, then take a special bus linking the two. The cablecar, called the "Teleférico", runs from 11.30 A.M. to 9 P.M.; one way costs 110 ptas., round trip 160 ptas. There is a pleasant restaurant and a snack bar at the Rosales station, with panoramic view.

There is also a zoo in the Casa de Campo Park. This is near the amusement park and sprawls out over 50 acres. Admission is 260 ptas. for adults, 130 for children of 3-8 yrs. There's also a children's zoo inside the regular zoo, charging a small additional admission. Bus 33 from Plaza de Isabel II takes you directly there. The zoo is open from 10 till sunset.

 SPORTS. Bullfighting comes first to mind though its popularity is now well on the decline and most *corridas* are patronized only by tourists and ageing *aficionados*. Madrid has two main rings, so be careful you get the right one. If you have a choice during your stay, don't miss the big Ventas bullring, which seats 25,000. A smaller bullring is the Vista Alegre in the Carabanchel Bajo region across the Manzanares river.

The season in Madrid runs from April to October. There is almost always a fight on Sunday, and often on Thursday as well. Starting times may vary from 4.30 P.M. until 6; bullfights and Mass are the only things in Spain that start on time, so be sure to be there early, for taxis are hard to get in the afternoon, and once the corrida has started, doors to the arena are closed. Pillows to sit on can be rented at the arena. Tickets for bullfights can be bought on the Calle de la Victoria, off the Carrera San Jerónimo, or on the latter street itself, near the Reina Victoria theater. The average Sunday *corridas* are now little more than a tourist spectacle—and not very good at that—but if you are intent on seeing a really good fight, try to be in Madrid around the middle of May during the San Isidro festivals; this will be your chance to see some of the best fights in Spain and tickets may well be hard to obtain.

Pelota is definitely something you shouldn't miss. Played at nights, on brightly illuminated cement courts, enclosed on three sides, with the spectators protected by netting on the other, it is the hardest, fastest ball game in the world. It is also a betting game, in which you get fast action for your money. If you want to try your luck, put 50 or 100 pesetas on Red or Blue and trust to luck. The handiest pelota court in Madrid is the Frontón Madrid, at Dr Cortezo 10. There is a session at 6 P.M. Mon.-Fri. and at 5.15 on Saturdays. Closed Sundays.

Football (soccer) is now Spain's number one sport and has far surpassed bullfighting or pelota in popularity. It may be seen between September and May in the huge Santiago Bernabéu Stadium on the Castellana, home of Real Madrid, which holds 130,000 spectators, or in the Vicente Calderón Stadium, home of Madrid Atlético, near the Manzanares river. The final of the 1982 world cup was played in the Bernabéu Stadium on July 11. If you want to see **basketball** or even **baseball** (it's not unknown in Spain), check with your hotel porter on games that may be scheduled—depending of course, on the season. **Horse races** take place at the Hipodromo de la Zarzuela, on the Ctra de La Coruña, except in the summer months. **Car racing** at the Jarama Track, on the road to Burgos.

If you want exercise yourself, there is a fashionable and luxurious **golf** club, the Real Club de la Puerta de Hierro, on the Carretera de El Pardo. (Membership fees are prohibitively high, however.) Golf de Somosaguas, tel. 212-16-47. Also Nuevo Club de Golf, Golf Las Matas, km 26 Coruña highway, tel. 630-08-

20. For latter, membership not required, only a club card made out by your hotel. Club has pick-up service. There are plenty of places to **swim**—the Hotel Plaza and Hotel Emperador pools, for instance, and at El Lago, Avenida de Valladolid 37. Also outside of town at Madrid Beach (Playa de Madrid) on the banks of the Manzanares; or consult the hotel porter. You can play **tennis** also at the golf club, or at the Casa del Campo; 15 all-weather courts.

Ice skating is at the Real Club in the Ciudad Deportiva, Paseo de la Castellana 259. There are two sessions daily, 11–1.45 and 5–11.45. Admission is 300 ptas. plus 50 ptas. to hire skates.

Greyhound racing is at the Canódromo Madrileño; buses leave from the Plaza Ramales. For **rowing,** there is the lake in the Retiro Park and the lake in the Casa de Campo, a much larger park across the Manzanares. In the winter, there is **skiing** in the sierra at Navacerrada. For **flying** enthusiasts, there exists the Royal Aero Club, with its airport at Cuatro Vientos; offices are at Carrera San Jerónimo 19.

 CHURCHES. If your interest in Madrid churches is as a worshipper, you may find one to which you would like to go among these: *Catholic, La Paloma,* Toledo 98; *San Ginés,* Arenal 13; or one of the newest, *Santa Rita,* Gaztambide 73 (architect Fisac) or *San Juan de la Cruz,* on the Plaza of that name. The Roman Catholic English-speaking parish is at the Chapel of Nuestra Señora de la Merced, Alfonso XIII 165. *Anglican,* the British Embassy church at Nuñez de Balboa 41. For other Protestant denominations, inquire at your embassy. *Jewish,* synagogue at Balmes 3.

 SHOPPING. Once, and not so very long ago, shopping in Madrid was an adventure with all the risk, thrill, disappointment and (sometimes) achievement, of the unexpected and the hazardous. Today, this is changed. Madrid is no longer the place of unusually exciting buys, where treasures can be discovered and incredible bargains made.

But if the thrill of the hunt has gone, the city does now offer something almost as good, a "safari" into a shoppers' dreamland. The large number of well-stocked stores selling everything imaginable, the glittering curio shops with their wares piled helter-skelter on dusty shelves, the richness and abundance of authentic works of art and, above all, the love and price with which local goods are manufactured, makes shopping in Madrid one of the chief attractions for anyone visiting this booming capital. Prices for most items are now on a par with those in England and the States.

Business hours. The siesta lasts from 1.30 until 5 in the summer, 2 to 4.30 in the winter, but main stores usually open from 9 to 1.30 and 4.30 to 8; schedule changes occasionally, so consult your hotel porter. Department stores now don't close at lunchtime.

Main Shopping Areas. Madrid has two main shopping areas. The first is in the center of town where the principal shopping streets are Gran Vía, the Calles de Preciados, del Carmen and Montera and the Puerta del Sol. The second, and more elegant area—and naturally more expensive—is in the Salamanca district bounded by Serrano, Goya and Conde de Peñalver. There is another up-and-coming area in the north of town around Calle Orense and the Azca shopping center between Orense and the Castellana.

Department Stores. On the whole, visitors will generally find the best bargains in the department stores, in anything from souvenirs to furniture. Moreover, chances are you'll feel more at ease picking through the counters at your own speed than struggling to make yourself understood with the small shopkeepers. Virtually all department stores have interpreters available. The following is a list of the main stores.

Galerías Preciados is the longest-established department store in Madrid. Its main building is on the Plaza Callao, right off the Gran Vía. Within the two seven-story buildings you'll find almost anything you may need. Another Galerías branch is located in Calle Arapiles near the Glorieta de Quevedo, and still another on Calle Goya, corner Conde de Peñalver. Each of the three Galerías has a cafeteria, open from 10 A.M. till 9 P.M. The Callao branch of Galerías is highly recommended for tourist souvenirs. Also outstanding are the Spanish ceramics, rugs, glassware and other handicrafts. Remains open throughout lunchtime.

El Corte Inglés in many ways is similar to Galerías and is its main competitor. There are four Corte Ingleses in Madrid: Calle Preciados, right near the Puerta del Sol; another one at the corner of Goya and Alcalá (also near the Goya *Galerías*); a third in the Urbanización Azca between the Castellana and Orense, and the fourth on the corner of Calle Princesa and Calle Alberto Aguilera. All have cafeterias. Quality of wares at the Corte Inglés is somewhat higher than that of Galerías. Best bet here, perhaps, are their leather goods. Remains open throughout lunchtime. The Preciados branch is probably the best.

Sear's, located on Calle Serrano, corner Ortega y Gasset, this American-named store features a wide variety of Spanish as well as foreign goods in its five stories of showrooms. It has a good toy selection. There's a cafeteria on the top floor, but without a view. Prices tend to be slightly higher than the Corte Inglés or Galerías Preciados, and it is usually less crowded. As the store has changed hands and, at presstime, was closed—possibly temporarily—we suggest you check on its status locally before planning a visit.

Celso Garcia is a smaller, more intimate department store on Calle Serrano, three blocks away from Sear's. Rather more expensive than the aforementioned, it also has higher-quality goods and more exclusive taste. There is a huge new branch in the Azca shopping center on the Castellana.

Special Shopping Areas. One of the most interesting and colorful of the Madrid shopping areas is one you should save for a Sunday morning. It's the **Rastro** or Flea Market, which stretches down the Ribera de Curtidores from

El Cascorro statue, and extends over a maze of little side streets branching out from either side. Here, on a Sunday morning, you'll see an incredible display of secondhand odds and ends, spread out artistically on blankets on the ground.

The central area, Curtidores, is much more "elegant." Here canvas booths have been set up to sell everything under the sun. Most of these, though, are cheap articles which are of little interest to the tourist, except for picture-taking.

If you want to try your hand at bargaining (which is a must here), there are booths selling everything conceivable. Buy with care, though, and don't carry money exposed. *Serious warning.* This place is an infamous hangout for pickpockets, who take advantage of the crowd's pushing and jostling. Women should leave pocketbooks behind and no one should take their passports or more money than they would mind losing.

From a buyer's viewpoint, the most interesting part of the *Rastro* is a series of galleries which line the street behind the booths. In dark shops built around picturesque patios, you can find all the antique dealers of Madrid represented. These shops, unlike the booths, are open all week during regular shopping hours, as well as on Sunday mornings. Here you can find old paintings and wood carvings, porcelain, furniture and jewelry. Also, in the Nuevas Galerías, Shop 45, you'll find a lapidary with unset precious, semi-precious and imitation gems which are well worth a look.

If you are a **stamp collector,** don't miss the *Stamp Fair,* held each Sunday and holiday morning from about 10 to 2 under the archways of the Plaza Mayor.

Secondhand books can be bought all year round from the bookstalls on the Cuesta Claudio Moyano, near the Atocha railroad station. With a little browsing, you'll find curiosities and first editions. And if you're in Madrid at the end of May and the beginning of June, you can visit the National Book Fair, held in the Retiro Park from 10 A.M. to 10 P.M. daily. Here, Spanish booksellers offer both their newest releases and old standards—all at a 10% discount.

For **handicrafts** and **Toledo ware,** you will find literally hundreds of shops all over Madrid, many of which are reliable, some less so. Try the department stores first, particularly the Corte Inglés and Galerías Preciados. Then you might try *Artespaña,* the official Spanish government handicraft shop. They have branches at Gran Vía 32, Hermosilla 14 and Plaza de las Cortes 3. They have a wonderful assortment of all things Spanish—wood carvings, handwoven rugs, embroidered tablecloths, Majorcan glassware, attractive stone ornaments for gardens and rustic Spanish furniture. Artespaña will ship goods throughout the world and, being government run, has reliable and reasonable prices.

Toledo wares are particularly good at *Artesanía Toledana,* Paseo del Prado and at *El Escudo de Toledo,* next door in Plaza Cánovas del Castillo. In both these stores you'll find a large selection of daggers, swords, chess boards, paintings, fans, Lladró porcelain, guns and leather wine bottles. For **Granada wares,** marquetry, inlaid mother of pearl and so on, try *Artesanía Granadina,* Marqués de Casa Riera.

Ceramics are a time-honored Spanish craft. Among the best examples are the exquisitely colored Manises lustrous glaze from Valencia, the more ornate designs from Granada and the blue and yellow Talavera pottery and pretty greens from Puente del Arzobispo. They can be found in most of the large department stores where you can also find the famous Lladró porcelains. These delicate figures are made in the Lladró factory at Tabernes Blances just to the north of Valencia. Among specialist ceramic shops are:

La Cerámica de Talavera, Calle Lagasca 44. Specializes, as the name indicates, in Talavera ceramics.

Talleres de Arte Grande, Serrano 56 and San Bernado 99. A world of ceramics, handicrafts, gifts etc. Exclusive and expensive.

Casa Talavera, Isabel la Católica 2, is a small old-timer in back of Gran Vía with good selection of all types of ceramics.

Cerámicas Arriba, Claudio Coello 16. Authentic ceramics from one of the few artisans still left in Spain.

The following areas are good for **antiques:** the Rastro, Calle del Prado, Carrera de San Jerónimo, Plaza de las Cortes, Plaza de Santa Ana.

For **fans,** try either the department stores or, for really superb examples, try the long established *Casa de Diego* in the Puerta del Sol.

Shoes. A chapter apart are Spanish shoes for both men and women. You'll find them made of sturdy, yet flexible leather, handcrafted in the latest styles and colors. The Spanish last is long and narrow so be very sure of trying your choice on carefully. Prices have gone up considerably, so unless shoes are very comfortable, don't buy them. If you are looking for something special, or have a foot that's difficult to fit, you can have shoes custom-made, though they will take at least a week to complete. Otherwise take a stroll along the Avenida José Antonio and Calle Serrano, where numerous shoe shops vie for attention.

 USEFUL ADDRESSES. *Spanish Tourist Office,* Torre de Madrid in the Plaza de España, and at Barajas airport. *City Tourist Office,* Plaza Mayor 3. *American Embassy,* Serrano 75, (tel. 276 3600). *British Embassy,* Fernando el Santo 16, (tel. 419 1528). *Main Post Office,* Plaza Cibeles. *Telephone Exchange,* Gran Vía at the Red San Luis. *Airport information,* (tel. 226 6192). *Infoiberia* (tel. 411 2545). *Iberia,* Cánovas de Castillo 4, (tel. 221 8230). *TWA,* Gran Vía 66, (tel. 248 0004). *British Airways,* San Bernardo 17 (tel. 248 7801). *Police Station,* Calle de Los Madrazo.

British-American Hospital, Juan XXIII 1, in the University City, (tel. 234 6700). *Emergency Dentist Service,* (tel. 244 5207). *American Express,* Plaza de las Cortes 2, (tel. 222 1180). *Wagon-Lits Cooks,* Alcalá 23, (tel. 221 1159). *Spanish Youth Hostels Head Office,* Ortega y Gasset 17, (tel. 401 9501). *Lost property,* for items lost in city buses, Alcántara 26; in taxis, Plaza de Chamberí 4; in metro, the lost and found at Cuatro Caminos station.

Laundromats, Juan Ramón Jiménez 28 and Manuela Malasaña 19, the latter open from 8 A.M. to 10 P.M.

Auto-tow service, Juan de Olías 15, (tel. 216 5427). Should your car get towed away by the authorities, call 266 6700 to find out where to pick it up and pay a fine. *Car hire:* the most central offices of the main car hire companies are: Atesa, Gran Vía 59 (tel. 248 9793); Avis, Gran Vía 60, (tel. 248 4203); Europcar,

San Leonardo 8, (tel. 241 8892); Hertz, Gran Vía 88, (tel. 248 5803); Ital, Princesa 1, (tel. 241 2290). *Central Reservation* numbers are Atesa, (tel. 450 2062); Avis (tel. 457 97 06); Budget (tel. 279 3400); Europcar, (tel. 456 6013); Hertz (tel. 242 1000); Ital (tel. 402 1034).

American Visitors' Bureau, Gran Vía 68, (tel. 247 0333). One flight up, all sorts of services for English-speaking tourists (shopping escorts, stenographers, interpreters, information, etc.). *Authorized Guides Association,* Duque de Medinacelli 2, (tel. 231 4699).

OLD AND NEW CASTILE

The Essence of Iberia

Enveloping the province of Madrid on the south and the east, four other provinces make up, with Madrid, the region of New Castile—Toledo, Ciudad Real, Cuenca and Guadalajara. To the west and north of Madrid are the provinces of Old Castile—Avila, Segovia, Burgos and Soria, with Valladolid, Palencia and La Rioja on either side of Burgos. The province of Santander is also historically part of Old Castile but as it forms a geographical entity with other provinces on the Cantabrian coast, we have included it in our Atlantic Coast chapter.

You will note, by the way, that the names of the Spanish provinces are the same as the names of their capital cities. (There are a few exceptions to this rule, the three Basque provinces, Navarre, La Rioja, Asturias, the Balearics and the Canaries.)

New Castile, a vast tableland watered by the large rivers Tagus and Guadiana, is flatter than Old Castile, though both are on the Meseta plateau, and at heights from 500 meters to 1,000 meters (1,640 to 3,280 feet). This area is sparsely populated and arid, though vast acreages of wheat stretch to the horizon, and there are large fields of saffron. Only near the forested mountains are there leaping torrents and lakes, and the slopes are good only for sheep raising. Castile occupies most of the center of Spain, stretching from the Cantabrian coast in the north to Andalusia in the south.

To the north, the Guadarrama mountains offer excellent winter sports, clear air, and an atmosphere ideal for a rest cure. Beyond the circle of resorts that constitute the immediate hinterland of the capital, the other showplaces of Old and New Castile are all easily accessible from Madrid. One way to get to know the heart of Spain is to establish yourself in Madrid and make your excursions from there.

If possible, avoid Castile during the height of what is normally considered the vacation season—that is, July and August. Central Spain at this time is hot and sun-baked. But it is not mild in winter. The Castiles with their high altitude can be bitterly cold. Spring and autumn are far and away the best for this region. The autumn weather is consistently better, but spring is the season of most of the fiestas, and, of course, of the Easter celebrations.

Castile's Epic History

Castile arose in Christian Spain in the 10th century, through a rebellion against the Kings of Asturias and León, initiated by Count Fernán González and carried on by his sons. The Kingdom of Castile was established in 957 and rights of succession granted. From a principality, Old Castile finally came to include all of central Spain until, in 1037, León and Castile were united. From then on, new territories were added, Toledo being captured in 1085, completing the region now known as New Castile.

In 1230, Castile was recognized as the representative kingdom for all Spain. Castile held its responsibilities in high regard, helping other rulers in their campaigns against the Moors, and the border castles bear witness to the region's warring abilities.

Three important contributions were made by Castile to the civilization of Spain. The first was an innovation in the legal system by which local customs as laws were adopted, in opposition to the written code. The second was the rise of a popular literature, the *Romancero,* which related past and present history in poetry and song. The most important, perhaps, concerns language. Castile started early to build its language on fixed principles, and by the 10th century, it ranked with

Latin as a popular tongue. By the 15th century, Castilian had been adopted in León and Aragón and had supplanted the Mozarabic dialects of the south of Spain.

Exploring Old Castile

The provinces of Old Castile curl about the core of the capital to the west and the north. They are most often visited from Madrid, with the exception of Burgos, which is apt to be a stop on the road between Madrid and France. But the other two of the top three attractions of this region, Avila and Segovia, are usually made the object of excursions from the capital.

As it is easy to see each of the towns in this area on separate trips from Madrid, there is no particular order in which they are likely to be visited. We might as well start, therefore, with Avila, sharing a border with Toledo in New Castile, and swing round clockwise through Segovia, Valladolid, Palencia, Burgos and Soria, until we close the circle at La Rioja (capital, Logroño), whose border is with Guadalajara, at the other extreme of the provinces of New Castile.

Mountains and Roman Roads

If you approach Avila from the north, you will travel through a hilly district, strewn with huge granite boulders and many evergreens, to make your last stage across an arid region. But if you come from Madrid, as you probably will, you run first through a countryside dotted with neat villages, then enter a valley enclosed by the foothills of the Guadarrama, and finally come to an area of bleak mountains.

Some 50 kilometers (37 miles) from Madrid, the Guadarrama range extends along a northeast–southwest axis, and with the Gredos range, divides Spain's huge central plateau into Old and New Castile. These mountains, standing out so distinctly in the soft rays of the setting sun, were featured in many of Velázquez's paintings. The Guadarrama range, below which a toll-tunnel provides a substantial shortcut, is the center of many summer activities. Trains and good roads have transformed the area into a vast park for the Madrileños. In winter, the area around Navacerrada Pass (1,860 m, 6,102 ft) is good for skiing. In summer, you can take excursions from here to the nearby valleys of Fuenfría and Paular, where you will find a 15th-century Carthusian monastery (now a hotel). Climbing up Mount Peñalara, the highest of the Guadarrama range (2,430 m, 7,973 ft), isn't difficult; the Pedriza and the Cabrera range, farther east, also offer good climbing possibilities for the alpinist.

The Sierra de Gredos, separated from that of Guadarrama by the Avila plateau, might be called the sportsman's paradise. Here, within easy access of the parador at Gredos, are the game and fishing preserves, where horses are furnished and mountain climbing may be enjoyed. There is excellent trout fishing in the River Tormes, which runs close to the scenic road from Avila to Barco de Avila, the latter a pleasant summer resort surrounded by ramparts.

Before the Puerto del Pico pass, with its well-preserved Roman road, another branch traverses the Sierra de Gredos to the Monastery of Yuste and Plasencia. Mombeltrán possesses a lovely 15th-century Gothic church, a 16th-century hospital and a splendid 14th-century Albuquerque castle. Arenas de San Pedro deserves a lengthy stop, not only for its Palace of the Infant Don Luis de Borbón, the Castle of the Triste Condesa, the Monastery of San Pedro de Alcántara and a 14th-century Gothic church, but also as a center for excursions to the picturesque mountain villages of Candelada and El Arena, or to the stalactite Grotto of Aguila.

Avila

The dramatically walled city of Avila, 1,219 meters (4,000 feet) above sea level and the highest provincial capital in Spain, is eminently worth visiting, for its historical associations and for its distinctive, unspoiled character. The winter climate is fiercely cold but the summers are not oppressively hot.

Roman Avila was converted to Christianity as early as the first century, and occupied by the Moors until reconquered by Count Raymond of Burgundy who brought it permanently under Christian control. Until the 16th century it was simply a prosperous town; then it assumed an aura of saintliness it still preserves to a remarkable degree.

This is due to Saint Teresa, the mystic whose personality lives today as vividly as it did in the 16th century, when she dedicated herself to the Way of Perfection, and trod barefoot the rocky roads of Spain. Teresa was a great administrator and founded thirty-two religious institutions for both men and women in different parts of Spain.

One itinerary that the traveler can follow is to the places glorified by Saint Teresa. These are the Convent of Nuestra Señora de Gracia, where she was educated; the Encarnación, where she made her profession and became Prioress; the Convent of St Joseph, which was the first establishment of the Carmelite Reform; and finally, the Convent of Saint Teresa, which stands on the site of her birthplace. Her room has been converted into a chapel, with a statue of her by Gregorio Hernández; then next to this is a room where relics are kept—her finger, rosary and walking stick.

A visit to Avila is best begun by a tour of the walls that enclose the city. There has been some restoration but this has not lessened their grandeur. They were begun in 1090 by Count Raymond on order of his father-in-law, King Alfonso I, who decided to repopulate Avila with settlers from other provinces. Among the new citizens were master builders who undertook the work with enthusiasm, making these walls the most complete military installation in Spain in the Middle Ages. They entirely enclose the city, measuring more than two and a half kilometers (1½ miles), and contain 88 towers, nine gateways and several posterns. They are at their most impressive viewed from the lookout Los Cuatro Postes on the Salamanca road. In spring you will see storks nesting in the turrets of the walls. A good place to look is in the part of the walls close to the Raimondo de Borgoña parador.

There are many interesting churches, convents and fortified palaces. The cathedral resembles a castle more than a place of worship. It was begun in the 12th century and completed in the 15th. There are two important entrances, the Gate of the Apostles, with its pointed arch and statue of the Savior surrounded by reposeful figures, and the west doorway, of baroque design. The interior is vast and dim, giving a general Gothic impression.

The church of San Pedro stands in the center of the city. It is Romanesque, with a beautiful rose window. The basilica of San Vicente, Romanesque and Gothic of the 12th to the 14th centuries, is outside the walls, erected on the spot where the saint was martyred. In the center of the chapel of the convent of Santo Tomás, 15th-century Gothic, is the alabaster tomb of Prince Juan, only son of Ferdinand and Isabella. The reredos and three cloisters are exceptionally fine, providing a worthy setting for the Museum of Oriental Art.

Further north, Arévalo and Madrigal de las Altas Torres are worth a short stop for their notable architecture.

Castles in Spain

The province of Segovia, separated from Madrid by the Guadarrama mountains, is famous for its castles, Romanesque architecture, and a Roman aqueduct. The outstanding sights, beside Segovia itself, are the towns of Pedraza and Sepúlveda, the castles of Coca and Fuentidueña, the palaces of Riofrío and La Granja.

The quickest way to reach Segovia from Madrid is to take Route N-VI which leads right into a toll speedway running as far as Adanero. You leave at the San Rafael exit, and then proceed along a good highway as far as Segovia. If there's not much traffic, you can drive the distance in about one hour.

Should you opt for a more leisurely, and far more rewarding, route, turn off at the Navacerrada exit. A narrow, curving highway leads to the resort village of Navacerrada. You can then make the steep descent to La Granja, with its beautiful palace and gardens, and the small village nestling nearby. After that it's straight sailing right into Segovia.

A lesser detour can be made by taking the indicated left turn on the road from San Rafael to Segovia for a visit to the magnificent Riofrío Palace, built by Elizabeth Farnese, widow of Philip V, in the neo-classical style round a central patio, but never finished. It houses a Hunting Museum. *Note:* the palace is very cold inside, and the guided tour quite lengthy, so take a wrap or jacket. The vast grounds are filled with roaming deer, which come up to your car. For a small toll drive right through the oak forest, a delightful short cut to Segovia.

Besides the Alcázar in Segovia, there are seven important castles in the region, reached by a few short detours over roads that are occasionally rather rough. Coca, already important in Roman times and the birthplace of Emperor Theodosius the Great, was built in the 15th century by Bishop Fonseca in flamboyant Gothic but shows strong mudéjar influence. Cuellar, of the 15th century, was restored, so its style is Gothic with mudéjar additions. In the 16th century a sumptuous palace was added, which once accommodated the Duke of Wellington. Twenty-nine kilometers (18 miles) east, mighty Fuentidueña is reached by a bridge over the Duratón. The view of Sepúlveda, 32 kilometers (20 miles) up the Duratón, is most impressive. The Gonzales Castle, that withstood not only many a Moorish siege but also the repeated assaults of Napoleon's armies, towers above narrow, tortuous streets, with Romanesque churches and noble palaces. Pedraza, still a walled town, is the reputed birthplace of the Emperor Trajan. Over the pretty Plaza Mayor rises a steep crag crowned by the stout walls of the 15th-century castle. Turegano was constructed in the 15th century as the fortress-castle of the bishops of Segovia. Eighteen kilometers (11 miles) east of the village of Navacerrada, on a superb site, stands the finest castle of them all—Manzanares el Real (15th century). Its crenelated walls and tower recall the heroic times of the Reconquest.

Segovia

Segovia stands 998 meters (3,276 feet) above sea level, between two small streams, the Eresma and the Clamores. The first thing that will strike you about Segovia is the enormous, and still undamaged Roman aqueduct. The romantic-looking Alcázar fortress-palace rises like a huge ship on the crest of an 80-meter-high (262-foot) rock. The best view of it is from near the circular 13th-century church of the Knights

Templar, just outside the town. Segovia's 16th-century cathedral is considered one of the finest in Spain.

Segovia has been an important city for 2,000 years. It was the center of Celto-Iberian resistance to Roman conquest, but was occupied by the Romans and razed in the year 80 B.C. It was the capital of Alfonso El Sabio (1284), Isabella was proclaimed queen here in 1474, and here Ferdinand, her husband, swore to preserve the independent rights of Castile.

Segovia's streets are crooked and picturesque, with the cathedral built at the highest point. On entering the city, the Alcázar is not visible, but a sudden turn, and there it is poised as if ready to take off in flight. Burnt down in 1862, it was rebuilt in a fairy-castle style, decorated with huge murals, but furnished with many genuine period pieces. No less striking is the Roman aqueduct, one of the best preserved Roman remains in the world. Built of huge, uncemented boulders, it joins two somewhat distant hills. It is 823 meters (900 yards) long and its 148 arches are over 9 meters (30 feet) high. In the center, a dip in the earth made the use of two tiers of arches necessary, and at this point it towers 27 meters (90 feet) above ground level. Water is brought from the hills sixteen kilometers (10 miles) away and still flows over the ancient aqueduct today.

Romanesque Churches, Gothic Cathedral

Those searching for beauty instead of grandeur will seek out the churches, for Segovia is a Romanesque city, untouched for six centuries. Most of them were built during the 12th and the beginning of the 13th centuries and are characterized by their outer galleries, which resemble arcades and give light and air to an otherwise heavy style. The idea may have been to keep the churches cool, but it added a new beauty to following styles. The finest examples are San Martín and San Millán, the latter showing some Moorish influence in its decorations. Others include San Esteban, with a graceful tower (restored), San Andrés with brick arches; San Lorenzo, a beautiful exterior; San Clemente, which has fine porticos, apses and tower; and San Juan de los Caballeros, today a studio for ceramics, founded by Zuloaga. Deserving special mention is Vera Cruz, consecrated in 1208, one of the most notable churches of the Knights Templar in Europe.

The 16th-century cathedral was the last Gothic building to be erected in Spain, replacing the original church destroyed by the *Comuneros*. Among the works of art are a *Pietà* by Juan de Juni (1571) and a collection of valuable 17th-century Flemish tapestries in the Chapter Hall under a fine coffered ceiling. In the Capilla Mayor stands a neoclassical marble reredos by Sabatini, in the Capilla del Sagrario a Christ

SEGOVIA
(NOT TO SCALE)

1 Alcázar
2 Monastery of El Parral
3 San Esteban Church
4 Cathedral
5 Post Office
6 Casa de Los Picos
7 San Millán Church
8 Roman Aqueduct
≋ Scenery
▯ Feudal Palace
✝ Church or Convent

by Churriguera above a ceramic altar; above all is the feeling of soaring height conveyed by the cathedral's interior, despite a somewhat compact exterior aspect. There are some wonderful stained-glass windows.

In front of Segovia's cathedral is the delightful Plaza Mayor, with a monument commemorating Juan Bravo, a local hero, Spain's equivalent of William Tell.

The Monastery of El Parral is one of the many famous convents still standing in Segovia. It was founded by Henry IV and is now a national monument. There are also the Clarisas de San Antonio el Real, a Dominican Convent established by the same king, and a Jesuit seminary. In touring the city do not miss the Plaza del Azoguejo mentioned by Cervantes. Formerly a rendezvous for thieves and knaves, it is now the market place.

Even new structures adhere to Segovia's architectural peculiarity (which, by the way, preserves its unity); this is the *esgrafiado,* a façade decoration that can best be seen on the entrance gates to the Alcázar, embellished with small pieces of coal!

Don't miss the walk on top of the city ramparts—it affords you a complete view of one of the finest old cities in the world. If you have a car, or don't mind a longer walk, leave from the aqueduct and make your way along the Ronda de Santa Lucia below the ramparts. Near the Carmelite Convent, burial place of St. John of the Cross, is a magnificent spot from which to photograph the Alcázar perched on top of a rock above the meeting place of the Eresma and Clamores streams. Then return to the city along the Carretera de los Hoyos.

Excursions from Segovia

The palace of La Granja de San Ildefonso, 11 kilometers (7 miles) from Segovia, 85 (53 miles) from Madrid, was built by the homesick Philip V to remind him of his beloved Versailles. It has become one of the showpieces of Spain. Originally the site was occupied by a hermitage built at the order of Henry IV of Castile. Later, it was purchased by Ferdinand and Isabella and presented to the Monastery of El Parral, when a farm (*granja*) was started nearby. And there it is, just as the first Bourbon king of Spain had it made to his liking—statues, fountains, châteaux, retreats, trimmed hedges, formal gardens—an exquisite bit of France in a Spanish wood; Philip V and his Queen, Elizabeth Farnese, are buried in the palace's collegiate church.

Thirty-one kilometers (19 miles) along the road to Valladolid, there is Santa María la Real de Nieva, with its famous relic, the Buried Virgin.

Valladolid, Province of Kings

Valladolid is another province rich in castles and ancient architectural remains, overshadowed, as usual, by the provincial capital, a city of 300,000 inhabitants in the heart of the endless wheat fields of the plateau, 193 kilometers (120 miles) north of Madrid. At an altitude of 692 meters (2,270 feet), the climate is somewhat harsh in summer and winter, but the Pisuerga river provides enough water to enable the beautiful gardens in and around the town to thrive despite the otherwise arid nature of the country.

In September, Valladolid celebrates the *Ferias Mayores,* or Great Fair; but if you happen to be in the vicinity during Easter week, do not miss the Semana Santa processions. Even for those not particularly interested in religious festivals, it is a great artistic experience to see passing before you, along the city streets, the fabulously beautiful statues created by famous *imagineros castellanos* so long ago. It was in Castile that this distinctive type of polychrome religious sculpture originated. Valladolid saw its beginnings and today preserves the finest examples of this work.

As is the case with many Spanish cities, the early history of Valladolid is dominated by one man. He was Count Pedro Ansurez, the town's governor and benefactor in the time of Alfonso VI. He provided it with its name, Belad Walid, an Arabic phrase meaning "the town of the governor". During much of the 13th century, Valladolid was the residence of the governors of Castile. The Cortes met here ten times, but in 1560 Philip II finally established the capital in Madrid. Napoleon set up his headquarters here in 1809.

Shades of Columbus and Cervantes

Wandering around this pleasant city of many arcades, you find, in front of the 16th-century La Magdalena church, the rebuilt house where Columbus died in 1506, the old home of Cervantes, which is now a museum, and the Atheneum, located in the house of José Zorilla, author of *Don Juan Tenorio.* One of Spain's most popular dramas, the latter is performed all over the country every year in November.

Los Pimenteles, the birthplace of Philip II, still stands, as does Las Aldabas, where Henry IV was born. Among many other palaces is the Casa de los Viveros, where Ferdinand and Isabella were married in 1469. Not all the events in Valladolid were happy ones, however. Just off the Plaza Mayor, used in ancient times for a bullring and for *autos da fé,* is the small square of the Ochavo, where you may see the spot upon which Don Alvaro de Luna, minister and favorite of King Juan II, was beheaded in 1453.

The cathedral, of late Renaissance style, was begun by Juan de Herrera and continued by Diego de Praves, while the upper part of the façade was added by Churriguera in his own individual baroque, but never completed. Juan de Juni's splendid reredos stands out in the classically austere interior of 32 Corinthian columns. The Collegiate Church next door is now the Diocesan Museum with lovely reredos, jewelry and above all the silver monstrance by Juan de Arfe, which is 1.82 meters (6 feet) high and weighs 63 kilograms (140 pounds). Almost facing the magnificent entrance arch is El Salvador with a Flemish reredos; backing onto the cathedral stands Santa María Antigua, founded in the 11th century and reconstructed in the 13th, whose Romanesque tower is an architectural gem.

Nearby Las Angustias is famous for its high altar designed by Velázquez, alas only the lesser Cristóbal, and Juan de Juni's *Vírgen de los Cuchillos* (Our Lady of the Knives). Beyond the Archiepiscopal Palace, the church of La Cruz and the house of the painter Berruguete, rises the fortress-like 15th-century San Benito, whose Renaissance cloisters have become the *Auditorio Patio Herreriano* for theatrical performances.

If you walk toward the river you come to the circular Convent of Santa Ana, founded by Philip II and rebuilt by Sabatini; three Goyas and a sculpture by Fernández adorn the church. Opposite is San Lorenzo; this by no means completes the list of churches, monasteries and palaces.

For those who love books, the College of Santa Cruz, founded by Cardinal Mendoza in 1479, contains a library of rare volumes. Across the Plaza Santa Cruz the austere building of the University is enlivened by a baroque portal. Courses for foreigners are given here during July and August, in literature, history and folklore, with excursions to historic cities.

This still leaves Valladolid's two greatest monuments, both on the prodigious Plaza San Pablo, adjoining the palace of Philip II. The façade of the 15th-century Dominican Monastery of San Pablo resembles in its plateresque profusion a Gothic reredos; it is rivaled by the entrance and cloisters of the College of San Gregorio, now Spain's outstanding National Museum of Sculpture, built between 1488 and 1496 for Bishop Alonso de Burgos, confessor of Ferdinand and Isabella; his coat of arms appears in the center of the façade. Inside is a patio of exquisite design, its lower, twisted columns upholding an open, lavishly carved gallery.

Here is displayed that polychrome sculpture to which Spanish artists brought a brilliant and original genius. Abandoning marble and bronze, these creators worked with wood—pine, oak and cedar—and added color. The method of execution was peculiar to Spain. Once the figure had been carved from wood, it was polished and the polychrome was applied by painters who specialized in this art. The process was highly technical and the results have never been equaled elsewhere.

The interior of San Gregorio is well adapted for these exhibits. The spacious rooms are rich in statues, carvings and fragments. Juan de Juni is represented by his touching *Entombment,* and Gregorio Fernández by the *Pasos;* both are carried in the Holy Week processions, but remain here during the rest of the year.

Excursions from Valladolid

If this formidable array of miscellaneous architecture should prove insufficient, there are castles and churches galore beyond the capital. Only eleven kilometers (seven miles) down the Pisuerga rise the cylindrical towers of mighty Simancas, a Moorish castle reconstructed by Alfonso III. Since the reign of Charles V it has served as the General Archive of the Kingdom and over 30 million documents are kept in its fifty-two rooms. Beautifully renovated, it's a splendid sight from the old road, but is bypassed by the new.

Medina de Ríoseco in the northern Tierra de Campos abounds in churches ranging from Gothic to baroque, while Villalón goes in for mudéjar and plateresque. A rectangular keep with four turrets was added in the 15th century to guard Fuensaldaña Castle; Mota del Marqués and Torrelobatón are as impressively stern reminders of the embattled past as Iscar and Portillo, where Don Alvaro de Luna was imprisoned.

South of the Duero, Olmedo, immortalized by Lope de Vega in his *Gentleman of Olmedo,* has preserved its ramparts and numerous churches. Nava del Rey not only possesses a Gothic-Renaissance church, but also produces excellent wines of the sherry type in the enormous vineyards which extend over this part of the province.

At Medina del Campo, the churches of San Antolín and San Martín contain reredos sculptured in part by Berruguete and Becerra. Other tokens of past glory are the Casa Blanca, the Casa Consistorial, and the Dueñas family mansion. Above all don't miss the superb castle of La Mota; it is marvelously well preserved, with a deep moat, towers, drawbridge and barbican. Here Isabella the Catholic breathed her last. It later served as a state prison, holding at various periods such choice inmates as Hernando Pizarro, Rodrigo Calderón and Cesare Borgia.

Along the course of the Duero, Peñafiel Castle was built in the 10th century, but the present unusual silhouette of a ship run aground dates from the 14th. At Valbuena de Duero stands the 12th-century Cistercian Monastery of St Bernard.

The Mad Queen and the Mapmaker

Lastly, Tordesillas, where Queen Joan (Juana la Loca), mad daughter of Ferdinand and Isabella and mother of the Emperor Charles V, lived out her distraught existence long after the death of her husband, Philip I of Spain. The story goes that she was so passionately in love with him that, when he died young, she refused to let his body be buried and carried the open coffin with her on her travels for three years before being confined at Tordesillas. She lived here for forty-nine years, a long time to stay in prison, even when the view over the Duero is unrivaled.

Prior to that, when Spain and Portugal were busily dividing up the "new world to be discovered," it was at Tordesillas, in 1494, that they reached an agreement, amending an earlier arbitral decree issued by the Borgia Pope Alexander VI. As a result, much of Latin America was settled by Spaniards, whereas Brazil became Portuguese, largely through an error in calculation, either involuntary or deliberate, committed by a certain cartographer named Amerigo Vespucci . . . yes, the very one.

The restored Convent-Palace of Santa Clara was originally the residence of King Pedro I. The mudéjar style is particularly striking in the patio—sometimes referred to as the Alhambra of Castile—and in the gilt-adorned chapel. The tomb of the founder, Friar Fernando de la Cueva, is a further fine example of 15th-century mudéjar art. Here also are the musical instruments of the Mad Queen, but her apartments were in an adjoining palace, of which, after a fire in 1974, only the church and tower of San Antolín remain.

The Communal Bull

In this part of the country the big fiestas are held in September. In small towns that can't afford arenas, a makeshift bullring is set up in the Plaza Mayor, where bull and fighters confront one another—for no celebration is complete without the gory encounter between man and beast. All exits from the square are barred off, it is surrounded by wood panels resembling campaign-billboards, sand is sprinkled on the ground, and then, on with the corrida! Everybody chips in to buy the bull; the people living in the square invite their friends to come and watch from windows and balconies.

This particular kind of bullfighting is governed by a set of regulations that make it something quite different from what the average visitor sees. It begins with a few ordinary passes at the bull in the improvised arena, and the banderillas are put in place. But the bull is then let loose to run through the town, perhaps even into the countryside if he can make it. The entire male population, on foot or on horseback, dashes off in pursuit, bent on killing the bull. The putting to death has to be done within established limits and rules; no firearms or poisons are allowed. The amateur matadors are usually armed with spears. Whoever strikes down the bull is borne in triumph and is awarded a prize and the bull automatically becomes the property of the community having jurisdiction over the territory in which the bull gets slaughtered. If he escapes beyond the town limits it's the neighbors who will do the feasting!

Palencia

The province of Palencia owes its wealth of old monasteries to the position it occupies across the famous pilgrimage route which led from France across northern Spain to the tomb of St. James the Apostle (in Spanish, Santiago) at Santiago de Compostela.

The lowlands of the River Pisuerga form the western boundary of Palencia; it is separated from Santander by the Cantabrian range. In general the landscape and climate of the region—called Tierra de Campos—is a blend of the dry Castilian plateau and the less severe north. There is a direct train service from Madrid to Palencia and also from the north, but travelers from Galicia must change at Venta de Baños.

In the 12th century the city of Palencia was the seat of the Castilian kings and the Cortes. It was reduced in importance by Charles V, however, who never forgave it for its part in the revolt of the Comuneros. The cathedral was begun in the 14th century, with an unusual plateresque altar and stone sculptures by Gil de Siloé. Next in importance is the church of San Miguel, 13th-century Gothic. The Plaza Mayor is typical and the city abounds in *alamedas* and gardens.

If you can give up a day, do not neglect *Las Rutas Románicas,* a little tour along the Pilgrim's Way which includes Fromista, with its Benedictine Monastery of San Martín, continuing to Villalcázar de Sirga, on a third-class road. Its Alcázar was a royal grant to the Knights Templar and in the Santiago Chapel, in the church of Santa María la Blanca, is the solitary tomb of a knight of the times. A fine reredos and some superb carved tombstones make the visit to this church—too important for the town's present-day population—more than worthwhile. Coming back through Carrión de los Condes, court of kings and seat of counts, you will visit the church of Santa María de la Victoria del Camino and other buildings. Only eight kilometers from Palencia is the Castle of Paradilla del Alcor; and nearby, in the village of Antillo del Pino, stop for one of the finest overall views in this part of Old Castile.

Burgos, the Shield of Castile

Castile of the Middle Ages, with its wealth of architecture, comes to life in the province of Burgos; a varied and rich land irrigated by the headwaters of the Ebro river. Burgos is reputed to speak the purest Castilian in Spain, which is understandable, since the language had its origin here, becoming the national tongue only later. The tradition of Burgos as the cradle of the best Spanish is carried on by the Burgos Institute, which gives special courses in the language for foreigners during August and September.

The city of Burgos straddles the River Arlanzón halfway between Madrid and San Sebastián. Though the Gothic character of the inner core has been preserved, many of the 150,000 inhabitants are engaged in industrial projects that have created dreary suburbs. The Holy Week processions are beautiful, especially on Good Friday. If you are in Burgos during Corpus Christi, visit the Monasterio de las Huelgas the next day for the procession called *Corpillos*.

Burgos was founded in the 9th century by a Castilian count. For a time it was the royal residence and the capital of Old Castile. It joined the Comuneros against Charles V, but appeased his wrath by erecting the triumphal Arco de Santa María, a curious gateway with towers, pinnacles, and statues. Many battles of the War of Independence were fought nearby and, during the Civil War, it was the headquarters of General Franco.

Burgos has two glories. One of the country's finest Gothic cathedrals, whose twin spires rise up to greet you long before you reach the city, stands here. In addition, it is the city of El Cid, the national hero who embodies the Spanish idea of chivalry. His equestrian statue in the city center is one of Burgos' great landmarks.

The first stone of Burgos cathedral was laid in the reign of Saint Ferdinand III by Bishop Mauricio in 1221 and the work was continued for the next thirty years. The façade and towers were finished in the 14th century; Juan de Colonia executed the Condestable Chapel and the tracery of the spires in the 15th century; the dome dates from the 16th century. The exterior, of the most exuberant flamboyant Gothic, culminates in the fine 13th-century sculpture on the Sarmental and Coronería gateways.

The interior of the cathedral is imposing in its grandeur and can be studied only superficially during a first visit. The Condestable Chapel, for example, is so large and elaborately decorated that it leaves you breathless. The Escalera Dorada, a flight of double steps with heavy gilt balustrades leading to the Puerta de la Coroneria, and the door itself were designed by Diego de Siloé. The reredos in the Chapel of Santa Ana is by his son, Gil de Siloé; the whole church, in fact, is a treasure house of sculpture by famous artists. Do not miss the superb ironwork. This craft reached its highest point in the Spanish Gothic. The cloister on the southeast side of the cathedral is 13th-century Gothic, and contains many statues of interest. It's advisable to engage a guide, since the greatest treasures are locked up. Two of the cathedral's more intriguing features are the bizarre image of Christ covered in a cow hide in the Santo Cristo Chapel, and high up in the nave just inside the West Door, the famous Papamoscas (flycatcher) Clock - watch the bird open its mouth as it strikes the hour.

Other churches and important places to see in Burgos are San Esteban, San Nicolás with a stunningly beautiful altarpiece by Simón de Colonia (1505), San Gil; the celebrated Casa del Cordón of the 15th century, where Columbus was received by Ferdinand and Isabella when he returned from his second voyage to America; and the Marceliano Santa María museum in the ruined cloisters of the Monastery of San Juan.

Three splendid Gothic monuments lie on the outskirts. To the west, the convent of Las Huelgas Reales, originally a summer villa of the kings of Castile, was converted into a majestically endowed convent for noble ladies by Alfonso VIII in 1187. The Gothic church is flanked by Romanesque cloisters and mudéjar chapels. The kneeling figures of Alfonso and his wife, Eleanor, daughter of Henry II of England, are on either side of the altar in the main chapel, while their tombs are behind the double screen that conceals the nuns from the public. Here also you will see the banner captured from the Moors in the Battle of Las Navas de Tolosa (1212). The collection of medieval fabrics may be unique, but is rather tattered.

Closer to the river is the Hospital del Rey, another foundation of Alfonso VIII, now a sadly neglected old men's home, but the Puerta de Romeros and the Casa de Romeros are plateresque at its best.

The Cartuja de Miraflores in the eastern suburbs is approached by a drive lined with poplars and elms. It was founded in 1441 by Juan II, the poet king, and rebuilt by Simón de Colonia. The reredos of its Isabelline Gothic church is by Gil de Siloé, gilded with the first gold brought back from America. Gil, one of the greatest wandering artists of the Middle Ages, carved the tombs of Juan II, his queen, Isabel of Portugal, and Prince Alfonso in alabaster by order of Queen Isabella.

El Cid

Five kilometers farther on is the Monastery of San Pedro de Cardeña where El Cid took leave of his wife before going into exile.

The exploits of El Cid Campeador (lord champion)—whose actual name was Rodrigo Díaz de Vivar—are immortalized in the greatest Spanish epic poem, *El Cantar del Mío Cid.* You can visit El Solar del Cid, the site of the house where he was born and see the coffer he filled with sand instead of treasure won from the Moors. He left the coffer as security for a loan, but when it was opened, the sand was found to have turned miraculously to gold. See the church of Santa Agueda, which lives in history because it was here that the Cid made the new King Alfonso VI swear that he had had no part in the death of his brother Sancho during the siege of Palencia. Finally, in the transept of the cathedral, is his tomb, beside that of his wife, Doña Jimena.

The whole of Castile is dotted with too many noble castles, churches and monasteries to enumerate. The 58 kilometers (36 miles) south to the most renowned, the Benedictine Monastery of Santo Domingo de Silos with its marvelous 11th-century cloister pass through Quintanilla de las Viñas, proud of its Visigothic church; and the ancient town of Covarrubias, in whose collegiate church two outstanding works of art can be seen: a triptych of Diego de Siloé and a polychrome sculpture by Berruguete. The walls of historic Lerma enclose a ducal palace and a 17th-century collegiate church.

Beyond the Ebro, the Castle of Medina de Pomar looks down on an Alcázar, a convent and the old Jewish quarter, and near the summer resort of Villacayo stands the 11th-century Romanesque Abbey of Tejada.

Soria, the Undiscovered and La Rioja, Vineyard of Spain

Most travelers bypass the provinces of La Rioja and Soria, although neither is far from the main road from San Sebastián to Madrid, and both are logical stops on the way to Zaragoza.

Soria might be called the "Red City," from the color of its sunbeaten soil, from which bricks and tiles are made. Lying on a plateau on the right bank of the Duero, it came under the rule of Castile in 1136, during the reign of Alfonso VII. There are several fine Romanesque churches—San Juan de Rabanera, San Pedro, the French-inspired Santo Domingo, and Nuestra Señora de la Mayor—but the most important is San Juan del Duero, with its ancient cloister.

Only seven kilometers north of Soria is the ancient city of Numancia, celebrated for its heroic resistance to the Romans. Destroyed by them in 134 B.C., its remains were discovered in 1854 by Eduardo Saavedra. There is, however, precious little to see. But the Numantine Museum in Soria is filled with artifacts from the excavations and is well worth a visit.

Medinaceli, seventy-two kilometers (45 miles) south of Soria, was an important stronghold of the Moors and contains tombs of the Medinaceli family, who, in the Middle Ages, were claimants to the Spanish throne. Their ancient castle still stands, and so does the Roman arch of the 2nd or 3rd century, the only one with a triple archway surviving in Spain. The village is picturesquely perched atop a hill and is well worth a visit, especially for those traveling the Madrid–Barcelona road.

Logroño, capital of the newly-named province of La Rioja, is beautifully situated on the Ebro, crossed here by two bridges, one of stone, constructed in the 13th century by Juan de Ortega. It was dominated first by the Romans, then by the Saracens. In 1076 it came under the rule of Alfonso I of Castile, and in 1521 the city defeated the invading army of the French. The finest table wines in Spain come from this beautiful province, which is equally rich in game and the sport afforded by its clear rivers, alive with trout and freshwater crayfish, called *cangrejos*.

Other places to visit in La Rioja are Calahorra, one of the oldest Iberian towns on the peninsula, once used as a refuge against the Romans; Santo Domingo de la Calzada, whose early Gothic cathedral is dominated by a baroque tower; inside is a lovely 13th-century reredos and—unique in Christendom—a white cock which crows lustily during the service from a cage opposite the saint's tomb; and Santa María, containing a handsome cloister and tombs of the kings of Castile.

Exploring New Castile

The provinces of Guadalajara, Cuenca and Ciudad Real form the eastern and southern boundaries of New Castile, and each has its arresting features and individual characteristics that mark it for special attention. While the terrain of these provinces varies, you are still in the plateau country, averaging over 457 meters (1,500 feet) above sea level, and in Ciudad Real you are in La Mancha, a word derived from the Arabic *manxu* meaning "dry and arid". In some places, the earth is green with verdure, and in others, the ground has cracked and sunk.

Two main highways from Madrid to Andalusia pass through this region, one by way of Toledo and the city of Ciudad Real, and the other leading through Aranjuez, Manzanares and Valdepeñas, famous for its wines and bodegas.

Toledo—the National Monument

Of all the names of the provinces that make up the region of New Castile, Madrid, Toledo, Ciudad Real, Cuenca and Guadalajara, the name that rings with the clash of tempered steel is Toledo, and in the province of Toledo, the city of Toledo overshadows all the rest.

Toledo is like a huge tapestry that depicts all the elements that have contributed to the development of the civilization of Spain. It is history recorded in stone by those who could not read or write, but history more eloquent than anything inscribed in books and, unlike words, never to be misunderstood by posterity. Architects made the plans, but it is the hand of the workman and the craftsman-artist, weaving his imagination into the stones, that tells the story. It is said that the Gothic has never been successfully restored in our day because the ancient artisan fashioned his work with pride, and the spirit that permeates his labor of love cannot be recaptured by us. Time mellows and softens harsh corners, but it is not time that has wrought the charm of Toledo. Every building speaks to you with its own voice.

Most visitors make Toledo, an hour and a half by bus southwest from Madrid, a one-day excursion from the capital, which is a pity. It is true that you can get a telescopic view of Toledo in one day and visit its main points of interest; but a longer stay opens up rewarding glimpses of nooks and corners typically Moorish in their atmosphere, evoking the spirit of the ancient city. Besides which, a more leisurely trip gives you a chance of stopping halfway between Madrid and Toledo at the villages of Illescas, to see the five remarkable El Grecos in the church of the convent of San Francisco de la Caridad. If you are able to stay overnight, you will also find that, when the tide of visitors subsides (and the streets of Toledo can be swamped during the height of the season) the city regains its ancient character.

The best time to visit Toledo is in the spring or fall, because in summer it is scorched by the sun and in winter it is swept by icy winds. The most important festivals take place during Easter week and Corpus Christi (Thursday after Trinity Sunday), when beautiful damasks and tapestries drape the balconies and windows of the town while a stately procession of priceless works of religious art, taken from the churches, wends its way through the city streets. Here the pasos, those exquisitely carved and brilliantly colored religious statues, so characteristic of Spain, are seen in an appropriate setting.

Architecture and History

The two great influences that characterize the Spanish scene, Christian and Moorish, are expressed in the architecture and art of Toledo. It is especially rich in buildings of the late 15th and 16th centuries. While Christian and Moorish styles overlap in many cases, others emerge as fairly pure examples of their types. There is nothing of the Moor in the cathedral and it is difficult to trace any Christian influence in the mosque, now called El Cristo de la Luz, which, together with the Convento de la Fé and the Mezquita de la Tornerías, are the oldest Córdoba-type edifices in Toledo.

The Sinagoga del Tránsito reveals Christian, Moorish and of course, Jewish influences. The interiors of the buildings are full of peerless works of art. The tombs, so wonderfully preserved, cannot be matched in their conception and exquisite detail. Particularly notable is the fine ironwork. The old iron founders were artists, but did not allow their imaginations to run riot. The results show harmony and boldness, but also great restraint.

As the Roman Toletum, Toledo was already a municipality in the year 192. In 418, it was occupied by the Visigoths, who transferred their court here in 567. Church councils were held and it became the center of religious and political struggles. For 373 years (712–1085), the city was under Moslem rule, and the inhabitants adopted the speech and habits of their conquerors, although keeping their Christian religion, thus becoming Mozárabes. In 1085, Alfonso VI reconquered the city.

Under Alfonso X, the famous School of Translations was created, which made Toledo one of the leading centers of medieval learning. The Moors, Mozárabes, Christians and Jews combined to make it the richest commercial and industrial city of those times. During the first years of the 16th century, Toledo was the head of the Castilian Comuneros movement against Charles V, and the city was defended nobly by Juan de Padilla and his wife, Maria de Pacheco, who continued to fight after his death. Although Toledo remained the capital of the monarchy, the kings spent much time away from the city and, in 1561, Philip II established the court at Madrid. Toledo has always kept the title *Ciudad Imperial y Coronada* (Imperial and Crowned City).

The church became all-powerful in Toledo and many of the most important events in Spanish history of the 16th century are connected with the cardinals of Toledo, who are the primates of Spain.

Austerity and Comfort

The exceptional situation of Toledo adds to its beauty considerably. The surrounding landscape offers a direct contrast to the austerity of the city. The earth, of a reddish shade, is rolling and steep in some places; and the country homes are surrounded by broad cultivated fields and fruit orchards.

The first impression of the city itself is one of austerity, silence, and absence of human life, for it remains as the Moors built it—houses rising straight up (many without windows on the street), barred gates presenting an appearance of prisons. It is only after investigation that you find agreeable lived-in patios behind those formidable walled homes and realize the barriers are a necessary protection from the elements.

The whole city is a tortuous network of cobbled alleys, so steep and narrow in places that only a patient donkey can get around them, or a man on foot. Small wonder that Toledo has been declared a national monument.

The Cathedral and Other Churches

The magnificence of the cathedral cannot be expressed in words. Originally the site of a Christian church, then a mosque, the first stone was laid by San Fernando in 1227 and it was completed in 1493. It is pure 13th-century Gothic with the usual Spanish variations. Gloom, vastness and energy are its predominant characteristics, but it is full of medieval romance.

The exterior is dominated by a tower 91 meters (300 feet) high and the flying buttresses, finials, great rose windows, and huge doors add to the impression of its immense size. Of the eight doors, those called *Reloj* (clock), 13th century, and *Los Leones* (lions), end of 15th century, are Gothic, *Presentación* is Renaissance and *Llana* (plain) is neo-classic. The interior has five naves supported by 84 columns. The main chapel is florid Gothic with a massive wood retable, gilded and painted in richest style. Its entrance grill is gorgeous with reliefs, coats of arms, and figures. Below is the Chapel of Santo Sepulcro, with three vaults and many stone statues. The plateresque choir is completely decorated both inside and out; the stalls are among the finest in Spain— twenty-five of them were carved by Berruguete.

Among the cathedral's many chapels, note the Mozarabic, which contains a remarkable painting by John of Burgundy. Mass is celebrated here every day according to the Mozarabic ritual. The Capilla de San Ildefonso has an 18th-century retable by Juan de Mena, and the

TOLEDO
(NOT TO SCALE)

1 Sta Cruz Museum
2 Cathedral
3 Post Office
4 Cristo de la Luz
5 San Roman
6 Santo Tomé
7 Tránsito Synagogue
8 El Greco Museum
9 Sta María La Blanca
10 San Juan de los Reyes
11 Cambrón Gate
12 Tavera Hospital (Museum)

◯ Church or Convent

〰 Scenery

Capilla de Santiago has the 15th-century sepulchers of Don Alvaro de Luna and his wife. One of the unique features of the cathedral is the 18th-century *transparente* by Narcisco Tomé. He opened up the ceiling of a cupola with a rose window and arranged it so that it seems transparent, allowing the light to stream down on the religious group below.

Notable works of art in the cathedral include El Greco's *Christ Stripped of his Garments.* In the Capilla de Tesoro (treasury), which is full of relics of untold value, is the famous *Custodia,* by Enrique de Arfe, which is carried in the processions on Corpus Christi. It is a supreme example of the goldsmith's art, 3 meters (10 feet) high and weighing 170 kilograms (375 pounds). The monstrance it encloses is made of the first gold ever brought from America by Columbus.

The only other important Gothic church in Toledo is San Juan de los Reyes, built by Ferdinand and Isabella in 1477, and originally destined to receive their sepulchers. Hanging on the façade are iron chains brought here by the Christians freed from Moorish dungeons by the Catholic Monarchs during their conquests. The church façade was completed in the 16th century by the famous Covarrubias. If you don't respond to all this, make your visit worthwhile by seeing the cloister, a flamboyant masterpiece of rare elegance.

The church of Santa María la Blanca was formerly a synagogue, built in the 12th or 13th century. Reconstructed in the 14th, it became a Christian church in the 15th, but the interior still gives the appearance of a mosque, with its hall divided into five naves by white columns and Moorish arches. The capitals and pediments are decorated with texts from the Koran. St Vincent Ferrer preached here. Perhaps the most famous church in Toledo, formerly a synagogue, is that of El Tránsito. It was built in 1360–6 with the money of Samuel Levi, treasurer of Pedro the Cruel, and contains magnificent mudéjar plaster decorations of the 14th century.

The chapel of Santo Tomé was built in the 14th century and totally reconstructed in the 18th. The beautiful tower still keeps most of its character, however. Its most precious possession is one of El Greco's famous apocalyptic paintings, *The Burial of the Count of Orgaz,* depicting an event which took place in this church.

El Greco's House and Toledo's Museums

The Casa del Greco is a museum restored in 16th-century style by the late Marqués de la Vega-Inclán and stands on the site of a former palace, part of which was once inhabited by the artist. The house has an attractive garden-patio, some rooms furnished with authentic pieces from the time when Domenico Theotocopulos (El Greco) lived in Toledo, and a collection of some of the artist's later works.

Several museums have been opened in Toledo. Among them are the Visigothic and Church Museum, located in the church of San Román, containing Visigothic remains, the famous "Concilliorum Collectio" book, votive crowns and so on, the Sephardic Museum in the Tránsito Synagogue, and the Contemporary Arts Museum in a delightful old house in Calle Bulas 13.

The historic Palacio de Lerma, or Hospital de Tavera, and the Hospital de Santa Cruz have also been converted into museums and thrown open to the public. The former, a 15th-century feudal mansion, was once the home of the Lerma family; it contains some wonderful works of art. Santa Cruz was designed by the same architect as the Hostal de los Reyes Católicos at Santiago de Compostela and is now the Municipal Museum of Toledo.

Sightseeing Walks

Toledo is as much a museum of the Spanish spirit out-of-doors, as it is behind the often forbidding walls that rise on every side. One of the best ways to encompass this unique city is to wander its streets, dipping into the treasuries of art and religion at will. Here is a walk around the old city that is easily divided into segments and which should help to reveal some of the secrets of Toledo. The walk starts outside the old city walls on the road from Madrid. Looking south, toward the city that is, the remains of the Roman amphitheater are away to the right and, on the road itself, you'll see the vast Hospital de San Juan Bautista, founded by Cardinal Tavera in 1541. The Cardinal's tomb, the work of Berruguete, is inside as are a reconstructed 16th-century pharmacy and a magnificent collection of paintings which includes works by Titian, El Greco, Tintoretto and Ribera, among them the latter's famous *Bearded Woman*. The building itself was completed by El Greco's son.

Beyond the Hospital is the 9th-century Moorish city gate, the Puerta Vieja de Bisagra and beyond that is the Renaissance Puerta Neuva de Bisagra, dating from 1550. Just past the gate and a little to the right is the brick 13th-century church of Santiago del Arrabal. Its tower, however, is a little older and is Moorish. Beyond the church is the Puerta del Sol. Though rebuilt by the Crusaders in the 14th century, its original mudéjar gate house dates from the 12th century. Just to one side of the Puerta del Sol is the little Ermita del Cristo de la Luz. It was built by the Arabs as a mosque in the 10th century and the date 980 can still be seen on the facade. It was converted into a church in the 12th century.

The main road from the Puerta del Sol bears right and leads to the Plaza de Zocodover, a pretty little triangular square with cafés and arcades that is the center of city life. It was damaged in the Civil War but subsequently restored and its original character carefully preserved. It is a most delightful spot in which to stop and rest before continuing the next stage of the walk.

At the southeastern corner of the square, the Cuesta de Alcazar leads, as its name suggests, to the fort of the Alcazar, a massive square building that stands resolutely on the highest point in the town. The first fort was built on this site in 1085 and was altered and enlarged almost continuously by the royal family until Charles V entirely rebuilt it in the 16th century. It was severely damaged in the Civil War when it was besieged by the Republicans for over two months. Extensive restoration has returned it to its former condition.

Retracing your steps back to the Plaza de Zocodover, you'll find the Arco de Sangre about half way along on the right (eastern) hand side, a Moorish gate much damaged in the Civil War and subsequently much restored. Beyond it is the Hospital de Santa Cruz, a delightful Renaissance building. It was built between 1505 and 1544 by a succession of architects for Cardinal Mendoza and stands on the site of a much older palace; the splendid Visigothic capitals in the cloister are from the original building. The interior, which is in the shape of a huge cross, is now a museum. Most exhibits date from the time of the Charles V.

Below the Hospital and to the northeast is the Puente de Alcántara, which spans the rocky banks of the Tagus. There has been a bridge on this site since Roman days, though the original Roman structure was destroyed by the Moors in the 9th century. The present bridge replaced that built by the Moors and dates from 1259, though it was substantially rebuilt in the late 15th century. The square tower at its west end contains a statue of San Ildefonso by Berruguete. At the far end of the bridge is the rather stern Castilo de San Servando. This was fortified especially for the defense of the bridge in the 11th century.

Back in the Zocodover, take the Calle del Comercio down to the most splendid and conspicuous of all Toledo's treasures, the glowering golden mass of the Cathedral (already described). Opposite the great church is the 18th-century Archbishop's Palace. On the southern side of the square is the Ayuntamiento or City Hall, the lower part of which is occupied by the Biblioteca Provincial. Around the opposite, that is the eastern, side of the cathedral is the Plaza Mayor. Sadly, it does not really live up to its name, but just to the north of it in the Calle de las Tornerias are the remains of a mosque on Visigothic foundations.

Return to the Plaza de Zocodover and refresh and prepare yourself for the last lap, for which you will need a good street map. Head down Calle Comercio again, taking the second street on your right, Toledo de Ohio, which leads into Calle de la Plata: follow this to the Plaza San Vicente. Diagonally opposite you, along Cardenal Lorenzana you pass on your right the former 18th-century University. Continue across Plaza Tendillas and along Esteban Illán till you arrive at the Plaza Padilla. Below you to the north west lies the Convent of Santo Domingo El Antiguo, dating from 1576 and the burial place of El Greco. To the south of the square, down the Calle San Roman, are a number of little churches, the most important of which is San Roman, now the home of the Visigoth Museum. Its tower was built in 1166 but the body of the building dates from about 1230. Its particular combination of Moorish and Christian elements makes it one of the prettiest and most interesting mudéjar buildings in Spain.

At the eastern end of the Calle San Roman is an attractive and shady little square, the Plaza Padre Meriana. Leading out of the square is the Calle de Alfonso XII which bends and snakes its way down to the Calle de Santo Tomé, one of the city's main thoroughfares and packed with tempting souvenir shops. Beside the Hostería Aurelio bar, turn down the narrow Travesía de Santo Tomé where, in the Plaza del Conde de Fuensalido, you will find the Chapel of Santo Tomé, home of El Greco's awesome and magnificent painting, *The Burial of Count Orgaz.* To your left as you leave the chapel is the 15th-century Palace of the Counts of Fuensalida, distinguished as much for being the place where Isabel of Portugal, wife of Charles V, died as for its attractive architecture.

Leaving the square via Calle Juan de Diós and yet more souvenir shops, and turning left, you come to El Greco's House, a much restored museum containing the artist's "supposed" studio, a collection of his works or copies of his originals and several rooms furnished with 16th-century furniture. Below El Greco's House on the right, is the Sinagoga del Tránsito, rather austere but very beautiful, home of the Sephardic Museum. Then turn right along Reyes Católicos (or Sta. María la Blanca as some maps call it) to the Synagogue of Santa María la Blanca, and further on at the end of this street to the final stop on this tour around Toledo, the splendid Gothic church of San Juan de los Reyes.

One final "must" to complete your appreciation of this lovely city, is the *panorámica.* Drive or hire a cab to take you along the Carretera de Circunvalación on the opposite side of the Tagus, crossing over the Puente San Martín and returning via the Puente de Alcántara. The view of the city standing like an impregnable island fortress amidst the waters of the Tagus is one of the most spectacular in Spain and one immortalized by El Greco in his *Storm Over Toledo* now in the Metropolitan Museum, New York.

Note. As we said, visitors to Toledo should be warned that it can become almost unbearably crowded during the day. For this reason we recommend you stay overnight, if possible at the excellent parador, not only to avoid the middle of the day crowds but also to see the floodlighting which turns the city into a place of magic.

The Knight of the Doleful Countenance

South on N401, across the National Park of Las Tablas de Daimiel, between the valleys of the Guadiana and the Jabalon, we come to Ciudad Real, a town that, sadly, has lost its former splendor. Originally a royal village founded by Alfonso X in 1225, it was elevated to the status of a city in 1420. With the expulsion of the Moors, it declined rapidly. There are two churches of interest; the Byzantine-inspired San Pedro, which dates from the 14th century, and the 16th-century Gothic cathedral of Santa Maria de Prado.

Southeast from Ciudad Real on C415 is the little town of Almagro, one time base of the Knights of Calatrava. Its castle stands further south. The wooden houses on the vast Plaza Mayor provide an unusual frame for the elegant 16th-century town hall while the Corral de Comedias is Spain's only surviving 17th-century theater courtyard. It is highly reminiscent of its Elizabethan counterparts. A short way out of town is the Dominican Monastery of the Assumption, remarkable for its great church and the superb double galleries of Renaissance cloister and plateresque stairway, doors and windows.

Further east on C415, beyond Valdepeñas, Villanueva de los Infantes's lovely classical Plaza Mayor and fine houses seem unjustly neglected by tourists.

Northeast of Ciudad Real, N420 crosses N-IV at Puerto Lápice where a signpost indicates the border of La Mancha. For *aficionados* of Cervantes, the road taken by Don Quixote on his three expeditions has been carefully reconstructed. Few will care to follow it to its conclusion on the eastern seaboard, but with a few deviations from the main road in La Mancha, some of his most amusing adventures may be re-lived. His home, and starting point, was in Argamasilla de Alba, a village of little importance, but the house of his lady love, Dulcinea, in El Toboso, northeast of Alcazár de San Juan, has produced enough romantic interest to have been declared a national monument. This modest mansion of the 16th century, Casa de la Torrecilla, was the home of Ana Martinez Zarco, whom the Spaniards have cast for the part of Dulcinea. There is an interesting Don Quixote library in the town hall.

Cuenca

N420 continues northeast from Alcázar de San Juan via Mota del Cuervo to Belmonte, a small fortified settlement that still has its original walls and city gates. Over it broods the imposing mass of its 15th-century castle, whose interior is partly in mudéjar style. N420 crosses an arid, grayish plateau as far as Olivares, where it thrusts into the lush green valley of the Júcar. When the road rejoins the river, it is between twisting and steep rock walls jutting up from the valley. Above, the wooden balconies of Cuenca's Casas Colgadas (Hanging Houses) are suspended over the abyss that has been carved by the River Júcar's devious meanderings.

The ancient city of Cuenca was recaptured from the Moors by Alfonso VIII in 1177. The impressive Gothic cathedral contains magnificent *rejas* (grilles) and, in the Treasury, there are two El Grecos and a unique 14th-century Byzantine diptych. The Calle de Obispo Valero leads to the new town while another route ascends the ravine of the Júcar to the picturesque small squares of Merced and Descalzos, and back through a rocky gateway to the Plaza Mayor.

The Museum of Abstract Spanish Art, the first of its kind in the nation, is housed in several of the 15th-century Casas Colgadas. Founded by the Filipino artist Fernando Zobel, it consists of numerous representative works by Spanish artists.

Thirty six kilometers (22 miles) north, mostly along the steep banks of the Júcar, is the Ciudad Encantada, the Enchanted City, where centuries of atmospheric action on the limestone has produced the fantastic illusion of houses, streets, flowers, vegetation, and even human beings, mysteriously frozen into stone. Less than three kilometers on at Rincon de Una is a fine amphitheater of natural rock.

Guadalajara

Guadalajara is a Moorish word meaning "valley of stones". The province is separated from Soria by the Guadarrama mountains, and the Tagus river flows through it. A chain of large dams and reservoirs has been constructed, a tremendous feat of engineering which may be viewed with the impressive scenery around, by taking the *Ruta de los Pantanos* (Reservoirs Route) excursion.

The city of Guadalajara is fifty six kilometers (35 miles) northeast of Madrid on the N-II (currently being widened into a motorway) which leads to Zaragoza. Originally settled by the Moors, it was subsequently conquered by a companion of El Cid. Thereafter, it was long dominated by the powerful Mendoza family who, in the 15th century, built the Gothic-mudéjar Infantado Palace where Philip II married his third wife, Elisabeth de Valois. Today the palace contains a Museum of Fine Arts, reached through the attractive Gothic arches of the Lion's Court.

Further evidence of the once-dominant Mendoza family can be found in the 14th-century church of Santa María de la Fuente where one of the early members of the family is buried. Another church, however, 16th-century San Ginés, contains the bulk of the Mendoza tombs. Two other churches in the town are of interest, San Nicolás, which has an especially elaborate and splendid altar, and Santiago, whose Gothic-mudéjar magnificence has lately been restored to its former splendor.

Twenty one kilometers (13 miles) off the N-II and 128 kilometers from Madrid (80 miles) is Sigüenza. Its churches, monasteries, palaces and mansions have contrived to give the town an atmosphere of rare harmony, from its alcázar (now a parador) on the hill all the way down to the banks of the Henares river.

Sigüenza's cathedral is an impressive building, more fortress than church. It was begun in 1150, though not completed until the following century. Among its works of art is the beautifully sculptured tomb of Martín Vázquez de Arce known as El Doncel, who was slain at Granada in 1486. It is an exceptionally lovely tribute from Isabella the Catholic to her page and shows him quietly reading a book.

PRACTICAL INFORMATION FOR CASTILE

WHAT TO SEE. The number one excursion in the immediate neighborhood of Madrid is to the great monastery of El Escorial and the nearby war memorial in the Valley of the Fallen. Aranjuez comes next, but if your time is limited this is possibly a place you might want to pass up in favor of more rewarding sorties further afield. However, the one place that no one will want to miss is Toledo. After that, your own interests will dictate your itinerary.

Segovia is probably the second most interesting city in the region, Ávila the third. Catholics may put Ávila ahead of Segovia, as the city of Santa Teresa, while those interested in Roman remains will stick to Segovia as second place to be visited after Toledo, for its great aqueduct.

If you are interested in architecture, the cathedral of Burgos is the finest in the two Castiles, with that of Toledo a close second. The cathedrals of Segovia and Sigüenza follow; those of Palencia and Ávila are also worth a visit. Ávila, in addition, possesses unbroken 11th-century walls. Valladolid is an interesting city, but one you can easily skip if pressed for time.

If you are a Cervantes enthusiast, you may want to visit La Mancha, perhaps to try to follow the route Don Quixote and Sancho Panza took. Though La Mancha itself is hardly changed since the time of Cervantes, there is little to see as far as the route of Don Quixote goes. About all that is left are the windmills at La Mota del Cuervo and Cryptana and a small prison in Argamasilla de Alba, the putative birth-place of Quixote. *La Venta de Don Quijote* in Puerto Lapice is a picturesque inn, which is reputed to have been the spot where Don Quixote was dubbed knight. In El Toboso, of Dulcinea fame, there is a museum located in what is thought to be Dulcinea's house, and a library devoted largely to Don Quixote in the town hall.

No one should miss an excursion to Cuenca to see the famed hanging houses; it is a genuinely charming place. An oddity is the Enchanted City near Cuenca; an illusion produced by the fantastic shapes into which time and weather have carved the soft limestone hills.

HOTELS AND RESTAURANTS

AGUILAR DE CAMPOO (Palencia). *Valentín* (M), Avda. del Generalísimo 21, tel. (988) 12 21 25. 47 rooms; with bar and garden.

ALARCON (Cuenca). *Parador Marqués de Villena* (E), Avda. Amigos Castillo, tel. (966) 33 13 50. Small historic building, only 11 rooms; with garden and garage. *Claridge* (M), on Madrid-Valencia road, tel. (966) 33 11 50. 36 rooms, pool, tennis and garden.

ALCALA DE HENARES (Madrid). *El Bedel* (M), San Diego 6, tel. (91) 889 3700. 51 rooms, bar.

Restaurant. *Hostería del Estudiante* (M), Colegios 3, tel. 888 0330. Located in 16th-century building, atmospheric décor.

ALFARO (La Rioja). *Palacios* (M), on the Zaragoza road, tel. (941) 18 01 00. 86 rooms, pool.

ALMAGRO (Ciudad Real). *Parador de Almagro* (E), Ronda de San Francisco, tel. (926) 86 01 00. 55 rooms. Located in the 16th-century convent of Santa Catalina; pool and gardens.

ALMURADIEL (Ciudad Real). *Los Podencos* (M), tel. (926) 33 90 00. Pleasant comfortable roadside inn, on the main N-IV before Despeñaperros pass.

ARANDA DE DUERO (Burgos). *Los Bronces* (M), tel. (947) 50 08 50. A modern hotel with 29 rooms and garden. *Montehermoso* (M-I), tel. (947) 50 15 50. 54 rooms and garden. Both are on the main Madrid-Burgos road, out of town. *Tres Condẹs* (M-I), tel. (947) 50 24 00. This is the newest, 35 rooms, bar.

Restaurants. *Casa Florencio* (M), Arias de Miranda 14, tel. 50 02 30. Good roast lamb. *Mesón de la Villa* (M), Plaza Mayor 1, tel. 50 10 25. One of the best places for Castilian roasts, typical decor in a basement in main square. Closed Mon.

ARANJUEZ (Madrid). *Las Mercedes* (M), on the main highway, tel. (91) 891 0440. 37 rooms, pool and garden. *Infantas* (I), Infantas 4, tel. (91) 891 1341. A simple hostel, but clean, modern and good.

Restaurants. *La Mina* (E-M), Príncipe 21, tel. 891 1146. Going for over 50 years, its specialties include asparagus and strawberries (both typical of Aranjuez) and *Faisán al Real Sitio* (pheasant) for which it is famous. *La Alegría de la Huerta* (M), just on the Madrid side of the river. Garden dining and good value. *Casa Pablo* (M), Almibar 20, tel. 891 1451. Excellent Castilian food in mesón setting. *La Rana Verde* (M), overlooking the Tagus.

ARNEDILLO (La Rioja). *Balneario* (E), Balneario, tel. (941) 39 40 00. 181 rooms, pool, tennis and gardens.

ARNEDO (La Rioja). *Victoria* (M), General Franco 103, tel. (941) 38 01 00. 48 rooms. Pool, garden and tennis.

AVILA. *Palacio de Valderrabanos* (E), Plaza de la Catedral 9, tel. (918) 21 10 23. In 15th-century mansion opposite the cathedral. Luxuriously appointed and highly recommended. *Parador Raimundo de Borgoña* (E), Marqués de Canales y Chozas 16, tel. (918) 21 13 40. Beautifully located in a reconstructed 15th-century palace which forms part of Avila's famous city walls. *Cuatro Postes*

(M), Ctra Salamanca 23, tel. (918) 21 29 44. Modern, just outside town, wonderful view of the walled city. *Don Carmelo* (M), Paseo Don Carmelo 30, tel. (918) 22 80 50. Opposite San Antonio park. *Reina Isabel* (I), José Antonio 17, tel. (918) 22 02 00. 44 rooms. *Rey Niño* (I), Plaza de José Tome 1, tel. (918) 21 14 04. Good value right in the heart of town.

Restaurants. The *Parador* (E), Castilian cuisine, try their *cocidos* or the *yemas de Santa Teresa. Cuatro Postes* (M), wide choice and good service. *Mesón El Sol* (M), Avda 18 de Julio 25, tel. 22 12 66. Recommended for good meat dishes. *El Torreón* (M), Tostado 1, tel. 21 31 71. Near cathedral, with downstairs "cave" restaurant, clean and well run. *Piquio* (I), Estrada 4, tel. 21 31 14. Popular for over 30 years; veal, lamb and suckling pig specialties. *El Rastro* (I), Plaza del Rastro 4, tel. 21 12 19. Typical Castilian inn.

BURGOS. *Landa Palace* (L), tel. (947) 20 63 43. Located in an historic building out of town on road to Irun, with 33 rooms, pool and gardens. Praised by readers for its charm and magnificent marble bathrooms. *Almirante Bonifaz* (E), Vitoria 22, tel. (947) 20 69 43. Slightly asceptic. *Condestable* (E), Vitoria 8, tel. (947) 20 06 44. Comfortable and central. *Corona de Castilla* (M), Madrid 15, tel. (947) 23 82 12. Modern, but in dull part of town. *España* (M), Paseo del Espolón 32, tel. (947) 20 63 40. Central and fairly recent; on a pleasant promenade with sidewalk cafés. Recommended is *Fernán Gonzáles* (M), Calera 17, tel. (947) 20 94 41. Overlooking river and city. *Norte y Londres* (I), Plaza Alonso Martínez 10, tel. (947) 20 05 45. Central and friendly, old world charm.

Restaurants. The restaurant at the *Landa Palace* (E) is probably the best in town. *Ariaga* (M), Laín Calvo 4, tel. 20 20 21. Founded over 65 years ago; delightful with linen tablecloths, ancient, respectful waiters and especially good fish dishes. *Casa Ojeda* (M), Vitoria 3, tel. 20 90 52. In magnificent old Castilian house, in part tastelessly modernized; good for traditional Castilian cooking. *Gaona* (M), Paloma 41, tel. 20 61 91. Colorful with typical mesón ambience; good for shellfish and game. *Pinedo* (M), Paseo del Espolón 1, opposite Hotel España, delightful turn-of-century cafe with restaurant upstairs. *Rincón de España* (M), Nuño Rasura 11. Not far from cathedral; large outdoor summer terrace and indoors a more stylish, sophisticated restaurant. Good choice of dishes. *Mesón de la Cueva* and *Mesón del Cid* are both (M-I) and opposite cathedral entrance. Atmospheric and fun if a little touristy. *Villaluenga* (I), Laín Calvo 20, is superb value for a quick cheap meal.

CALAHORRA (La Rioja). *Parador Marco Fabio Quintiliano* (E), Era Alta, tel. (941) 13 03 58. 67 rooms, beautiful décor and good facilities.

CERVERA DE PISUERGA (Palencia). *Parador de Fuentes Carrionas* (E), tel. (988) 87 00 75. A new parador with 80 rooms, beautifully situated in mountain setting overlooking a reservoir. Good view of Picos de Europa from balcony.

CHINCHON (Madrid). *Parador Nacional* (E), Avda Generalísimo 1, tel. (91) 845 8378. In a delightful picturesque town. 38 rooms in an historic house; pool.

CIUDAD REAL. *Castillos* (M), Avda. del Rey Santo 8, tel. (926) 21 36 40. 131 rooms, parking. *El Molino* (E), tel. (926) 22 30 50. 18 rooms, on the road to Carrión (N420).

COVARRUBIAS (Burgos). *Arlanza* (M), Plaza Mayor 11, tel. (947) 40 30 25. 38 rooms in historic building; a semi-parador.

CUENCA. *Torremangana* (E), San Ignacio de Loyola 9, tel. (966) 22 33 51. Modern hotel in new part of town, 111 rooms. *Cueva del Fraile* (M), tel. (966) 21 15 71. 40 rooms, located in a restored 16th-century building, 7 km out of town on road to Buenache. *Xucar* (M-I), Cervantes 17, tel. (966) 22 45 11. 28 rooms. *Avenida* (I), Avda José Antonio 39, tel. (966) 21 43 43. 33 rooms, central.
Restaurants. *Mesón de las Casas Colgadas* (E-M), tel. 21 18 22. The best restaurant in town; located in the hanging houses. *Figón de Pedro* (M), Cervantes 13, tel. 22 68 21. Typical décor, regional dishes and good daily specials. A real Cuenca tradition. *Los Claveles* (I), 18 de Julio 32, tel. 21 38 24. Going for over 30 years; décor and dishes are typical of La Mancha. Closed Thurs.

EL ESCORIAL (Madrid). *Victoria Palace* (E-M), Juan de Toledo 4, tel. (91) 890 1511. 89 rooms, pool, gardens. Near the monastery, pleasant, friendly, recommended. *Miranda Suizo* (M-I), Floridablanca 20, tel. (91) 896 0000. A charming, stylish old hotel on main street. *Cristina* (I), Juan de Toledo 6, tel. (91) 890 1961. Charming house next to Victoria Palace; 16 rooms. *Jardín* (I), Leandro Rubio 2, tel. (91) 896 1007. Simple hostel with 22 rooms and pleasant garden.
Restaurants. *Charolés* (E), Floridablanca 24, tel. 896 0491. One of the most elegant, on a pleasant terrace overlooking Floridablanca. Serves a good selection of meat dishes. *Mesón La Cueva* (E), San Antón 4, tel. 890 1571. An atmospheric mesón founded in 1768 with several small rustic dining rooms. El Escorial's best known restaurant. *Doblón de Oro* (E-M), Plaza de la Constitución 5, tel. 896 0741. Outdoor dining in alleyway and in the square. *Fonda Genara* (E-M), Plaza San Lorenzo, tel. 896 0291. Elegant restaurant with theatrical décor. Located in an 18th-century theater which won one of Premio Europa Nostra's five annual prizes for skillful restoration.
Alaska (M), Plaza San Lorenzo, tel. 896 0241. Dining on an attractive outdoor terrace, Castilian décor. *Mesón Serrano* (M), Floridablanca 4, tel. 890 1704. Good Spanish dishes either indoors or in the garden in the back. *Castilla* (M), Plaza de la Constitución 2 (tel. 896 1006). Tables outside in the square in summer.
Cafetería del Arte (I), Floridablanca 14, tel. 890 1721. A good range of dishes at all prices. Also snacks and sandwiches. *El Caserío* (I), Reina Victoria 2. Some tables on the sidewalk, local décor. *Miranda Suizo* (I), Floridablanca 20. This

hotel has a good dining room serving some very reasonably priced *platos combinados.*

LA GRANJA DE SAN ILDEFONSO (Segovia). *Roma* (M), Guardias 2, tel. (911) 47 07 52. A 16-room hostel.
Restaurants. *Canónigas* (E), Edificio Canónigas, tel. 47 11 60. Recommended. *La Hilaria* (M), 2.5 km out in Valsaín, tel. 47 02 92. *Maribén* (M), Cuartel Nuevo 2, tel. 47 07 69. Pleasant *mesón. Madrid* (I), simple tavern restaurant with outdoor setting.

GUADALAJARA. *Pax* (M), on main Madrid-Barcelona highway, tel. (911) 21 18 00. 61 rooms, pool, tennis and gardens. *España* (I), Teniente Figueroa 3, tel. (911) 21 13 03. 33 rooms, old but renovated.
Restaurants. *La Murciana* (M), Miguel Fluiters 21, tel. 21 30 11. Typical décor. *El Ventorrero* (M), López de Haro 4, tel. 21 25 63. Rustic décor.

GUADARRAMA (Madrid). *Manila* (M-I), tel. (91) 854 0395. Deluxe hostel with 14 rooms. *Miravelle* (M-I), on main highway, tel. (91) 850 0300. 13-room hostel with parking and garden.

HONRUBIA DE LA CUESTA (Segovia). *Las Campanas del Milario* (I), on the highway, tel. (911) 54 30 00. A 7-room motel; pleasant for coffee, meals or overnighting.

LA LASTRILLA (Segovia). *Puerta de Segovia* (M), on highway, tel. (911) 41 20 60. 4 km from Segovia, 100 rooms. Pool, garden and tennis.

LOGROÑO (La Rioja). *Los Bracos* (E), Bretón de los Herreros 29, tel. (941) 22 66 08. A new hotel with 72 rooms. *Carlton Rioja* (E), Gran Vía 5, tel. (941) 24 21 00. The best hotel, large and modern. *Gran Hotel* (M), General Vara de Rey 5, tel. (941) 21 21 00. A pleasant old-timer with garden and garage. *Murrieta* (M), Marqués de Murrieta 1, tel. (941) 22 41 50. 113 rooms, modern. *El Cortijo* (M-I), Crta. del Cortijo, tel. (941) 22 50 50. A modern hotel with pool, tennis, garden.
Restaurants. *Mesón de la Merced* (E), Marques de San Nicolas 136, tel. 22 10 24. Excellent restaurant located in an old bodega. *Asados González* (M), Carnicerías 3, tel. 21 12 96. Known also as *La Chata,* this serves the best roast goat in Spain. *Cachetero* (M-I), Laurel 3, tel. 21 21 24. A meal in this Logroño legend is a must; much frequented by artists, bullfighters and the famous. *La Vinoteca* (I), San Juan XIII 14, tel. 22 42 64. Half shop, half restaurant; hundreds of different cheeses and smoked meats, Rioja wine.

MANZANARES (Ciudad Real). *Albergue Nacional* (E-M), on N-IV highway, tel. (926) 61 04 00. 50 rooms, garden, pool. *El Cruce* (M), on the N-IV, tel. (926) 61 19 00. 37 rooms, pool and garden. *Manzanares* (I), tel. (926) 61 08 04. 23 rooms, garden.

MAQUEDA (Toledo). *El Cazador* (M), on highway, 30 rooms, pool and garden.

MEDINA DE POMAR (Burgos). *Las Merindades* (I), Plaza Somovilla, tel. (947) 11 08 22. 23 rooms, 3-star hotel with very low rates.

MEDINA DE RIOSECO (Valladolid). *Los Almirantes* (M), San Francisco 2, tel. (983) 70 01 25. 30 rooms, pool, good views.

MEDINA DEL CAMPO (Valladolid). *La Mota* (M-I), Fernando el Católico 4, tel. (983) 80 04 50. 40 rooms. *Reina Isabel* (I), Isabel la Católica 3, tel. (983) 80 02 50. 14 rooms. *San Roque* (I), on N-VI, tel. (983) 80 06 12. 30 rooms.

MIRAFLORES DE LA SIERRA (Madrid). *Palmy* (M), Eusebio Guadalix 17, tel. (91) 624 3712. 23 rooms. *Refugio* (M), Fuente del Gazapo, tel. (91) 624 42 11. 48 rooms, pool, garden.

MIRANDA DE EBRO (Burgos). *Don Cesar* (M), on highway, tel. (947) 31 18 43. 124 rooms, garden and bar. Reader complains it is shabby.

MONZON DE CAMPOS (Palencia). *Castillo de Monzón* (M), tel. (988) 80 80 75. 10 rooms. *El Caballero* (I), tel. (988) 80 80 77. 39 rooms.

MOTA DEL CUERVO (Cuenca). *Mesón de Don Quijote* (M), Francisco Costi 2, tel. (966) 18 02 00. Pool, gardens, restaurant, excellent value. Good base for exploring Quixote country.

MOTILLA DEL PALANCAR (Cuenca). *Hotel del Sol,* (I), on Madrid-Valencia highway, tel. (966) 33 10 25. Excellent rooms at budget prices.

NAVACERRADA (Madrid). Winter sports area. *La Barranca* (E-M), tel. (91) 856 0000. A new hotel with pool, gardens and many facilities. *Arcipreste de Hita* (M), Praderas de San Sebastián, tel. (91) 856 01 25. Pool, gardens, many amenities; good value. *Doña Endrina* (M-I), Avda de Madrid, tel. (91) 856 0200. 40 rooms. *Las Postas* (M-I), tel. (91) 856 0250. 21 rooms. All these are in the village.

At the pass (Puerto de Navacerrada) are *Venta Arias* (M), tel. (91) 852 1100; *Pasadoiro* (M), tel. (91) 852 14 27; *El Corzo* (I), tel. (91) 852 0900.

NAVARREDONDA DE GREDOS (Avila). *Parador de Gredos* (E), 2.5 km outside, tel. (918) 34 00 48. Beautifully located in the Gredos mountains, this was the first of the government-run paradores; Alfonso XIII chose the site in 1926. The parador has since been refurbished and enlarged.

LAS NAVAS DEL MARQUES (Avila). *San Marcos* (I), Plaza Ciudad Ducal, tel. (91) 897 0101. 16 rooms, tennis and garden. A 3-star hotel with very reasonable rates.
Restaurant. *Magalia* (M), Paseo de las Damas, tel. 897 0210.

OROPESA (Toledo). *Parador Virrey Toledo* (E), Plaza del Palacio 1, tel. (925) 43 00 00. A magnificent castle-cum-palace built in 1402 on a site believed to have had a castle since 1716 B.C. Commands a beautiful view over surrounding countryside and mountains of the Sierra de Gredos.

PALENCIA. *Castilla la Vieja* (E-M), Casado del Alisal 26, tel. (988) 74 90 44. 87 rooms, central. *Rey Sancho de Castilla* (M), Avda Ponce de León, tel. (988) 72 53 00. 100 rooms, pool and tennis. *Monclús* (M), Menéndez Pelayo 3, tel. (988) 74 43 00. 40 rooms, central. *Roma* (I), Alonso Fernández de Madrid 8, tel. (988) 74 57 00. 23 rooms.
Restaurants. *Casa Damián* (E), Martínez de Azcoitia 9, tel. 74 46 28. Good typical food. *Lorenzo* (M), Avda. Casado del Alisal 10, tel. 74 35 45.

PANCORVO (Burgos). *El Molino* (M), on main highway, tel. (947) 35 40 50. 48 rooms, pool and gardens.

EL PAULAR (Madrid). *Santa María del Paular* (E), tel. (91) 869 32 00. A refurbished monastery, set in pine forests, high in the mountains.

PUERTO LAPICE (Ciudad Real). *El Aprisco* (I), on highway, tel. (926) 57 61 50. A modern, cozy roadside inn with pool, good for overnighting. *El Puerto* (I), tel. (926) 57 60 00. Also on highway. Another good motoring inn.
Restaurant. *La Venta del Quijote* (M), tel. (926) 57 61 10. Delightful village inn, supposedly where Don Quijote was dubbed knight. Roaring fireplace in winter, dining in courtyard in summer. Try their *olla* or roast lamb and the *queso manchego,* a specialty of the region, and Spain's best cheese.

SANTA MARIA DE HUERTA (Soria). *Albergue Nacional* (E-M), tel. (975) 32 70 11. 40 rooms, garden.

SANTO DOMINGO DE LA CALZADA (La Rioja). *Parador Nacional* (E), Plaza del Santo 3, tel. (941) 34 03 00. An historic building with 27 rooms.

SEGOVIA. *Parador Nacional* (E), tel. (911) 41 50 90. Modern parador in beautiful setting a little way out of town on road to Valladolid. The most expensive. *Los Linajes* (E), Dr. Velasco 9, tel. (911) 41 55 78. Delightful modern hotel built in Castilian style with splendid views. In the heart of old town close to San Esteban church. *Gran Vía* (E-M), Ezequiel González 24, tel. (911) 42 73 61. 57 rooms. *Acueducto* (M), Padre Claret 10, tel. (911) 42 48 00. Ageing, with balconies overlooking the famous aqueduct. *Las Sirenas* (M), Juan Bravo 30, tel. (911) 41 18 97. Right in the center of town; a good luxury hostel overlooking San Martín church.

Restaurants. *Mesón de Cándido* (E), Plaza del Azoguejo 7, tel. 42 59 11. One of the best-known restaurants in Spain, located in a 15th-century building. Reserve a table early to get one at the windows facing the aqueduct. Specialties are paella, roast lamb and above all, suckling pig. *Casa Duque* (E-M), Cervantes 12, tel. 41 17 07. Dating back to 1895, it boasts fine food by any standards.

El Bernardino (M), Cervantes 2, tel. 41 31 75. Traditional Castilian restaurant, serving local specialties. *Garrido* (M), Ruiz de Alda 2, tel. 41 40 74. Recommended by locals. *La Oficina* (M), Cronista Lecea 10, tel. 41 14 88. Another typical spot; downstairs is a friendly tavern, upstairs are two delightful dining rooms brimming with paintings and knick-knacks. *Solaire* (M), Santa Engracia 3, tel. 41 34 19. Pleasant indoor and outdoor dining, good service and food. *La Taurina* (M), Plaza Mayor 1, tel. 41 30 08. Typical Segovian décor; owner is an ex-*torero* who will feed you well.

El Abuelo (I), Alhóndiga 1. Typical cellar like tavern with a wide range of menus to choose from.

SIGÜENZA (Guadalajara). *Parador Nacional* (E), tel. (911) 39 01 00. Located in a building whose origins go back to Visigoth days. It began as a Visigoth castle, became a Moorish fortress, and finally, an episcopal palace. A truly impressive building in an interesting medieval town.

SORIA. *Parador Antonio Machado* (E-M), Parque del Castillo, tel. (975) 21 34 45. This is probably the best in town; 14 rooms, garden. *Alfonso VIII* (M), Alfonso VIII 10, tel. (975) 22 62 11. 55 rooms, central. *Caballero* (M), Eduardo Saavedra 4, tel. (957) 22 01 00. This is Soria's newest hotel, central with bar and good amenities. *Mesón Leonor* (M), Paseo de Mirón, tel. (975) 22 02 50. 32 rooms, many facilities.

TALAVERA DE LA REINA (Toledo). *León* (M), on highway to Extremadura, tel. (925) 80 29 00. 30 rooms. *Talavera* (I), Avda Gregorio Ruiz 1, tel. (925) 80 02 00. 80 rooms, parking and bar.

Restaurant. *El Arcipreste* (M), Bandera de Castilla 14, tel. 80 40 92. Typical decor.

EL TIEMBLO (Avila). *Las Jaras* (M), Embalse de Burguillo. Next to the Burguillo reservoir; open April-Sept. only. *Los Toros de Guisando* (M-I). A pleasant top hostel.

TOLEDO. *Parador Conde de Orgaz* (E), Paseo de los Cigarrales, tel. (925) 22 18 50. A modern parador built in typical Toledo style and beautifully located with a magnificent view of Toledo and the Tagus. The best (and by far most expensive) hotel in town. *Cardenal* (E), Paseo de Recaredo 24, tel. (925) 22 49 00. Attractive historic setting built into the city walls; much praised restaurant, though we have had complaints of ageing facilities and rude reception.

Alfonso VI (M), General Moscardó 2, tel. (952) 22 26 00. Excellent hotel next to Alcázar, with Castilian-style décor. *Carlos V* (M), Escalerilla de la Magdalena 3, tel. (925) 22 21 00. 55 rooms, good accommodations in modern hotel right in center. *Maravilla* (M), Barrio Rey 5–7, tel. (925) 22 30 00. 18 rooms, in heart of town, surrounded by good restaurants. *Almazara* (M-I), Ctra Piedrabuena 47, tel. (925) 22 38 66. Charming setting outside city with splendid views. Old world charm and friendly service. Recommended. Open April-Oct. only. *Imperio* (I), Cadenas 7, tel. (925) 22 76 50. Modern hotel in center with good simple accommodations.

Restaurants. *Aurelio* (E), Plaza del Ayuntamiento 8, tel. 22 77 16. Typical décor; popular restaurant. *Hostal del Cardenal* (E), Paseo de Recaredo, tel. 22 08 62. Managed by Botín of Madrid, this is Toledo's best restaurant. Interesting food and pleasant service. *Venta de Aires* (E), Circo Romano 25, tel. 22 05 45. A little out of town, a deluxe and recommended restaurant, moderately priced for its standard. Its specialty is partridge, which is a specialty of the city in general. Cozy and rustic, indoors in winter, outdoors in large garden in summer.

Casa Aurelio (E-M), Sinagoga 6, tel. 22 20 97. Highly recommended by readers; atmospheric specialties are partridge and quail. *La Tarasca* (E-M), Comercio 8. Elegant, stylish restaurant with a good menu. *Casa Plácido* (M), Santo Tomé 4, tel. 22 26 03. Moderate, clean and pleasant. *Cigarral Monterrey* (M), Ctra. Piedrabuena 42, tel. 22 69 50. A bit out of town, a popular terraced restaurant. *Los Cuatro Tiempos* (M), Sixto Ramón Parro 5, tel. 22 50 21. Pleasant and cozy in heart of town. *La Cubana* (M), opposite Alcántara park, tel. 22 00 88. Over the Alcántara bridge; recommended. *Emperador* (M), Ctra del Valle 1, tel. 22 46 91. Just out of town, with lashings of atmosphere. Recommended.

Hostería Aurelio (M-I), corner of Santo Tomé and Travesía del Conde. Good tapas and reasonably priced meals, just round corner from Chapel of Santo Tomé. *Venta Carranza* (I), Ctra Piedrabuena 39, tel. 22 30 69. Restaurant with terrace, just out of town. Service and standards unreliable, however. *El Patio* (I), Plaza de San Vicente 4 on the corner of Calle de la Plata. Attractive typical décor, dining in tiled patio.

TORDESILLAS (Valladolid). *Parador Nacional* (E), on the N620, tel. (983) 77 00 51. Modern parador with 73 rooms, pleasant location, pool. *El Montico* (E), on the N620, tel. (983) 77 07 51. Good hotel, 34 rooms; with pool, tennis and garden.

VALDEPEÑAS (Ciudad Real). *Meliá El Hidalgo* (E), on the N-IV, tel. (926) 31 16 40. More bungalows, with pool and garden. *Vista Alegre* (I), on N-IV, tel. (926) 32 22 04. 17 rooms. *Cervantes* (M-I), Seis de Junio 46, tel. (926) 32 26 00. A good 2-star hostel, in town.

VALLADOLID. *Conde Ansúrez* (E), María de Molina 9, tel. (983) 35 18 00. A good hotel with 76 rooms; fairly central. *Felipe IV* (E), Gamazo 16, tel. (983) 22 77 35. Modern, 132 rooms, bar, parking, bingo among its many facilities; somewhat impersonal. *Olid Meliá* (E), Plaza de San Miguel 10, tel. (983) 25 42 00. Valladolid's best hotel. Good service, excellent (but expensive) restaurant; in quiet area of town.

Inglaterra (M), María de Molina 2, tel. (983) 22 22 19. Fairly central, nice location, 47 rooms. *Roma* (M), Héroes del Alcázar 8, tel. (983) 22 23 18. 38 rooms, central.

Restaurants. *Mesón la Fragua* (L), Paseo de Zorrilla 10, tel. 33 71 02. Top cuisine and old world charm. *El Cardenal* (E), Plaza de Tenerías 18, tel. 33 80 33. Reputedly best for food, elegant setting and lovely view of river. *La Goya* (E), Puente Colgante 29, tel. 23 12 59. Garden dining, on the other side of Pisuerga river. *Mesón Panero* (E), Marina Escobar 1, tel. 22 14 67; also a restaurant at Recoletos 3, tel. 22 98 33. Good menu and wine list; every year a week is set aside for Valladolid regional specialties. *Mesón La Viña* (E-M), Ferrari 5, tel. 22 07 20. Cozy, dining room upstairs. *Oscar* (E-M), Ferrari 1, tel. 22 90 23. Another well recommended restaurant.

Machaquito (M), Calixto Fernández de la Torre 5, tel. 22 82 57. Simple setting, top food, good value. *Mesón Cervantes* (M), Rastro 6, tel. 22 60 76. Good simple homely fare. *Astur Vasco* (I), Atrio de Santiago 5, tel. 22 82 30. Extremely good value. *El Caballo de Troya* (I). Correos 1, Quaint mesón, good food, pleasant setting.

VILLACASTIN (Segovia). *Albergue Nacional* (E-M), on the N-VI, tel. (911) 10 70 00. Small, 13 rooms, a worthwhile base and very good for food.

SHOPPING. Toledo is the tourist's paradise when it comes to shopping for gifts and mementos to take home. The fame of its embossed leather is second only to the greater renown of its damascened (inlaid) steel.

Centuries ago Toledo steel was esteemed as the best in the world for producing strong, flexible blades. The inlay work of gold on steel, for which the Toledo steelmakers were famous, is still carried on here, and the city's stores literally bulge with examples, of everything from inexpensive earrings to full-size swords and family shields. Also of interest here are beautiful ceramics, pottery, and hand-embroidered linens. Stop off at the ceramic roadside stalls just outside town on the road to Madrid. Marzipan is a specialty of Toledo; it is delicious and makes a good small gift.

USEFUL ADDRESSES. Tourist Offices: **Aranjuez;** Plaza Santiago Rusiñol. **Avila;** Plaza de la Catedral 4. **Burgos;** Plaza Alonso Martínez 7. **Ciudad Real;** Toledo 27. **Cuenca,** Colón 34. **El Escorial;** Floridablanca 10. **Logroño,** Miguel Villanueva 10. **Palencia;** Calle Mayor 149. **Segovia;** Plaza

Mayor 10. **Soria;** Plaza Ramón y Cajal. **Toledo;** Puerta de Bisagra. **Valladolid,** Plaza Zorrilla 3.

CAR HIRE. Avila; *Tapia,* Padre Victoriano 2. **Burgos;** *Hertz,* Vitoria 115; *Ital,* General Vigón. **Cuenca;** *Araque,* Colón 58; *Rodríguez,* Parque de San Julián 17. **Segovia;** *Galvan,* Puente de Muerte y Vida 6; *Sierramar,* Avda. Fernández Ladreda 11. **Soria;** *Talleres Valero,* Termancia 7; *Juan Novillo,* San Benito 5. **Toledo;** *Autos Arevalillo,* Calle de la Plata 4; *La Imperial,* Santa Justa 5. **Valladolid;** *Atesa,* Padre Manjón 5; *Avis,* Felipe II 3; *Hertz,* Panaderos 25; *Ital,* Muro 16.

NAVARRE AND ARAGON

Bulls, Mountains and Miraculous Virgins

East of Castile lie Navarre, a single province, and Aragón, made up of three: Huesca, Zaragoza (Saragossa) and Teruel. In Navarre, there is only one name that will ring a bell for most people, that of Pamplona, which attracts tourists at one time during the year and for one reason—the running of the bulls. Zaragoza is the capital of Aragón, and on the Madrid-Barcelona route, while Teruel is virtually *Terra Incognita* for foreigners, though some of them may have stopped, more or less accidentally, at its capital city on the way between Madrid and Valencia. This area might be visited from several points: from Barcelona, Madrid or San Sebastián, or from across the border in France.

Like all the provinces bordering on the Pyrenees, Navarre and Huesca can be recommended for summer visits because of their cool moun-

202

tain climate. They also offer a good choice of mountain resorts, which are even more popular for winter sports.

Navarre

The history of Navarre, one of the four Christian kingdoms into which northern Spain was divided during the period when the Moors held the south, has always been linked with that of the neighboring Basque country. Isolated castles, imposing monasteries, Romanesque or Gothic churches in walled towns, witness Navarre's stormy past; but it is equally visited for the natural beauty of its Pyrenean scenery, as exemplified in Roncesvalles, famed from the *Song of Roland* and one of the loveliest crossings into France; the Irati and Salazar valleys, leading to the higher crossing at Puerto de Larrau; or the Baztan valley. Because it was so small a kingdom, it became only one modern province and is an exception to the general rule that Spanish provinces are named for their capital cities. Navarre has kept its ancient name instead of taking that of its chief city, Pamplona.

The Running of the Bulls

Pamplona's big moment comes at the time of the Fiesta de San Fermín, between July 6 and 14. The cross streets along the route from the corral to the bullring are shut off, and while tourists and other non-combatants watch from windows and balconies, the bulls are coursed through the main streets of the town to the bullring. Ahead of them run the youths of Navarre, ducking and dodging the charges of the infuriated animals for the edification of their girl friends. This is the place that provided background for Ernest Hemingway's *The Sun Also Rises* (or *Fiesta*, depending on which edition you read) and you will know, if you read the book, that Pamplona is set in good fishing country. Its attractions include a 15th-century Gothic cathedral, whose 14th-century cloisters are outstanding, 13th-century San Nicolás, 14th-century San Cernín, the citadel and ramparts, and the Navarre Museum, which has a fine collection of medieval church murals.

Forty-three kilometers (27 miles) southwest by N-III, Estella on the Ega river was in the late 12th century the residence of King Sancho the Wise, whose palace is an unusually fine example of Romanesque civil architecture. No less remarkable is the church of San Pedro de la Rúa with lovely cloisters, the palaces of the nobles and churches down to the 16th century. One and a half kilometers south is the Benedictine abbey of Irache, eight kilometers (5 miles) north the Cistercian abbey of Iranzu, and twenty kilometers (13 miles) east Puente la Reina is graced by old churches and a bridge over the Arga.

Forty-three kilometers (27 miles) southeast from Pamplona by N240, Sangüesa features the church of Santa María with a superb Romanesque portal, several 12th- and 13th-century churches, the royal palace of the same period, the 15th-century palace of the Duque de Granada and a bridge over the Aragón river. Eight kilometers west rises the 13th-century castle of Javier, where St Francis Xavier, Apostle of the Indies and Japan, was born in 1506. Now a Jesuit college, the castle is well worth a visit.

Across the thirteen-kilometer long artificial lake of Yesa, formed by the damming of the Aragón and popular with campers, the 11th-century monastery of Leyre, Spain's first large Romanesque building, has been well restored.

Aragón

Aragón, together with Catalonia, was united to Spain when its King Ferdinand married Isabella, Queen of Castile and León, in the 15th century, but, as with other Spanish medieval kingdoms, its frontiers are still remembered by the inhabitants, who possess their own separate customs and traditions.

Today Aragón consists of the provinces of Huesca, Zaragoza and Teruel, which together form a strip little more than 160 kilometers (100 miles) wide, but which thrusts 400 kilometers (250 miles) south from the central Pyrenees almost to the Mediterranean port of Valencia.

The outstanding natural and architectural sites of Huesca, touristically the most attractive province, can be included in one roundtrip. The N240 climbs northwest from the capital via Ayerbe and then follows the Río Gállego to Santa María. Here, it meets the N330 which turns northeast, skirting the Reservoir de la Peña, famous for its trout and dominated by Spain's most important Romanesque castle, Loarre, perched on a crag.

After leaving the Gállego, a further eleven kilometers of a branch west (left) lead to the monastery of San Juan de la Peña. Set among green meadows the *new* monastery is a fairly recent structure (1714). Another one and a half kilometers down the mountain the *old* monastery is distinguished by its 10th-century lower church, its upper church, which was hollowed into the rock in the 13th century, and the well preserved though roofless cloister, the pantheon where the heroes of Aragón were buried. Lastly, there is the setting itself. Right in the heart of a mountain wilderness, the enclosure stands on uneven ground, overhung dramatically by a huge mass of rock.

And there is a legend. The Holy Grail was kept here because San Juan de la Peña was used as a Christian fortress to resist the Arab invaders. In 713 Zaragoza fell into their hands, then Huesca; the inhabitants fled to the Pyrenees. Amongst them were two young men, Voto and Félix. The former, who was a keen huntsman, was pursuing a stag when the cornered animal leapt over the edge of a precipice and the huntsman, feeling that he was about to topple over too, commended his soul to John the Baptist. Miraculously, he was held there on the very edge of the precipice. When he went in search of the shattered remains of the stag, he came upon the body of a hermit who had died in the cave beneath the crag. From the inscription that the hermit had carved on the stone before he died, the young man learned that the cave was dedicated to John the Baptist. Voto and his brother promptly renounced the world and went to live in the cave which had such miraculous associations for them. History was enacted here, too. It was in this monastery that men took the oath to fight against the Moslem invader.

The N330 passes over the 1,080-meter high Puerto de Oroel on the remaining 16 kilometers (10 miles) to Jaca, an important crossroads and a good base for exploring the region.

Jaca and the Pyrenees

A favorite residence of medieval Aragonese kings, the ancient town of Jaca is still surrounded by the walls built in 1592 together with the imposing citadel, upon foundations dating from 194 B.C. The 10th-century Romanesque cathedral is flanked by the plateresque town hall, the Museum of Romanesque Art and a Benedictine convent; two bridges, Romanesque San Miguel and Gothic San Cristobal, span the Río Aragón.

Fourteen kilometers (9 miles) north on N330 is Canfranc, the customs station with France, while right on the border is Candanchú, 1,676 meters (5,500 feet) above sea level and a popular summer and winter sports resort; to the east, beyond Panticosa, some of the highest peaks in the Pyrenees tower 3,298 meters (11,000 feet) into the usually cloudless blue sky.

Owing to the mountains it is necessary to return to Jaca and then turn east on the C134 which follows the railroad to Sabiñánigo where there are some fine samples of mudéjar architecture. From there, the northern section of the C136 climbs the lovely Valle de Terna to the thermal spa of Panticosa, recommended for bronchitis and rheumatism, but now even more important as a winter sports center. A more elegant spot, however, is El Formigal above Sallent de Gállego on the way to France. C140 branches east (right) to the beautiful National Park and game reserve of Ordesa, where a wealth of wildlife may be seen amid completely unspoilt magnificent scenery.

From the parador at Valle de Pineta, below Monte Perdido, which is 3,355 meters (11,000 feet) high, it is possible to return on C138 along the Ara and Cinca rivers to Barbastro which has a 16th-century cathedral, an episcopal palace and an interesting town hall on the colonnaded Plaza Mayor, and then west (right) to Huesca on the N240. The southern section of C136 connects Sabiñánigo over the Puerto de Monrepos, 1,262 meters (4,200 feet) directly with Huesca.

Huesca

If you are approaching Huesca from the north, the first glimpse you will get is of the cathedral, built over the mosque that took the place of the original church. The alabaster altar piece is very fine indeed. The cloister, which dates further back, is Romanesque, except for one Gothic wing. Works by Goya, Guido Reni, Gilarte and Crespi Carducci are among the masterpieces exhibited in the museum. But the finest section of all is devoted to the primitives.

The House of Culture (a community center) is situated within the old Sertoria, or university, which was restored in the 17th century. You can still see a piece of the original Roman wall. San Pedro el Viejo, which is a national monument, was erected over the remains of a pagan temple; it is one of the oldest churches in Spain, and has a Romanesque cloister and the tombs of Ramiro II and Alfonso I of Aragón. Other interesting sites in the town are the churches of San Agustín, San Miguel and San Lorenzo. The Renaissance architecture of the town hall has served as a model for much of the inner town, which thus presents an unusually harmonious character.

Today Huesca has a history going back to 400 B.C. It was liberated from the Moors in 1096. During the Civil War it was in the front line for the entire two and a half years as a Franco stronghold, and suffered considerable damage. It has been somewhat over-restored.

Between Huesca and Zaragoza, no halts are suggested, except perhaps for the ancient village of Almudévar, which has a strange and disproportionately large church and the ruins of a castle.

Zaragoza

Zaragoza (written Saragossa by English-speaking peoples and pronounced Tharagotha by the Spaniards) is the capital of Aragón, seventy-two kilometers (45 miles) by road or rail from Huesca. In that relatively short distance, however, the green of the Pyrenees foothills has given way to a desolate, tawny-colored plateau, blasted by shade temperatures of over 38°C (100°F) in summer, swept by icy winds in winter and, in years of drought, the peasants would gladly exchange a liter of wine for a liter of water to save their dying cattle.

Yet despite the desolation of its immediate surroundings, Zaragoza is, and always has been, a city of great strategic importance. Its name is a corruption of Caesar Augustus, who made it his headquarters while carrying out the campaigns that were to end the two centuries of struggle necessary for Rome to subdue Spain. The great Charlemagne arrived at its walls in the year 777, but was unable to take the city. Liberated from the Moors in 1118, it immediately became the capital of the Kingdom of Aragón. Its year-long resistance to Napoleon in 1808–9 is an example of the great courage and endurance of which the Spaniards are capable.

Being almost exactly equidistant between Madrid and Barcelona, it is an obvious stopping place for travelers by road or rail.

Zaragoza possesses a university founded in 1587, and is the home of Spain's most famous officers' training academy. Don't be surprised to see fiercely mustached, booted and spurred individuals standing around licking ice-cream cones.

Zaragoza is near the home of Francisco de Goya (1746–1828), and therefore possesses many of the works of the man whom many consider the greatest of all Spanish artists.

Of far greater interest than the cathedral—despite some Goya frescos and a Tapestry Museum—is the 18th-century Basilica del Vírgen del Pilar, set upon the banks of Spain's largest river, the Ebro, a site traditionally chosen by St James the Apostle. With its cupolas and blue tiling, its baroque magnificence seems at first sight to belong to Baghdad rather than Aragón. Inside, the tremendous sweep of its 129-meter-long (422-foot) and 64-meter-long (211-foot) nave makes you feel as though you are in some strange underground city. The Virgin herself is a small 15th-century carving, not over 30 centimeters (one foot) high, set on a silver-inlaid jasper pillar, itself deeply worn by 250 years of kisses from the devout, and partly covered by an incongruous Olympic flag. Goya contributed to the frescoes in the choir of the chapel; there is an incredible wealth of jewels, gold plate and priceless Flemish and Spanish tapestries to be seen in the treasury, many of which accompany the little Virgin on her ceremonial procession through the city on October 12. The Basilica also contains two paintings by Velázquez.

The modern administrative buildings that have gone up along the spacious Plaza del Pilar blend in remarkably well, and the pinkish brown of the brick provides a pleasing unifying element between the Roman ramparts on one end and the Lonja, the 16th-century Exchange, on the other. The octagonal mudéjar tower of San Pablo rises above the old quarter, which is graced by Renaissance and baroque palaces.

The other architectural highlight of Zaragoza is the newly restored Castle of Aljafería, situated in particularly ugly surroundings. It began life as an 11th-century Moorish palace, then became the residence of the Christian kings after the Reconquest and finally was a center of the Inquisition. The walls still serve as a reminder of an age when gold came flowing in from the New World.

The Provincial Museum of Fine Arts, in addition to a special room devoted to Goya, contains a *St. Francis* of El Greco. Goya fans should not miss his frieze illustrating the life of the Virgin, in the 16th-century Cartuja d'Aula Dei, thirteen kilometers (8 miles) outside the town.

The main road from Zaragoza to Madrid passes through Calatayud, with interesting mudéjar church towers, to Alhama de Aragón 114 kilometers (71 miles) further on, where almost on the borders of the province, there is a welcome release from the desolation of the scenery. By branching off for nineteen kilometers (12 miles) to Nuévalos, you can reach the famous 12th-century Monasterio de Piedra, well worth a visit. Cistercian austerity is softened by the exceptional oasis of gardens that surrounds it. Such a wealth of greenery comes as a complete surprise in the inner aridity of this part of Aragón.

Teruel

N330 from Zaragoza to Teruel leads through the best Aragonese vineyards to Daroca, whose medieval walls measure almost two kilometers in length, and enclose 100 towers and churches of all styles. It is one of the oldest towns in Spain. The Corpus Christi procession and ensuing popular fiestas here take on extraordinary proportions.

Teruel, on the River Turia, is 185 kilometers (115 miles) from Zaragoza, and is the smallest of the three provincial capitals of Aragón. It stands 915 meters (3,000 feet) above sea level, and provides an interesting halt on the way to the coast, some 105 kilometers (65 miles) away.

The town's chief fame is due to its medieval lovers, Diego Marcilla and Isabela de Segura, who, separated by their parents, both died of broken hearts. In death, their mummified bodies are united in the church of San Pablo. There are other sights in this ancient city: Los Arcos, an aqueduct constructed by a French engineer, Pierre Vedel, in the 16th century, and the church of Santa María (with a mudéjar belfry), of the same epoch. San Martín and its Arab tower are older, dating from the 13th century.

Teruel changed hands twice during the Civil War, and was the point from which, in 1938 Franco made his decisive thrust down to the sea, fatally cutting Republican territory in two.

A worthwhile excursion is a visit to Albarracín, thirty-two kilometers (20 miles) to the west. This small Moorish fortified town, perched in the mountains 1,100 meters high (3,600 feet), remains purely medieval. Its church has a number of fine 16th-century Flemish tapestries. A little way to the southeast is Callejón del Plou, where there are prehistoric cave paintings of red bulls; at Navazo, there are other paintings of human but snakeheaded figures against a background of black and white bulls. Although these paintings belong to the dawn of time, they still retain an extraordinary vividness of color and movement.

For most people, however, the road leads to the south, through Viver to Segorbe, eighty-seven kilometers (54 miles) from Teruel, from which the Mediterranean is only half an hour away by car. This walled town, set between two castle-crowned peaks, is rich in reminders of its Roman past.

The Northwest

Having explored the areas to the southwest and southeast of Zaragoza and, earlier, the area to the northeast, all that remains now is the northwest, the road to Tudela and Pamplona.

Before actually reaching Tudela, it is a good idea to take the turning (it is on the left if you are coming from Zaragoza) to Magallón and Borja. Early in the 12th century it was given to Don Pedro de Atares, the founder of a family which was later destined to become famous—the Borgias. It is now just a sleepy market town that the tourist passes through on his way to the Monastery of Veruela. The monastery is located on the outskirts of the village of Vera (the road is terrible).

On setting out, the motorist should not rely on the old road signs, as they may lead him well astray. His best plan is to ask for the road to Veruela and Vera.

Veruela dates back to 1146. It looks like a fortress from the outside. The first Borgia, Don Pedro de Atares, its founder, handed it over to the Cistercians. The Jesuits were banished from Spain in 1932, but they have been back at the monastery since 1940. The church is magnificent; the cloister has been partly rebuilt. The restoration of the Chapter House has been accomplished most successfully. Features worth noticing are the many tombs and the ambulatory.

In Tarazona, the 15th-century cloister of the 12th-century cathedral has been successfully restored. Brick is equally pleasingly used in the other mudéjar churches, while the former Lonja, now the town hall, is decorated with Renaissance reliefs of the Labors of Hercules.

N121 branches northeast, back to Navarre, where Tudela's 12th-century cathedral is a particularly interesting example of the transition from Romanesque to Gothic; there is a superb carving on the doorway depicting the Last Judgment. Unfortunately, the effect is lost, as it is not set far enough back for you to see it in perspective. The town itself is bustling and alive. Everything about the place has a quaint charm that is most appealing. The Plaza de los Fueros is quite delightful, with its wrought-iron balconies.

When you cross the Romanesque bridge over the Ebro (17 arches and 380 meters (1,247 feet) long), you return to dreary hillocks, dotted with grayish plants and tufts of thyme. Continue north on N121 to Caparroso, where C124 branches east (right) following the River Aragón for sixteen kilometers (10 miles) to Carcastillo and the Cistercian abbey of Nuestra Señora de la Oliva, set right in the heart of the vineyards. This region has a wealth of interesting buildings. Carlos II, the Wicked, added a Gothic nave and gate to the 12th-century fortress church of San Martin de Unx. The 12th-century church of Ujué, a few kilometers to the north of Oliva, is built over an unusual crypt and possesses a fine portal and beautiful 16th-century reredos.

Back on N121, Olite's parador is part of the erstwhile residence of the kings of Navarre. Bridging the transition from the 14th to the 15th centuries, Carlos III built a castle in the French style, with a touch of mudéjar polychromed woods, ornate pavements and *azulejos*. The royal chapel became the church of Santa María; more ancient (11th century) and more beautiful is the church of San Pedro, whose Romanesque cloisters and portal are finely worked.

Tafalla, six and a half kilometers to the north, likewise possesses a Santa María and San Pedro, moreover convents of San Francisco and of the Immaculate Conception. Eleven kilometers northwest, stout towers strengthen the walls enclosing Artajona's Gothic San Saturnino and San Pedro with the miraculous statue of Our Lady of Jerusalem.

PRACTICAL INFORMATION FOR ARAGON AND NAVARRE

WHAT TO SEE. The most interesting city in this area is Zaragoza, Jaca is second; Pamplona is visited for the bulls and also has an interesting cathedral. Panticosa will give you a spa vacation in the Pyrenees. Candanchú can be a center for a fishing trip in the summer or winter sports in winter. The National Park of Ordesa is a game preserve, with a state-run mountain refuge where you may stay, amid wonderful scenery. Southwest of Jaca, the legendary Monastery of San Juan de la Peña is a worthwhile excursion. For Roman remains, there is Segorbe; for an old walled town, Daroca. Probably the most compelling attraction in this region is provided by prehistoric painted caves near Teruel. For an old abbey set in fine fountain-studded grounds, visit the Monastery of Piedra, near Calatayud. Main ski centers besides Candanchú are Benasque, Burguete, Sabiñanigo and Sallent de Gallego, all provided with cablecars.

HOTELS. For the San Fermin festivals in Pamplona, hotel rooms are impossible to find if you have not booked long in advance. Between July 4 and 15, the dates of the festivals, do not expect to find even the most humble room in the most meagre pension. The town will be booked to bursting point and beyond.

Many of the spa towns in the Pyrenees have hotels which are only open in the summer. The ski resort hotels, however, stay open all year round and you'll find that these resorts make beautiful summer vacation spots.

HOTELS AND RESTAURANTS

ALCAÑIZ (Teruel). *Parador de la Concordia* (E), Castillo de los Calatravos, tel. (974) 83 04 00. 12 rooms in converted Calatrava castle, just outside town.

ALHAMA DE ARAGON (Zaragoza). Spa for rheumatism and catarrh. *Termas y Parque* (E), General Franco 20, tel. (976) 84 0011. 110 rooms, with pool, tennis and gardens. *Balneario Guajardo* (I), General Franco 3. 86 rooms, pool and garden.

ALSASUA (Navarra). *Alaska* (M), 10 km out of town on Burgos-San Sebastián road, tel. (948) 56 01 00. 25 rooms, garden and pool, good views.

BALNEARIO DE PANTICOSA (Huesca). *Gran Hotel* (M), tel. (974) 48 71 61. 72 rooms, tennis and garden. *Mediodía* (M), tel. (974) 48 71 61. 52 rooms, with tennis, and garden.

BIELSA (Huesca). *Parador Monte Perdido* (E), Valle de Pineta, tel. (974) 50 10 11. 14 km from the village, a modern parador with 16 rooms and superb views of the surrounding mountains.

CALATAYUD (Zaragoza). *Calatayud* (M), García Olaya 17, tel. (976) 88 13 23. 63 rooms, garden and parking.

CANDANCHU (Huesca). *Edelweiss* (E), on N123, tel. (974) 37 32 00. 76 rooms. *Pirineos* (E), tel. (974) 37 30 00. Apartment hotel, very expensive in skiing season. *Candanchu* (M), tel. (974) 37 30 25. 48 rooms.

DAROCA (Zaragoza). *Daroca* (I), Mayor 42, tel. (976) 80 00 00. 20 rooms.

EJEA DE LOS CABALLEROS (Zaragoza). *Cinco Villas* (M), Paseo del Muro 10, tel. (976) 66 03 00. 30 rooms, comfortable.

ELIZONDO (Navarra). *Baztán* (E), tel. (948) 58 00 50. 84 rooms, with pool and gardens.

FITERO (Navarra). *Palafox II* (M), Extramuros, tel. (948) 77 61 00. 48 rooms, pool and garden. *Balneario Bécquer* (M), 3 km outside village, tel. (948) 77 61 00. 218 rooms, pool, tennis and garden. *Balneario Palafox* (I), 3 km outside, tel. (948) 77 61 00. 55 rooms, pool, tennis and garden.

HUESCA. *Pedro I de Aragón* (E), Parque 34, tel. (974) 22 03 00. 52 rooms, centrally located. *Montearagón* (M), on N240, tel. (974) 22 23 50. 27 rooms, parking, pool and garden amongst other facilities. *Mirasol* (I), Ramón y Cajal 29, tel. (974) 22 37 60. Small family-run hostel right in center; spotless and good value.
   Restaurants. *Navas* (M), San Lorenzo 15, tel. 22 47 38, is the best. *Sauras* (I), Zaragoza 2, tel. 21 12 74, is a long-standing tradition.

ISABA (Navarra). *Isaba* (E-M), on highway, tel. (948) 89 30 00. Pleasantly situated with parking and garden. Rates are (M), Sept.-June.

JACA (Huesca). *Gran Hotel* (E-M), Paseo del General Franco 1, tel. (974) 36 09 00. 80 rooms, with pool, tennis and garden. *Conde de Aznar* (M), General Franco 3, tel. (974) 36 10 50. 23 rooms. *La Paz* (I), Mayor 41, tel. (974) 36 07 00. 34 rooms.

Restaurants. *La Cocina Aragonesa* (E), Cervantes 5, tel. 36 10 50. One of the best, delicious desserts. *José* (M), La Salud 10, tel. 36 16 18. Very popular; good paella.

NUEVALOS (Zaragoza). *Monasterio de Piedra* (I), tel. (976) 84 90 11. At the monastery, 61 rooms, with pool and tennis. *Las Truchas* (I), tel. (976) 84 90 40. On the Cillas-Alhama road, 36 rooms, pool, mini golf and tennis.

OLITE (Navarra). *Parador Príncipe de Viana* (E), Plaza de las Teobaldas 2, tel. (948) 74 00 00. 48 rooms, in historic castle, gardens.

PAMPLONA. During the San Fermines, July 5-14 prices are very much higher than normal. *Los Tres Reyes* (L), Jardines de la Taconera, tel. (948) 22 66 00. A luxury hotel with 168 rooms, pool and garden amongst its many amenities. *Ciudad de Pamplona* (E-M), Iturrama 21, tel. (948) 26 60 11. 117 rooms, good amenities. *Nuevo Hotel Maisonnave* (M), Nueva 20, tel. (948) 22 26 00. 164 rooms. *Orhi* (M), Leyre 7, tel. (948) 24 58 00. 55 rooms. *Eslava* (M), Plaza Virgen de la O, tel. (948) 22 22 70. 28 rooms. *Yoldi* (M), Avda de San Ignacio 11, tel. (948) 22 48 00. 46 rooms. A bit oppressive looking, but friendly. *Valerio* (I), Avda. de Zaragoza 5, tel. (948) 24 54 66. A 2-star hostel with 16 rooms, and serving meals.
Restaurants. *Hostal del Rey Noble* (E), Paseo Sarasate 6, tel. 21 12 85. Excellent food in cozy setting. *Josetxo* (E), Estafeta 73, tel. 22 20 97. Well known for good food, especially seafood and fish specialties. *Cafetería Tres Reyes* (M), below the Tres Reyes hotel, has good, medium priced food. *Vista Bella* (M), Jardines de la Taconera, tel. 25 05 81. Pleasantly located in a park.

RIBAFORADA (Navarra). *Sancho El Fuerte* (M), on N232, tel. (948) 86 40 25. 133 rooms, with pool; a very reasonable 3-star hotel.

SABIÑANIGO (Huesca). *La Pardiña* (M), Sta. Orosia 36, tel. (974) 48 09 75. 64 rooms, pool, and garden. *Mi Casa* (M-I), Avda. del Ejército 32, tel. (974) 48 04 00. 72 rooms. *Alpino* (I), General Franco 58, tel. (974) 48 07 25. 18 rooms.

SALLENT DE GALLEGO (Huesca). Ski center, so prices of the first two are (L) in winter. *Formigal* (E), tel. (974) 48 80 00. 108 rooms, the best. *Eguzki-Lore* (E), tel. (974) 48 80 75. 32 rooms. *Nievesol* (M), tel. (974) 48 80 34.

SOS DEL REY CATOLICO (Zaragoza). *Parador Fernando de Aragón* (E-M), tel. (976) 88 80 11. 66 rooms, a regional style parador.

TERUEL. *Reina Cristina* (E), Paseo del Generalísimo 1, tel. (974) 60 68 60. A 3-star hotel, central with 62 rooms. *Parador Nacional* (E-M), 2 km out of town, tel. (974) 60 18 00. Modern parador with 40 rooms, just north of town, mini golf and garden. *Civera* (I), Avda Sagunto 37, tel. (974) 60 23 00. 73 rooms, garden. *Alpino* (I), tel. (974) 60 61 58. 32 rooms. 5 km. east on N234.

TUDELA (Navarra). *Morase* (M), Paseo Marqués de Vadillo 13, tel. (948) 82 17 00. 3-star hostel with 26 rooms. *Santamaría* (M), Frauca 20, tel. (948) 82 12 00. 56 rooms, central. *Tudela* (I), Ctra de Zaragoza, tel. (948) 82 05 58. 18 rooms.

ZARAGOZA. *Corona de Aragón* (L), Avda Cesar Augusto 13, tel. (976) 22 49 45. Modern and with àll the amenities of a deluxe hotel. *Gran Hotel* (L), Costa 5, tel. (976) 22 19 01. Excellent older hotel, only 4 stars but rates are (L). *Palafox* (L), Casa Jiménez, tel. (976) 23 77 00. The latest addition to Zaragoza's deluxe hotels. *Don Yo* (L-E), Bruil 4, tel. (976) 22 67 41. 181 rooms. *Ramiro I* (E), Coso 123, tel. (976) 29 82 00. *Rey Alfonso I* (E), Coso 17, tel. (976) 21 82 90. *Goya* (E-M), Cinco de Marzo 5, tel. (976) 22 93 31. Modern and spacious with restaurant. *Oriente* (E-M), Coso 11, tel. (976) 22 19 60.

Europa (M), Alfonso I 19, tel. (976) 22 49 01. 54 rooms. *París* (M), Pedro María Ric 14, tel. (976) 23 65 37. 62 rooms. *Conde Blanco* (I), Predicadores 84, tel. (976) 44 14 11. 83 rooms. *Gran Vía* (I), Gran Vía 38, tel. (976) 22 92 13. 30 rooms. *Los Molinos* (I), San Miguel 28, tel. (976) 22 49 80. 40 rooms.

About 10 km out on the road to Madrid is an excellent modern roadside hotel with pool and good restaurant, *El Cisne* (M), tel. (976) 33 20 00.

Restaurants. *Los Borrachos* (E), Sagasta 64, tel. 27 50 36. Delicious food and good service. Game and fish specialties. Recommended by readers as one of the best restaurants in Spain. *El Cachirulo* (E), tel. 33 16 74. 4 km out of town on N232 to Logroño, superb food, Aragonese atmosphere and folk music. *Savoy* (E), Coso 42, tel. 22 49 16. Excellent. *Costa Vasca* (E), Valenzuela 13, tel. 21 73 39. Top Basque dishes. *Horno Asador Goyesco* (M), Manuel Lasala 44, tel. 35 68 71. Excellent cuisine and typical Aragonese décor. *Mesón del Carmen* (M), Hernán Cortés 4, tel. 21 11 51. An old time favorite with authentic Aragonese cooking. *Casa Colás,* Mártires 10. Just one of the many budget restaurants and tascas on this street and the streets leading off it. *Taberna Aragonesa* (I), Hernán Cortés 8, tel. 22 62 60. Another budget spot.

USEFUL ADDRESSES. Tourist Offices. **Canfranc** (Huesca); Fernando el Católico 3. **Huesca;** Coso Alto 23. **Jaca;** Plaza Calvo Sotelo. **Pamplona;** Duque de Ahumada 3. **Teruel;** Tomás Nogués 1. **Zaragoza;** Plaza de Sas 7.

CAR HIRE. Pamplona; *Atesa,* Sanguesa 24, *Avis,* Iturralde y Suit 5, *Hertz,* Hotel Tres Reyes. **Zaragoza;** *Atesa,* Avda Valencia 3, *Avis,* Fernando el Católico 9, *Hertz,* Luis del Valle 26, *Ital,* Mariano Barbasán 16.

THE WESTERN PROVINCES

Unknown Spain

In Spain's Far West, pressed for most of its length against the Portuguese border, and separated at either end by one province's width from the sea (on the north, Asturias; on the south, Huelva), lies a row of five provinces. These are, from north to south, León, Zamora, Salamanca, and the two provinces that make up Extremadura: Cáceres and Badajoz. They are not obvious tourist provinces, like Andalusia, but they are among the most attractive in Spain, and precisely because they are less visited, you will find in them an atmosphere more unadulteratedly Spanish. In the whole of Spain you will find few places offering more beauty and outstanding interest than Salamanca; and, for sheer picturesqueness, Caceres is altogether unique.

So far as weather is concerned, the best time to visit this area is the same as for most of the rest of the non-coastal regions of Spain—spring and fall, with fall less subject to rain. An exception might be made for the Sierra de Gredos, discussed in connection with the Old Castile province of Avila, which extends also into Cáceres. This attractive mountain range offers a pleasant summer playground.

León and Pajares

León, almost exactly 320 kilometers (200 miles) by road from Madrid and 840 meters (2,750 feet) above sea level, is the gateway to the northern and northwestern provinces of Asturias and Galicia.

In the 11th century León was the capital of Christian Spain, but with the liberation of Toledo in 1085 the warrior court moved there, so as to be nearer to the still enslaved provinces of the south. With the unification of the kingdoms of León and Castile, the latter became dominant, and the old city slowly declined in importance. Although it is full of 10th-, 11th- and 12th-century churches, monasteries and convents, León is unique in two ways—first, the almost incredibly beautiful 13th-century stained-glass windows of the cathedral. There are 230 of them, 12 meters (40 feet) high, and once within the dark interior of the perfect Gothic building, you will find yourself walking in a patterned maze of glowing colors of an unearthly depth and intensity. The second is the 11th-century church of San Isidro el Real, housing the body of the saint; its vault possesses the most beautiful wall-paintings of the 12th century in Spain.

León also has the former convent of San Marcos, today a five-star hotel of great charm, and the church of Nuestro Señor de Camino.

Sixty kilometers (38 miles) north of León, N630 climbs to the famous 1,356-meter (4,450-foot) Pajares Pass (with a gradient of one in seven on the far side), which marks the border between the provinces of León and Asturias. Here there is a comfortable and attractive parador, and though it is in the opposite direction to that in which we are now theoretically heading, it might be worth a visit for the matchless view afforded in spring and autumn over the mountains of Asturias.

Pajares, however, is more conveniently visited if you are going beyond León to the coast. For that matter, if you are not in a hurry to reach Zamora, 145 kilometers (90 miles) from León, then we recommend a similar diversion on the other side of it, after you have passed the attractive old town of Benavente on your way westward to Puebla de Sanabria. There is an albergue here, but, even more important, it is only a few kilometers to the loveliest mountain lake in Spain, where tree-covered hills crowd down to the water's edge. Here you are already in the province of Zamora, though still 108 kilometers (67 miles) from the city.

Zamora

The little city of Zamora is perched defensively upon a steep hill, and it was here Doña Urraca, wicked daughter of King Ferdinand I, shut herself in to resist the besieging forces of her brother Sancho in 1072. Just outside the defiant walls of Zamora she had Sancho murdered. Under his younger brother Alfonso, there began the second great wave of the Reconquest, led by the gigantic, almost legendary figure of El Cid Campeador.

Sightseers in Zamora feel almost as if they had been whisked off to the Orient. The Arabs have left their stamp here through the intermediary, so to speak, of the Mozárabes; the latter were a paradoxically united group of both Christians and Moslems who staged an uprising against the Eastern potentates in Córdoba without waiting for the Reconquest. This bit of history explains why Zamora was constantly war-torn.

The distinguishing feature of the local Palace of Justice is its shield, ornamented by the figure of a monkey, which has led to its being referred to disrespectfully as the Casa de los Momos, or House of Grimaces. The Holy Week Museum is installed in a restored palace close to the church of Santa María la Nueva. The cathedral is unfortunately disfigured by a ponderous tower that throws its proportions off kilter. In Zamora, you will derive a certain consolation from the mellow Flemish tapestries that are the pride of the museum: they hang in the charming cathedral cloister. Beforehand, pay a little visit to the choirstalls; the work of Rodrigo de Alemán, they are full of wickedly amusing, natural touches. Visit also the interior of San Claudio's church and of Santiago El Viejo, the scene of the solemn ceremony in which El Cid received his knighthood. (That, of course, didn't keep him from being expelled from the town later on.) The beautiful Renaissance parador of the Condes de Alba y Aliste should not be missed.

Not far from El Cid's 11th-century house, a 15-arch stone bridge spans the river and brings you to the Cabanales suburb. Try to find time to see Santo Domingo, Santa María de la Orta (the order of the Knights Hospitaler), Santo Tomé and Santiago del Burgo. Before leaving the subject of churches, we should also mention San Pedro de la Nave (a quarter of an hour away), founded in Visigothic times.

Zamora was an old frontier fortress, and you cannot drive the sixty-five kilometers (40 miles) to Salamanca through this pleasantly hilly countryside, with the dark mountains of the north Portuguese province of Braganza occasionally visible far to the west, without realizing that this is frontier country. Crumbling but still formidable medieval castles face west towards their troublesome neighbors, who broke away from

Spain only in the 12th century, and the people, too, have something of the frontiersman's unmistakable air—lean, handsome, wiry, and always alert, yet still delightfully courteous to the foreigner.

Head east for Toro and its Roman bridge, 30 kilometers distant halfway between Zamora and Tordesillas. At Santa María la Mayor, see the wooden retable, and also the "Virgin of the Fly," for which the great Queen Isabella is said to have posed.

Salamanca

Your first glimpse of the ancient city of Salamanca is unforgettable. Beside you flows the swift River Tormes, and beyond it rise the old houses of the city topped by the golden walls, turrets, domes and spires of the cathedral. Salamanca's history goes back to the time of Hannibal, and a Roman bridge still spans the river. Like León it suffered almost total destruction in the ebb and flow of the centuries-long struggle to eject the Moors, and its great days began only when Alfonso XI of León founded the University in 1223 (much enriched later by Alfonso the Wise who bequeathed it his own huge library of 100,000 volumes and manuscripts).

Several different buildings make up the university. Opposite the main entrance lies the Rectory, housed in the former Hospital del Estudio, which was founded in 1413. The chapel is used as an assembly hall and has a strikingly beautiful polychrome coffered ceiling.

On the other side of the blind passageway you will see the 17th-century Escuelas Menores, which served as a kind of university preparatory school. The walls of the charming cloistered courtyard of green lawns are covered with *vitores* testifying to the enthusiasm of successful candidates. The façade of the main building is a tapestry in stone. A double doorway leads through the vestibule, whose ceiling is adorned with an interlaced mudéjar design into the Patio de Escuelas; the chapel and lecture rooms are clustered around the lower Gothic cloister, from which a majestic staircase ascends to the upper loggia, distinguished by a lovely coffered ceiling; the famous library is on this floor.

Higher up the Calle Serranos spreads the larger Pontifical University La Clerecía, the former Jesuit College whose church is typical of the order's styles; nearby is the Dominican Theological University.

Lastly, there is the Casa Rectoral, its second floor now housing the Unamuno Museum. The great philosopher lived here from 1900 to 1914.

Not content with three universities, Salamanca also possesses two cathedrals. The three-meter-thick (10-foot) walls of the Old were built by the Cid's chaplain, Don Jerónimo de Perigueux, in the early 12th

SALAMANCA
(NOT TO SCALE)

1 Plaza Mayor
2 Post Office
3 Monterrey Palace
4 Purísima Church
5 Ancient Irish College
6 University
7 New & Old Cathedral
8 La Clerecia
9 Casa de Las Conchas
10 Las Dueñas Convent
11 San Esteban Monastery
12 Casa de Las Muertes
✝ Church or Convent

century. In the center of the 53-panel reredos stands the *Vírgen de la Vega,* patroness of Salamanca, a 13th-century copper statue adorned with Limoges enamels. The lovely cloister is surrounded by numerous chapels. Most of the works of Salamanca's greatest painter, Fernando Gallego, are in the Diocesan Museum, beside a superb triptych and many other treasures. Though outmoded by 1513, the Cathedral Chapter clung to Gothic and after some two hundred years the graceful vaults and towers of the New Cathedral were at last finished. The interior is rather bare, except for the baroque choir and some of the chapels.

Across the Plaza, the 18th-century Anaya Palace backs on the 16th-century convent of Las Dueñas, remarkable for its double cloisters and a façade facing the even more extravagant stone filigree of the church of San Esteban; the latter belongs to a Dominican monastery, where the Cloister of the Kings should be seen.

On the way back to the center you pass the Renaissance Palaces of Orellana and La Salina, next to the 15th-century Torre del Clavero. Don't miss the famous Casa de las Conchas, whose unusual shell decorations and Ave María Grille hide a lovely court.

The Plaza Mayor

The Calle de la Compañía passes the doorway of San Benito; the richly decorated Monterrey Palace stands opposite the convent of Las Agustinas (Purísima Church), which houses Ribera's famous painting *The Immaculate Conception* . . . in fact, there are about thirty superb buildings, all worth studying. But you should keep the best for the last: the Plaza Mayor, Spain's most perfect, begun in 1729 and completed in 1755 with Churriguera's Royal Pavilion. The Town Hall is a harmonious part of the arcaded buildings round the trapezium-shaped square, used for bullfights till the last century, but now given over to open-air cafés. Sitting surrounded by such perfection you simply don't feel like moving away. It is a touch of splendor, right in the heart of this really delightful university town.

A Roman bridge spans the Tormes; part of its 26 arches has been rebuilt. The tower that used to adorn it vanished in the last century.

If your visit is in September for Salamanca's fiesta (you might easily come especially from Madrid, only 214 kilometers (133 miles) away, for this), be sure to book well in advance, as hotels are crowded then. This is also a good time for a side excursion in the province of Salamanca, to the shrine of Peña de Francia, eighty-five kilometers (53 miles) from the city, nearly 1,830 meters (6,000 feet) above sea level—and cool after the noise and excitement of Salamanca's *fiesta mayor.*

Ciudad Rodrigo

If you are on your way to Portugal, you should pause at the ancient town of Ciudad Rodrigo eighty-seven kilometers on N620 from Salamanca. Named after its liberator from the Arabs, Count Rodrigo Gonzales Girón, it contains some beautiful 16th-century manorial houses near the picturesque Plaza Mayor. The British Dukes of Wellington are also Lords of Ciudad Rodrigo, as it was here that the Iron Duke inflicted a decisive defeat upon the forces of Napoleon in 1808. Wellington's troops were drunk with blood, gunpowder and alcohol, and they proceeded to sack the city, which burned for a week. The depredations as a whole were charged up to the French, however. Spaniards are fond of repeating in a tone of voice like that of Job on his pallet, "The Arabs polished, Napoleon demolished."

The city walls lining the banks of the Agueda are still standing. The fortress is now a parador. The more recent (16th century) Casa Montarco has retained more of its original flavor. Don't miss the cathedral, whose construction began in the 12th century. Rodrigo de Alemán studded the country with carved choirstalls of mystical or pagan inspiration. The ones he designed for Ciudad Rodrigo's cathedral will astound you by the starkness of their realism. The Chapel of Cerralbo houses a fine Ribera painting.

If you drive to the Monastery of Peña de Francia on the C525, branching south off the N620 to Ciudad Rodrigo, you get the maximum of sightseeing by returning via Miranda del Castañar, with castles and mansions, San Martín del Castanar below a soaring fortress, and through the oak and chestnut forests of the Sierra to Bejar, distinguished by a 16th-century ducal palace and the beautifully landscaped gardens of El Bosque. There you join the N630 to Salamanca, but on no account miss La Alberca.

The whole town has been classified a national monument. To visit it, go down to the calvary cross and continue on foot through the narrow passageways which are paved with steps. Practically all the houses have stables on their ground floors, and the upstairs living quarters are profusely blooming with living plants. Below are the shadowy valleys of Las Batuecas, where prehistoric cave paintings and small hermitages emphasize the primeval landscape.

In a southeasterly direction from Salamanca, you can take a pleasant side trip to Alba de Tormes nineteen kilometers (12 miles) on C510. Perched high on a hill, its castle dominates the low-lying flatlands.

St. Teresa died in 1582 in the Carmelite convent on the opposite shore of the Tormes, spanned by the twenty arches of the medieval bridge. Devoted hands have sought to reconstruct the setting of her last days on earth for the edification of visitors. A century later, a famous writer also died here—Pedro Calderón de la Barca, one of Alba de Tormes' native sons. His plays—*Life is a Dream, The Doctor in His Honor*—are still performed wherever the theater is revered.

Extremadura, Land of the Conquistadores

The region of Extremadura, lying between Castile and Andalusia, partakes of the characteristics of both Kingdoms. Its landscapes are big and broad, with limitless horizons even when vast plains are broken by hills and valleys. Two of Spain's great rivers, the Tagus and the Guadiana, water these lands and then flow on through Portugal to meet the Atlantic Ocean. The Sierra de Gata and the Sierra de Gredos form natural mountain barriers to the north as do the slopes (gentle at this point) of the Sierra Morena to the south. The poet José María Gabriel y Galán has immortalized this scenery in simple and effective verse.

Asters and peonies grow wild, with rock roses on the hillsides where eagles nest. Fruit trees thrive, sheep roam the slopes, and in some sections acorns furnish food for pigs. Delicious jams are made from the fruits, and ham and sausage from the pork. Extremadura is famous for these products.

Time stood still in these harsh lands, whose population was drained to the Americas. Only recently has Spain's second wave of prosperity produced even in the remote west the large blocks of flats, whose deadening concrete sameness encroaches on the walled towns, fine churches and stately manor houses from which the Conquistadores sailed forth. After briefly touching down in Cuba, Hernán Cortés conquered Mexico with a handful of troops, lost it during the *Noche Triste*, and recaptured it, only to lose it again. Francisco Pizarro, the illiterate hog-raiser from Trujillo, conquered the Incas in Peru, while Pedro de Valdivia from Villanueva de la Serena added Chile to the Spanish possessions. Vasco Núñez de Balboa, to whom Queen Isabella was so attached that she didn't want him to sail, crossed the unexplored continent and 'claimed' the Pacific Ocean for his sovereigns. Another native of Jerez de los Caballeros, Hernando de Soto, thrust northward following the Mississippi upstream and became one of the first white men to set foot in what is now the United States. By the time violent death had overtaken them, they had brought Spain great wealth and vast territories.

If you are lucky you will run into a local fiesta that, in its naive charm, will be unlike anything that you have ever seen before. In Extremadura, celebrations that take place on the Feast of the Holy Cross on May 3 and at carnival time are among the best known, and weddings and baptisms retain traditional aspects long forgotten in other parts of the country. The local dances show the influence of Andalusia; the *seguidilla* is the most popular. Some Extremaduran dances are reminiscent of the Scottish sword dance and people say that they were learned from Wellington's Scottish troopers.

Whether you enter Extremadura from the north, continuing on N630 from Salamanca, or come in from Madrid, via Talavera de la Reina and Oropesa, on N-V, you enter the province of Cáceres; but coming from Madrid, your first good-sized town is Trujillo, while on the route we are following, it will be Plasencia.

Plasencia and Yuste

The location of Plasencia is somewhat similar to that of Toledo. It lies on a fertile, craggy promontory with the River Jerte flowing below and surrounding it on three sides. An important city in Roman times, it was reconquered from the Moors by Alfonso III of Castile in 1180. He built its double line of walls with their sixty towers, which are, however, almost entirely hidden by encroaching houses.

The cathedral, begun in 1498 in flamboyant Gothic, was finished in unmistakable Renaissance. The interior is of noble proportions and contains some rare works of art. The choirstalls, carved by Rodrigo Alemán, have been declared "the most Rabelaisian in Christendom."

Other churches worth seeing are the 15th-century Gothic San Nicolás and San Ildefonso, both containing beautiful tombs; San Pedro, a blend of Romanesque and mudéjar; and the convent of San Vicente, whose sacristy is decorated with rare antique tiles. Still showing signs of former grandeur are the medieval manors, notably the Casa de Dos Torres, with its 13th-century door, and the Casa de las Bóvedas, which has a lovely garden.

The monastery of Yuste was founded in 1414, ravaged by the French in 1809, and party restored by its present owner, the Marqués de Mirabel. Forty-eight kilometers (30 miles) east of Plasencia in the wooded foothills of the Sierra de Gredos, Yuste possesses no scenic or architectural features which might explain its choice by the ruler of the largest part of Christendom. Yet Charles V declared this part of the country to be "perpetual spring." In 1555, when only 55 years old, tired of kingly responsibilities, he renounced his empire and retired to this bleak heart of Spain. The Emperor seems to have been torn between a desire for monastic simplicity and his gluttony, as well as between renunciation of the world and the anxiety over the Dutch policy of his son and heir, Philip II, to which he gave famous vent during a visit by the latter. Charles V died here in 1558 and his body rested in Yuste until 1574, when it was removed to the Escorial.

Cáceres, Trujillo and Alcántara

If you wish to visit a living example of a feudal town, stop off at Cáceres, with its steep, narrow, twisted streets, its medieval palaces, towers and temples. It was rebuilt by the Moors who called it Qazrix and whose ramparts still encircle the old city, topped by a dozen of the original thirty towers. Joined to the Kingdom of León by Alfonso IX in 1227, the whole of the walled city has remained intact with its fortified late palaces, of which those of the Golfines, Pereros, Sánchez-Paredes and Solís, as well as the Cigüeñas Tower, are outstanding.

The visit is best begun from the vast Plaza Mayor beneath the Bujaco Tower; ascend the stairway to the Arco de la Estrella. Below the patio of the baroque Veletas Mansion, which houses the Provincial Museum, is a large Moorish cistern. Opposite, on the highest point, stands the church of San Mateo, originally a mosque.

The 16th-century tower of Santa María looks over the modern statue of San Pedro de Alcántara on the delightful Plaza de Santa María, flanked by the Episcopal Palace, the Casa de Ovando and the Mayoralgo Palace with its mudéjar patio. Some further architectural gems lie outside the walls, the Renaissance Santa Clara Convent on the one end, the Godoy Palace, facing the church of Santiago on the other. The whole town, old and new, spreads below the sanctuary of the Vírgen de la Montaña, from which the view extends to the distant peaks of the sierras.

Pizarro, conqueror of Peru, was born in Trujillo, forty-eight kilometers east of Cáceres, and the palace of the Marqueses de la Conquista built with treasure brought back from the New World, still stands in the Plaza Mayor, one of the loveliest, with its 16th-century palaces, and the equestrian statue of Pizarro, executed like its duplicate in Lima by the American sculptor Charles Carey Rumsey. Pizarro's tomb is in the church of Santa María de la Concepción.

Steep narrow lanes climb to the well-preserved Moorish castle. The convent of San Miguel and Santa Isabel was founded by Queen Isabella; triumphal arches recall victorious battles. Fernando Gallego carved the twenty-five panels of the reredos in the 15th-century church of Santa María la Mayor.

Alcántara, derived from El Kantara, the Arabic word for bridge, is perched on a rocky point forty-eight kilometers northwest of Cáceres. In the early 13th century, it was rescued from the Moorish clutch by the Knights of Calatrava, who lived in the San Benito monastery. There are also elegant mansions, Santa María de Almocover and the bridge built under Trajan's reign during the second century; its strikingly pure arches are made of granite blocks assembled without any cement.

On the highway from Ciudad Rodrigo to Cáceres, there's an interesting stop at Coria which has kept its original walls, the best preserved in all of Roman Europe—483 meters (1,585 feet) long and 8 meters (25 feet) wide, with watch-towers 4 meters (13 feet) high. The castle and the cathedral are well worth the trip: the cathedral's single nave is Spain's largest.

Guadalupe

The monastery of Guadalupe lies in an alpine setting seventy-seven kilometers (48 miles) east of Trujillo and is well worth a visit. Let the monks be your hosts for the night or stay in the parador, a converted convent. Before getting down to exploring the vast monastery, spend a few minutes wandering through the little village with its quaint and archaic pillared houses. The monastery is the home of men who pay eternal homage to a physical representation of the Virgin which sits on a throne, with jewel-crowned head, protected by fortress-like walls. All the great of Spain have passed before her shrine.

The discovery of Our Lady of Guadalupe was a miracle of the 13th century. The Virgin appeared to a cowherd, blinding him by her brilliance, telling him to look for a statue of her that had been buried in the vicinity under a bramble bush. This statue, said to have been carved by Saint Luke, was unearthed and a chapel built on the spot, which gave way to a bigger church founded by Alfonso VI, endowed later, with benefices added. The façade of the church faces the village and its interior has baroque decorations added in the 18th century. The magnificent 16th-century grilles were made by Giraldo de Merlo and Jorge Manuel Theotocópulos, the son of El Greco. The vestry is built like a church, with a chapel to St Jerome decorated with superb paintings by Zurbarán. The vestry behind the altar contains sculpture by La Roldana and nine paintings by Luca Giordano. It is impossible to describe the jeweled robes, chalices, gold-and-silver-embroidered vestments, and other treasures that exist here in such profusion. A unique feature of the monastery is its mudéjar cloister with its open pavilion decorated in brickwork and colored tiles.

Mérida and Badajoz

But this has taken us far east of our north–south route, to which we must now return. Pursuing it from either Trujillo or Cáceres brings us, in eighty-four kilometers (52 miles) from the former or seventy-one from the latter, to the city of Mérida in the province of Badajoz, where more important traces of the Roman epoch remain than in any other place in Spain, including a magnificent theater where classic dramas are still performed at night against a uniquely well-preserved backdrop of Corinthian columns.

Until quite recently, this Roman theater was buried under tilled land. It is twenty-two meters (71 feet) high and seats 4,000 on the partially restored marble tiers. The Archeological Museum is already Spain's most important, but further excavations are in progress.

In addition to this main Roman site, there is a very worn Arch of Trajan, and on the outskirts the high arches of the aqueduct, known locally as Los Milagros (the Miracles), a smaller bridge over the Albarrega and a truly monumental one over the Guadiana.

Forty-three kilometers (27 miles) east at Medellín, Hernán Cortés, the most dashing of the Conquistadores, was born in 1485. Unlike Pizarro, Cortés came from a prominent family and had studied at Salamanca. The pedestal of his equestrian statue bears the names of his heroic exploits: Mexico, Tabasco, Otumba, Tlaxcala. Across the Guadiana, spanned by a 17th-century bridge, rises a mighty castle protected by the square Homage Tower.

Another fourteen kilometers takes us through well-irrigated farmland to Villanueva de la Serena, birthplace of Chile's conqueror, Pedro de Valdivia, commemorated by a bronze statue. Other attractions are the baroque Asunción church, the convents of the Concepción and of the Franciscans, a number of hermitages and the 16th-century Town Hall.

Further east the Guadiana and its tributaries have been dammed up in a series of artificial lakes, which provide excellent fishing, especially at Lake Cijara in the 25,000-hectare National Reserve.

The last station on the trail of the Conquistadores is the birthplace of Nuñez de Balboa and Hernando de Soto. The mansions and dazzling white houses of Jerez de los Caballeros, topped by the slender towers of numerous churches and ringed by ancient walls, lie in a broad plain framed by gentle hills planted with olive and cork trees, on the southern confines of Extremadura.

The charming small town of Zafra with its arcaded squares and white washed houses is one of the oldest in Extremadura and is well worth a short visit or even an overnight stay. Its 15th-century castle was built by Lorenzo de Figueroa and has a notable patio attributed to Juan de Herrera, architect of the Escorial. This splendid building which once gave hospitality to Hernán Cortés, is now a remarkable parador with a well stocked tourist information office in its entrance. Take a stroll through the nearby streets to see the Plaza Grande and Plaza Chica which have been expertly restored and boast several picturesque houses and noble façades.

Way over to the west, close to the border with Portugal, Olivenza is a graceful town showing a strong Portuguese influence in the Manueline style Gothic architecture of its two churches, Santa María Magdalena and Santa María del Castillo, and its early 14th-century castle.

Finally we come to Badajoz, capital of Spain's largest province. Though traces of its important role in Roman and Moorish times are still in evidence, today Badajoz is a rather run-down town which offers little to lure the tourist miles from his route; though should you be passing through on your way to Portugal, it perhaps justifies a visit of an hour or so. It must be said at this stage that its inhabitants are amongst the friendliest and most welcoming in Spain. On the left bank of the Guadiana, it is credited with a continuous, clear summer sky and a short winter. Founded by Romans as Pax Augusta, it reached its greatest importance in Moorish times as capital of the taifa, or kingdom; and the Alcazaba, residence of the Moorish kings, still dominates the walled section from the La Muela hill. The castle's battlements enclose the octagonal Espantaperros (Dog scarer, dog being a Moorish term of abuse for Christians) Tower, and the Archeological Museum within the fortifications.

Just below the fortifications lies the sadly dilapidated Plaza Alta which, until it was allowed to fall into its present state of decay, must have ranked high amongst those picturesque squares for which Spain is famous. It is worth spending a few mintues here if only to reflect on the motive that drives thousands of Spaniards to abandon their traditional homes in favor of the monstrous, faceless apartment blocks which now desecrate the outer limits of so many of their beautiful cities.

Other places to see in the lower town are: the cathedral, in some ways more akin to a fortress than a church, the intimate Plaza de Cervantes, with the writer's statue, the former gateway to the walled city, the Museum of Fine Arts, the Puerta de las Palmas, the bridge across the Guadiana and the lovely gardens that afford sweeping views over Vauban's fortifications.

PRACTICAL INFORMATION FOR THE WESTERN PROVINCES

WHAT TO SEE. Of the cities in this region, Salamanca is incontestably the most important. It is one of the great cities of Spain, and is, indeed, the most frequently visited from Madrid of all the places in this area. Cáceres, an old feudal town, and Trujillo also are interesting as evocations of the past. Mérida is the first center of Spain for Roman remains, with its Roman theater, circus and 64-arch bridge. Lovers of architecture and of stained glass cannot afford to miss León, which might be called the Chartres of Spain, both because its cathedral ranks with the finest in the country and because the stained glass in it, like that of Chartres of the 13th century, is one of the glories of Spain. The cathedral of Plasencia, though interesting, cannot be compared with León, but it possesses an unusual curiosity in its Rabelaisian carved choir stalls. Two monasteries of great interest exist in this area, those of Guadalupe and Yuste, and visits to the shrine of Peña de Francia, near Salamanca, and the sanctuary of La Virgen de la Montaña, at Cáceres, will take you to some exceptionally beautiful heights. Nature lovers are also recommended to seek out Pueblo de Sanabria and Ribadelago de Franco on the shore of a lake. For winter sports, try Puerto de Pajares.

A real "must" in this region is an excursion to the village of La Alberca, 8 km from Peña de Francia (a well-known vantage point) and near to Ciudad Rodrigo. A national monument, its picturesque houses and regional costumes are delightful. Candelario, another picturesque village (4 km southeast of Bejar), is perched 1,125 meters (3,000 ft.) high in the mountains.

HOTELS AND RESTAURANTS

ALBA DE TORMES (Salamanca). *Benedictino* (I), Benedictinas 6, tel. (923) 30 00 00. 44 rooms, parking and garden.

LA ALBERCA (Salamanca). *Las Batuecas* (I), Fuente Canal. A 2-star hotel with 24 rooms, parking and garden.

BADAJOZ. *Gran Hotel Zurbarán* (E), Paseo de Castelar 6, tel. (924) 22 37 41. Excellent modern hotel with pool, close to river and overlooking a pleasant park. *Lisboa* (M), tel. (924) 23 82 00 and *Río* (M), tel. (924) 23 76 00 are both in Avda Elvas across the river. Lisboa is well recommended by a reader and Río has pool. *Conde Duque* (M-I), Muñoz Torrero 27, tel. (924) 22 46 41. Smallish, modern, central. *Cervantes* (I), Tercio 2, tel. (924) 22 51 10. Recommended 3-star hostel in pretty Plaza Cervantes.

Restaurants. *Caballo Blanco* (E), Avda. General Rodrigo 7A, tel. 23 42 21. Modern and elegant in outskirts. *Los Gabrieles* (M), Vicente Barrantes 21, tel. 22 00 01. Recommended by locals. *Manila* (M), corner of Plaza San Francisco. Good restaurant upstairs, downstairs good (I) *tapas* and *platos combinados*. *El Sótano* (M), Virgen de la Soledad 6, tel. 22 00 19. Central and popular.

BEJAR (Salamanca). Near the pass in the Sierra de Bejar. *Colón* (M), Colón 42, tel. (923) 40 06 50. Garden, bar and good low rates.

BENAVENTE (Zamora). *Parador Rey Fernando II de León* (E), tel. (988) 63 03 00. 30 rooms, in an historic building with parking and garden.

CACERES. *Alcántara* (E-M), Avda. Virgen de Guadalupe 14, tel. (927) 22 89 00. 67 rooms. *Extremadura* (E-M), Avda. Virgen de Guadalupe, tel. (927) 22 16 00. 69 rooms, with parking, pool and gardens. *Alvarez* (M), Moret 20, tel. (927) 21 39 00. Friendly oldish hotel right in center with good accommodations; well recommended. *Ara* (M), Juan XXIII 3, tel. (927) 22 39 58. 62 rooms, with bar and parking, good facilities for a 1-star hotel though not right in center.

Restaurants. *Hostería del Comendador* (E-M), Ancha 6, tel. 21 30 12. Located in a palace in the old walled city. *Nuestra Señora de la Montaña* (M), tel. 22 10 58. At the shrine 1 km out of town. Magnificent food and great views. *Figón Eustaquio* (M), Plaza San Juan 14, tel. 21 31 47. Local color, rustic décor.

CIUDAD RODRIGO (Salamanca). *Parador Enrique II* (E-M), Plaza del Castillo 1, tel. (923) 46 01 50. Located in a 15th-century castle, with pleasant garden. 28 rooms. *Conde Rodrigo* (M), Plaza Salvador 7, tel. (923) 46 14 04. Highly recommended by reader.

GUADALUPE (Cáceres). *Parador Zurbarán* (E), Marqués de la Romana 10, tel. (927) 36 70 75. In an old convent, 20 rooms, pool and garden. *Hospedería del Monasterio* (M), Plaza Juan Carlos 1, tel. (927) 36 70 00. Accommodations in the monastery itself, 38 rooms.

Restaurant. *Mesón El Cordero* (I), Convento 11, tel. 36 71 31. Good views and typical décor.

JARANDILLA DE LA VERA (Cáceres). *Parador Carlos V* (E-M), tel. (927) 56 01 17. A late 14th–early-15th-century castle-cum-palace, where Charles V spent 15 months before retiring to the monastery at Yuste.

LEDESMA (Salamanca). *Balneario* (M), tel. (923) 57 02 50. 168 rooms, pool and gardens.

LEON. *San Marcos* (L), Plaza de San Marcos 7, tel. (987) 23 73 00. 258 rooms, in an elegant, magnificent old stone palace. Many amenities. *Conde Luna* (E), Independencia 5, tel. (987) 20 65 12. 154 rooms, with parking, pool, tennis, gardens, bar among its numerous facilities. *Olidén* (E-M), Plaza Santa Domingo 5, tel. (987) 22 75 00. 50 rooms. *Quindos* (M), Avda. José Antonio 24, tel. (987) 23 62 00. 96 rooms. *Ríosol* (M), Avda de Palencia 3, tel. (987) 22 36 50. 141 rooms, bar. *París* (I), Generalísimo 20, tel. (987) 23 86 00. 77 rooms, in historic building; bar.

Restaurants. *Mesón Conde Luna* (E), General Lafuente 1, tel. 21 70 21. *Novelty* (E), Independencia 2, tel. 25 09 90. Elegant and luxurious. *El Aperitivo* (M), Fuero 3, tel. 21 26 33. *La Bodega Regia* (M), Plaza San Martín 8, tel. 23 94 90. Typical local décor. *El Emperador* (M), Santa Nonia 2, tel. 21 71 40. *Los Candiles* (I), Independencia 11, tel. 21 70 73. Comfortable and pleasant. *Casa Pozo* (I), Arco de Animas 3, tel. 22 30 90. Popular with locals and serves good hearty food; pleasant service.

MERIDA (Badajoz). *Parador Vía de la Plata* (E), Plaza Queipo de Llano 3, tel. (924) 30 15 40. 53 rooms, in a magnificent old convent in town center. *Emperatriz* (M), Plaza de España 19, tel. (924) 30 26 40. 41 rooms; in medieval palace. *Motel Las Lomas* (M), on N-V, tel. (924) 30 37 47. 35 rooms. *Texas* (M), on N-V, tel. (924) 30 29 40. 44 rooms.

PLASENCIA (Cáceres). *Alfonso VIII* (E-M), Alfonso VIII 32, tel. (927) 41 02 50. Excellent value; recommended.

PONFERRADA (León). *Hotel Del Temple* (E), Avda. de Portugal 2, tel. (987) 41 00 48. In an historic building, with pool, tennis, bar, and charming décor. *Conde Silva* (M), on the N-VI, tel. (987) 41 04 07. 60 rooms; recommended.

PRADORREY (Leon). *Motel Pradorrey* (E), at km 331 on the N-VI, tel. (987) 61 57 29. Good for overnighting.

SALAMANCA. *Parador Nacional* (E), Teso de la Feria, tel. (923) 22 87 00. A recent parador with 108 rooms. Stands on far side of the Tormes with good views of city. *Gran Hotel* (E), Plaza del Poeta Iglesias 3, tel. (923) 21 35 00. Very comfortable, with plenty of old world charm and a magnificent medieval dining room. *Jardín Regio* (E), 3 km outside, tel. (923) 20 02 50. Many amenities including pool. *Monterrey* (E), Azafranal 21, tel. (923) 21 44 00. Pleasant, old style hotel, very central. *Alfonso X* (M), Toro 64, tel. (923) 21 44 01. Backs on to Monterrey with whom it shares the same management and dining room. *Condal* (M), Santa Eulalia 2, tel. (923) 21 84 00. Good modern hotel, central.

Ceylán (I), Plaza del Peso 5, tel. (923) 21 26 03. *Emperatriz* (I), Compañía 4, tel. (923) 21 92 00. In an historic building near La Clerecía. *Pasaje* (I), Espoz y Mina 11, tel. (923) 21 20 03. Connected to Plaza Mayor via a passage on west side of square.

Restaurants. *Feudal* (E), Plaza Poeta Iglesias 3, tel. 21 35 00. In the Gran Hotel, serves superb meals in old-world setting. *Nuevo Candil* (E), Plaza de la Reina 2, tel. 21 50 58. One of Salamanca's best restaurants; set menu is reasonably priced. *Venecia* (E-M), Plaza del Mercado 5, tel. 21 67 44. Another leading restaurant. *Chez Victor* (E-M), Espoz y Mina 22, tel. 21 31 23. Authentic French cuisine.

El Candil (M), Ruiz Aguilera 10, tel. 21 72 39. A popular, atmospheric bodega dedicated to good eating. Same management as El Nuevo Candil. *El Mesón* (M), Plaza Poeta Iglesias 3, tel. 21 72 22. Typically Castilian décor and cuisine, next to the Gran Hotel. *La Posada* (M), Aire 1, tel. 21 72 51. Excellent restaurant, popular with locals, near Condal hotel. *Río Plata* (M), Plaza del Peso 1, tel. 21 90 05. Small and atmospheric, a good find. *Roma* (I-M), Ruiz Aguilera 8, tel. 21 72 67. Atmospheric with good food and service.

TORO (Zamora). *Juan II* (M), Plaza del Espolón 1, tel. (988) 69 03 00. 42 rooms, pool and garden.

TRUJILLO (Cáceres). *Gran Hotel El Conquistador* (M), tel. (927) 32 01 50. 46 rooms, pool, garden and bar. *Las Cigueñas* (M), tel. (927) 32 06 50. 78 rooms, garden. Both are just out of town on road to Madrid.

Restaurant. *Fonda la Troya* (I) in Plaza Mayor. A real find, belonging to the Spain of yesteryear. Look for the "fonda" sign and go upstairs where granny rules with a stern hand. There is no menu and no set prices—you eat what you're given and pay what she charges but it won't be more than 600 for a 5-course feast with wine. Enormous salads and the best *tortillas* in Spain await you at your table and they're on the house.

VILLAFRANCA DEL BIERZO (León). *Parador Nacional* (E), Avda. de Calvo Sotelo, tel. (987) 54 01 75. A modern parador with 40 rooms, parking and garden.

ZAFRA (Badajoz). *Parador Hernán Cortés* (E), Plaza Corazón de María, tel. (924) 55 02 00. Located in a majestic fortified palace, one of the most remarkable paradores in Extremadura; built between 1437 and 1443. Hernán Cortés, conqueror of Mexico, lived here before leaving for the New World. 28 rooms, with pool and gardens; in center of town. *Huerta Honda* (E-M), Avda. López Asma, tel. (924) 55 08 00. Modern hotel built in attractive Andalusian style with atmospheric mesón type restaurant. Central and near the parador.

ZAMORA. *Parador Condes de Alba y Aliste* (E), Plaza de Cánovas, tel. (988) 51 44 97. One of the most magnificent paradores in Spain. Located in the old part of town in a converted medieval palace which still contains many antiques. 19 rooms, with garden and pool. *Dos Infantas* (E-M), Cortinas de San Miguel 3, tel. (988) 51 28 75. Modern, with 58 rooms. *Cuatro Naciones* (M), Avda. José Antonio 7, tel. (988) 51 22 75. Modern, rather antiseptic hotel, but clean and comfortable. *Rey Don Sancho* (M), 2.5 km out on N630, tel. (988) 52 34 00. 76 rooms.

Restaurants. *Paris* (E-M), Avda. de Portugal 14, tel. 51 43 24. Elegant, good food. *La Rueda* (M), Ronda de la Feria 19, tel. 52 77 91. On edge of town on the road to León; a rustic-style meson. *Rey Don Sancho* (M). A modern café and restaurant in the Avenidas Park. *Valderrey* (M-I), Benavente 7. Bar serving good tapas, and a pleasant restaurant; in street between Santa Clara and San Torcuato.

 USEFUL ADDRESSES. Tourist Offices. **Badajoz;** Pasaje de San Juan 2, behind the City Hall in Plaza de España. **Cáceres;** Plaza Mayor. **Ciudad Rodrigo;** Puerta de Amayuelas 6. **León;** Plaza de Regla 3. **Merida;** Teniente Coronel Asensio 9. **Salamanca;** Gran Vía 11, and there is a city tourist office information booth in the Plaza Mayor. **Trujillo;** Plaza Mayor. **Zamora;** Santa Clara 20.

CAR HIRE. León; *Hertz,* Rodríguez del Valle 12, *Ital,* Condesa Sagasta 36. **Salamanca;** *Hertz,* Avda de Portugal 131 and at the station.

SPAIN'S ATLANTIC COAST

Basques, Asturians and Galicians

The northern coast of Spain, that rectangle that looks west across the open Atlantic and north across the Bay of Biscay, is familiar to many tourists. Still, only a small proportion penetrate all the way to the western coast, but the Basque country, the section closest to France, contiguous with that other land of the Basques across the border, has been visited by hundreds of thousands who have never traveled more deeply into the Iberian Peninsula.

This is the result of geographical position, for vacationists without time to cover the comparatively great distances of Spain can swoop across the French border and make the swing around a part of the coast region, visit the Basque country in a few days, and enjoy San Sebastián for a weekend.

Considering its size, there is unusual variety in Atlantic Spain, which includes at least four quite distinct regions: Vascongadas, the Basque country, made up of the three provinces of Guipúzcoa, Vizcaya and Alava; Santander, now officially known as Cantabria, politically and historically a part of Old Castile; Asturias with the single province of Oviedo; and Galicia, which is composed of four provinces, Lugo, La Coruña, Pontevedra and Orense.

Exploring the Atlantic Coast

Although heavily populated and full of individuality, Vascongadas is a tiny region—only some 145 km (90 miles) from east to west and 72 from north to south—and communications are amongst the best in Spain.

Here we should just mention the current terrorist situation in the Basque Country. Bombings, kidnappings and assassinations carried out by ETA, the Basque separatist movement, are fairly frequent throughout the region, but they are directed at the police, banks and prominent businessmen and not normally against tourists. The danger to tourists would seem to be minimal.

Let us briefly sum up what the area has to offer that cannot always be found in other parts of Spain.

Firstly, in San Sebastián, there is a city expressly created for the tourist, with every kind of comfort for a pleasant summer holiday and boasting two of the best beaches in Spain. Because it is only a few kilometers from the French frontier, it is a place that is used to the peculiar habits of foreigners and where foreigners, therefore, can feel at home. Secondly, the Basque country, with its northern sea, temperate heat, and rugged coast. Thirdly, the rough and ready Basque himself, with his passion for all forms of outdoor sport, large meals, hard liquor and hard work, is far easier for the Anglo-Saxon to understand than the proud, passionate, but austere Castilian.

No one knows for certain the origin of the Basque race and language, but it is believed that the Basques are the descendants of the original Iberians, who inhabited the peninsula even before the Celts arrived some 3,500 years ago, and were driven by successive waves of conquerors, Phoenician, Roman, Visigoth and Moorish, into the fastnesses of the Pyrenees and, by one of those inexplicable twists of history, somehow survived as a distinct entity. In any case, they are not Spaniards in appearance, origin, character or language.

In appearance they tend to be short, wide of shoulder and hip, barrel-chested, and with the typical mountaineer's short, sturdy legs. They are huge eaters and drinkers, hard working, and shrewd, superb natural singers like the Welsh, and talk a language which, to the novice, sounds as if it is composed exclusively of the letters U, G, LL, RR, TH and ZZ.

Guipúzcoa

From the French frontier onward, it's an uninterrupted chain of superb beaches, of which the most famous is San Sebastián. San Sebastián is only 20 kilometers from the French frontier at the River Bidasoa, which is spanned by the bridge that links Spanish Irún with French Hendaye.

It is a pleasant city, designed to provide the tourist with an ideal setting in which to pass the summer months. It is never excessively hot and the streets are wide, and fresh with the breezes of Biscay. There are luxurious shops, hotels, restaurants, bars and nightclubs, and all the sightseeing is within a day's run. This is one of those cities which amply lives up to its long reputation for a lovely setting and really excellent amenities.

For serious sightseeing we can recommend the magnificent collection in the San Telmo Museum, or a trip to Hernani, an attractive town where the church shelters some beautiful (and little-known) gilded wood carvings. Also of interest are two old churches—the exuberantly baroque Santa María and the 16th-century San Vicente, both in the old town, between Mount Urgull and the Alameda.

But before reaching San Sebastián, shortly after Irún, it's worth a detour to Fuenterrabía to see its medieval citadel and castle of Charles V, now a parador, and interesting harbor.

Other places of interest along the coast, not far from San Sebastián, are Deva, with a fine bathing beach, the charming little ports of Zumaya and Guetaria. Nearby Zarauz is a most pleasant and attractive bathing resort. To the west are the picturesque fishing villages of Ondárroa, Lequeitio and Bermeo, while inland, at Loyola, is the austere monastery and baroque church built around the house where St Ignatius, founder of the Jesuit order, was born in 1491.

There are many other places worth stopping at. The modern basilica of Aránzazu fits in ideally with the wooded hills surrounding it. At Azpeitia, in the mountains, you will see some very pretty houses. There is also Elgoibar, which has a lovely gateway, the manor house of Val de l'Espina at Ermua, the church of Santa María de Galdácano, Vergara, Azcoitia, Oñate and a great many other places.

One word of warning, however: rain is frequent all the year round on this north coast!

Vitoria

Vitoria (137,000 inhabitants), capital of the province of Alava, is
only sixty-five kilometers (40 miles) by road from Bilbao, and 116 from
San Sebastián via Tolosa. Although only some fifty-six kilometers in a
direct line from the coast at its nearest point, Vitoria is 536 meters
(1,760 feet) above sea level. The gray stone houses with high bay
windows, combined with a tendency to Scotch mists, call to mind an
English country town, more than anything Spanish.

It is an interesting little town set in beautiful country. In the town
hall you can still see the special knife—the Machete Vitoriano—over
which the Attorney General must place his hands while he is sworn
into office, this being a reminder that he will be beheaded if he fails to
give satisfaction!

There are Van Dyck and Rubens paintings side by side with a
12th-century Virgin in the cathedral of Santa María, but of greater
importance to the locals is the jasper White Virgin of Vitoria in the
12th-century church of San Miguel. She is carried through the streets
in procession, with much bell ringing followed by fireworks, on August
12. The high altar before which she stands is unusually beautiful.

It was the king of Navarre, Sancho VI, who founded Vitoria in 1181
on the site of the ancient city of Gazteiz (to which name it has now
reverted amongst Basque-speaking people). The old and the new towns
are quite separate. The Provincial Museum contains canvases by Ribera and Alonso Cano, together with some interesting modern works.
The former Plaza Vieja has become the Plaza de la Vírgen Blanca.
There is a monument there to commemorate the terrible defeat inflicted
by Wellington on Napoleon's forces on June 21 1813, just outside the
town. The famous Machete used to be preserved inside a niche in the
apse of San Miguel. The Plaza del Machete backs on to the church. In
that square stands the palace of Villasuso, displaying a very fine coat
of arms.

It is worth taking some short side trips into the countryside around
Vitoria as much of the real charm of Vascongadas lies in its ancient
mountain villages, and any road inland will take you through half a
dozen that have not changed materially since Columbus borrowed the
money from great Queen Isabella to discover America, and thus
inaugurate the European dollar gap.

Bilbao

Bilbao, with a population of something under half a million, is the
largest city in the Basque country, and became its administrative capi-

tal during the Civil War. It lies some eleven kilometers from the sea, but ships of 4,000 tons can navigate the River Nervión to the city docks.

Iron ore is mined in the locality, and the largest blast furnaces in Spain are to be found around Bilbao. It is an industrial center and port far more than a tourist resort, but in the summer months the luxurious villas of the residential suburbs of Santurce and Portugalete fill with guests from Madrid.

Bilbao is relatively modern, being founded as late (for Spain) as the year 1300 and is less overpoweringly endowed with ancient buildings than is commonly the case in Spain. However, art is not lacking here; do not fail to visit the quite exceptional collection of Grecos, Riberas and Goyas in the Museo de Bellas Artes, in the park halfway up the Gran Vía—particularly the Goyas.

If archeology interests you, you might visit from Bilbao the prehistoric caves of Basondo. If, on the other hand, you are an enthusiastic oyster eater, then steal off by yourself to the little fishing village of Plencia, twenty-nine kilometers from Bilbao where, as well as enjoying the oysters, you can see the 13th-century castle of Butrón. Then there is Pedernales Bay (with the Chacharramendi Islands) backed by Mount Urguiola, which is crowned with old palaces. Bilbao's most frequented beach is at Algorta.

Guernica, which was completely rebuilt after the Civil War and has been immortalized by Picasso's portrayal of its sufferings, is about thirty-two kilometers to the northeast of Bilbao. The countryside you pass through is wooded with a sprinkling of meadows; it is like a miniature Switzerland, except around Amorebieta, which is spoilt by industrialization.

Other musts near here are Mundaca and the extraordinary panorama of the Nervión estuary, especially at low tide. Most important of all, you should go on north a few more miles till you reach Bermeo, the prettiest fishing port of Spain. You see houses set in tiers on the steep cliff, washing drying at the windows and the fleet of gaily colored fishing boats, all neatly lined up in the harbor. It is a painter's dream. But remember that it is advisable to go there before September 15th. The fishermen depart after that date for their annual season of deep-sea fishing and the three docks are then pathetically empty.

You can return to Bilbao by way of Mungula and Miranda, an area of woods and mountains and, alas, factories. From a tourist's point of view, the scenery is not striking. Most cars turn off to the right on reaching Mungula and return to the coast.

While we are northwest of Bilbao, drive past the castle of Santurce, just to sample the delicious grilled sardines, or *sardinas asadas,* in the street, before going on to Castro Urdiales. The latter is a compulsory stop and is the oldest town on the coast. The Vikings destroyed the ancient Flaviobriga, which dated from Roman times. A fortress was built, and a fort was also erected in the little cove of Urdiales, where the lighthouse dominates the castle. Whatever you do, be sure to visit Nuestra Señora de la Anunciación, a splendid ocher-colored building. When Cesare Borgia escaped in 1506 from the castle of La Mota at Medina del Campo, where he had been held captive, it was in Castro Urdiales that he found a temporary refuge.

At Laredo, which has a curious 13th-century church, Charles V used to come and worship after his abdication.

Santander (Cantabria)

If you are looking for a summer vacation with swimming, fishing, hunting, tennis, golf, yachting and all the other pastimes dear to the heart of a sportsman, you will find it in the province of Santander, now officially designated Cantabria. Situated in the north of Spain, its shoreline bordering the Bay of Biscay (the only province belonging to Castile with an outlet to the sea) it is dotted with bathing beaches. The terrain of the province varies from warm, fertile valleys rich in fruit trees to the snow-capped mountains of the Picos de Europa. During the season there is good skiing and other winter sports.

Mention should be made of the spas of this region, which have been little publicized and offer relief from afflictions ranging from arthritis to respiratory troubles. Many of them are only a short distance from the city of Santander. Solares is twenty-four kilometers away. Its waters are especially beneficial for stomach disorders.

The province of Santander is also rich in small villages, each with its own personality, and, of course, there are the prehistoric paintings discovered in the caves of Altamira in 1875. Much of the folklore of this region has been lost, but romerías are still held locally.

The city of Santander is first mentioned historically only in 1068, when it was called the Port of San Emeterio. Later, the city was converted into a fortress, and given an arsenal and shipbuilding yards. Its commerce flourished in medieval times, especially after the discovery of America, and its ships contributed to the reconquest of Seville. In recent times, two catastrophies, which necessitated almost total reconstruction, have made Santander perhaps the most modern Spanish city today, one practically devoid of ancient remains. (The only significant one is the 12th-century crypt of the former cathedral.) The atmosphere of Santander is distinctly nautical, with its docks and old fishing quarter.

Santander has three excellent beaches: Magdalena, nearest to town; El Sardinero, smartest, equipped with good hotels and all nautical paraphernalia for holidaymakers; and finally Mataleñas, near the beautiful camping site of Bellavista.

Prehistoric Altamira

Even for those not historically or artistically minded, a visit to the caves of Altamira is a must, just as a reminder that there were people living over 13,000 years ago who were advanced enough to make colored pigments and draw amazing pictures of the animals that existed at that time. These decorations were made when most of the northern part of Europe was still in the glacial period, with only a small strip of land visible in Spain between the mountains and the Bay of Biscay. Men dressed in skins, and retired to caves at night to protect themselves from the wild beasts. Even then, a desire for beauty burned in the breasts of these prehistoric nomads, expressing itself in the ornamentation of their homes. These artists, with only charcoal, ocher and hematites, were able to make every shade of yellow, red and gray.

The first cave was discovered in 1875, another in 1928. Perhaps the most expressive observation about them was made by a Frenchman who called them "The Sistine Chapel of the Ice Age." The caves are twenty-nine kilometers west of Santander and three kilometers from Santillana del Mar. But . . . we are afraid there has to be a note at this point.

The huge crowds of people that have flocked to the caves over the last few years have seriously endangered the paintings. The problems of atmospheric control, dust, general wear and tear on the rock surfaces and a whole host of other factors totally inimical to the safety of these enormously important works, forced the authorities to close the caves completely from 1977 to early 1982. It now appears, however, that the condition of the paintings has improved as a result of this closure. But at the time of writing it was still uncertain whether the caves would be opened to tourists on a regular basis, so we would advise readers to contact the Spanish National Tourist Office for details regarding the latest situation. There are, however, three caves at nearby Santillana del Mar which are open to the public, as well as the caves at Puente Viesgo, twenty-three kilometers away.

Santillana del Mar

Santillana del Mar is an old village that would still be fast asleep if it were not for these prehistoric discoveries. Nothing has happened here since the 15th century, yet it still remains fresh and lovely. Some of the finer houses are adorned with heraldic coats of arms and emblems, some quite ancient and illustrious. Be sure to visit the 12th-century collegiate church, the most important Romanesque building in the region. The tomb of Santa Juliana (a corrupt form of whose name the town bears) stands in its center. In summer, concerts are given in the exquisite cloisters. The former palace of Carreda Bracho has been turned into a really delightful parador. Santillana del Mar is an adorable little village. The inhabitants add mischievously, "This is the town of the three lies. It has never been holy (*santa*) and it is not flat (*llana*) and the sea (*mar*) is six kilometers away!"

There is scarcely a village or town in the province of Santander that is not distinctive from some point of view. Mention can be made of only a few. Comillas, a small port with two beaches and a pontifical university, Noja with the beach of La Isla, Reinosa, near the Romanesque churches of Bolmir and Retorillo, Potes with beautiful scenery and a medieval tower, Limpias, for its famous crucifix.

Here in the inaccessible mountains of northern Spain, the Christian Spaniards took refuge from the Moors in the 8th century and began the reconquest of Spain. This range spreads over three provinces; the highest peaks are under perpetual snow. They are a challenge to mountain climbers, who have opened many clubs in the vicinity, where guides are available. From the Refugio de Aliva on the Picos, excursions are organized all year.

Asturias and Galicia

Finisterre—world's end—was Galicia's name until the discovery of America, for west of it lay nothing but the ocean, and if you were so foolish as to sail on, you could expect to slip over the edge and plunge down into the abyss.

Along the coast of Asturias and Galicia, the sea is often rough and cold (though the deep estuaries are sheltered and calm), and the landscape inland is as green and lush as southern Ireland. Here you find barren mountains, variable skies, and ancient, gray stone towns nestling among tall trees.

Although some visitors may find the northwest insufficiently Spanish to fit in with their previous notions, in fact it is far more Spanish than is typically Moorish Andalusia. For it was precisely to Asturias that the most doggedly independent of the Spanish people withdrew when the Moorish invasion in the 8th century swept over their country and on, almost to the gates of Paris.

Grimly barricaded behind mountains that rise from 1,525 to 2,440 meters (5,000 to 8,000 feet), they learned through hunger, cold and hardship the spiritual austerity and physical courage that are still such marked national characteristics. Pelayo, who was descended from the Goths, swore an oath with other princes to fight against the Moslem invaders. They won their first victory in 718; the Reconquista had begun. It was to end 800 years later with the capture of Granada.

In a cave near Covadonga, you will find the sarcophagus of the valiant knight and the statue of the Virgin, who assisted in the defeat of the Moors. Two other excursions can be recommended, one to Cangas de Onís and including the gorge of the Sella, the Roman bridge and the wonderful *corniche* of Panes (spoilt to some extent, unfortunately, by poor road conditions), and the other to the Lake of Enol, where the traveler can gaze from the Mirador de la Reina at one of the loveliest views in the world.

Asturias was never conquered and Galicia was early liberated from the Moors. Although neighboring León was the setting for desperate advances and retreats for a century and a half, it then became the Christian capital of Spain, remaining so until it gave place to Burgos. Thus, the northwest's claim to be more truly Spanish than any other part of Spain seems to be historically justified.

Although both provinces are primarily agricultural, the coal mines of Asturias are of vital importance to the economy of the whole country, while the great Galician port of El Ferrol is Spain's chief naval and shipbuilding base. The ports of La Coruña and Vigo, also in Galicia, and the smaller Asturian port and seaside resort of Gijón are all thriving commercial towns, but once away from the sea, these are provinces with fat cattle, excellent salmon and trout fishing, pine-clad hills, and occasional snow-capped mountains.

Oviedo

Oviedo, the capital of Asturias, was Spain's capital for a while in the 8th century, and possesses a fine Gothic cathedral containing the cross that was carried into the Battle of Covadonga by Don Pelayo; it was later covered with gold and precious stones.

The cathedral is linked with the history and foundation of the city; there was a hermitage there from the beginning of the 8th century. The present building which belongs to a later date (14th to 16th century), is one of the most representative examples of Gothic art. The Chapel of the Chaste King was intended as a royal burial place. Its stairway, the Cámara Santa, is famous.

Several of the buildings in Oviedo are pre-Romanesque in style; this is also called *Ramiresque,* after King Ramiro I, who originated it. This pre-Romanesque style is very austere and is found nowhere else. At the beginning of the 9th century, only the capital, Oviedo, was enriched by splendid buildings. But only a century later the countryside round about and the small town became fired with ambition to do things on a grand scale.

The façade of the university was built in 1598. Inside you can see paintings by Ribera and Zurbarán. There is also an *Apostolado* by El Greco in the ducal palace of El Parque.

The inland area between Llanes, Gijón and Oviedo is interesting. Places to visit are San Antolín de Bedón (monastery dating from the 10th and 11th centuries), Santiago de Gobiendes, Priesca (San Salvador, consecrated in the 10th century), Villaviciosa at the head of the Ría, San Juan de Amandi (12th century), San Salvador de Valdediós (9th century), Naranco with its Santa María (formerly a palace, only later converted into a church) and San Miguel de Lillo.

Gijón, which is nearly as big as Oviedo, is an industrial town and at the same time a port (the new port is at El Musel, a few kilometers farther on), a university town and a holiday resort. The large beach of San Lorenzo has excellent bathing and an attractive esplanade. There are certainly plenty of opportunities for taking a dip and acquiring a tan on the coast of Asturias. From Llanes to Salinas, with Ribadesella and Colunga lying in between, summer visitors will find everything they need for an enjoyable holiday.

Luarca has a savage beauty which distinguishes it from its rivals, a splendid beach, and the prettiest little fishing port you can imagine. Cudillero and Navía will not disappoint you, either. The last little Asturian town, Castropol, is perched on a promontory.

Before setting out to explore the surrounding province, spend half an hour in the offices of the Spanish Tourist Department to learn about the latest variations in local bus and train communications, for these change considerably, with the time of year. Ask how best to visit Cangas de Onís, nearby Covadonga, Cabo (cape) de Peñas, and the mountain lake of Enol, or the fine bathing beaches of Ribadesella.

Discovering Galicia

Galicia, consisting of the four provinces of Lugo, La Coruña (Corunna to the British, and no nonsense with the Spanish 'ñ'), Pontevedra and Orense, is considerably larger than Asturias, and, consequently, unless you have a car, requires more planning in order to explore it comfortably on a short holiday.

One road from Castropol skirts the inlet to Ribadeo, then to Mondoñedo, a somber town with an imposing cathedral. It dates from the 13th century, but as usual a great number of alterations were carried out in the 16th and 18th centuries. The road then bends round to the west toward Villalba, but at Mondoñedo you can return to the Lugo road, via Ríotorto. This allows you to stop at Meira, where you will find the pure lines of Cistercian architecture at the monastery, originally under Benedictine supervision. (From the 12th century, it came under the rule of Clairvaux.) The church (13th century) is very beautiful.

Except for a Napoleonic interlude, Lugo has rested in relative peace for the last 1,000 years, and stands today, still surrounded by well over a kilometer of high medieval walls, perched on a hill overlooking the River Miño. There is quite a wide road around the walls and about fifty semi-circular towers. A surprise awaits you in the cathedral—the passages between the naves are walled up, but the choir, at least, is surrounded by glass. The chapels all around are overloaded with a lavish display of rococo bric-à-brac.

The 14th-century Santo Domingo is one more of the countless beautiful churches that are so thickly spread over the whole country. Near the bridge over the Miño are the ruins of Roman sulphur baths, where the medicinal water still gushes out at 43°C (110°F).

It is ninety-seven kilometers (60 miles) from Lugo to La Coruña, and the road (N-VI) runs through pleasant, hilly country. Your trip will take you from 483 meters (1,584 feet) above sea level, the altitude of Lugo, all the way down to zero, since La Coruña is on the coast.

The tourist who is anxious to see everything will take N540 from Lugo, then C547 to Mellid, taking a look at the magnificent ruins of the ancient and imposing monastery of Sobrado de los Monjes (782), twenty-four kilometers north of Mellid. It was immense at one time and was *the* leading religious authority in Galicia. It was, of course, Cistercian. The present church dates from the 17th century. It is the cloisters that will hold the visitor's attention; they are abandoned and are overgrown with a romantic covering of weeds, filling one with nostalgia and an awareness of history. Few Galician churches are as beautiful as the church at Sobrado. The sacristy deserves a glance and the kitchen is just as it was in the 15th century.

Betanzos, nearer the coast, has retained much of its medieval character and is a very interesting town. Fernán Pérez de Andrade, who lived in the 14th century, was undoubtedly a man of good taste, for he has left a splendid palace for us to visit.

As you have to pass through Betanzos if you are going to La Coruña, you might as well go to nearby El Ferrol del Caudillo. General Franco was born there, and it would appear to be one of the finest natural harbors in the world. There is not much we can say about it, except that the parador is very comfortable. It is the region itself that is charming, with its white-washed houses; the windows are framed in dark gray stone and the woodwork is painted green, or sometimes blue. The old houses often have a glazed balcony or loggia with small panes of glass added on to the front.

North of El Ferrol, you may wish to explore one of the least frequented corners of Spain, where lonely beaches, often made up of "black" sand, stretch eastward toward Asturias. Picturesque Vivero and the smaller fishing villages of Valdoviño, Cedeira and Ortigueira all have their simple hostels and *fondas*.

La Coruña

An important port, especially for oil shipments, La Coruña is a mixture of modern and historical buildings—with the modern not always in the best of taste. The wooden balconies of the old houses with their small panes of glass are a distinctive feature. It can also boast a fair number of restaurants offering the fine seafood for which Galicia is famous. And, indeed, this city (of 190,000 inhabitants) does have a history. Romans, Visigoths, Arabs, Charles V and Napoleon—as you will see later on—have all left some trace behind them. So have the sardines and the canneries which have made it rich. There is a fine, large harbor. A few centuries ago, it witnessed the preparation of the most powerful fleet of that era. Philip II was so proud of it that he christened it the Invincible Armada, but it never returned. It was defeated by a storm and by the fire-ship plan thought up by an ingenious Englishman, Sir Francis Drake, possibly while bowling.

La Coruña is built on a narrow point jutting out into the Atlantic, and is surrounded by sandy bathing beaches. The showpiece is its Hercules' Tower, which dates from the time of Breogan and was restored by the Emperor Trajan—himself, by the way, born in Spain—for use as a lighthouse. Breogan was a Celtic chieftain, who erected the tower in celebration of his tribe's removal to Ireland.

The tomb of Sir John Moore, the British general who was fatally wounded in his retreat to La Coruña before Napoleon's Marshals Soult and Ney, is in the beautiful San Carlos gardens.

Those with a taste for sightseeing may enjoy a visit to the Convent of San Francisco, where King Charles I of Spain called a meeting of the Cortes in 1520 in order to raise the funds necessary to ensure his election as the Holy Roman Emperor, under his better-known title of Charles V.

Santiago de Compostela

The showpiece of Galicia is undoubtedly Santiago de Compostela, the holy city, one of the three chief places of pilgrimage of the Middle Ages.

It is possible to follow the pilgrims' route, the Camino de Santiago, down from France, across the north of Spain to Santiago. It is, in fact, a fascinating exercise in medieval tourism. Unbelievable as it may seem,

The Cathedral of Santiago de Compostela, for long one of the major pilgrim destinations of Europe

The Palacio Almudaina,
in Palma, a favorite meeting
place that has been carefully
reconstructed

**Fresh morning vegetables—
the "Flea Market" in Palma,
Majorca**

The Patio de los Leones in the
Alhambra, one of the chief
masterpieces of Moorish Spain

the crowds that "took the cockleshell" and made the journey sometimes numbered as many as two million in a year.

Some guidebooks generously allow the traveler three hours to explore Santiago de Compostela. Setting aside sentiment, faith and the
ever-present possibility of falling in love with this very beautiful city,
one can acquire a really lasting impression by merely visiting the enormous rectangular Plaza del Obradoiro, magnificently framed by the
cathedral, the Hostal de los Reyes Católicos, the San Jerónimo College
and the Rajoy Palace, now the city hall. By stretching things, you could
add a quarter of an hour for a stroll through the city and another fifteen
minutes for a short walk in the park known as Paseo de Herradura,
which offers a superb view of the city.

On the other hand, one could well spend a day in and around the
great cathedral and it would be a day worth remembering. The west
entrance, known as the Fachada del Obradoiro, approached from the
plaza by a quadruple flight of steps, is a wonderfully ornate masterpiece. The south door, or Puerta de las Platerías, Silversmiths' Door,
dating from 1104, faces the Casa del Cabildo and is partly concealed
by the Clock Tower, but you can see that the huge corbel on the left
is in the form of a cockleshell—the sign of St. James the Apostle which
all pilgrims who visited here carried. The marble outer shafts are
carved with tiers of figures in a bewildering confusion. At the east end
is the Puerta Santa (1611), open only when St. James's Day falls on a
Sunday. The north door is less notable.

When the visitor enters the cathedral (from the front, or Obradoiro,
side), he is struck by the gigantic but harmonious proportions of the
three naves. Walk under the Pórtico de la Gloria, the work of the famed
Maestro Mateo and one of the crowning achievements of 12th-century
sculpture. In the crypt beneath the Capilla Mayor, a silver urn contains
the remains of the Apostle, and his two disciples, St. Theodore and St.
Athanasius. The *botafumeiro*, normally kept in the library, is the large
censer which is lit on special occasions and, despite its great weight,
hung from the roof and sent swinging over the heads of the congrega-
tion. It takes six men to keep it in motion.

Next to the cathedral is the Archbishop's Palace, one of the most
beautiful to be found even in this land of ancient palaces. The town is
ringed with historic monasteries, churches and pilgrims' hostels.

The feast day of St. James, July 25, is Santiago de Compostela's big
moment, but a moment that begins the night before and that continues
for a week. This is the time to come (making sure you have hotel
accommodation first), if you want to participate. However, it is distinctly not the time to come if you want to be able to move leisurely
about the cathedral and along the arcaded streets of the ancient city.

The visit is now over for hurried travelers. But others might be interested in two monuments left from the 6th century: the Church of San Felix de Solovo, the oldest in Santiago (for it pre-dates the discovery of the Apostle's remains), which was rebuilt in the 12th century; and the San Martín Pinario Monastery (599). On Plaza Quintana facing the cathedral, there is the immense bare wall of San Pelayo de Ante-Altares. To its left stand two charming old houses, of which one, the baroque Casa de la Parra, is famous.

Tradition has it that Saint Francis of Assisi himself founded the monastery that bears his name. After seeing this, to do a thorough job, you might stroll along Rua del Villar (to glance at the Casa del Déan) and Rua Nova; then stop for a moment in front of the portal of Los Canónigos, and, on Plaza de Platerías, in front of the imaginative delirium of the baroque decoration displayed by the Casa del Cabildo.

If you are lucky enough to be staying overnight, be prepared for the town to change into a colorful, fascinating maelstrom as darkness falls. Like many other Spanish towns, Santiago has a character all its own, and it comes roaring out at night.

At the Gates of Portugal

To the south of Santiago, the indentations along the Atlantic coast become more and more marked. There is a succession of deep inlets, called *rías,* and estuaries that seem to go on forever. These are the lush green fjords, where the air smells of iodine and salt. It is a region of delightful houses and courteous people.

After Santiago, Pontevedra, fifty-six kilometers south, has to be an anticlimax. Though it dates back to Roman times and is rich in antiquities, with a fine 16th-century church, Santa María la Mayor, the town is not particularly interesting. Nonetheless, the city has some charming old sections to it, and its historical museum is well worth a visit. A stroll through the ancient streets surrounding the museum can be most rewarding. There is, of course, the doorway of Santa María la Mayor made of glittering gray granite. And there are the ruins of an ancient cloister all covered in greenery. Your main memory is of the extremely odd contours of the Peregrina chapel. Pontevedra is notable chiefly for its beautiful position at the head of the Ría, a deep bay cutting far into the land.

It is from Pontevedra, by a corniche road that offers some of the most beautiful coastal scenery in Spain, that one reaches the resort paradise of the island of La Toja, with its balmy climate, fine bathing, and many mineral springs. There are a great many beaches along the way. In the villages, you come past old *pazos* or palaces and seigniorial mansions, especially in Villagarcía and Cambados. Also notice the traditional *hórreos* on each property, where farmers formerly stored their grain, looking like boxes supported on six stone pillars, with the inevitable cross on each side of the roof. On the Ría, you will see a strange type of craft—like a raft with a hut on it—moored to the bottom by means of a cage made of stakes. These are mussel beds. On the island of La Toja there are three hotels, one of them a famous deluxe resort, and a little bit of everything else besides, including gardens, cafés, beaches, minigolf, a casino and pigeon shooting—in fact, everything that man has devised for his vacation happiness. The light is magnificent and there is one scene you should not miss—the fisherman walking on the waters at low tide, pushing his boat with his hands.

There are two monasteries to see on the way—the monastery of Poyo, which is almost on the outskirts of Pontevedra on the road to La Toja, and the monastery at Arménteira, a little farther away, beyond Combarro.

Little remains of the first one, which is Benedictine. The present church dates from the 16th century and the cloister from the 18th. But the trip is particularly worth making for the wonderful view you get of the Ría and also for the sake of the choirs which can be heard there on Saturday evenings. The building occupied by the Galician novices stands beside the church. (Remember that women are forbidden to enter.)

The second monastery, at Armenteira, is Cistercian, and dates back to 1162. It is long abandoned, but its magnificent Romanesque architecture, including church, cloisters and monkish dependencies, has now been tastefully restored.

Vigo

The thriving port of Vigo is twenty-seven kilometers south of Pontevedra, and is one of the best places in Galicia to choose as a holiday center—particularly for visitors not possessing a car. From Vigo, there are excellent bus communications and you can cross the wide bay by ferry to Cangas de Morrazo, Santa Tecla and the Portuguese frontier.

You seldom see a port so miraculously endowed by nature as that of Vigo. A series of islets defends the entrance to the deep roadstead. Here again, we come across the name of Sir Francis Drake, who captured and plundered the town so prettily built in the form of an amphitheater. As a result of the Franco-Spanish differences with Britain during the war of the Spanish Succession, legend says the sea bed here is covered with a layer of gold. A British squadron attacked a convoy, heavily laden with treasure from America, sending all its ships to the bottom.

A stay in Vigo is pleasant and restful. There are no historical monuments to visit and the tourist can relax. But it is worth going up to the Castro or fortress, from where you can get a magnificent panoramic view of the city.

Orense

Orense, the most distant from La Coruña of the four provincial capitals of Galicia is, like Lugo, of Roman origin, and contains excellent thermal springs.

Orense's name comes from *oro* (gold), not the gold from the New World which was both a blessing and a curse to Spain, but the gold from the Sil, that was panned there. It is a more modest town today but you can nevertheless spend a pleasant hour or two strolling through the streets of the old town. The cathedral, unfortunately, is stifled by the walls of the houses surrounding it. There you can see a fairly successful replica of the Door of Glory in Santiago, but this one is called the Door of Paradise. Calvo Sotelo whose murder triggered off the Civil War in 1936, represented Orense in the Spanish parliament.

South of Orense is Celanova, with its extraordinary monastery of San Salvador, which is Benedictine and goes back to the 10th century. All that remains of it is the Chapel of San Miguel, a unique example of the Mozarabic style in Spain that has survived intact.

And there is the inevitable Cistercian monastery—Santa María la Real de Osera is about sixty-four kilometers away. The original buildings were almost entirely destroyed by fire in 1552. The new buildings are in Renaissance and baroque styles. The chapter house is the part to visit in particular.

Go and see it even if you have had a surfeit of churches and monasteries—go and see it for the sheer pleasure of driving through the delightful Galician countryside. You may have seen the grain storehouses in Asturias, perched high on pillars. Here you will see the *hórreos*. They are smaller and more elongated—curious structures, sometimes very old and worm-eaten. There they stand beside the houses, each one like a sarcophagus piously preserved by the head of the family. And yet, all they contain is maize. There are many forests of pine and eucalyptus and accompanying sawmills. And in Galicia you will see a sight that no longer exists anywhere else in Spain, not even in Andalusia, for here the women toiling in the fields, are clad from head to toe in black peasant garb, with long flowing skirts and thick knitted stockings; a scene more reminiscent of the 19th than late-20th century. But, however attractive the countryside, the traveler is reluctant to leave Galicia for yet another reason—the cooking here is the best in Spain.

PRACTICAL INFORMATION FOR THE ATLANTIC COAST

WHAT TO SEE. The three great attractions of this area are the beautiful medieval town of Santillana del Mar; Santiago de Compostela, the great medieval pilgrimage center, where Spain's patron saint, St. James the Apostle, is buried in one of Spain's greatest cathedrals; and San Sebastián, the top playground of the north. There is also one of those quieter playground paradises of the type known only to the few in this part of Spain—the firths and fjords (*rías*). There is a whole cluster of spas, notably Solares, in the Santander region. This is an area that offers much to the art lover, especially those who like Romanesque architecture and medieval sculpture, not to mention the glories of Santiago de Compostela and Santillana. There are some paintings in San Sebastián and Bilbao, some wood carvings at Hernani, near San Sebastián, and a 13th-century castle at Butrón, near Bilbao. Otherwise, the chief attractions of the regions are its sports. Nature lovers should visit Fuente Dé in the Picos de Europa, which has an excellent *parador*.

HOTELS AND RESTAURANTS

ARGOMANIZ (Alava). *Parador Nacional* (E-M), tel. (945) 28 22 00. 54 rooms, in a historic palace with garden.

BAYONA (Pontevedra). *Parador Conde de Gondomar* (E), Monterreal, tel. (986) 35 50 00. Pleasant location, 128 rooms, pool, gardens and tennis.

BILBAO. *Villa de Bilbao* (L), Gran Vía de López de Haro 87, tel. (94) 441 6000. A top class hotel with all amenities. *Aranzazu* (E), Rodríguez Arias 66, tel. (94) 441 3200. Good hotel with many amenities. *Carlton* (E), Plaza Federico Mayua 2, tel. (94) 416 2200. A much older 4-star hotel, but still one of the best. *Ercilla* (L), Ercilla 37, tel. (94) 443 8900. Large and modern with many amenities. 4-star hotel but its rates are high.

Avenida (M), Hurtado de Saracho 2, tel. (94) 412 4300. A good 3-star hotel with several amenities. *Conde Duque* (M), Campo Volantín 22, tel. (94) 445 6000. *Nervión* (M), Campo Volantín 11, tel. (94) 445 4700. 351 rooms.

Cantábrico (I), Miravilla 8, tel. (94) 415 2811. 51 rooms, parking. *San Mamés* (I), Luis Briñas 15, tel. (94) 441 7900. 36 rooms. *Zabalburu* (I), Plaza Martínez Artola 8, tel. (94) 443 7100. 27 rooms, parking.

Restaurants. *Guria* (E), Barrencalle Barrena 8, tel. 415 0434. With an atmosphere that matches the excellence of its food. *Victor* (E-M), Plaza Nueva 3, tel. 415 1678. On the first floor; recommended. *Urkia* (M), Ronda 31, tel. 415 1607.

CAMBADOS (Pontevedra). *Parador del Albariño* (E), Cervantes, tel. (986) 54 22 50. 63 rooms, regional décor, gardens.

CANGAS DE ONIS (Asturias). Popular resort town with the Spanish. *Ventura* (M), Ctra Covadonga, tel. (985) 84 82 00. 16 rooms, garden and bar.

CASTRO URDIALES (Cantabria). Charming fishing port between Santander and Bilbao. *Las Rocas* (E), on the beach, tel. (942) 86 04 04. 61 rooms, bar, bingo and good facilities. *Miramar* (M), near beach, (942) 86 02 00. 33 rooms, bar. *Vista Alegre* (M), Barrio Brazomar, tel. (942) 86 01 50. 20 rooms, pleasant location.

COLOMBRES (Asturias). *San Angel* (E), on Santander-Oviedo highway, tel. (985) 41 20 00. 77 rooms, pool, gardens, bar. Superb ocean views. *Mirador de la Franca* (M), Playa de la Franca, tel. (985) 41 21 45. 52 rooms.

COMILLAS (Cantabria). Beautiful town with a lovely beach about 1 km away. *Casal del Castro* (M), San Jerónimo, tel. (942) 72 00 36. 45 rooms, with tennis, gardens and bowling green. Open mid-June to mid-Sept. only. *Joseín* (M), Santa Lucía 27, 23 rooms. *Paraíso* (M-I), a 3-star hotel with very low rates.

CORCUBION (La Coruña). *Motel El Hórreo* (E), Santa Isabel, tel. (981) 74 55 00. 40 rooms, pool and bar; on the estuary.

LA CORUÑA. *Atlántico* (E), Jardines de Méndez Núñez, tel. (981) 22 65 00. 200 rooms, bar; recommended. *Finisterre* (E), Paseo del Parrote, tel. (981) 20 54 00. This is the best hotel in town; beautiful location on the bay that commands a sweeping view. Pool, gardens, sauna, tennis, bingo. *España* (M), Juana de Vega 7, tel. (981) 22 45 06. 80 rooms. *Riazor* (M), Andén de Riazor, tel. (981) 25 34 00. Located only a few streets from center; comfortable, clean rooms. Snack bar, no restaurant. *Almirante* (M-I), Paseo de Ronda, tel. (981) 25 96 00. 20 rooms. *Los Lagos* (I), tel. (981) 28 62 99. 35 rooms, parking, pool, tennis and gardens. *Santa Catalina* (I), Travesía de Santa Catalina 1, tel. (981) 22 66 09. A modern hostel, central and close to good restaurants in Olmos.
Restaurants. Virtually all the restaurants are on Calles Galera, Olmos and Estrella.
Cochinillo de Oro (E), Pardo Bazán 5, tel. 27 58 00. Under the same manage-

ment as the famous *Cándido* in Segovia and was opened by the great man himself. This is a recent restaurant serving the famous Segovian specialty of *cochinillo asado,* roast suckling pig. *Naveiro* (E), San Andrés 129, tel. 22 28 48. Specializes in Galician cooking. *El Rápido* (E), Estrella 7, tel. 22 42 21. Excellent display of shellfish but prices are vastly inflated.

Os Arcados (Playa Club) (E-M), on Riazor Beach, tel. 25 00 63. Good, with sea view but tends to cater for groups rather than individuals. *El Coral* (E-M), Estrella 5, tel. 22 27 17. Recommended, especially for shellfish. *Duna-2* (E-M), Estrella 2–4, tel. 22 70 43. One of the best restaurants in town and very popular with locals. Excellent management organizes special weeks of regional cooking, when chefs from different parts of Spain are invited to prepare their regional specialties. *Fornos* (E-M), Olmos 25, tel. 22 16 75. This once famous restaurant is now under new management and not so highly thought of as it once was, but it is still recommended, particularly for seafood.

O Meson (M) and *Mesón de la Cazuela* (M) are both on Callejón de la Estaca, just off Avda. de la Marina. Typical décor and outdoor terraces. *Gasthof* (I) on Avda. de la Marina, is an outdoor café, serving good snacks and *platos combinados,* in pleasant surroundings overlooking port. *Tala* (I), Galera 29, also serves light meals, snacks and tapas.

COVADONGA (Asturias). *Pelayo* (E-M), tel. (985) 84 60 00. 55 rooms; oldish hotel with garden. An ideal mountain retreat. Excursions to the mountain lakes leave from its steps.

DEVA (Guipúzcoa). *Miramar* (M), José Joaquín Aztiria, tel. (943) 60 11 44. 60 rooms, parking, comfortable.

EIBAR (Guipúzcoa). *Arrate* (M), Ego Gain 5, tel. (943) 71 72 42. 89 rooms, bar and bingo.

ESPINAMA (Cantabria). *Parador Río Deva* (E-M), 3.5 km out of town, tel. (942) 73 00 01. 78 rooms, very peaceful, with fabulous views.

EL FERROL DEL CAUDILLO (La Coruña). *Almirante* (E), Frutos Saavedra, tel. (981) 35 84 44. 122 rooms. *Parador Nacional* (E-M), Almirante Vierna, tel. (981) 35 34 00. 30 rooms, built in regional style.

FUENTERRABIA (Guipúzcoa). Near French border, small beautiful old town, with colorful Basque houses. *Guadalupe* (M), Ciudad de Peñíscola, tel. (943) 64 16 50. 34 rooms in pleasant location, pool. *Alvarez Quintero* (M), Alvarez Quintero 7, tel. (943) 64 22 99. 14 rooms. *Parador El Emperador* (M), Plaza Armas del Castillo, tel. (943) 64 21 40. Superb medieval citadel, 16 rooms. *Provincial de Jaizquíbel* (I), Monte del Jaizquíbel, tel. (943) 64 11 00. Small, quiet and well situated up a mountain.

GIJON (Asturias). *Hernán Cortés* (E), Fernández Vallín 5, tel. (985) 34 60 00. Old hotel right in center. Close to beach; both have high, almost (L) rates. *Príncipe de Asturias* (E), Playa de San Lorenzo, tel. (985) 36 71 11. *Parador Molino Viejo* (E), Parque de Isabel la Católica, tel. (985) 35 49 45. Modern copy of an old Asturian windmill, only 6 rooms, a little way out of town. *Robledo* (M), Alfredo Truán 2, tel. (985) 35 59 40. 132 rooms, in center. *León* (M), Ctra. de la Costa 11, tel. (985) 37 01 11. 85 rooms, fairly central. *Pathos* (M), Contracay 5, tel. (958) 35 25 46. Not a bad choice as only two streets from beach, but rather functional and unexciting.

Restaurants. *El Faro* (E), Avda. García Bernardo, tel. 36 04 29. A 4-fork restaurant on far side of Piles Canal. *Parador Molino Viejo* (E) also serves good meals. *Bella Vista* (M), Avda. García Bernardo, tel. 36 29 36, in El Piles. *Mercedes* (M), Libertad 6, tel. 35 01 39. One of the best restaurants in this somewhat gastronomically unexciting town. Wood-paneled rustic décor, family-type atmosphere; good solid fare. *El Trole* (M), Alvarez Garaya 6, tel. 35 00 48. *Rincón de Antonio* (I), Ezcurdia 24, tel. 35 99 03. Good for seafood and cider, in tavern setting.

GUETARIA (Guipúzcoa). **Restaurant.** *Kaia* (E), General Arnao 10, tel. 83 24 14. Good for fish and seafood, decorated in country style, with good views of the sea and coast.

LAREDO (Cantabria). Virtually a French colony and a pleasant beach resort. *El Ancla* (E), González Gallego 10, tel. (942) 60 55 00. 25 rooms, garden and bar. *Cosmopol* (E), Avda. de la Victoria, tel. (942) 60 54 00. 60 rooms, garden. *Risco* (E), La Arenosa 1, tel. (942) 60 50 30. 20 rooms, garden. Located on mountainside; has a good restaurant and splendid view over the bay.

LLANES (Asturias). *Don Paco* (E), Parque de Posada Herrera, tel. (985) 40 01 50. 42 rooms, in historic building, with parking and garden. *Montemar* (M), Genaro Riestra, tel. (985) 40 01 00. 2-star hotel with 40 rooms and garden. *Peñablanca* (M), Pidal 1, tel. (985) 40 01 66. 30 rooms, central and pleasant. *México* (I), Avda de México, tel. (985) 40 10 57. 20 rooms, a hostel with garden.

LUARCA (Asturias). *Gayoso-Hotel* (E), Paseo de Gómez 4, tel. (985) 64 00 54. 3-star hotel with 26 rooms.

LUGO. *Lugo-Husa* (E), Avda Ramón Ferreiro, tel. (982) 22 41 52. 169 rooms, the best in town. *Méndez Núñez* (M), Reina 1, tel. (982) 23 07 11. 94 rooms, central. *Miño* (I), Tolda de Castilla 2, tel. (982) 22 01 50. 50 rooms.

ORENSE. *San Martín* (E), Curros Enriquez 1, tel. (988) 23 56 11. Best in town; good amenities. *Sila* (M), Avda. de la Habana 61, tel. (988) 23 63 11. *Barcelona* (I), Avda. Pontevedra 13, tel. 22 08 00. Pleasant location, overlooking a square in the old part of town. *Padre Feijoo* (M), Pl. Eugenio Montes 1, tel.

22 31 00. Highly recommended for value. *Parque* (I), Parque de San Lázaro 24, tel. 23 36 11. Very central, close to cafés and shops.

Restaurants. *San Miguel* (E), San Miguel 12, tel. 22 07 95. The best in town, excellent shellfish. *Carroleiro* (M), San Miguel 10, tel. 22 05 66. Delightful old world décor and charm, good service; recommended. *Martin Fierro* (M), Avda. Sáenz Diez 65, tel. 23 48 20. A modern, elegant restaurant with a terrace overlooking river. Specializes in Argentinian *parrilladas.* *Mesón As Caracochas* (M), Bedoya 45, tel. 22 10 45. Pleasant mesón-type décor, good menu. *Pingallo* (M), San Miguel 6, tel. 22 00 57. The most reasonably priced of the restaurants on this street.

OVIEDO. *La Reconquista* (L), Gil de Jaz 16, tel. (985) 24 11 00. A 5-star hotel with many amenities. *La Jirafa* (E), Pelayo 6, tel. (985) 22 22 44. 80 rooms. *Ramiro I* (E), Calvo Sotelo 13, tel. (985) 23 28 50. 82 rooms. *Regente* (E), Jovellanos 31, tel. (985) 22 23 43.

La Gruta (M), Alto de Buenavista, tel. (985) 23 24 50. 55 rooms. *Principado* (M), San Francisco 6, tel. (985) 21 77 92. *Barbón* (M-I), Covadonga 7, tel. (985) 22 52 93. 40 rooms. *España* (M-I), Jovellanos 2, tel. (985) 22 05 96.

Restaurants. *Casa Fermín* (M), Avda del Cristo 23, tel. 23 99 50. Fine reputation for good food. *Marchica* (M), Dr. Casal 10, tel. 21 30 27. Near the Galerías Preciados; recommended. *Pelayo* (M), Pelayo 15, tel. 22 00 04. A fairly elegant restaurant, with a cafeteria next door, right next to La Jirafa hotel.

PAJARES (Asturias). *Parador Puerto de Pajares* (M), tel. (985) 49 60 23. 5 km from the pass; 28 rooms in beautiful mountain setting.

PASAJES DE SAN JUAN (Guipúzcoa). **Restaurant.** *Casa Cámara* (E-M), San Juan 79, tel. 35 66 02. Tops for seafood.

PONTEVEDRA. *Parador Casa del Barón* (E), Maceda, tel. (986) 85 58 00. Magnificent palace right in town. *Rías Bajas* (E), Daniel de la Sota 7, tel. (986) 85 51 00. 100 rooms; in town center. *Virgen del Camino* (M), Virgen del Camino 55, tel. (986) 85 59 04.

Restaurants. *Calixto* (E-M), Benito Corbal 14, tel. 85 62 52. Probably the best in town. Also good is the *Parador* (E-M). *Casa Digna* and *Casa Rua,* both (M) and both on Avda das Carbacerias at bottom of Campo de la Torre. Both have tables outside as well as modern indoor dining rooms. On the street alongside the river though the view is not spectacular. *Casa Durán* (I), Virgen del Camino, is a possibility. Convenient for Virgen del Camino hotel.

PUERTOMARIN (Lugo). *Parador Nacional* (M), tel. (982) 54 50 25. A modern parador with 10 rooms and garden. Closed at presstime, so check.

REINOSA (Cantabria). *Vejo* (M), Avda. Cantabria 15, tel. (942) 75 17 00. Modern, 71 rooms with pool, garden and tennis. *Corza Blanca* (I), on Reinosa-Tres Mares road, tel. (942) 75 10 99. 44 rooms.

RIBADEO (Lugo). *Parador Nacional* (E), Amador Fernández, tel. (982) 11 08 25. Modern parador with 47 rooms. *Eo* (M), Avda. de Asturias 5, tel. (982) 11 07 50. Pool, gardens and good views of the mountains.

RIBADESELLA (Asturias). *Gran Hotel del Sella* (E), tel. (985) 86 01 50. 71 rooms, pool, tennis, bar and garden. *La Playa* (M), La Playa 42, tel. (985) 86 01 00. 12 rooms, garden.

SAN SEBASTIAN. *Costa Vasca* (E), Avda Pío Baroja 9, tel. (943) 21 10 11. The newest 4-star hotel, 203 rooms. Generally well appointed, but rather characterless. A ten-minute walk down a steep hill from Ondarreta beach. *Londres y Inglaterra* (E), Zubieta 2, tel. (943) 42 69 89. One of the best but also the most expensive, with gracious old world charm, excellent service and splendid views. *María Cristina* (E), Paseo República Argentina, tel. (943) 42 67 70. An old stand-by but service and accommodations are not what they used to be, and the hotel's creaking age is becoming increasingly apparent. *Monte Igueledo* (E), on Mount Igueledo, tel. (943) 21 02 11. Finely sited atop mountain, a 20-min. drive up winding road, high taxi fare. Though rooms have superb view, the hotel is rather characterless. *Orly* (E), Plaza de Zaragoza 4, tel. (943) 46 32 00. 63 rooms; central and popular. *San Sebastián* (E), Avda. de Zumalacarregui 20, tel. (943) 21 44 00. Near Ondarreta beach, with pool and gardens. Rooms facing the highway are hot and noisy.

Avenida (M), Ctra a Igueledo, tel. (943) 21 20 22. 47 rooms, pool and gardens. *Niza* (M), Zubieta 56, tel. (943) 42 66 63. Off Plaza Zaragoza, near beach, with old world charm; 41 rooms, some are rather expensive. *Parma* (M), General Jauregui 11, tel. (943) 42 88 93. Impeccably clean, with sea views, modern décor and deluxe bathrooms. *Gudamendi* (I), Barrio de Igueledo, tel. (943) 21 41 11. Pleasant setting on Mount Igueledo, garden, 30 rooms.

Restaurants. *Akelarre* (E), on top of Mount Igueldo, tel. 21 20 52. Magnificent views and food. *Arzac* (E), Miracruz 21, tel. 27 84 65. Just in the outskirts on road to Fuenterrabía, offers extraordinary, unusual and excellently prepared food in an intimate cottage setting. *Nicolasa* (E), Aldamar 4, tel. 42 17 62. Elegant, well-known restaurant. *Txomin* (E), Avda Infanta Beatriz, tel. 21 07 05. Near Ondarreta beach, offers top food in rustic setting.

Aita Mari (M), Puerto 23. Famous seafood restaurant in old town. *La Cueva* (M), Plaza de la Trinidad, in port area. *Clery* (M), Plaza de la Trinidad. Pleasant outdoor dining in the port. *Juanito Kojua* (M), Puerto 14, is famous throughout Spain for its succulent seafood. Simple décor, with upstairs and downstairs dining rooms. Popular, so expect to wait.

California 27 (I) and *Dover* (I) cafeterias at Avda. de la Libertad 27 and 21 both do good inexpensive snacks and *platos combinados.*

SANTANDER. *Real* (L), Paseo de Pérez Galdós 28, tel. (942) 27 25 50. Once one of the finest hotels in Europe. Luxury restaurant. *Bahía* (E), Alfonso XIII 6, tel. (942) 22 17 00. One of Santander's leading hotels. *María Isabel* (E-M), Avda. de García Lago, tel. (942) 27 18 50. At the end of Sardinero beach, with splendid views, large balconied rooms, pool and garden. *Rex* (E-M), Avda Calvo Sotelo 9, tel. (942) 21 02 00. 53 rooms, modern. *Roma* (E-M), Avda. de los Hoteles 5, tel. (942) 27 27 00. 44 rooms, tennis, garden, near Sardinero beach. *Sardinero* (E-M), Plaza de Italia 1, tel. (942) 27 11 00. Close to beach. All the above rise 1,000–1,500 ptas. in July-Sept. Reader-recommended is the 2-star hostel *Europa* (I), across the street from Sardinero beach. Excellent value, and run by friendly, helpful owners.

Restaurants. *La Sardina* (E), Dr. Fleming 3, tel. 27 10 35. High standards, specializing in nouvelle cuisine. *Chiqui* (M), Manuel García Lago, tel. 27 20 98. On Sardinero beach, probably the best in town. *Mar de Castilla* (M), Estación Marítima, tel. 21 19 62. At the ferry station with oceanside view. *El Molino* (E), 13 km out on Torrelavega road, tel. 27 63 00. Delightful restaurant in old windmill. Outstanding food with emphasis on nouvelle cuisine Cantabrica. *El Vivero* (M), Poblado Pescadores, tel. 23 01 33. In fishing port, specializes in seafood and fish.

Albo (I), Peña Herbosa 15, tel. 27 50 02. Cozy and intimate with good service. *Mesón Los Arcos* (I), Hernán Cortés 3, tel. 23 11 62. A typical mesón. *Los Peñucas* (I), Marqués de la Ensenada, tel. 22 94 45. In fishing port area, one of the best. *Posada del Mar* (I), Juan de la Cosa 3, tel. 27 10 51. Excellent meals in rustic setting. Try their fish soup and *merluza posada*. *El Recreo* (I), Somorrostro 2, tel. 22 07 67. Simple food, near cathedral.

SANTIAGO DE COMPOSTELA. *Reyes Católicos* (L), Plaza de España 1, tel. (981) 58 22 00. Elegant and sumptuous, one of the most magnificent establishments in Spain. Two dining rooms, bars, seafood restaurant, garden and nightclub. Housed in a converted hospital built by Ferdinand and Isabella at the close of the 15th century, skillfully modernized without destroying any of the original medieval atmosphere.

Husa Santiago (E), new, 2 km out on road to La Estrada, tel. (981) 59 79 72.

Peregrino (E), Avda. Rosalía de Castro, tel. (981) 59 18 50. Modern hotel, a little way out of town on road to Pontevedra. Pool, gardens, bar, but a little austere. *Santiago Apostel* (E), La Grela 6, tel. (981) 58 71 38, new, just out of town on the Lugo road. *Compostela* (E-M), General Franco 1, tel. (981) 58 57 00. Centrally located and close to old town. Another famous hotel in historic building. Rooms are old fashioned but comfortable. Hotel is famous for its student banquets. *Gelmírez* (M), General Franco 92, tel. (981) 59 11 00. 138 rooms, central. *Universal* (I), Plaza de Galicia, tel. (981) 59 22 50. Modern and central. There are also many good hostels if accommodations prove hard to find; ask at the tourist office.

Restaurants. *Chitón* (E), Rua Nova 40, tel. 58 51 44. Elegant dining in the heart of the old town. *Don Gaiferos* (E), Rua Nova 23. Elegant, modern décor. *Vilas* (E), Rosalía de Castro 88, tel. 59 10 00. Opened in 1915 this restaurant has served top Galician cuisine ever since. *Tacita de Oro* (E-M), General Franco (Hórreo) 31, tel. 59 32 55. Well patronized by locals, convenient to Gelmírez hotel, though not in the old town.

El Caserio (M) and *Victoria* (M) both on Calle Bautizados, serve good Galician dishes. *San Clemente* (M), San Clemente 6, tel. 58 08 82. A pleasant restaurant overlooking the old town, some tables on sidewalk. Excellent shellfish. Next door is *Trinidad* (M), also good.

If you walk down the Calle del Franco you will find literally hundreds of restaurants; take your pick. *El Franco* (E-M) at no. 28 is one of the best, *San Jaime* (I), Raiña 4, is a delightful 1st-floor restaurant overlooking the Plaza Fonseca. Local Galician dishes, simple and charming; serves Ribero wine in white china bowls.

Santiago has many delightful cafés. *Alameda* (M), on corner of Calle del Franco and Avda. Figueroa, has tables on the sidewalk and is very popular in the early evening. It also has a restaurant serving meals and *platos combinados.* *Derby* (E-M), on the corner of Plaza Galicia, is a delightful old-world café with charm and good service. *Fonseca* (I) in Plaza Fonseca at the top of Calle del Franco, has tables in the square, and serves generous free tapas with your drinks.

SANTILLANA DEL MAR (Cantabria). *Parador Gil Blas* (E), Plaza Ramón Pelayo 8, tel. (942) 81 80 00. In an 18th-century manor house in one of the most picturesque and well preserved villages in Spain. 45 rooms, garden and parking. *Los Infantes* (M), Avda. Le Dorat 1, tel. (942) 81 81 00. 31 rooms. In seigniorial style in keeping with the village. *Altamira* (I), Cantón 1, tel. (942) 81 80 25. A budgeteer's dream come true. Cozy, rustic décor, and large rooms.

Restaurant. *Mesón de los Blasones* (M-I), Plaza de Gándara, tel. 81 80 70. Serves delicious food at reasonable prices in a charming atmosphere and with good service. Reader recommended.

LA TOJA (Pontevedra). *Gran Hotel* (L), tel. (986) 73 00 25. Located between the sea and the pinewoods, this is a magnificent establishment which has everything – marvelous situation, lovely surroundings, tennis courts, golf links, swimming pool, and a private beach. It also houses the island's casino.

Loujo (E), tel. (986) 73 02 00. A 4-star hotel with golf, tennis and pool. Open June-Sept. *Balneario* (M), tel. (986) 73 01 50. A one-star hotel, with 43 rooms, pool, golf, tennis and gardens. Open July and Aug. only.

TORRELAVEGA (Cantabria). *Marqués de Santillana* (M), Marqués de Santillana 6, tel. (942) 89 29 34. 32 rooms. *Saja* (M), Alcalde del Río 22, tel. (942) 89 27 50. 45 rooms, parking. *Regio* (I), José María de Pereda 34, tel. (942) 88 15 05. 24 rooms.

TUY (Pontevedra). *Parador San Telmo* (E), 1 km out of town, tel. (986) 60 03 09. 16 rooms. Characteristic local building; pool and gardens.

VERIN (Orense). *Parador de Monterrey* (M), 4 km out of town, tel. (988) 41 00 75. A modern parador with 23 rooms, pool and gardens.

VIGO (Pontevedra). *Bahía de Vigo* (E), Cánovas del Castillo 5, tel. (986) 22 67 00. Comfortable, well equipped rooms. *Ciudad de Vigo* (E), Concepción Arenal 4, tel. (986) 22 78 20. Modern, with 101 rooms. *Samil Playa* (E), on Samil beach about 6 km out of town, tel. (986) 23 25 30. With pool, tennis, sauna and disco. Above are all very expensive July-Aug.

Ensenada (E-M), Alfonso XIII 35, tel. (986) 22 61 00. 109 rooms, modern. *México* (M), Vía Norte 10, tel. (986) 41 40 22. 112 rooms. *Niza* (M), María Berdiales 32, tel. (986) 22 88 00. 39 rooms. *Estación* (I), Alfonso XIII 47, tel. (986) 21 56 12. 22 rooms. *Lisboa* (I), José Antonio 50, tel. (986) 41 72 55. 93 rooms.

Restaurants. *El Castro* (M), Manuel Olibie 31, tel. 41 08 39. Set in a park. *El Mosquito* (M), Plaza Villavícencio 4, tel. 21 35 41. Good for seafood.

VILLALBA (Lugo). *Parador Condes de Villalba* (E), Valeriano Valdesuso, tel. (982) 51 00 11. 6 rooms in lovely medieval castle.

VITORIA (Alava). *Canciller Ayala* (E), Ramón y Cajal 5, tel. (945) 22 08 00. A large modern hotel, the best in town. *General Álava* (M), Avda. de Gasteiz 53, tel. (945) 22 22 00. Large and modern with gardens and bar. *Páramo* (I), General Alava 11, tel. (945) 23 04 50. 40 rooms, central.

Restaurants. *Dos Hermanas* (M), Postas 27, tel. 25 88 52. Established over 100 years ago; good vegetables, seafood and osso buco. *Mesón Nacional* (M), Ortiz de Zarate 5, tel. 23 21 11. *El Portalón* (E), Correría 151, tel. 22 49 89. Set in a 15th-century house, rustic style, this is one of the favorites.

VIVERO (Lugo). *Las Sirenas* (M), Sacido Covas Vivero, tel. (982) 56 02 00. 25 rooms, garden, near beach and good views. *Tebar* (I), Nicolás Cora 70, tel. (982) 56 01 00. 27 rooms, recent.

ZARAUZ (Guipúzcoa). A very pretty Basque seaside town, with a lovely clean sandy beach. *La Perla* (E-M), Avda. Navarra 1, tel. (943) 83 08 00. 72 rooms. *Zarauz* (E-M), Avda. de Navarra 4, tel. (943) 83 02 00. 73 rooms, parking, garden. *Paris* (M), tel. (943) 83 05 00. Popular hotel with pool.

 USEFUL ADDRESSES. Tourist Offices. **Bilbao;** Alameda Mazarredo. **La Coruña;** Dársena de la Marina. **Gijón;** General Vigón 1. **Lugo;** Plaza de Soledad 15. **Orense;** Curros Enríquez 1. **Oviedo;** Cabo Noval 5. **Pontevedra;** General Mola 1. **San Sebastián;** Reina Regente. **Santander;** Jardines de Pereda. **Santiago de Compostela;** Rua del Villar 81. **Vigo;** Jardines Elduayen. **Vitoria;** Parque de la Florida.

British Consul. **Bilbao;** Alameda Urquijo 228, tel. 415 7600. **Vigo;** Plaza de Compostela 23, tel. 21 14 50.

CAR HIRE. Bilbao; *Avis* at airport and Dr. Areilza 34; *Hertz* at airport, station and Nicolás Achucarro 10; *Ital* at airport and Euskalduna 9. **La Coruña;**

Avis, Plaza de Vigo; *Hertz* at airport and station; *Ital,* Juan Flórez 47. **Gijón;** *Avis,* Plaza Piñole 3, *Hertz,* Anselmo Cifuentes 12. **Pontevedra;** *Autoservicio,* Santa Clara, *Motolux,* Riestra 19. **San Sebastián;** *Atesa,* Plaza de Zaragoza 2, *Avis,* Triunfo 2, *Hertz,* Marina 2. **Santander;** *Atesa,* Aparcamiento Alfonso XIII, *Avis,* Nicolás Salmerón 3, *Hertz,* Alcázar de Toledo 6. **Santiago de Compostela;** *Atesa,* Hostal Reyes Católicos, *Avis,* República de El Salvador 10; *Hertz,* Avda. de Lugo 145. **Vigo;** *Avis,* Uruguay 12. *Hertz,* Felipe Sanchez 110.

Colònia Güell — Gaudí

BARCELONA

A Busy Port with an Elegant Accent

With a population of over three million, Barcelona, second largest city in the country, has an international flair and sophistication lacking in most other regions of Spain. Its high cultural level, industrial muscle and thriving maritime commerce—cemented by a language of its own —have long made Barcelona a formidable rival to Madrid, often surpassing the capital in industrial production and intellectual achievement. This has given the citizens of Barcelona a local pride—they feel that they are essentially different from the rest of Spain.

Through the centuries Catalans, and especially the citizens of Barcelona, have forged a reputation for themselves in industriousness while remaining appreciative of the pleasures of life. Like the Basques, they take great pride in their own culture. The Catalan language (they will argue fiercely that it is *not* a dialect of Castilian or French) is commonly spoken in most households, more now than in the thirty-five years when it was outlawed by the Franco regime. You will hear people speaking Catalan in the streets and shops; plays are put on in Catalan, a newspaper is printed in that language, and there is a Catalan radio and television station.

The ordered cosmopolitanism of Barcelona will immediately be evident to the tourist as he explores the city. Many streets are cobbled and lined with trees as in France, and there are French-type cafés with glass-enclosed terraces in the winter which invite you to while away an hour. Drivers tend to be more careful than in Madrid, zebra crossings for pedestrians are usually respected and red lights not jumped. The food, too, is essentially different from Madrid's. You'll often be served more imaginative dishes and desserts than in the rest of the Peninsula. Tea rooms and pastry shops reminiscent of France and Germany lure afternoon idlers in the elegant section of town. This polish, however, goes hand in hand with a taste for local specialties in the portside taverns; the *paella* served there rivals in excellence that made in Valencia.

The pace of life in Barcelona is very different from other parts of Spain, with a greater emphasis on home values. Though the city is certainly not lacking in nocturnal entertainment, the Catalans themselves rather frown on the goings-on around the port area and are reputed to be early risers and early-to-bed solid citizens, and you may find that meals are somewhat earlier here than elsewhere in the country, and certainly earlier than in Madrid.

The city lies between two mountains, Tibidabo and Montjuich, but sprawls a good deal, so you will find yourself resorting to taxis, buses or the Metro (subway). The Ramblas, the traditional main street, continues to be a hive of activity at all hours of the day and night, but no really centralized section can be pinpointed: cinemas, clubs and restaurants are scattered all around the city. The Paseo de Gracia perhaps comes closest to being an entertainment and shopping nexus.

As a large port city, there are the seamier sides as well, which makes for greater diversity and contrasts than in cities of the interior. You can opt for the luxury shops and restaurants on and off the Paseo de Gracia or plunge into the backstreet turmoil of the Barrio Chino or the streets adjacent to the Plaza Real.

The climate of Barcelona is extremely mild—witness the palm trees in some streets and squares. In summer, weather can be uncomfortably hot and muggy, and air-pollution is a mounting problem. Beaches near Barcelona are not recommended for bathers who value their health, but thirty-two kilometers north on the Costa Brava and to the south at Casteldefels and Sitges, well-equipped but overcrowded resorts provide escape-valves. In winter, the people of Barcelona head towards such popular resorts in the Pyrenees as La Molina and Baqueira-Beret for some wonderful skiing.

A Little History

Barcelona's history dates back to its founding by the Phoenicians. This Greek colony was subsequently occupied by the Carthaginians in 237 B.C., who called it Barcino (after the ruling House of Barca). Later the Romans changed its name to Julia Faventia Augusta Pia Barcino and made it the capital of the Roman province of Layetania. After a spell as capital of the Goths, it was conquered in 713 by the Moors, who in turn were ousted by the Franks. Under the Counts of Barcelona, starting in 874, the city attained its independence.

In the 11th century, Ramón Berenguer I compiled a sort of constitution, the *Usatges,* which proclaimed the region's autonomy and sovereignty, but in 1137 Catalonia became part of Aragón. During the 14th and 15th centuries the city prospered immensely thanks to its maritime trade, for Aragón then ruled over such Mediterranean colonies as the Balearics, Sardinia, Sicily and the Kingdom of Naples. Finally, in 1474 when Isabella of Castile married Ferdinand of Aragón, Barcelona became part of united Spain, and ceased to be a capital.

However the tradition of independence has always remained uppermost in the life of Catalans and on numerous occasions over the past centuries the region has revolted against the central authority of Madrid. Catalans have jealously guarded their language and culture and still only reluctantly think of themselves as Spaniards.

During the Civil War, Barcelona was a stronghold of the Republic, and base for many anarchists and communists. It resisted the approach of Franco's troops till very nearly the end of the conflict. Franco rigorously suppressed Catalan separatism and the Catalan language. But since the establishment of regional autonomy in 1979, the Catalans have been making headway in reinstating their customs and language. And in March 1980 they voted for their first home-rule parliament since the Civil War. The Catalan Nationalist Party, led by Jordi Pujol, won the largest number of seats.

Sightseeing in Barcelona

Barcelona offers the tourist a great variety of sights ranging from some excellent museums to the weird architectural vagaries of Antonio Gaudí. A good spot to start your wanderings is the Plaza de Cataluña, the large, somewhat amorphous square which is the intersection of several important streets.

The Ramblas

If you leave the Plaza de Cataluña by way of the Ramblas, you reach a section of the city which is a fascinating amalgam of earthy taverns and atmospheric squares and alleys. The Ramblas, which changes its name every block or so, is a lively, thronged promenade flanked by trees, running through the center of this area. It is lined with bookshops, flower stalls, stands with bird cages and fish tanks and is one of the most colorful streets in the whole country. The traffic roars down either side of it, while the middle section is happily still devoted to the needs of pedestrians. The Ramblas is always bustling with an endless stream of flaneurs, tourists, sailors and businessmen. The activity is such that you don't know where to look first, whether at the stalls, the crowd, the bootblacks and lottery-ticket sellers, the cafés, or at the venerable old buildings lining the street.

All the way along, cross streets beckon you to plunge deeper into the maze-like area. In contrast to the elegance of the section north of the Plaza de Cataluña, the Ramblas is lined mostly with inexpensive hotels, hooker clubs, snack bars and old cafés. Intermingled with these are historic monuments such as the church of Nuestra Señora de Belén on the right, on the corner of Calle Carmen, and opposite it the Baroque Palacio de Moya, built in 1702, and the Palacio de la Virreina, at number 99, built by a viceroy of Peru in 1778. This now contains the Museum of Decorative Arts. A little further down on the right you reach a famous Barcelona landmark, the Liceo Opera House, one of the oldest and largest in Europe and long the pride of the city. It was built in 1845–7 and holds an audience of 5,000.

The Plaza Real

One of the narrow side streets on the left leads to the Plaza Real, a porticoed square in the Mediterranean style, surrounded by cafés and restaurants serving shellfish and other refreshments. Several tall palm trees in the center of the square add a touch of tropical voluptuousness. The Plaza Real is especially lively on summer evenings, when the outdoor cafés are jammed with customers sitting till the wee hours of the morning. Just behind the Plaza, on the Calle Escudellers, is a cluster of bars and restaurants teeming with visitors and Spaniards of every description. Some of Barcelona's oldest and most atmospheric restaurants are located here, including Los Caracoles, famous since the turn of the century for its seafood, paellas and, of course, snails.

On the other side of the Ramblas you can plunge into the area of narrow streets known as the Barrio Chino, though the Chinese have long since departed. It swarms with somewhat shady nightclubs; single men usually get inviting nods from the ladies who frequent the little bars in the humid lanes, but it is also an area which contains some excellent budget restaurants.

The Port

At the bottom of the Ramblas lies the Plaza Puerta de la Paz, the port area, with its bronze statue of Columbus perched on a high column; energetic souls can climb to the top for a fine view of the port and the city. Anchored in the water nearby is a replica of the *Santa María,* Columbus's flagship, and on the right of the Ramblas is the excellent Maritime Museum chronicling the importance of Barcelona as a world port. The museum is housed in the medieval Reales Ataranzanas, the remains of a fort built by Jaime the Conqueror. In it are displayed old maps, model ships, compasses and other seafaring paraphernalia.

On the left, going down the wide Paseo de Colón which flanks the port where you can sometimes see battleships anchored, you come to the Plaza del Duque de Medinaceli, with a pretty fountain, and the Comandancia General, formerly the Convent of the Mothers of Mercy (1846), with a pretty patio. The façade dates from 1929. Behind it is the baroque church of La Merced (1775), with a Renaissance portico from a previous church.

La Merced contains the image of Barcelona's patron saint, the 16th-century Virgin of Mercy. Further down the Paseo de Colón, on the corner of the Via Layetana, is the Post Office, built in 1926. Straight ahead lies the Avenida La Argentera, site of the Lonja (Stock Market) rebuilt in 1763. This, the Ramblas and the narrow streets behind the Plaza Real and the cathedral, are the most walkable parts of town.

The Cathedral

Returning to our starting point at the Plaza de Cataluña, shoppers can plunge into purchases at the Corte Inglés department store on the north side of the large square. Those who want to continue the sightseeing should walk down the Puerta del Angel, past the Galerías Preciados department store, to one of the glories of Barcelona, its superb Gothic cathedral, one of the finest in the country.

The cathedral is set in the so-called "Gothic" quarter of the city, a fascinating labyrinth of medieval streets and mansions, ideally suited for leisurely explorations. The present cathedral (known to the locals as La Seu) stands on the site of an earlier church, the Basilica of Santa Eulalia, which dated from A.D. 878. Work on the present structure was begun in 1298 under the kings of Aragón, and was completed around

1450. Such master builders as Jaime Fabré of Majorca and Master Roque are credited among its architects.

The two octagonal towers at either side of the transepts date from the 14th century, whereas the neo-Gothic façade on the Plaza Cristo Rey is modern (1892), as is the recent spire. The three rather somber naves measure 76 by 34 meters (249 by 111 feet), rising to a height of 23 meters (76 feet). The choirstalls by Matías Bonafe (the lower sections) and Lochner and Friedrich, two Germans of the late 15th century (for the upper sections) are astounding examples of the glories that wood-carving attained in the Middle Ages. See also the main altar, the crypt of Santa Eulalia, twenty-nine chapels and especially the magnificent cloister built in the Italian Renaissance style, finished by Roque in 1448, with capitals depicting scenes from the Bible.

Leaving the cathedral by the main door you come out into the Plaza Cristo Rey. To your left is the 15th-century Casa del Arcediano, home of the city's archives, while to the right is the Pía Almoína mansion, now the Diocesan Museum and containing splendid examples of Catalan Gothic workmanship. On Sunday mornings, people gather here to dance the traditional sardana, a living symbol of the tenacious regionalism of Catalonia.

The Gothic Quarter

Next, stroll through the Gothic Quarter, a warren of narrow streets with old churches and palaces dating from the 14th century. Go on down the Calle del Obispo Iruria at the side of the cathedral towards the Plaza de San Jaime. An alleyway off to the left leads to four Roman columns, remains of a temple dedicated to Augustus. On the west side of the plaza is the 15th-century Palau de la Generalitat. Facing it across the square is the Ayuntamiento, whose facade dates from 1400; inside it you can see the famous Salón de Ciento and the impressive mural of José María Sert in the Salón de Crónicas. Behind the Ayuntamiento, on the Bajada San Miguel, you will come across the Centelles Palace (15th century).

Wander at will through the maze of narrow streets and then make your way to the Plaza del Angel between Jaime I and Via Layetana. From here head towards the Plaza del Rey, bordered by Santa Agueda, a 14th-century Gothic chapel built into the old Roman walls, the Casa Padellás, home of the museum of the City of Barcelona, and the 16th-century Palace of the Viceroys of Catalonia. Stairs lead out of a corner of this square to the Palacio Real Mayor, originally the Palace of the Counts of Barcelona. It was here in the 14th-century Tinell banqueting hall that the Catholic Monarchs received Columbus on his return from his first trip to the Americas. Today it houses the Federico Marés Museum, which contains sculpture from the 12th to the 18th centuries.

The Museums of Modern Art and Natural History

A short walk from the Gothic Quarter, across the broad Vía Layetana, will bring you to the Ciudadela Park, containing a cluster of museums as well as the very pleasant though small City Zoo. Within the park are the Numismatic, Modern Art and Natural History Museums.

The Museum of Modern Art is something of a misnomer, since it actually includes paintings from the late 18th century to the present. Most of the paintings are of local fame, but it is revealing to study the late 19th-century and early 20th-century works produced in Barcelona, which proved a transition period between the Impressionists and modern nonfigurative trends. They evoke a golden period of painting and bohemianism in Barcelona. These were the years Picasso lived here. There are also works by such excellent painters as Fortuny, Rusiñol, Casas, Nonell, Zuloaga and Sunyer, many of them unjustly neglected.

The Natural History and Numismatic Museum, a large sprawling building, is nearby.

The Picasso Museum

Leaving the Ciudadela Park, go down the Calle de la Princesa and turn left at the Calle Montcada, which takes you to the Picasso Museum. Though originally the collection was rather anemic, it has been added to over the years and is now one of the world's foremost museums on the artist who spent many of his formative years in Barcelona. In 1970, the artist donated some 2,500 works to the museum, despite pressures from the French government to keep the works in that country. The collection includes paintings, engravings and drawings ranging over his entire creative life, some dating back as far as 1895 when Picasso was only nine years old. Of special interest are his variations on Velázquez's *Las Meninas* and his sketches of Barcelona.

Barceloneta

The nearby Via Layetana will take you to the Plaza de Antonio López and a street leading to the Paseo Nacional, the main thoroughfare of the Barceloneta section of the city. This old residential workers' and fishermen's quarter was originally built in 1755 and, although rather scruffy and run-down, is worth a visit at lunchtime for its no-frills restaurants along the Paseo Nacional and the side streets, many of them specializing in seafood. As you walk past you will see people sitting outdoors, their plates piled high with shrimps, while others, often whole families, are digging into a paella.

The restaurants range from humble diners to elegant old favorites. On the Calle Maquinista is a cluster of favorites, including the Pañol and Ramonet taverns. The latter is a lively haunt where the Catalans delight in ali-oli sandwiches (with tomato and garlic), smoked ham and *butifarra*. The rafters are so thickly hung with sausages and hams that the ceiling vanishes.

After lunch at Barceloneta, or maybe at the Siete Puertas, an old turn-of-the-century favorite on the Paseo de Colón, at the entrance to Barceloneta, you can take the cablecar at the opposite end of the Paseo Nacional up to Montjuich Park, which has splendid views.

Montjuich Park and its Museums

Commanding a strategic position in Montjuich Park, laid out in 1929–30 by Forestier for the International Exhibition, is the spectacular castle. The citadel was built in 1640 by those in revolt against Philip IV. It was stormed several times, the most famous assault being in 1705 by Lord Peterborough for the Archduke Charles of Austria. In 1808, the castle was seized by the French under General Dufresne during the War of Independence. Later, in 1842, Barcelona was bombarded from its heights. The castle houses a Military Museum. Outside is a pleasant terrace and a restaurant commanding magnificent views of the city and its surroundings.

The most important of the cluster of museums in the Park of Montjuich, which includes the Archeology Museum and the Joan Miró Foundation, is the Museum of Catalan Art and Ceramics in the Palacio Nacional. It contains an extraordinary collection of Catalan Romanesque and Gothic art treasures, such as can be seen nowhere else in the world. The murals—a superb collection—reredos and medieval sculptures represent the zenith of this genre in Spain. More conventional baroque and Renaissance paintings, virtually all of a religious nature, are well represented too, but it is the Romanesque works which make a visit obligatory. Among the highlights is the concave fresco Pantocrator from the church of San Clemente de Tahull.

The exhibits in the Archeological Museum date from prehistoric times to the 8th century and include many artifacts found in the Balearics as well as some from the diggings at Ampurias, the large Greek and, later, Roman colony on the Costa Brava. The Roman items are mostly frescoes and mosaics. Classical plays are performed in the nearby Greek Theater in summer.

Another major attraction on Montjuich is the Pueblo Español, a delightful miniature village, with each Spanish province represented.

The Pueblo is a kind of Spain-in-a-bottle, with the local architectural styles of each province faithfully reproduced, enabling you to wander from the walls of Avila to the wine cellars of Jerez, tasting the local wines, watching glass being blown, pottery being shaped and fabrics being printed. In all, there are seventy shops featuring regional handicrafts and wares.

Montjuich Park is made additionally attractive by the presence of several fine restaurants, ideal for al fresco dining on warm summer nights, as well as a large well kept amusement park.

Leaving the park by its main exit you come to a huge fountain, one of the great prides of the city, which on festive occasions and weekends in summer is made to play colored fantasies while floodlights illuminate the large Palacio de las Naciones behind it. A wide esplanade leads past the fair buildings used for the many exhibitions and trade fairs which Barcelona hosts. Coming out on the rather ugly Plaza de España, you are face to face with Las Arenas bullring, built in Moorish style, though it is no longer used for bullfights. From here you can take the subway back to the Plaza de Cataluña.

The Incomparable Gaudí

One of the major attractions of Barcelona, and one which is often the sole reason for a visit by those interested in architecture, is the work of Antonio Gaudí, who was tragically run over by a tram in 1926. His most famous building is the Church of the Sagrada Familia (Holy Family), still under construction even though he began work on it in 1881. If you have never seen any of his work you should make a visit to at least one of his buildings a must. The Catalan worked more as a sculptor than an architect, changing his ideas frequently as the work progressed; molding huge masses of material with a fluidity and freedom that turned towers into candles shrouded in molten wax, staircases into swooping parabolas, doorways into troglodytes' caves.

Other specimens of Gaudí's exciting architecture are the crypt of the Güell Colony in San Baudillo, two apartment buildings, the Casa Milá and the Casa Batlló in the Paseo de Gracia, and the Palacio Güell, off the Ramblas on the Carrer Nou de la Rambla, which is now the site of the Museum of Spanish Theater (containing period dolls, posters, and mementos of Barcelona's artistic past). Perhaps most fascinating, because you can inspect it at close range on Sundays, is the Güell Park, an art nouveau extravanganza where the strange shapes have been put at the service of a park-playground, with a mosaic pagoda, undulating benches and fantastic-shaped architectural effects.

After an exhausting day of sightseeing, a welcome respite is a trip to Tibidabo Mountain for a superb panoramic view of the whole city. The fun fair and cafeterias somewhat spoil this beautiful spot.

PRACTICAL INFORMATION FOR BARCELONA

 HOW TO GET ABOUT. The least expensive way to travel from the airport to the city center is to take the airport train to Sants Station, just north of the Plaza de España. The train runs from early in the morning to about 11 P.M. Late at night there are buses between the airport and city. Or you can take a taxi; a taxi ride from the airport into town will cost you what is on the meter (about 1,100 ptas.) plus 90 ptas. and extra for luggage.

Modern Barcelona, north of the Plaza de Cataluña, is largely built on a grid system, though there is no helpful numbering system as in the U.S. However, the old part of town—the Gothic Quarter and the Barrio Chino, which are on either side of the Ramblas—is quite different altogether. Here the narrow streets wind and twist in all directions. It is an area which can only be explored on foot, so before you plunge into this fascinating labyrinth, best arm yourself with a good street map.

BY TAXI. Distances between places of interest in Barcelona are not especially great so a taxi ride should not work out too expensively. Taxis available for hire show a *Libre* sign in daytime and a small green lamp at night. When you begin your ride a standard charge of about 48 ptas., will be shown on the meter. There are further small supplements for each suitcase, for night fares (10 P.M. to 6 A.M.), for rides on Sundays and public holidays, for rides from a station and the port (about 35 ptas.), and for going to or from a bullring or football match (about 50 ptas.). Make sure your driver turns down the flag when you start your journey.

BY METRO. The subway system is already fairly extensive and is currently being further enlarged. This is the cheapest form of public transport and probably the easiest to use. You pay a flat fare no matter how far you travel. As of mid 1983 tickets cost 25 ptas., 30 on Sundays, or else you can buy a *tarjeta multiviaje* costing 155 ptas. for nine rides. The Plaza de Cataluña is the best connecting station for lines in all directions.

BY BUS. Most of the bus routes pass through the Plaza de Cataluña; again there is a flat fare system and again it's a little higher on Sundays (30 ptas. and 35 ptas. in mid 1983). A *tarjeta multiviaje* costs 195 ptas. and is good for nine rides. It can be bought from the transport kiosk in Plaza Cataluña (opposite Calle Vergara) where you can also obtain maps of the bus and metro system. To go to the beach at Casteldefels, take the UC from outside the University or the quicker, and slightly more expensive but less frequent, T11.

To go up Mount Tibidabo, take the 17 bus from Plaza Cataluña (or the subway) to Avda. de Tibadabo, from which a special tram *(tramvia blau)* runs to the funicular station. To reach the Parque Güell, take bus 10, 24 or 31.

STREET NAMES. As in many other Spanish towns, several of Barcelona's streets have had their names changed recently. In Barcelona this can be even more confusing for the tourist as both Catalan and Castilian (Spanish) names are used as well as the old and new names; it all depends which map you are using. To try and lessen this confusion, the following should be of help: Avda. Generalísimo Franco is now Avda. Diagonal; Avda. de José Antonio Primo de Rivera is now Gran Vía de las Corts Catalanes; Calle del Marqués del Duero is now Avda. del Paralelo; Paseo de General Mola is now Paseo de San Juan; Plaza de Calvo Sotelo is now Plaza de Francesc Maciá; Calle General Sanjurjo is now Calle de Pi i Margall; Calle del Conde de Asalto is now Carrer Nou de la Rambla; Calle de General Primo de Rivera is now Carrer Ample; the top part of Via Layetana is now Pau Claris; Martínez Anido is now Paseo de Picasso.

 HOTELS. As might be expected in a city of the size and importance of Barcelona, there are many hotels of all types and in all price ranges, from the truly luxurious to the more modest. The following is our selection.

Deluxe

Avenida Palace, Gran Vía 605 (tel. 301 9600). 211 rooms. Central and with all amenities. Elegant, well kept, old-world style hotel.

Diplomatic, Pau Claris 122 (tel. 317 3100). 213 rooms. Pool, shops. Modern, elegant and efficient.

Presidente, Avda. Diagonal 570 (tel. 200 2111). 161 rooms. Modern and with splendid view over city.

Princesa Sofia, Pio XII (tel. 330 7111). 505 rooms. With pool, shops and bingo.

Ritz, Gran Vía 668 (tel. 318 5200). 197 rooms. In a class by itself; with summer garden, topnotch restaurants, old-world charm. One of the best and most elegant hotels in Europe. On the corner of Calle Lauria.

Sarriá Gran Hotel, Avda. Sarriá 50 (tel. 239 1109). 314 rooms. Modern, in the Plaza Francesc Maciá area.

Expensive

Arenas, Capitán Arenas 20 (tel. 204 03 00). 59 rooms, Garden.

Balmoral, Vía Augusta 5 (tel. 217 87 00). 94 rooms. Central and with parking.

Colón, Avda. Catedral 7, tel. 301 1404. 161 rooms. In the Gothic Quarter overlooking cathedral square. Oldish, a little gloomy but with a charm and intimacy of its own. Parking.

Condor, Vía Augusta 127 (tel. 209 4511). 78 rooms. Parking and good amenities. In elegant area just beyond Diagonal.

Cristal, Diputación 257 (tel. 301 6600). 150 rooms. Good location, close to center, on corner of Rambla Cataluña.

Gala Placidia, Vía Augusta 112 (tel. 217 8200). A luxurious, suites-only hotel, though officially classed only as 3-star.

Gran Hotel Calderón, Rambla de Cataluña 26 (tel. 301 0000). Garage, pool, sun terrace and cafeteria, but there have been complaints about service and food.

Majestic, Paseo de Gracia 70 (tel. 215 4512). 350 rooms. Pool and shops.

Royal, Ramblas 117, tel. 301 9400. 108 rooms. Near the top of the Ramblas just down from Plaza Cataluña. Well recommended by readers.

Covadonga, Avda. Diagonal 596, tel. 209 5511. Stylish older hotel with 76 rooms.

Moderate

Expo Hotel, Mallorca I–35 (tel. 325 1212). 432 rooms. Parking, pool and bingo. Modern and professional but lacking in character. Self-service cafeteria only and located in a rather dull part of town opposite Sants station.

Gaudí, Carrer Nou de la Rambla 12 (tel. 317 9032). 71 rooms. Modern and nicely decorated. Situated opposite Gaudí's Palacio Güell, just off the Ramblas.

Gótico, Jaime I 14 (tel. 315 22 11). 73 rooms. In the heart of Gothic Quarter just down from Plaza San Jaime.

Gran Vía, Gran Vía 642 (tel. 318 1900). 48 rooms. Elegant old hotel between Paseo de Gracia and Pau Claris.

Habana, Gran Vía 647 (tel. 301 0750). Genteel and old fashioned establishment on an elegant street.

Montecarlo, Rambla de los Estudios 24 (tel. 317 5800). Elegant old hotel with turn of the century décor, beautiful chandeliers, lounge, new furniture, garage and coffee shop.

Oriente, Ramblas 45 (tel. 302 2558). Impressive lobby and mezzanine and elegant 1920s style; modernized rooms. Rooms on front could be noisy.

Suizo, Plaza del Angel 12 (tel. 315 4111). 44 rooms. Just off Via Layetana, on edge of Gothic Quarter, overlooking Jaime I metro.

Inexpensive

Antibes, Diputación 394 (tel. 225 8250). 65 rooms. Parking.

Bonanova Park, Capitán Arenas 51 (tel. 204 0900). 60 rooms. In fashionable area on far side of Diagonal.

Continental, Ramblas 138 (tel. 301 2508). 28 rooms. At very top of Ramblas near Plaza Cataluña. Stylish old building with elegant canopies.

Internacional, Ramblas 78 (tel. 302 2566). 53 rooms. Friendly, old-fashioned hotel right opposite Liceo Opera House.

Mesón Castilla, Valdoncella 5 (tel. 318 2182). 53 rooms. Pleasant old hotel, centrally located in old part of town.

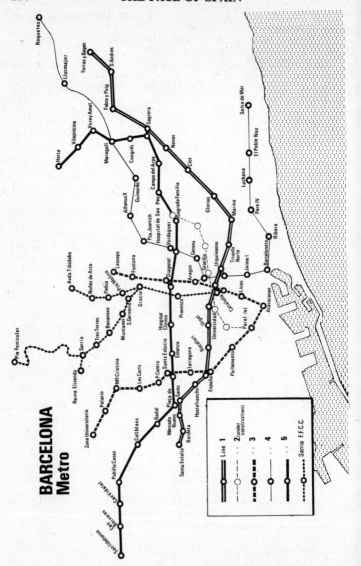

BARCELONA Metro

Line 1
2 (under construction)
3
4
5
Sarria F.F.C.C.

RESTAURANTS. Barcelona is well endowed with fine restaurants. Catalan cooking is wholesome with hearty portions and the paellas here rival those of Valencia and Alicante. Snails are also a specialty while pasta is more popular in Catalonia than in any other part of Spain, especially canelloni. The seafood, needless to say, is excellent. Barcelona has long been a notorious port; should you come across street walkers near any of our recommended restaurants, rest assured, they (the restaurants) are quite respectable inside!

Many Barcelona restaurants are closed Saturday night and Sunday, so do check in advance. Many close for a month in summer, usually August.

Deluxe

Amar Lur, Mallorca 275 (tel. 215 3024). Probably Barcelona's most elegant restaurant, situated in a luxurious house with private garden, and serving la Nouvelle Cuisine Basque.

Chalet Suisse, Diagonal 493 (tel. 259 1923). Swiss cuisine, so good meat and, of course, fondues.

Finisterre, Diagonal 469 (tel. 230 9114). Catalan specialties served in style.

La Masiá de Esplugas, at the end of Diagonal (tel. 371 3742). Outdoor dining and dancing.

Orotava, Consejo de Ciento 335 (tel. 302 3128). Tops for seafood; posh setting.

Reno, Tuset 27 (tel. 200 9129). High reputation for elegance and haute cuisine. Recommended for business entertainment.

Vía Veneto, Ganduxer 10 (tel. 250 3100). Highly recommended for the best in food and professional service.

Expensive

Agut d'Avignon, Trinidad 3 (tel. 302 6034). Hidden at the end of the first alley on the right off Avinyó leading out of Fernando. Rustic atmosphere, a favorite with politicians, Catalan cuisine and game specialties in season.

Bali, near the amusement park on Montjuich (tel. 241 3609). Indonesian restaurant specializing in *Rijsttafel.*

La Dida, Roger de Flor 230 (tel. 207 2391). Specializes in meat cooked over a charcoal fire.

La Font del Gat, Paseo Santa Madrona (tel. 224 0224). Magnificently set on Montjuich in a large villa with patio. The dining takes place among fountains and flowers. Expensive but worth it. Catalan specialties.

Il Giardinetto, Granada 22 (tel. 218 7536). A fashionable Italian restaurant.

Hogar Gallego, Via Layetana 5 (tel. 319 9077). An old favorite. Galician cooking specializing in seafood. Wonderful display of tapas at the bar.

Jaume de Provença, Provença 88 (tel. 230 0029). Ideal for business lunches. Haute cuisine specialties include baby eels rolled in smoked salmon.

Petit Soley, Plaza Villa de Madrid 4 (tel. 302 6164). Typical dishes amid lovely gardens with excavated Roman statues.

La Venta, Plaza del Funicular (tel. 212 6455). Delightful turn-of-the-century spot with tile floors, marble-topped tables, pot-bellied stove. Good for indoor and outdoor dining. Located at end of Dr. Andreu near funicular station.

Moderate

El Abrevadero, Vilá y Vilá 77 (tel. 241 3893). Claims to be the oldest restaurant in Barcelona. Catalan cooking with a famous Monday *cocido.*

Amaya, Ramblas 24 (tel. 302 6138). Basque food and famous for its meat dishes. Despite the ladies of the night who hang around outside, this is a good respectable restaurant.

Can Miserias, Conde Borrell 106 (tel. 254 78 37). Good regional specialties.

Can Sole, San Carlos 4 (tel. 319 5012). Plenty of old-world charm with a nice tavern atmosphere. Specializes in seafood. Recommended.

Los Caracoles, Escudillers 14 (tel. 302 3185). Famous Barcelona restaurant with wonderful décor and atmosphere. Specialty is snails.

Casa Leopoldo, San Rafael 24 (tel. 241 3014). Meat and seafood dishes from Galicia. In the heart of the Barrio Chino.

Culleretes, Quintana 5 (tel. 317 6485). In narrow street sandwiched between Boquería and Fernando, just off Ramblas. This is a real find. Three dining rooms, walls hung with photos of visiting celebrities. Do not be put off by the hookers outside. The charcoal-roasted chicken is recommended.

Joanet, Paseo Nacional 66 (tel. 319 5023). This charming restaurant (formerly *El Puerto*) in the Barceloneta area has been catering to diners since 1888. Excellent hors d'oeuvres and seafood.

Siete Puertas, Paseo Isabel II 14 (tel. 319 3033). Delightful restaurant with loads of old-world charm. Extremely popular.

Tibet, Ramiro de Maetzu 34 (tel. 214 5045). At the back of the Parque Güell, quaintly perched on top of a cliff. Catalan cooking with good spit-roasted meat.

Inexpensive

Agut, Gignas 16 (tel. 315 1709). Good value Catalan cooking in the heart of the Gothic Quarter.

El Bell Lloc, Legalidad 74 (tel. 219 7338). Charming, clean and inexpensive.

Can Lluis, Cera 49, tel. 241 1187. Over 100 years old, very popular.

Flash Flash, La Granada 25, tel. 228 5567. Trendy modern décor, serving 101 omelets until 1.30 A.M.

Mesón de las Ramblas, Ramblas 92. Pleasant bistro popular with tourists. Good value *menu del día.*

La Ponsa, Enrique Granados 89 (tel. 253 1037). A family-run restaurant serving Catalan food.

FAST FOOD. *Beefeater,* General Mitre 108. Pub atmosphere and huge steaks. *El Drugstore,* Paseo de Gracia 71, open from 7 A.M. to 5 A.M. for snacks and self-service meals. *Drugstore David,* Tuset 19, specializes in a dozen different types of hamburger and is popular with the young set. *Kentucky Fried Chicken,* Aribau 16 and also Calle Fontanella. *McDonalds,* Pelayo 62, on the corner of Ramblas. *La Oca,* Plaza Francesc Maciá 10. Smart trendy café, rather expensive, serving *platos combinados,* club sandwiches and pastries; also take-away snacks. *Topics,* Diagonal 474, is a good self-service cafeteria.

BARS. The best and most interesting and characteristic bars are to be found in the Barceloneta port area and in the Gothic Quarter, especially around the Calle Escudillers and the Plaza Real where on summer evenings thousands of people gather to eat shrimps and drink wine or huge liter glasses of beer.

 NIGHTLIFE. Barcelona has long had a reputation as a center of wild and wooly nightspots. But surprisingly for a city of its size, there is no really respectable high-class nightclub along the lines of, say, Paris' *Lido* or *Crazy Horse.* While we list a few possible places below, check before reserving a table as some of the shows might well offend the more sensitive. Most of the seemier night spots are found in the Barrio Chino and around the tawdry Para-lel.

Barcelona, probably more so than any other Spanish city, has not been slow to take advantage of the liberal climate regarding censorship laws, which has spread fast throughout post-Franco Spain.

NIGHTCLUBS.
Apolo, Paralelo 61 (tel. 241 4005). Musical shows are the order of the day in this rather run-down theater.

Barcelona de Noche, Tapias 5 (tel. 241 1167). Claims to have a "sexi-show." But check it out first.

Bodega Bohemia, Lancaster 2 (tel. 305 5081). Live shows in an atmospheric tavern with a touch of nostalgia for the old days.

Burbujas, Calvet 36 (tel. 209 5186). Two shows nightly. One of the more respectable ones.

Caesar's, Avda. de Roma 2 (tel. 325 4872). Dinner and shows with well known artistes.

El Molino, Vilá y Vilá 93 (tel. 241 6383). A famous old theater where you will enjoy an evening of hilarious burlesque and vaudeville. Unusual and inexpensive.

Victoria, Paralelo 69 (tel. 241 3985). Comic and musical revues; ideal for those whose Spanish isn't up to regular theater.

FLAMENCO. Catalans often consider this Andalusian spectacle anti-Catalan so Barcelona is not richly endowded with Flamenco spots and those that are in business are aimed right at the tourist market.

The best bets are *El Cordobés,* Ramblas 35 (tel. 317 6653) and *Los Tarantos,* Plaza Real 17 (tel. 302 5150). The latter is quite good. Entrance including one drink starts at around 1,700 ptas.

DISCOS. Barcelona is packed with discos. Some good ones are: *Bocaccio,* Muntaner 505; *Equilibrio,* Plaza Pie del Funicular; *Studio 54,* Avda Paral-lel 64. The latter is the largest and probably the most "in" at present.

CINEMA. Although most international movies are dubbed into Spanish, there are about half a dozen *cines de arte y ensayo* which often show films in their original language. These are all listed in the weekly *Guía del Ocio* (also an excellent guide to restaurants and all forms of nightlife). The official Filmoteca is at Travesera de Gracia 63 and shows three films a day in their original (often English) language.

MUSIC. Barcelona has one of the world's finest opera houses, with a seating capacity of 5,000. The Gran Teatro del Liceo stands on the Ramblas and the corner of San Pablo (Sant Pau). The box office for advance bookings is in San Pablo (tel. 302 6019). In winter there is an international opera and ballet season from November till February.

Concerts are held regularly in the *Palau de la Música,* Amadeo Vives 1 (tel. 301 1104), with both local and international artists.

In the summer concerts are held on Wednesday evenings in the patio of the *Antiguo Hospital de la Santa Cruz* on Calle Hospitalet. The International Theater Festival is held in the *Teatre Grec* in Montjuich in July and August. Performances of popular song and dance.

  MUSEUMS. Barcelona is well endowded with a number of fine museums. Most charge an admission fee though some are free on Sundays. Most are closed on Mondays.

Archeological Museum, Parque de Montjuich. Open Tues. to Sat. 10 to 2 and 6 to 8; Sun. and public holidays 10 till 2 only. Roman mosaics and display of finds from Ampurias.

Bullfighting Museum, Monumental Bullring. Open 10 to 1 and 3.30 to 7; on days when there is a corrida, from 10 till 1.30 only.

Decorative Arts Museum, Palacio de la Virreina, Rambla de las Flores 99. Open Tues. to Sat. 9 to 2 and 4.30 to 9; Mon. 4.30 to 9 only; Sun. 9 to 2.

Gaudí Museum in Parque Güell. Open Sun. and holidays only, 10 to 12 and 4 to 7.

Joan Miró Foundation in Montjuich Park. Works by Miró and others. Open Tues. to Sat. 11 to 8; Sun. 11 to 2.30.

Maritime Museum in Reales Atarazanas in Puerta de la Paz. Huge collection of naval souvenirs, model ships, old maps, coins, etc. Open 10 to 1.30 and 4 to 6.30, Sun. 10 to 1.30 only.

Military Museum in Montjuich Castle. Well-arranged. Open 10 to 2 and 5 to 8 (7 in winter); Sun. 10 to 8 (7 in winter).

Modern Art Museum in Ciudadela Park. Paintings from 18th to early-20th centuries. Many canvases evoke the era when Picasso lived in Barcelona. Open Tues. to Sat. 9 to 7.30; Sun. 9 to 2; Mon. 3 to 7.30.

Museum of Catalan Art, Palacio Nacional, on Montjuich. Open 9.30 to 2. Closed Mon. Houses the greatest collection of Catalán art in the world, as well as an interesting selection of Spanish ceramics.

Museum of the History of Barcelona in the Casa Padellás in the Plaza del Rey. Open Tues. to Sat. 9 to 2 and 5 to 8.30; Mon. 5 to 8.30 only; Sun. 9–2.

Picasso Museum, Montcada 15. Good collection of the artist's work housed in three historic palaces. Open Mon. 4.30 to 8.30; Tues. to Sat. 9.30 to 1.30 and 4.30 to 8.30; Sun. 9.30 to 1.30.

Science Museum, Teodor Roviralta 55. Open daily 10 to 8. The first of its kind in Spain. Includes a Planetarium with functions at 1 and 6 Mon. to Sat. and every half hour on Sundays.

Theater Museum, Nou de la Rambla. Open 11 to 2 and 6 to 8, Sun. 11 to 2 only. Interesting collection of dolls, posters and memorabilia located in Gaudí's Palacio Güell.

Wax Museum, Rambla de Santa Mónica 4. Open every day 11 to 1.30 and 4 to 7.30 (8 on Sat. and Sun.).

 PARKS AND GARDENS. The closest to the center of town is the *Parque de la Ciudadela* where you will find the zoo and the Museums of Modern Art and Natural History; there are some pleasant gardens and fountains and this is an agreeable place to spend siesta time should you not be at the beach. The *Parque Güell* in the northwest of the city is a delightful place to visit on Sunday afternoons. It was begun by Gaudí whose idea was to build a kind of garden city to demonstrate his ideas on town planning. However, his death cut the project short and only a few early constructions can be seen but these constitute a superb art nouveau extravanganza and the park is well worth a visit, not only for Gaudí's incredible mosaics but also for the view over the city to the Mediterranean. Gaudí's house, now the Gaudí Museum, can be visited on Sundays.

There is a splendid view of the city from *Montjuich* reached by taxi or buses 1, 13 or 101, and here you can visit the Museum of Catalan Art, the Military Museum, the Archeological Museum and the Joan Miró Foundation. There is a good amusement park, the model Spanish village and at weekends the beautiful Monjuich fountains.

Tibidabo mountain is 530 meters (1,745 feet) high and can be reached either by funicular (see page 271) or by a winding road affording spectacular views of Barcelona and the Mediterranean. On the top is a basilica, another fun fair, and nearby the monastery and palace of Pedralbes.

 SPORTS. Bullfights in Spain are ordinarily to be seen from the end of March to October. The main ring is the Monumental on Gran Vía and Carlos I. Las Arenas ring is rarely used now. Tickets can be bought from the official ticket office at Muntaner 24 or from below the Teatro Principal in the Ramblas (which also sells soccer tickets).

Good **football** (soccer) is to be seen in Barcelona, where games are usually played Sundays, either at the Nuevo Campo de Barcelona or at Campo de Sarriá. **Pelota** is played at Frontón Principal Palacio, Plaza del Teatro 27.

Golf may be played at the San Cugat club, 18 holes, about 14 km from the center of town, the Prat Club, and at least three others in the surrounding area

(Sitges, San Andrés de Llaveneras and Vallromanos). For **tennis,** there are the Clubs Barcino, La Salud, Pompeya, El Turó, and the Real Club de Tenis Barcelona. Rental courts at Andrés Gimeno off the highway in Castelldefels, and at Can Melich at Sant Just Desvern (take SJ bus at Plaza Universidad for latter). **Bowling** at the Boliche, Diagonal 508. **Ice skating** at Roger de Flor 168, 11–2, 6–12; Sunday 10–1, 4–7, 8–11. Another at Barcelona Football stadium, 10–1, 4–7.30, 10.30–1; Sunday 10–1, 4–9.

 SHOPPING. The best shopping streets are the Paseo de Gracia (the Fifth Avenue of Barcelona); Avda. Diagonal between calle Ganduxer and Paseo de Gracia; Gran Vía between Balmes and Vía Layetana; Rambla Cataluña (below Plaza Cataluña it is referred to as Las Ramblas); the area between Ramblas and Vía Layetana; and Calle Tuset, with small boutiques, several good ones in the Drugstore David.

If you're feeling adventurous, you might wander over to the Mayor de Gracia area, just above and north of Paseo de Gracia. This is really a small, almost independent *pueblo* within a large city, a warren of small, narrow streets, changing name at every corner, and filled with tiny shops where you'll find everything from old-fashioned tin lanterns to real feather dusters.

For **antiques,** your best bet is to wander in the area around the cathedral in the Barrio Gótico. Calle de la Paja and Calle Baños Nuevos have one antique shop after another. There you'll find old books, maps and furniture. On Thursday mornings, there is an antiques market in the Cathedral Square, and sometimes you can find bargains at Els Encants market at Plaza de las Glorias.

Artespaña, the government-run Spanish **handicraft** shop, Diagonal 419 and Rambla Cataluña 121.

Best for **souvenirs** is the *Pueblo Español,* where you'll find everything from embroidered linens, mantillas, fans, olive-wood objects, Majorca pearls, ceramics, hand-painted fabrics, typical sandals, to hand-carved boats, all at the same or lower prices than in the souvenir shops on the Ramblas.

Barcelona, like Madrid, has its **flea market,** or, rather, markets known as *Els Encants.* The Belle Caire market, Plaza de las Glorias Catalanas, operates all day every day except Tues. and Thurs. The San Antonio market, in the Calles de Urgel, Borrell and Validomat, is open all week, but Sun. A.M. mostly for second-hand books.

Major **department stores** are: *El Corte Inglés,* Plaza Cataluña with a newer larger one on the Diagonal (nearest metro, María Cristina); *Galerías Preciados,* Puerta del Angel, Plaza Francesc Maciá and Meridiana 352.

 USEFUL ADDRESSES. *Spanish Tourist Office,* Gran Vía 658. *City Tourist Office,* Plaza San Jaime (Sant Jaume). *Train Stations:* Término, Avda. Marques de Argentera; Paseo de Gracia, an underground station where Aragón meets Paseo de Gracia; Sants-Central, at the end of Avda. de Roma. Information, reservations and tickets are available from any of the above stations. *Bus Station:* most buses to destinations within Spain leave from Estación del Norte, Avda. Vilanova; to the Costa Brava, from Paseo Colón 3; to Lérida and Andorra from Ronda Universidad 4. For buses to Madrid, inquire at Paralelo 15, and to Bilbao at the Expo Hotel, Mallorca 1–35, near Sants Station. For bus journeys outside Spain, *Iberbus,* Bergara 2 (tel. 318 5746) have services to France, Italy, Belgium and Holland; *Via Tourisme,* Pau Claris 117 (tel. 302 5675) have buses to France, Belgium, Holland, Germany and London.

Iberia, Rambla de Cataluña 18 (tel. 325 7100); Plaza de España (tel. 325 6000); Mallorca 277 (tel. 215 3820). *British Airways,* Paseo de Gracia 59 (tel. 215 2112). *Wagon Lits Cooks,* Paseo de Gracia 8 (tel. 317 5500). *American Consulate,* Vía Layetana 33, (tel. 319 9550). *British Consulate,* Diagonal 477, (tel. 322 2151). *Hospital of the Foreign Colonies,* Alegre de Dalt 87, (tel. 213 2012). *Main Post Office,* Plaza de Antonio López. *Telephone Exchange,* Plaza de Cataluña on the corner of Fontanella. *Car Hire,* Atesa, Lauria 46, (tel. 317 1798); Avis, Casanova 209, (tel. 209 9533); Hertz, Tuset 10, (tel. 217 8076); Ital, Travesera de Gracia 71, (tel. 209 7544).

CATALONIA

Gateway to the Mediterranean

Catalonia (in Spanish *Cataluña,* in Catalan, *Catalunya*) constitutes a bridge between France and Spain. Barcelona's Prat de Llobregat airport handles some four million passengers annually. The quickest access by road is on the Perpignan–Barcelona toll-road crossing the border at La Junquera, though more attractive crossings into Catalonia, whether by road or rail, are over the Pyrenees at Puigcerdá or along the Côte Vermeille in Roussillon (French Catalonia) to Port Bou, where the railroad turns inland to Figueras, while the road meanders along the Costa Brava to Cadaqués.

Roussillon, Catalonia and the Balearic Islands had a common history in the Middle Ages, and this community of fate has been reflected in their architecture, customs, dances, music habits and costumes. It is, of course, mirrored above all in the common language, which is

different from Castilian. Catalan is related to Provençal, with an ad-
mixture of harsh intonation that robs it of the soft, musical cadences
of Provençal, but at the same time adds vigor and dynamism to it.
Catalan is spoken from Perpignan to Valencia and, with variations, in
the Balearic Islands. It has some affinities with French.

Of the industry of the Catalans, there can be no doubt: they boast
of their modern factories, especially for textiles, which rank with the
finest in the world. Also, they are much more commercially minded
than other Spaniards. Catalonia, with Barcelona as its cultural center,
was one of the greatest seats of nautical, maritime and astronomical
knowledge during the Middle Ages, and Catalans were famous for their
seafaring exploits.

Wine, oil, fruit and cork have been the staples of Catalonia for
hundreds of years, and, with the exception of cork which has been
ousted by plastics, they still are today. Food is the least exotic here of
all the Spanish provinces and the least strange to foreign palates and
stomachs. The Catalans take pride in the preparation of their food;
travelers often find that the cuisine in many Catalan places can stand
comparison with that of France.

Spanish Catalonia, divided today into the four provinces of Girona
(formerly Gerona), Barcelona, Tarragona and Lleida (formerly Lerida), has enjoyed a turbulent, rich history that has scattered its monuments throughout the province with a truly generous hand. Geography
and the quirks of historical development have contributed largely to the
distinct character of Catalonia, which differs in so many respects from
that of the kingdoms of central Spain. The mountains stretching along
the Ebro and the desert-like plains of Aragón separate Catalonia from
central Spain; consequently, Catalonia looked toward the Mediterranean as its natural outlet, and so acquired maritime characteristics.

Barcelona's Hinterland

The environs of Barcelona abound in places of great interest to lovers
both of landscape and of antiquity—San Cugat del Vallés, with a lovely
Benedictine abbey; Tarrasa, the ancient Egara, which has charming
examples of pre-Roman architecture; Llobregat river with a Roman
bridge. But the main site, easily reached from the Martorell freeway
exit, is the world-famous monastery of Montserrat, where medieval
legend placed the Holy Grail, a claim contested by many other places.

The countless legends that surround Montserrat, which inspired
Wagner's opera *Parsifal,* are undoubtedly rooted in the fantastic and
strangely unreal appearance of this mountain. It juts up abruptly some
1,135 meters (3,725 feet) above the valley of the Llobregat river and is
outlined with monoliths that look like immense stone figures. The best

view of the supernatural wall is to be had from some distance away on the road to Manresa.

Founded in A.D. 880, the monastery has some 300 Benedictine monks today. Each year, thousands of pilgrims go there to see its chief treasure, the Black Virgin of Montserrat, which is supposed to have been carved by St Luke. But even the vast monastic complex is dwarfed by the grandeur of the jagged mountain peaks. From the highest, called San Jerónimo and accessible by cablecar, a large section of the coast and the entire range of the eastern Pyrenees are visible on a clear day. Except for the church and the Virgin's Sanctuary, you cannot visit the monastery, and the village itself is swamped by tourism. El Greco, Correggio and Caravaggio are represented in the monastery museum, while the music-lover will have an unforgettable experience listening to the Escolanía, the boys' choir founded 700 years ago, singing at morning mass, at the Salve and at the end of vespers.

The granite Sierra de Montseny, away to the northeast, deserves a separate excursion, to include the drive up from San Celoni, near the freeway, to the Santa Fé hermitage, from where there are sensational views. The road to Montseny itself traverses the entire sierra to Tona on N152, while the branch to Viladrau and Arbucias winds along the sierra's northern slopes.

Around Catalonia

In moving farther from Barcelona for the explorations of Catalonia, there are three directions from which to choose—ignoring the Costa Brava, which will be treated later. Southward along the coast is for the beaches near Barcelona or the inland toll-road for Tarragona and Valencia; westward into the province of Lleida is also the way to Madrid, or, if you turn north from its capital, to Andorra. Northward takes you to the playgrounds of the Pyrenees, their spas, their resorts, in winter their ski centers, and to the ancient town of Puigcerdá. The most traveled of all these routes is the coastal road south.

Costa Dorada

A freeway leads past the Prat de Llobregat airport to the important resort of Castelldeféls, but then the overcrowded coastal road narrows to Sitges, to which the people of Barcelona flock for bathing. It is an attractive town, proud of its flowers, which carpet the streets during the Corpus Christi processions. There is an excellent beach at Sitges, the fishing is good, and if you are a golfer, you can play on the local links. The town has several museums; most interesting is the Cau-Ferrat, founded by the artist Rusiñol, which contains some of his own paintings, but a greater attraction is provided by two canvases of El Greco. Connoisseurs of wrought ironwork will be delighted to find here a beautiful collection of *cruz terminal,* crosses once erected to delimit town boundaries.

Unless bound for the coastal resorts of Villanueva y Geltrú, Cubellas, Calafell or Torredembara, motorists are advised to avoid the traffic jams on the overcrowded N340, not least because the parallel freeway offers an attractive alternative through vineyards and olive groves.

The A2 freeway, as it branches west to Lleida, passes two superb monasteries. The first is the Cistercian monastery of Santes Creus, founded in 1159. The three austere aisles and the unusual 14th-century apse combine with the newly restored cloisters and the courtyard of the royal palace to make a complex of great beauty.

Another turning off the highway leads to Montblanch, whose ancient gates are too narrow for cars. A walk through its narrow streets reveals Gothic churches with lovely stained glass windows, a 16th-century hospital and fine medieval mansions. Eight kilometers further on is the second monastery; that of Santa María at Poblet. Its simple lines, uncluttered surfaces and lovely arches proclaim Cistercian origins.

And indeed Poblet, at the foot of the Prodes Mountains, is the most complete and representative masterpiece of Spanish medieval monastic architecture. Started in 1153, it took three centuries to complete. The monastery suffered extensive damage in the 1835 revolution, and monks of the reformed Cistercian order have successfully carrried out the difficult task of restoration. Monks and novices pray again before the splendid retable over the tombs of the Catalan rulers, sleep in the cold, austere dormitory, eat their frugal meals in the stark refectory, while a fountain plays in the rose garden. The cloister is outstanding for lightness and severity, two elements that you rarely find so deftly blended as at Poblet.

Tarragona

Tarraco, renamed Colonia Julia Tarraconensis by Julius Caesar in 45 B.C., was one of Rome's principal strongholds in Spain (it has only about 110,000 inhabitants today whereas in Roman times it had a quarter of a million) and, even before reaching it, you pass by the triumphal arch of Bara, unrestored and undamaged, which dates back to the 3rd century B.C. English engineers constructed in 1707 the glacis on which the Archeological Promenade skirts the formidable 3rd-century B.C. Ibero-Roman ramparts above the "cyclopean" walls, containing blocks of stone so huge that is is impossible to explain how they could have been raised before the age of machinery, even by employing thousands of slaves. Visigothic, Moorish and Catalan towers guard the Roman gates.

From the sea Tarragona looks like an evocation of, and a scene from, the Middle Ages; viewed from the air, it presents a picture of wonderful clarity. In Roman times, it was regarded as one of the empire's finest urban creations; its wine was already famous and its population was the first in Spain to gain Roman citizen status. Signposts indicate Scipio's tower, the amphitheater and the perfectly preserved three-tier aqueduct some 4 kilometers outside the city, while the Praetorium stands next to a medieval masterpiece built from the stones of these Roman monuments.

A flight of steps leads up to the cathedral, which is 13th century. Though never finished, the clustered columns of the stark interior contrast dramatically with the idyllic cloister round the rose garden. The showpiece of the rich treasury is a rare Gothic tapestry. From the "Mediterranean Balcony" at the head of the main avenue, the Rambla Nova, the view extends over a series of fine beaches.

Just off the highway, seventy-seven kilometers (48 miles) to the southwest is Tortosa, nestling since Roman times in a superb setting on the left bank of the Ebro. The 14th-century cathedral and the 16th-century college of St. Aloysius Gonzaga rise majestically above the medieval quarter. The soil around here is very rich, producing superb fruit and vegetables. A particularly lovely drive follows the Ebro upstream to the dam at Flix and to the last of the impressive chain of artificial lakes formed by the Ebro, Cinca and Segre, and finally, through idyllic olive groves and green hills, to Lleida.

Lleida

The motorway west from Barcelona leads to Zaragoza and eventually to Madrid after passing through the least known of the four provinces of Catalonia—indeed, the principal place of interest between Barcelona and Lleida occurs before the provincial border is passed. In Igualada, you might enjoy stopping to look at the old people's home, with its curious Gaudí-esque façade of unhewn stone and pebbles.

In its own distinctive way, Lleida equals many another provincial capital. Though it is an industrial town, the old quarters of the city are picturesque, and certain streets are shut off to traffic to make things easier for pedestrians and shoppers. The streets are all bursting with life, full of bright sunshine and welcome shade. Some streets have the protective *toldos* stretched across to ward off the heat of the sun's rays.

From whichever direction you approach Lleida, you see the upper part of a mighty building rising above what looks like a fortified castle atop a hill on the banks of the Segre river. This is the ancient La Séo

Cathedral—deconsecrated, converted into a fort, burned, and pillaged. The recent restoration has entirely recaptured the majesty of this grandiose edifice, all the more deeply impressive for having survived disaster. You may admire the cleverly conceived square cloister, and the intricate fretwork portals and columns. To top it all you have a glorious, sweeping view out over the plain.

Though Lleida lies on the main east–west road (N-II) from Barcelona to Madrid, scenically far more rewarding is the narrow C1313 via Balaguer up the lovely Segre valley and then along the artifical lake into tiny Andorra, a grand shopping center in a glorious setting.

Side Trip to Andorra

The way to Andorra lies through the little town of Séo de Urgel—the only way to go in winter, for snow can block the passes from France, and then Andorra may only be entered from Spain. Séo de Urgel is unimportant now—though its cheese is very popular—but in the 13th century, the date from which its old cathedral stems, it was of sufficient note to justify being given two co-princes. The Bishop of Urgel was one, the Count of Foix, the other. And today Andorra still, nominally at least, is ruled by these two co-princes, the Bishop and the President of France to whom the Count of Foix ceded the title. The Councils of the Valleys of Andorra really govern themselves and so are independent of the powers that theoretically hold them in feudal fief.

If you slip into this patriarchal and minute country, with its deep gorges and savage mountain scenery, there are two places that are most likely to attract you—Andorra la Vella, the capital, and Les Escaldes, a spa, better equipped even than the capital to put up visitors. The visit offers a rare combination of natural beauty and strictly practical benefits, as the duty-free status of Andorra makes it a shopper's paradise—provided you hold a foreign passport you are simply waved through the customs. The only snag is parking, as the narrow valley, hemmed in by majestic mountains on all sides, literally has not enough space to accommodate the uninterrupted influx of cars.

You may escape from this traffic into the idyllic upper valleys, or pass through Andorra entering France over the highest road pass in the Pyrenees, blocked by snow half the year and thus ideal skiing terrain. Or you may keep on C1313 which turns east (right) just before the Andorran frontier, following the Segre for fifty more splendid kilometers to another border crossing at Puigcerdá, which can also be reached directly from Barcelona via Vich and Ripoll.

Puigcerdá was once the capital of the Cerdagne, a Pyrenean land straddling the present Franco-Spanish frontier. High in the mountains, it has a nine-hole golf course and is a center for the summer and winter vacation resorts of the Pyrenees—Super-Molina (Spain's top winter sports resort), Nuria, Camprodon, and Puigcerdá itself, and the spa of Ribas de Fresser.

The Green Catalonia

Travelers interested in discovering for themselves the real Catalonia, the one that is seldom available to tourists in a rush, should try another itinerary that is highly recommended. Between the frontier and Barcelona, there is a roundabout route from Figueras, due west on C260 and C150 to Olot and Ripoll, then veering obliquely south on N152 via Vich to bring you to the capital of the province.

Here, you will see land that is carefully tilled and productive, a living green refutation of the proverbially arid reputation of Spanish soil. The landscape is endlessly changing, alternating between hills and wooded dales. On a sheer basalt cliff overhanging the Fluvia River, Castellfullit juts out like the prow of a ship. The road passes through the rather disappointing town; what looks from afar like a story-book village loses its charm close-up. Don't plan to stop anywhere before San Juan de las Abadesas, where the church possesses a handsomely carved wood calvary cross.

The general appearance of villages, particularly in Catalonia, has been undergoing a curious change. New capital resulting from the tourist industry has been invested in storage silos built along outlines closely resembling those of the generally square church steeples, somehow reminiscent of Tuscany. Everywhere, new camping grounds and swimming pools have mushroomed. If you're bent on finding the old-world atmosphere of Spanish rural existence, you will have to avoid the international traffic sweeping down to Barcelona and stick to back roads.

Probably the most pleasant sights in the Catalonian countryside are the farms. The multitude of buildings of austere grayish or pinkish stone, with their staggered levels of rooftops and ubiquitous square towers, give the farmhouses an immutable, centuries-old look of fortresses, exactly the way they must have looked in more heroic times.

Churches confer dignity on the villages. Church architecture is pretty much the same everywhere here: Romanesque—either real or imitation—with baroque façades added on. The tiniest village boasts its main square, framed by arcades, and a *rambla,* or promenade (from *rable,* a species of tree), where it is fun to sit and watch the villagers stroll up and down during the sacred evening *paseo* . . . or to stroll with them.

Olot has managed to preserve most of its original flavor. Even its new quarters catch your eye, with their modern church that flaunts a springboard-shaped steeple and a gigantic monk's head sculptured by Iloret on its façade. This is the church of St. Peter the Martyr, whose name has been extended to the surrounding neighborhood.

The town of Ripoll was considerably disfigured by turn-of-the-century industrialization. It commands a halt, nevertheless: the 11th-century monastery of Santa María is worth a visit. The portal is one of the outstanding achievements of Romanesque art and so are the cloisters with their double colonnades.

Vich sits in the middle of the plain at the confluence of the Guri and the Heder rivers, 488 meters (1,600 feet) above sea level: it's the business and industrial center for the region. It possesses a handsome baroque cathedral (St Peter's), whose Byzantine tower dates back to the 11th and 12th centuries, and an interesting museum. The cathedral is decorated with very powerful modern murals painted twice by José María Sert because the first series was destroyed in the Civil War.

If you wish to detour here, take N141 to Moya—notice its church tower with the odd "lobster-claw" fretwork—and then go on to Manresa, where you will catch your first glimpse of the fantastic ridge of Montserrat, looming up to your left.

Instead of passing thorough Moya and Manresa, you can keep to N152 through La Garriga, a charming medieval town set in a rich agricultural valley, and in a few more kilometers find yourself once more in Catalonia's first city, Barcelona.

PRACTICAL INFORMATION FOR CATALONIA

WHAT TO SEE. Dominating every other attraction of Catalonia is the great and lovely city of Barcelona itself —particularly since the outstanding single touristic attraction of this region, the Holy Grail Monastery of Montserrat, is an easy excursion from Barcelona. After Barcelona as a lodestone for visitors comes the stretch of summer playland called the Costa Brava, the Rugged Coast (see separate chapter). Besides Barcelona, other cities you might like to visit are the old coastal city of Tarragona with its Roman amphitheater and aqueduct; Manresa, for its remarkable 14th-century church, noted for its stained glass, and Vich, for its cathedral, cloisters, and museum. The monastery of Poblet, though less well known, ranks for interest with those of Montserrat and Guadalupe. Barcelona's summer playgrounds are at Castelldeféls and Sitges, whose beautiful beaches lie south of the capital.

For winter sports, La Molina, near the French frontier, is a top skiing place. This Pyrenean region, of which Puigcerdá was the ancient capital, is pleasant for summer loafing. There are a few spas in Catalonia, such as Caldas de Malavella and Caldas de Montbúy.

A worthwhile excursion that can be made from Catalonia is to the little country of Andorra, reached from Seo de Urgel, in the Pyrenees.

HOTELS. The hotels of the Costa Brava resort towns as well as those of Girona and Figueras are dealt with in a separate chapter. There are six paradores in this area; at Cardona and Vich in Barcelona province, at Arties, Seo de Urgel and Viella in Lleida province; and at Tortosa in Tarragona province.

HOTELS AND RESTAURANTS

AMETLLA DEL VALLES (Barcelona). *Del Valles* (E), Autovía de la Ametlla, tel. (93) 843 0600. 54 rooms, pleasant.

ANDORRA. Tiny republic perched in the Pyrenees, easily approached from Seo de Urgel. At **Andorra la Vella:** *Andorra Park* (E), tel. (9738) 20979. Quiet, secluded setting, pool, tennis. *Eden Roc* (E), Avda. Dr Mitjavila, tel. (9738) 21000. *President* (E), Avda. Santa Coloma, tel. 22922. 88 rooms plus suites. *Sasplugas* (E), Avda. del Co-Princep Iglesias, tel. (9738) 20311. With good views. *Andorra Palace* (M), Prat de la Creu, tel. (9738) 21072. Tennis, pool, mountain views. *Serola* (M), Ctra Santa Coloma, tel. (9738) 20647. 56 rooms.

At **Les Escaldes:** *Les Comtes d'Urgell* (M), tel. (9738) 20621. 200 rooms. *Roc Blanc* (M), Plaza del Co-Princeps 5, tel. (9738) 21486. 96 rooms.
At **La Massana:** *Rutlan* (E), tel. (9738) 35000. Pool, good views.

ARENYS DE MAR (Barcelona). *Raymond* (M), Paseo Xifre 1, tel. (93) 792 1700. 33 rooms. *Carlos I* (I), Rial Canalias, tel. (93) 792 0383. 100 rooms, pool. *Impala* (I), Urb. Montmar. tel. (93) 792 1504. 52 rooms, pool and tennis. *Titus* (I), tel. (93) 791 0300. 44 rooms, pool and garden.
Restaurants. *Portinyol* (E), Escollera de Levante, tel. 792 0009. Good views of beach and good seafood. *Hispania* (E-M), Real 54, tel. 791 0457. An excellent restaurant a little bit out of the center.

ARTIES (Lleida). *Parador Don Gaspar de Portola* (E), tel. (973) 64 08 01. 40 rooms, in mountain setting.

BALAGUER (Lleida). *Conde Jaime de Urgel* (E), Avda Pedro IV, tel. (973) 44 56 04. 60 rooms, a semi parador with pool and many amenities. *Mirador del Segre* (I), General Vives 3, tel. (973) 44 57 50. 33 rooms.

BARRUERA (Lleida). *Manantial* (E), Caldas de Bohí, tel. (973) 69 02 93. 119 rooms, located in historic building, with pool, mini golf, gardens and bar.

CALAFELL (Tarragona). *Kursaal* (E), Avda San Juan de Díos 119, tel. (977) 69 23 00. 4-star hotel with 39 rooms. *Canadá* (M), Mosén Jaime Soler 44, tel. (977) 69 15 00. 106 rooms, pool, garden and bar. *Miramar* (M), Rambla Costa Dorada 1, tel. (977) 66 23 04. 201 rooms, garden.

CALDAS DE ESTRACH (Barcelona). *Colón* (E), Paz 16, tel. (93) 791 0351. 82 rooms, pool, mini golf, bowling green, bar. *Jet* (I), Pasaje Francisco Riera 24, tel. (93) 791 0651. A good value 3-star hotel.

CALDAS DE MONTBUY (Barcelona). *Balneario Broquetas* (M), Plaza España 1, tel. (93) 865 0100. 84 rooms, in historic building, with pool, mini golf and garden. *Balneario Termas Victoria* (I), Barcelona 12, tel. (93) 865 0150. 91 rooms, pool and garden.

CALELLA (Barcelona). Not to be confused with Calella on the Costa Brava. *Mont Rosa* (M), Paseo de las Rocas, tel. (93) 769 0508. Modern, 120 rooms with terraces, private beach. *Las Vegas* (M-I), Zona Riera Faro, tel. (93) 769 0850. Excellent, 94 rooms. *Amaika* (I), Barcelona, tel. (93) 769 1412. Large, 3-star hotel, with very moderate rates. *La Maresma* (I), on edge of town, tel. (93) 899 0800. 50 rooms, pool and tennis, low rates.

CAMBRILS (Tarragona). *Augustus I* (M), Ctra. Salou, tel. (977) 38 11 54. 243 rooms, pool and gardens. *Centurión Playa* (M), Ctra. Salou, tel. (977) 36

14 50. Another large, modern hotel. *Motel La Dorada* (M), on N340, tel. (977) 36 01 50. 37 rooms, good rates. *Cesar Augustus* (I), Ctra. Salou, tel. (977) 38 18 12. 120 rooms, pool and gardens; same management as Augustus I.

CAMPRODON (Girona). *Güell* (I), Plaza de España 8, tel. (972) 74 02 16. 43 rooms, parking. *Rigat* (I), Plaza del Doctor Robert 2, tel. (972) 74 00 13. 74 rooms, pool, mini golf, garden and bar.

CARDONA (Barcelona). *Parador Condes de Cardona* (E), tel. (93) 869 1275. 65 rooms, in ancient castle of Dukes of Cardona; good food and service.

CASTELLDEFELS (Barcelona). Seaside resort just south of Barcelona. *Rey Don Jaime* (E), Torrebarona, tel. (93) 665 1300. The top hotel, 64 rooms, with pool, tennis and gardens. *Bel-Air* (M), Paseo Marítimo 169, tel. (93) 665 1600. 38 rooms, golf, mini golf and tennis among its many amenities. *Mediterráneo* (M), Paseo Marítimo 294, tel. (93) 665 2100. 47 rooms, good view. *Neptuno* (M), Paseo Garbi 74, tel. (93) 665 1450. 38 rooms, pool. *Playafels* (M), Playa Ribera de San Pedro, tel. (93) 665 1250. 34 rooms, golf, garden and private beach. *Rancho* (M), Paseo de la Marina 212, tel. (93) 365 1900. 60 rooms, pool and tennis. *Elvira* (I), Calle 22 de la Pineda 13, tel. (93) 665 1550. 31 rooms, garden. *Rialto* (I), Paseo Marítimo 70, tel. (93) 665 2058. 14 rooms, garden and parking.

COMARRUGA (Tarragona). *Gran Hotel Europe* (E), Avda. Palfuriana, tel. (977) 66 18 50. Modern with pool, tennis and mini golf among the many amenities. *Brisamar* (M-I), Plaza Hermanos Trillas, tel. (977) 66 17 00. 102 rooms, pool and tennis, some very reasonable rooms. *Casa Mari* (M-I), Villafranca 8, tel. (977) 66 17 50. 106 rooms, pool.

LA GARRIGA (Barcelona). *Blancafort* (M), Baños 55, tel. (93) 871 4600. 50 rooms, pool, tennis and mini golf.

IGUALDA (Barcelona). *América* (E), tel. (93) 803 1000. 52 rooms, garden.

LA JUNQUERA (Girona). Frontier town. *Puerta de España* (M), on N–II, tel. (972) 54 01 20. 26 rooms. *Frontera* (I), on the N–II, tel. (972) 54 00 50. 28 rooms. *Goya* (I), on N–II, tel. (972) 54 00 77. 35 rooms. *Junquera* (I), on N–II, tel. (972) 54 01 00. 28 rooms, central.

LLEIDA (formerly Lérida). *Condes de Urgel II* (E), Avda. de Barcelona 17, tel. (973) 20 23 00. Quite large, and popular with tour groups. *Condes de Urgel* (M), Avda. de Barcelona 2, tel. (973) 20 23 00. Under same management as above, but much smaller, 34 rooms, with pool and bar. *Jamaica* (M-I), Ctra de Zaragoza, tel. (973) 22 15 40. 24 rooms. *Principal* (M-I), Plaza Pahería 8, tel. (973) 24 09 00. 42 rooms, central.

Restaurants. *Sheyton Pub* (E), Avda. Prat de la Riba 39, tel. 23 81 97. Best in town, with an English atmosphere. *Forn del Nastasi* (M), Salmerón 10, tel. 22 45 10.

LLIVIA (Girona). *Llivia* (M), Ctra. de Puigcerda, tel. (972) 89 60 00. 63 rooms, pool, tennis and bar.

MALGRAT DE MAR (Barcelona). *Malgrat* (I), tel. (93) 761 0216. 24 rooms. *Monte Playa* (I), Paseo Marítimo, tel. (93) 761 0508. 183 rooms, garden.

MANRESA (Barcelona). *Pedro III* (M), Muralla Sant Francesc 49, tel. (93) 874 3650. A central, 3-star hotel.

MATARO (Barcelona). *Castell de Mata* (E), on N–II, tel. (93) 790 1044. 52 rooms in historic building, pool, mini golf, garden and bar. *Colón* (I), Colón 6–8, tel. (93) 790 4492. 55 rooms.

LA MOLINA (Girona). Winter sports resort. *Palace* (E), Supermolina, tel. (972) 89 20 16. 32 rooms, with pool, tennis and garden. *Adsera* (E-M), tel. (972) 89 20 01. 35 rooms, in center, pool and garden. *Roc Blanch* (I), on road to station, tel. (972) 89 20 75. 22 rooms, central. *Solineu* (I), Avda. Supermolina, tel. (972) 89 20 16. 54 rooms, pool, tennis and bowling green.

MONTSENY (Barcelona). *San Bernat* (M), Montaña Finca el Clot, tel. (93) 847 3011. 18 rooms, in quiet location with excellent views of the mountains.

MONTSERRAT (Barcelona). *Abad Cisneros* (E), Plaza de Montserrat, tel. (93) 835 0201. 41 rooms. *Monasterio* (I), Plaza Movestir, tel. (93) 835 0201. 34 rooms. Both under same management.

PRATS Y SAMPSOR (Lleida). *Moixaró* (M), Ctra. Bellver-Alp, tel. (973) 89 02 38. 32 rooms, pool and garden; the only hotel here.

PUIGCERDA (Girona). Some 1,200 meters above sea level, delightfully situated and cool at night. *Puigcerda Park Hotel* (M), Ctra. Barcelona, tel. (972) 88 07 50. 54 rooms, in town. *Chalet de Golf* (M-I), tel. (972) 88 09 71. A few kilometers out of town along the beautiful Segre valley; with 16 rooms and golf course. *Hotel del Lago* (M), Avda. Dr Piguillén, tel. (972) 88 10 54. 16 rooms, with pool, golf, tennis and bowling green. *María Victoria* (M), Florenza 9, tel. (972) 88 03 00. 50 rooms, in town. *Martínez* (I), Ctra. de Llivia, tel. (972) 88 02 50. 15 rooms.

RIALP (Lleida). *Condes del Pallars* (E), Ctra. Esterri de Aneu, tel. (973) 62 03 50. 103 rooms, pool, tennis, mini golf and garden.

RIBAS DE FRESSER (Girona). *Cataluña Park* (I), Mauri 9, tel. (973) 72 71 98. 22 rooms, pool and garden.

SALARDU (Lleida). *Montarto* (E), Baqueira-Beret, tel. 18. 166 rooms, pool and bar.

SALOU (Tarragona). *Salou Park* (E-M), Calle 31, tel. (977) 38 02 08. Comfortable with pool and good view. *Calavina* (M-I), tel. (977) 38 01 50. 70 rooms, pool. *Las Vegas* (M-I), Alfonso V, tel. (977) 38 06 54. 275 rooms, with pool. *Delfín Park* (I), Calle Mayor, tel. (977) 38 03 08. 244 rooms, pool. *Picnic* (I), tel. (977) 38 01 58. 43 rooms with pool. *Planas* (I), Planas Bonet 2, tel. (977) 38 01 08. 100 rooms.
    Restaurants. *Casa Soler* (M), Virgen del Carmen, tel. 38 04 63. *Miramar* (M), Espolón del Muelle, tel. 38 27 67.

SAN BAUDILLO DE LLOBREGAT (Barcelona). *El Castillo* (I), Antiguo Castillo, tel. (93) 661 0700. Very reasonable 3-star hotel, with pool, mini golf and tennis. Close to Barcelona airport.

SAN CARLOS DE LA RAPITA (Tarragona). *Miami Park* (M), Avda. del Generalísimo 33, tel. (977) 74 03 51. 80 rooms.

SAN HILARIO DE SACALM (Girona). *Suizo* (E-M), Plaza Verdaguer 8, tel. (972) 86 80 00. 39 rooms, central. *Solterra* (M), Paseo Font Vella 22, tel. 37. 42 rooms, pool and garden. A 4-star hotel with very reasonable rates.

SAN POL DE MAR (Barcelona). *Gran Sol* (E-M), tel. (93) 76 00 51. 45 rooms, tennis. *Torre Martina* (I), tel. 84. 35 rooms, pool; a 3-star hotel with low rates.

SAN VICENTE DE MONT-ALT (Barcelona). *Clipper* (M), Marítimo 21, tel. (93) 791 0800. 103 rooms, pool, garden.

SEO DE URGEL (Lleida). *Castell Motel* (E), on highway, tel. (973) 35 07 04. 39 rooms. *Parador Nacional* (E-M), tel. (973) 35 20 00. A modern parador with 85 rooms, in center.

SITGES (Barcelona). Crowded, popular seaside resort; fashionable among the young. *Calipolis* (E), Avda. Sofía, tel. (93) 894 1500. Pleasant modern hotel. *Terramar* (E), Passeig Maritim, tel. (93) 894 0050. Right on the beach, old world charm, spacious garden, pool, golf and tennis. *Antemare* (E-M), Avda. Tercio, tel. (93) 894 0600. 72 rooms with pool. *Los Pinos* (M), Passeig Maritim, tel. (93) 894 1550. 42 rooms, pool, golf and garden. *Galeón* (M-I), San Francisco 44, tel. (93) 894 0612. 47 rooms, pool, garden. *Sitges Park* (I), Jenis 12, tel. (93) 894 0250. 79 rooms, in historic building, pool and garden.

Restaurants. *El Greco* (E), Passeig de la Ribera 72, tel. 894 2906. On quay; cozy with rustic English décor. *Fragata* (M), Passeig de la Ribera 1, tel. 894 1086. Also on quay. *Vivero* (M), Paseo Balmins, tel. 894 2149. On the beach, tops for seafood.

SOLSONA (Lleida). *Gran Sol* (M), Ctra. de Manresa, tel. (973) 811 1050. 82 rooms, pool, golf and tennis. Located in historic building.

TARRAGONA. *Imperial Tarraco* (E), Rambla Vella 2, tel. (977) 20 30 40. Historic building with good views of city; pool, mini golf and tennis among its many facilities. *Lauria* (E), Rambla Nova 20, tel. (977) 20 37 40. Good hotel with many amenities including pool. *Astari* (M), Vía Augusta 97, tel. (977) 20 38 40. 50 rooms, pool and garden. *París* (M), Maragall 4, tel. (977) 20 33 40. 2-star hotel with 45 rooms. *Sant Jordi* (M), Vía Augusta, tel. (977) 20 40 46. 40 rooms.

Restaurants. *Náutico* (E), in the port, tel. 21 00 62. Good for seafood. *Sol Ric* (E), Vía Augusta 227, tel. 20 10 26. Very pleasant terrace garden, well known to locals. Regional cuisine; highly recommended.

TORTOSA (Tarragona). *Parador Castillo de la Zuda* (E-M), tel. (977) 44 44 50. 82 rooms, located in ancient castle.

VALLFOGONA DE RIUCORP (Tarragona). *Balneario* (M), on outskirts, tel. (977) 88 00 25. Pool and bowling green, in quiet setting.

VICH (Barcelona). *Parador Nacional* (E), 14 km outside, tel. (93) 888 7211. Modern parador with 31 rooms. Pleasantly situated.

VIELLA (Lleida). *Tuca* (E), Ctra Betrén, tel. (973) 64 07 00. 4-star hotel with 118 rooms. *Parador Valle de Arán* (E-M), 2 km out of town, tel. (973) 64 01 00. Modern parador with 135 rooms, pool. Located in the Lleida Pyrenees with beautiful views over mountains. *Arán* (I), Avda. José Antonio 1, tel. (973) 64 00 50. 44 rooms.

VILLANUEVA Y GELTRU (Barcelona). *César* (I), Ferrer Pi 9, tel. (93) 803 0704. 3-star hotel, with 21 rooms, garden. Low rates.

USEFUL ADDRESSES. Tourist Offices. Barcelona; Gran Vía de las Corts Catalanas 658. **Girona;** Ciudadanos 12. **Tarragona;** Rambla Nova 46.

CAR HIRE. Tarragona; *Avis* at Reus airport and Rambla Nova 125; *Hertz,* Vía Augusta 91; *Europcar,* Avda Andorra 10; *Ital,* Rambla Nova 32; *Budget,* Rovira Virgili 20.

THE COSTA BRAVA

Sun, Sand and Sweet-Smelling Pines

The Costa Brava, or "rugged coast", is an extraordinarily beautiful stretch of jagged shoreline that begins at Blanes, northeast of Barcelona, and runs from there past 145 kilometers (90 miles) of coves and beaches blessed by the Mediterranean sun to the Franco-Spanish frontier town of Port Bou. Every step of it is a delight.

Little by little it has been discovered, and the growth of its popularity during the last twenty years has been nothing short of phenomenal. Where once there were only ten hotels along the coast, there are today hundreds, all with modern facilities and most with sea-view terraces; apartment blocks have sprung up like mushrooms.

This unprecedented expansion of facilities for millions of visitors every year has inevitably encroached upon the natural beauty of the coast, yet the fantastically brilliant blue of the sea by day still contrasts with red-brown headlands and cliffs, and so do the distant lights of the sardine fishing fleet that reflect across the wine-colored waters at dusk. Neat umbrella pines till march briskly to the fringes of white sandy beaches. At least they do when they can find their way through the concrete and cars.

Around the Costa Brava

Girona, the Costa Brava's airport, handling over a million passengers annually, lies on the toll-road from France, and is connected with all the coastal resorts by regular bus services. Yet Barcelona is still the most popular starting point because so many visitors combine some sightseeing with a seaside holiday. Blanes, only sixty-five kilometers (40 miles) northeast of the Catalan capital, is the first stop on this itinerary and can be reached by train or bus as well as by car.

Blanes is the largest and least recommendable town on the Costa Brava, with a resident population of over 16,000. Its accessibility makes it popular with Spanish vacationers though industry is given precedence over tourism.

Blanes is built around the gentle curve of a bay. The open walk facing the sea and known as the Maestranza provides a pleasant locale for the typically Spanish institution of the paseo, a leisurely promenade in the cool of the evening. The bay itself is more for mooring the gaily painted boats of the fishing fleet than for bathing, but there are delightful, coarse-grained sand beaches for swimming at the head of the neighboring *calas*—deep-sea inlets—of La Forcanera and San Francisco.

The town itself is dominated by the medieval castle of St. John, which is perched on the summit of a decoratively pointed hill a little way inland. The outbreak of the Civil War was the signal for an orgy of church burning by the Republicans both here and elsewhere in Catalonia, and the thousand-year-old church of Santa María la Antigua was one of the few survivors.

Besides an attractive botanical garden and an aquarium, you may also wish to visit the picturesque fishermen's quarters of S'Auguev and La Mossanada. Fiestas are celebrated on July 24 and 25, in honor of St. James, patron saint of Spain, and again on August 21. The daily fish auction, held at the north end of the beach at 5.30 P.M., is interesting.

From Blanes, the coastal road leads north again for five kilometers to the popular resort of Lloret de Mar. Shortly after leaving Blanes, there is a side road to the right over a hill thick with vines and umbrella pines leading to the wide sweep of the Playa de Fanals.

On July 24–25 fishermen in gaily decked boats of every size and shape pay their respects to their patron saint in the hermitage of Santa Cristina. This is the famous procession known as *S'Amorra*. The religious part of the festival over, the fishermen stay on to sing, drink, and dance the sardana all night long under the vast branches of Europe's largest umbrella pine, which is festooned with colored lights. They also have a dance of their own, of Moorish origin, the *morrotxas* (the *x* in Catalan is pronounced like *ch* in Spanish). For the rest of the year, visitors content themselves with an excellent golf course.

Lloret de Mar has jumped into the front rank and is now the largest hotel and residential center of the Costa Brava. Apart from a Roman ruin it has a superb, sandy beach. The whole atmosphere of the place seems to have been inspired by the image in the local hermitage of the Virgen de Alegría—Our Lady of Happiness. Though the huge masses of people who have invaded her once quiet territory would no doubt make her wonder just how the modern world goes about looking for its happiness!

Tossa de Mar

It is thirteen kilometers from Lloret to Tossa de Mar, the road running parallel to the sea through small woods of oak, pine and cork trees, with clearings for vines that produce the extremely strong, slightly sweet, white wine of the district. This drive is worth doing for itself alone. The views, though often crowded, are just as often very beautiful.

Tossa was probably the first place on the Costa Brava to attract foreigners, even in the days before the Civil War; and it is also the town that has suffered most from commercialization.

Again, the center of the beach at Tossa is occupied by the fishing fleet, but its northern end just opposite the tawny-colored rock island of Illa, is clean. However, it is better to go just round the corner to the Mar Menuda beach. At the other end of Tossa beach is a headland upon which are the fairytale 12th-century fortifications of the Vila Vella or Old Town, and it is these that give Tossa its special beauty. Playa Llorell and Cala Morisca beaches are further south, and usually less crowded, because of their distance from Tossa. Remember to climb up to the 14th-century Gothic church to enjoy the narrow, 17th-century streets of the Vila Vella. The view back to the beach, seen through an arch of one of the three great towers of the still older fortifications—the Tower of the Hours, the Tower of Homage and the Jonas Tower—is surely among the loveliest.

San Felíu de Guixols to Palamós

It is only twenty-three kilometers from Tossa to San Felíu de Guixols but, if you take the incredibly beautiful coast road (there is an easier but longer one inland), prepare yourself for one sharp corner after another as the narrow road winds round the heads of innumerable deep-cut inlets in a way that makes driving real work. Translucent blue fingers of water thrust deep into the red rocky cliffs to which all-too-many hotels cling precariously.

San Felíu de Guixols has numerous *simpático* little bars and restaurants, a bullring and many hotels, but there is no beach worthy of the name. This is no problem, however, because a bus service runs to and from S'Agaró, the cream of Costa Brava resorts, only three kilometers away; people who cannot afford S'Agaró hotel prices stay in San Felíu and commute to the S'Agaró beach.

Now that it has lost its lucrative cork industry (owing to the advent of plastics), San Felíu lives from its port, its fishing, and its tourist trade. According to an old tradition, it was founded by Charlemagne, but there was a community there long before then. It was called Jecsalis, from which the present name of Guixols is derived.

S'Agaró is one of the showpieces of the Costa Brava, and you must not fail to walk along the kilometer or so of sea wall, beginning below the Hostal and ending at the magnificent Concha beach. This lovely little walk is invisible from either the popular bathing beach or the Hostal. S'Agaró is the creation of one man, José Ensesa, who bought the land and built upon it his idea of a perfect seaside resort. From S'Agaró you can visit some intriguing villages which lie inland; for instance, Lagostera and Caldas de Malavella with ruins of Roman thermal baths.

Beyond S'Agaró there comes the long sweep of the Bay of Palamós, where there is a break in the coastal cliffs so typical of the Costa Brava, and here, the resort of Playa de Aro continues to grow. Its many hotels are full of visitors who come to enjoy the bathing from the perfect, sandy beach which is over a kilometer long. Calonge, nearby, also has good hotels.

San Antonio de Calonge, three kilometers from Palamós, was once a small hamlet. It is now a lively resort well endowed with hotels. However, you may want to travel on to the attractively placed little town that rises steeply from the end of the low-lying bay.

In actual fact, Palamós is more attractive in outward appearance than it proves upon closer inspection, partly, at least, because it has been so repeatedly knocked about by war. Barbarossa and a Turkish fleet blew it to bits in 1543, the French did the same in 1694 and 1814, and the British had a go at it in 1772. Just for good measure, it was both bombed and shelled from the sea by the forces of General Franco in the 1936–9 Civil War. It is a fairly important commercial center, and has a fishing fleet that will make you reach for your camera—especially when the light is right. The neighboring beach of La Fosca is smaller, and has lovely, shallow water for swimming.

From the rather ugly little inland town of Palafrugell a number of roads radiate, leading to some of the most delightful of all the Costa Brava resorts—Calella, Llafranch, Cape San Sebastián, Tamariu and Aiguablava. None is more than six kilometers away, and each has its own beach and distinct personality. Tamariu, where the umbrella pines fringe the silver-white strand, is probably the most beautiful.

Llafranch, sheltered from the northeast by 150-meter-high (500-foot) Cape San Sebastián, and continuously inhabited for some 3,000 years, was an Iberian settlement in pre-Greek and Roman times. From the 18th-century hermitage, with its baroque sanctuary, set near the lighthouse that crowns the cape, you can see far along two of the loveliest stretches of the entire coast, both of them well worth the climb. The Botanical Gardens at Cape Roig can also only be reached from Palafrugell, via Calella. A bit difficult to find, these gardens are worth a visit by those who are interested in the flora of the Mediterranean.

The coast between Cape San Sebastián and Aiguablava is imposing in its rugged magnificence, but can be appreciated only from the sea. Here are several delightful little beaches, a number of deep calas, and the fantastic Gisbert Cave, which pierces the rock for 244 meters (800 feet) even more dramatically than the famous Blue Grotto of Capri.

Aiguablava—Catalan for blue water—is scenically the loveliest of resorts, and has the added advantage of a parador; its beach of Fornells epitomizes what Mediterranean bathing should be—deep, clear, blue water, sheltered by two headlands to form a natural yacht basin.

The neighboring town of Bagur, with its ruined medieval castle, contains a number of fine porched houses, built during the last century by those who went to Cuba to make their fortunes and returned rich to end their days in comfort in the place of their birth. The beaches of Sa Tuna, Sa Riera and Aiguafreda, however, are well over a kilometer away, which accounts for the fact that, touristically, Bagur has not advanced as much as might be expected. Nevertheless, there are a few hotels including the beautifully positioned and luxurious Aiguablava.

Anyone interested in earthenware will go inland for about fourteen kilometers as far as La Bisbal, built round the 14th-century episcopal palace-fortress above the River Daró. It supplies all the markets in the country with pottery. This excursion can easily be extended to the 11th-century Lombard-Romanesque monastery church of San Miguel at Cruilles just over a kilometer further on, returning via the 14th-century Sarriera castle at Vulpellach, the Iberic town and 11th-century church at Ullestret, the triple walls pierced by twelve gates of Peratallada, and the square towers of Pals below a well-preserved 14th-century castle. Pals, moreover, possesses the second of the Costa Brava's excellent golf courses.

North to Ampurias and Cadaqués

The southern half of the Costa Brava ends here. Northward the coastal character changes considerably until you reach Rosas. Suddenly, the road emerges from the cork and pine woods and runs between long, straight avenues of plane trees across a flat and well-watered plain with irrigation streams and ditches that intersect the rice paddies and almond groves.

This is the plain of the Lower Ampurdan. Until medieval times, an arm of the sea enabled even large ships to reach such fascinating old towns as Torroella de Montgri and Castelló de Ampurias, but gradually the silt brought down by the Rivers Ter, Fluvia and Muga cut them off from their profitable maritime trade.

Torroella de Montgri was a Royal Borough as early as 1272, and was originally surrounded by medieval walls. The Castle of Montgri on its hilltop was built between 1294 and 1301 by Jaime II of Aragón and Catalonia, but was never finished as the outer walls and four round corner towers attest.

Estartit is important as a holiday resort, with a marina berthing over 1,000 craft and extensive accommodation for tourists. Estartit's beach is of fine white sand, one of the best on the coast. It extends for more than five kilometers.

The mass of the Medas Islands, off the coast, offer scuba divers some of the best diving in these parts. La Escala is given over mainly to fishing and the construction of boats, including the rather portly craft known as *vacas,* cows. It lies at the southern extremity of the huge sandy Bay of Rosas, next door to the really magnificent Greco-Roman ruins of the city of Ampurias, which is unquestionably the Costa Brava's number one sightseeing feature, and right by the beach.

The original trading settlement was built on the site now occupied by the attractive medieval village of San Martín de Ampurias, then an island, by Greeks from Marseille, who named it Paleopolis. During the wars against the Phoenicians in the 5th century B.C., it was decided to build a fortified settlement a couple of kilometers away on the mainland, which was called Neapolis, and it was this site that was rediscovered in 1908, and which has now been fully excavated.

More recently, a large Roman city, about ten times the size of Neapolis, and belonging to the 2nd and 3rd centuries A.D., was unearthed on its outskirts; it is filled with many matchless mosaic pavements and household ornaments. Excavation work may go on for years to come. Visit the museum on the site and allow plenty of time to explore the lower (Greek) town and upper (Roman) town, from which there is a magnificent view over the Bay of Rosas. Tape machines sited near the museum enable you to hear the history of Ampurias in one of several languages for just a few pesetas. We should point out that, if you don't have time to visit Ampurias, a great deal of the best material uncovered there has been taken to the museums in Barcelona and Girona.

At Castelló de Ampurias visit the crumbling, but still quite startlingly beautiful, 13th-century church of Santa María. Although stripped by the Republicans in 1936 of all but the superb 15th-century alabaster retable of Vicente Borrás and a few finely carved tombs of the medieval Counts of Ampurias, it is still quite remarkable. This once rich and powerful walled city has shrunk today, but the citizens are proud of their 16th-century plaza, their 13th-century palace of the Counts of Ampurias, the seven-arched, 14th-century bridge, and the two huge 15th-century convents, which however, do not equal the 11th-century convent of San Miguel de Fluvía further south.

Rosas is ten kilometers from Castelló de Ampurias, at the northern end of its great bay and at the foot of the Rodes mountains, an outlying spur of the mighty Pyrenees. It is the only Costa Brava resort that faces due west, and so is justly famous for the way each summer sunset sets aflame every windowpane in the town. The old town and port cluster round the ruins of an 11th-century fortress for protection against the swift and deadly Barbary slave raids that continued all along Spain's Mediterranean coast right into the last century. For centuries fishing was the port's life-blood, but its current popularity as a tourist center has taken over. At Rosas, the fish are auctioned in the traditional manner. Once, at least, you should make a point of going down in the early evening to see the boats returning and watch the catches being unloaded and auctioned.

The Canyelles Petits beach, as a matter of fact, is better for bathing and if you wish to explore on foot round the corner of Punta Falconera, you will find a whole series of moderately unspoiled little calas, where bathing is still delightfully adventurous, such as Llado, Rustella, and the mile-deep Cala Morisca.

Cadaqués

To reach Cadaqués, eighteen kilometers away by road, you have to drive over a 458-meter (1,500-foot) pass through the Sierra Alseda, but for some of the way, you will be running through almond and olive groves, and the road is good. As a town, Cadaqués is one of the most attractive of all the Costa Brava resorts, with its whitewashed houses. Its tiny beach is of a special kind of reddish blue slate, used most decoratively in houses, walls and streets, but uncomfortable to sit on, and agonizing to walk over in bare feet. Fortunately, there are a few small sandy beaches along the sides of Cabo Créus, the legend-filled headland of Cape Cross, but reached mostly only on foot, over the headland. Cadaqués has a 16th-century parish church strikingly situated, and many steep, immensely picturesque streets.

The town became an artists' haunt in the 50s, with Salvador Dali building a house there, ornamented with huge, egg-shaped garden decorations, opposite the Port Lligat Hotel. It retains a good deal of its slightly bohemian atmosphere and its moderate inaccessibility makes it attractive for those wanting to get away from things.

Further on, you can reach one of the Club Méditerranée's vacation camps, famous for its skin-diving school; it is tucked away in a corner of Cabo Créus.

There remain only Puerto de la Selva, Puerto de Llansá and the frontier village of Port Bou, and, although pleasant enough, they are all unremarkable. However, if you feel like a full hour's climbing, you might ascend the nearly 610-meter (2,000-foot) summit of Cape Cross, from Puerto de la Selva, where you will find the ruins of the 10th-century monastery of San Pedro de Roda, complete with prehistoric dolmens, anchorites' caves and haunted grottos. The marvelous view all the way from Ampurias in the south to the French Gulf of Lions in the north makes the effort well worthwhile. Alternatively, and far easier, you can drive all the way up to the monastery along the sightseeing road leading out of Villajuiga.

Inland to Figueras and Girona

Before turning inland from our tour of coastal resorts to take a brief look at Figueras and Girona, it is perhaps worth suggesting here that the water-level route into Spain from France can be blistering hot in summer, whether you come by train or car. Much more pleasant is the road and rail route from Toulouse in France, through such charming old towns as Foix and Ax-les-Thermes, to the frontier at Puigcerdá, some 1,067 meters (3,500 feet) up in the Pyrenees. After passing through the lovely Segre valley, this route climbs still further before gradually descending the foothills and turning south at Ribas de Fresser for Barcelona.

Tourists bound for Cadaqués or Rosas frequently enter Spain by way of Cerbère and Port Bou (C252). When you reach Llansá, *don't* take the fork road to Cadaqués, unless you want a horrific (though scenically stunning) drive through Puerto de la Selva on a very narrow road: continue inland on C252 to the Rosas signpost. The main road continues to Figueras, where it links with the toll-road to Girona.

Figueras is of no great moment despite the imposing bulk of the 18th-century fortress castle of San Fernando, capable, so they say, of containing an army of 10,000 men with 500 horses. The town also possesses a Dalí Museum.

While Figueras is unexciting, Girona is a city of really exceptional interest. Its most famous view is of the houses that line the River Oñar, their windows always draped with an unimaginably colorful array of drying laundry!

Girona is a town full of fine, historic buildings, the most imposing of which is the cathedral, reached up a noble flight of 36 steps. Its 18th-century baroque façade conceals the 11th-, 12th- and 14th-century building. Inside, its architecture is unusual in that it possesses only a single 60-meter-long, 23 meter-wide, and 34 meter-high nave (200-foot-long, 75-foot-wide and 110-foot-high). It contains many priceless tapestries and a 14th-century silver altar.

Girona was a town long before the Romans named it Gerunda, but its greatest historical glory was when it suffered no less than three sieges by 15,000 of Napoleon's best troops. In 1809, it held out for six months, the citizens forming themselves into regular battalions, one of them composed exclusively of women.

The church of San Pedro de Galligans which houses the provincial museum, was built by Charlemagne in the 9th century. Along the Paseo Arquelológio are the church of San Lucas, the Capuchin convent, the Arab baths, the gates of San Cristóbal and San Daniel. Sections of cyclopean walls contain stones 3 meters square, which defy all explanation of how they were placed there before the invention of mechanical devices. But probably the most impressive of all Girona's many sights are the Easter week processions, when barefoot penitents walk the narrow, ancient streets, carrying candles and wearing black hoods that conceal all but their eyes, which, illuminated by the tapers, gleam with an uncanny light.

PRACTICAL INFORMATION FOR THE
COSTA BRAVA

WHAT TO SEE. Most people come to the Costa Brava to enjoy a relaxing holiday basking in the sun and swimming, sailing and water skiing, rather than for serious sightseeing. However, there are a few things of interest in this area should you be able to lure yourself away from the temptations of the beach for an hour or two. Girona (formerly Gerona) is one of the oldest cities in Catalonia and dates back to Roman times; its cathedral is well worth a visit as are many of its churches. At Figueras you can visit the Salvador Dalí museum though the selection of paintings is rather limited. Ampurias has impressive Greco-Roman remains.

HOTELS. The vast majority of hotels on the Costa Brava have sprung up with amazing rapidity during the last fifteen years or so; they tend to be the concrete highrise type which, sadly, one has come to expect in the over-developed coastal regions of Spain. In their favor, however, they are mostly well provided with modern amenities, all rooms have private bathrooms, and many are close to the beach. The Costa Brava, together with the Costa Blanca and Costa del Sol, is one of Spain's biggest package-deal holiday regions; so don't be surprised if the 3-star hotel of your choice is totally booked up for the whole season, or if the hotel set-up is more geared to dealing with groups than with individuals. At any rate, most resorts have a wide choice of hotels, you shouldn't have too much trouble finding suitable accommodations.

The majority of hotels on the Costa Brava are only open from March/April through Sept./Oct., so if you are planning a stay in winter, check first. For modest accommodations, most of the resorts also have many simple hostels and pensions, for the most part not included in our recommendations.

For those travelers seeking something a little out of the ordinary, there is the *parador* at Aiguablava or the deluxe *Gavina* at S'Agaró. For golf enthusiasts there is the *Golf Costa Brava* at Santa Cristina de Aro; and for those who enjoy older hotels, the *Trías* at Palamos.

HOTELS AND RESTAURANTS

All Costa Brava resorts are in the province of Girona; when telephoning any of these resorts from outside Girona province, first dial the area code of (973); if you are already in Girona, dial only the number.

AIGUABLAVA. *Parador Costa Brava* (E), tel. 62 62 62. Beautifully located modern parador with 80 rooms. Idyllic setting; its large terrace, shaded by pine trees, is an ideal place for an evening drink after a day on the beach.

BAGUR. *Aiguablava* (E), tel. 62 20 58. Without doubt, one of Spain's finest hotels, with superb management and delightful situation; amenities include pool and tennis courts, and a short walk to the sea. *Bonaigua* (M), on Fornells beach, tel. 62 20 50. 47 rooms, with a good view. *Bagur* (I), Calle de Coma y Ros 8, tel. 31 22 07. 30 rooms. *Sa Riera* (I), tel. 62 30 00. 41 rooms, parking and garden.

BLANES. *Park Blanes* (E), S'Abanell, tel. 33 02 50. Close to beach with pool, mini golf and tennis. *Horitzo* (M), Paseo Marítimo 11, tel. 33 04 00. 121 rooms. *Consul Park* (I), Avda. Villa de Madrid, tel. 36 16 50. 225 rooms, pool and garden.

CADAQUES. *Llane Petit* (E), Dr Baltomens 36, tel. 25 80 50. 35 rooms, close to beach. *Playa Sol* (E), Playa Pianch 5, tel. 25 81 40. 49 rooms, overlooking beach. *Rocamar* (E), Virgen del Carmen, tel. 25 81 50. On a cliff, 1 km from town; 80 rooms, pool and tennis. *Port Lligat* (I), Port Lligat, tel. 25 81 62. 30 rooms, pool. *S'Aguardá* (I), Portal de la Fuente, tel. 25 80 82. 27 rooms.
Restaurants. *Es Baluard* (M), Riba Nemesio Llorens 2, tel. 25 81 83. *Don Quijote* (M), Avda. Caridad Seriñana, tel. 25 81 41. Pleasant bistro, with terrace and vine-covered garden. *La Gaviota* (M), Narciso Monturiol 14, tel. 25 81 87. Decorated with Dalí paintings; must book.

CALDAS DE MALAVELLA. *Balneario Vichy Catalán* (M), Dr Furest 8, tel. 47 00 00. Historic building, pool, tennis and pleasant gardens. *Balneario Prats* (I), San Esteve 7, tel. 47 00 61. 76 rooms, pool.

CALELLA. *Duing* (E), Barrio San Roc, tel. 30 00 50. 37 rooms, pool, tennis and gardens. *Alga* (E-M), tel. 30 00 58. 54 rooms, pool, tennis, gardens. *Garbi* (M-I), Calle del Mirto, tel. 30 01 00. 30 rooms, pool, garden. *Port Bo* (I), Gelpi 4, tel. 30 02 50. 46 rooms, tennis. Low rates for a 3-star hotel.

CALONGE *Park Hotel San Jorge* (E), Ctra. de Palamos, tel. 31 52 54. One of the best on the Costa Brava. Pool and tennis amongst its many amenities. *Cap Roig* (E-M), Ctra de Palamos, tel. 31 52 08. Large hotel, with pool and tennis. *Condado de San Jorge* (M), Ctra. de Palamos, tel. 32 71 16. 36 rooms, pool.

LA ESCALA. *Nieves Mar* (M), Paseo del Mar, tel. 77 03 00. 80 rooms, garden, tennis. *Voramar* (M), Paseo de Luis Albert 2, tel. 77 01 08. 40 rooms, pool and bar.
Restaurant. *Els Pescadors* (M), Port d'en Perris 3, tel. 77 07 28. Good for fish and seafood.

ESTARTIT. *Bell Aire* (M), Rocamaura 6, tel. 75 81 62. 78 rooms, with good views. *Coral* (I), Plaza de la Iglesia 1, tel. 75 82 00. 59 rooms, garden. *Miramar* (I), Avda de Roma 7, tel. 75 86 28. 61 rooms, tennis and parking.

Restaurant. *Eden* (I), Victor Concas 2, tel. 75 80 02. Dining to music.

FIGUERAS. *Pirineos* (E), Ronda Barcelona 1, tel. 50 03 12. 53 rooms. *President* (E), Ronda Ferial 33, tel. 50 12 04. 75 rooms, parking. *Ampurdán* (M), on highway, tel. 50 05 62. 48 rooms, garden, parking. *Durán* (M), Lasanca 5, tel. 50 12 50. Much patronized by the French who appreciate its excellent cooking. *Rallye* (M), Ronda de Barcelona, tel. 50 13 00. 15 rooms, garden. *Ronda* (I), Ctra. de la Junquera, tel. 50 39 11. 36 rooms. *Trave* (I), Balmes, tel. 50 05 91. 69 rooms, pool, garden.

Restaurants. *Ampurdán Hotel* (E), highly recommended by readers for huge portions of delicious food. *Durán hotel* (M), one of the best in Catalonia. *Viarnes* (M), Pujade del Castell 23, tel. 50 07 91. Well recommended.

FORNELLS DE LA SELVA. *Fornells Park* (M), on N–II, tel. 47 61 25. 36 rooms, garden and pool.

GIRONA. *Costabella* (M), on N–II, tel. 20 25 24. 22 rooms. *Inmortal Gerona* (M), Ctra. Barcelona 31, tel. 20 79 00. 76 rooms, fairly central, parking. *Ultonia* (M), Avda. Jaime I 22, tel. 20 38 50. 45 rooms, in town. *Europa* (I), Julio Carreta 21, tel. 20 27 50. 26 rooms, parking.

12 km out of town, on the autopista A17 at exit 8, is *Novotel-Gerona* (E), 82 rooms.

Restaurants. *Rosaleda* (E-M), Paseo de la Dehesa, tel. 21 36 68. Pleasant location in a park. *Casa Marieta* (I), Plaza Independencia 5, tel. 20 10 16. Good value.

LLAFRANCH. *Terramar* (E), Cipsele 1, tel. 30 02 00. An old hotel, the best in town, with good views. *Levante* (M), Paseo Francisco Blanes 3, tel. 30 03 66. 20 rooms, a 2-star hotel. *Paraíso* (M), Paraje Font D en Xeco, tel. 30 04 50. 55 rooms, pool and gardens. *Casamar* (I), Francisco de Blanes, tel. 30 01 04. 24 rooms, pleasant.

LLANSA. Good beach resort, with modest hotels only. *Grimar* (M), Ctra. de Port Bou, tel. 38 01 67. 38 rooms, garden. *Mendisol* (M), Grifeu beach, tel. 38 01 00. 32 rooms, parking and garden. *Berna* (I), at the port, tel. 38 01 50. 38 rooms, parking and garden. *Grifeu* (I), Ctra. de Port Bou, tel. 38 00 50. 33 rooms.

LLORET DE MAR. Brash, sophisticated resort, with hundreds of hotels and hostels; it is only possible to mention a few of them here. *Monterrey* (E), Ctra. Hostalrich-Girona, tel. 36 40 50. The biggest of the 4-star hotels, 229 rooms, pool, tennis and garden. *Rigat Park* (E), Playa de Fanals, tel. 36 52 00. Spanish-style hotel, pleasantly situated, with private beach, pool and gardens. *Roger de*

Flor (E), Turo del Estelat, tel. 36 48 00. Good views, 15 mins. from beach and center. Pool, gardens, located in historic building. *Santa Marta* (E), Playa de Santa Cristina, tel. 36 49 04. 3 km from town, in beautiful gardens; pool, tennis and many other amenities. *Tropic* (M), Camprodón y Arrieta, tel. 36 51 54. 40 rooms, centrally located, pool. This is by far the smallest and cheapest of the 4-star hotels.

Among the numerous 3-star hotels are the following. *Eugenia* (M), Ctra Hostalrich-Tossa, tel. 36 44 00. 118 rooms, pool and gardens. Rates are (I) outside July-Sept. *Rosa Mar* (M), Avda. 2 de febrero, tel. 36 43 50. 169 rooms, pool, bingo. *Capri* (I), Avda. 2 de febrero, tel. 36 45 62. 155 rooms, pool, garden. *Flamingo* (I), Fernando Agulló, tel. 36 51 88. *Ifa Hotel Lloret* (I), Serria del Barral, tel. 36 46 08. 81 rooms, pool, garden. *Mercedes* (I), Avda. Mistral 16, tel. 36 43 12. 88 rooms, pool, garden, bar. *Metropol* (I), Prat de la Riba 2, tel. 36 41 62. 86 rooms. *Santa Rosa* (I), Serria del Barral, tel. 36 43 62. 134 rooms, pool, garden and bar.

Among the modest hotels are *Montecarlo* (I), Avda. 2 de Febrero, tel. 36 49 08. 94 rooms, garden. Pleasantly situated in pine wood. *Mundial* (I), Buenaventura Leal 17, tel. 36 43 50. 98 rooms, pool, garden and parking; good value. *Oasis Park* (I), Playa de Fanals, tel. 36 50 21. 428 rooms, pool, golf, mini golf, tennis and bar. Very good value. *Perelló* (I), Areny 7, tel. 36 46 62. 40 rooms, 5 mins. from beach.

PALAMOS. *Trías* (E), also (M) and (I), 70 rooms. Paseo del Mar, tel. 31 41 00. One of the very few Costa Brava old timers, with attractive gardens and pool. *San Luis* (M), Avda. 11 septiembre 61, tel. 31 40 50. 24 rooms. *San Juan* (I), Mayor de San Juan 30, tel. 31 42 08. 31 rooms, pool and garden.

PLAYA DE ARO. *Aromar* (E-M), Paseo Marítimo, tel. 81 70 54. 105 rooms. *Columbus* (E-M), Paseo del Mar, tel. 81 71 66. 111 rooms, with pool, tennis, mini golf and gardens. Only hotel with pool in town. *Cosmopolita* (E), also (M) and (I) rooms, Pinar del Mar 1, tel. 81 73 50. 88 rooms, garden, private beach. *Costa Brava* (M), Punta d'en Ramis, tel. 81 73 08. 46 rooms, parking. *Rosamar* (M), Virgen del Carmen, tel. 81 73 04. 62 rooms, garden. *La Masía* (I), Avda. Santa María de Fanals 7, tel. 81 75 00. 38 rooms, parking, mini golf; very good service. *Miramar* (I), Virgen del Campo, tel. 81 71 50. 45 rooms, parking.

Restaurants. *Montbar* (E), Pinar del Mar, tel. 81 71 31. *La Grillade* (M), Pinar del Mar 14, tel. 81 73 33. French cuisine.

PUERTO DE LA SELVA. A pretty little place. *Porto Cristo* (M-I), Mayor 41, tel. 38 70 62. 54 rooms, central and pleasant. *Amberes* (I), Selva de Mar, tel. 38 70 30. 18 rooms, close to harbour, simple and pleasant.

ROSAS. *Almadraba Park* (E), Playa Almadraba, tel. 25 65 50. 66 rooms, just outside town, on beach. *Canyelles Platja* (E-M), Playa Canyelles, tel. 25 65 00. 110 rooms, by beach, with garden and parking. *Coral Playa* (E-M), Playa del Rastrillo, tel. 25 62 50. 128 rooms, parking and garden. *Moderno* (M), Paseo

Marítimo 15, tel. 25 65 58. 57 rooms, parking, overlooking sea. *Mariam Platja* (M-I), Paraje Salate, tel. 25 61 08. 101 rooms. *Montecarlo* (M-I), Avda del Caudillo 1, tel. 25 66 73. Central, 126 rooms. *Monterrey* (M-I), Urb. Santa Margarita, tel. 25 66 76. 138 rooms. *Mediterráneo* (I), Paraje Salata, tel. 25 63 00. 67 rooms, pool.

Restaurants. *Hacienda El Bulli* (E), tel. 25 76 51. A few km southeast in Cala Montjoy, this restaurant is well worth the journey. Excellent cuisine, unusual dishes. *El Cazador* (M), Plaza San Pedro 8, tel. 25 60 33.

S'AGARO. Smartest resort with the most luxurious hotel on the Costa Brava. *Hotel de la Gavina* (L), Plaza de la Rosaleda, tel. 32 11 00. Super-deluxe hotel with 73 rooms. Palatial setting amid tree-shaded lawns; has a Louis XV suite with genuine period furniture. Pool, bowling alley, tennis, dining in Candlelight Room.

SAN ANTONIO DE CALONGE. *Rosa dels Vents* (E), Paseo del Mar, tel. 31 42 16. 58 rooms, garden, overlooking sea. *Rosamar* (E-M), Paseo del Mar 33, tel. 31 41 65. 63 rooms, garden, overlooking sea. *Reymar* (M), Paraje Torre Valentina, tel. 31 53 04. 49 rooms, garden and parking. *Príncipe Ben Hur* (M-I), Playa de Torre Valentina, tel. 32 73 54. 20 rooms, parking, by the beach. *Aubi* (I), San Antonio 253, tel. 31 47 06. 55 rooms, tennis, garden and parking. *Lys* (I), Ctra de Palamos, tel. 31 41 50. 22 rooms, parking.

SAN FELIU DE GUIXOLS. A lovely old fishing village behind the tourist façade. *Reina Elisenda* (E), Passeig dels Guixols 20, tel. 32 07 00. 70 rooms, with garden and good amenities. *Caleta Park* (E-M), on San Pol beach, tel. 32 00 12. 105 rooms. *Curhotel Hipócrates* (M), Paraje las Forcas, tel. 32 06 62. 103 rooms, pool and parking. *Montjoi* (M), San Elmo, tel. 32 03 00. 62 rooms, pool, garden, overlooking harbor, good service. *Murla Park* (M), Guixols 22, tel. 32 04 50. 88 rooms, pool, bar, bingo. *Panorama Park* (M), Travesía de Roig 1, tel. 32 07 54. 69 rooms, garden. *Gesoria* (I), Campmany 3, tel. 32 03 50. 34 rooms, tennis, garden. *Montecarlo* (I), Montaña de San Elmo, tel. 32 00 00. On a cliff with wonderful views.

Restaurants. *S'Adolitx* (M), Mayor 13, tel. 32 18 53. Pleasant decor and patio. *Casa Buxo* (M), Mayor 18, tel. 32 01 87. Pleasant and intimate.

SANTA CRISTINA DE ARO. *Golf Costa Brava* (E), by the Costa Brava golf club, tel. 83 70 52. Pool, 8 tennis courts, golf, all in a peaceful location.

Restaurant. *Los Pañolles* (M), on C250, tel. 83 70 11. Rustic décor.

TAMARIU. Ideal for those in search of peace, sailing and perfect bathing. *Hostalillo* (E), Perica 8, tel. 30 01 58. 72 rooms with TV. *Jano* (I), Paseo del Mar 5, tel. 30 04 62. 51 rooms. *Tamariu* (I), Paseo del Mar 3, tel. 30 01 08. 24 rooms, parking.

TOSSA DE MAR. A resort of reasonably high standard, which can be crowded in summer particularly the pebble beach. *Mar Menuda* (E), on Mar Menuda beach, tel. 34 10 00. 28 rooms, pool, tennis, gardens. *Vora Mar* (E-M), Avda. de la Palma, tel. 34 03 54. 53 rooms, garden and good amenities. *Gran Hotel Reymar* (M), on Mar Menuda beach, tel. 34 03 12. A 4-star hotel, and the best in town, but rates are moderate. 131 rooms, pool, bowling and gardens. *Costa Brava* (M-I), tel. 34 02 24. 102 rooms, pool. *Delfín* (M-I), Costa Brava 2, tel. 34 02 50. 63 rooms. *Diana* (I), Plaza de España 10, tel. 34 03 04. 21 rooms, in historic building. *Tonet* (I), Plaza Iglesia, tel. 34 02 37. In local style near the cathedral square. 36 rooms, an excellent bargain.

Restaurants. *Bahía* (M), Socorro 4, tel. 34 03 22. On beach with terrace dining; good seafood. *María Angela* (M), Paseo del Mar 10, tel. 34 03 58. Near walls of old town, excellent seafood.

 USEFUL ADDRESSES. Girona, Tourist Office, Ciudadanos 12. Hotel Information Center, Parque de la Dehesa, next to the N–II highway, tel. 20 30 01. Police Station, Avda. de Jaime I 17. Emergency Hospital, Plaza Hospital 5, tel. 20 14 75.

There are Municipal Tourist Offices in the City Halls of the following resorts: Blanes, Lloret de Mar, Tossa de Mar, San Felíu de Guixols, Playa de Aro, La Escala, Rosas; and at Palamós at Paseo 18 de Julio 9; at Palafrugell in Calle Vilar.

CAR HIRE. Figueras; *Autos Alquiler New Car,* San Lázaro 36; *Autos Sant Jordi,* Pedro III 16; *Miguel Pau,* San Juan Bautista 17. **Girona;** *Avis,* at the airport and Ctra. de Barcelona 35; *Ital,* San Juan Bautista de la Salle 38, *New Car,* Lorenzana 42; *Rent a Car,* Canónigo Dorca 15.

SOUTHEAST SPAIN

Costa del Azahar and Costa Blanca

Following the successful practice that every bit of coast must be labeled with an attractive trade name, the shores of the provinces of Castellón de la Plana and Valencia have been officially baptized Costa del Azahar—not a bad choice, as the fragrant perfume of the orange blossom *(azahar)* pervades the whole countryside. The Costa Blanca, less originally named after the dazzling white light which after all is not restricted to that particular stretch of coast, lumps together the seaside of Alicante, Murcia and parts of Almería as far south as Cape Gata, two wide arcs divided by Cape Palos.

The northern 320 kilometers (200 miles) used to be known as the Levante—a rather vague term simply meaning "east." In ancient times the Levante was a favored place for Phoenician trading ships, and it is interesting to note that the inhabitants today still have a strongly

Semitic cast of countenance, not found elsewhere in Spain. The Phoenicians never attempted the conquest of Spain, merely contenting themselves with trading posts, to which the Ibero-Celts themselves brought the minerals the Phoenicians sought, but it was as they sailed along this stretch of coast, and gazed uneasily at the menacing mountains, that they gave to the country its present name—Spagna, meaning "the hidden land."

South and west of the Levante lie the two modern provinces that represent the medieval kingdom of Murcia—Murcia and Albacete. The latter is of little interest to tourists beyond the fact that the shortest road from Madrid to the Costa Blanca runs through it, as well as the less frequented and thus much quicker inland route via Jaén to Granada. The main road linking the Levante with Andalusia runs through Murcia.

Exploring the Southeast

The Levante is best approached by the Barcelona—Valencia—Alicante toll-road, though the narrow coastal road is scenically superior, entering Castellón, the first of the two great orange-growing provinces, at Vinaroz, a little town that once belonged to the Knights Templar, and is still famous for its wine. Just beyond it, outside Benicarló, and within sight of the parador, is the promontory upon which is built the strangely romantic fortress town of Peñiscola. Roadways lead to this town of highrise apartments, modern hotels, shops and restaurants. Seen from afar, Peñiscola is dramatically picturesque, but nothing can equal this first view and wandering about this 3,000-year-old city is disappointing.

The highway and railway leave the sea after Peñiscola to pass the ruined castle of Chisvert, but to return at the fine bathing beaches of Oropesa with its Torre del Rey, a model of 16th-century military architecture, and Benicasim (a Moorish name), six kilometers from the idyllic Carmelite monastery at the Desierto de las Palmas, Desert of Palms being merely an original way to indicate the scarcity of that tree among the pines and cypresses.

Castellón de la Plana is small for a provincial capital, but bustling with movement in the wide avenues. The 14th-century Gothic church of Santa María contains paintings by Zurbarán, while San Augustín is decorated with colorful tiles; the town is overlooked by the 40-meter-high (130-foot) belfry.

Next comes Villareal at the mouth of the River Mijares, with its disproportionately large church and on the Seco, closer to the sea, Burriana, with a fine Gothic church.

The first place of interest after entering the province of Valencia is Sagunto, the ramparts of whose medieval castle extend for over a kilometer across the hilltop of the ancient acropolis. These enormous fortifications which can be seen from a distance give the best view over the ruins of the Roman town which includes a theater capable of holding 7,000 spectators. Sadly, this splendid site is ruined by gigantic steel mills and cement factories.

Valencia

Sagunto is only twenty-three kilometers (14 miles) from Valencia, the third city of Spain. Valencia is the obvious capital of the Levante, being roughly equidistant from its two bigger sisters, Barcelona and Madrid. Though of surprisingly little maritime importance, Valencia has mushroomed into a hugh town of characterless highrises which sadly swamp the lovely old nucleus on the right bank of the Río Turia.

Valencia was liberated from the Moors by that legendary figure El Cid at the end of the first wave of the Reconquest in 1094 but, at his death, it again became an Emirate, and was not permanently in Christian hands until 1238. Don Jaime I, the Conquistador King of Aragón, retook the city for Catholic Spain following a four months' siege, won with the help of troops commanded by the Archbishop of Narbonne (France). It was a true holy war—the Moors, who had been subjugated definitively by the Spaniards at the end of the 15th century were now forced to choose between exile or conversion to Christianity. Some pretended to submit and were henceforth known as Moriscos, others resisted. Accused of nefarious relationships with the Berbers, not to mention conspiracy, they were expelled from Spain in 1609.

The city picked the wrong side in the War of the Spanish Succession at the beginning of the 18th century. Later it rebeled against Napoleon, and was considerably damaged by Marshal Suchet before it surrendered in January 1812.

Valencia lies on the River Turia, which enters the sea at the large port of El Grao, some three kilometers east. To the north are the Levante and Malvarrosa beaches, south lie Nazaret and Pinedo, followed by the less crowded El Saler backed by the La Dehesa pine wood, Recati, El Perello and the string of the Las Palmeras beaches.

Valencia's historical buildings cluster round the 14th-century cathedral, which is entered by three portals, respectively Romanesque, Gothic and rococo; but this mixture of styles has been done away with in the interior, where Renaissance and baroque marbles have been removed, as is now the trend in Spanish churches, in a successful restoration of the original pure Gothic. There is a large treasury; one side chapel features a Goya picture of St. Francis Borgia surrounded by devils waiting eagerly for the saint's demise. Before a superb Florentine Gothic retable stands a small dark vessel, supposedly the Holy Grail, used at the Last Supper. It is amazing just how often the Holy Grail pops up in Spain. There must have been quite an industry in Grail manufacture at one time.

The unfinished octagonal 15th-century belfry, affectionately known as Miguelete, faces across the Plaza de Zaragoza—provided, oh bliss, with a large underground parking area—the much finer hexagonal 17th-century tower of Santa Catalina. San Martín, at the corner of the plaza and the main shopping street, Calle San Vicente, contains another Goya and a fine late Gothic sculpture of the patron saint. The basilica of the Virgen de los Desamparados (Virgin of the Unsheltered) adjoins the cathedral near the porch which has accommodated a meeting of the water tribunal every Thursday since 1350, and where all decisions regarding the irrigation of the local crops are still made. The paramount importance of water is emphasized in the very name of the Marqués de Dos Aguas, the fantastic façade of whose nearby rococo palace—now the Ceramics Museum—centers on the figures of the *Two Waters* by Hipólito Rivero who died demented—not really surprising after you have seen the sculptures. Do not leave Valencia without a visit to this magnificent Ceramics Museum.

The 15th-century Lonja de Mercadero, with its Orange Court, is probably architecturally the most satisfying of the historic buildings. The splendid 14th-century arch of the Torres de Serranos spanned a gate in the walls—which surrounded the old town till 1865—leading to one of the three bridges across the Turia. The Museum of Fine Arts in the San Pío V buildings on the north bank is considered one of the finest in Spain.

The Golden Apples of the Hesperides

The coastal road to the southern beaches runs on the thin strip of land (La Dehesa) which barely separates the sea from the Albufera Lagoon, rimmed with rice-fields and pleasant pinewoods. There are large-scale duck shoots in the fall. A short distance farther on, the road rejoins N332, near the Cullera rock.

Before continuing on this most attractive road farther south toward Alicante, it is necessary to mention oranges—those golden apples that Hercules was sent to capture from nearby Majorca in legendary times.

Following years of experiment, it was found possible to spread the orange harvest over five months—from late November until the end of April—so that in spring, you will see both flower and fruit growing simultaneously on the same tree. As you drive along this road at night, the waves of perfume from the blossoms are almost overpowering.

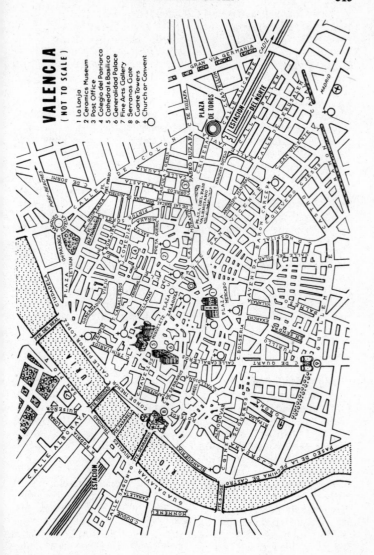

VALENCIA
(NOT TO SCALE)

1 La Lonja
2 Ceramics Museum
3 Post Office
4 Colegio del Patriarca
5 Cathedral & Basilica
6 Generalidad Palace
7 Fine Arts Gallery
8 Serranos Gate
9 Cuarte Towers
† Church or Convent

Some forty-eight kilometers (30 miles) from Valencia, the toll road to Alicante passes Játiva, which is well worth seeing. This is the home town of the Borjas, better known outside Spain by the Italian form of their name, Borgia. Their castle, set on the slopes of Mount Bernisa, is exactly what one has always pictured whenever one hears the phrase "castles in Spain".

By the coast road (N332) via Gandía and Villajoyosa, it is 190 kilometers (118 miles) from Valencia to Alicante. After leaving behind the righthand fork to Játiva, you will find yourself driving through muddy rice-fields, except where the green of the rice itself shows above the surface of the water—tawny hills ahead mark the beginning of the Levante's loveliest province, Alicante, and the Costa Blanca.

Let yourself revel one last time amid the charms of the orange-country, for which the town of Gandía is the flourishing business center. In the palace of the Dukes of Gandía, St. Francis Borgia was born. You can visit the 17th-century state rooms and the cell in which he scourged himself. Other worthwhile buildings are the convent of Santa Clara, the monastery of San Jerónimo, the collegiate church, the town hall and the former university.

If you look at a map of Spain you will notice the great spur of Cape Nao that drives out into the Mediterranean toward the island of Ibiza, only about 100 kilometers away. Turning that corner is to turn from a coast that looks toward Italy and find yourself on one that mirrors Africa. In the course of a few kilometers, the scenery changes from one of oranges and rice to one of olives and palms, from a variable, if benign, climate, to tawny aridity.

The Costa Blanca

The popular name for the stretch of coast between Cape Nao and Cape Gata is the Costa Blanca, or "white coast," including the towns of Alicante and Cartagena as well as numerous attractive beach resorts which have, unfortunately, expanded at an uncontrolled rate, creating a kind of sub-Miami growth of endless concrete hotels and apartment houses. These catered to a surge of interest in cheap holidays which is already on the decline and will inevitably leave in its wake a chain of tasteless architecture and over-developed towns.

One can get away from the worst of the property developer's excesses, however, and enjoy what is still a sun-worshippers' paradise. Here you are in the land of the carnation, a flower so prevalent that it even faintly perfumes the local wine, and here, too, you come to one of those strange but lovely places with which the entire Costa Blanca is strewn—the Peñon of Ifach (or Ifach Rock). It is located five kilometers away to the left of the main road, beyond the town of Calpe, which was utterly deserted for nearly one hundred years after Barbary pirates killed or carried off as slaves the entire population in the 17th century. The 305-meter (1,000-foot) monolith of the Peñon rises sheer from the sea into the sky, the summit conveniently accessible through a tunnel. Legend tells of the goatlike spirits that pluck to their deaths those unwise enough to scale these heights at the full of the moon. At the foot of the Peñon are two perfect sandy bathing beaches.

Back on the coastal road, which plunges periodically through tunnels in the rock, the next town we come to is Altea, an old and picturesque fishing village with white walls and blue tiled domes. Although now a developing resort, it has retained much of its charm, especially in the old quarter around the church, and is a favorite haunt of artists. Then comes Benidorm, a hugely overdeveloped resort though some praise must be given to its two splendid beaches, and hidden somewhere amongst the concrete blocks the original pretty village still survives. Then come Villajoyosa and San Juan, Alicante's summer resort; both of little interest but with fine beaches.

Alicante

Alicante, terminal of the toll-road, is dominated by the vast Moorish castle of Santa Bárbara, set on a rocky peak. From the palm-lined harbor, ships sail regularly to the Balearic Islands and Algiers. A glory of the city is its date-palm avenue, the Explanada, with some of the only date-palms in Europe upon which the fruit ripens.

Although definitely torrid in the summer, escape from the nineties in the shade is unusually easy as, only twenty-three kilometers from Alicante, there are pine woods at a height of over 1,220 meters (4,000 feet), with views across terraced vineyards to the sea.

Twenty-three kilometers along the inland N340 leads to Elche, with a palm forest, first planted by the Moors for the dates; it is from here that the whole of Spain is provided with the yellow palm fronds used for Palm Sunday processions.

The origins of this town are ancient, even for Spain, and the remarkable stone bust known as the Dama de Elche (in Madrid's Archeological Museum) is one of the earliest examples of Iberian sculpture. The Mystery Play performed in Elche church on the Feast of the Assumption (August 15) draws many visitors. Its 14th-century music is unique.

Palm and orange groves are scattered through market gardens up to Orihuela, on the banks of the Segura, halfway to Murcia. Enjoy strolling through Orihuela's winding little streets, and don't miss the Gothic cathedral (whose handsomest portal, however, happens to be Renaissance), the church of Santiago, and above all, the striking architectural cluster formed by the Santo Domingo monastery with its two magnifi-

cent double-storied Renaissance cloisters, and the old unversity buildings.

Alicante possesses several excellent beaches, followed by a string of
seaside resorts along the coastal N332 to Cartagena; first Santa Pola,
from which you may want to take a short excursion to primitive
Tabarca Island, eleven kilometers distant, where old fortifications and
reputed treasure offshore lure the curious. Torrevieja, further south, is
a rapidly developing resort heavily patronized by Spaniards; the *haban-
era* dance originated here and there is an annual summer music festival.
Continuing southward, you will reach Mar Menor (Smaller Sea), a
huge lagoon fringed by high-rise hotels, nearly closed off from the
Mediterranean by a narrow spit of land.

Murcia

Soon after Orihuela, N340 enters the province of Murcia and roughly follows the course of the Segura, though the foothills of the Sierra
de Carrascoy often intervene between road and river. This is the driest
region of Spain and possibly of Europe, with less than twenty days of
rain annually, but near the life-giving rivers whose waters irrigate three
crops a year.

The capital, Murcia, lies in the rich Segura valley. Roman statues
and coins were found near the present site, and it was with Roman
bricks that the Moors built the 8th-century Murcia, which was only
liberated and annexed to the crown of Castile in 1243. The Murcian
dialect contains many Arabic words and, in appearance, many of its
inhabitants clearly reveal their Moorish ancestry.

Though begun in the 14th century, the cathedral received its magnificent plateresque façade as late as 1737. But the Gothic Door of the
Apostles dates from the 15th century, as also the splendid Isabelline
chapel of the Marqués de los Vélez, with carvings by Francisco de
Salcillo. Other works by this popular sculptor of the 18th century,
pieces of an astonishing intensity, are in the Jesus Hermitage (Ermita
de Jesús), now a museum, whence they are taken for Holy Week
processions. Little is left of the old town except some dilapidated
houses rising straight from the river, which you might follow to the
malecón, the old dike built by the Romans to hold back the Segura's
waters. It stretches out through palm trees and market gardens, the
fertile *huertas,* so perfectly irrigated ever since the days of the Moors.
You can also see out over Murcia and the huertas from the Cresta del
Gallo, or Cockscomb.

Murcia is visited chiefly by tourists on their way from Alicante
southwest to Granada, via Lorca, a romantic-looking town of small
churches and convents, with a 13th-century castle, the baroque collegi-

ate church and Guevara palace, and picturesque Holy Week processions. But Murcia can also be reached from Madria via Albacete.

Albacete

From Madrid to Albacete, via Ocaña and Mota del Cuervo, is 250 kilometers (155 miles). Albacete is an agricultural town specializing in wines and saffron. Just over nine hundred meters (3,000 feet) above sea level, it has a picturesque 15th- and 16th-century quarter on the crest of a hill, known as Alto de la Villa, and the Hermitage of San Antonio is a good example of 17th-century architecture.

Taking N430, the southerly of the two routes from this important road junction to Valencia, you soon see the imposing 15th-century fortress-prison-castle of Chinchilla de Monte Aragón away on your left and, if the day is clear, the distant Sierra de Alcaraz rising to nearly 1,830 meters (6,000 feet), to the south. Chinchilla is an old pottery town producing attractive ware.

But most of the 146 kilometers (91 miles) of N301 from Albacete to Murcia run adjacent to the bleak uplands of La Mancha, where Don Quixote went adventuring, and the scenery is impressive rather than attractive. However, once across the provincial border and into Murcia, and through the Roman fortress town of Cieza, dominated by its feudal castle, the road drops some 823 meters (2,700 feet) to green farmland.

From Murcia the road runs south for fifty kilometers to the sea at Cartagena, founded by the Carthaginians in the 3rd century B.C. and, as Spain's principal Mediterranean naval base, the scene of numerous battles, the more recent of them being raids by Sir Francis Drake in 1588, naval engagements during the Napoleonic Wars, and a rebellion in 1873.

Apart from its value as a port, Cartagena has survived through 22 centuries for the same reason that attracted the Phoenicians, namely its silver, lead, iron, zinc and copper mines. It dominates the 177 kilometers of Murcian seashore from the modern resort of La Manga to Aguilas. The Holy Week celebrations here are especially interesting.

In the southernmost part of the Costa Blanca N332, bad and narrow but unfrequented, winds through an extraordinary landscape of pointed rocks and broken hills, to touch the coast at the resorts of Mazarrón and Aguilas.

PRACTICAL INFORMATION FOR SOUTHEAST SPAIN

WHAT TO SEE. The region's outstanding site is the ancient fortress town of Peñíscola, sometimes called Spain's Mont St. Michel, parts of which are 3,000 years old. The most interesting cities are Valencia and Alicante; "queen" of the Costa Blanca is Benidorm. Pilgrims will want to see the Holy Grail in Valencia. Students of history will stop at Sagunto with its archeological ruins, whose population committed suicide rather than yield to Hannibal. Jativa is interesting, too. Nature lovers may visit the palm forest of Elche. For bathing, Ifach, Benidorm, Gandía, Mar Menor, or Alicante are best. Lake Albufera is outstanding for duck shooting.

There are some spectacular festivals in this region too, though expect hotel rooms to be at a premium at these times. In Valencia between March 12–19 you can see the falla celebrations—floats, effigies, bonfires and fireworks in the streets; in Alcoy around St. George's Day, April 23, street battles between Moors and Christians; and in Elche on August 14–15 the famous mystery play takes place in honor of the feast of the Assumption.

HOTELS. Some of the coastal towns in this area, such as Benidorm, are now long established resorts and are well supplied with modern hotels; other, more recent resorts are only now being developed. Rates in 3-star hotels on the coast tend to be very reasonable. This is principally due to the large number of package-deal holiday operators using them.

HOTELS AND RESTAURANTS

ALBACETE. *Los Llanos* (E), Avda. España 9, tel. (967) 22 37 50. 102 rooms, pool. *Parador de la Mancha* (E-M), on the N301, tel. (967) 22 94 50. 70 rooms, in regional style, pool, mini golf, tennis, gardens. *Albar* (M), Isaac Peral 3, tel. (967) 22 52 08. 51 rooms. *Bristol Gran Hotel* (M), Marqués de Molins 1, tel. (967) 21 37 87. A 3-star hotel with 69 rooms; centrally located.

Restaurant. *Las Rejas* (M), Dionisio Guardiola 7, tel. 22 72 42. Good typical mesón.

ALCOCEBRE (Castellón). *Las Fuentes* (E), on Las Fuentes beach, tel. (964) 41 03 25. 50 rooms, with pool, tennis, gardens and many amenities.

Restaurant. *El Tridente* (E), on Las Fuentes beach, tel. 41 03 25. Luxurious with a magnificent view over the sea.

ALCOY (Alicante). *Reconquista* (E-M), Puente San Jorge 1, tel. (965) 33 09 00. 77 rooms.

ALFAZ DEL PI (Alicante). *Park Hotel Panorama* (I), Pintor Albir Altea, tel. (965) 88 81 00. A 3-star hotel with very reasonable rates; 54 rooms, pool, mini golf and gardens.

ALICANTE. *Gran Sol* (E), Avda. Méndez Núñez 3, tel. (965) 20 30 00. 150 rooms. Modern skyscraper right on the main street. *Meliá Alicante* (E), Playa del Postiguet, tel. (965) 20 50 00. 547 rooms. A vast apartment complex with all amenities and very high rates, overlooking the beach. *Colegio Oficial Farmacéuticos* (M), Gravina 9, tel. (965) 21 07 00. 46 rooms. Charming old hotel between Expl. de España and the Plaza Ayuntamiento. *Covadonga* (M), Plaza de los Luceros 17, tel. (965) 20 28 44. Good modern hotel in pleasant square in elegant part of town. Very reasonable rates. *Maya* (M), Manuel Penalva y Don Violante 5, tel. (965) 26 12 11. 200 rooms, pool, some suites. *Palas* (M), Cervantes 5, tel. (965) 20 93 10. 48 rooms. Pleasant hotel with charm on the corner of Expl. de España. Nearby in the old town is another charming old hotel, the *Residencia Palas* (M), Plaza Ayuntamiento 6, tel. (965) 20 66 90. 53 rooms. *La Balseta* (I), Manero Molla 9, tel. (965) 20 66 33. 84 rooms. Modern hotel just off Portal de Elche. *La Reforma* (I), Reyes Católicos 7, tel. (965) 22 21 47. 52 rooms. Modern.

Restaurants. *Delfín* (E), Explanada de España 14, tel. 21 49 11. Modern restaurant, one of the best in town. *Quo Venit* (E), Plaza Santísima Faz 3, tel. 21 66 60. Atmospheric décor in a delightful square in the old town. *La Roda* (M), next to Quo Venit, is a colorful mesón. Both have tables on the sidewalk. *La Epoca* (E-M), San Isidro 8. Elegant and stylish. Tucked away between Méndez Núñez and Sanjurjo. *La Goleta* (M), Explanada de España 8, tel. 20 03 38. Plain simple décor with old world air. *Rincón Castellano* (I), Manero Molla 12, opposite Balseta hotel. Charming mesón with check tablecloths and friendly service. Castilian specialties include roast pork and lamb. Excellent *menu del día*. For typical mesón-type eating there is a cluster on the Calle Sanjurjo, including the *Mesón de Labradores, Mesón del Pollo,* and *Mesón de la Chuleta,* all (M-I) and serving local dishes.

ARCHENA (Murcia). *Termas* (E), tel. (968) 67 01 00. 70 rooms in old building, with garden. *Madrid* (I), 62 rooms, garden.

BENICARLO (Castellón). *Parador Nacional* (E-M), on N340, tel. (964) 47 01 00. Modern parador with 108 rooms, pool and garden.

BENICASIM (Castellón). *Azors* (M), Paseo Marítimo, tel (964) 30 03 50. 88 rooms, overlooking sea, pool, mini golf, tennis and garden. *Orange* (M), Gran Avenida, tel. (964) 30 06 00. 415 rooms, pool, mini golf, tennis, garden and many other amenities. *Bonaire* (M-I), Paseo Marítimo, tel. (964) 30 08 00. 79 rooms, pool, mini golf, tennis. *Miami* (I), Partida Masía Frailes, tel. (964) 30

00 50. 44 rooms, pool and tennis. *Tramontaña* (I), Paseo Marítimo, tel. (964) 30 03 00. 65 rooms, overlooking sea, garden.

BENIDORM (Alicante). *Gran Hotel Delfín* (L), Playa de Poniente, tel. (965) 85 43 00. A luxury hotel though rates are only (E). 87 rooms, pool, tennis, tropical gardens, with old Spanish-style furniture. *Cimbel* (E), Avda. Europa, tel. (965) 85 21 00. 144 rooms. *Los Dalmatas* (E), Estocolmo 4, tel. (965) 85 19 00. Aztec décor, 270 rooms, pool and garden. *Don Pancho* (E), Avda. Mediterráneo, tel. (965) 85 29 50. 251 rooms, pool, garden.

Avenida (M), Martínez Alejos 5, tel. (965) 85 41 08. 4-star hotel with 93 rooms, open April-Oct. only. *Belroy Palace* (M), Avda. del Mediterráneo 13, tel. (965) 85 02 03. Also 4-star, 102 rooms. *Costa Blanca* (M), Playa de Levante, tel. (965) 85 54 50. 190 rooms, pool and gardens, 4-star.

There are over 30 3-star hotels, all with very reasonable rates. To mention just a few: *Brisa* (I), Playa de Levante, tel. (965) 85 54 00. 70 rooms, by beach, pool. *Didac* (I), Vía Emilio Ortuno, tel. (965) 85 15 49. 100 rooms, pool, garden, by beach. *Los Dunes* (M), Playa de Levante, tel. (965) 85 24 00. 110 rooms, pool, close to beach. *Haway* (I), Viena, tel. (965) 85 04 00. 230 rooms, pool, tennis, minigolf. *Los Pelicanos* (M), Gerona, tel. (965) 85 23 50. 476 rooms, pool, tennis.

Of the many 2-star hotels, with very reasonable rates, the following are good value: *Dynastic Park* (I), Avda. Rincón de Loix 17, tel. (965) 85 36 00. 114 rooms, pool, mini golf, tennis, garden. *Montemar* (I), San Pedro 16, tel. (965) 85 06 00. 89 rooms, central. *Planesia* (I), Plaza de San Jaime 5, tel. (965) 85 54 66. 36 rooms, central. Good view over sea and beaches.

Restaurants. *El Cisne* (E), on Valencia-Alicante highway, tel. 85 14 81. 4 km out, recommended by readers for fine food and service. Rustic décor and pleasant tree-shaded garden. *Tiffany's* (E), Avda. Mediterráneo, Edificio Coblanca 3, tel. 85 44 68. One of the top restaurants. Modern with musical entertainment while you dine. *Aitona* (M), Ruzafa 1, tel. 85 30 10. Rustic décor. *La Caserola* (M), Rincón de Loix, Avda. Bruselas 7, tel. 85 17 19. Good French food; dining on terrace with flowers. *Hogar del Pescador* (M), Paseo de Colón, is good for typical tapas near the municipal gardens. *Mesón Felipe V* (M), Horno 1. Beautiful restaurant with outdoor terrace and delicious food.

CALPE (Alicante). *Venta la Chata* (M), Ptda. de la Cometa, tel. (965) 83 03 08. 17 rooms, a charming roadhouse. *Paradero Ifach* (I), Explanada del Puerto 50. On the beach, a little out of town. 29 rooms, tennis. *Rocinante* (I), Ptda. Estación 10, tel. (965) 83 12 08. 28 rooms, pool.

Restaurants. *Paradero de Ifach* (M), the best of several here, a charming restaurant-hotel with wonderful view and good food. *Puerto Blanco* (M), 2 km south of town, tel. 83 09 77. Well recommended.

CARTAGENA (Murcia). *Cartagonova* (E-M), Marcos Redondo 3, tel. (968) 50 42 00. 127 rooms, parking. *Mediterráneo* (M), Puerta de Murcia 11, tel. (968) 50 74 00. 46 rooms. *Alfonso XIII* (I), Paseo Alfonso XIII 30, tel. (968) 52 00 00. Modern. 239 rooms.

Restaurant. *Mare Nostrum* (M), Alfonso XIII, tel. 52 21 31. At the port, good for seafood and fish.

CASTELLON DE LA PLANA. *Hotel del Golf* (E), Playa del Pinar, tel. (964) 22 19 50. Just out of town on the beach at El Grao; modern, with 127 rooms, golf course, mini golf, tennis and gardens. *Mindoro* (E), Moyano 4, tel. (964) 22 23 00. 114 rooms, in town. *Myrian* (M), Obispo Salinas 1, tel. (964) 22 21 00. 24 rooms with TV and radio, parking. *Turcosa* (M), Avda. de Buenavista 1, tel. (964) 22 21 50. 70 rooms, 5 km out in El Grau. *Doña Lola* (I), Lucena 3, tel. (964) 21 40 11. Pleasant small hotel across from station. Ask for a room at the back.

Restaurants. *Club Náutico* (M), Escollera Poniente, tel. 22 24 90. With good views of port. *Brisamar* (I), Buenavista 26, tel. 22 29 22. *La Tasca del Puerto* (I), Avd. del Puerto 13, tel. 22 20 88. Good for seafood.

CULLERA (Valencia). *Sicania* (E), Playa del Raco, tel. (96) 152 0143. 117 rooms, private beach, tennis and gardens. *Bolendam* (I), Avda. Cabanal 17, tel. (96) 152 0089. 39 rooms; open April-Sept. only. *Safi* (I), Faro de Cullera, tel. (96) 152 0577. 31 rooms, parking, garden.

Restaurant. *Balcón de Cullera* (M), tel. 152 2444. On way up to the Sanctuary. Good view over the sea.

DENIA (Alicante). *Denia* (M), Ptda. Suertes del Mar, tel. (965) 78 12 12. 280 rooms, pool and gardens. *Los Angeles* (M-I), Playa de las Marinas, tel. (965) 78 04 58. 60 rooms, parking, garden. *Las Rotas* (I), Ptda. Les Rotes 47, tel. (965) 78 03 23. 23 rooms, tennis, garden.

ELCHE (Alicante). *Huerto del Cura* (E), Federico García Sanchiz 14, tel. (965) 45 80 40. A semi-parador, with 59 rooms, delightfully set in palm grove, good restaurant, pool, mini golf, tennis and many other amenities. *Cartagena* (M), Gabriel Miró 12, tel. (965) 46 15 50. 34 rooms, central. *Don Jaime* (I), Avda. Primo de Rivera 5, tel. (965) 45 38 40. 64 rooms, central.

Restaurants. *Els Capellans* (M), Federico Sanchiz 14, tel. 45 80 40. At the Huerto del Cura hotel amid the famous palm grove. Very good paellas and fish. Outdoor dining beside the pool. *Parque Municipal* (M), Paseo de la Estación, tel. 45 34 15. Set in park, with outdoor terrace and dining under the palms; a favorite with locals.

GANDIA (Valencia). *Bayren I* (E), Paseo de Neptuno, tel. (96) 284 0300. By lovely beach and orange groves; 164 rooms, pool and garden. *Los Robles* (E-M), tel. (96) 284 2100. 240 rooms. *Tres Anclas* (E-M), tel. (96) 284 0566. Modern, on the beach. *Tres Delfines* (M), tel. (96) 284 1400. 136 rooms, on beach, pool and garden. *Bayren II* (M), Mallorca Playa, tel. (96) 284 0700. 125 rooms. *San Luis* (M), Paseo de Neptuno 6, tel. (96) 284 0800. 72 rooms. *Porto* (M), María Angeles Suárez, tel. (96) 284 1723, 135 rooms, by beach. *Safari* (M-I), Legazpi

3, tel. (96) 284 0400. 113 rooms, pool, garden. *Gandía Playa* (I), Devesa 17, tel. (96) 284 1300. Modern, 90 rooms, by beach, pool.

JAVEA (Alicante). *Parador Costa Blanca* (E), tel. (965) 79 02 00. Modern parador with 60 rooms. Beautifully located overlooking beach; pool and garden.
   Restaurant. *Austriaco Umberto* (M-I), Paseo Amanecer de España, at Arenal beach, tel. 79 38 04. Good food with wonderful Austrian cakes. Good value *menu del día.*

LORCA (Murcia). *Alameda* (M), Museo Valiente 8, tel. (968) 46 75 00. Central, 43 rooms.

LA MANGA DEL MAR MENOR (Murcia). A newish seaside, golfing and sports resort, with good swimming. *Cavanna* (M), tel. (968) 56 36 00. 407 rooms, pool, tennis, garden. *Doblemar Casino* (E), Gran Vía de la Manga, tel. (968) 56 39 10. 485 rooms, pool, garden and a casino. *Galua-Sol* (E), tel. (968) 56 32 00. 170 rooms, overlooks sandy beach, pool, tennis, bowling. *Entremares* (M), Gran Vía de la Manga, tel. 56 31 00. 245 rooms, pool, tennis, bowling.
   Restaurants. *Dos Mares* (M), Plaza Bohemia, tel. 56 30 93. With good views of the sea. *El Mosqui* (E-M), 3 km out at Cabo de Palos, tel. 56 30 06. Boat-shaped restaurant serving excellent *paella* and *caldero.*

MURCIA. *Hispano II* (E), Lucas 3, tel. (968) 21 61 52. A 3-star hotel with 35 rooms. *Siete Coronas Meliá* (E), Ronda de Garay 3, tel. (968) 21 77 71. 108 rooms, 4-star, good amenities; this is the best in town. *Conde de Floridablanca* (M), Corbalán 7, tel. (968) 21 46 26. 60 rooms, in historic building. *Majesti* (M), San Pedro 5, tel. (968) 21 47 42. Central right by the Mercado de Verónica; recommended. *Rincón de Pepe* (M), Apostoles 34, tel. (968) 21 22 39. 122 rooms. *Fontoria* (I), Madre de Diós 4, tel. (968) 21 77 89. 127 rooms, a 3-star hotel with very reasonable rates.
   Restaurants. *Rincón de Pepe* (E), Apostoles 34, tel. 21 22 39. An established tradition in Murcia, famous for its good fun and quaint setting. *Hispano* (M), Lucas 7, tel. 21 61 52. Traditional Spanish dishes and *nouvelle cuisine.* Pleasant terrace and bar.

ORIHUELA (Alicante). *La Zenia* (E), tel. (965) 32 02 00. 200 rooms, pool. *Montepiedra* (M-I), Dehesa de Campoamor, tel. (965) 32 03 00. 64 rooms, pool, garden.

OROPESA (Castellón). *Neptuno Stop* (M), on Barcelona road, tel. (964) 31 03 75. Motel with 21 rooms and pool. *El Cid* (I), *Las Playetas* (I), tel. (964) 30 07 00. 52 rooms, by beach, pool, tennis, bowling, garden. *Koral* (I), Paseo Marítimo, tel. (964) 31 04 14. 147 rooms. *Oropesa Sol* (I), Ctra. del Faro 97, tel. (964) 31 01 50. 50 rooms, by the beach.

PEÑISCOLA (Castellón). *Hostería del Mar* (E), tel. (964) 48 06 00. Across road from beach, slightly out of town. 73 rooms, very pleasant with local décor, garden and small pool. *Cartago* (M), tel. (964) 48 01 00. 26 rooms, garden, tennis, bowling. *Papa Luna* (M), tel. (964) 48 07 60. Modern with 230 rooms. A new hotel highly recommended by a reader is *Benedict XIII* (I) on hill above town with garden, pool and tennis. Tasteful décor and caring attention.

Restaurants. *Hostería del Mar* (M), serves good dinners in its Banqueting Hall. Delightful setting, in old part of town. *Casa Severino* (M-I), Príncipe 1, tel. 48 01 16. Splendid terrace with ocean view.

PLAYA SAN JUAN (Alicante). *Sidi San Juan Palace* (L), Pda Cabo la Huerta, tel. (965) 65 13 00. Luxury hotel with pool, minigolf, tennis, disco. *Almirante* (M), Avda. Niza 38, tel. (965) 65 01 12. 68 rooms, central, near beach.

PUERTO DE MAZARRON (Murcia). *Dos Playas* (E), tel. (968) 59 41 00. 100 rooms, pool, garden, bingo. *Bahía* (M), Playa de la Reya, tel. (968) 59 40 00. 57 rooms, garden. *Durán* (I), Playa de la Isla, tel. (968) 59 40 50.

PUERTO LUMBRERAS (Murcia). *Parador Nacional* (M), on N340, tel. (968) 40 20 25. Modern parador with 60 rooms, pleasant garden, and good food. *Riscal* (I), Avda. Pedro García Rubio, tel. (968) 40 20 50. 27 rooms, garden.

PUZOL (Valencia). *Monte Picayo* (L), tel. (96) 142 0010. Luxury hotel with 86 rooms, pool, mini golf, tennis; well situated with excellent views and peaceful surroundings. Casino and nightclub.

EL SALER (Valencia). On the coast, 10 km south of Valencia. *Sidi Saler Palace* (L), on the beach, tel. (96) 367 4100. 276 rooms, a luxury hotel with tennis, golf and pool amongst other amenities. *Parador Luis Vives* (E), on Alicante road, tel. (96) 323 68 50. Modern parador by the beach with 58 rooms; pool, golf, mini golf and garden. *Patilla II* (M), Los Pinos 8, tel. (96) 367 1558. 28 rooms, garden.

SANTA POLA (Alicante). *Pola Mar* (E-M), Playa de Levante 6, tel. (965) 41 32 00. 76 rooms, by beach. *Rocas Blancas* (M), tel. (965) 41 13 12. Pool.

SANTIAGO DE LA RIBERA (Murcia). *Lido* (I), Conde Campillo 1, tel. (968) 57 07 00. 32 rooms, on beach. *Ribera* (I), Explanada de Barnuevo 10, tel. (968) 57 02 00. 38 rooms, simple, on beach.

TORREVIEJA (Alicante). *Berlín* (M), Torre del Moro, tel. (965) 71 15 37. 50 rooms, pool, minigolf, garden. *Mar Bella* (I), Avda. Alfredo Nobel 8, tel. (965) 71 08 28. 30 rooms, by beach.

VALENCIA. *Astoria Palace* (E), Plaza Rodrigo Botet 5, tel. (96) 322 9590. 207 rooms. Modern hotel with many amenities, in central, pleasant square. *Reina Victoria* (E), Barcas 4, tel. (96) 321 1360. 92 rooms. Central and elegant. *Dimar* (E), Gran Vía Marqués de Turia 80, tel. (96) 334 1807.

Excelsior (M), Barcelonina 5, tel. (96) 321 3040. 65 rooms. Old but good, just off Pza. Rodrigo Botet. Pleasant cafeteria. *Inglés* (M), Marqués de Dos Aguas 6, tel. (96) 321 4555. 63 rooms. Old world charm, overlooking Ceramics Museum. *Llar* (M), Colón 46, tel. (96) 322 7296. 51 rooms. Modern, opposite Galerías Preciados. *Metropol* (M), Játiva 23, tel. (96) 321 4485. 109 rooms. Another good old world style hotel, opposite bullring and train station.

Bristol (M-I), Abadía San Martín 3, tel. (96) 322 4895. Central, hidden in narrow street by church of San Martín. *Continental* (M-I), Correos 8, tel. (96) 321 7218. 43 rooms. Just behind post office, off main square. *Europa* (I), Ribera 4, tel. (96) 322 0589. In a central, almost traffic free, street. *Internacional* (I), Bailén 8, tel. (96) 321 4565. 55 rooms. By train station.

Restaurants. *Los Viveros* (E), Jardines del Real, tel. 369 2350. Wonderful food in charming setting in a park. Dining on tree-shaded terrace. *El Condestable* (E), Artes Gráficas 15, tel. 369 9250. Excellent French restaurant. *Les Graelles* (E), Plaza Galicia 11, tel. 369 9039. *Mesón del Marisquero* (E), Felix Pizcueta 7, tel. 322 9791. Rustic décor; specializes in seafood.

El Ateneo (E-M), Plaza del País Valenciano 18, tel. 321 0154. An old Valencia tradition with excellent dining and service. *Comodoro* (E-M), Transís 3, tel. 321 3815. Select restaurant close to Astoria Palace hotel; dinner only. *Lionel* (E-M), En Llop 4, tel. 321 5634. Just off Pza País Valenciano; recommended. *Nederland 1814* (M), Pza Rodrigo Botet. Stylish modern décor; (I) *tapas* and sandwiches.

For a vast selection of (M) restaurants, stroll along Calle Moisén Femades which is full of atmospheric bars. Try *Alcázar, Río Sil* or *Palacio de la Bellota*.

Casa Cesareo (I), Guillén de Castro 15, tel. 321 2214. Opposite San Agustín church; a dull location on a busy street, but atmospheric interior. Excellent value. Best for lunch. *Barrachina* (I), Plaza del País Valenciano 2. Famous throughout Spain. Spectacular bar snacks - sausages, *pepitos* and *empanadas*.

USEFUL ADDRESSES. Tourist Offices. Albacete; Avda. de España 3. **Alicante;** Explanada de España 2. **Castellón;** Plaza María Augustina 5. **Murcia;** Alejandro Seiquer 4. **Valencia,** Calle de la Paz 46.

CAR HIRE. Alicante; *Avis* at airport and Expl. de España 3; *Hertz* at airport and station; *Ital,* Segura 21; *Budget,* Padre Vendrell 16. **Benidorm;** *Budget,* Edificio Cervantes, Avda de Europa. **Castellón;** *Budget,* Escultor Viciano 5. **Murcia;** *Hertz,* at airport; *Europcar,* Gran Vía 10; *Ital,* Dr. Fleming 10. **Valencia;** *Avis* at airport and Isabel la Católica 17; *Budget,* Plaza los Pinazo 5; *Hertz* at airport and Segorbe 7; *Ital,* Isabel la Católica 19.

SEVILLE

Prelude to Andalusia

The place to begin a visit to Andalusia is Seville, perhaps the one city in Spain that no one should miss. Whether you use Seville as a base from which to visit the rest of Andalusia, or visit it for itself alone, you really should go there. Partly because Seville is one of the few cities on earth that really live up to their image.

Start your visit there with an hour spent on a café terrace, sipping *sangría* and munching shrimps, watching the crowds pass by. There is something in the air of Seville that will immediately communicate itself to you. A sense of romance, a sense of joie de vivre, a sense of color and life. The Sevillians sitting around you, smoking their cigars and fingering their tiny glasses of sherry, will be watching the passing crowd too. It is a local pastime, *the* local pastime, for every Andalusian has learned the great Arab maxim, "Life is much shorter than death", and he intends to relish every last bit of life before death takes a hand.

The Cathedral and Giralda Tower

Seville's cathedral can only be described in superlatives. It is the largest in Spain (and the largest Gothic building in the world), the highest, and the richest in decoration, and great works of art. When Saint Ferdinand delivered Seville from the Moors, the city set about replacing its 12th-century mosque with a grandiose monument, befitting its proud and opulent station. In order to hasten the building begun in 1402, the canons renounced their incomes and lived in ascetic privation. Nothing was too fine for the church: sculptured portals, Flemish altar screens, stained-glass windows, wrought-iron grilles, marble floors, bronze candelabra. The centuries have brought further treasures in the form of votive offerings, the finest canvases of Zurbarán and Morales, and two beautiful Murillos, the *Immaculate Conception* and *Saint Anthony.*

Inside the cathedral is a shrine containing precious relics of Seville's liberator, Saint Ferdinand. Another glorious mausoleum beneath the high vaults is that of Christopher Columbus. The great explorer knew triumph and disgrace, and found no repose even in death. He died at Valladolid, bitterly disillusioned. His body was first buried at Santo Domingo, then at Havana, and brought to Seville only when Spain had lost the last vestige of the New World he had discovered. The details of Columbus' long and tragic life are better understood after a study of the General Archives of the Indies in the Casa Lonja collection of New World documents, built by Juan Herrera, the architect of the Escorial, opposite the cathedral. Since Seville adorned her immense shrine with gold and precious woods brought from Peru and the West Indies, it is only just that Columbus should share a place among them.

Every day the bell of this colossal monument that summons the faithful to prayer rings out from a Moorish minaret. For when they had razed the old mosque, the Sevillians could not bring themselves to destory the admirable tower of Abou Yakoub, a splendid example of Arabic art and one of the marvels of Seville. It has been topped by a five-story bell tower capped by a mammoth statue of Faith, so ingeniously mounted that its great bulk turns with the slightest breeze. This is the giraldillo ("something that turns") whence the magnificent tower gets its name, La Giralda. The platform at 70 meters (230 feet) is reached by a gently sloping ramp wide enough for two horsemen to pass abreast. From this splendid site you can see the iridescent panorama of Seville, the pattern of gardens and the loop of the river.

The Guadalquivir quays no longer shelter graceful sailing vessels of the past, but freighters loaded with wood, lead or minerals. The port has long since lost the regal position it held when the Tribunal of the Indies met in Seville, and when the Portuguese, Magellan, came there to embark on his first trip around the world. For many years the port was paralyzed by encroaching sand, but when the Tablada Canal was dug in 1926, ocean-going vessels were brought again to Seville's shores.

The Alcázar

The Tower of Gold (Torre del Oro), whose yellow cupola is reflected in the Guadalquivir, was formerly linked to the Alcázar by a subterranean passage, for the palaces of Arab kings served also as fortresses. High rough walls served to defend exquisitely decorated interiors. Pedro the Cruel installed himself in the Alcázar and had it restored at great expense, but rather too hastily, for there are disturbing elements such as badly executed Christian inscriptions among the Moslem motifs. The Catholic Monarchs added their own halls and embellishments to the delicate columns of the Patio de las Doncellas, where the sultans received their tribute of young virgins. Charles V built a small palace and the hall where the splendid tapestries depicting his triumphal expedition to Tunis are exhibited. The apartment in which the Spanish monarchs frequently resided in the 19th century and where Queen Isabella II was born was restored in 1977. Two gardens, enclosed in high walls covered with bougainvillaea, are adorned with a grotto and fountains.

Santa Cruz

The old Jewish area of Santa Cruz, with its twisting, winding little white byways, is a perfectly conceived set for an operetta. Old houses mingle with souvenir and antique shops. Every whitewashed garden wall has its wrought-iron lantern and its casual overflow of vines. Every window hides behind a pot-bellied iron grille bristling with spikes. But through open doors you catch glimpses of inviting patios that remind you that Murillo once lived in one of these charming dwellings and is buried in the lovely Plaza de Santa Cruz. Nearby his house has now been opened as a small museum. He must have loved the unstudied artistry of his flagstone patio, brightened with masses of potted plants and copper vessels, and enlivened by a fountain. A particularly beautiful patio can be seen at number 2, Callejon del Agua.

La Caridad

Love is an all-important question in Seville, the city of Don Juan. He was actually called Miguel de Mañara. He was rich, licentious, careless of his life and his wealth. Leaving the scene of a drunken orgy he encountered a funeral procession and saw, with horror, that the partly decomposed corpse was his own. He accepted the apparition as a sign from God. Andalusians, with all their love of life, have a morbid preoccupation with death, and a taste for the tragic and sanguinary. It is evidenced in their passion for bullfights and in their gruesome statues of Christ and the martyrs. Miguel de Mañara renounced his worldly goods and joined the brotherhood of the Caridad, whose unsavory task it was to collect the bodies of executed men and give them burial. He died in this fine baroque almshouse, the Caridad, where his portrait can still be seen. But the chief attraction—and a sinister one—is two paintings by Valdes Leal, commissioned by Miguel de Mañara. They realistically represent the Triumph of Death: a skeleton in knightly armor and a bishop in his coffin devoured by worms.

Murillo said that one had to hold one's nose when looking at this canvas. His own paintings cover the Caridad walls with Virgins and cherubs. He is the painter of Seville, as El Greco is that of Toledo and Goya that of Madrid. He has painted the burning tenderness of Seville in the eyes of his Virgins as he has captured the piquancy of Santa Cruz's street urchins.

All of Seville's churches are interesting in their own way, some are obviously reconstructed mosques, others are Spanish baroque. The chapels are naively cluttered with artificial flowers. Golden lamps illuminate figures by Roldán and Montanés. There are Christs and Virgins with names of touching lyricism: *Our Lady of Solitude* and *Jesus of Great Omnipotence,* the *Virgin of Sorrow* and *Christ Expiring.* The neighborhood parishes render to each saint a particular homage, but none is more revered than the Virgin of Hope. She is familiarly known as the Macarena, because her church, San Gil, adjoins the Macarena Gate, a remnant of the old Roman wall. As familiar to the Sevillian as the features of his sweetheart are those of the Macarena. She is the matadors' protector and few bullfighters would dream of entering the arena without addressing a prayer to her.

Pilate's House

A visit to Seville would be incomplete without 30 minutes or an hour at the Casa de Pilatos, residence of the Marquis of Medinaceli. The Duke of Tarifa, a 16th-century ancestor of the present inhabitant,

SEVILLE
(NOT TO SCALE)

1 Giralda & Cathedral
2 Alcazar
3 Archives of The Indies
4 San Telmo Palace
5 Tobacco Factory (New University)
6 Post Office
7 Bull Ring
8 La Caridad
9 City Hall
10 Old University
11 Fine Arts Museum
12 Casa de Pilatos
13 Las Dueñas Palace
✟ Church or Convent

returned from a pilgrimage to the Holy Land and built this mansion in the style of Pontius Pilate's residence there, or so he thought. The vast patio, the fine stucco work, and the un-blue azulejos (though *azul* means 'blue') are much more mudéjar than Roman, even to the untrained eye. On the upper floor the furnished apartments of the Medinaceli family contain some lesser known works of Goya, Murillo and Velazquez.

Other notable buildings in Seville are the 16th-century city hall, a fine example of Spanish plateresque, and the baroque 18th-century palace of San Telmo.

María Luisa Park

The María Luisa park was once the gardens of the San Telmo palace. These were redesigned in 1929 for the Ibero-American exhibition, and today its sunken gardens with pools, and fountains and ceramic tiles provide welcome shade from Seville's summer heat. Many of the pavilions from the 1929 exhibition still remain and are used as consulates and private schools. Be sure to see the Plaza de España, the vast semi-circular brick building which was Spain's pavilion in the 1929 fair. The ceramic tiles adorning it represent every provincial capital in Spain and the four bridges you'll see represent the four medieval kingdoms of the Iberian peninsula. At the far end of the park is the Plaza de América, an ideal place to spend siesta time watching the children feed the hundreds of white doves which fly around its ceramic fountains.

Holy Week and Its Processions

The citizen of Seville is a habitual night-owl, and, during Holy Week he seldom sleeps at all. By Palm Sunday every balcony is hung with palm branches from Elche. The faithful are busily acquiring merit by freshening up the statues, brushing Caiphas' velvet robe, combing Saint John's sheepskin, and ironing the linen for the communion rail. Seville's streets and alleys become crowded with parades that continue until Good Friday. Out of their niches come all the carved stations of the cross: Jesus before Pilate or in the Garden, groups of as many as twenty sumptuous figures, richly clothed and armed, surrounded by handsome trees, rugs and draperies. These *pasos* are mounted on platforms and carried through the city by five or six dozen bearers.

Each parish offers at least one paso and one figure of Christ or Mary to the parade. These are carried under an embroidered canopy, among flaming tapers and silver lamps. The sumptuousness of the statues is unbelievable, Madonnas are dressed in capes of satin or damask, encrusted with pearls and strands of gold; diadems glitter with precious

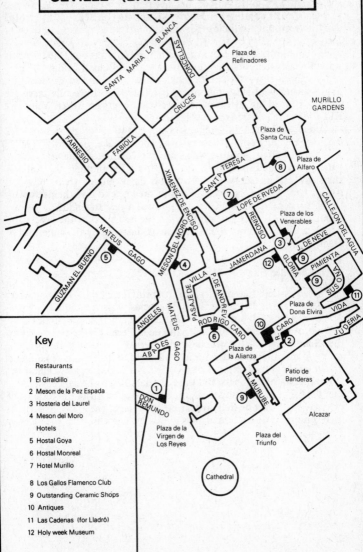

SEVILLE (BARRIO DE SANTA CRUZ)

Plaza de Refinadores

MURILLO GARDENS

Plaza de Santa Cruz

Plaza de Alfaro

Plaza de los Venerables

Plaza de Dona Elvira

Plaza de la Alianza

Patio de Banderas

Alcazar

Plaza de la Virgen de Los Reyes

Plaza del Triunfo

Cathedral

SANTA MARIA LA BLANCA
DONCELLAS
CRUCES
FARNESIO
FABIOLA
XIMENEZ DE ENCISO
SANTA TERESA
LOPE DE RVEDA
REINOSO
J. DE NEVE
CALLEJON DEL AGUA
PIMIENTA
GLORIA
JAMERDANA
SUSONA
VIDA
JUDERIA
R. CARO
MATEUS GAGO
GUZMAN EL BUENO
MESON DEL MORO
PASAJE DE VILLA
P. DE ANDREV
RODRIGO CARO
ANGELES
ABADES
MATEUS GAGO
DON REMUNDO
R. MURUBE

Key

Restaurants

1 El Giraldillo
2 Meson de la Pez Espada
3 Hosteria del Laurel
4 Meson del Moro

Hotels

5 Hostal Goya
6 Hostal Monreal
7 Hotel Murillo

8 Los Gallos Flamenco Club
9 Outstanding Ceramic Shops
10 Antiques
11 Las Cadenas (for Lladró)
12 Holy week Museum

stones. Great Spanish ladies have emptied their jewel caskets to shower the Virgin with gifts. Among this splendor move hooded barefooted penitents, each wearing a rope around his waist and carrying a lighted candle. According to their order, these pilgrims wear cowls of linen or heavy pleated satin of scarlet, blue, purple or gray.

The first procession begins on Palm Sunday afternoon, the last ends with the last streaks of sunset on the evening of Good Friday. In spite of its elaborateness, the spectacle is monotonous, and so an incongruous assortment of extra mummers is introduced. In Seville these are Roman centurions, at Lorca, Biblical characters and even Mahomet and Cleopatra. There is also a torero parade.

Added to the general excitement are the songs of gypsies and the constant popping of firecrackers. Make no mistake, this Holy Week is a boisterous affair. Visitors who have rented comfortable seats in the gallery can watch indefinitely one tableau after another; the Andalusians are ecstatic, comfortable or not. They munch their nuts and candy, wrap their exhausted infants in shawls, and give themselves up to this supreme moment. They have waited a year to lend their joy and agonized tears to this Passion Play. In the last hours of the procession you hear their tortured songs, the *saetas,* inspired by the sufferings of Jesus.

The Seville Fair

The week-long fair takes place in springtime (after Easter), when Seville is wearing her finest dress of acacias, wisteria and early roses. A vast livestock exhibition draws breeders and their finest animals from every province. Along the Explanada de la Feria, on the right bank of the Guadalquivir, little wooden and canvas houses are improvised, where families receive friends day and night, with abundant food and drink, music and laughter. There is always a barrel organ, a guitar or, at least, a pair of castanets. But the essential thing is the dance. Andalusian dancers can be found in all the smoke-laden, dusty dance halls of the city. They may be thin, ardent performers, or they may be surprisingly plump, but they are always agile and graceful.

PRACTICAL INFORMATION FOR SEVILLE

WARNING. In recent years Seville has become notorious for purse snatching and stealing from parked and even moving cars. Take extra care with your belongings at all times and never leave anything in a parked car. The situation is now so bad that we recommend you carry only a small amount of cash on you and maybe a credit card; leave your passport and traveler's checks in the hotel safe.

 HOW TO GET ABOUT. Seville, with its labyrinth of narrow streets, can be a difficult city to find your way about in and is best negotiated on foot. Fortunately all the main sites, except possibly for the park, are fairly close together. Arm yourself with a city map and mark your hotel on it, it may not be so easy to find at the end of a day's sightseeing!

BY TAXI. If you do get lost, or are feeling weary, then take a taxi. They are plentiful and not too expensive. Make sure the driver puts his meter on at the start of the ride. As of mid-1983, fares were as follows: meter starts at 48 ptas., and goes up 3 ptas. each 15 seconds. Supplements are: suitcases 15 ptas., Sundays and holidays 30 ptas., night fares 12–6 A.M. 35 ptas., leaving a station 30 ptas., to or from the airport 100 ptas. There is a 25% surcharge on rides to or from the bullring or football ground, and on all trips during the April Fair. No extra charge during Easter Week. Taxis take up to four people.

BY BUS. Local buses are blue and cream and charge a flat fare of 25 ptas. Microbuses cost 35 ptas. single ride. A *bonobus* good for 10 rides can be bought for 195 ptas. normal bus, 300 ptas. microbuses, from the *taquillas* in Plaza del Duque, Plaza Madalena and between the cathedral and archives where you can also get a plan of the system. Taking a bus can be confusing, however. Due to Seville's complicated one-way system, many buses return along a different route from their outward journey, so ask if you're uncertain.

BY CARRIAGE. *Coche caballos* (horse-drawn carriages) add a touch of local color to Seville's streets. A good place to hire one is in Plaza Virgen de los Reyes, outside the cathedral entrance. Four or five people can ride together. If you don't like the price quoted, be sure to bargain, but always agree your price before your ride begins. A recommended route for a buggy ride is through the María Luisa Park visiting the Plaza de España and the Plaza de América.

BY METRO. A metro system is being constructed, but is unlikely to be open by 1984.

STREET NAMES. The following street names have recently been changed. Avdas. Queipo Llano and José Antonio are now Avda. de la Constitución. Plaza de la Falange is now Plaza San Francisco. Plaza General Franco is now Plaza de la Magdalena. Plaza 18 de Julio is now Plaza de la Concordia. Plaza Calvo Sotelo is now Puerta de Jerez.

HOTELS. During Easter week and the Seville fair at the end of April hotel rooms are virtually impossible to find, many having been booked for as much as a year in advance. Rates are about double at this time and you will probably be obliged to take half or even full board terms.

Many of Seville's hotels are located in narrow streets and may be extremely hard to find if you are arriving for the first time in your own car. In which case we advise that one of you take a taxi which you can follow in your own car to the hotel. In Easter week many of the streets in the center of town may be closed to traffic altogether; most hotels will then have porters with trolleys who will collect your luggage from your car or taxi.

To telephone a Seville number from outside Seville province, use the prefix 954.

Deluxe

Alfonso XIII, San Fernando 2 (tel. 22 28 50). Reopened in 1979 after three years of renovation and although some of the old splendor of this historic building has gone, much of its beauty and old world charm remain, including the beautiful central patio and magnificent ceramic tiles. Centrally located next to Seville university, and near the cathedral and Alcázar, this is undoubtedly the best hotel in town; but service is not always reliable, sadly.

Luz Sevilla, Martín Villa 2 (tel. 22 29 91). 142 rooms, centrally located, close to shopping area, with air-conditioning, solarium, boutiques, good restaurant and other amenities. Closed at presstime and its future uncertain, so check.

Expensive

Colón, Canalejas 1 (tel. 22 29 00). 261 rooms. Popular old-style hotel.

Doña María, Don Remondo 19 (tel. 22 49 90). Small, tasteful rooms furnished with antiques; roof-top swimming pool with good view of Giralda. Highly recommended. No restaurant.

Inglaterra, Plaza Nueva 7 (tel. 22 49 70). 120 rooms. Recently rebuilt, modern hotel located in central square. The gourmets go here for fine cuisine and excellent service.

Los Lebreros, Luis Morales 2 (tel. 25 19 00). 439 rooms all have balconies equipped with rotating canopies to provide choice of *sol* or *sombra*. One of Seville's newest hotels, with room for 1,000 guests; airconditioning and pool. Located slightly out of town on the Málaga road.

Macarena, San Juan Ribera 2 (tel. 37 57 00). Opposite basilica of the famous Virgin. Readers complain it is shabby and very noisy.

María Luisa Park, Carrero Blanco 26 (tel. 45 60 11). Attractive setting in shady park beside casino and open air restaurant. Check if open.

Nuevo Lar, Plaza de Carmen Benítez 3 (tel. 36 07 00). Good standards and well recommended though it tends to cater for groups.

Pasarela, Avda. de la Borbolla 11 (tel. 23 19 80). Recent and close to María Luisa park. Garage and sauna; television in all rooms.

Porta Coeli, Eduardo Dato 49 (tel. 25 18 00). 247 rooms. With shops, some suites and bingo. Located a little out of town center.

Moderate

Alcázar, Menéndez Pelayo 10 (tel. 23 19 91). Modern hotel on busy road, overlooking Murillo and Alcázar gardens.

América, Jesús del Gran Poder 2 (tel. 22 09 51). Modern hotel centrally located close to shops on Plaza del Duque.

Becquer, Reyes Católicos 4 (tel. 22 89 00). A pleasant, modern hotel with bar and lounge. Good service.

Corregidor, Morgado 17 (tel. 38 51 11). Pleasant and reasonably central.

Don Paco, Jerónimo de Córdoba 4 (tel. 22 49 31). Caters mainly for the package tour trade and when full can be very noisy and the dining room service harassed, to say the least. At other times it is pleasant enough and has a roof-top pool, but beware the paper thin walls of the rooms!

Fernando III, San José 21 (tel. 21 73 07). Located on edge of Barrio Santa Cruz, with rooftop patio and pool. Recommended.

Fleming, Sierra Nevada (tel. 36 19 00). 84 rooms. Garden and some suites. Good service.

Internacional, Aguilas 17 (tel. 21 32 07). An old-world 2 star hotel in the narrow streets of old Seville near Casa Pilatos.

Inexpensive

Ducal, Plaza de la Encarnación 19 (tel. 21 51 07). 51 rooms and close to shops. Reader recommended.

Montecarlo, Gravina 51 (tel. 21 75 03). 26 rooms. Old fashioned hotel in a picturesque house.

Murillo, Lope de Rueda 7, (tel. 21 60 95). 61 rooms. Right in heart of Barrio Santa Cruz. Picturesque and highly recommended. Cannot be reached by car but a porter with a trolley will collect your luggage from your taxi.

Niza, Reyes Católicos 5, (tel. 21 54 04). Old fashioned and friendly but the rooms are beginning to show their age.

Sevilla, Daioz 5, (tel. 22 08 52). 30 rooms. In typical Sevillian house with garden overlooking picturesque square. Central.

 RESTAURANTS. Seville has many atmospheric restaurants in the medium to expensive price range but surprisingly few in the inexpensive category. This may be due to the abundance of *mesones* and *bodegas* all over town which serve a vast range of tapas at the bar but do not provide tables or waiter service. Many of the locals eat this way, particularly in the evenings. Remember that traditionally lunch is the main meal and tends to be a rather lengthy affair. Few Sevillians begin lunch before 2.30 and many are still at the table as late as 4.30. If you are pressed for time, however, most restaurants begin serving around 1 when they will be less crowded and therefore speedier.

Expensive

La Almoraina at Los Lebreros hotel is tops for elegance.

El Burladero at the Colón hotel is a long-standing Seville tradition with atmospheric décor and bullfight ambience.

Albahaca, Plaza Santa Cruz (tel. 22 07 14). Newly opened, lovely setting in old Jewish quarter, with atmosphere and creative dishes.

Casa Senra, Becquer 41 (tel. 22 30 24). An old favoite near the Macarena Gate. Excellent seafood. Try the tasty *gazpacho* and sole.

La Raza, Avda Isabel la Católica (tel. 23 51 04). Open air dining in María Luisa Park. Fairly chic but service can be slow.

Mesón Don Raimundo, Argote de Molina 26 (tel. 22 33 55). Located in an old convent and serving Andalusian specialties and wine from the owner's vineyard. Atmospheric and popular with locals.

Paco Ramos, Reyes Católicos 21 (tel. 21 75 74). New. There is a French flavor to the cuisine and the standards and service are excellent if the prices somewhat high by Spanish standards.

Moderate

Los Alcázares, Miguel de Mañara 10 (tel. 21 31 03). Close to entrance to Alcázar with typical Sevillian décor and beautiful ceramics.

Bodegón Torre del Oro, Santander 15 (tel. 21 31 69). Rustic atmosphere, good food and popular with Americans.

El Giraldillo, Plaza Virgen de los Reyes 2 (tel. 21 45 25). Typical, colorful mesón, opposite entrance to cathedral. Popular with both tourists and locals.

Hostería del Laurel, Plaza Venerables 5 (tel. 22 38 66). Typical Andalusian décor in heart of Barrio Santa Cruz. Recommended.

La Isla, Arfe 25 (tel. 21 20 28). Well recommended for seafood and super paellas; praised by readers.

Mesón del Moro, Meson del Moro 6 (tel. 21 21 71). A touch of the Moors here. A wide choice of pricey dishes but the *menu del día* is very reasonable.

El Puerto, Betis 59 (tel. 21 17 25). Excellent location on the edge of the Guadalquivir, and reasonable prices.

Río Grande, Betis 70 (tel. 27 18 31). Huge outdoor terrace beside the Guadalquivir with splendid view of the city.

San Francisco, Plaza San Francisco 10, tel. 22 20 56. Another recently opened restaurant, in an old house in the central square. Its original menu is a pleasing mixture of French and Spanish inventiveness, a little pricey.

Inexpensive

La Cueva de la Pez Espada, Rodrigo Caro 18. Colorful tavern in Barrio Santa Cruz, between Plaza Doña Elvira and Alianza. Friendly service.

Los Duendes, Conteros 45. Atmospheric popular spot close to the cathedral. Go early or expect to wait. Food is average but prices are low. Fun décor.

El Mesón, Dos de Mayo 26 (tel. 21 30 75). Typical Sevillian bodegón with lashings of atmosphere. Photos of famous diners in inner room.

Mesón Tenorio, Mateus Gago 9, near the cathedral. Reader recommended. Bullfight décor and marvelous paella.

 NIGHTLIFE. Seville's nightlife is at its best in its **flamenco** shows. Entrances including one drink are around 1400 ptas. Best are *El Arenal,* Rodo 7, (tel. 21 64 92) and *Las Trochas,* Ronda de Capuchinos 23 (tel. 35 50 28). Others are *Los Gallos,* Plaza Santa Cruz 6, (tel. 21 31 98) and *La Cochera,* Menendez Pelayo 42 (tel. 36 40 97). Very popular is *El Patio Sevillano,* Paseo de Colón 11, (tel. 21 41 20) which caters mainly for coach parties. It has a mixture of regional Spanish dances and flamenco. Another popular flamenco club catering mainly for groups is *Don Felipe,* Avenida Felipe II 4, (tel. 23 39 40).

DISCOS. *El Dragón Rojo,* Betis 59, (tel. 27 20 07), is rather small but has reasonable prices. *El Coto,* Luis Montoto 118, (tel. 25 19 00), beneath Los Lebreros hotel is the best and well recommended. Its opening hours are somewhat erratic so check before you go there. *Holiday,* Jesús del Gran Poder 71, (tel. 21 88 77), is a vast club which sometimes puts on floor shows.

SEVILLANOS. If you would like to hear some typical Sevillian songs, then try the *Garbanzo Palace Bar,* Menéndez y Pelayo 18, (tel. 23 51 10). Shows begin around 11.30 P.M. and entrance including one drink costs around 400 ptas. This is a favorite with locals.

 MUSEUMS. Most state-owned museums and galleries are closed on Mondays. Most are free to students with an International Student Card. Although many museums are advertized as free on one day a week, this is only to Spaniards with IDs; tourists will have to pay. Most of Seville's museums are centrally located and can easily be visited on foot. Although we give opening hours and entrance prices below, this is only a guide. Prices rise frequently and hours vary from summer to winter year to year, so be sure to check.

Alcázar and gardens, entrance in Plaza del Triunfo. Built in mudéjar style by Pedro I in 14th century on the remains of a Moorish palace. Spain's second most beautiful Moorish palace after Granada's Alhambra. Open 9 to 12.45 and 4.30 to 7 (3 to 5.30 in winter), adm. 120 ptas. Open mornings only on Sun. and holidays.

Archives of the Indies, Avda. de la Constitución. Interesting collection of documents on the discovery, conquest and colonization of America, housed in the Casa Lonja built by Juan de Herrera, architect of El Escorial. Open Mon. to Sat., 10 to 1. Conducted tours in Spanish only. Free.

Basilica of the Macarena, near the Macarena Gate. Modern basilica where the famous statue of Our Lady of Hope, known as *La Macarena,* is kept. The procession of La Macarena takes place on Holy Thursday and is the most beautiful of all Seville's Easter processions. Open 9.30–12.30 and 5.30–8. There is an admission charge to see the treasure, and donations may be expected.

Cathedral and Giralda, entrance in Plaza Virgen de los Reyes. Open 10.30 to 1 and 4.30 to 6.30 (3.30 to 5.30 in winter), adm. 100 and 25 ptas respectively.

Convent of Santa Paula, Calle Sta Paula. Recently opened, 16th- and 17th-century paintings and furniture. Open 9 to 1 and 4 to 7.

Hospicio de los Venerables Sacerdotes, in square of same name in Barrio Santa Cruz. Baroque church with notable works of art, beautiful patio and housing the Museum of Holy Week. Open 10 to 2 and 4 to 8. Entrance 25 ptas.

Hospital of Charity, Calle Temprado. Founded in 17th century by Miguel Mañara, better known as Don Juan. Famous paintings by Murillo and Valdés Leal and main altar by Roldán. Open 10 to 1.30 and 3.30 to 7. Adm. 35 ptas or give a donation.

Museum of Archaeology, Plaza de América, in the Renaissance Pavillion in María Luisa Park. Open 10 to 2. Closed Mon. Adm. 150 ptas.

Museum of Contemporary Arts, Santo Tomás. In 18th-century house alongside Archives of the Indies, and now the home of 20th-century Spanish painting and sculpture. Open 10 to 1 and 5 to 9 weekdays, 10 to 1 Sun., closed Mon.

Museum of Fine Arts, Plaza del Museo. Good collection of Murillo, Valdés Leal and Zurbarán housed in an old convent. After the Prado, this is Spain's most important art gallery. Open 10–2 and 4–7; Sun. 10–2 only. Closed Mon. Adm. 150 ptas. The upper floor is (still) closed for restoration.

Museum of Popular Arts and Customs, Plaza de América in María Luisa Park. Open 10 to 2. Closed Mon. Temporary exhibitions open from 10.30 to 2 and 5 to 8.

Pilate's House, Plaza Pilatos. Home of the Duke of Medinaceli, this beautiful palace is built in mudéjar style and is sumptuously decorated with ceramic tiles. Should not be missed. Open 9 to 1 and 3 to 6.30. Adm. to ground floor 100 ptas; upper floor can only be visited in guided tours, furnished apartments of Medinaceli family, a further 50 ptas.

Temple of Jesús del Gran Poder, in street of same name. Famous statue by Juan de Mesa. Open 9.30–1.30 and 7–9.

Tower of Gold, near San Telmo Bridge. 13th-century tower which once guarded entrance to harbour, now houses the Naval Museum. Good view from roof. Open 10 to 2, on Sun. 10 to 1, closed Mon. Adm. 15 ptas.

 PARKS AND GARDENS. María Luisa Park. This is probably the prettiest park in Spain, with a fascinating mixture of formal designs and wild vegetation. Also fountains, cafés, small sequestered nooks, where one may sit and read or dream. Its beautiful villas were built for the Hispanic-American exhibition of 1929, each pavilion representing a different Latin American country.

Not to be missed is the magnificent *Plaza de España,* a vast governmental building, with sumptuous tile decorations, a kind of outdoor museum in itself.

This was Spain's pavilion for the 1929 fair. Equally worthwhile is the *Plaza de América* at the other end of the park where hundreds of white pigeons gather to be fed in its beautiful gardens and tiled fountains.

Also beautiful are the *Murillo Gardens* on the edge of the Barrio Santa Cruz and the delightful gardens of the *Alcázar* with their patios, flowering shrubs and ornamental pools and fountains. The latter can be visited on a ticket to the palace.

SHOPPING. Seville's main shopping streets are in the area bounded by the Calles Sierpes, Tetuan, and Velázquez, the Plaza de la Madalena and the Plaza del Duque. The *Corte Inglés* **department store** in Plaza del Duque stays open during siesta hours and has a cafeteria on the top floor. *Galerías Preciados* is in Plaza de la Madalena.

Antiques and **ceramics** are best in the Barrio Santa Cruz. Try the antique shops in Rodrigo Caro between the Plazas Alianza and Doña Elvira. Good ceramic shops are in Romero Murube, on the corner of Vida and Callejón del Agua, and in Calle Gloria where we would specially recommend *Cerámicas Sevilla* at no. 5. It specializes in hand-painted plates by local artists.

For **fans**, try *Casa Rubio*, Sierpes 56. For **folk costumes** try *Establecimiento Lina*, Plaza Santa Cruz 12; and for **flamenco** dresses, *Pardales* at Cuna 23. Children's flamenco dresses are usually cheapest in the souvenir shops around the cathedral. **Lace** mantillas and tablecloths as well as woven and embroidered cloths are good at *Feliciano Foronda*, Alvarez Quintero 52. A good **souvenir** shop with a wide selection of Lladró porcelain is *Las Cadenas*, Calle Vida in the Barrio Santa Cruz. For a good selection of regional artisan work, try *Cosas de Andalucía* at Hernando Colón 17.

Artespaña, the Spanish government **handicraft** shop is at Rodríguez Jurado 4, just off Avda. de la Constitución.

USEFUL ADDRESSES. *Tourist Office*, Avda. Constitución 21. *American Consulate*, Paseo de las Delicias 7, (tel. 23 18 85). *British Consulate*, Plaza Nueva 8, (tel. 22 88 75). *Post Office*, Avda. Constitución 32. *Telephone Exchange*, Plaza Nueva 3. *Police Headquarters* (lost passports), Plaza de la Gavidia, (tel. 22 88 40).

Renfe Office, Zaragoza 29. *Cádiz Railroad Station*, Avda. de Cádiz. *Córdoba Railroad Station*, Plaza de Armas. *Bus Station*, José María Osborne, (lines to all destinations except Huelva and Badajoz. Buses to Huelva leave from Segura 18, and to Badajoz from Arenal 3). *Airport*, 12 km out on road to Córdoba, (tel. 51'06 77). Iberia is the handling agent for all foreign airlines in Seville. *American Express*, agent is Viajes Alhambra, Teniente Coronel Segui 3 (tel. 22 44 35 and 21 39 96).

ANDALUSIA AND ITS TWO COASTS

Costa del Sol and Costa de la Luz

Andalusia is the fabulous land that armchair tourists mistake for Spain. If you believe the travel posters, every girl is called Carmen, wears a carnation in her hair, spends her days swooning over a matador bloodying up a bull and her nights swooning over guitar serenades wafted to her window through the heavy perfume of orange blossoms. Somewhere in the background a fountain plays seductively and the Alhambra looms against the sky. The more sophisticated may add the specter of a hooded penitent or one of Murillo's little beggars.

The odd thing is that Andalusia really *is* rather like that. In spite of a century of blatant advertising, comic opera settings and terrible tourist souvenirs that turn up all over the world, Andalusia remains mysterious, original, incredibly romantic and reeking with atmosphere. In fact, supremely worth visiting, for the first—or the fifty-first—time.

If you're happy to do no more than visit Seville's cathedral, Cordoba's mosque and Granada's Alhambra, you'll get along without too much trouble or difficulty. The roads are adequate, there'll be sherry and serenades; you can buy a black lace mantilla. All the beautiful Spanish postcards you've ever seen will come to life for you. And in a week you can tour the entire region and enjoy it very much. But that is not the only way, or even the best way.

For there is so much to see in Andalusia—too much for a mere week's stay. To know and understand Andalusia fully would take not a week, but a lifetime. For Andalusia has everything. There is the glamor of candlelight reflected upon gold brocade, the hooded, barefoot figures of marching penitents, and the sudden wailing lament of impromptu flamenco saetas sung as the Holy Week processions pass through the darkened streets of Seville, Granada or Málaga. There is the comfort and sophistication of great seaside hotels on the Costa del Sol and Costa de la Luz, respectively Andalusia's Mediterranean and Atlantic shores, backed by fortress towns half as old as time, and vast tawny sierras where eagles wheel toward the unclouded sun. Andalusia is fierce, virile, beautiful, and pagan—it is *never* dull!

Huelva and the Discovery of the New World

West of Seville, the Odiel and Tinto rivers flow through the dreary plains, dyed red by copper deposits. Huelva, between the two busy rivers, is still an active port. A huge monument to Columbus by the American sculptress, Mrs Whitney, stands in the estuary, but it is from Palos, now a fishing village higher up the Tinto, that Columbus' three caravels departed for America.

The coastal road continues east for only forty-five kilometers (28 miles) to Mazagón, an up-and-coming coastal resort at the beginning of the endless sands of the Playa de Castilla, which is backed by the 1,300 square kilometers (500 sq. miles) of the Coto Doñana (Doñana Nature Reserve) extending east to Las Marismas, a paradise for the ornithologist.

So Huelva is necessarily approached from Seville. The road passes through several nice little towns, such as Sanlúcar la Mayor, La Palma del Condado, and Niebla, an ancient settlement on the Tinto, all of them with interesting churches in a blend of mudéjar and Gothic styles. Niebla still has its original walls, with their four Moorish gateways also revealing Roman and Visigothic traces. Equally deserving of a visit, Santa María la Granada is a curious 10th-century Mozarabic church, once converted into a mosque and subsequently enhanced by Gothic and mudéjar adjuncts.

Huelva was founded by the Phoenicians; the bulk of its humming industry comes from the exportation of copper ore and from canneries. But a visit to the old monastery at La Rabia, at the confluence of the Odiel and the Tinto, will repay the more historically minded. In 1484, Christopher Columbus, down on his luck and practically at the end of his rope, found refuge and assistance here. The monks who had taken him in grew to realize the significance of his scientific investigations, and interceded on his behalf with the king and queen. Those heroic times have left vivid traces in the church, the room in which Columbus conferred with the monks, the cloister and the patio. The return to the main roads leads through Palos and extensive vineyards to Moguer with its splendid 14th-century Santa Clara monastery.

Beyond Huelva N431 continues forty-eight kilometers to Ayamonte, a small fishing hamlet next door to Portugal. The way to the frontier is paved with endless, shining beaches, including La Antilla and Isla Cristina.

En Route to Córdoba

The Guadalquivir, which the Arabs called the Great River, was once navigable as far as Córdoba. Galleys moored at the splendid ports along the river banks. Today, you can see the imposing ruins at Itálica, founded by Scipio, and the birthplace of three emperors, Hadrian among them. Vestiges of castles, sanctuaries and thermal baths remain at Arva. But the most moving Roman ruin is the necropolis at Carmona, with 900 family tombs chiseled out of the rock. Its walls are decorated with leaves and birds, and pierced with niches for urns. An adjoining small museum with archeological finds, completes the picture.

Carmona itself is a small and typically Moorish town that has managed to preserve its naturalness. As you wander through its narrow, twisting streets, bordered by unpretentious little houses punctuated here and there by an occasional palace, with the bright sunlight playing in and out among the intricacies of wrought-iron balconies, suddenly you come upon the extraordinary San Pedro church, begun in 1466; its interior is an unbroken mass of sculptures and gilded surfaces. Nearby stands the Gothic church of Santa María, designed by the architect of Seville's cathedral, and embellished by primitive paintings, a triptych, and a calvary cross. For a great view out over the town, climb up to the Alcázar, the once proud Moorish citadel with its scattered ruins.

Not so long ago, there was nothing but an expanse of wasteland as far as you could see along this route. Vast agricultural projects, however, have already changed the desolate aspect of the plain that was fertile enough when the Romans and Arabs cultivated it with dogged labor. One of Spain's most urgent problems, the rehabilitation of this sterile ground, has been tackled energetically.

Ecija, a dazzling white cluster, passed successively through Greek, Roman, Visigothic and Moorish hands. You will find plenty of Renaissance and baroque palaces to see here. Gothic art is also represented in the Santa María and Santiago churches. At Santa Cruz, dominated by its high-standing Moorish tower, there is a Greco-Byzantine icon, presented in the 6th century by St. Gregory the Great to the local bishop, while several china monuments and fountains add a far-eastern flavor to the reputedly hottest town in Europe.

Córdoba

If you visit the ancient city of the caliphs in midsummer, you will find it blanched, torrid and still, under an unrelenting sun. You may seek a breath of fresh air on the river banks, but you won't find it. So try to visit Córdoba earlier or later; but if you have no choice, it is still a worthwhile trip to see the old Arab mills and the arches of a Roman bridge, which testify together to the city's rich history.

Originally, Córdoba was only an olive oil center, but a strange destiny was in store for this curve of the Guadalquivir. Its lush fields saw the ferocious encounter of Caesar and his rival Pompey the Younger, in which 22,000 soldiers perished. Later, under Arab domination, there were intrigues and struggles among the emirs, often settled by means of poison, dagger or silken strangler's cord. Retaken by Saint King Ferdinand, the city suffered additional misfortunes as a Christian frontier town. Again, during the Napoleonic invasion, the name of Córdoba had tragic implications.

There is, of course, a modern Córdoba, arising from the activity of the Sierra copper mines and electric equipment factories. Just go down to the Plaza de José Antonio, with its bustling cafés and alfresco restaurants.

But the great drawing card of Córdoba is the 8th-century mosque (Mezquita). Despite continuing restoration, the outside still presents a dilapidated aspect. Grass grows between its paving stones, the mosaics are chipped, the walls cracked by a scorching sun. It began as a Roman temple erected in honor of Janus and is now dedicated to the Virgin. Abdu'r Rahman intended it to surpass all other Arab mosques in grandeur.

Crossing the threshold, you are immediately confronted with evidence of the magnificent Moorish civilization. Some 850 columns rise in a forest of onyx, jasper, marble and granite, reflecting all the colors of the rainbow in oblique rays of light. The ceiling is of carved and delicately tinted cedar. Topping the pillars are capitals remaining from the Visigoth church that was razed to make a place for the mosque. Many of the bronze and copper lamps that illuminate the building were made from church bells carried from Santiago de Compostela by Christian slaves.

The pilgrims' knees have worn away the stone floor in many places. The *maksoureh,* a kind of anteroom (which now precedes the "new," 11th-century, mihrab), was reserved for the caliphs and their guests. Its central part, with its delicate mosaic and plasterwork, is a masterpiece of oriental art.

The Legacy of the Moors

To the eternal glory of the caliphs, it may be said that they made Córdoba not merely rich and powerful, but one of the greatest centers of art and philosophy of their epoch. In this city, where Seneca studied, there developed a stream of illustrious thinkers, among them Averroes, the great Arabian scholar, and the Jewish philosopher, Maimonides. One emir was as proud of his mastery of algebra as he was of the beauty of his favorites. Dazzling and erudite, this was the Córdoba that brought marble from Tarragona and Carthage for its mosque, and perfumed wood from Lebanon for its chamber of odalisques. This was the Córdoba whose citizens refused to disturb a stone of their wonderful mosque after Saint Ferdinand had driven out the Moors, but blessed the building and consecrated it to the Virgin. Alas, three centuries later, a clergy more zealous than esthetic decided to erect a church in the midst of the Moorish columns. The citizens fought bitterly against this outrage, and even threatened the lives of workers who undertook the demolition. But Charles V had given his consent to the construction, and so, at great expense, the *crucero* was built. It is a splendid baroque affair, and would be stunning were it not a heavy, awkward mass in this airy forest of columns.

The mosque is best seen during a summer sunset, when its tawny walls are gilded by the dying rays of light. In her niche on the nearby street of Cardenal Herrero, the Virgin of Lanterns stands demurely behind a lantern-hung grille, rather like a lovely lady awaiting a serenade.

But you can sense most deeply the city's somnolent pace on the Plaza de los Dolores (the Square of Sufferings), surrounded by the Convento de Capuchinos. Eight lanterns hanging from twisted wrought-iron brackets shed their light on a calvary scene. It is a secret spot where convent walls and flowers gleam in the dusk.

Your imagination is staggered by the varied styles along Córdoba's meandering byways, where a hint of Moorish languor still lingers. The Roman bridge near the mosque was rebuilt by the Moors. The ruins down by the water's edge are old Arab mills; on the far shore, the old fort of La Calahorra is also Arab. San Pablo church is the most intact and precious treasure of the 13th century, while the 15th century is exemplified by the residence of the Cavaliers of Santiago on Valdelas-granas Square, replete with mudéjar charm. Look for the Calle del Buen Pastor, where you find the two patios and the coffered ceiling of the convent of Jesús Crucificado, the quintessence of 16th-century mudéjar art. Nor can you ignore the baroque church of San Hipólito on the Paseo del Gran Capitán, although its style doesn't really do much to enhance it.

Shades of Don Quixote haunt the Plaza del Potro, where the inn is reputed to have extended hospitality to Cervantes' hero. Here, too, is the Fine Arts Museum, housed in a former Charity Hospital founded by the Catholic kings, and the delightful museum of Julio Romero de Torres, the Córdoban artist who died in 1930.

You will also find in Córdoba one of Spain's most famed synagogues: this one together with those of Toledo are the only surviving synagogues in the country. Standing in the heart of the old Judería, or Jewish quarter, it proudly bears its resplendent stucco ornamentation and its 14th-century Hebrew inscriptions.

Las Ermitas and Medina Azahara

There is a nice, typically Spanish contrast in two wholly dissimilar sidetrips that you can make in the surrounding area. One is to Las Ermitas, a few kilometers to the northwest on the Sierra slopes, where several hermits continue to perpetuate the early traditions of the original church, identical to those observed by the members of the faithful who established themselves here in the 4th century! Today, their membership is scattered, but they bide their time, saying prayers and tilling the soil, like the true peasant-monks that they are.

The second sidetrip, in a completely opposite mood, takes you to the site where once stood a splendid oriental monument built for a beloved woman: about eleven kilometers west of Córdoba are the ruins of Medina Azahara, a palace erected by a 10th-century caliph for his favorite. The Hall of the Ambassadors has been rebuilt and in a small museum, a few relics of the vanished marble have been collected. According to the storytellers of the time, there were no fewer than

4,300 columns of gleaming white, green and pink marble supporting an inlaid wood ceiling.

The Road to Granada

The quickest route from Córdoba to Granada, N432 allows for a sidetrip from Alcalá la Real to Montefrío with its Gothic-Renaissance church and castle built into the Moorish fortress, the early 18th-century pure plateresque San Antonio and the late 18th-century neoclassical circular church of the Encarnación. Five kilometers away, at Peñas de los Gitanos, is one of the rare remains of the late paleolithic Iberian period, the settlement of Hipo-Nova.

N331 via Antequera links up with the Seville-Granada road, whilst the longest but most rewarding way is through Andújar, Bailén and Jaén. Turn off at Andújar up a beautiful winding road for thirty-two kilometers, to the fantastic mountain-top shrine of Nuestra Señora de la Cabeza. The church is set above the stark ridges of the Sierra Morena, wildly remote, in forests famous for wild board shooting, so completely out of the 20th century as to be mildly alarming. During the Spanish Civil War, the Falangists and members of the Guardia Civil settled in for a last stand in this sanctuary, which they thought would be relatively easy to defend. Completely shut off, the garrison withstood an eight months' siege, towards the end of which the provisions parachuted in by the Nationalist forces failed to cope with the increasing problem of famine. It was finally forced to surrender to the Republicans, who set the sanctuary on fire. (The present shrine is a reconstruction.)

Bailén is the road junction at which one turns south to Jaén and Granada. Napoleon's troops were defeated here in 1808, on July 16, while on another July 16—in the year 1212—the decisive Battle of the Reconquest was fought on the plain of Las Navas de Tolosa, to the north of Bailén. A crusade instigated by Pope Innocent II brought together troops from Castile, Aragón and Navarre fighting side by side with Germans, Frenchmen and Italians. The Moslem forces, commanded by Emir Mohammed Abou Abd Allah, stood ready for the fray. When the clash between cross and crescent got under way, the outcome seemed dubious for some time, until the Moors abandoned the fight and this part of Andalusia was restored to Christendom.

If you entered Andalusia on the N322, you passed through the silvery sea of vast olive groves which stretches from the superbly rugged outlines of the Sierra de Alcaraz and the Sierra de Segura to Ubeda and Baeza. If not, continue east of Bailén to Ubeda to rejoin the Granada road at Jaén, a sidetrip of some ninety-seven kilometers (60 miles), but actually only fifty-one kilometers more than the direct route.

Ubeda is worth the detour. Its winding streets spill out abruptly into the resplendent Santa María Square with the superb El Salvador church. The parador, a former palace with period-style furnishings, is the ideal place to stay for absorbing the feeling of the town. The cloister of Santa María, the Convent of La Trinidad and the Casa de las Cadenas (House of the Chains . . . it was once a prison) are all very interesting, and at every turn you encounter stately residences and churches basking in the subtle interplay of superb sunlight effects. St. John of the Cross died here, at the end of the 16th century. Ubeda is no mere resurrection of the past: it *is* the past, continuing to live on in rare serenity, the likes of which are not to be found in many places.

From Ubeda you will come to Baeza, once the seat of a small university and still a treasure house of early Renaissance and plateresque architecture. Be sure to see the fabulous Benavente Palace which shelters a seminary behind its Gothic facade and curious gallery.

Jaén, unlike most Andalusian cities, has more dignity than charm. Just as its austere pines and chestnut trees replace the palm and olive groves of the south, so are its citizens more taciturn than their neighbors. The people of Jaén tell the story of two brothers unjustly condemned to death by King Ferdinand IV. Before the victims were hurled to death from the sinister precipice of Peña de los Carvajales, they called upon heaven to avenge them. Their properly vindictive Spanish God almost immediately summoned the king to his own Last Judgement. The road winding down to Granada through increasingly green country provides a promising introduction to the serene languor of the Granada plateau.

Granada

When Boabdil, the last Moorish king of Granada, surrendered the city to Ferdinand and Isabella, he left his palace by the Puerta de Los Siete Suelos (Gate of the Seven Sighs) and asked that this gate be sealed forever. His heart-broken sobs found a lasting echo in Arab hearts, for of all Spain, the Moors deplored most the loss of Granada, and mourn it still in their evening prayers. Of all their treasured cities Granada was their chief delight.

As their standard was raised on the tower of the Alhambra, the Catholic Monarchs knelt among their soldiers and monks to thank God for victory. That January day in 1492 was for them a day of pure, transcendent joy. They wished to be buried in Granada, and built the flamboyant Gothic Royal Chapel where they have lain side by side since 1521, later joined by their daughter Juana la Loca. Though the

Catholic Monarchs are remembered throughout the sanctuary—their statues on bas reliefs and pillars, their escutcheons on walls, their banners among vaults, and their crown and scepter in the sacristy— their grandson, Charles V, decided it was too small a chapel for so much glory. He commissioned Diego de Siloé to design a huge cathedral which was not finished until 1667. But even this Renaissance masterpiece, in spite of stained-glass windows, paintings by El Greco and Ribera, carvings by Alonso Cano, and an admirable portal in the Great Chapel, like all the rest of Granada's monuments, is overshadowed by the glorious silhouette of the Alhambra. It dominates the entire city, Moorish and Christian alike; from the Madraza, opened by Yusuf I as a university in the 14th century, the adjoining Alcaicería, once the silk exchange and now a market for local handicrafts, the Gothic splendor of Santo Domingo, the Renaissance of San Jerónimo, where the Gran Capitán Gonzalo de Córdoba is buried, San Juan de Diós, still used as a hospital, while the restored Hospital Real is now part of the University, the 17th-century University building itself, to the Cartuja monastery whose baroque sacristy has been called the Christian Alhambra because of its delicate stucco work.

The Alhambra, Seat of Caliphs and Kings

Signs indicate the narrow street that mounts a stiff grade to the cool vale where Wellington had elm trees planted to add a bit of English greenery to the Andalusian scene. Soon you reach the first door of the first wall, and cross the threshold straight into the Arabian Nights.

Luckily the entrance tickets provide a plan with the itinerary, otherwise it would be difficult to know where to begin. You find your eyes roving from lacy walls, painted ceilings, and scintillating domes to multicolored tiles and gold mosaics. Sometimes a breath of air strays in from a garden or the dripping of a fountain carries a touch of welcome coolness. You are in a realm of little columns, festooned arches and mysterious inscriptions. The Pool of Myrtles leaves a clear picture of turquoise green among black bushes.

Each of the towers of the Alhambra has its secret, each stone the trace of a name or a drop of blood. It was this fascinating riddle that held Washington Irving so long in Granada, attempting to capture every secret nuance. An Arab proverb says that God gives to those he loves a means of living in Granada.

The Alhambra's delights are not grasped in one visit, they increase with closer acquaintance. The most antique vestige in the Alhambra is the 9th-century Moorish fortress of the Alcazaba. The great hulk of its watchtower still stands out impressively. The very first Cross of the Reconquest was proudly erected on its terrace, from which you can

enjoy a sweeping panorama of the city. The two towers overlooking the
Square of the Cisterns date from more recent times. The sorting of these
souvenirs is simple: first come the defense structures, the outer walls
with their huge square towers and fortified doors. Next, around the
Court of Myrtles, the official residence. This contains the Hall of Bene-
diction, under a cedar cupola. The walls are covered with the inscription "Allah alone is Conqueror". Next is the Ambassadors' Hall, the
scene of many lavish receptions given by the Moorish kings under its
polychrome cedarwood cupola. Then comes the Council Room, or
Mexuar, which Charles V used as a chapel.

Finally, radiating from the Lions' Court, the private apartments: the
Sala de las Dos Hermanas, which was the harem, decorated with two
marble slabs so alike that they have given the room its name, the Hall
of the Two Sisters; the Room of Secrets, with its whispering alcoves;
the marble baths, perforated like incense burners for escaping steam
and perfumes; and the Sala de los Abencerrajes, where a sultan, jealous
either of his throne or of his favorite, had 36 princes beheaded and
watched their blood flow into the Fountain of Lions.

The Hand and the Key

The history of the Alhambra is woven through seven centuries. It
begins with the Arab epoch, full of intrigues of the seraglio, the pomp,
conspiracy and voluptuousness of the court. Its leading figures are
poets, emirs, assassins, alchemists, eunuchs and spies. On the first door
of the ramparts, called the Puerta de la Justicia, the Arabs wisely
carved the hand of Fatima, whose five fingers evoke the five laws of the
Koran. On the second door, a key was engraved. And the legend was
that the Alhambra would remain inviolable until the day when the
hand of the first door took the key that opened the second. The prophe-
cy was fulfilled. Dissolute and cruel, the kings of Granada were so
engrossed in their quarrels and viciousness that they forgot the great
rules imposed by Allah. Through destructive internal warfare, they
themselves opened the door to the invader.

The Catholic Monarchs were at once enraptured and scandalized by
the subtle splendors of the Moorish palace, built in the most fragile of
materials—clay. They attempted to live there, but Christian habits did
not conform easily to the exotic setting. Charles V upset the order of
the gardens and chambers by superimposing a huge, square Renaissance palace on the Cerro del Sol. Though less incongruous than his
church within the mosque of Córdoba, the palace was never finished
and the Alhambra was abandoned for centuries. Water grew stale in
the pools, the fragile stucco garlands crumbled, and the ancient royal
palace became a refuge for every stray dog, beggar, gypsy and tramp,

who made themselves comfortable among the mosaics and marbles. When Wellington entered Spain on his Napoleonic hunt, he was delighted with Granada, sent all the indigents flying, and himself appropriated the apartments of Charles V. Washington Irving, Alexandre Dumas and other romantic 19th-century writers constructed a world of moonlight and ghosts among the ruins. A world largely irrelevant to the truth of the past. Today, the Alhambra has been expertly restored to a convincing semblance of past glory among its terraces and gardens; the circular court of Charles' palace provides a magnificent setting for the Annual Festival of Music and Dance, part of the *Festivales de España,* held in late June, while the upper floor houses the Fine Arts Museum.

The Generalife

The Alhambra, as its Arabic name indicates, is ocher-red. The Generalife (*Gennat-al-Arif,* "Garden of the Builder") is white. Standing on the hill nearest their palace, it was the summer residence of the caliphs. Every detail was conceived with an eye to cool, relaxed repose. Its perfect proportions rely on understatement and intimacy—a design for sweet privacy. The battlements are not all decorated, serving merely as white frames for the landscape spread below them. The deep blue sky and a land studded with delightful bouquets of gardens stretch away into the distance. The gardens of the Generalife, fragrant with roses and jasmine, are hedged in by yew trees. Open to the sky, the great reception hall is animated by a constant shower of crystal drops from slender fountains that play above a mirror of sparkling water and water even flows down the handrails of the upper garden's staircase. The open-air theater is backed by stately cypresses.

At dusk the ravine of the Darro is already bathed in shadows; you can hear the shallow torrent roar under tiny bridges, but the streets of the Alcaicería are still hot. Narrow streets part dilapidated, part hiding beautiful cármenes (Granada's private villas with fragrant gardens) wind up the slopes of Albaicín, which retains its original Moorish atmosphere, though the numerous mosques have long been converted into baroque churches. The plaza in front of the church of San Nicolás affords the loveliest view of the sunset on the Alhambra's ocher walls and on the snowcapped peaks of the Sierra Nevada. This is a sight that never ceases to astonish the visitor—the golden Andalusian sun caressing those incredible white summits.

The Gypsies

Suddenly the night is a profound blue, and one by one, the lamps on Sacromonte begin to twinkle. The hour has come for a stroll among the gypsy caves.

Granada's symbol is an open pomegranate, because the city opens on a triple hill with all the beauty of this exotic fruit, which the caliphs imported from the Orient. But the name Granada derives from the word *garnathah,* mountain cave, for the Sacromonte is riddled with caverns. They might have sheltered early Christians, for when searchers were looking there for the emirs' buried treasures they found, instead, a vast collection of bones. Some of these they assumed belonged to San Cecilio, the city's patron saint, and so the hill was sanctified and a monastery built on its summit.

You begin the ascent of the Sacromonte near the picturesque and mildly dangerous gypsy quarter. The *cuevas* (or caves) that penetrate the chalky cliff are like the grottos of Arab legends, spread with thick, richly colored rugs and gleaming with copper utensils. The women never vary their traditional dance dress, a tight gown split to the waist, with a long flounced train. They wear their black hair plastered to their heads; all have long, sultry eyes, olive-colored skin, and fire in their blood. Each family is a tribe in itself, and the minute you venture into the Sacromonte, filthy, handsome children drag you off to the family lair, whether you like it or not. You will sit through a performance given by mama, sisters, aunts and cousins, all intent on playing guitars and dancing—sometimes not too well. It may be costly, for the children are extremely tenacious, and you must cross their grimy paws with a good bit of silver in order to gain your freedom. Meanwhile, the interior of the cave is worth studying. You will see grandfather's photograph hanging on the wall beside the Virgin Mary and an assortment of banderillas retrieved from bullfights. But don't be so carried away by the scene that you forget your purse. Many of these gypsies are thieves and scarcely bother to hide the fact. So never carry more money to the Sacromonte than you can well lose, avoid the too-private party, and go, preferably, with a Spaniard you can trust to show you about the place. Your visit will be more interesting, and will be less likely to end badly.

To admire gypsy art and crafts at leisure, and souvenirs of Empress Eugénie, wife of Napoleon III, visit the museum in the noble old Casa de los Tiros, which also accommodates the Tourist Bureau.

From Seville to Granada

The 258 kilometers (about 170 miles) of N334 and N342 take you from Seville's sweltering plains to Granada's more temperate hills at the foot of the Sierra Nevada, by the shortest route.

Like so many of its sister cities in Spain, Osuna is rich in both Moorish and Roman history, particularly the latter. However, the city bears the distinctive stamp of the 16th century, as exemplified by its collegiate church on the hilltop. There you will find an exquisite two-story patio, plus the tombs of the Dukes of Osuna, descendants of the Borgia Pope Alexander VI, set in a crypt constituting a remarkable Renaissance pantheon.

Several roads meet outside and bypass Antequera, but it is well worth the small detour if you remember what particular stage this town represented in the Reconquest. Following the great Christian victories over the Moors in the 13th century, the latter maintained themselves for another 200 years in Granada. The spirit of Reconquest entered into a state of hibernation. One of its chief awakenings occurred in 1410 with the capture of Antequera from the Arabs, who left a mighty fortress on the town heights.

Near Antequera are the Menga Galleries, a prehistoric site where huge dolmens form arches. The mystery of their origin is as unfathomable as that of all other similar monuments of the dim past. The famous Swiss architect, Le Corbusier, inscribed the visitors' book: "To my predecessors."

N342 continues through picturesque countryside with many rocks and canyons. The Genil river divides Loja's narrow, winding lanes of white houses dominated by a 9th-century Moorish fortress, 16th-century San Gabriel has exquisite mudéjar ceilings attributed to Diego de Siloé; Santa María, the Santa Clara monastery and the Hospital de la Misericordia are also interesting. The Genil flows through a wild gorge where waterfalls hurtle down between the rocks.

Descending onto Granada's richly irrigated plain, the road passes Santa Fé, founded in 1491 during the siege of Granada as a campsite for the Christian troops. Here the last bastion of the Moslem world was surrendered to Ferdinand and Isabella, and here the Catholic Monarchs granted Columbus the ships to discover the New World.

Roads from Granada

Most of eastern N342—linking at Puerta Lumbreras with N340 to the Costa Blanca, Murcia and the terminus of the motorway at Alicante—lies within the borders of Andalusia. The only town of note, Guadix, nestles under an imposing Renaissance cathedral.

Before bursting into indignant denunciation of the cave dwellings at Purullena, go and look inside one or two. They are warm in winter, cool in summer, have electricity, and are rent-free. Perhaps they are not so healthy or romantic as a caravan—but they are a great deal more comfortable. Recently there has been a boom in this troglodyte real estate. Many of the cave homes, which only a few years ago cost as little as 25,000 pesetas, are now selling at over half a million pesetas. There is even a troglodyte disco for the young of Purullena; once a country inn serving food and drink to the mule trains on their way to Granada, this cave is now equipped with the latest disco equipment and film projectors and can hold up to five hundred people.

The road runs through wild mountain scenery, with crumbling fortresses set upon vast ocher-colored crags, to the provincial border at Las Vertientes.

An attractive choice of roads leads south from Granada to the Costa del Sol. N321 branches after Loja to Málaga; C340 passes the 4th-century Roman hypogeum and a Moorish tower at Gabia la Grande just outside Granada, as well as the Moorish baths of Alhama, a spa for rheumatic diseases, beautifully situated between the Tejeda and Zafarraya ranges above a large artificial lake, before hitting the coast at Vélez-Málaga. In the west, you might branch off N342 at Guadix, to Almería on N324 between the rugged ranges of the Sierra de Baza and the Sierra Nevada. To tackle the latter by plunging into the magnificent mountain scenery, descending to the coast via Ugíjar and Berja in the Alpujarra range, is too adventurous for the average motorist. By far the shortest (72 kilometers) and hardly less scenic route is on N323 from Granada to Motril, through the western foothills of the Sierra Nevada which, however, more than justifies a special visit.

The Sierra is one of the prime beauties of Granada. This mountain range rises behind the city like the background of a mural, cleaving the blue depths of the sky with its snowy heights. Fifty-five kilometers (34 miles) of one of Europe's most magnificent mountain roads lead to lakes, meadows, wild torrents, and to the snow-capped Mulhacén (3,500 meters, 11,477 feet), Spain's highest peak, while the road itself reaches an altitude of 3,050 meters (10,000 feet) at Pico de Veleta, in the heart of the mountains. Ski-lifts and cablecars facilitate skiing from a choice of hotels and refuges the year round.

The Costa del Sol—Motril to Almería

When you reach sea level at Motril, you are in the center of the sugarcane country. Motril was another of the Moorish strongholds, and possesses a fine, early 16th-century collegiate church.

Situated halfway between Málaga and Almería east and west respectively, Motril has developed into a leading beach resort of the Costa del Sol, which stretches from Cape Gata to Tarifa.

The road to Almería passes the rapidly developing resorts of Torrenueva, Castel de Ferro, Adra on an elevation between two beaches, bypasses Roquetas and rejoins the coast at Aguadulce.

Almería is the capital of the grape industry. As late as November you will see the peasant women delicately packing the huge green clusters destined for the Christmas tables of Paris, London or Stockholm. Almería is dominated by the imposing Alcazaba fortress built by the Caliph Abdu'r Rahman, entered by the Gothic gate of the Reyes Católicos and provided with a bell tower by Carlos III. The fortifications, in whose garden a musical festival is held in the second half of August, command a sweeping view over the port and city, whose core still consists of distinctly oriental flat-roofed houses in a maze of narrow, winding alleys, though now framed by modern blocks of flats.

Buttressed towers give the 16th-century Gothic cathedral the look of a castle, despite the Renaissance façade. Other landmarks are the 18th-century Renaissance churches of Santo Domingo and Santiago. One small mosque has survived by being consecrated as San Pedro.

Motril to Málaga

If you turn westward at Motril toward Málaga, along the recently widened but still cluttered coastal road, you'll see some delightful scenery—giant cliffs, tropical sugarcane plantations, and date palm trees outlined against the sea.

Twenty-one kilometers' ride from Motril brings you past wonderful seascapes, to Almuñecar, a fishing village since Phoenician times, 3,000 years ago. Here, too, is a ruined Moorish castle, where once the kings of Granada kept their treasure.

Thirty-four kilometers beyond that is the little town of Nerja, with a fantastic lookout place, known as the Balcony of Europe, set high above the sea, and a huge stalactite cave discovered in 1959 by a shepherd boy looking for his ball, which has been converted into an auditorium for concerts, ballet performances and similar entertainments. The cave, a kind of underground cathedral, contains the world's longest known stalactite (200 feet). Once past the Torrox lighthouse, you see on your right the village of Torrox, a terraced town overlooking its vineyards—it is only half an hour now to the end of this lap of your journey. The nearby beaches of El Morche, El Faro, Peñoncillo and Caceite together make up about eight kilometers of sand.

Málaga

Málaga is a fast expanding city, attractive in its center and eastern approaches, yet hideous in the urban sprawl of its western outskirts where the huge high-rises marching determinedly towards Torremolinos now encroach on its traditional sugar cane fields. Málaga's wine, fruit and sugar commerce rivals that of the Levantine and Catalan coasts. The city is lively, prosperous and busy, with attractive villas among exotic foliage. You can dine in the old fortress of Gibralfaro or at one of the fishermen's restaurants on the beach, where Malagueña soup is served along with grilled red mullet.

This thriving city, protected by mountains from the inclemencies of the north, is, with San Sebastián, Palma de Mallorca and Alicante, one of the great seaside capitals of Spain, though most tourists head for Torremolinos and Marbella further down the coast rather than the city itself. Statistics show that its winter climate is equaled in hours of sunshine by only one other European town—in southern Sicily.

Málaga cathedral was begun in the 16th century, but it has never been finished, and lacks a second tower to balance the single existing 68-meter-high (224-foot) one, with its fifteen bells. Almost miraculously the lovely wood carvings of the enclosed central choir, the work of the 17th-century artist, Pedro de Mena, survived the Civil War unharmed. The wood is occasionally carved wafer-thin to express the fold of a robe or the shape of a finger, and must surely be among the greatest masterpieces of its kind. Besides the choir stalls, there are canvases by Alonso Cano, who was also the architect of the cathedral, by Morales, Van Dyck and Andrea del Sarto.

If you have shopping to do, the best shops are in Calle Larios, not far from the Renaissance cathedral. Or you can walk through the park (or more exactly, the parks, for they are divided into a series of gardens of different types) to the old Moorish Alcazaba, with its own lovely flower gardens set among the grim 11th-century walls of the fortress which now houses the Archaeological Museum. Over three thousand years of history are perpetuated in the walls of this fortress. From the heights on which the Gibralfaro Castle stands, you can look down over Málaga and the port.

West from Málaga

Leaving Málaga and traveling westward along the coastal road, past fields of sugarcane, we come to Torremolinos (the main highway now bypasses it, so turn off at the indicated place), not all that long ago merely a small village, with the asset of an eight-kilometer-long beach. Overdeveloped and a prey to the packaged tour operators, Torremolinos is also the leading foreign colony in Spain. Swarms of English, French and American residents, as well as the hordes of tourists, crowd its streets in season. Shops and restaurants, nightclubs and bars, at every price from luxury to budget, make this one of the most incredible examples of 20th-century tourism run riot.

Benalmádena and Fuengirola are somewhat simpler; each has several kilometers of rather grubby sandy beach. An interesting detour of only a few kilometers is to drive inland from either Torremolinos or Fuengirola to the hillside village of Mijas. This picturesque mountain village with its narrow streets of whitewashed houses affords breathtaking views over the Mediterranean. The town has become something of an artists' colony, retirement haven and tourist paradise; it offers splendid souvenir shopping for, in particular, leather, woven rugs, Lladró and ceramics.

Marbella has grand hotels, scattered over no less than four beaches. Its cafés and shops reflect a much more up-market tourism than elsewhere on the coast. All around are luxurious residential estates in well-selected beauty spots, comprising hotels, bungalows, golf-courses and other vast sporting facilities. The recently constructed marina at Puerto Banus, just west of Marbella, is a sight in itself. The picturesque waterfront, huge vulgar yachts, array of beautiful people and swinging scene that goes on late into the night in its 100 or so restaurants, rivals even St. Tropez in trendy glamor.

A road climbs from Marbella to the *refugio* at Ojén among the peaks of the Sierra Blanca. Another branch, C339, affording some splendid views and safe driving, winds from San Pedro de Alcántara up through wild, eagle-haunted scenery to Ronda. Yet the most spectacular if longer approach to that fascinating town is from further south, shortly after San Roque, C341 up the Guadarranque valley past the church of Nuestra Señora de los Angeles till you enjoy near Gaucín a truly breathtaking view over a large section of the coast to the mighty rock of Gibraltar and distant Africa.

Continuing west along the coast, which is now swinging southward, we pass through Estepona, once a charming little port and now just about the last of the development sprawl westward. It has an immense, fine sand beach and a seafront promenade over a kilometer long. The four-lane highway ends when the road turns inland to San Roque. This little town was built within sight of Gibraltar by the Spaniards, who chose to evacuate the fortress when it was captured by the British in 1704. From here it is thirteen kilometers, along an avenue of eucalyptus, to the port of Algeciras, but only eight kilometers to La Linea and Gibraltar. (At presstime there was still no access from Spain to Gibraltar. Visitors wishing to visit Gibraltar from Spain have to take the ferry or hydrofoil to Tangiers in Morocco and travel back to Gibraltar.)

Algeciras and Cádiz

Algeciras is the southern rail terminus, and the port from which three ferries sail daily in just over two hours across to Tangier in North Africa, even more frequently to Ceuta, with smaller Melilla Spain's last foothold in North Africa. Though endowed with a 15th-century cathedral and fortress, Ceuta's 170,000 inhabitants and the crowds of visitors, mostly daytrippers, are only interested in the town's free port status, which makes it a shoppers' paradise a mere hour's sailing from Algeciras. The customs inspection there is very thorough, not for tax-free purchases of tourists, but for Moroccan hashish. The crossing is shorter than that through Tangier (only an hour) and is, of course, less expensive. A crack, ultra-modern boat train connects with Madrid, an overnight run, and, in season, there is also car-ferry train service from Madrid. Across the bay towers Gibraltar.

Through hills dotted with motel colonies and camping sites, we reach Tarifa, Spain's southernmost point, and may, on a clear day, see, across the narrow Straits of Gibraltar, the coast of Africa, with the foothills of the Rif low on the horizon. Tarifa, a charming white town, is well worth a short stop, just to stroll through the spotless streets, flowered gardens, and explore the Alcázar. Though the castle is now a military base, it can be visited at specified hours.

The Costa de la Luz

After Tarifa, the sea is no longer the warm, gentle Mediterranean, but the Atlantic, and we lose sight of it for a while, for N340 runs through vast wheat fields. Along that coastline which we cannot see is Cape Trafalgar, where Nelson found victory and death in 1805. At certain times of the year, the tuna swarm along the coastal waters here. They are fished for with nets; the small boats close in with their nets, tightening the circle while the men lash out at the fish. The tuna are massacred in a furious mêlée; their blood dyes the ocean purple.

The road next passes the foot of the steep hill upon the crown of which clusters the romantic-looking town of Vejer (well worth the three-kilometer detour), and after passing the white village of Chiclana and several branches to bathing beaches reaches San Fernando, the huge industrial zone that surrounds and pollutes the entire inlet.

Cádiz

The historic port of Cádiz is built upon a long narrow peninsula; it claims to be the oldest continuously inhabited settlement in western Europe. Drake bombarded the city in 1587, and the Duke of Essex sacked it in 1596, probably in revenge for its contribution to the "Invincible Armada" that was to have conquered England; little of the ancient town survives, therefore. The historic castle of Medina Sidonia, the Armada's commander, is not far inland.

Once you cross the narrow isthmus into the city, you immediately see why Cádiz is called "the cup of silver," for the atmosphere sparkles with a radiant sort of dust, brilliant as mica. The city is African in appearance, with palm trees, white houses, cupolas, and street stalls piled with oranges. But its most striking features are the churches in their green gardens and the silvery harbor.

This admirable, landlocked haven has made Cádiz a typical, busy, brawling southern port. The picturesque rabbit warren of its narrow back streets and delightful squares is noisy each night with singing and hands clapping out the unmistakable beat of flamenco.

The city possesses a small but worthwhile art collection (works by Zurbarán and Ribera) in its Museo de Pinturas, Plaza de Mina 5. The small oratory of Santa Cueva contains several lesser-known works by Goya, and in Santa Catalina Chapel, sadly no longer open to visitors, there is a deeply moving tribute to Murillo's memory; with various others of his works, here hangs Murillo's last painting, entitled *The Mystic Marriage of St. Catherine.* While working on it, the artist fell from his scaffolding and died of his injuries, in 1682. Also of interest is the church of San Felipe Neri, where the Cortes of Cádiz were held and where the 1812 Constitution was proclaimed.

The composer Manuel de Falla, one of Cádiz's native sons, lies buried in the crypt of the neo-classical cathedral.

From Cádiz, we turn north again, on the last segment of our Andalusian circle, north to Jerez and Seville, our starting point. The toll-road crosses the bay on a bridge to Puerto Real and bypasses the points of interest. So back to N-IV, down the isthmus through San Fernando with its formidable grille windows, past the attractive little town of Puerto de Santa María, from which sherry used to be shipped before the railway linked Jerez with Cádiz, and past the gleaming salt marshes of the flat river delta of the Guadalquivir.

We encounter now a chalky desert region, where the Moors and the Visigoths fought the famous battle of Guadalete in 711, settling the rulership of all but the remote northern provinces of Spain for the next 500 years. This land and the river are as charged with history as the Guadalquivir was charged with the blood of men who fought on its banks to defend the peninsula from Islam. There is little to break the monotony of brambles and scrub grass—only an occasional isolated castle or a flight of wheeling eagles. And then we reach the orderly vineyards that announce Jerez de la Frontera.

Jerez de la Frontera

The home of sherry is surrounded by immense vineyards. Their grapes have funded a host of beautiful churches and palaces. Jerez is justly proud of its famous heady wine, flamenco dancers and *cante jondo* singers, improvisers who give vent to restrained, tragic passion in subtle modulations.

A visit to the bodegas of González Byass is an exciting experience even if you do not care for sherry, for there you will see casks signed by visiting notables—royalty, writers, bullfighters, musicians—and perhaps taste a few drops from the 1850 cask. If you do, you will not like it. It is almost like vinegar. But a drop or two in your ordinary 14-year-old wine will make it taste like nectar.

At the Harvest Festival in the second week in September, the grapes are blessed in a colorful pageant in an exquisite setting, the triple staircase and portal of the 17th-century collegiate church whose five naves are crowned by an octagonal cupola flanked by a Moorish tower. Amongst other outstanding religious buildings are the Convent of Santo Domingo, Isabelline San Miguel with its splendid lateral chapels, reredos and plateresque gate, mudéjar San Dionisio and Gothic Santiago. They are all flanked by the Renaissance and baroque palaces of the Marqueses de Montana, de Bertemati, Requelme and de Campo Real.

However, despite these notable buildings the town is sadly run down at present from a tourist's point of view—roads are being carved up throughout the center, there are few hotels for a town of its size, even, though with two notable exceptions, fewer restaurants worthy of mention, and there is no longer even a tourist information office, which perhaps speaks for itself. A general air of depression, even unpleasancy, prevails—drunks (a rare sight in Spain) abound in the bars as do obvious drug addicts; and it is on Jerez's ever increasing drug problem that the numerous purse snatchings and muggings that occur in its streets are largely blamed. Despite this gloomy picture a City Council scheme is underway to restore Jerez's heritage and encourage a new pride in its citizens (their words, not ours). We sincerely hope it will be successful in restoring this once charming town to its rightful image. In the meantime, by all means stop off here to visit the bodegas and even—so long as you watch your purses—for a quick glance around, but we do not recommend a longer stay.

Six kilometers east of Jerez, be sure to see the famous 15th-century Carthusian monastery of La Cartuja. Its elaborate Renaissance façade contrasts dramatically with its austere Gothic interior and vast cloisters. Once a stud farm, its strain of horses is still the pride of the annual Horse Fair and is perpetuated in the famed Spanish Riding School in Vienna.

Twenty-four kilometers west through seemingly endless expanses of the renowned manzanilla vineyards you reach Sanlúcar de Barrameda, at the mouth of the Guadalquivir. In 1498 Columbus sailed from here on his third voyage to the Americas; twenty years later Magellan steered his ships out of the same harbor on the start of his world-circling exploit. The Church of Nuestra Señora de la O, with its splendid panelling, mudéjar gate and 18th-century reredos and which antedates both these intrepid explorers, has now been declared a national monument. The main palaces in the town, all of which are worth seeing, are those of the Orléans-Bourbons and the Condes de Niebla. The Castle of Santiago guards the river mouth.

Fine beaches extend along the town's southern promontory to Chipiona, where the Roman general Scipio the "African" built a beacon tower. Further south past many fine sandy beaches lies Rota, a white village below a medieval castle, and now a U.S. naval base and popular summer resort.

One final trip that is well worth making leads in a different direction. East from Jerez and towards Málaga the road passes through the picturesque mountain town of Ronda.

Roads to Ronda

N342 leads first of all to Arcos de la Frontera, perched dramatically on a wild crag and crowned by a castle above the gorge of the Gaudalete river. Santa María in the Plaza España in the old town is a fascinating blend of architectural styles and here also is the parador and a balcony with splendid views. Further on towards Ronda you will see silhouetted against the sky to your right the virtually impregnable Arab fortress of Zahara de la Sierra, which held out until 1483 against the Christian forces. Zahara is perhaps the most typical and worthwhile of the so-called "White Towns" of this route; another is Grazalema (warning: do not attempt the tortuous winding 531 route over the

Puerto de la Paloma between Zahara and Grazalema, stick to the more conventional approaches).

A final rewarding detour before reaching Ronda, would be to the little known Pileta Caves beyond Benaojón, reached through some magnificent mountain scenery. A guardian from the farm down in the valley will show you round the caves but the system for contacting him is primitive and typically Spanish. Your patience, however, will be well rewarded by the prehistoric wall paintings and the caves' weird stalactite and stalagmite formations.

Ronda was the last stronghold of the legendary Andalusian bandits and scene of the last great rising of the Moors against Ferdinand and Isabella. Its setting is unforgettable, perched above a rocky cleft over ninety meters (300 feet) deep, spanned by three bridges.

Ronda, one of the oldest towns in Spain, has always attracted artists and writers: two famous admirers were Goya and Hemingway. If the Rondians have often sheltered bandits and snapped their fingers at customs officers, it is because they had only one road to guard, and that a narrow mule path. Well protected in the midst of eroded cliffs, it has always been difficult to reach.

Ronda's outstanding feature is the spectacular bridge, the Puente Nuevo (1761), from whose lantern-lit parapet you can have a paralyzingly first-hand view of El Tajo, the gorge dividing the town. Deep down in the chasm are the two other bridges, Puente Viejo and Puente San Miguel, the former on Roman foundations.

The older section of town, called Ciudad, lies south of the gorge. Its Collegiate Church, once a mosque, was later rededicated to the Virgen de la Encarnación and successive restorations added the three late Gothic naves and baroque altar. Look also for the Casa del Rey Moro, an 11th-century residence of the Moorish ruler of the area, and the Casa de Mondragón, home of several early Spanish monarchs. The residence of the Marqués de Salvatierra, also in Ciudad, is occasionally open to visitors. In the new (15th- and 16th-century) part of town, called Mercadillo, are the town hall, the Paseo de la Merced gardens, a spectacular cliffside walk and the 200-year-old bullring, the second oldest in Spain, which has changed little since it was built in 1784. The ring is open to visitors and bullfights are held here just once a year during the September fiesta. Ronda is considered the cradle of modern bullfighting and mementoes of its famous 18th-century son, Pedro Romero, father of the art, loom large all over town.

PRACTICAL INFORMATION FOR ANDALUSIA

 WHAT TO SEE. The highlights of Andalusia are its colorful, lovely old cities. In order of importance, the ones you should try and get to see are: Seville, for its cathedral, the Giralda tower, the Alcázar and its gardens and the Santa Cruz quarter; Granada for, of course, the Alhambra and its cathedral; Córdoba for the mosque; Málaga for the beaches; Cádiz, where Drake singed the King of Spain's beard in 1587; Jerez de la Frontera, the home of sherry; and last, but certainly not least, Algerciras, a rather ugly town, but an important jumping off point for North Africa.

Not far from the cathedral city of Jaén are the once important Renaissance towns of Ubeda and Baeza, which are certainly worth visiting.

Marbella, on the Costa del Sol, is a favorite international playground; Torremolinos attracts the larger crowd. There is a pleasant spa, Marmolejo, in the province of Jaén, quiet and ideal for a rest. Lovers of the antique can seek out the traces the Romans left at Itálica and Carmona, between Seville and Córdoba, or visit the old Spanish mountain town of Ronda; or the prehistoric caves near Antequera and at Nerja, near Málaga. Other beautiful stalactite caves are the Gruta de las Maravillas in Aracena in the north of Huelva province. There is a famous shrine near Andújar. Sportsmen may hunt wild boar not far from there. If you are an *aficionado,* you will be interested to know that Seville has the oldest and most famous 18th-century bull ring in Spain, La Maestranza (Andalusia also has the second oldest, at Ronda), and is the second city for bullfights in Spain, except at fiesta time, when it is the first.

 HOTELS. The most highly developed region of the Costa del Sol is between Málaga and Marbella where concrete blocks shot up with alarming rapidity 10–15 years ago, completely transforming what were once sleepy Andalusian fishing villages. The popularity of this area for package holidays has waned somewhat over the last few years and you should now have no great difficulty in finding accommodations, or in realizing that you are, in fact, in Spain—the fish-and-chip and sauerkraut-and-frankfurter eating fraternity are now on the way out, and though many foreign tourists still visit the coast they have been joined in the last few years by an almost equal number of Spanish holiday makers.

From Marbella to Estepona there has been some interesting resort development in recent years, happily much more in keeping with traditional Andalusian architecture. Accommodations here tend to be more stylish.

Of late there have been quite a few developments around Almería, until recently a more neglected part of the Costa del Sol. Roquetas de Mar, Aguadulce and Dalía are just a few of these "urbanizations". Resorts are also being developed along the Costa de la Luz in Cádiz and Huelva provinces. Hopefully none of these will take on the alarming proportions of the Torremolinos sprawl.

Inland from the coast, the choice of hotels is much the same as elsewhere in non-coastal Spain. The major cities, being of great touristic interest, are all well supplied with both modern and old hotels. The range of *paradores* in Andalusia is excellent, there being no fewer than 16 in the whole region.

HOTELS AND RESTAURANTS

AGUADULCE (Almería). *Satélites Park* (M), tel. (951) 34 06 00. Large, modern hotel with pool, shops and many other facilities.

Restaurant. *Mesón El Abuelo* (M), Calle del Alamo, tel. 34 16 53. Typical tavern.

ALGECIRAS (Cádiz). *Octavio* (E), San Bernardo 1, tel. (956) 65 24 61. 80 rooms, all with airconditioning, television, garage; some suites. *Reina Cristina* (E), Paseo de la Conferencia, tel. (956) 65 00 61. Justly famous hotel with lovely tropical garden and terrace with view of Gibraltar and the mountains of Africa beyond; also with tennis, pool, nightclubs.

Alarde (M), Alfonso XI 4, tel. (956) 66 04 08. 68 rooms, modern and central. *Las Yucas* (M), Agustín Bálsamo 2, tel. (956) 66 32 50. 33 rooms, modern. *Término* (I), Avda. Villanueva 6, tel. (956) 67 14 90. Simple and clean, with views of port.

Restaurants. *Iris* (M), San Bernardo 1. *Manolo* (M), Ruiz Zorrilla 2, good for seafood. *La Rioja* (M), Avda. Virgen del Carmen 19.

ALMERIA. *Gran Hotel Almería* (E), Reina Regente 4, tel. (951) 23 80 11. Good service, comfortable and with many amenities. *La Parra* (E), Ctra. Nacional 340, tel. (951) 34 05 04. Modern hotel in picturesque location, with pool, garden, golf and tennis.

Alborán (M), El Alquián el Toyo, tel. (951) 22 58 00. 103 rooms, with pool, tennis, garden and shops. *Costasol* (M), Almería 58, tel. (951) 23 40 11. 55 rooms, central. *Hairan* (M), Vivar Téllez 80, tel. (951) 24 20 11. 40 rooms. *Indalico* (M), Dolores Sopeña 4, tel. (951) 23 11 11. Comfortable and recommended. *Embajador* (I), Calzada del Castro 4, tel. (954) 25 55 11. 67 rooms, reasonable and convenient to station.

Restaurants. *Club del Mar* (M), Muelle 1, tel. 23 50 48. In Salmerón Park with view of port. *Rincón de Juan Pedro* (M), Plaza del Carmen 6, tel. 21 25 01. Excellent food in pleasant rustic setting. *Sol y Mar* (M), in the port past the Club de Mar, on the road to Málaga. Good food.

Casino (I), is a good budget bet, modern and pleasant with good seafood and paella. *Imperial* (I), Puerta de Purchena 5, tel. 23 51 65. Modest but famous for food.

ALMUÑECAR (Granada). *Carmen* (I), Avda. General Galindo 8, tel. (958) 63 14 13. 18 rooms, close to beach. *Goya* (I), Avda. General Galindo, tel. (958) 63 05 50. 24 rooms, by beach. *La Najarra* (I), Avda. General Galindo, tel. (958) 63 08 73. 30 rooms. All these hotels are very modest.

Restaurant. *Los Geranios* (M-I), Placeta de la Rosa 4, tel. 63 07 24. In an attractive square, dining on three floors all with typical Andalusian décor.

ANDUJAR (Jaén). *Hotel Del Val* (I), just outside on Madrid road, tel. (953) 50 09 50. Pool, gardens, night club, good food in modern restaurant.

ANTEQUERA (Málaga). *Parador Nacional* (E-M), García del Olmo, tel. (952) 84 17 40. Comfortable, with pleasant garden and views and good food.

ARCOS DE LA FRONTERA (Cádiz). *Parador Casa del Corregidor* (E), Plaza de España, tel. (956) 70 05 00. 21 rooms, in the heart of the old town. Check if open. *Mesón la Molinera* (M-I), 6 km out of town on road to El Bosque, very reasonable accommodations in bungalows, pool and garden.

AYAMONTE (Huelva). *Don Diego* (M), Ramón y Cajal, tel. (955) 32 02 50. 45 rooms. *Parador Costa de la Luz* (E-M), El Castillito, tel. (955) 32 07 00. 20 rooms, pool, garden and airconditioning in rooms.

BAILEN (Jaén). *Parador Nacional* (E-M), tel. (953) 67 01 00. 86 rooms, modern with pool. *Motel Don Lope de Sosa* (M), tel. (953) 67 00 58. 27 rooms, garden and good restaurant. *Zodiaco* (I), tel. (953) 67 10 58. 52 rooms, modern with good restaurant. All three are on main highway, NIV.

LOS BARRIOS (Cádiz), near Algeciras. *Guadacorte-Meliá* (E), tel. (956) 66 45 00. 118 rooms; one of the best hotels in the area with many facilities including pool, tennis and gardens. *La Posada del Terol* (M), Barriada de Palmones Playa, tel. (956) 66 18 62. 24 rooms, pool.

BENALMADENA COSTA (Málaga). *Triton* (L), tel. (952) 44 32 40. 190 rooms, pools, tennis, sauna, private beach. *Alay* (E), tel. (952) 44 14 40. 2 pools, beach, good service, recommended. *Costa Azul* (E), tel. (952) 44 28 40. 312 rooms. *Riviera* (E), tel. (952) 44 12 40. 173 rooms, many airconditioned, and overlooking beach; pool, tennis, night club and many other facilities. *Delfín* (I), tel. (952) 44 30 40. 252 rooms, near beach, with gardens and pools. All are located on main highway.

LOS BOLICHES (Málaga), *see* Fuengirola.

CADIZ. In the old town: *Atlántico* (E), Parque Genovés 9, tel. (956) 21 23 01. Parador in magnificent position on headland. *Francia y París* (M), Plaza Calvo Sotelo 2, tel. (956) 21 23 18. Highly recommended old-world hotel. Of the modern hotels on the isthmus, *Isecotel* (E), Amílcar Barca 35, tel. (956) 23 54 01, has large elegant apartments overlooking beach. *San Remo* (M-I), Paseo Marítimo 3, tel. (956) 23 22 02, also overlooks beach.

Restaurants. *El Anteojo* (E-M), Alameda de Apodaca 22, tel. 21 36 39. Elegant and modern; upstairs is a panoramic dining room with view over bay, downstairs a pleasant terrace. *El Faro* (E-M), San Felix 15, tel. 21 10 68. Locals say this is the best; especially good seafood. *Curro El Cojo* (M), Paseo Marítimo 2, tel. 23 31 86. Recently opened elegant restaurant near Isecotel. Superb meat dishes, mainly pork based, no fish at all. *Español* (M), Duque Victoria 6, tel. 21 18 93. Good food. *Meson La Piconera* (M), San Germán 5, tel. 22 18 84. Atmospheric spot. Also several (M-I) restaurants in the Plaza San Juan de Dios. All in the old town except Curro El Cojo.

LA CAROLINA (Jaén). *La Perdiz* (E), tel. (953) 66 03 00. Good hotel with pool at top of Despeñaperros pass on main N-IV.

CAZORLA (Jaén). *Parador El Adelantado* (M), 27 km from village, tel. (953) 72 10 75. 22 rooms, in a superb situation high in the mountains, in a game reserve; good shooting. *Cazorla* (I), Plaza del Generalísimo 4, tel. (953) 72 02 03. 22 rooms, modest, the only hotel in village.

CORDOBA. *Gran Capitán* (E), Avda América 3–5, tel. (957) 22 19 55. Excellent, though on a busy street. Tops is *Meliá Córdoba* (E), Jardines de la Victoria, tel. (957) 29 80 66. 99 rooms, pleasant, many amenities including pool and nightclub, best rooms at back. *Parador La Arruzafa* (E), Avda. de la Arruzafa, tel. (957) 27 59 00. Modern hotel with fine, old Moorish garden.

El Califa (M), Lope de Hoces 14, tel. (957) 29 94 00. Modern and central. *Los Gallos* (M), Avda. de Medina Azahara 7, tel. (957) 23 55 00. 105 rooms, many amenities, including pool. *Maimónides* (M), Torrijos 4, tel. (957) 22 38 56. Attractive and well recommended, beside the mosque.

Colón (I), Alhaken II 4, tel. (957) 22 62 23. 40 rooms. *Marisa* (I), Cardenal Herrero 6, tel. (957) 22 63 17. Typical Andalusian house, on north side of mosque. *Selu* (I), Eduardo Dato 7, tel. (957) 22 38 65. 105 rooms.

Restaurants. *El Caballo Rojo* (E), Cardenal Herrero 28, tel. 22 38 04. Atmospheric with excellent readers' reports. Close to mosque. *Castillo de la Albaida* (E), Ctra. Trassierra, tel. 27 34 93. About the best in town, but 4 km from center. Located in a 14th-century castle, it is a magnificent place to dine in old world surroundings.

Almudaina (M), Plaza de los Santos Mártires 1, tel. 22 43 36. Attractive location in an old school overlooking the walls of the Alcázar right at entrance to Judería. Andalusian patio, Cordoban décor and cooking. *El Churrasco* (M), Romero 16, tel. 29 08 19. A favorite with the Cordobeses, especially for succulent grilled meats. *Mesón del Conde* (M), Medina y Corella, tel. 22 30 83. Large patio, good food in narrow street beside mosque. *Los Patios* (M), Cardenal Herrero 16. Self-service cafeteria-style spot, but in beautiful setting—outdoor dining in patio decorated with hundreds of flowerpots.

Andalucía (I), José Zorrilla 3. Popular, budget dining. *La Hostería* (I), Sevilla 2. Old fashioned, pleasant and inexpensive. *Plata* (I), Victoriana Rivera 10. Dining on the sidewalk on a side street off main square.

For a typical tavern, try *Mesón de la Luna,* Calleja de la Luna. Charming setting, terrace, gardens and fountain.

DALIAS (Almería). *Golf Hotel Almerimar,* tel. (951) 48 09 50. 38 rooms, near beach, with pool, golf, tennis and many other facilities.

ESTEPONA (Málaga). *Atalaya Park* (E), tel. (952) 81 16 44. About midway between Marbella and Estepona, with 18-hole golf course, private beach, pool, all sports facilities, nightclubs, and all other delights of an excellent resort hotel. *Golf El Paraíso* (E), tel. (952) 81 28 40. Revolving restaurant, disco, beach, tennis and golf. *Santa Marta* (M), tel. (952) 81 13 40. An older favorite, with gardens and garage. All three are on the main highway.

Restaurants. *El Molino* (E), Urb. El Saladillo, tel. 80 09 49. Rustic décor and good French cuisine. *Le Castel* (M), in Bahía Dorada, tel. 80 05 46. French-run and renowned in the area for fine food and good service. *Costa del Sol* (M), San Roque, tel. 80 11 01. Colorful, French restaurant with excellent *menu del día.* Specialties include home-made terrine and asparagus mousseline, coq au vin, seafood thermidor and entrecôt Bordelaise. Highly recommended. *The Yellow Book* (M), on highway, tel. 80 04 84. Outstanding service and excellent food. Specialties include mushrooms in seafood sauce, chicken Killara and steak and kidney pie. Good selection of steaks. Closed Mon.

FUENGIROLA (Málaga). *Las Palmeras* (E), Príncipe de España, tel. (952) 47 27 00. 535 rooms, all facilities including golf, tennis, bowls and bingo. Near beach.

Angela (M), Príncipe de España, tel. (952) 47 52 00. 261 rooms, with pool, gardens, tennis and disco. *Florida* (M), Paseo Marítimo, tel. (952) 47 61 00. Pleasant setting with own garden and reasonable rates. *Mare Nostrum* (M), on highway, tel. (952) 47 11 00. Attractive curved layout enables every room to get the sun. Pool, private beach, mini golf, tennis, bowling green and many other amenities. *Torreblanca* (M), on highway, tel. (952) 47 58 50. Pool, private beach, and just outside village of same name. *La Concha* (I), on highway, tel. (952) 47 10 00. 63 rooms, comfortable, tennis and open-air dining, on beach in Los Boliches.

Restaurants. *Los Claveles* (E), Ctra. de Cádiz, tel. 47 32 64. French and Belgian specialties and good service. Try the *Sole del Jefe* in shellfish sauce or one of the 8 varieties of steak. Closed Mon. *El Conquistador* (E), Plaza Constitución 20, tel. 47 01 45. Good ambience and pleasant service. Try the Snails Burgundy and the Sole Champagne or Steak Conquistador. Closed Thurs. *La Langosta* (E), Calvo Sotelo 1, Los Boliches, tel. 47 50 49. Excellent restaurant with long standing reputation for top quality. Specialties include lobster, sole and steak. Highly recommended.

Sin Igual (M), Ctra de Cádiz, Los Boliches, tel. 47 50 96. Small and some-what lacking in atmosphere, but serving good food, with many Greek dishes. Recommended are their soups and spinach pancakes, shish kebab and lamb chops. *La Sirena* (M), Calvo Sotelo 18, Los Boliches, tel. 47 50 46. An atmos-pheric Thai restaurant serving good spicy food. Try the Thai coffee. Closed Tues. *Van Gaalen's* (M), Paseo Marítimo, tel. 47 56 94. Elegant with seafood specialties. Try the Seafood Zarzuela or the Sole Hija Pascuale. Closed Mon.

Bélgica Antigua (I), Avda. del Ejército, tel. 47 15 96. A simple, good value bistro with friendly service and good *menu del día*. *La Cazuela* (I), Miguel Márquez 8, tel. 47 46 34. Good value, small, popular and often crowded. Good are the Chicken Kiev, pork chop and apple sauce, and Pepper Steak.

GRANADA. *Alhambra Palace* (E), Peña Partida 2, tel. (958) 22 14 68. Fully modernized, in historic house with beautiful views, close to Alhambra. *Carmen* (E), José Antonio 62, tel. (958) 25 83 00. 166 rooms, central and comfortable. *Luz Granada* (E), Calvo Sotelo 18, tel. (958) 20 40 61. 174 rooms, many amenities, but readers report it impersonal, geared to tour groups. *Meliá Grana-da* (E), Angel Ganivet 7, tel. (958) 22 74 00. Central, though there have been complaints about noise and service. *Parador San Francisco* (E), Alhambra, tel. (958) 22 14 93. Spain's most popular parador, magnificently located in an old convent within the Alhambra walls. Only 26 rooms, book at least 6 months ahead.

Brasilia (M), Recogidas 7, tel. (958) 25 84 50. Modern, central and comfort-able but aseptic. *Guadalupe* (M), Avda. de los Alijares, tel. (958) 22 34 23. 43 rooms. Up near Generalife, with good food. *Generalife* (M), Alixares del Generalife, tel. (958) 22 55 06. Pleasant new hotel with pool way up on Alham-bra hill. *Kenia* (M), Molinos 65, tel. (958) 22 75 06. 19 rooms, quiet, formerly a private villa, personalized service. *Victoria* (M), Puerta Real 3, tel. (958) 25 77 00. Old-world charm, period dining room, in heart of town. *Washington Irving* (M), Paseo del Generalife 2, tel. (958) 22 75 50. Pleasant location near Alhambra, garden and many amenities.

Inglaterra (I), Cetti-Meriem 6, tel. (958) 22 15 59. Old Andalusian house with period charm, right in center. *Macia* (I), Plaza Nueva 4, tel. (958) 22 75 35. Modern, in pleasant, central square. *Montecarlo* (I), José Antonio 44, tel. (958) 25 79 00. 63 rooms, central. *Sudán* (I), José.Antonio 60, tel. (958) 25 84 00. Old-world charm, pleasant, and good food. *Universal* (I), Recogidas 16, tel. (958) 22 34 10. 55 rooms, central.

Restaurants. *Sevilla* (E), Oficios 14, tel. 22 12 23. The best, beside the cathe-dral in the Alcaicería with typical Granadino décor and wonderful tapas bar. *Torres Bermejas* (E), Plaza Nueva 5, tel. 22 31 16. Excellent restaurant, closed Sun.

Alcaicería (M), Oficios 8, tel. 22 43 41. In heart of old Arab quarter. Decorat-ed in smart Arab style; excellent food. *Colombia* (M), Antequeruela Baja 1, tel. 22 74 33. On Alhambra hill, guitar music. *Cunini* (M), Pescadería 9, tel. 22 37 27. Recommended for seafood and fish. *Los Leones* (M), José Antonio 10, tel. 25 50 07. Central and recommended. Closed Tues. *Los Manueles* (M), Zaragoza

2, tel. 22 34 15. Atmospheric, with ceramic tiles, and smoked hams hanging from ceiling. Outdoor dining. *Las Vidrieras* (M), Recogidas 59, tel. 25 27 81. Recommended.

Meson Andaluz (M), Cetti Meriem 10. Pleasant service and a wide choice of dishes. *Nueva Bodega* (I), Elvira 35. A budgeteer's delight.

GUADIX (Granada). Interesting for the caves (6.5 km north) in which many people still live. *Comercio* (I), Mira de Amezcua 3, tel. (958) 66 05 00. 21 rooms, simple. *Mulhacén* (I), Ctra. de Murcia 43, tel. 66 07 50. 40 rooms, a pleasantly located hostal with garage.

HUELVA. *Luz Huelva* (E), Alameda Sumdheim 26, tel. (955) 25 00 11. Many amenities, but impersonal and geared to businessmen. No restaurant. *Tartessos* (M), Avda. Martín Alonso Pinzón 13, tel. (955) 24 56 11. 105 rooms, some suites. *Costa de la Luz* (I), José María Amo 8, tel. (955) 25 64 22. 35 rooms.

Restaurants. *La Cinta* (M), Arquitecto Pérez Carasa 23, tel. 21 32 11. *Otra Montaña* (M), Avda Martín Alonso Pinzón 24, tel. 21 35 64. *Las Tinajas* (M), Alfonso XII. Excellent seafood and tapas. *Victor* (I), Rascón 35, tel. 21 70 35. Outside town on Cádiz road in Sanlúcar la Mayor, is *Venta Pepe Pazos* (I). Try the *sopa de picadillo,* a meal in itself.

JAEN. *Parador Castillo de Santa Catalina* (E), Castillo de Santa Catalina, tel. (953) 23 23 87. Beautifully situated, converted castle with monastic-style, balconied rooms. *Condestable Iranzo* (M), Paseo de la Estación 32, tel. (953) 22 28 00. 147 rooms, several amenities including disco, shops and bingo. *Xauen* (M), Plaza de Dean Mazas 3, tel. (953) 23 40 91. 35 rooms, garage, central. *Rey Fernando* (M-I), Plaza de Coca de la Piñera 7, tel. (953) 21 18 40. 36 rooms, with garage, old fashioned. *Europa* (M-I), Plaza de Belén 1, tel. (953) 22 27 00. 36 rooms, no breakfast. *Reyes Católicos* (I), Avda. de Granada 1, tel. (953) 22 22 50. 28 rooms. *La Yuca* (I), 5 km out on highway, tel. (953) 22 19 50. 23 rooms, pleasantly located, garden and gas.

Restaurants. Best and most spectacular meals in the parador, perched on top of a mountain commanding a magnificent view of city. *Jockey Club* (M), Paseo de la Estación 20, tel. 21 10 18. The most luxurious. *Mesón Nuyra* (M), Pasaje Nuyra, tel. 23 41 17. Typical mesón in central pedestrian street.

JEREZ DE LA FRONTERA (Cádiz). *Jerez* (L), Avda. Alvaro Domecq 41, tel. (956) 33 06 00. Recent, pool, gardens and other amenities. *Capele* (E), Gen. Franco 58, tel. (956) 34 64 00. 30 rooms. *Motel Aloha* (M), outside town, tel. (956) 33 25 00. 27 rooms, pleasant location, pool. *El Coloso* (I), Pedro Alonso 13, tel. (956) 34 90 08. Friendly oldish hotel, simple and adequate.

Restaurants. *El Bosque* (E), Alcalde Alvaro Domecq 26, tel. 33 33 33. Lovely setting in park. *Tendido 6* (E-M), Circo 10, tel. 34 48 35, opposite bullring, specializes in seafood. Popular at lunchtime, so book. *La Posada* (M), Arboledilla 2, tel. 33 34 20. Tiny restaurant with even smaller menu but the daily specials are lovingly chosen.

LANJARON (Granada). *Miramar* (M), Generalísimo Franco 10, tel. (958) 77 01 61. 60 rooms, good location, pool and garden. *Andalucía* (M), Generalísimo Franco 15. 57 rooms, pool and garden. *Nuevo Palas* (M-I), Gen. Franco 28, tel. (958) 77 01 11. 30 rooms, pool. *Paraiso* (I), Gen. Franco 18, tel. (958) 77 00 12. 30 rooms, garden.

LOJA (Granada). *El Mirador* (I), on the main road, tel. (958) 32 00 42. 60 rooms. Recently enlarged and modernized. Good view; useful for motorists. **Restaurant.** *El Mirador* (M), caters for coach parties, but food is excellent.

MALAGA. *Málaga Palacio* (L), Cortina del Muelle 1, tel. (952) 21 51 85. Málaga's most elegant hotel, very central, 228 rooms. All amenities, though there have been complaints of poor service. *Bahía* (M), Somera 8, tel. (952) 22 43 05. 44 rooms, central. *Casa Curro* (M), Sancha de Lara 7, tel. (952) 22 72 00. Central, modern and comfortable. *Los Naranjos* (E-M), Paseo de Sancha 29, tel. (952) 22 43 16. 38 rooms, short distance from center on pleasant avenue. *Parador de Gibralfaro* (E), on mountain top, 3 km from center, tel. (952) 22 19 02. Beside Moorish castle, beautiful view over bay. *Las Vegas* (M), Paseo de Sancha 28, tel. (952) 21 77 12. In residential area with panoramic dining room, pool and gardens.

Astoria (I), Comandante Benítez 3, tel. (952) 22 45 00. 61 rooms, garage. *Lis* (I), Córdoba 7, tel. (952) 22 73 00. 53 rooms, central. *California* (I), Paseo de Sancha 19, tel. (952) 21 51 65. On pleasant avenue short distance from center. *Olletas* (I), Cuba 1, tel. (952) 25 20 00. 66 rooms.

10 km out on road to Torremolinos, and close to airport, in *Guadalmar* (E), Urb. Guadalmar. Pleasant, tennis, pool, gardens, disco; but you need a car, it's a long way from anywhere except the golf course.

Restaurants. *La Alegría* (E), Marín García 18, tel. 22 41 43. Specializes in shellfish. *Calycanto* (E), Avda. Pintor Sorolla 51, tel. 21 59 14. *Skorpios* (E), Ventaja Alta, tel. 25 84 94. On road up to Gibralfaro.

Antonio Martín (M), Paseo Marítimo, tel. 22 21 13. Very popular, dining on terrace, in harbor area. *Cortijo de Pepe* (M), Plaza de la Merced 2, tel. 22 40 71. Typical Andalusian décor, good value. *Guerola* (M), Esparteros 8, tel. 22 31 21. Central, tables outdoors in summer; menu is more original than most. *Casa Pedro*, Quitapenas 121, on El Palo beach, tel. 29 00 13. Famous for seafood and fish. Huge dining room overlooking ocean, very popular, extremely crowded on Sun. for lunch. *La Cancela* (I), Denis Belgrano 3, tel. 22 31 25. Pleasant, typical and popular with locals. Good food, dining on sidewalk in summer.

On Pedregalejos and El Palo beaches (Málaga-Nerja road) there is a cluster of excellent seafood beach restaurants in summer. Seafood straight off the boats.

MARBELLA (Málaga). *Don Carlos* (L), tel. (952) 83 11 40. Located 13 km east of Marbella on road to Málaga. 16 acres of landscaped grounds between beach and hotel. 2 dining rooms, coffee shop, cocktail lounge. *Golf Hotel Nueva Andalucía* (L), tel. (952) 81 11 45. Luxurious and small (22 rooms) hotel in an isolated position, surrounded by golf course. *Marbella Club* (L), tel. (952) 77

13 00. Out of town on road to Cádiz. Officially a 4-star hotel, its prices are nevertheless deluxe. 76 rooms, beautiful gardens, pool and bungalow accommodations. *Meliá Don Pepe* (L), Finca Las Marinas, tel. (952) 77 03 00. Just outside town on road to Cádiz. Super deluxe hotel with every possible amenity. But ask for room facing sea; larger rooms face onto parking lot, road and bleak mountains. *Los Monteros* (L), tel. (952) 77 17 00. On road to Málaga, with 18-hole golf course, tennis, pools, horseback riding: an admirable hotel—the most expensive in Spain!

Puente Romano (L), tel. (952) 77 01 00. On road to Cádiz. A spectacular hotel and apartment complex. The "village" located between the Marbella Club and Puerto Banús incorporates a genuine Roman bridge in its beautifully landscaped grounds, which run from the road side down to the beach. The style is Andalusian mountain and apartments are luxurious. There are two pools, full hotel services for those requiring them, and an enormous disco.

Andalucía Plaza (E), tel. (952) 81 20 40. Located in front of Puerto Banús, 6 km out on Cádiz road. 3 golf courses, 5 pools and much convention business, which does not always favor the individual traveler. *El Fuerte* (E), Llano de San Luís, tel. (952) 77 15 00. Centrally located in interesting old building, with pool, gardens and tennis. Recommended. *Marbella-Dinamar Club* (E), tel. (952) 81 12 43. On Cádiz road, near Puerto Banús, with private beach, pool, sauna, tennis. Formerly the Marbella Holiday Inn, now under new management.

Artola (M), tel. (952) 83 13 90. 5 km out on road to Málaga. 64 rooms, golf and tennis. *Las Chapas* (M), tel. (952) 83 13 75. Some way out on Málaga road. Pool, tennis, and features a ring for teaching bull-fighting with hornless calves. *Estrella del Mar* (M), tel. (952) 83 12 75. On Málaga road. 98 rooms, by beach, many facilities including pool, sauna and bowling. *Guadalpín* (M), tel. (952) 77 11 00. About 1.5 km out on road to Cádiz, with bar, gardens and restaurant; good value.

Aifil (I), Avda. Ricardo Soriano 19, tel. (952) 77 23 50. 56 rooms, in town. *Club Pinomar* (I), tel. (952) 83 13 45. On road to Málaga. 431 rooms, many amenities including pool, mini golf, tennis and bowling. Good value. *Don Miguel* (I), Camino del Trapiche, tel. (952) 77 28 50. 501 rooms, in town, a 3-star hotel with low rates and many amenities, pool. *Lima* (I), Avda. Antonio Belón 2, tel. (952) 77 05 00. 64 rooms, very central.

Restaurants. *Cenicienta* (E), Avda. Cánovas del Castillo, tel. 77 43 18. One of the best restaurants in area. The *Gambas Duque de Alba* and the crêpes are recommended. *El Corzo Grill* (E), in Los Monteros Hotel, tel. 77 17 00. Elegant gourmet dining to piano music. *La Fonda* (E), Plaza Santo Cristo 10, tel. 77 25 12. Highly personalized Andalusian tavern in heart of town. *Marbella Club Hotel* (E), tel. 77 13 00. Grills in delightful garden setting. *El Refugio* (E), Crta. de Ojén, tel. 77 18 48. Pleasant terrace and garden, perfect service and unbeatable cuisine. 3 km north of Marbella on C337. Highly recommended.

Chez Charlemagne (M), 8 km out on Málaga road, tel. 83 11 05. French specialties, lovely garden and terrace. *Mesón del Conde* (M), Avda. José Antonio 18, tel. 77 10 57. Friendly, simple but attractively decorated Swiss restaurant. Good fondue and *Boeuf Bourguignon*. *Mesón del Pasaje* (M), Pasaje 5, tel. 77

12 61. One of best moderate restaurants in town. Victorian décor, very popular. *Mena* (M), Plaza de los Naranjos 10, tel. 77 15 97. Good seafood and pleasant terrace. *Metropol* (I), Ricardo Soriano 29, tel. 77 11 39. In center of town, good, typical cuisine and pleasant décor.

At **Puerto Banus** you'll be hard pressed to chose from the array of restaurants that grace the waterfront. The following are recommended: *Beni* (E), Muelle Benabola, tel. 81 16 25; *Taberna del Puerto Pepito* (M), Muelle Ribera; *Taberna del Alabardero* (M), Muelle Benabola, tel. 81 40 26.

MIJAS (Málaga). *Mijas* (E), Urb. Tamisa, tel. (952) 48 58 00. Beautifully located hotel with Andalusian décor. Rose garden, terrace, pool and outdoor lunchtime buffets.

Restaurants. *El Padrastro* (E), Paseo del Compás, tel. 48 50 00. Stunning view and good food. *La Alegría de Mijas* (M), Pasaje del Compás, tel. 48 57 20. Specialty is partridge. *Escudo de Mijas* (M), Pescadores, tel. 48 50 25. French restaurant with magnificent view and excellent cuisine. *Mirlo Blanco* (M), Plaza Queipo de Llano 13, tel. 48 57 00. Specializes in Basque cooking. Try the *Txangurro,* a crab meat specialty. Steaks are good too, and so is the *Soufflé Grand Marnier. Molino del Cura* (M), Ctra. de Mijas, tel. 48 58 13. Excellent service and ambience. Specialties from South America, China, India and Spain.

La Bóveda del Flamenco (I), just off village square below Mirlo Blanco. Good value *platos combinados. Casa los Jamones* (I), good typical cooking.

MOJACAR (Almería). *Parador de los Reyes Católicos* (E), tel. (951) 47 82 50. 2.5 km out of town. 98 rooms, pool and gardens. *Indalo* (M), Ctra. de Carboneras, tel. (951) 47 80 01. 308 rooms, pool, tennis and disco. *Mojácar* (M), Mirador de la Puntica, tel. (951) 47 81 50. 60 rooms, pool and bowling. Perched atop the village with glorious views. *El Moresco* (M), tel. (951) 47 80 25. 147 rooms, pleasant central location, pool.

NERJA (Málaga). *Parador de Nerja* (E), tel. (952) 52 00 50. 5 km outside town. 40 rooms, pool, pleasant gardens with view of sea. *Balcón de Europa* (M), Paseo Balcón de Europa 5, tel. (952) 52 08 00. 105 rooms, central and pleasant. *Portofino* (I), Puerta del Mar 2, tel. (952) 52 01 50. 12 rooms, a delightful small hotel in fine situation with excellent French-Italian cuisine.

Restaurants. *Rey Alfonso* (E-M), Balcón de Europa. Recommended. *Cueva de Nerja* (M), 4 km out near caves, tel. 52 06 33. *Pepe Rico* (M), Almirante Ferrándiz 28, tel. 52 02 47. Good food.

PUERTO DE SANTA MARIA (Cádiz). *Fuentebravia* (E), Playa de Fuentebravia, tel. (956) 85 17 17. 90 rooms, near Rota, one of the most pleasant hotels on the coast. *Meliá Caballo Blanco* (E), on road to Cádiz, tel. (956) 86 37 45. Nicely furnished, bungalows in garden, pool, beach nearby. *Puertobahía* (M), Playa de Valdelagrana, tel. (956) 86 27 21. Good amenities, close to beach.

Restaurants. *El Resbaladero* (M), Micaela de Aramburu 18, tel. 86 26 22. Located in the old fish market, well known for fish and seafood dishes. *Venta*

Millán (M), Cante de los Puertos 12, tel. 86 30 73. Excellent seafood and service in an intimate atmosphere. Reader-recommended.

PUNTA UMBRIA (Huelva). *Pato Amarillo* (M), Urb. Everluz, tel. (955) 31 12 50. 120 rooms, some suites, pool and disco. *Pato Rojo* (M), Avda. Oceano, tel. (955) 31 16 00. 60 rooms, magnificent view.

Restaurant. *La Pequeña Alhambra* (M), Ancha, tel. 31 18 29. Moorish décor inspired by the Alhambra in Granada.

RONDA (Málaga). *Reina Victoria* (E), Jerez 25, tel. (952) 87 12 40. Spectacularly placed in gardens on the very lip of a gorge, commanding an impressive view; pool. *Polo* (M), Mariano Xouviron 9, tel. (952) 87 24 47. Good old-style hotel. *Royal* (M), Virgen de la Paz 52, tel. (952) 87 11 41. Pleasant.

Restaurants. *Don Miguel* (E), Villanueva 4, tel. 87 10 90. Dining on terrace overlooking gorge; the best. Atmospheric mesón décor. *Pedro Romero* (M), opposite bullring with - yes, bullfight décor. *Mesón Santiago* (I), Marina 3, tel. 87 15 59.

ROQUETAS DEL MAR (Almería). *Playasol* (E-M), Urb. Playa Serena, tel. (951) 32 08 25. Central with pool, mini golf, tennis and disco. *Alis* (M), Avda. Mediterráneo, tel. (951) 32 03 75. Pool and gardens. *Roquetas Park Hotel* (M), Pez Espada, tel. (951) 32 02 50. 291 rooms, pool, gardens and close to shopping center. *Sabinal* (M), Avda. de las Gaviotas, tel. (951) 32 06 00. 416 rooms, pool and gardens. *Zoraida Park* (M), Pez Espada, tel. (951) 32 07 50. 495 rooms, pool, mini golf, garden and disco.

ROTA (Cádiz). *Caribe* (E), Avda. de la Marina 62, tel. (956) 81 07 00. 42 rooms, some suites, pool. *Parque Victoria* (E), Avda. Juan Ramón Jiménez, tel. (956) 81 15 00. 22 rooms, only classed as a 2-star hotel, but prices are fairly high. *Playa de la Luz* (M), Arroyo Hondo, tel. (956) 81 05 00. 285 rooms, many amenities including pool.

SALOBREÑA (Granada). *Salobreña* (M), tel. (958) 61 02 61. 4 km out on road to Málaga. 80 rooms, pool and gardens. *Salambina* (I), tel. (958) 61 00 37. 1 km out on Málaga road. 13 rooms, simple.

Restaurants. *Salomar 2000* (M), tel. 61 08 30. 2 km out of town, near beach. Outstanding French cuisine. *Mesón Durán* (I), tel. 61 01 14. Beside the sea, 3.5 km out on road to Málaga. Typical décor.

SAN PEDRO DE ALCANTARA (Málaga). *Golf Hotel Guadalmina* (E), Hacienda Guadalmina, tel. (952) 81 17 44. A bungalow-hotel near the beach, with pool, tennis, golf and many other amenities. *Alcotán* (I), tel. (952) 81 15 48. On main highway. 84 rooms, pleasant location, pool and gardens. *El Pueblo Andaluz* (I), tel. (952) 81 16 42. Andalusian style, well situated off main road; pool and riding.

Restaurant. *Los Duendes* (E-M), Lagasca 44, tel. 81 18 56. Good lobster.

SAN ROQUE (Cádiz). *Motel San Roque* (I), tel. (956) 78 01 00. 37 rooms, pool. *Río Grande* (I), tel. (956) 78 60 25. 22 rooms, pool and garden, rock bottom rates.

Restaurant. *Don Benito* (M), Plaza de Armas 10, tel. 78 07 78.

SANLUCAR DE BARRAMEDA (Cádiz). Attractive Andalusian town at mouth of Guadalquivir. *Guadalquivir* (M), Calzada del Ejército, tel. (956) 36 07 42. 81 rooms, central, bingo.

SEVILLE. See *Practical Information* for Seville.

SIERRA NEVADA (Granada). *Meliá Sierra Nevada* (E), Sierra Nevada-Prado Llano, tel. (958) 48 04 00. 221 rooms, nightclub and restaurant. Rates are those of a deluxe hotel, almost double other hotels in area. *Nevasur* (E), Estación de Deportes de Invierno, tel. (958) 48 03 50. 50 rooms. *Parador Sierra Nevada* (E), tel. (958) 48 02 00. 35 km from Granada, at an altitude of 2,500 meters. 32 rooms. *Sol y Nieve* (E), Prado Llano, tel. (958) 48 03 00. 70 rooms. A vast complex with boutiques, pools, tennis, skating; in short, the lot.

Restaurants. *Por Qué No?* (E), Nevada Center, Edificio América. *Cunini Sierra Nevada* (M), San José 1, tel. 48 01 70. Fish and seafood specialties.

SOTOGRANDE (Cádiz). *Tenis Hotel Sotogrande* (L), tel. (956) 79 21 00. Off main highway near Guadiaro. The Sotogrande estate, the fruit of the planner's dream of an international leisure community, lies between the beach and the foothills of the Sierra Almenara. It offers magnificent sports facilities, 3 golf courses, riding, polo, tennis, pelota and shooting. There is a long, wide sandy beach and a large yachting center. Highly recommended, for sporty types.

TARIFA (Cádiz). *Balcón de España* (E-M), tel. (956) 68 43 26. 32 rooms, pool. *Mesón de Sancho* (M), tel. 68 49 00. A bungalow-hotel off the main road with pool.

Restaurant. *Chez Nous* (M), Puerto del Bujeo, tel. 66 15 18. Half way between Tarifa and Algeciras. English owned and housed in an old stage coach station with excellent food service. Reader recommended.

TORREMOLINOS (Málaga). *Meliá Torremolinos* (L), Avda Carlota Alessandri 109, tel. (952) 38 05 00. Usual luxurious Meliá standards. *Pez Espada* (L), Vía Imperial, tel. (952) 38 03 00. Stylish old favorite in nice location beyond Carihuela, happily reopened again after some years. *Cervantes* (E), Las Mercedes, tel. (952) 38 40 33. Busy, cosmopolitan hotel in heart of town. *Meliá Costa del Sol* (E), Huerta Nueva, tel. (952) 38 66 77. Apartment complex at Bajondillo Beach at end of Paseo Marítimo. *Parador del Golf* (E), tel. (952) 38 12 55. Modern parador at Málaga golf course halfway between Málaga and Torremolinos.

Don Pablo (M), tel. (952) 38 38 88, *Don Pedro* (M), tel. (952) 38 68 44, and *Isabel* (M), tel. (952) 38 17 44, are all modern resort hotels on the Paseo

Marítimo at Bajondillo beach. *Príncipe Sol* (M) at the end of Paseo Maritimo, tel. (952) 38 41 00, is a little out of the ordinary with eastern style and marvelous buffets. *Amaragua* (M), tel. (952) 38 46 33, and *Jorge V* (M), tel. (952) 38 11 00, are both good, just beyond Carihuela; and close by is *Los Nidos* (I), tel. (952) 38 04 00. *El Pozo* (I), Casablanca, tel. (952) 38 06 22, is a pleasant Andalusian house in center.

Restaurants. *Caballo Vasco* (E), Casablanca, tel. 38 23 36. Delicious Basque cuisine, well attended by the family owners. *Las Pampas* (E), just off Casablanca. Argentinian restaurant serving superb steaks.

Florida (M), Casablanca 15, tel. 38 73 66. Hot and cold buffet at fixed price and small à la carte menu. Dancing to live music. *Hong Kong* (M), Cauce, tel. 38 41 29. Chinese and Indian specialties. *León de Castilla* (M), in Pueblo Blanco off Casablanca, tel. 38 69 59. Large, elegant Spanish cooking, good wines; rustic décor. *La Rioja* (M), in Pueblo Blanco off Casablanca. Atmospheric dining with good wines. *Viking* (M), Casablanca 1, tel. 38 10 41. Cozy and intimate spot with good Danish food. *El Atrio* (M), is a delightful small French restaurant in Plaza de los Tientos in Pueblo Blanco. *La Cava* (M), also in Pueblo Blanco, is recent and stylish and offers a more original menu than most.

La Cacerola (I), María Barrabino. English dishes such as steak and kidney pie and lemon meringue. *La Luna* (I), San Miguel. Two flights up with terrace and rustic décor. Very popular. *Pizzería La Barraca* (I), corner of Casablanca and Fandango. Informal and charming.

On **Bajondillo** Beach are several good fish restaurants. *Hawaii Playa* and *El Yate de Cordobés* are both reader recommended.

The real gourmet area of Torremolinos is the *Carihuela.* To reach the Carihuela, turn left off the highway at Las Palomas hotel and make your way down to the beach and the Calles de Bulto and Carmen. It is fun to stroll along the promenade and choose your own restaurant from the many that line the beach, but here are a few suggestions:

El Cangrejo (M), Bulto 25, tel. 38 04 79. One of the best displays of seafood in Spain. Be sure to book. Even if you are not intent on full scale dining, you should visit its bar to sample some of the magnificent shellfish *hors d'oeuvres.* *Casa Prudencio* (M), Carmen 43, tel. 38 14 52. Also well-known for its seafood. *Casa Guaquín* (M-I), Carmen 37, tel. 38 45 30 and *La Concha* (M-I), at Bulto 35 are both pleasant bistros with a wide choice of menu.

UBEDA (Jaén). *Parador Condestable Dávalos* (M), Plaza Vázquez Molina, tel. (953) 75 03 45. Elegant hotel, 25 rooms. Located in 16th-century palace with beautiful patio. *Consuelo* (I), Avda. Ramón y Cajal 12, tel. (953) 75 08 40. A simple one-star hotel.

USEFUL ADDRESSES. Tourist Offices. **Algeciras;** at the port. **Almería;** Hermanos Machado, Edificio Multiple. **Baeza;** Plaza del Pópulo. **Cádiz;** Calderón de la Barca 1. **Cazorla;** José Antonio 1. **Córdoba;** Hermanos González Murga 13. **Granada;** Casa de los Tiros, Pavaneras 19. **Huelva;** Plus

Ultra 10, 2nd floor. **Jaén;** Arquitecto Bergés 3. **Málaga;** Larios 5. **Ronda;** Plaza de España 1. **Torremolinos;** Edificio la Noguelera 516. **Ubeda;** in the City Hall in the Plaza del Ayuntamiento.

British Consulates. **Algeciras;** Avda. Franco 11, tel. 66 16 00. **Málaga;** Calle Duquesa de Parcent 4, tel. 21 75 71. U.S. Consulate, in **Fuengirola,** tel. 46 18 65.

CAR HIRE. Algeciras; *Avis* and *Hertz,* Villanueva 1; *Europcar,* Cañonero Dato 4. **Almería;** *Avis,* Canónigo Molina Alonso; *Hertz* at Station and Avda. Calvo Sotelo; *Budget,* Paseo de Almería 47. **Cádiz;** *Avis,* Avda. Cayetano del Toro 16; *Hertz,* Condesa Bermeja 5; *Ital,* Cuesta de las Calesas 41. **Córdoba;** *Avis* at airport and Plaza de Colón 28; *Ital,* José María Herrero 26; *Europcar,* Antonio Maura 3. **Granada;** *Avis* at airport and Recogidas 31; *Hertz* at airport and Luis Braille 7; *Ital,* Pza. de Cuchilleros 12. **Jerez de la Frontera;** *Avis* at airport and Sevilla 25; *Hertz,* Julio Ruiz de Alda 29; *Budget,* Plaza de Silos 16. **Málaga;** *Avis* at airport and Cortina del Muelle 13; *Hertz* at airport, station and Alameda Colón 17. **Torremolinos;** *Avis,* Complejo Comercial El Congreso; *Hertz,* Edificio Montemar, several others all along Avda Montemar.

THE ROCK OF GIBRALTAR

Tariq's Mountain

The future of the tiny British Crown Colony fondly nicknamed Gib
remains unclear. When Spain, which lays claim to Gibraltar on both
geographical and historical grounds, applied for membership of both
the EEC and NATO, the contentious issue of Gibraltar proved a major
stumbling block. In particular the question of the Spanish/Gibraltar
border, closed by Franco in June 1969, has remained unanswered. The
British, while happy to see the border reopened—indeed their side of
the border has always remained symbolically open—are unwilling and
to some extent unable to cede the rock to the Spanish, not least because
the vast majority of Gibraltarians are determined to retain their colonial status. Gibraltar is also a vital NATO port. The Spanish, full members of NATO since May 1982, will clearly find it acutely embarrassing
to use the port while Gibraltar itself remains in British hands. Funda-

mentally, however, they consider it an absurd anachronism that a part of Spain, as they see it, should remain in the hands of a foreign government, even if it is a friendly one. If anything, it is this final fact that makes the problem all the more difficult.

At presstime the situation was still unresolved. The reopening of the border, scheduled for June 1982, was postponed until the end of that year, largely due to the Falklands crisis. The opening of the border however, has only been partial, for only Spaniards may cross into Gibraltar from the mainland, foreigners are still barred from reaching the rock this way. We advise you to check on the current situation but should it remain unchanged, your only access to Gibraltar will be via ferry or hydrofoil from Algeciras to Tangiers in Morocco, and from there to Gibraltar—a very round about trip indeed!

In ancient times, Gibraltar was one of the two Pillars of Hercules that marked the western limit of the known world; its position dominating the narrow entrance to the Mediterranean led to its seizure by the Moors in 711 as a preliminary to the conquest of Spain. Incidentally, they held it for longer than either the Spaniards or the British have ever done, a fact to which tribute is paid unconsciously whenever anyone pronounces its name, for Gibraltar is a corruption of Jebel Tariq, or Tariq's Mountain—Tariq was the Moorish commander who built the first fort of Gibraltar.

For nearly 750 years, Tariq was held by the Moors, until the Spaniards captured it in 1462 on the Feast Day of St. Bernard, now the colony's patron saint. The English, heading an Anglo-Dutch fleet in the War of the Spanish Succession, captured the Rock in 1704, after three days of fighting. After several years of skirmishing in the vicinity, Gibraltar was ceded to England by the Treaty of Utrecht in 1713. With the exception of the Great Siege, when a Franco-Spanish force battled at its ramparts for three years (1779–82), Gibraltar has lived a relatively peaceful existence ever since. During the two world wars, it served the Allies well as an important naval and air base.

Though this is British territory, traffic keeps to the right, and you are forbidden to use horns or klaxons. The local substitute is to beat violently on the side of the car, or shout. Actually, both of these rules are of little practical value, since in most of the narrow, almost sidewalkless, streets, jammed from curb to curb with peddlers, handcart men, boys on bicycles and pedestrians of all nationalities, you progress where and how you can. The inhabitants use minute, speedy British cars, which weave miraculously in and out of the crowds, somehow avoiding mass slaughter.

It is not surprising that Gibraltar is always crowded. Much of its geography is perpendicular, which would restrict its capacity even if it were much larger than it is—about five kilometers long by just over one kilometer wide.

Why should tourists fight their way into this crowded area, to sweat under the muggy prevailing wind, the energy-stealing Levante? Sights are not many, but the whole place is a spectacle in itself, with its remnants of a Moorish castle, its red-tiled roofs and pink houses, influenced by Spain, its police wearing the old-fashioned helmets of the London policemen, and its colorful, noisy, teeming, polyglot, permanent and temporary population. The main reason is the free port status, which in combination with the low exchange rates, makes goods about the cheapest in Europe.

You must go to the upper Rock to visit the famous Barbary apes, the only wild apes in Europe, who are believed to know a passage under the sea from the caves of Gibraltar to the caves near Tetuán, in Morocco, on the other side of the 16 kilometers of water that constitute the Straits of Gibraltar. Legend also says that while the apes remain, Britain will continue to hold the Rock. Nobody puts any stock in that, of course, yet during the war, when the number of apes and Britain's fortunes were dwindling simultaneously, no less a person than Winston Churchill issued orders for maintenance of the ape contingent. Their numbers were built up, Britain's fortunes turned, coincidentally or not, as you may choose to believe, and to this day, they roam the heights.

The famous Galleries of the Rock were carved out during the Great Siege, and although the only attack on Gibraltar since then was by aircraft in 1940, over thirty-two kilometers of tunnel were excavated during World War II, in preparation for a possible invasion.

Not far away from the stolid apes, you can explore the famous caves, especially the latest to be discovered, St. Michael's, revealed during fortification work in 1942, with their stalactites, underground lake, and mysterious subterranean breeze (perhaps coming from Africa?). This extraordinary underground amphitheater is used for concerts during the annual Arts Festival. Or visit the little fishing village of Catalan Bay, populated by descendants of Italian fishermen who came here in the 18th century. Catalan Bay has been Italian ever since. Or you can visit Trafalgar Cemetery, where the dead of that battle are buried (but not Nelson, who went home in a barrel full of brandy).

THE BALEARIC ISLANDS

Majorca, Minorca, Ibiza and Formentera

Until comparatively recent times, this group of sixteen islands was officially divided (as it was originally by the Romans) into two groups, one consisting of Majorca, Minorca, Cabrera and seven uninhabited ones, and the other, the more western group, of Ibiza, Formentera and four other islets, which were known as the Pityuses or Pine Islands. Today, however, this whole area, a geological continuation of the Andalusian mountain range, is included under the name of the Balearic Isles.

Although each island has its own local Mallorquín patois with a strong French influence, the language, basic customs and race are akin to Catalan, and not Spanish. The islanders, despite their stormy history as the pawns in the struggle between overwhelmingly more powerful peoples, have yet contrived to preserve a distinct character and personality.

A Little History

They provided Hannibal (reputedly born on the small island of Conejera, northwest of Ibiza) with his only regiment of stone-slingers, which won fame in many battles with Rome. Even earlier, in the semi-mythical times of the Greek Argonauts, it was in Majorca that Hercules found the Golden Apples (oranges), and there that the last High Priestesses of the Mother Cult held court in the mysterious depths of the Caves of Drach, one of the five official gateways to the underworld of the Ancients.

The Vandals seized the islands from the Romans in A.D. 455 and, except for a brief Byzantine reconquest under Belisarius, held them until the Moors took over in 798. For four centuries, Palma was the home port of particularly skillful and bloodthirsty pirates, who ravaged the coast as far as Italy and menaced communications. It was not until 1229 that Jaime of Aragon broke the Moorish hold upon the islands and made them an independent kingdom. Many of the islands' finest old buildings date from this period of independent Mallorquín kings. Under its fourth king Majorca was conquered by Pedro IV of Aragón in 1343, and the Balearics became part of Spain. In the War of the Spanish Succession, Majorca escaped the wrath of Marlborough and the British fleet by siding with the Austrian Pretender against Louis XIV's grandson Philip V, but Minorca was occupied continuously by the British, except for an interval of 17 years, from 1708 until 1802.

Majorca lies roughly 210 kilometers (130 miles) south of Barcelona, and 225 east of Valencia. Port Mahón, capital of Minorca, is roughly 161 kilometers (100 miles) northeast, and Ibiza 113 kilometers (70 miles) southwest of Palma. Ibiza, the southernmost of the islands, is only 105 kilometers (65 miles) from the mainland, its nearest ports of contact being Valencia and Alicanti.

Weather Matters

All year round, Majorca has an especially fine climate, though winters can be cold and damp. Generally speaking, Ibiza is hotter and Minorca colder than Majorca in all seasons, but these are relative differences. The swimming season runs from April to November.

In Palma de Mallorca, the best seasons are May–June and September (though the entire island is a mass of pale pink almond blossoms in February). Such rain as there is, falls mostly in March–April and October–November. Palma itself can be almost uncomfortably hot in

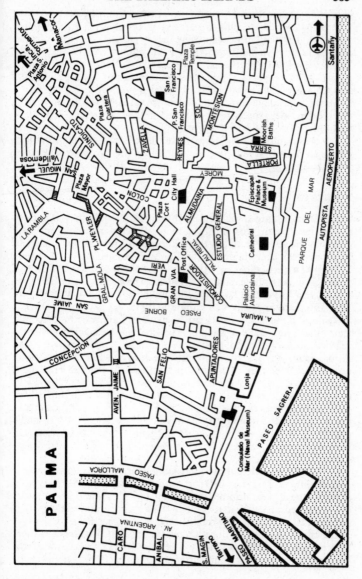

July–August, but the countryside is cooler, especially by the sea. Along the southern coast of Majorca, the season is from April until October, inclusive. The northern coast, being more exposed, is for the summer only, with the notable exception of Formentor, which lies in a huge, sheltered bay at the northeast tip of the island. Here you can swim in March and November. The huge open beaches of Pollensa, Alcudia and Cala Ratjada in the northeast are also summer-only centers.

Minorca's climate is totally different from that of its big sister, with changeable skies, cooler temperatures, and greener vistas. It is at its best only from May to September.

Ibiza, the hottest of the three (it can be blistering in midsummer), allows swimming at any time of the year. As the locals say, "Majorca looks to Spain, Minorca looks to France, and Ibiza looks to Africa."

Majorca

The Balearics are among the most touristically developed islands in the Mediterranean, with plenty of modern accommodations and easy accessibility, giving many northern Europeans their first experience of Mediterranean sun. Majorca is the big sister, being some 97 kilometers long by 80 wide, and having a population of about 600,000, almost half of which lives in the capital city, Palma. The floating population increases year by year. In fact, Majorca arguably welcomes more visitors than any place in Spain: 4¼ million in 1982!

Visitors to the island by sea are likely to be impressed by their first view of some outstanding landmarks including the magnificent 13th-century Gothic cathedral, the nearby almost contemporary Lonja (the former exchange) and the Convent Church of San Francisco, with its exquisite cloisters, and the 14th-century Castle of Bellver, stronghold of the kings of Majorca in medieval times. In the center of the bay, a low cliff rises immediately above the port, and from here to the Bellver, or western end of the bay, known as El Terreno, are the countless hotels, brilliantly illuminated at night, in witness of the island's popularity. When arriving by air the approach to the city is rather less impressive, along a modern dual highway until one reaches the waterfront and city center.

In Palma itself, there remain areas of picturesque, narrow, winding 17th-century streets. You will find a stroll through the old town quite as rewarding as the obligatory visits to the cathedral and Bellver Castle.

The cathedral looks at its best from the sea because only from a distance is it possible to appreciate its majestic proportions. The central of the three great naves, forested by 14 graceful 17-meter- (56-foot) high pillars, is 74 meters (244 feet) long and 46 (150 feet) wide, and although it is rather dark and austere in appearance, it contains many treasures. Here are the tombs of two of Majorca's four kings, and also of the anti-Pope Clement VII, who died in 1447, all illuminated by one vast and beautiful rose window. It was built between 1230 and 1601, the cloisters being 18th-century baroque. Expressive sculptures adorn the fine Gothic doorway which faces out toward the sea, while the interior of the cathedral and its museum contain many pictures, carved stalls, altar pieces and gold plate.

Of special interest to Americans is the monastery of San Francisco, from which Junipero Serra, a native of Majorca, departed for California, where he founded the city he named for his alma mater.

Almost next door to the cathedral is the huge Bishop's Palace and the small Castillo de la Almudaina, residence of the Moorish kings before their Christian successors constructed warlike Bellver.

It is a long and hot climb to Bellver—as no doubt an attacking enemy was intended to discover—so take a taxi. Even then, you still have to climb up a circular stone stairway to reach the top of the tower. The view along the coast and inland across pine forests and almond groves makes the effort well worth while. The castle was built by King Jaime II at the beginning of the 14th century and contains a most attractive circular courtyard.

Also worth seeing in Palma is the Lonja, a former exchange. Started in 1426, it is one of the most interesting examples of the Spanish Gothic style, remarkable for the clearcut elegance of its lines. Almost next door is an interesting Maritime Museum.

But Palma, though it is there if you want it, is not primarily a place for serious sightseeing. It is, however, emphatically a place to wander in, sit and enjoy a drink or a good seafood lunch or, especially, shop. The leatherwork of Majorca is excellent, as are the ceramics, glasswares, artificial pearls, woodcarvings and wrought ironwork. These are of the best quality and very reasonable.

There are numerous good bathing beaches strung along the nineteen kilometers of the Bay of Palma, but due to poor planning during the early boom days of tourism development a number of high-rise resorts of garish character and lack of any charm were allowed to grow. Other parts of the island provide a refreshing contrast to these awful commercial centers.

Excursions Around Majorca

For visitors with an urge to explore, Majorca lends itself to a number of half-day and full-day excursions, all of which can be made from Palma. The first of these takes you westward to Calamayor, Palma Nova, the superb beach at Paguera, Andraitx, Camp de Mar and

Puerto de Andraitx. This excursion can be combined, in a single day, with the second one, below.

The second itinerary takes a full day, northwest to Bañalbufar and Estallenchs for the best coastal scenery, then back to Valldemosa and on north through Deya to Sóller and Puerto de Sóller. You can return by a different route over a mountain pass to visit Alfabia, the Moorish gardens near Buñola. Total distance 121 kilometers (75 miles).

The third, also all day, heads northeast through Inca to Alcudia, then on to Formentor in the extreme northeast before returning via Pollensa, the monastery at Lluch and the spectacular coastal scenery around La Calobra. Total distance, 170 kilometers (100 miles).

The fourth turns east from Palma for Manacor, Porto Cristo and the fabulous Caves of Drach, Son Servera and the Caves of Artá, and back, at the end of the day, via Inca. Total distance, 193 kilometers (120 miles). This distance can be reduced by returning from Artá to Palma via Manacor.

A fifth excursion turns south through Lluchmayor (with a short detour to the mountain monastery of Randa), to Campos, Santañy, Cala d'Or and Cala Marsal. Total distance, 158 kilometers (98 miles).

These trips, of course, include only the highlights of Majorca. The island has any number of half-hidden little bays and romantic mountain villages that can be discovered only by settling down outside of Palma and exploring a particular region in detail. Despite its great and growing popularity, Majorca, fortunately, is just large enough for this kind of discovery still to be possible. One still undeveloped spot is Petra, 40 kilometers from Palma, with its Fray Junipero Serra, a museum-library honoring the founder of California's chain of Spanish missions. Next door is the house where Father Serra was born in 1713.

Although Majorca has few railway lines, these (with the exception of the one to Sóller) are not to be taken seriously by anyone except an antiquarian. Do your exploring by road, either on one of the excursion buses that visit most places of interest or, ideally, by hired car. If hiring a car, note that gas (petrol) stations are closed on Sundays and holidays and that use of seat belts is obligatory.

Palma West to Puerto de Andraitx

This excursion takes you through all the new holiday resorts from the fashionable Terreno at the west end of Palma Bay, to Bendinat, Calamayor, C'as Catalá, Illetas and Palma Nova, from where there is a rapid boat service direct to Palma every hour. This region, rich in pine forests, is full of historical associations, but much of it has been spoiled by touristic and property development.

Palma Nova and Magalluf are huge developments of hotels and apartment blocks, conjured out of thin air. There was absolutely nothing there about a decade ago except the hills sweeping down to the sand and the sea. It is the symbol of what modern Majorca is all about.

The road (locally known as the *camino de la muerte* owing to the large number of weekend motor accidents) crosses a broad headland to return to the sea at the great Paguera beach, Fornells, and, branching off to the right, Camp de Mar. This last has a particularly fine sandy beach, and from it, a wooden bridge heads to a tiny, rocky island. On the island is a café-bar-restaurant justly famous for its deliciously fresh lobsters and prawns. Back on the main road you will be four kilometers from the little agricultural town of Andraitx, and another four from Puerto de Andraitx, a picturesque little fishing village and, now, marina with a growing number of good hotels and restaurants. From here, once you are clear of the deep rocky bay, the coast is magnificent. From Puerto de Andraitx one can make a delightful six kilometer walk to the fishing village of San Telmo, where one can hire a boat to reach the island of Dragonera.

There is an alternative inland route home from Andraitx through Capdella and Calvia, through hilly country green with almond groves.

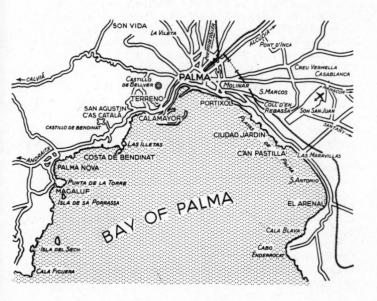

Palma North to Puerto de Sóller

Crossing the island at its narrowest point, the road from Palma winds north and slightly west for some twenty-seven kilometers (17 miles), twisting through orange groves and around mountains in such a way that you will need an hour to reach the sea and Bañalbufar. En route, you pass the fine old manor house of Son Forteza, near Esporlas, where there are some fine 18th-century mansions that once belonged to Spanish nobles. Esporlas itself, set picturesquely above the bed of a dry river, is famous for its especially lightweight woolen skirts, banded with bright color. Nearby, La Granja is an 18th-century farm with lovely gardens and restaurant which also presents folkdance shows and handicraft displays.

Bañalbufar is also attractive, though its wealth is not from tourists. The land is steeply terraced for the cultivation of a winter crop of potatoes and a summer crop of the strongest flavored tomatoes in all Spain, much in demand for use in ketchup.

Just beyond Bañalbufar you come to a ruined stone lookout tower, reached by a narrow stone bridge. This is known as the Tower of the Owls, and from it you can see the finest stretch of majestic coastal scenery anywhere in the Mediterranean. If you want to save yourself a twisting 18-kilometer ride south of Estallenchs to Andraitx, you can get a fair idea from here of what the remaining stretch is like, and then return eight kilometers to the crossroads for Valldemosa. However, if all the narrow twists and turns do not put you off, go on the exciting trip to the south as far as the belvedere of Ricardo Roca; the spectacular view is worth it.

Valldemosa

A great deal of sentimental nonsense has been written about Valldemosa (principally by German and French authors), because Chopin and George Sand spent a miserable winter here in 1838. This whole cult is false, chilly, and quite unmoving. True, the boom of the church clock can be recognized in Chopin's Prelude, Opus 28, No. 2, but the cells where the famous lovers stayed seem phoney today. The two pianos used by the great composer, together with the fresh white rose that is laid each morning on the keyboard, may be authentic, but George Sand's "silk" stockings are surely 20th-century nylon. Those who get a thrill from contemplating the scene of an illicit affair, even after more than a century, might recall that while the lovers stayed here, Chopin's consumption got worse, and the locals stoned George Sand until she gave up wearing trousers in public. At least the lovely little flower-filled garden outside Chopin's cell is genuine and charming, and so is the view down into the wooded valley. Valldemosa also boasts several aristocratic residences, and a Chopin Festival, held in August.

The scenery beyond Valldemosa grows more enchanting with every kilometer until you reach Deya, whose inhabitants still gather on the beach at the sound of a conch shell, the signal of the fishing fleet's return. Deya has long been the home of the British poet and novelist Robert Graves.

The coast beyond Deya is haunted by the late Archduke Salvador of Habsburg, who wrote an extremely influential six-volume work on the Balearics, and built himself two large houses here, high above the sea, together with a special carriage road leading to his private anchorage. The house "San Marroig", with the Archduke's paintings and personal possessions, is now open to the public. In winter concerts of Baroque music are held every Sunday at 5.30 P.M.

Sóller itself probably will not detain you for long, but it is only five kilometers to Puerto de Sóller, one of the few safe ports along the whole ninety-seven-kilometer length of the island's iron-bound northern coast. It is more than safe; it is almost closed off, so that you cannot see the open sea from the port, only the neat, circular bay itself, surrounded by the ubiquitous hotels. A delightful way to reach Sóller is by the little antique train which runs five times daily from Palma. In Sóller this connects with an equally antique tram to the Puerto.

By car you can return to Palma over a 610-meter (2,000-foot) pass, from which there is a fine view. As you descend, you will see the gnarled and twisted shapes of thousand-year-old olive trees, seeming to writhe as if in agony. You can make a pleasant stop in the lovely old Moorish gardens of Alfabia, or turn aside to the old town of Bunyola with its impressive Baroque church.

Or, alternatively, you can take the road that leads up the valley from Sóller to Fornalutx, a peaceful mountain village, and beyond to the Puig Mayor, at 1,440 meters the highest mountain on the island. This used to be a trip that could be done only on foot or donkey, but now the road curls right up to the top, giving breathtaking views back to the sea. Once over the top you can return to Palma via Inca.

Palma Northeast to Formentor

The journey from Palma through Inca to the north coast provides an excellent opportunity of getting to know the varied character of the landscape of Majorca. At the first town clear of Palma, Santa María, you can sample a glass of delightful anisette in a bodega full of local color and run by a Franciscan convent called Minimos.

Inca is an easy drive of 24 kilometers from Palma along the road to Alcudia, and can also be reached by daily train or bus from Palma. It is famous for its characterful market on Thursdays, its old shops, its folk dances, particularly those to be seen at Corpus Christi and on August 2, and for its 13th-century church of Santa María la Mayor—worth visiting, despite the defacing 18th-century additions. Most visitors stop off at the Cellar Ca'n Ripoll, where twelve vast and ancient olive-wood casks, each holding 4,000 liters of the excellent local wine, suggest Switzerland or Bavaria rather than Spain. The wine varies from the sweet muscatel to a dry red that tastes like a medium sherry. Try the roast suckling pig, or any other of the numerous delightful tasty tapas they have to offer. This region owes a good deal of its prosperity to the large shoe factories and to the leather industry in general.

Around Inca, the soil is so good and the water so plentiful that farmers can raise up to five crops a year from the same field. One result is that both men and women work seven days a week from dawn till dusk all the year round. Another is that they are relatively rich, which is hardly surprising. Everywhere the landscape is dotted with the typical Mallorquin windmills, used to draw up this precious water, although motor pumps have now mostly taken over the job.

Alcudia is some fifty-three kilometers from Palma, situated on the southern of the two lobster-like claws in the extreme northeast. It is an ancient town, site of a Phoenician settlement and later of the main Roman settlement on the island. It has a fine Roman theater and restored medieval walls and gates. Alcudia was the last stronghold of the Moors when Jaime the Conqueror landed in the west of the island. Its name means 'the hill' in Arabic. Its streets are most picturesque, but few stop to look at the old town, although its markets, held on Tuesday and Sunday mornings, attract many tourists in summer.

Puerto de Alcudia lies in the northern corner of the huge sweep of the Bay of Alcudia—thirty-two kilometers of almost white-sand unbroken beach, though the road swings inland at C'an Picafort less than halfway along. Inland, it is flat and swampy (there is an important migratory bird sanctuary here), but the number of appartment blocks and summer villas here has boomed. Smaller and less commercially developed, is the Bay of Pollensa, north of Alcudia. The bays of Alcudia and Pollensa are famous for sailing and windsurfing. Each has good marina facilities, hotels, restaurants, nightclubs and holiday apartments. Near C'an Picafort there is a good, but commercial, camping site.

Pollensa, Formentor and Lluch

Puerto de Pollensa has been a favorite vacation spot on the island for many years. The water here sparkles because there is nearly always a breeze, and thus it is seldom uncomfortably hot.

The ten-kilometer drive to Formentor, over a tawny-colored headland, is one of the most beautiful in the world, with glimpses of a romantic island set in a sea so blue as to seem impossible. Alternatively, motor-boats take passengers from Puerto de Pollensa to Formentor's superbly sheltered, pine-girt bathing beach, and bring them back for lunch. If you go to Formentor by road, and can spare the time, continue for thirteen kilometers to Cala Figuera and the lighthouse at Cabo Formentor, which is the island's wildly beautiful northeastern tip.

After returning to Puerto de Pollensa, take the road for Pollensa, but do not fail to turn off to the right (just before reaching the town) for five kilometers to Cala San Vicente with its delightful views and pleasant restaurants. Pollensa itself is an ancient little town, with a baroque church by a tree-shaded market square, narrow streets and fine old houses. There are splendid views from the Calvary (365 steps) and Puig, the hill facing Pollensa. After Pollensa, the road runs for eighteen kilometers through mountainous country to the attractive and ancient monastery of Lluch.

Lluch has both a strong personality all its own and a wonderful sense of timeless peace. The small image of the Virgin of Lluch, Majorca's patron saint, was found miraculously in 1208, and is the object of pilgrimages from all over the island. The surrounding countryside, with several strange triple crosses, or Calvarios, crowning the hills, is unforgettable.

If you have some extra time, drive the fourteen kilometers each way up the incredible corniche road to Calobra. The country is so wild here, on the lower slopes of 1,450-meter-high (4,756-foot) Puig Mayor, that you might be in the remotest Atlas Mountains, but if it is scenery you want (and your nerve and engine are to be relied upon) then you will not be disappointed. (This point can also be reached from Sóller.)

From Lluch, the road runs past the Sanctuary of Cristo Rey to Inca and thence back to Palma.

To the Caves of Drach

The straight run of fifty-one kilometers from Palma eastward to Manacor provides a good general impression of the rich agricultural central part of the island. Before Manacor, in Algaida, is an old hand-blown glass factory, Gordiola. Manacor is Majorca's second largest town and manufactures furniture and ceramics. Once there, you should not miss the great cultured pearl and gold filigree shop in the main square, the rectangular 15th-century parish church, or the 13th-century Torre del Palau, once part of a palace of the kings of Majorca.

The sea is only about nineteen kilometers further on at the delightful little resort of Porto Cristo, where there is an excellent bathing beach at the edge of the sheltered waters of the cala. Another kilometer brings you to the huge and famous Cuevas del Drach (Dragon Caves).

To describe adequately the nightmare splendors of this extraordinary freak of nature would be impossible. The weird stalactites and stalagmites are really extraordinary. After walking for a kilometer or so through tunnels, caves and grottoes, you reach a large underground lake, beside which seats are arranged for two thousand people in a natural auditorium. This is said to be the largest underground lake in Europe.

The lights go out, and after a breathless pause, a faintly illuminated boat, propelled by muffled oars and containing a small orchestra of stringed instruments playing terribly sugary classics, glides across the deep, totally still water. You can leave by boat across the lake (high in the roof you can see the roots of a tree straggling through from the surface) and then climb a long flight of stone steps, having spent nearly two hours underground. Although interesting, the caves are usually overcrowded with tourists, which can spoil the magic.

Eight kilometers north of Porto Cristo, the road forks to reach Cala Millor and the lovely beaches of Son Servera. Then, after an inland sweep to avoid an impassable headland, you reach the sea again, high above the exquisite beach of Cala Cañamel, to enter the Caves of Artá. While those of Drach were only rediscovered some 60 years ago (they were well known in ancient times), the Caves of Artá have been visited since the 18th century. They are more somber, as the rock is almost black, less fanciful, but "architecturally" even more impressive, giving you the impression of being inside a vast baroque cathedral. The Hall of the Flags, or Sala de las Banderas, is, for example, about 40 meters (130 feet) high.

Retracing your route six kilometers back, the road forks north to Capdepera, with its magnificent 14th-century castle, and Cala Ratjada, the island's easternmost point, where the sleepy little port has been turned into a topnotch resort. Indeed, so has a lot of this part of the coast. Now the amenities at Cala Millor and Cala Bona are catching up with the areas nearer to Palma. One of the main attractions has been the great sandy sweep of Artá Bay.

The way back to Inca, through olive, almond and pomegranate groves, is as varied and beautiful as any of the inland roads.

Palma to the Southeast

This excursion appeals to visitors seeking something off the beaten track. It runs along the little-known south coast of the island: Palma–Lluchmayor–Monastery of Randa–Lluchmayor–Campos–Santañy (where the railway ends)–Cala Figuera–Santañy–Alquero Blanco–Calonge–Cala D'Or–Calonge–Felanitx–Porreras–Lluchmayor–Palma; nearly 160 kilometers (100 miles) of alternately peaceful and majestic scenery.

At Lluchmayor, King Jaime III of Majorca was killed by Pedro IV of Aragón, the kingdom of Majorca then being permanently joined to the kingdom of Aragón (14th century). Randa, to the north of Lluchmayor, was where the celebrated theologian, philosopher and alchemist, Ramón Lull, lived and worked in the 13th century. He was the author of *Ars Major,* which explained "how to discover the truth."

None of the towns along this route—Lluchmayor, Santañy, Felanitx—has any remarkable sights to show, but they do have the essential feel of the island about them. The high spots are the superb bathing beaches and surroundings of Cala D'Or, Cala Santañy, Cala Marsal and a dozen others that pierce a stretch of not more than thirteen kilometers of coast, with Cala D'Or at the center.

A detour of six kilometers each way from Lluchmayor to the monastery of Randa is in order merely to obtain a view over the whole southwestern part of Majorca, and forty-eight kilometers away to the little island of Cabrera, a view you will not readily forget.

Minorca

Although Minorca is second in size among the Balearic Islands—roughly fifty kilometers long by twenty wide, with a shoreline of over 200 kilometers—it possesses a much more temperate climate than any of the other islands, and so is greener than Ibiza or parts of Majorca. Besides frequent ships from Barcelona and Palma, there are frequent daily scheduled air services, complemented by direct charter flights from England. The excellent main road runs like a backbone for 45 kilometers from the capital, Port Mahón in the southeast, to the former capital of Ciudadela in the northwest.

There is another good road about halfway across the island, which runs north from this main lateral road, from Mercadal, for eight kilometers to the port of Fornells. For the rest, if you wish to explore the extremely lovely coastline, with its many splendid beaches, there are roads which run off the main highway, and lead down to the sea. They are not the best in the world, but adequate. By and large, exploration is more fun by boat than by car. This is rather difficult to arrange, but is well worth the effort.

The Minorcans tend to have a more relaxed attitude to life than the Majorcans and have been less tempted by the riches offered by mass tourism. Local industries are leathercraft and the making of world famous costume jewellery, in addition to agriculture, which covers a greater proportion of the island than in Majorca. A faint echo of the British period can be caught in the two gin distilleries and a small-scale industry in the making of reproduction furniture. The British flavor of the 18th-century architecture has by now been almost completely mellowed by the local influence. The island has charm and a distinctly different flavor to the other Balearic islands. It offers, increasingly, new hotels, good restaurants and varied nightlife encouraged by tourism, but still operates at a gentler pace.

Some History

All over the island, you will come across prehistoric dolmens, taulas or talayots, rock- and earth-works, believed to have been erected some 4,000 years ago, that at Talati resembling a miniature Stonehenge. Phoenicians, Greeks, Carthaginians (these last led by Hannibal's brother Magon) preceded the Romans, who conquered the island in 122 B.C. and named the capital Portus Magonis, and all left something of their cultural heritage. The Fine Arts Museum has a finely displayed collection of coins, ceramics, glass and statuary in a huge 18th-century building in Port Mahón.

The Vandals, Byzantines (under Belisarius), Moors and, briefly, Catalans, obtained possession, until it was unified under the independent Kingdom of Majorca in the 14th century. It was not until Ferdinand and Isabella that Minorca became part of Spain, late in the 15th century.

Barbarossa, the Turkish pirate (or admiral, according to whether you are reading Christian or Turkish history), sacked both Mahón and Ciudadela in 1558, and the island was seized by the British fleet in 1708. This was confirmed by the Treaty of Utrecht in 1713. The French ousted the British in 1756 for seven years and a Franco-Spanish force did so again in 1782, this time for 16 years. Nelson occupied it for four years until Britain finally left after the Treaty of Amiens in 1802.

The British influence is noticeable in their fortress city of Georgetown, now called Villa-Carlos, at the entrance to the great harbor, where the windows are of the horizontal sash type unknown elsewhere in Spain, where the French window is universal.

Fishing is wonderful round Minorca, and the inhabitants are proud of having invented mayonnaise sauce to go with it.

Minorca's Different Colors

Minorca as a whole is most strangely unlike Majorca, lacking much of the latter's golden-beige of the old, and blue-and-white of the new, buildings. Here the predominant colors are white, green and terra-cotta, from the walls, shutters and roofs of the houses. You cannot fail to be struck by the sense of unassailable calm, combined with a faint trace of 18th-century English dignity, both softened by a purely southern grace.

The superb natural harbor leading to Mahón is hardly equaled in size by any other Mediterranean port, and it is completely sheltered. Because of the harbor's excellence, in fact, naval officers of the newly born United States of America trained here from 1802 until 1845, when the Naval Academy in Annapolis was opened!

During their long occupation the British spent a million pounds on fortifying the entrance to the harbor, and even constructed a secret underground passage between San Felipe and Fort Marlborough, which it may interest the historically minded to inspect. The Golden Farm on the north side of the harbor was the home of Nelson during his brief stay on the island.

There is more of historic interest to see in the former Moorish capital of Ciudadela than in Port Mahón, including several very fine 17th-century palaces (notably those of the Marqués de Menas Albas and the Count of Saura), and a 14th-century cathedral, while the fine old town hall and the churches of San Agostino, San Francisco and Nuestra Señora del Rosario all add an enchantingly medieval atmosphere to the little town. Down by the port, a number of picturesque harbor-side restaurants cater to the yachtsmen and summer tourists.

If you turn off the Mahón-Ciudadela road at Ferrerías and drive 8 kilometers south you come to the small resort of Santa Galdana where two large hotels now cater to tourists. Once a delightful cove with calm waters and a good sandy beach surrounded by a pinewood, this is one of the few places in Minorca to have suffered at the hands of the developers. Although the setting still retains some charm, the water is now polluted and unpleasant odors waft over the crowded beach.

Santo Tomás a few kilometers down the coast offers much better bathing with a clean sea and fine sandy beach. But probably the best bathing beach on Minorca is that of Son Bou reached by a good stretch of road from Alayor. The water here is clean and excellent for swimming or wind-surfing and acres of fine sand stretch away into the distance. Although popular, it is never too crowded.

Other readily accessible beaches include Cala Mezquida, five kilometers from Port Mahón, and Cala de Alcaufar, Es Grau, Arenal d'En

Castell, Punta Prima and Cala'n Porter, all within twenty-four kilometers of Mahón.

Minorca's highest hill is 360-meter (1,180-foot) Mount Toro, from which, on a clear day, you can see almost the entire outline of the island. At the top, which can be reached by car, is a charming old monastery and a huge, open-air statue of Christ. In Minorca there is less opportunity than in Majorca for those who are in search of excitement, but the island does offer more than adequate comfort, a gentle beauty and a deep sense of peace.

Ibiza

The smallest and most southern of the Balearic Big Three is about thirty-five kilometers long by twenty-six wide. It still preserves some of the pine forests for which the Greeks called it *Pitiousa,* the Pine Island, but now blended with almond, olive and fig groves, even occasional palms; the sun seems to burn more fiercely from an almost-always cloudless sky.

The hordes of antiquity had more than a nodding acquaintance with the island of Ibiza; Phoenicians, Romans, Byzantines, Moors and, finally, the soldiers of Aragon and Spain, all were on the premises at one time or another. Each succeeding occupant bequeathed a new name to the island, and yet we are not at all surprised to discover how these different names resemble one another: Aivis, Ebysos, Ebusus, Yebisah, Ibiza . . . the island derives its own distinctive personality from the subtle blending of these sundry civilizations. Over a long span of centuries, up until quite recent times, visitors to Ibiza were few and far between, and hence the island preserved its customs and traditions intact. The busy airport has put an end to this isolation, Ibiza being less than half an hour's flying time from Valencia, barely an hour from Barcelona, twenty minutes from Palma.

The island has 45,000 inhabitants (only 5,000 less than in far larger Minorca), of whom almost 19,000 live in the capital, locally known as La Ciudad—the city. The island's highest point is 472-meter (1,550-foot) Atalaya de San José, and it is generally far more hilly than placid Minorca.

The City

The city rises steeply from the water's edge, blindingly white, fascinatingly uneven as to roof levels, its walls splashed everywhere with the violent scarlet of geranium, carnation or purple bougainvillaea. This, you will feel at once, is what people who have never been there mean when they talk longingly of the perfect Mediterranean, escapist island.

A dazzling genuine medieval fortress crowns the city's heights—this is the D'Alt Vila, or upper town, built up and added to by Charles V and Philip II. The lower town, nestling snugly below, is a spread of cubic buildings shining forth in all their whitewashed intensity. Only three entrance-gates give access to the upper town, which is enclosed by ramparts. Choose the best-preserved of these gateways, the Portal de las Tablas, which you can reach from the Plaza del Mercado. Two Roman statues, which were excavated during the building of the walls, placed in niches, guard the passage on both sides.

The D'Alt Vila abounds in natural observation points, the largest of which is Cathedral Square, where you will also find the castle and the Bishops' Palace. Many budding young artists have studios in the fine old residences, most of which have been restored here and there. The D'Alt Vila is also where the city's best restaurants are located. Some have tables placed outdoors on the quaint, cobblestone streets and squares. The port area is rather more tawdry. There are some cheap hole-in-the-wall eateries and bars, and a few cheap hotels. All better hotels are out of town at the beaches. Try to visit the Museo Puig des Molins which contains a unique collection of Phoenician artifacts recovered from excavations of the necropolis of Ereso. After browsing through the tourist shops here, you'll likely head back to the D'Alt Vila or to nearby Figueretas.

The Rest of the Island

The only towns beside the city are Santa Eulalia del Rio and San Antonio Abad. The latter is now the island's most important tourist center, due to its burgeoning hotels, pleasant esplanade and numerous bars, restaurants and discos. San Juan Bautista lies five kilometers inland from the up-and-coming little resort of Portinaitx del Rey in the extreme north. Buses (there is no railway) link them together and all distances are short, so there is little need to hire a car for traveling between the towns. However it is worthwhile for exploring the more remote spots in the northeast and southwest of the island. These can also be reached by sea, which can be arranged inexpensively by local travel agencies.

Ibiza's coast is cliff-like for the most part, but deeply penetrated by calas, or inlets, where the water is marvelously calm, and at the head of which there is usually a sandy beach circled by pine trees. Some of the best of these calas are just north of Santa Eulalia, notably Playa dés Caná, Cala Nova, Cala Llena and Cala Mestilla. All are perfect for diving and underwater fishing. Just north of San Antonio is Cala

Grassio and, west of it, is the delicious Cala Bassa, from which you can see the sizable, but now uninhabited, island of Conejera.

Anyone with archeological interests should not fail to visit the extraordinary necropolis of Ereso, which you will find at a nearby spot called Puig des Molins, by going through Portal Nou. Santa Eulalia del Río was founded in about 700 B.C. by the Carthaginians, and its triple fortifications were familiar to the earliest voyagers. Its principal sight is the extraordinary African kraal-shaped church.

The road to the salt marshes (Las Salinas), on the southern part of the island, passes through San Jorge: the church here and the one in the picturesque village of San José are Ibiza's two most delightfully typical churches, definitely among the sights to be seen. After following the beaches of En-Bossa, you reach the marshes, which were worked by the early Carthaginians, who also exploited salt mines on Formentera. It's quite a show to see the salt being extracted and loaded onto the narrow-gauge industrial railway.

Codolar beach, to the west of southernmost La Canal, and not far from the airport, provides ample stretches of unrationed sand.

Cave paintings and ceramic objects believed to date from 1800 B.C. indicate that the island itself has been inhabited since the dawn of civilized time. But for most visitors, Ibiza is less an exercise in sightseeing than an adventure in sea, sun and underwater mysteries.

Formentera

Every day, large motor-boats chug out of Ibiza harbor and make the eighteen-kilometer crossing to Formentera in an hour or so. The route lies through a straggle of uninhabited islands, and you will probably be convoyed all the way by a school of porpoises and flying fish.

Looking westward, you will glimpse the incredibly romantic island of Vedrá, rising for 366 meters (1,200 feet) sheer from the water. Its only inhabitants are blue lizards.

Once among the salt pans of Formentera's only port, Cala Savina, an old bus makes it up the five sloping kilometers to the "capital" of San Francisco Xavier. There is not much trace of 20th-century technology in all Formentera's sixteen kilometers of length by two-and-a-half width, but there are several good hotels and some spotlessly clean pensions where you need spend only a reasonable amount of pesetas a day, and that will include plenty of the excellent local wine.

The island is really two highish peaks linked by an eight-kilometer-long, narrow, low-lying waist, on both sides of which are unbroken and untouched sweeps of beach. The smaller, higher, eastern knob, known as La Mola (192 meters, 630 feet), has plentiful water and, as a result, grazing for the cows that produce the exquisite Formentera cheeses.

Here also grow the grapes famous since Roman times. The hilltops are sprinkled with busy windmills, grinding the rich corn that covers the whole island in the spring.

PRACTICAL INFORMATION FOR THE BALEARIC ISLANDS

HOW TO GO. Most European capitals are connected by air to Palma, capital of Majorca. *British Airtours* have inclusive holiday flights from various British airports to Palma, Ibiza and Minorca. *Iberia* also has daily flights between London (Heathrow) and Palma, and several flights weekly from London to Mahón, on Minorca, and to Ibiza. All British travel agents have budget charter flights, and Iberia and *British Airways* offer special excursion fares. Financial savings are especially worthwhile with charter flights from Gatwick or Luton during the slacker seasons. Flight time from London to Palma is 2 hours.

Iberia flies from New York, Miami and Los Angeles to Madrid, you can then connect for Palma in less than an hour. It also maintains regular services between Spanish mainland cities and the Balearics. From Barcelona or Valencia it takes about 35 minutes to reach Palma.

Iberia has services from Marseille and from Nice to Palma and operates flights between the islands. All air services are crowded during the Christmas, Easter and summer seasons and reservations should be made well in advance.

From the airport into Palma you can take either a taxi (about 800 ptas.) or the public bus service which operates half-hourly to the city center. A taxi to the main nearby resort of Arenal will cost around 500 ptas., to a northern resort, such as Pollensa, about 4,000 ptas.

To reach the islands by boat, *Compañia Trasmediterránea* have the following passenger and car ferry services to Palma: daily from Barcelona (8 hrs); from Valencia daily (11 hrs); from Alicante thrice weekly (13 hrs). It also links Palma and Ibiza (4 hrs), and Barcelona-Port Mahón (Minorca), both thrice weekly. There is also a car ferry link between Sete, in southern France, and Minorca, during the summer only. If traveling with a car, note that embarcation and booking conditions in Barcelona port can be chaotic, so reserve well ahead and arrive early to claim your place. Ferries are often full during high, summer season.

HOW TO GET ABOUT MAJORCA. There are several daily bus services between the various resorts throughout the island and the capital, Palma, which make a whole day excursion cheap and easy.

There is a delightfully old-fashioned train that goes through the mountains to Sóller. Another line goes a long way around from Palma to Inca.

Car hire is from: *Atesa,* Antonio Ribas 33, *Avis* and *Hertz,* both on Paseo Marítimo at nos. 16 and 13, *Ital,* Avda Conde de Sallent 13, all in Palma. Or from any of the hundreds of other firms all over the island. Avis, Hertz and Europcar have booths at the airport and it is usually not necessary to book in advance. One can pay by credit card. It is also possible to hire motorscooters and bicycles.

Sightseeing coaches, run by reliable travel agencies such as *Iberia, Marsans, Melía* etc., pick you up at your hotel and take you to Valldemossa Monastery, Formentor and Pollensa, the caves of Artá and Drach, Sóller, etc. There are also a number of boat tours out of such places as Palma or Alcudia.

The other islands. Transportation here is simply a question of car, bus, taxi, bicycle, donkey or your own two feet. All the important roads are good; but away from the few highroads, the road surfaces can be diabolical, with the danger from potholes exacerbated by wandering troops of sheep, goats and peasants. It's wise to try to find out if what looks like a road might not turn into a cart-track just over the hill.

You can rent cars in all the main towns. In Ciudadela, Menorca, *Avis* are in Conquistador 81 and *Hertz* at Calvo Sotelo 42. In Mahon, Menorca, *Avis* are at the airport; *Hertz* at Vassallo 14. In Ibiza, *Avis* and *Hertz* are both at the airport; *Atesa* at Canarias 6.

 HOTELS. Many of the Balearic hotels, especially on the smaller islands and in the less developed resorts, are only open from April through October and tend to be *very* full during the high summer season, July and August. Be sure to check first if you are planning a winter break. Many of the larger modern hotels deal mainly with package-tour groups; they often have their own discos and provide entertainments and sporting facilities. Most of the hotels have their own dining rooms and many holiday-makers eat in their hotels rather than in restaurants, which is a pity as there are excellent restaurants of many styles and price levels on the island. We have recommended specific restaurants where we know them to be worthwhile, but exploring on one's own can result in some excellent alternatives. Try the characterful local cuisine: grilled meats, pork, lamb and rabbit, also seafood.

Hotel prices in the Balearics tend to be cheaper than mainland cities, but similar to mainland resorts. To telephone any of our hotels from outside the Balearics, the area dialing code is (971). Within the islands, just dial the number.

FORMENTERA

A tiny rather plain island with good beaches, but there is not much to see or do. In recent years the island has become a haven for topless—and bottomless—sun worshippers.

SAN FRANCISCO JAVIER. *La Mola* (E), on Mitjorn beach, tel. 32 00 50. Large hotel in very peaceful surroundings, with view of sea, tennis, pool. *Formentera Playa* (M), on Mitjorn beach, tel. 32 00 00. *Sa Volta* (M), near Es Pujols beach, tel. 32 01 20. 18 rooms. *Italia* (I), Playa Mitjorn.

SAN FERNANDO. *Rocabella* (M), on Es Pujols beach, tel. 32 01 85. 40 rooms, good in its category.

IBIZA

A pleasant small island good for beach holidays. Ibiza town is colorful and worth a visit, but otherwise there is not a lot to see. If you want a quiet, restful holiday, avoid the overdeveloped resort of San Antonio Abad. For peace and quiet, the best places are probably San Miguel and Portinatx in the north of the island.

IBIZA. *El Corsario* (M), Poniente 5, tel. 30 12 48. 14 rooms in an interesting old building, perched atop the D'Alt Vila; pleasant accommodations and superb views.

At **Figueretas Beach,** 1.5 km away: *Los Molinos* (E), Muntaner 60, tel. 30 22 50. 147 rooms, pool. *Ibiza Playa* (M), by the beach, tel. 30 28 04. 124 rooms, pool, gardens, and a good view of the sea. *Cenit* (I), Archiduque Luis Salvador, tel. 30 14 04. 62 rooms, good views and quiet situation.

At **Playa d'En Bossa:** *Torre del Mar* (E), tel. 30 30 50. 217 rooms, modern, with nightclub and other amenities. *Algarb* (M), tel. 30 17 16. 408 rooms, pool. *Goleta* (M), tel. 30 21 58. 252 rooms, pool, gardens and nightclub. *Tres Carabelas* (M), tel. 30 24 16. 245 rooms, pool, gardens and nightclub.

At **Talamanca beach:** *Playa Real* (E-M), tel. 30 09 00. 237 rooms, pool and mini golf. *Argos* (M), tel. 30 10 62. 106 rooms, pool, gardens and good views.

Restaurants. *L'Altrium* (E-M). Recommended. *Celler Balear* (M), Avda. Ignacio Wallis, tel. 30 10 31. Opposite the San Antonio bus stop, local décor, good for fish and seafood; try the *zarzuela de mariscos* or the *rape marinera. El Vesubio* (M), Navarra 19, tel. 30 00 26. A good Galician restaurant at Figueretas beach.

PORTINATX. Excellent though crowded beach on the northern coast set among pinewood hills. *El Greco* (M), tel. 33 30 48. 242 rooms, pool, a package hotel. *Presidente Playa* (M), tel. 33 30 14. 270 rooms, pool, the other package hotel here. *Cigüeña Playa* (M-I), Cala Portinatx, tel. 33 30 44. 84 rooms, simple, pool and garden, and right on the beach. *Oasis* (M), on the beach, tel. 33 30 70. 38 rooms, simple hostel. *Portinatx* (I), Playa de Portinatx, tel. 33 30 43.

SAN AGUSTÍN. *Bergantín* (M), on S'Estanyol beach, tel. 34 09 50. 155 rooms, pool. *Elsa* (I), Ses Fontanelles, hostel. *Els Pins* (I), Cala de Bou, tel. 34 05 50. 170 rooms, pool, tennis, garden. *Riviera* (M), Bahía de San Antonio, tel. 34 08 12. 168 rooms, pool and garden.

SAN ANTONIO ABAD. Unattractive and brash resort, with dirty sea and poor beaches, though there is plenty of transport to better beaches nearby. Lively nightlife and full of souvenir shops. *Nautilus* (E), Punta Pinet, tel. 34 04 00. Excellent hotel with 168 rooms and pool. *Palmyra* (E), Dr. Fleming, tel. 34 03 54. 120 rooms, pool and gardens, on the beach.

There are many 3-star hotels, some moderate ones are: *Arenal* (M), Dr. Fleming, tel. 34 01 12. 131 rooms, pool, tennis and garden. *Gran Sol* (M), Es Calo des Moro, tel. 34 11 08. 138 rooms and pool. *Hawaii* (M), Isaac Peral, tel. 34 05 62. 210 rooms, pool and garden. *Ses Sevines* (M), Playa San Antonio, tel. 34 00 66. 133 rooms, tennis, garden. *Tanit* (M), Cala Gracio, tel. 34 13 00. 386 rooms, 2 restaurants. Some rooms are (I). *Hostel Maricel* (I), Avda. Dr. Fleming, tel. 34 09 77.

Restaurants. A very good range available, mostly serving international menus. *El Yate* (E), Paseo Marítimo 22, tel. 34 00 99. Near the port, with rustic décor. *Celler El Refugio* (M), Bartolomé Vicente Ramón 5, tel. 34 01 29. An atmospheric restaurant. *S'Olivar* (M), San Mateo 9, tel. 34 00 10. Pleasant, with a garden, serving Spanish dishes.

SANTA EULALIA DEL RIO. A sizeable resort and a pleasant town, but the local beaches are not too good. There are ferries to better beaches nearby. *Fenicia* (E), Ca'n Fita, tel. 33 01 01. 191 rooms, just across the river from the town, with pool, tennis, garden and nightclub. *La Cala* (M), San Jaime 76, tel. 33 00 09. 74 rooms, pool and garden, with a matchless view. *Los Loros* (M), Ses Estaques, tel. 33 08 61. 262 rooms, in lovely quiet setting, with pool and garden. *Miami* (M), Playa Es Cana, tel. 33 02 01. 370 rooms, pool, garden, nightclub. *Tres Torres* (M), Ses Estaques, tel. 33 03 26. 112 rooms, pool and nightclub. *S'Argamasa* (M), Urb. S'Argamasa, tel. 33 00 51. 159 rooms, pool, tennis, garden. Located 10 km north of town in a peaceful location, with private beach.

Restaurants. The following are all recommended and good value: *El Naranjo* (M), *La Posada* (M), and *The Owl and the Pussycat* (M).

SAN VICENTE. At north end of island. *Hacienda Na Xamena* (E), Hacienda, tel. 33 30 46. 54 rooms, with pool and nightclub. A very good hotel but the rates are extremely high, above those of many luxury hotels. *Imperio Playa* (M), Cala San Vicente, tel. 33 30 55. 210 rooms, pool, nightclub.

MAJORCA

There is more to see and explore on Majorca than on any other of the Balearic islands, and there are plenty of good beaches and many activities both for day and nighttime. It also offers fine, varied scenery around the coasts and in the hills and farmlands of the interior.

EL ARENAL. A noisy, brash package resort just to the east of Palma. There is a good sandy beach but the town is unpleasant and untypical except of the worst kind of resort. Discos, souvenir shops and snack bars abound. All in all, the town is best avoided in the height of the season, though it might be all right in winter when there are fewer bodies steaming on the beach, and fewer holiday-makers drinking themselves into a two-week stupor. It does, however, have all the facilities for a good family holiday, if small children are involved, with a good safe beach and various entertainments. There is an openair market, with folk dances, every Tuesday and Saturday.

Garonda Palace (E), Avda. Nacional, tel. 26 22 00. About 6 km from Palma, 110 rooms, pool. *Playa de Palma-Sol* (E-M), Ctra. Arenal 11, tel. 26 29 00. 113 rooms, pool, garden. *Acapulco* (M), Ctra. Arenal 11, tel. 26 18 00. In historic building, by beach, pool, garden, nightclub. *Riviera* (M), Polígono 94, tel. 26 06 00. 74 rooms, pool, near beach. *Copacabana* (I), Berlín 65, tel. 26 04 12. 112 rooms, set in a garden with pines, a little way from the sea. Pool and tennis. *Hostel Royal* (I), San Bartolome 3, tel. 26 36 47.

BAÑALBUFAR. This village is 26 km northwest of Palma near some of the most beautiful coastal scenery in all Majorca. *Mar y Vent* (M), José Antonio 49, tel. 61 00 25. A 3-star hostel with 15 rooms and pool.

CA'N PASTILLA. A very noisy resort, 6 km from busy Palma airport; has very crowded summertime beach. *Alexandra-Sol* (E), Avda. de los Pinos 73, tel. 26 23 50. 156 rooms, pool, garden and nightclub. *Linda* (M), Torre Redonda, tel. 26 29 90. 189 rooms, pool, tennis and mini golf. *Gran Hotel El Cid* (I), Ctra. El Arenal, tel. 26 08 50. 216 rooms, pool, mini golf, tennis.

CA'N PICAFORT. An ugly resort town on the northern coast, full of concrete hotels, souvenir shops and snack bars, but there is a good long sandy beach. *Granero* (M), Via Diagonal, tel. 52 71 25. 211 rooms and good facilities. *Gran Vista* (M), Ctra. Artá-Alcudia, tel. 52 73 46. 277 rooms, 2 pools, mini golf, garden, nightclub and huge recreational area. *Exagón* (M), Ronda de la Plata, tel. 52 70 76. 285 rooms, pool, tennis, mini golf, nightclub. *Tonga* (M), Ctra. Artá-Alcudia, tel. 52 70 00. 322 rooms, pool, mini golf, garden and nightclub. One redeeming feature for the resort is its horse-riding facilities, with good cross-country excursions being available.

CALA BONA. Once an unspoilt fishing village but now overwhelmed by neighboring Cala Millor. Mixed rocky and excellent sandy beach. *Gran Sol* (M), Francisco Oliver Nabot, tel. 56 72 75. 58 rooms, near beach, pool, mini golf, tennis, garden. *Levante* (I), Calabona, tel. 56 71 75. 137 rooms, pool, garden, nightclub.

CALA D'OR. 70 km from Palma on the east coast, this is a pleasant resort with an attractive indented coastline and sandy beach, good bistros, cosmopolitan atmosphere and worthwhile horse-riding. *Cala Esmeralda* (E), Urb. Cala Esmeralda, tel. 65 71 56. 151 rooms, pool and garden. *Gran Hotel Tucán* (E), Bulevard, tel. 65 72 25. 155 rooms. *Cala Gran* (M), on the beach, tel. 65 71 00. 72 rooms, pool and garden. *Rocador* (M), Marqués de Comillas, tel. 65 70 76.

95 rooms, near beach, garden. *Rocamarina* (M), Urb. Es Forti, tel. 65 78 32. 207 rooms, with pool and garden. *Cala d'Or* (I), Avda Bélgica, tel. 65 72 49. 27 rooms and garden, above a pretty bay. *Corfu* (I), Urb. Cala Egos, tel. 65 76 00. 214 rooms, garden and nightclub. A 3-star hotel with low rates. *Skorpios Playa* (I), Polígono 27, tel. 65 71 51. 163 rooms, pool and garden.

CALA FORNELLS. A beautiful small bay with bathing from rocks, 25 km from Palma, on the west coast close to Andraitx. *Coronado* (E), on the beach, tel. 68 68 00. 110 rooms, garden. *Cala Fornells* (M), tel. 68 69 50. 85 rooms.

CALA MAYOR. Just east of Palma. *Nixe Palace* (L), Calvo Sotelo 269, tel. 40 38 11. A five-star hotel with 132 rooms. In historic building with pool and nightclub. *Santa Ana* (E), Gaviota 9, tel. 40 15 12. 190 rooms, pool.

CALA MILLOR. A big purpose-built resort with a large sandy beach and good hotels, situated between the Caves of Drach and those of Artá, not far from Son Servera. *Borneo* (E-M), Urb. El Dorado, tel. 56 70 51. 200 rooms, pool, mini golf, on the beach. *Flamenco* (E-M), San Lorenzo, tel. 56 73 01. 220 rooms, on the beach. *Playa Cala Millor* (E-M), Urb. Sa Manica, tel. 56 70 75. 242 rooms, pool and garden, by the beach. *Biniamar* (M-I), Urb. Son Moro, tel. 56 78 51. 108 rooms. *Don Juan* (M-I), on the beach, tel. 56 73 00. 134 rooms, pool and tennis. *Osiris* (M-I), Wa Penal, tel. 56 73 25. 213 rooms, by the beach, pool and garden. *Alicia* (I), on road between Cala Millor and Cala Bona, tel. 56 77 01. 166 rooms, mini golf and garden.

CALA MOREYA. Pleasant small beach. *Colombo* (M), tel. 57 09 49, medium size. *Playa Moreya* (I), tel. 57 01 00. 257 rooms, pool, garden.

CALA MURADA. Good beach and located near the picturesque villages of Porto Colon and Porto Cristo on the east coast. *Cala Murada* (M), tel. 57 31 00. 77 rooms, tennis and garden; 5 mins. from sandy beach in this well planned villa development. *Valparaiso* (M-I), Solar F, tel. 57 30 55.

CALA RATJADA. In the extreme northeast, with an easy access to picturesque Capdepera with its castle, and to the caves of Arta. Fairly pleasant resort with 2 beaches and attractive harbor. *Aguait* (M), Avda. de los Pinos, tel. 56 34 08. 188 rooms, pool, garden and rocky bathing. *Serrano* (M), Son Moll, tel. 56 33 50. 46 rooms, pool, and an Andalusian-style wine cellar. *Son Moll* (M), Tritón, tel. 56 31 00. 118 rooms, garden, by beach. *Bella Playa* (I), Cala Guya, tel. 56 30 50. 143 rooms, pool, garden and spacious lounge. 4-min. walk to sandy beach. *Cala Gut* (I), Ctra. del Faro, tel. 56 31 66. 44 rooms, pool and garden. Peacefully surrounded by pines, near a rocky beach.

Restaurant. *Ses Rotges* (M), Alsedo, tel. 56 31 08. French cuisine with rustic décor.

CALA SANTAÑY. Picturesque and peaceful, popular with the locals. *Pinos Playa* (M), Costa D'En Nofre, tel. 65 39 00. 98 rooms. Very good bathing from fine sandy beach.

CALA SAN VICENTE. A small resort on the rugged northwest coast. There are two pretty coves, bathing is from rocky beaches but there are underwater currents. *Molins* (M), on the beach, tel. 53 02 00. 90 rooms, with tennis and garden. Well located with good cuisine and good amenities. *Cala San Vicente* (I), Capitán Jergens, tel. 53 02 50. 44 rooms, tennis and garden. *Don Pedro* (I), on the beach, tel. 53 00 50. The largest hotel here, garden. *Simar* (I), Capitán Jergens, tel. 53 03 00. 107 rooms, pool and nightclub.
Restaurants. For good seafood, the *C'al Patro* (M) and *Vora-Mar*.

CALAS DE MALLORCA. A badly planned urban development on a rocky head amid scrub land, with possibly the tiniest beach in Majorca. Many of the hotels are some way from the "beach." *Los Chihuahuas* (E), Cala Antena, tel. 57 32 50. 216 rooms, pool, tennis, bowling, nightclub and many other amenities. *Los Mastines* (E), Cala Antena, tel. 57 31 25, 260 rooms, pool, tennis, mini golf, nightclub. *Los Canarios* (M), tel. 57 32 00. 215 rooms, pool and garden. *Balmoral* (I), tel. 57 31 02. 102 rooms, pool, garden, mini golf, nightclub. *Samoa* (I), tel. 57 30 00. 331 rooms, pool, tennis, mini golf, bowling and nightclub.

LA CALOBRA. A beautiful spot in the north of the island; can be reached most easily by boat from Puerto Soller. *La Calobra* (M), on the beach, tel. 51 70 16. 55 rooms, garden.

CAMP DE MAR. Small resort 3 km from Andraitx and 26 km from Palma. There is a small sandy beach surrounded by pinewoods. *Lido* (M), tel. 67 11 00. 116 rooms, garden, by the beach. *Playa* (M), tel. 67 10 25. 239 rooms, pool, garden and nightclub. *Villa Real* (M), Ctra. del Puerto, tel. 67 10 50. 52 rooms, by the beach.

CANYAMEL. Charming resort, free from usual commercialization; excellent beach; near town of Capdepere in east of the island. *Playa de Canyamel* (M), 112 rooms and good amenities. *Caballito Blanco* (I), tel. 56 38 50. 90 rooms. The *Torre de Canyamel* is an interesting restaurant in a 12th-cent. tower, Mallorcan specialties.

COSTA DE LOS PINOS. A small and stylish villa development with just one hotel. Small narrow beach surrounded by pinewoods and orchards. *Eurotel Golf Punta Roja* (E), tel. 56 76 00. 240 rooms, with extensive sports facilities including a 9-hole golf course.

DEYA. Small village on hilltop surrounded by mountains, about 32 km north of Palma. A famous artist center. Sea bathing is from rocks a few km away. *Es*

Moli (E), tel. 63 90 00. 77 rooms, pool, in delightful grounds with beautiful views. Excellent food. *Costa D'Or* (I), Lluch Alcari, tel. 63 90 25. Very cheap but delightful. A villa set amongst pines and olives, with 41 rooms, and tennis court. *Can Oliver* and *Can Quet* are (I) reasonable pensions.

FELANITX. Village in the interior to the east of the island, pleasant center for touring. *Robinson Club Cala Serena* (E), tel. 65 78 00. 210 rooms, on beach, with pool and nightclub. *Ponent* (M), on Cala Ferrera beach, tel. 65 72 34. 104 rooms, pool. *Tamarix* (I), Cala Ferrera, tel. 65 78 51. 40 rooms, garden.

FORMENTOR. Almost at the northeast tip of Majorca, 68 km from Palma, a long rugged peninsular with a long narrow sandy beach. *Formentor* (L), tel. 53 13 00. A luxury hotel wonderfully located among exquisite gardens, with magnificent views of sea and mountains plus one of the most attractive beaches in the Mediterranean. 131 rooms, mini golf, tennis. Excellent restaurant.

ILLETAS. About 8 km west of Palma, with excellent views of the bay but a very limited beach. *Mar-Sol* (L), tel. 40 25 11. Deluxe hotel with 136 rooms and all amenities. Kosher food available. *Bon Sol* (E), Po Adelfas 8, tel. 40 20 00. Good views and genuine Spanish décor. 73 rooms, pool, tennis, mini golf, garden. *Bonanza* (E), Po Adelfas, tel. 40 11 12. 138 rooms, pool, golf and tennis. *Illetas* (M), tel. 23 35 45. 67 rooms, pool, garden. Built on a series of rock terraces above the sea, good food.

INCA. Majorca's second-largest town, a center for the leather industry but uninteresting for sightseeing. No worthwhile hotel. **Restaurant.** *Celler Ca'n Amer* (M), Miguel Durán 39, tel. 50 12 61. One of Spain's most famous restaurants, set in an attractive wine cellar. Try the succulent roast suckling pig.

MAGALLUF. Synthetic high-rise resort of little merit, on Palma bay, 18 km west of Palma. *Atlantic* (E), Po Ballena, tel. 68 02 08. 80 rooms, by the beach and surrounded by palm trees. *Barbados-Sol* (E), Notario Alemany, tel. 68 05 50. Enormous hotel with pool, tennis, mini golf and nightclub. *Meliá Magalluf* (E), Notario Alemany, tel. 68 10 50. 242 rooms, pool and garden. *El Caribe* (M), on the beach, tel. 68 08 08. 53 rooms, garden. Pleasantly traditional for the area.

PAGUERA. Large resort 24 km west of Palma, with reasonable beach and some older buildings amongst the usual concrete blocks. *Villamil* (E), Ctra. Andraitx, tel. 68 60 50. Set amid pines above the sea. 103 rooms, pool and tennis. Very expensive. *Sunna* (E-M), Gaviotas, tel. 68 67 50. 75 rooms, pool and garden. *Bahía Club* (M), Ctra. de Andraitx, tel. 68 61 00. 55 rooms, attractive gardens. *Carabela* (M), Ctra. Andraitx, tel. 68 64 08. An older hotel with 44 rooms. *Cormorán* (M), Puchet, tel. 68 66 54. 72 rooms, pool and garden.

Bella Colina (I), Atalaya 4, tel. 68 69 00. Just above the sea, quiet and modern. 36 rooms, pool and garden. *Gaya* (I), Calle Niza. A 3-star hotel by the beach, with 45 rooms, pool and garden.

There are many reasonable international restaurants. In the club of the *Beverley Hotel* one can watch an excellent flamenco show, presented nightly.

PALMA DE MALLORCA. Capital city, port and tourist center. A fascinating, colorful place, but there is no beach. It is the best place to stay if you are going on a winter holiday. There is lots of nightlife and good shopping. Although a tourist attraction it has managed to retain its Spanish flavor with many ancient buildings and narrow streets.

Valparaíso (L), Francisco Vidal, tel. 40 04 11. 138 rooms, in residential quarter, with recent, impressive garden and superb views of bay. Rates are super high. *Victoria-Sol* (L), Joan Miró 21, tel. 23 43 42. 159 rooms, pool, fabulous views, renowned for its cuisine. Near the nightclub area but avoid rooms overlooking Tito's Club.

Bellver-Sol (E), Paseo Marítimo 106, tel. 23 67 44. 393 rooms, pool and nightclub. *Melia Mallorca* (E), Monsenor Palmer 2, tel. 23 27 40. 239 rooms. Overlooking the harbor in good central position with all facilities. *Palas Atenea-Sol* (E), Paseo Ing. Gabriel Roca, tel. 28 14 00. 370 rooms. Recommended.

La Caleta (M), Marqués de la Cenia 61, tel. 23 09 51. 19 rooms, pool. *Constelación* (M), Corp Mari 27, tel. 40 04 61. A modern hotel with 40 rooms, pool and garden. *Costa Azul* (M), Paseo Marítimo 87, tel. 23 19 40. 140 rooms, pool and garden. *Majórica* (M), Garita 9, tel. 40 02 61. 149 rooms, pool and garden. *Mirador* (M), Paseo Marítimo 10, tel. 23 20 46. 78 rooms, with a sea view. *Saratoga* (M), Paseo de Mallorca 6, tel. 22 72 40. 123 rooms, pool and garden. Recommended.

Araxa (I), Alférez Cerda 22, tel. 23 16 40. 79 rooms, a pleasant lawn and trees, pool. *Augusta* (I), Francisco Vidal, tel. 40 26 93. A 3-star hotel with low rates in residential area; 88 rooms, pool, tennis and garden. *Bonanova* (I), Francisco Vidal 5, tel. 23 59 48. 80 rooms, pool; a comfortable place near El Terreno, very low rates, perfect for budget travelers. *Madrid* (I), Garita 28, tel. 40 01 11. A 2-star hotel with 84 rooms, pool and garden. *San Carlos* (I), Cam Morro 16, tel. 40 39 11. 73 rooms all facing the sea, pool and garden.

Restaurants. Palma is very well supplied with good restaurants ranging in style from Spanish, Mallorquine, international, Italian, French—even Chinese. Fish is one of the main specialties of the island, as are dishes of pork, rabbit and the wide range of local vegetables. *El Patio* (E), Consignatorio Schembri, for top cuisine. *Portalon* (E), Calle Bellver, in the Gomila area, much frequented by knowledgeable Spaniards. *Violet* (E), in 17th cent. mansion. *Zanglada* (E), in the old part of town, *nouvelle cuisine,* excellent.

Ancora (M), located by the Club de Mar, *nouvelle cuisine.* *Chez Sophie* (M), Apuntadores 24, tel. 22 60 86. Recommended for good French cooking. *El Duende* (M), Cecilio Metelo 5, a bistro with a small but excellent menu. *Gina's* (M), Plaza de la Lonja 1, tel. 21 72 06. Good Italian and Spanish dishes in bistro setting. *La Pizzeria* (M), Calle Bellver 31, has topnotch Italian food; there's a large garden with trees and fountain for al fresco dining. *La Casita* (I), on Joan Miró, with top French-American food in simple setting. *Celler Sa Premsa* (I), Plaza Obispo de Palou. One of the oldest, and still one of the best, budget bargains. In a cavernous bodega, it serves simple Spanish fare in congenial surroundings at very low prices. Small and cheap, but serving excellent Mallorquine food is *Payes* (I), on Filipe Bauza.

Nightclubs. Among the most popular discos in Palma is the one in the *Club de Mar,* Paseo Marítimo. The best live show is at *Tito's,* Pl. Gomila, which lives up to its reputation. 18 km west of Palma in Magalluf there is an elegant casino which has a 1,000-seat supper club. For the latest news on the disco scene and details of current events, artistic and cultural, consult the local English language newspaper *The Bulletin.*

PALMA NOVA. 13 km west of Palma, this is another brash resort, crammed with concrete tower hotels and tawdry souvenir shops. There is a good sandy (but crowded) beach if you don't mind the bodies and the blaring music. It is near the Marineland oceanarium.

Cala Blanca-Sol (E), Paseo Duque de Estremera, tel. 68 01 50. Elegant hotel, 161 rooms, pool. *Comodoro* (E), Paseo Calablanca, tel. 68 02 00. 83 rooms, pool, garden, nightclub; close to good bathing. *Punta Negra* (E), Predio Hostalet, tel. 68 07 62. 58 rooms, pool, beside a cove. *Hawaii* (M), Urb. Torre Nova, tel. 68 11 50. 206 rooms, by beach, pool and nightclub. *Honolulu* (M), Avda. Magaluf, tel. 68 04 50. 216 rooms, pool. *Palma Nova* (M), Miguel Santos Oliver, tel. 68 14 50. 209 rooms, pool, mini golf and nightclub. *Canaima* (I), Paseo del Mar, tel. 68 00 62. 62 rooms, pool. *Torrenova* (I), Avda. de los Pinos, tel. 68 16 16. 254 rooms, pool.

PORTO CRISTO. The fishing village ambience is almost wrecked by dozens of daily tourist coachloads, but side streets offer some respite. Small beach and pleasant harbor. Close to the Drach caves, limited nightlife. *Drach* (I), Ctra. de Cuevas, tel. 57 00 25. 52 rooms, pool. *Estrella* (I), Curriean 16, tel. 57 01 50. 41 rooms, pool, garden. *Perelló* (I), San Jorge 30, tel. 57 00 04. Simple, with 95 rooms.

Restaurant. *El Patio* (M), specializing in fish dishes and international cuisine.

PUERTO DE ALCUDIA. Now becoming a pleasant major resort, with superb beach and good facilities. The yacht harbor is surrounded by cafés and restaurants. *Nuevas Palmeras* (E), Avda. Minerva, tel. 54 54 50. An apartment hotel with 114 rooms, close to beach. *Princesa* (E), Avda. Minerva, tel. 54 69 50. Another apartment hotel, 102 rooms all with TV, pool. *Fortuna Playa* (M), Urb. Las Gaviotas, tel. 54 59 94. 210 rooms, pool, garden. *Jupiter* (I), Dr. Davison, tel. 54 56 00. 463 rooms, pool, mini golf, bowling garden. *Saturno* (I), Dr. Davison, tel. 54 57 00. 315 rooms, pool, tennis, garden.

Restaurants. *Loro Verde* (M), specializes in grilled meats and lobster. *Miramar* (M), a good place for fish dishes, overlooking the harbor. *S'Albufera* (M), excellent grills, vast portions. *Meson Los Patos* (I), specializing in Mallorquine cooking.

PUERTO DE POLLENSA. A delightful fishing port-cum-resort with stately Spanish villas and small hotels round a pleasant bay. There are many good restaurants around the yacht marina.

Daina (E), Teniente Coronel Llorca, tel. 53 12 50. 60 rooms, pool. *Pollensa Park* (M), Urb. Uyal, tel. 53 13 60. This is the only really big hotel. 316 rooms, pool, tennis, mini golf, garden, nightclub. *Sis Pins* (M), Anclada Camarasa 229, tel. 53 10 50. 55 rooms, close to beach. *Miramar* (I), Anclada Camarasa 39, tel. 53 14 00. 69 rooms, tennis and garden. *Uyal* (I), Paseo de Londres, tel. 53 15 00. Historic building, pool and gardens. *Raf* (I), Paseo Coronel Llorente 28, tel. 53 11 95. 25 rooms, close to beach.

Restaurants. *Bec Fi* (M), good for grills. *Ca'n Pacienci* (M), between Pollensa and Puerto Pollensa, tel. 53 07 87. *Cellar Cavostra* (I), Mallorquine food.

PUERTO DE SOLLER. Small fishing port with natural harbor in the north of the island. Day-trippers from Palma tend to crowd the small beach. *Edén* (I), Es Traves, tel. 63 16 00. Overlooking harbor, 152 rooms, garden and bowling. *Es Port* (I), Antonio Montis, tel. 63 16 50. In a converted medieval manor house, 3 min. from beach. 96 rooms, pool, garden. *Espléndido* (I), Marina Es Traves, tel. 63 18 50. 104 rooms, very low rates, two terraces for dining. *Mare Nostrum* (I), Marina, tel. 63 14 12. 58 rooms, garden.

Restaurant. In the main town of Soller, away from the harbor, *El Guia* (M), for fish and local dishes.

SANTA PONSA. Brash resort with good, but small, beach; within easy reach of Palma. *Golf Santa Ponsa* (L), tel. 68 05 20. 18 rooms, and an 18-hole golf course. *Santa Ponsa Park* (E), Puig del Teix, tel. 68 15 62. 269 rooms, by beach, pool and garden. *Bahía del Sol* (M), Avda. Jaime I, tel. 68 09 00. 162 rooms, by beach. *Casablanca* (I), Via Rey Sancho 11, tel. 68 12 00. 87 rooms, by beach, pool, garden. *Isabela* (I), Puig del Teix, tel. 68 06 58. 156 rooms, pool, garden, nightclub.

SON VIDA. An attractive development in the hills behind Palma with good views towards Palma bay. *Son Vida* (L), Castillo de Son Vida, tel. 23 23 40. About 30 km from Palma. Located in an old castle, 171 rooms, some of which have the original period furniture. Extensive grounds, pool, restaurant, tennis and golf course. *Racquet Club* (E), tel. 28 00 50. 8 km from Palma in beautiful setting. 51 rooms, pool, tennis and garden.

VALLDEMOSA. Characterful old town in spectacular mountain scenery; famous for visit by Chopin and George Sand. Only one small hostal, *C'An Mario,* but worthwhile touring destination.

Restaurant. *C'an Pedro* (M), Archiduque Luis Salvador, tel. 61 21 70. Typical mesón with good value dining.

MINORCA

A much quieter island than Majorca. There are some good beaches, many of them at the end of dirt paths. There has been quite a lot of development recently but not on such a large scale as in Majorca. Villas tend to be more popular than hotels here and there are fewer package-tour travelers than on Majorca.

CALA GALDANA. *Audax* (E), tel. 37 31 25. Facing beach, in a secluded position. 244 rooms. *Los Gavilanes* (M), tel. 37 31 75. 375 rooms, pool, nightclub.

CALA'N PORTER. *Playa Azul* (I). 108 rooms, by the beach, with pool and garden.

CIUDADELA. *Cala Blanca* (E-M), Urb. Cala Blanca, tel. 38 04 50. 147 rooms, near small sandy beach. Pool and garden. *Esmeralda* (E-M), Paseo San Nicolás, tel. 38 02 50. 132 rooms, in town itself, pool, tennis and garden. *Almirante Farragut* (M) with some (I) rooms, Urb. Los Delfines, tel. 38 28 00. 472 rooms, near beach, pool, tennis and nightclub. *Calan Blanes* (M), tel. 38 24 97. 103 rooms, garden. *Ses Voltes* (M), Cala de Santandria, tel. 38 04 00.
Restaurants. The best restaurants are at the port. *Casa Manolo* (M), tel. 38 00 03, is the best. *La Payesa* (M), tel. 38 00 21, is also good. *El Comilón* (M), Paseo Colón. Wide choice of menu and pleasant interior patio. *Casa Quinto* (I), Alfonso III, is simple and popular.

FORNELLS. Delightful small fishing port on north of island, well known for its fish restaurants serving lobster specialties. *Casa Garriga* and *Es Plá*, both (M), are two of the best.

MAHON. 4 km inland from the open sea, Mahón has a perfect natural harbor. Not many people stay here but it is usually crowded with visitors in the daytime. A far quieter place than either Palma or Ibiza towns.
Port Mahón (E), Paseo Marítimo, tel. 36 26 00. 60 rooms. Stands on a cliff directly above the yacht club, with a good view over the harbor. Very comfortable, with pool, garden and nightclub. *Capri* (M-I), San Esteban 8, tel. 36 14 00. 75 rooms. This is the only other hotel in town, though there are about half a dozen hostels.
Restaurants. *El Greco* (M), Dr Orfila 49, tel. 36 43 67. *De Nit* (M), Camina Ferranda 3, tel. 36 30 30, 2 km south at Llumesanas, possibly the best on the island. *Rocamar* (M), Fonduco 16, tel. 36 56 01. 1 km out in Cala Fonduco, lovely views, good for fish. *Chez Gaston* (I), Conde de Cifuentes 13, tel. 36 00 44. There is a whole host of good restaurants at the port.

PUNTA PRIMA. Quite a well established resort with lots of villas, and a medium-sized shady beach which gets rather crowded. *Pueblo Menorca* (M), tel. 36 18 50. 538 rooms, pool, garden and nightclub. A one-star hotel. *Xaloc* (M) with (I) rooms too, tel. 36 19 22. 58 rooms, pool, mini golf, garden.

S'ALGAR. A modern development, mainly villas, only a few hotels. Rocky bathing. *S'Algar* (M), tel. 36 17 00. 106 rooms, pool, garden, nightclub.

SANTO TOMAS. A very quiet development with a large sandy beach. *Santo Tomás* (E), by the beach, tel. 37 00 25. 60 rooms, pool, mini golf, tennis, garden amongst its many amenities. *Los Condores* (M), by the beach, tel. 37 00 50. 184 rooms, pool, garden and nightclub.

SON BOU. *Los Milanos* and *Los Pinguinos* both (M). Two large modern soulless hotels at end of beautiful beach.

VILLACARLOS. Stands on the cliffs above the inlet between Mahón and the sea. *Agamenon* (E-M), Paraje Fontanillas, tel. 36 21 50. 75 rooms, pool, by beach. *Rey Carlos III* (E-M), Miranda de Cala Corp, tel. 36 31 00. 87 rooms, by beach, pool. *Hamilton* (M), Paseo de Santa Agueda 6, tel. 36 20 50. This is by far the biggest hotel, with 132 rooms, pool and nightclub. *Hotel del Almirante* (I), on road to Mahón, tel. 36 27 00. 30 rooms in an 18th-century house.

Restaurants. There are many delightful restaurants at the harbor, best for evening dining only. Recommended is *La Lola* (M), serving Basque dishes.

 SHOPPING. Majorca has a number of specialties that provide charming, delightful, and even useful **souvenirs** and gifts to take home with you. Among them are the artificial Majorcan pearls, in soft colors, made into necklaces, bracelets, brooches and earrings—they are manufactured by *Majorica,* in Manacor; also **ceramics,** tiles, cups and plates, all brightly colored, with blue and red prevailing; embroidery; and wrought-iron articles of all kinds, from lamps to flower bowls. Wrought-ironwork is done with great taste and skill here, and extremely cheaply. Local handmade glassware is also popular.

Perhaps the best buys of all are in **leather.** Shoes, made largely in Inca, gloves, extremely reasonable and very soft, jackets and so on, are all easily available in most parts of the island, but choice and prices are usually better in Palma.

The two main areas to explore are the myriad of winding streets and staircases around the Plaza Mayor, crammed with tiny shops each vying for the visitor's attention, and the smart Avenida Jaime III which is packed from end to end with chic, attractive shops with special concentration on shoes and other couture items.

Markets are always great fun to visit, even if you're not buying. Palma is well supplied with them. Mercado Pedro Garau in the Plaza Pedro Garau is a riot of animals and food. The Flea Market held in the Rondo on Saturdays is a maze of everything from wood and leather to cast-off clothes and furniture. A lesser version is the Baratillo on Gran Vía. The main city market, selling almost everything, everyday, is located on Plaza Olivar.

The rest of the island is well supplied with market days. One of the biggest is at Inca on Thursdays; here you can find almost anything. Alcudia's is on Sun. and Tues.; Artá, Sun; Felanitx, Sun.; Lluchmayor, Fri.; Pollensa, Sun.; La Puebla, Sun.; and Sóller, Sat.

The other islands have less to offer in the way of shops. Leather, again, is a good buy usually, but less so than in Majorca. The main thing is to shop around, look long and carefully, and haggle whenever you can. All the islands have tourist traps that would make Long John Silver turn in his grave. If you are after typical souvenirs, go to the small shops that sell groceries or kitchen utensils. Locally produced spices or woodware can be cheap and excellent, but you will have to thread your way through a wilderness of plastic.

 USEFUL ADDRESSES. Tourist Offices. **Palma de Mallorca;** Avda. Jaime III 10, and at the airport. **Mahón** (Minorca); Plaza del Generalísimo 13. **Ibiza;** Vara del Rey 13.

British Consulates. **Palma;** Plaza Mayor 3D, tel. 21 24 45. **Ibiza;** Avda. Bartolomé y Tur 24, 9th floor, tel. 30 18 18. U.S. Consulate. **Palma;** Avda. Jaime III 26, tel. 22 26 60.

For boats to the mainland and between the islands, go to the *Transmediterránea* office on the quay in Palma; or ask at any of the tourist offices.

In Palma the Police Emergency number is: 092.

For day-to-day information on events and local cultural activities consult the English-language daily newspaper *The Bulletin*.

ENGLISH-SPANISH
VOCABULARY

LANGUAGE/30

For the Business or Vacationing International Traveler

In 24 languages! A basic language course on 2 cassettes and a phrase book . . . Only $14.95 ea. + shipping

Nothing flatters people more than to hear visitors try to speak their language and LANGUAGE/30, used by thousands of satisfied travelers, gets you speaking the basics quickly and easily. Each LANGUAGE/30 course offers:

- approximately 1½ hours of guided practice in greetings, asking questions and general conversation
- special section on social customs and etiquette

Order yours today. Languages available:

ARABIC	GREEK	JAPANESE	RUSSIAN
CHINESE	HEBREW	KOREAN	SERBO-CROATIAN
DANISH	HINDI	NORWEGIAN	SPANISH
DUTCH	INDONESIAN	PERSIAN	SWAHILI
FRENCH	ITALIAN	PORTUGUESE	SWEDISH
GERMAN	TURKISH	VIETNAMESE	TAGALOG

To order send $14.95 per course + shipping $2.00 1st course, $1 ea. add. course. In Canada $3 1st course, $2.00 ea. add. course. NY and CA residents add state sales tax. Outside USA and Canada $14.95 (U.S.) + air mail shipping: $8 for 1st course, $5 ea. add. course. MasterCard, VISA and Am. Express card users give brand, account number (all digits), expiration date and signature.
SEND TO: FODOR'S, Dept. LC 760, 2 Park Ave., NY 10016-5677, USA.

ENGLISH-SPANISH VOCABULARY

The most important phrase to know (one that may make it unnecessary to know any others) is: "Do you speak English?"—in Spanish *¿Habla Usted inglés?* If the answer is *No,* then you may have recourse to the list below.

Useful Phrases

ENGLISH	SPANISH
Good morning or good day	Buenos dias
Good afternoon	Buenas tardes
Good evening or good night	Buenas noches
Goodbye	Adiós
How are you?	¿Como está Usted?
How do you say in Spanish?	¿Como se dice en español?
Fine	Perfectamente
Very good	Muy bien, Muy bueno
It's all right	Esta bien
Good luck	Buena suerte
Hello	Hola (pronounced 'ola')
Where is the hotel?	¿Donde está el hotel?
How much does this cost?	¿Cuanto vale esto?
How do you feel?	¿Como se siente Usted?
How goes it?	¿Qué tal?
Pleased to meet you	Mucho gusto en conocerle
The pleasure is mine	El gusto es mío
I have the pleasure of introducing Mr . . .	Tengo el gusto de presentarle al Señor . . .
What's your address (phone numb	¿Cuál es su dirección (su número de teléfono)?
I like it very much	Me gusta mucho
I don't like it	No me gusta
Many thanks	Muchas gracias
Don't mention it	De nada
Pardon me	Perdone Usted, Perdóneme
Are you ready?	¿Está listo?
I am ready	Estoy listo
Welcome	Bienvenido
I am very sorry	Lo siento mucho
What time is it?	¿Qué hora es?
I am glad to see you	Mucho gusto en verle
I understand (or) It is clear	Entiendo (or) Está claro

Whenever you please	Cuando guste
Please wait	Espere, por favor
I will be a little late	Llegaré un poco tarde

Food and Drink

Meat	la carne
Fish	el pescado
Chicken	el pollo
Pork	el cerdo
Veal	la ternera
Lamb	el cordero
Turkey	el pavo
Duck	el pato
Sauce or gravy	la salsa
Juice	el zumo
Mustard	la mostaza
Pepper	la pimienta
Salt	la sal
Potato	la patata
Spinach	las espinacas
Beans	las judías
String beans	las judías verdes
Peas	los guisantes
Asparagus	los espárragos
Mushrooms	los champiñones
Carrot	la zanahoria
Lettuce	la lechuga
Radish	el rábano
Garlic	el ajo
Olive	la aceituna
Breakfast	el desayuno
Lunch	la comida
Dinner	la cena
Tea	el té
Coffee	el café
Chocolate	el chocolate
Milk	la leche
Ice cream	el helado
Cake	el pastel
Biscuit	la galleta
Orange juice	el zumo (jugo) de naranja
Ham and eggs (fried)	los huevos fritos con jamón
Scrambled eggs	los huevos revueltos

Hard-boiled eggs	los huevos duros
Poached eggs	los huevos escalfados
Toast	la tostada
Butter	la mantequilla
Marmalade, jam	la mermelada
Omelet	la tortilla
Honey	la miel
Bacon	el tocino
Ham	el jamón
Water	el agua
Fried	frito
Boiled	hervido
Roasted	asado
Raw	crudo
Well done (steaks)	bien hecho
Rare (steaks etc.)	poco hecho
Salmon	el salmón
Sardine	la sardína
Tuna	el atún
Lobster	la langosta
Crayfish	el langostino
Crab	el cangrejo
Clam	la almeja
Salted codfish	el bacalao
Sole	el lenguado
Oyster	la ostra
Beer	la cerveza
Brandy	el coñac
Soda	(el agua de) soda
Red wine	el vino tinto
White wine	el vino blanco

Days of the Week

Monday	el lunes
Tuesday	el martes
Wednesday	el miércoles
Thursday	el jueves
Friday	el viernes
Saturday	el sábado
Sunday	el domingo

Colors

Red	rojo
Blue	azul
Black	negro
White	blanco
Green	verde
Gray	gris
Yellow	amarillo
Orange	naranja
Brown	marrón

Adjectives

Dry	seco
Heavy	pesado
Light	ligero
High	alto
Low	bajo
Sweet	dulce
Bitter	amargo
Clean	limpio
Dirty	sucio
Expensive	caro
Inexpensive	barato
Up	arriba
Below	abajo

Clothing

Hat	el sombrero
Socks	los calcetines
Stockings	las medias
Dress	el vestido
Skirt	la falda
Blouse	la blusa
Underclothing	la ropa interior
Overcoat	el abrigo
Belt	el cinturón
Gloves	los guantes
Handkerchief	el pañuelo
Shoes	los zapatos
Shirt	la camisa
Sweater	el jersey

Medical

Aspirin	la aspirina
Band-aid	la tirita
Pharmacy	la farmacia
Doctor	el médico
Dentist	el dentista
Emergency	urgencia
Hospital	hospital/clínica
Ambulance	la ambulancia
I am ill	Estoy enfermo
I have pain in . . .	Me duele . . .
heart	el corazón
stomach	el estómago

In Spain medical supplies can be obtained at all times of the night at regular pharmacies which are "de guardia," and which rotate within a given neighborhood.

Motoring

A motorcar	Un coche—un automóvil—un auto
To hire a car	alquiler un automóvil—un auto
Body of the car	caja (carrocería) del auto
Fuel	el combustible
Gasoline (petrol)	la gasolina
Carburetor	el carburador
Driving wheel	el volante
Car frame	el chassis
Spring	el resorte—el muelle
A screw	un tornillo
Car axle	el eje del auto
Ball bearings	cojinetes de bolas
Wheel, front—rear	la rueda delantera—trasera
Tire	el neumático
Inner tube	la cámara de aire
To inflate	inflar, dar aire
Tire valve	la válvula de la cámara de aire
To repair	reparar
Valve	la válvula
Engine	el motor
Plug	la bujía
Spark	la chispa
Radiator	el radiador
Oil	el aceite
Accelerator	el acelerador
Brake	el freno

Tank	el tanque—el depósito
Gear box	la caja de cambio de velocidades
Head lamps	los faros
To start	poner en marcha
To stop	parar
The garage	el garage
To grease	engrasar
To wash	lavar

Numbers

The answers to many questions you ask will be given in numbers. Therefore you need to know what they sound like. We suggest you learn the numbers. Their pronunciations are given in parentheses.

1 uno, una (oono, oona)
2 dos (dohss)
3 tres (tress)
4 cuatro (kwahtro)
5 cinco (theenko)
6 seis (sayeess)
7 siete (seeaytay)
8 ocho (ocho)
9 nueve (nwayvay)
10 diez (dee-eth)
11 once (onthay)
12 doce (dothay)
13 trece (traythay)
14 catorce (katorthay)
15 quince (keenthay)

16 dieciséis (dee-eth ee sayeess)
17 diecisiete
18 dieciocho
19 diecinueve
20 veinte (vayntay)
30 treinta (traynta)
40 cuarenta (kwahrenta)
50 cincuenta (theenkwenta)
60 sesenta (sayssenta)
70 setenta (saytenta)
80 ochenta (ochenta)
90 noventa (noventa)
100 ciento, cien (thee-ento, thee-ayn)
1000 mil (meal)

INDEX

INDEX

The following abbreviations have been used in this index: E for Entertainment; H for Hotels, Paradores etc.; M for Museums; R for Restaurants; S for Sports.

MAP
OF
SPAIN

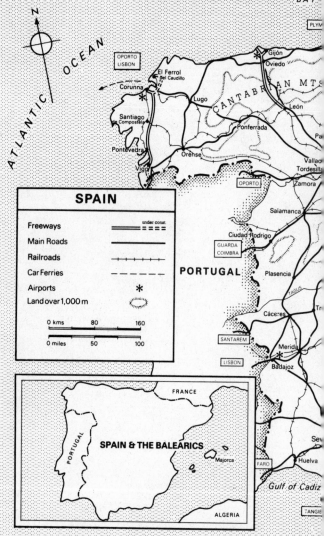

ATLANTIC OCEAN

N

BAY

PLYM

OPORTO
LISBON

El Ferrol
del Caudillo

Gijón

Oviedo

Corunna

CANTAB

AN MTS

Santiago
de Compostela

Lugo

León

Ponferrada

Pa

Pontevedra

Orense

Vallao

Tordesill

Vigo

OPORTO

Zamora

Salamanca

SPAIN

Freeways	under const.
Main Roads	
Railroads	
Car Ferries	
Airports	*
Land over 1,000 m	

0 kms	80	160
0 miles	50	100

Ciudad Rodrigo

GUARDA
COIMBRA

PORTUGAL

Plasencia

TAGUS

Cáceres

Tr

SANTAREM

Mérida

LISBON

Badajoz

FRANCE

PORTUGAL

SPAIN & THE BALEARICS

Majorca

FARO

Sev

Huelva

Gulf of Cadiz

ALGERIA

TANGIE

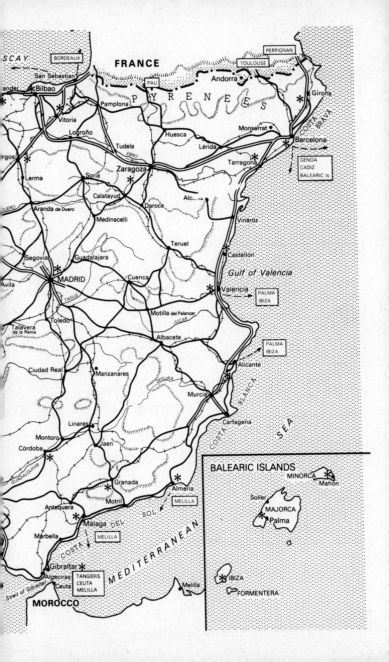